GLOBALIZATION AND INTERNATIONAL DEVELOPMENT

GLOBALIZATION AND INTERNATIONAL DEVELOPMENT
The Ethical Issues

EDITED BY H.E. BABER AND DENISE DIMON

broadview press

Library and Archives Canada Cataloguing in Publication

    Globalization and international development : the ethical issues / edited by H.E. Baber and Denise Dimon.

Includes bibliographical references.
ISBN 978-1-55481-012-3 (pbk.)

    1. Globalization—Moral and ethical aspects. 2. Economic assistance—Moral and ethical aspects.
I. Baber, Harriet Erica, editor of compilation II. Dimon, Denise, editor of compilation

HF1359.G583 2013   174   C2013-903974-0

Broadview Press is an independent, international publishing house, incorporated in 1985.

We welcome comments and suggestions regarding any aspect of our publications—please feel free to contact us at the addresses below or at broadview@broadviewpress.com.

North America
PO Box 1243, Peterborough, Ontario, Canada K9J 7H5
2215 Kenmore Ave., Buffalo, New York, USA 14207
Tel: (705) 743-8990; Fax: (705) 743-8353
email: customerservice@broadviewpress.com

UK, Europe, Central Asia, Middle East, Africa, India, and Southeast Asia
Eurospan Group, 3 Henrietta St., London WC2E 8LU, United Kingdom
Tel: 44 (0) 1767 604972; Fax: 44 (0) 1767 601640
email: eurospan@turpin-distribution.com

Australia and New Zealand
NewSouth Books
c/o TL Distribution
15-23 Helles Avenue, Moorebank, NSW, Australia 2170
Tel: (02) 8778 9999; Fax: (02) 8778 9944
email: orders@tldistribution.com.au

www.broadviewpress.com

Copy-edited by Martin Boyne

Designed by Chris Rowat Design, Daiva Villa

PRINTED IN CANADA

Contents

Introduction

> The problem of the twentieth century is the problem of the color-line—the relation of the darker to the lighter races of men in Asia and Africa, in America and the islands of the sea.
> —W.E.B. Du Bois

This book is a selection of readings that address the contemporary moral issues that arise from the division between the Global North and South—"the problem of the color-line" that W.E.B. Du Bois identified at the beginning of the twentieth century and which, on a scale that Du Bois could not have foreseen, is the problem of the twenty-first. It is interdisciplinary in scope, including articles by economists and other social scientists as well as philosophers. In addition to standard readings in ethical theory and topical essays by philosophers such as Anthony Appiah, Martha Nussbaum, Peter Singer, Thomas Nagel, and others, it contains essays by writers from other academic disciplines, including economists Amartya Sen, Joseph Stiglitz, and Thomas DeGregori. It also includes current empirical material from the World Bank, the IMF, United Nations agencies, and other sources, which will be informative to instructors as well as students, and which instructors and students need if they are to engage in a reasonable discussion of the ethical issues concerning globalization broadly construed. Each section concludes with a short list of recommended readings for instructors and students who wish to pursue in greater depth the topics considered. The selected readings are central to the topics covered in these sections and guide readers through the extensive literature in these areas.

Philosophers by and large are not comfortable with empirical facts, and quite often they do not know where to find data when they need it. That is perhaps why ethics courses (and ethicists) have traditionally focused on the *hard* ethical problems—the moral dilemmas that provoke chronic controversy even though the empirical facts are not in dispute. In such cases no provision of further information will resolve the disagreements. The hardest cases are fictional, because here philosophers can *stipulate* the facts of the story that are intended to pump subjects' intuitions. You are at the convergence of two trolley lines: on the siding there is one man tied to the track; on the mainline five men are tied down. The train is speeding down the mainline and cannot be stopped. You control the switch. Should you divert the train to the other track where only one man will be killed instead of five? Subjects who ask for additional factual information are smartly rebuffed: we do *not* know anything about the moral character or family responsibilities of the five men on the mainline; we do not know whether the one man on the siding is a famous violinist or which of the potential victims is the most likely to discover a cure for cancer. The provision of any further information would be irrelevant or misleading because the purpose of this exercise is to pump ethical intuitions about acts of omission and commission *given* this particular set of assumptions.

In real life it is most often issues in biomedical ethics that approximate these austere thought-experimental conditions. In what circumstances is abortion morally permissible? Is it ever morally wrong? If so, why and under what conditions? We know all the facts of fetal development but still disagree. No further empirical information will, or can, settle the dispute. Concern about how non-human animals ought to be treated is another source of such irresolvable moral controversies. We know all the relevant empirical facts about non-human animals, but we still disagree about how they ought to be treated in labs or in zoos, and whether it is morally permissible to kill them for food or for sport. These are hard ethical questions that cannot be answered by dint of further empirical information.

Some of the most pressing moral questions, however, in particular those concerning economic issues and public policy, are easy questions—from the moral point of view. The controversies that surround these questions concern matters of fact. So currently, in the US, the ongoing bitter disagreement about environmental policy is, at bottom, an empirical question: "hard" to the extent that it poses vexed questions about policy and about the role of government, but "easy" from the moral point of view in that it does require an answer to those purely moral questions, which, like the trolley problem, cannot be answered by provision of any empirical information. A highly vocal minority of Americans, led by their elected representatives, oppose regulations intended to reduce the emission of greenhouse gases into the atmosphere. Over one quarter of Americans hold that the federal government should not regulate the release of greenhouse gases, and an additional 4 per cent are unsure.[1]

Now there is a hard ethical question underlying environmental concerns: do we have any obligation to future generations? If we have no such obligation, we might as well enjoy ourselves now, use up all available natural resources, and trash the Earth: after us the deluge. But this carpe diem policy is not what drives most opponents of environmental regulations. The current controversy arises from a disagreement about the facts of the matter: 36 per cent of Americans believe that most scientists are unsure about whether global warming is occurring, and 46 per cent believe that if in

1 Polling Report, *Environment*, 2011, <http://www.pollingreport/enviro.htm>.

fact the Earth's temperature is rising, it is due to natural changes rather than human activities.[2] The disagreement here is about plain empirical facts—about whether climate change is in fact occurring and whether, if it is, it is caused by human activity.

Quite often, what appear to be disagreements of principle are actually factual disagreements. So debates about immigration, integration, and diversity are often assumed to arise from a conflict of interest between ethnic minorities wishing to preserve ancestral cultures and members of the larger society pressing them to assimilate. Advocates of "multiculturalism" defend the right of immigrants and members of ethnic minorities to retain their ancestral languages and cultures, while members of native majority populations complain that ethnic minorities "keep to themselves," and critics, such as David Goodhart, whose essay appears in this volume (ch. 44), worry that societies with significant immigrant and minority populations are "too diverse" to support a robust welfare state. But, when asked, acculturated immigrants and members of ethnic minorities complain that however acculturated they may be, they are not accepted.[3] Thus, during the 2005 riots in French immigrant suburbs, residents complained that they were excluded and tagged with identities that were alien to them. "How am I supposed to feel French when people always describe me as a Frenchman of Algerian origin?", journalist Nadir Dendoune complained. "I was born here. I am French. How many generations does it take to stop mentioning my origin?...I do not know a single youth in my estate who does not want to leave."[4]

Those who are worried about the supposed interests of immigrants and ethnic minorities defend the right of members of minority groups to retain "their" cultures and to resist assimilation. They rarely ask the empirical question: do members of minority groups *want* to retain "their" cultures? More fundamentally, are the languages and folkways of their ancestors *their* cultures? Why should I identify with a culture that is alien to me or learn an alien language that I have never even heard because it is my ancestors' language? How many generations does it take to stop mentioning my origin and imposing the burden of identifying with it on me? Anthony Appiah worries about ethnic "scripting" and the tyranny of authenticity, which imposes this burden on us, and Amartya Sen expresses reservations about multiculturalism understood as "plural monoculturalism" (ch. 47).

Before setting out to adjudicate between the interests of minorities and members of the dominant culture, we want to know what their interests are. Do immigrants *want* to "keep to themselves"? Do minorities *want* to preserve their ancestral cultures? There should not be any insurmountable difficulties in discovering the facts about what immigrants and members of ethnic minorities want: we can ask—and listen.

---

2 Ibid.
3 H.E. Baber, *The Multicultural Mystique: The Liberal Case against Diversity* (Amherst, NY: Prometheus Books, 2008).
4 Ibid., p. 73.

Sometimes, however, the facts are not easy to come by, since they concern the future course of events and the consequences of our actions. Garrett Hardin, in his classic 1974 article making "the case against helping the poor" (ch. 32), warned that the "population explosion" that preoccupied pundits of the period would be exacerbated by the Green Revolution and the provision of aid to poor countries. People, he predicted, would behave like yeast cells when more sugar was dumped into the medium in which they were growing: the more food they got, the faster they would reproduce until, reaching the limit of Earth's carrying capacity, they would start dying off. But Hardin was wrong. As it turned out, the richer people got—the more food and other resources they had—the more slowly they reproduced. In the decades following Hardin's Malthusian prognostication, population growth slowed. Currently, in affluent Europe and Japan, where virtually unlimited food is readily available, population growth is below the replacement rate of 2.1 children per woman. And in recent years it has declined in the Global South as well.

The most difficult questions that arise from the division between the Global North and South concern the causes of poverty, violence, and other ills that disproportionately plague the developing world and the consequences of our policies and practices. In 2005, the wealthiest 20 per cent of the world accounted for 76.6 per cent of total private consumption, while the poorest fifth accounted for just 1.5 per cent.[5] The poorest people live in the world's poorest countries. In 2006 world gross domestic product (GDP) was $48.2 trillion. The world's wealthiest countries, comprising approximately one billion people, accounted for $36.6 trillion (76%); low-income countries, roughly 2.4 billion people, accounted for just $1.6 trillion (3.3%).[6] In the US, average GDP per capita is $129 per person per day; globally, 895 million people live on less than 99 cents per day.[7] In chapter 7, Abhijit Banerjee and Esther Duflo describe the economic lives of the poor. And in chapter 8, Rebecca Mead, on the eve of Lula's election as president of Brazil, depicts the economic lives of the ultra-rich. What are the causes of growing global inequality, and of the persistence of extreme poverty? Has economic globalization contributed to the growth of economic inequality? Can it be made to work for the poor? Joseph Stiglitz (ch. 15), Matthew Zwolinski (ch. 17), and Benjamin Barber (ch. 18) discuss economic globalization and speculate about its likely consequences. Economists Daron Acemoglu and James Robinson (ch. 10), William Easterly (ch. 12), and Paul Collier (ch. 13) offer competing explanations for the persistence of poverty and suggest different remedies.

---

5 A. Shah, *Poverty Facts and Stats*, 1 September 2010, <http://www.globalissues.org/article/26/poverty-facts-and-stats>.
6 Ibid.
7 A.V. Banerjee and E. Duflo, *Poor Economics*, 2011, <http://www.pooreconomics.com/teaching-book>.

All agree that aid is part of the solution. But aid is not an unqualified good. Often it comes with conditions that have been detrimental to the interests of recipients. During the late twentieth century, the IMF and World Bank imposed "structural adjustment" conditions promoting "free market" policies on loans made to developing countries, which critics suggest harmed borrowers. Even apart from the pressure exerted on developing countries by these agencies to conform to neoliberal ideologies, the presence of NGOs in the Global South distorts local economies. Aid organizations compete with local businesses, and well-paid bureaucrats jack up housing prices. In addition, as Clifford Bob notes in his critique of these "merchants of morality," large, well-funded NGOs set the agenda of local organizations, which tailor their programs to be marketable. "Indeed," he notes, "many NGOs now offer training programs to build advocacy capacity, establish contacts, and develop media smarts":

> One of the most elaborate programs is the Washington, DC-based International Human Rights Law Group's two-year Advocacy Bridge Program, which aims to "increase the skills of local activists to amplify their issues of concern globally" and to "facilitate their access to international agenda-setting venues." Under the program, dozens of participants from around the world, chosen to ensure equal participation by women, travel to Washington for one week of initial training and then to Geneva for three weeks of on-site work at the UN Human Rights Commission. In their second year, "graduates" help train a new crop of participants.[8]

A number of critics worried about the detrimental effects of aid commend microentrepreneurship as a superior alternative. Therefore, in the years following Muhammad Yunus's 1983 establishment of the Grameen Bank, the world's first microcredit lender, there was widespread enthusiasm for the program. The Right, globally resurgent during the period, applauded Yunus's program because it promoted entrepreneurship and seemed to show that capitalism, albeit on a small scale, could improve the lot of the poor. The Left liked it because it supported small-scale, grassroots projects and empowered women. The United Nations declared 2005 the International Year of Microcredit, and in 2006 the Nobel Peace Prize was awarded to the Grameen Bank and to Muhammad Yunus as a pioneer in the microcredit movement. More recently, however, critics have expressed reservations about the benefits of microcredit. How effective are microcredit and entrepreneurship in lifting families in the Global South out of poverty? In chapter 24, Muhammad Yunus writes about how the Grameen Bank, the microcredit organization he founded, helped women in his native Bangladesh and elsewhere start small businesses, provide for their families,

---

8 C. Bob, "Merchants of Morality," *Foreign Policy* 129 (March/April 2002): 43.

and contribute to local economies. Aneel Karnani argues to the contrary in chapter 25 that "employment, not microcredit, is the solution," noting that "the key issue is whether microcredit helps eradicate poverty... [and] that while 'heart-warming case studies abound, rigorous empirical analyses are rare.'"[9]

Sometimes, however, empirical facts and analyses are not enough. Sometimes, even when we know the empirical facts of the matter, and are confident in our ability to assess the costs and risks of various courses of action, we are puzzled about how to weigh those costs, benefits, and risks. Growing genetically modified crops carries some risk of undermining biodiversity. Is that risk warranted given the benefits? Vandana Shiva, an advocate of "deep ecology," argues in an open letter to Oxfam (ch. 34) that promoting genetically modified crops "risks betraying the [Global] South." Thomas DeGregori (ch. 35) disagrees, noting that many residents of the Global South want no part of Shiva's program. And indeed Indian writer Ramachandra Guha depicts the activities of many Western-based environmentalists as a form of cultural imperialism promoted by "Green missionaries" that sets back the interests of the world's poor and indigenous people.[10] How should we weigh the diverse interests of environmentalists and farmers, Western sentimentalists, and the starving masses of the Global South? How much risk is it reasonable to assume?

Concerns about human rights pose similar puzzles. Authoritarian strong men, who still dominate a number of nations in the Global South, impose what we should regard as unwarranted restrictions on the freedom of their citizens. And traditional cultures embody practices that Westerners regard as unacceptable: in many parts of Africa, female genital mutilation is widespread, and throughout the non-Western world, wife-beating is, if not approved, both expected and acceptable. The practice of *sati*, in which recently widowed women immolated themselves on their husbands' funeral pyres was, though not common, significant in many parts of India, well into the nineteenth century. According to British East India Company records, there were 8,135 incidents recorded from 1813 to 1828.[11]

We know the response of colonial powers to such local customs during the heyday of colonialism in the nineteenth century, as articulated by Charles Napier, British governor of the Bombay Presidency in the mid-nineteenth century in response to Hindu priests defending the practice of *sati*:

> Be it so. This burning of widows is your custom; prepare the funeral pile. But my nation has also a custom. When men burn women alive we hang them,

---

9 A. Karnani, "Employment, not Microcredit, Is the Solution," pp. 800–04 in this volume.

10 R. Guha, "Radical American Environmentalism and Wilderness Preservation: A Third World Critique," *Environmental Ethics* 11 (1989): 71–83 (cited in "Environmental Ethics," *Stanford Encyclopedia of Philosophy* <http://plato.stanford.edu/entries/ethics-environmental>).

11 Datamation Foundation, "Hindi Bengali Widows through the Centuries," n.d., <http://www.datamationfoundation.org/women4.htm>.

and confiscate all their property. My carpenters shall therefore erect gibbets on which to hang all concerned when the widow is consumed. Let us all act according to national customs.[12]

It is difficult not to cheer Napier's response. Cultural preservation is all very fine and edifying, but not (as most of us think) at the cost of supporting the custom of bullying or forcing women to burn themselves alive. *Sati* was not in any case a universal cultural custom and, indeed, over the centuries, before colonialism, local rulers tried to suppress it. But what are we to say of other culturally embedded customs that impose hardships on members of the culture—in particular women and members of other disadvantaged groups? What are we to say about female genital mutilation, slavery, and caste systems? Too often multiculturalism privileges high-prestige members of non-Western societies or those whom Westerners regard as representative of the culture—the high-caste Hindu priests promoting *sati* or the young, lower-class males who constitute the Arab "street." They either ignore women, slaves, and outcasts or assume that members of these disadvantaged groups have a greater interest in cultural cohesion than in individual rights for themselves—that loyalty to the culture and social solidarity, including solidarity with husbands and masters, trumps personal gratification, freedom, or any other benefits they might obtain from colonial or neocolonial domination.

Seeing world affairs through the lens of nationalism, we assume that communal "self-determination," that is, rule by members of one's own ethnic group, is a good thing. But even assuming that it is good, all other things being equal, we can still ask *how* good it is, and when trade-offs are called for. Are oppressive indigenous regimes preferable to benign colonialism? When, if ever, is it permissible for nations to interfere in the internal affairs of other sovereign states, and by what means? Is colonialism ever morally acceptable? Dinesh D'Souza argues in chapter 21 that "colonialism was the transmission belt that brought to Asia, Africa and South America the blessings of Western civilization." Should the widows of India have resisted British attempts to abolish *sati* and thrown themselves on their husbands' funeral pyres as an expression of loyalty to their culture in order to resist white Western hegemony?

Even when the empirical questions have been answered, there is a residue of purely ethical disagreement. In 1947, the United Nations formulated a "universal declaration of human rights" (ch. 40), asserting such apparently uncontroversial principles as prohibitions on slavery and the slave trade and on torture, inhuman and degrading punishment, acceptance of the equality of all persons before the law, the right of fair hearing by impartial tribunals, and rights to nationality, property, freedom of thought, expression, and religion; in response, the American Anthropological Association withdrew from discussions on the grounds that no such declaration could be applicable

---

12 William Napier, *History of General Sir Charles Napier's Administration of Scinde* (London: Chapman and Hall, 1851).

to all human beings. Committed to cultural relativism, anthropologists have been unwilling to pass judgment on culturally based practices such as female genital mutilation, the killing of infants or the aged, and acts of communal violence that arise from long-standing, traditional inter-ethnic or inter-religious hostilities such as clashes between Hindus and Muslims in India or Tutsis and Hutus in Rwanda.

Reflecting on the folkways of her profession, anthropologist Carolyn Fluehr-Lobban (ch. 41) is critical about this stance. Citing practices such as female genital mutilation, honor killing, domestic violence, and ethnic cleansing, Fluehr-Lobban worries that cultural relativism undermines any serious commitment to human rights—and licenses repressive regimes to deflect international criticism of the abuse of their citizens.

Many students who will read this book believe themselves to be cultural relativists, and many instructors who will assign it as a class text believe that cultural relativism is naive. Since students typically imagine themselves to be relativists because they focus on easy cases for relativism, in particular differences in customs concerning sexual conduct, we present the hard cases, including female genital mutilation and honor killing. We include also a detailed, unsympathetic critique of cultural relativism by James Rachels (ch. 42) to explain why we not only condemn these customs but why we *ought* to. We hope that the readings we have included provide students and instructors with the basis for an informed dialogue about cultural relativism. In the first part of the book, to set the foundation for this dialogue, we include readings in what might be understood as ethical theory in the broadest sense by John Stuart Mill, John Rawls, Robert Nozick, Peter Singer, Michael Sandel, and Amartya Sen, in order to provide plausible alternatives to relativism.

Globalization, the increasing transnational integration of economic and social institutions, poses some of the least tractable moral dilemmas and is likely to demand some of the most vexed political decisions. This collection of data and readings from ethicists and from economists and other social scientists will introduce students to contemporary issues concerning globalization broadly construed and, we hope, inspire those who will grapple with these issues and contribute to these decisions.

I

Ethical Theory: Introduction

In *Utilitarianism*, John Stuart Mill argues that the foundation of morals is to be found in the "Greatest Happiness Principle," according to which "actions are right in proportion as they tend to promote happiness, wrong as they tend to produce the reverse of happiness."[1] By the time of Mill's writing, the principle of utility thus understood had a long history, going back to Hobbes, Locke, and Bentham, and even further to Epicurus.

Utilitarianism is a *consequentialist* ethical theory, according to which the rightness or wrongness of any action is judged wholly and solely by its consequences. On consequentialist accounts, actions are right if they have the best possible overall consequences—those which are most conducive to the well-being of all concerned. This raises two further questions. First, we want to know with whose well-being we should be concerned. We should certainly consider the welfare of living human beings, but should we care about future generations? Should we care about all sentient beings, including non-human animals? Should we care about non-sentient beings—trees, inanimate objects, or the earth's ecosystem in toto? Second, just considering sentient beings, i.e., humans and animals, which most consequentialists agree are beings whose welfare matters, what constitutes their well-being?

In addition to these questions, utilitarianism raises serious worries about how well-being ought to be distributed. Utilitarianism is popularly characterized as the doctrine that we ought to promote "the greatest good for the greatest number." But this does not give us any guidance about how the good, whatever it is, ought to be allocated. Should we aim for the greatest sum of well-being over the population, even if it is arbitrarily and inequitably distributed? Should we strive to obtain the highest

---

1 John Stuart Mill, *Utilitarianism*, pp. 12–19 in this volume.

average well-being, even if it does not yield the greatest sum of good overall? Mill's classic formulation of well-being is intuitively attractive, but the devil is in the details.

Contemporary liberals, libertarians, and communitarians have responded to Mill. One of John Rawls's main aims in his *Theory of Justice*, widely regarded as the twentieth century's most significant work of political philosophy, is to provide an alternative to utilitarianism. Utilitarianism, Rawls suggests, fails to take seriously the distinction between persons and so cannot provide the resources for any plausible principles of *distributive justice*, i.e., normative principles designed to guide the allocation of material benefits and burdens amongst persons. To arrive at such principles without allowing our own interests to prejudice our deliberations, Rawls suggests that we consider what principles would be adopted by rational individuals who, though aware of general facts about the world and human nature, knew nothing of their particular characters or circumstances. Thus situated, behind a "veil of ignorance," Rawls argues, we would accept the set of principles that he holds are constitutive of "justice as fairness." The first principle affirms basic political liberties: each person is to have equal claim to an adequate scheme of basic liberties insofar as it is compatible with the same scheme for all. The second principle applies primarily to social and economic institutions that are, first, to provide fair equality of opportunity to all, and second, to secure the greatest benefit for the least-advantaged members of society. Rawls's account of justice as fairness revived interest in political philosophy and applied ethics amongst philosophers in the Anglo-American tradition, and a good deal of the most significant later work in the field begins as a response to Rawls.

In *Anarchy, State and Utopia*, Robert Nozick proposes an alternative, libertarian understanding of justice. Repudiating the notion of distributive justice as an account of fair end-states, Nozick argues that a distribution of goods is just to the extent that it is brought about by free exchange from a just starting position. Nozick's principles of justice concern the *process* by which holdings are acquired and transferred, and the means by which past injustices in the acquisition and transfer of holdings are rectified rather than the pattern in which holdings are distributed as a result. According to Nozick, "liberty upsets patterns": there is no fair pattern of distribution *per se*, and any attempt to enforce an end-state principle to produce a pattern requires redistributive activities that undermine individual liberty and, typically, violate individual rights. In contrast to all "patterned" theories that aim at what purport to be just end-states, Nozick's "entitlement theory" deems a distribution just if it arises from legitimate processes of distribution.

Peter Singer suggests that Nozick's book is a "major event in contemporary political philosophy" because it is the only current viable non-utilitarian alternative to Rawls. Like Rawls's account, Nozick's entitlement theory is a rights-based approach in the tradition of Locke and Kant. Nozick's account, however, prohibits the compulsory redistribution of wealth from the rich to the poor—and Nozick has argued that Rawls, insofar as he is committed to respecting individual rights, cannot consistently support such a policy. If, however, we support compulsory redistribution, Singer, a utilitarian, suggests that utilitarianism is our best bet.

Communitarianism has been understood as a non-utilitarian alternative to both Rawlsian liberalism and the libertarian account popularized by Nozick. Whereas liberals and libertarians worry about the distinction between persons, communitarians are concerned about persons' connections with one another as members of communities delineated by time, place, circumstance, and history. They worry also that the universalism espoused by utilitarians, Rawlsian liberals, and libertarians reflects assumptions that are in fact Western and highly parochial. Michael Sandel argues that Rawlsian liberalism, as well as Nozick's entitlement theory and other libertarian accounts, rests upon an unrealistic, overly individualistic conception of the self as "unencumbered" by the historical context and communal attachments that form the identities of persons.

Fundamental to each of these non-utilitarian accounts is the recognition that classical utilitarianism does not provide an adequate account of distributive justice— an issue that is at the core of most discussions of globalization broadly construed. Intuitively, the fundamental problem of globalization is the recognition that a variety of goods—wealth, security, political participation, economic opportunity, access to natural resources, and the like—are unequally and, arguably, inequitably distributed.

Economist Amartya Sen argues that every serious moral theory demands "equality of *something*":

> Not only do income-egalitarians...demand equal incomes, and welfare-egalitarians ask for equal welfare levels, but also classical utilitarians insist on equal weights on the utilities of all and pure libertarians demand equality with respect to an entire class of rights and liberties. They are all "egalitarians" in some essential way.... To see the battle as one between those "in favor of" and those "against" equality (as the problem is often posed in the literature) is to miss something central to the subject.[2]

In his classic essay "Equality of What?", the Tanner Lecture on Human Values delivered at Stanford University in 1979, Sen canvasses the alternatives and argues that the equality that matters from the moral point of view is "basic capability equality": the equality of effective freedom to achieve a satisfactory level of valued states or "functionings." His book *The Idea of Justice* follows up the departures made in that essay.

Advocates of Sen's Capability Approach, including Martha Nussbaum, have attempted to provide lists of these valued states. Nevertheless Sen, insisting that his is an "approach" rather than a completed theory, has resolutely refused, suggesting provocatively that "basic capability equality can be seen as essentially an extension of the Rawlsian approach in a non-fetishist direction."

---

2 Amartya Sen, *Inequality Reexamined* (Cambridge, MA: Harvard UP, 1992), p. ix.

1. Utilitarianism*

John Stuart Mill

To inquire how far the bad effects of this deficiency have been mitigated in practice, or to what extent the moral beliefs of mankind have been vitiated or made uncertain by the absence of any distinct recognition of an ultimate standard, would imply a complete survey and criticism, of past and present ethical doctrine. It would, however, be easy to show that whatever steadiness or consistency these moral beliefs have attained, has been mainly due to the tacit influence of a standard not recognised. Although the non-existence of an acknowledged first principle has made ethics not so much a guide as a consecration of men's actual sentiments, still, as men's sentiments, both of favour and of aversion, are greatly influenced by what they suppose to be the effects of things upon their happiness, the principle of utility, or as Bentham latterly called it, the greatest happiness principle, has had a large share in forming the moral doctrines even of those who most scornfully reject its authority. Nor is there any school of thought which refuses to admit that the influence of actions on happiness is a most material and even predominant consideration in many of the details of morals, however unwilling to acknowledge it as the fundamental principle of morality, and the source of moral obligation. I might go much further, and say that to all those a priori moralists who deem it necessary to argue at all, utilitarian arguments are indispensable. It is not my present purpose to criticise these thinkers; but I cannot help referring, for illustration, to a systematic treatise by one of the most illustrious of them, the Metaphysics of Ethics, by Kant. This remarkable man, whose system of thought will long remain one of the landmarks in the history of philosophical speculation, does, in the treatise in question, lay down a universal first principle as the origin and ground of moral obligation; it is this: "So act, that the rule on which thou actest would admit of being adopted as a law by all rational beings." But when he begins to deduce from this precept any of the actual duties of

* Source: *Utilitarianism* (Indianapolis: Hackett, 1978). Or John Stuart Mill. *Utilitarianism*. Reprinted from *Fraser's Magazine* 7th ed. London: Longmans, Green, and Co., 1879, pp. 6, 11–12, 13–18, 26–28, 32, 34–36, 41–42, 49–51, 52.

morality, he fails, almost grotesquely, to show that there would be any contradiction, any logical (not to say physical) impossibility, in the adoption by all rational beings of the most outrageously immoral rules of conduct. All he shows is that the consequences of their universal adoption would be such as no one would choose to incur.

The creed, which accepts as the foundation of morals, Utility, or the Greatest Happiness Principle, holds that actions are right in proportion as they tend to promote happiness, wrong as they tend to produce the reverse of happiness. By happiness is intended pleasure, and the absence of pain; by unhappiness, pain, and the privation of pleasure. To give a clear view of the moral standard set up by the theory, much more requires to be said; in particular, what things it includes in the ideas of pain and pleasure; and to what extent this is left an open question. But these supplementary explanations do not affect the theory of life on which this theory of morality is grounded—namely, that pleasure, and freedom from pain, are the only things desirable as ends; and that all desirable things (which are as numerous in the utilitarian as in any other scheme) are desirable either for the pleasure inherent in themselves, or as means to the promotion of pleasure and the prevention of pain.

Now, such a theory of life excites in many minds, and among them in some of the most estimable in feeling and purpose, inveterate dislike. To suppose that life has (as they express it) no higher end than pleasure—no better and nobler object of desire and pursuit—they designate as utterly mean and groveling; as a doctrine worthy only of swine, to whom the followers of Epicurus were, at a very early period, contemptuously likened; and modern holders of the doctrine are occasionally made the subject of equally polite comparisons by its German, French, and English assailants.

When thus attacked, the Epicureans have always answered, that it is not they, but their accusers, who represent human nature in a degrading light; since the accusation supposes human beings to be capable of no pleasures except those of which swine are capable. If this supposition were true, the charge could not be gainsaid, but would then be no longer an imputation; for if the sources of pleasure were precisely the same to human beings and to swine, the rule of life which is good enough for the one would be good enough for the other. The comparison of the Epicurean life to that of beasts is felt as degrading, precisely because a beast's pleasures do not satisfy a human being's conceptions of happiness. Human beings have faculties more elevated than the animal appetites, and when once made conscious of them, do not regard anything as happiness which does not include their gratification. . . . It is quite compatible with the principle of utility to recognise the fact, that some kinds of pleasure are more desirable and more valuable than others. It would be absurd that while, in estimating all other things, quality is considered as well as quantity, the estimation of pleasures should be supposed to depend on quantity alone.

If I am asked, what I mean by difference of quality in pleasures, or what makes one pleasure more valuable than another, merely as a pleasure, except its being greater in amount, there is but one possible answer. Of two pleasures, if there be one to which all or almost all who have experience of both give a decided preference, irrespective of any feeling of moral obligation to prefer it, that is the more desirable pleasure. If one of the two is, by those who are competently acquainted with both, placed so far above the other that they prefer it, even though knowing it to be attended with a greater amount of discontent, and would not resign it for any quantity of the other pleasure which their nature is capable of, we are justified in ascribing to the preferred enjoyment a superiority in quality, so far outweighing quantity as to render it, in comparison, of small account.

Now it is an unquestionable fact that those who are equally acquainted with, and equally capable of appreciating and enjoying, both, do give a most marked preference to the manner of existence which employs their higher faculties. Few human creatures would consent to be changed into any of the lower animals, for a promise of the fullest allowance of a beast's pleasures; no intelligent human being would consent to be a fool, no instructed person would be an ignoramus, no person of feeling and conscience would be selfish and base, even though they should be persuaded that the fool, the dunce, or the rascal is better satisfied with his lot than they are with theirs. They would not resign what they possess more than he for the most complete satisfaction of all the desires which they have in common with him. If they ever fancy they would, it is only in cases of unhappiness so extreme, that to escape from it they would exchange their lot for almost any other, however undesirable in their own eyes. A being of higher faculties requires more to make him happy, is capable probably of more acute suffering, and certainly accessible to it at more points, than one of an inferior type; but in spite of these liabilities, he can never really wish to sink into what he feels to be a lower grade of existence. We may give what explanation we please of this unwillingness; we may attribute it to pride, a name which is given indiscriminately to some of the most and to some of the least estimable feelings of which mankind are capable: we may refer it to the love of liberty and personal independence, an appeal to which was with the Stoics one of the most effective means for the inculcation of it; to the love of power, or to the love of excitement, both of which do really enter into and contribute to it: but its most appropriate appellation is a sense of dignity, which all human beings possess in one form or other, and in some, though by no means in exact, proportion to their higher faculties, and which is so essential a part of the happiness of those in whom it is strong, that nothing which conflicts with it could be, otherwise than momentarily, an object of desire to them.

Whoever supposes that this preference takes place at a sacrifice of happiness—that the superior being, in anything like equal circumstances, is not happier than the inferior—confounds the two very different ideas, of happiness, and content. It is indisputable that the being whose capacities of enjoyment are low, has the greatest chance of having them fully satisfied; and a highly endowed being will always feel that any happiness which he can look for, as the world is constituted, is imperfect.

But he can learn to bear its imperfections, if they are at all bearable; and they will not make him envy the being who is indeed unconscious of the imperfections, but only because he feels not at all the good which those imperfections qualify. It is better to be a human being dissatisfied than a pig satisfied; better to be Socrates dissatisfied than a fool satisfied. And if the fool, or the pig, are a different opinion, it is because they only know their own side of the question. The other party to the comparison knows both sides....

According to the Greatest Happiness Principle, as above explained, the ultimate end, with reference to and for the sake of which all other things are desirable (whether we are considering our own good or that of other people), is an existence exempt as far as possible from pain, and as rich as possible in enjoyments, both in point of quantity and quality; the test of quality, and the rule for measuring it against quantity, being the preference felt by those who in their opportunities of experience, to which must be added their habits of self-consciousness and self-observation, are best furnished with the means of comparison. This, being, according to the utilitarian opinion, the end of human action, is necessarily also the standard of morality; which may accordingly be defined, the rules and precepts for human conduct, by the observance of which an existence such as has been described might be, to the greatest extent possible, secured to all mankind; and not to them only, but, so far as the nature of things admits, to the whole sentient creation....

... [W]hat the assailants of utilitarianism seldom have the justice to acknowledge, that the happiness which forms the utilitarian standard of what is right in conduct, is not the agent's own happiness, but that of all concerned. As between his own happiness and that of others, utilitarianism requires him to be as strictly impartial as a disinterested and benevolent spectator. In the golden rule of Jesus of Nazareth, we read the complete spirit of the ethics of utility. To do as you would be done by, and to love your neighbour as yourself, constitute the ideal perfection of utilitarian morality. As the means of making the nearest approach to this ideal, utility would enjoin, first, that laws and social arrangements should place the happiness, or (as speaking practically it may be called) the interest, of every individual, as nearly as possible in harmony with the interest of the whole; and secondly, that education and opinion, which have so vast a power over human character, should so use that power as to establish in the mind of every individual an indissoluble association between his own happiness and the good of the whole; especially between his own happiness and the practice of such modes of conduct, negative and positive, as regard for the universal happiness prescribes; so that not only he may be unable to conceive the possibility of happiness to himself, consistently with conduct opposed to the general good, but also that a direct impulse to promote the general good may be in every individual one of the habitual motives of action, and the sentiments connected therewith may fill a large and prominent place in every human being's sentient existence. If the impugners of the utilitarian morality represented it to their own minds in this its, true character, I know not what recommendation possessed by any other morality they could possibly affirm to be wanting to it; what more beautiful or more exalted developments of human nature any other ethical system can be supposed to foster, or what springs of action, not accessible to the utilitarian, such systems rely on for giving effect to their mandates.

The objectors to utilitarianism cannot always be charged with representing it in a discreditable light. On the contrary, those among them who entertain anything like a just idea of its disinterested character, sometimes find fault with its standard as being too high for humanity. They say it is exacting too much to require that people shall always act from the inducement of promoting the general interests of society. But this is to mistake the very meaning of a standard of morals, and confound the rule of action with the motive of it. It is the business of ethics to tell us what are our duties, or by what test we may know them; but no system of ethics requires that the sole motive of all we do shall be a feeling of duty; on the contrary, ninety-nine hundredths of all our actions are done from other motives, and rightly so done, if the rule of duty does not condemn them. It is the more unjust to utilitarianism that this particular misapprehension should be made a ground of objection to it, inasmuch as utilitarian moralists have gone beyond almost all others in affirming that the motive has nothing to do with the morality of the action, though much with the worth of the agent. He who saves a fellow creature from drowning does what is morally right, whether his motive be duty, or the hope of being paid for his trouble; he who betrays the friend that trusts him, is guilty of a crime, even if his object be to serve another friend to whom he is under greater obligations....

We not uncommonly hear the doctrine of utility inveighed against as a godless doctrine. If it be necessary to say anything at all against so mere an assumption, we may say that the question depends upon what idea we have formed of the moral character of the Deity. If it be a true belief that God desires, above all things, the happiness of his creatures, and that this was his purpose in their creation, utility is not only not a godless doctrine, but more profoundly religious than any other. If it be meant that utilitarianism does not recognise the revealed will of God as the supreme law of morals, I answer, that a utilitarian who believes in the perfect goodness and wisdom of God, necessarily believes that whatever God has thought fit to reveal on the subject of morals, must fulfill the requirements of utility in a supreme degree. But others besides utilitarians have been of opinion that the Christian revelation was intended, and is fitted, to inform the hearts and minds of mankind with a spirit which should enable them to find for themselves what is right, and incline them to do it when found, rather than to tell them, except in a very general way, what it is; and that we need a doctrine of ethics, carefully followed out, to interpret to us the will [of] God....

Again, defenders of utility often find themselves called upon to reply to such objections as this—that there is not time, previous to action, for calculating and

weighing the effects of any line of conduct on the general happiness. This is exactly as if any one were to say that it is impossible to guide our conduct by Christianity, because there is not time, on every occasion on which anything has to be done, to read through the Old and New Testaments. The answer to the objection is, that there has been ample time, namely, the whole past duration of the human species. During all that time, mankind have been learning by experience the tendencies of actions; on which experience all the prudence, as well as all the morality of life, are dependent.... It is a strange notion that the acknowledgment of a first principle is inconsistent with the admission of secondary ones. To inform a traveller respecting the place of his ultimate destination, is not to forbid the use of landmarks and direction-posts on the way. The proposition that happiness is the end and aim of morality, does not mean that no road ought to be laid down to that goal, or that persons going thither should not be advised to take one direction rather than another.
...

THE QUESTION is often asked, and properly so, in regard to any supposed moral standard—What is its sanction? what are the motives to obey it? or more specifically, what is the source of its obligation? whence does it derive its binding force? It is a necessary part of moral philosophy to provide the answer to this question; which, though frequently assuming the shape of an objection to the utilitarian morality, as if it had some special applicability to that above others, really arises in regard to all standards. It arises, in fact, whenever a person is called on to adopt a standard, or refer morality to any basis on which he has not been accustomed to rest it. For the customary morality, that which education and opinion have consecrated, is the only one which presents itself to the mind with the feeling of being in itself obligatory; and when a person is asked to believe that this morality derives its obligation from some general principle round which custom has not thrown the same halo, the assertion is to him a paradox; the supposed corollaries seem to have a more binding force than the original theorem; the superstructure seems to stand better without, than with, what is represented as its foundation. He says to himself, I feel that I am bound not to rob or murder, betray or deceive; but why am I bound to promote the general happiness? If my own happiness lies in something else, why may I not give that the preference?

If the view adopted by the utilitarian philosophy of the nature of the moral sense be correct, this difficulty will always present itself, until the influences which form moral character have taken the same hold of the principle which they have taken of some of the consequences—until, by the improvement of education, the feeling of unity with our fellow-creatures shall be (what it cannot be denied that Christ intended it to be) as deeply rooted in our character, and to our own consciousness as completely a part of our nature, as the horror of crime is in an ordinarily well brought up young person....

Now, society between human beings, except in the relation of master and slave, is manifestly impossible on any other footing than that the interests of all are to be consulted. Society between equals can only exist on the understanding that the interests of all are to be regarded equally. And since in all states of civilisation, every person, except an absolute monarch, has equals, every one is obliged to live on these terms with somebody; and in every age some advance is made towards a state in which it will be impossible to live permanently on other terms with anybody. In this way people grow up unable to conceive as possible to them a state of total disregard of other people's interests. They are under a necessity of conceiving themselves as at least abstaining from all the grosser injuries, and (if only for their own protection) living in a state of constant protest against them. They are also familiar with the fact of co-operating with others and proposing to themselves a collective, not an individual interest as the aim (at least for the time being) of their actions. So long as they are co-operating, their ends are identified with those of others; there is at least a temporary feeling that the interests of others are their own interests. Not only does all strengthening of social ties, and all healthy growth of society, give to each individual a stronger personal interest in practically consulting the welfare of others; it also leads him to identify his feelings more and more with their good, or at least with an even greater degree of practical consideration for it. He comes, as though instinctively, to be conscious of himself as a being who of course pays regard to others. The good of others becomes to him a thing naturally and necessarily to be attended to, like any of the physical conditions of our existence. Now, whatever amount of this feeling a person has, he is urged by the strongest motives both of interest and of sympathy to demonstrate it, and to the utmost of his power encourage it in others; and even if he has none of it himself, he is as greatly interested as any one else that others should have it. Consequently the smallest germs of the feeling are laid hold of and nourished by the contagion of sympathy and the influences of education; and a complete web of corroborative association is woven round it, by the powerful agency of the external sanctions.

This mode of conceiving ourselves and human life, as civilisation goes on, is felt to be more and more natural. Every step in political improvement renders it more so, by removing the sources of opposition of interest, and levelling those inequalities of legal privilege between individuals or classes, owing to which there are large portions of mankind whose happiness it is still practicable to disregard. In an improving state of the human mind, the influences are constantly on the increase, which tend to generate in each individual a feeling of unity with all the rest; which, if perfect, would make him never think of, or desire, any beneficial condition for himself, in the benefits of which they are not included....

The deeply rooted conception which every individual even now has of himself as a social being, tends to make him feel it one of his natural wants that there should be harmony between his feelings and aims and those of his fellow creatures. If differences of opinion and of mental culture make it impossible for him to share many of their actual feelings—perhaps make him denounce and defy those feelings—he still needs to be conscious that his real aim and theirs do not conflict; that he is not opposing himself to what they really wish for, namely their own good, but is, on the contrary, promoting it. This feeling in most individuals is much inferior in strength to their selfish feelings, and is often wanting altogether. But to those who have it, it possesses all the characters of a natural feeling. It does not present itself to their minds as a superstition of education, or a law despotically imposed by the power of society, but as an attribute which it would not be well for them to be without. This conviction is the ultimate sanction of the greatest happiness morality.... This it is which makes any mind, of well-developed feelings, work with, and not against, the outward motives to care for others, afforded by what I have called the external sanctions; and when those sanctions are wanting, or act in an opposite direction, constitutes in itself a powerful internal binding force, in proportion to the sensitive-ness and thoughtfulness of the character; since few but those whose mind is a moral blank, could bear to lay out their course of life on the plan of paying no regard to others except so far as their own private interest compels.

2. An Egalitarian Theory of Justice*

John Rawls

The Role of Justice

Justice is the first virtue of social institutions, as truth is of systems of thought. A theory however elegant and economical must be rejected or revised if it is untrue; likewise laws and institutions no matter how efficient and well-arranged must be reformed or abolished if they are unjust. Each person possesses an inviolability founded on justice that even the welfare of society as a whole cannot override. For this reason justice denies that the loss of freedom for some is made right by a greater good shared by others. It does not allow that the sacrifices imposed on a few are outweighed by the larger sum of advantages enjoyed by many. Therefore in a just society the liberties of equal citizenship are taken as settled; the rights secured by justice are not subject to political bargaining or to the calculus of social interests. The only thing that permits us to acquiesce in an erroneous theory is the lack of a better one; analogously, an injustice is tolerable only when it is necessary to avoid an even greater injustice. Being first virtues of human activities, truth and justice are uncompromising.

These propositions seem to express our intuitive conviction of the primacy of justice. No doubt they are expressed too strongly. In any event I wish to inquire whether these contentions or others similar to them are sound, and if so how they can be accounted for. To this end it is necessary to work out a theory of justice in the light of which these assertions can be interpreted and assessed. I shall begin by considering the role of the principles of justice. Let us assume, to fix ideas, that a society is a more or less self-sufficient association of persons who in their relations to one another recognize certain rules of conduct as binding and who for the most part act in accordance with them. Suppose further that these rules specify a system of cooperation designed to advance the good of those taking part in it. Then, although

---

* Source: *A Theory of Justice* (Cambridge, MA: Harvard UP, 1971), pp. 3–4, 11–15, 18–19, 60–62, 64–65, 100–04, 274–77.

a society is a cooperative venture for mutual advantage, it is typically marked by a conflict as well as by an identity of interests. There is an identity of interests since social cooperation makes possible a better life for all than any would have if each were to live solely by his own efforts. There is a conflict of interests since persons are not indifferent as to how the greater benefits produced by their collaboration are distributed, for in order to pursue their ends they each prefer a larger to a lesser share. A set of principles is required for choosing among the various social arrangements which determine this division of advantages and for underwriting an agreement on the proper distributive shares. These principles are the principles of social justice: they provide a way of assigning rights and duties in the basic institutions of society and they define the appropriate distribution of the benefits and burdens of social cooperation.

The Main Idea of the Theory of Justice

My aim is to present a conception of justice which generalizes and carries to a higher level of abstraction the familiar theory of the social contract as found, say, in Locke, Rousseau, and Kant. In order to do this we are not to think of the original contract as one to enter a particular society or to set up a particular form of government. Rather, the guiding idea is that the principles of justice for the basic structure of society are the object of the original agreement. They are the principles that free and rational persons concerned to further their own interests would accept in an initial position of equality as defining the fundamental terms of their association. These principles are to regulate all further agreements; they specify the kinds of social cooperation that can be entered into and the forms of government that can be established. This way of regarding the principles of justice I shall call justice as fairness.

Thus we are to imagine that those who engage in social cooperation choose together, in one joint act, the principles which are to assign basic rights and duties and to determine the division of social benefits. Men are to decide in advance how they are to regulate their claims against one another and what is to be the foundation charter of their society. Just as each person must decide by rational reflection what constitutes his good, that is, the system of ends which it is rational for him to pursue, so a group of persons must decide once and for all what is to count among them as just and unjust. The choice which rational men would make in this hypothetical situation of equal liberty, assuming for the present that this choice problem has a solution, determines the principles of justice.

In justice as fairness the original position of equality corresponds to the state of nature in the traditional theory of the social contract. This original position is not, of course, thought of as an actual historical state of affairs, much less as a primitive condition of culture. It is understood as a purely hypothetical situation characterized so as to lead to a certain conception of justice. Among the essential features of this situation is that no one knows his place in society, his class position or social status, nor does any one know his fortune in the distribution of natural assets and abili-ties, his intelligence, strength, and the like. I shall even assume that the parties do not know their conceptions of the good or their special psychological propensities. The principles of justice are chosen behind a veil of ignorance. This ensures that no one is advantaged or disadvantaged in the choice of principles by the outcome of natural chance or the contingency of social circumstances. Since all are similarly situated and no one is able to design principles to favor his particular condition, the principles of justice are the result of a fair agreement or bargain. For given the circumstances of the original position, the symmetry of everyone's relations to each other, this initial situation is fair between individuals as moral persons, that is, as rational beings with their own ends and capable, I shall assume, of a sense of justice. The original position is, one might say, the appropriate initial status quo, and thus the fundamental agreements reached in it are fair. This explains the propriety of the name "justice as fairness": it conveys the idea that the principles of justice are agreed to in an initial situation that is fair. The name does not mean that the concepts of justice and fairness are the same, any more than the phrase "poetry as metaphor" means that the concepts of poetry and metaphor are the same.

Justice as fairness begins, as I have said, with one of the most general of all choices which persons might make together, namely, with the choice of the first principles of a conception of justice which is to regulate all subsequent criticism and reform of institutions. Then, having chosen a conception of justice, we can suppose that they are to choose a constitution and a legislature to enact laws, and so on, all in accordance with the principles of justice initially agreed upon. Our social situation is just if it is such that by this sequence of hypothetical agreements we would have contracted into the general system of rules which defines it.

...It may be observed, however, that once the principles of justice are thought of as arising from an original agreement in a situation of equality, it is an open question whether the principle of utility would be acknowledged. Offhand it hardly seems likely that persons who view themselves as equals, entitled to press their claims upon one another, would agree to a principle which may require lesser life prospects for some simply for the sake of a greater sum of advantages enjoyed by others. Since each desires to protect his interests, his capacity to advance his conception of the good, no one has a reason to acquiesce in an enduring loss for himself in order to bring about a greater net balance of satisfaction. In the absence of strong and last-ing benevolent impulses, a rational man would not accept a basic structure merely because it maximized the algebraic sum of advantages irrespective of its permanent effects on his own basic rights and interests. Thus it seems that the principle of utility is incompatible with the conception of social cooperation among equals for mutual advantage. It appears to be inconsistent with the idea of reciprocity implicit in the notion of a well-ordered society. Or, at any rate, so I shall argue.

I shall maintain instead that the persons in the initial situation would choose two rather different principles: the first requires equality in the assignment of basic rights and duties, while the second holds that social and economic inequalities, for example inequalities of wealth and authority, are just only if they result in compensating benefits for everyone, and in particular for the least advantaged members of society. These principles rule out justifying institutions on the grounds that the hardships of some are offset by a greater good in the aggregate. It may be expedient but it is not just that some should have less in order that others may prosper. But there is no injustice in the greater benefits earned by a few provided that the situation of persons not so fortunate is thereby improved. The intuitive idea is that since everyone's wellbeing depends upon a scheme of cooperation without which no one could have a satisfactory life, the division of advantages should be such as to draw forth the willing cooperation of everyone taking part in it, including those less well situated. Yet this can be expected only if reasonable terms are proposed. The two principles mentioned seem to be a fair agreement on the basis of which those better endowed, or more fortunate in their social position, neither of which we can be said to deserve, could expect the willing cooperation of others when some workable scheme is a necessary condition of the welfare of all. Once we decide to look for a conception of justice that nullifies the accidents of natural endowment and the contingencies of social circumstance as counters in quest for political and economic advantage, we are led to these principles. They express the result of leaving aside those aspects of the social world that seem arbitrary from a moral point of view....

The Original Position and Justification

...The idea here is simply to make vivid to ourselves the restrictions that it seems reasonable to impose on arguments for principles of justice, and therefore on these principles themselves. Thus it seems reasonable and generally acceptable that no one should be advantaged or disadvantaged by natural fortune or social circumstances in the choice of principles. It also seems widely agreed that it should be impossible to tailor principles to the circumstances of one's own case. We should insure further that particular inclinations and aspirations, and persons' conceptions of their good, do not affect the principles adopted. The aim is to rule out those principles that it would be rational to propose for acceptance, however little the chance of success, only if one knew certain things that are irrelevant from the standpoint of justice. For example, if a man knew that he was wealthy, he might find it rational to advance the principle that various taxes for welfare measures be counted unjust; if he knew that he was poor, he would most likely propose the contrary principle. To represent the desired restrictions one imagines a situation in which everyone is deprived of this sort of information. One excludes the knowledge of those contingencies which sets men at odds and allows them to be guided by their prejudices. In this manner the veil of ignorance is arrived at in a natural way....

Two Principles of Justice

I shall now state in a provisional form the two principles of justice that I believe would be chosen in the original position....

The first statement of the two principles reads as follows.

First: each person is to have an equal right to the most extensive basic liberty compatible with a similar liberty for others.

Second: social and economic inequalities are to be arranged so that they are both (a) reasonably expected to be to everyone's advantage, and (b) attached to positions and offices open to all.... [The Difference Principle]

By way of general comment, these principles primarily apply, as I have said, to the basic structure of society. They are to govern the assignment of rights and duties and to regulate the distribution of social and economic advantages. As their formulation suggests, these principles presuppose that the social structure can be divided into two more or less distinct parts, the first principle applying to the one, the second to the other. They distinguish between those aspects of the social system that define and secure the equal liberties of citizenship and those that specify and establish social and economic inequalities. The basic liberties of citizens are, roughly speaking, political liberty (the right to vote and to be eligible for public office) together with freedom of speech and assembly; liberty of conscience and freedom of thought; freedom of the person along with the right to hold (personal) property; and freedom from arbitrary arrest and seizure as defined by the concept of the rule of law. These liberties are all required to be equal by the first principle, since citizens of a just society are to have the same basic rights.

The second principle applies, in the first approximation, to the distribution of income and wealth and to the design of organizations that make use of differences in authority and responsibility, or chains of command. While the distribution of wealth and income need not be equal, it must be to everyone's advantage, and at the same time, positions of authority and offices of command must be accessible to all. One applies the second principle by holding positions open, and then, subject to this constraint, arranges social and economic inequalities so that everyone benefits.

These principles are to be arranged in a serial order with the first principle prior to the second. This ordering means that a departure from the institutions of equal liberty required by the first principle cannot be justified, or compensated for, by greater social and economic advantages. The distribution of wealth and income, and the hierarchies of authority, must be consistent with both the liberties of equal citizenship and equality of opportunity.

It is clear that these principles are rather specific in their content, and their acceptance rests on certain assumptions that I must eventually try to explain and justify. A theory of justice depends upon a theory of society in ways that will become evident as we proceed. For the present, it should be observed that the two principles (and this holds for all formulations) are a special case of a more general conception of justice that can be expressed as follows.

> All social values—liberty and opportunity, income and wealth, and the bases of self-respect—are to be distributed equally unless an unequal distribution of any, or all, of these values is to everyone's advantage.

Injustice, then, is simply inequalities that are not to the benefit of all. Of course, this conception is extremely vague and requires interpretation.

As a first step, suppose that the basic structure of society distributes certain primary goods, that is, things that every rational man is presumed to want. These goods normally have a use whatever a person's rational plan of life. For simplicity, assume that the chief primary goods at the disposition of society are rights and liberties, powers and opportunities, income and wealth. These are the social primary goods. Other primary goods such as health and vigor, intelligence and imagination, are natural goods; although their possession is influenced by the basic structure, they are not so directly under its control. Imagine, then, a hypothetical initial arrangement in which all the social primary goods are equally distributed: everyone has similar rights and duties, and income and wealth are evenly shared. This state of affairs provides a benchmark for judging improvements. If certain inequalities of wealth and organizational powers would make everyone better off than in this hypothetical starting situation, then they accord with the general conception.

Now it is possible, at least theoretically, that by giving up some of their fundamental liberties men are sufficiently compensated by the resulting social and economic gains. The general conception of justice imposes no restrictions on what sort of inequalities are permissible; it only requires that everyone's position be improved....

Now the second principle insists that each person benefit from permissible inequalities in the basic structure. This means that it must be reasonable for each relevant representative man defined by this structure, when he views it as a going concern, to prefer his prospects with the inequality to his prospects without it. One is not allowed to justify differences in income or organizational powers on the ground that the disadvantages of those in one position are out-weighed by the greater advantages of those in another. Much less can infringements of liberty be counterbalanced in this way. Applied to the basic structure, the principle of utility would have us maximize the sum of expectations of representative men (weighted by the number of persons they represent, on the classical view); and this would permit us to compensate for the losses of some by the gains of others. Instead, the two principles require that everyone benefit from economic and social inequalities....

The Tendency to Equality

I wish to conclude this discussion of the two principles by explaining the sense in which they express an egalitarian conception of justice. Also I should like to forestall the objection to the principle of fair opportunity that it leads to a callous merito-cratic society. In order to prepare the way for doing this, I note several aspects of the conception of justice that I have set out.

First we may observe that the difference principle gives some weight to the consid-erations singled out by the principle of redress. This is the principle that undeserved inequalities of birth and natural endowment are undeserved, these inequalities are to be somehow compensated for. Thus the principle holds that in order to treat all persons equally, to provide genuine equality of opportunity, society must give more attention to those with fewer native assets and to those born into the less favorable social positions. The idea is to redress the bias of contingencies in the direction of equality. In pursuit of this principle greater resources might be spent on the educa-tion of the less rather than the more intelligent, at least over a certain time of life, say the earlier years of school.

Now the principle of redress has not to my knowledge been proposed as the sole criterion of justice, as the single aim of the social order. It is plausible as most such principles are only as a prima facie principle, one that is to be weighed in the bal-ance with others. For example, we are to weigh it against the principle to improve the average standard of life, or to advance the common good. But whatever other principles we hold, the claims of redress are to be taken into account. It is thought to represent one of the elements in our conception of justice. Now the difference principle is not of course the principle of redress. It does not require society to try to even out handicaps as if all were expected to compete on a fair basis in the same race. But the difference principle would allocate resources in education, say, so as to improve the long-term expectation of the least favored. If this end is attained by giving more attention to the better endowed, it is permissible; otherwise not. And in making this decision, the value of education should not be assessed only in terms of economic efficiency and social welfare. Equally if not more important is the role of education in enabling a person to enjoy the culture of his society and to take part in its affairs, and in this way to provide for each individual a secure sense of his own worth.

Thus although the difference principle is not the same as that of redress, it does achieve some of the intent of the latter principle. It transforms the aims of the basic structure so that the total scheme of institutions no longer emphasizes social effi-ciency and technocratic values....

...The natural distribution is neither just nor unjust; nor is it unjust that men are born into society at some particular position. These are simply natural facts. What is just and unjust is the way that institutions deal with these facts. Aristocratic and caste societies are unjust because they make these contingencies the ascriptive basis for belonging to more or less enclosed and privileged social classes. The basic structure of these societies incorporates the arbitrariness found in nature. But there is no necessity for men to resign themselves to these contingencies. The social system is not an unchangeable order beyond human control but a pattern of human action. In justice as fairness men agree to share one another's fate. In designing institutions they undertake to avail themselves of the accidents of nature and social circumstance only when doing so is for the common benefit. The two principles are a fair way of meeting the arbitrariness of fortune; and while no doubt imperfect in other ways, the institutions which satisfy these principles are just....

There is a natural inclination to object that those better situated deserve their greater advantages whether or not they are to the benefit of others. At this point it is necessary to be clear about the notion of desert. It is perfectly true that given a just system of cooperation as a scheme of public rules and the expectations set up by it, those who, with the prospect of improving their condition, have done what the system announces that it will reward are entitled to their advantages. In this sense the more fortunate have a claim to their better situation; their claims are legitimate expectations established by social institutions, and the community is obligated to meet them. But this sense of desert presupposes the existence of the cooperative scheme; it is irrelevant to the question whether in the first place the scheme is to be designed in accordance with the difference principle or some other criterion.

Perhaps some will think that the person with greater natural endowments deserves those assets and the superior character that made their development possible. Because he is more worthy in this sense, he deserves the greater advantages that he could achieve with them. This view, however, is surely incorrect. It seems to be one of the fixed points of our considered judgments that no one deserves his place in the distribution of native endowments, any more than one deserves one's initial starting place in society. The assertion that a man deserves the superior character that enables him to make the effort to cultivate his abilities is equally problematic, for his character depends in large part upon fortunate family and social circumstances for which he can claim no credit. The notion of desert seems not to apply to these cases. Thus the more advantaged representative man cannot say that he deserves and therefore has a right to a scheme of cooperation in which he is permitted to acquire benefits in ways that do not contribute to the welfare of others. There is no basis for his making this claim. From the standpoint of common sense, then, the difference principle appears to be acceptable both to the more advantaged and to the less advantaged individual....

Background Institutions for Distributive Justice

The main problem of distributive justice is the choice of a social system. The principles of justice apply to the basic structure and regulate how its major institutions are combined into one scheme. Now, as we have seen, the idea of justice as fairness is to use the notion of pure procedural justice to handle the contingencies of particular situations. The social system is to be designed so that the resulting distribution is just however things turn out. To achieve this end it is necessary to get the social and economic process within the surroundings of suitable political and legal institutions. Without an appropriate scheme of these background institutions the outcome of the distributive process will not be just. Background fairness is lacking. I shall give a brief description of these supporting institutions as they might exist in a properly organized democratic state that allows private ownership of capital and natural resources....

In establishing these background institutions the government may be thought of as divided into four branches.[1] Each branch consists of various agencies, or activities thereof, charged with preserving certain social and economic conditions. These divisions do not overlap with the usual organization of government but are to be understood as different functions. The allocation branch, for example, is to keep the price system workably competitive and to prevent the formation of unreasonable market power. Such power does not exist as long as markets cannot be made more competitive consistent with the requirements of efficiency and the facts of geography and the preferences of households. The allocation branch is also charged with identifying and correcting, say by suitable taxes and subsidies and by changes in the definition of property rights, the more obvious departures from efficiency caused by the failure of prices to measure accurately social benefits and costs. To this end suitable taxes and subsidies may be used, or the scope and definition of property rights may be revised. The stabilization branch, on the other hand, strives to bring about reasonably full employment in the sense that those who want work can find it and the free choice of occupation and the deployment of finance are supported by strong effective demand. These two branches together are to maintain the efficiency of the market economy generally.

The social minimum is the responsibility of the transfer branch.... The essential idea is that the workings of this branch take needs into account and assign them an appropriate weight with respect to other claims. A competitive price system gives no consideration to needs and therefore it cannot be the sole device of distribution. There must be a division of labor between the parts of the social system in answering to the common sense precepts of justice. Different institutions meet different claims. Competitive markets properly regulated secure free choice of occupation and lead to an efficient use of resources and allocation of commodities to households. They set a weight on the conventional precepts associated with wages and warnings, whereas the transfer branch guarantees a certain level of well-being and honors the claims of need....

---

1 For the idea of branches of government, see R.A. Musgrave, *The Theory of Public Finance* (New York: McGraw-Hill, 1959), ch. I.

It is clear that the justice of distributive shares depends on the background institutions and how they allocate total income, wages and other income plus transfers. There is with reason strong objection to the competitive determination of total income, since this ignores the claims of need and an appropriate standard of life. From the standpoint of the legislative stage it is rational to insure oneself and one's descendants against these contingencies of the market. Indeed, the difference principle presumably requires this. But once a suitable minimum is provided by transfers, it may be perfectly fair that the rest of total income be settled by the price system, assuming that it is moderately efficient and free from monopolistic restrictions, and unreasonable externalities have been eliminated. Moreover, this way of dealing with the claims of need would appear to be more effective than trying to regulate income by minimum wage standards, and the like. It is better to assign to each branch only such tasks as are compatible with one another. Since the market is not suited to answer the claims of need, these should be met by a separate arrangement. Whether the principles of justice are satisfied, then, turns on whether the total income of the least advantaged (wages plus transfers) is such as to maximize their long-run expectations (consistent with the constraints of equal liberty and fair equality of opportunity).

Finally, there is a distribution branch. Its task is to preserve an approximate justice in distributive shares by means of taxation and the necessary adjustments in the rights of property. Two aspects of this branch may be distinguished. First of all, it imposes a number of inheritance and gift taxes, and sets restrictions on the rights of bequest. The purpose of these levies and regulations is not to raise revenue (release resources to government) but gradually and continually to correct the distribution of wealth and to prevent concentrations of power detrimental to the fair value of political liberty and fair equality of opportunity. For example, the progressive principle might be applied at the beneficiary's end.[2] Doing this would encourage the wide dispersal of property which is a necessary condition, it seems, if the fair value of the equal liberties is to be maintained.

---

2 See Meade, *Efficiency, Equality and the Ownership of Property* (London: G. Allen & Unwin, 1964), pp. 56f.

3. The Entitlement Theory*

Robert Nozick

The term "distributive justice" is not a neutral one. Hearing the term "distribution," most people presume that some thing or mechanism uses some principle or criterion to give out a supply of things. Into this process of distributing shares some error may have crept. So it is an open question, at least, whether *re*distribution should take place; whether we should do again what has already been done once, though poorly. However, we are not in the position of children who have been given portions of pie by someone who now makes last minute adjustments to rectify careless cutting. There is no *central* distribution, no person or group entitled to control all the resources, jointly deciding how they are to be doled out. What each person gets, he gets from others who give to him in exchange for something, or as a gift. In a free society, diverse persons control different resources, and new holdings arise out of the voluntary exchanges and actions of persons....

The subject of justice in holdings consists of three major topics. The first is the *original acquisition of holdings*, the appropriation of unheld things. This includes the issues of how unheld things may come to be held, the process, or processes, by which unheld things may come to be held, the things that may come to be held by these processes, the extent of what comes to be held by a particular person, and so on. We shall refer to the complicated truth about this topic, which we shall not formulate here, as the principle of justice in acquisition. The second topic concerns the *transfer of holdings* from one person to another. By what processes may a person transfer holdings to another? How may a person acquire a holding from another who holds it? Under this topic come general descriptions of voluntary exchange, and gift and (on the other hand) fraud, as well as reference to particular conventional details fixed upon in a given society. The complicated truth about this subject (with place-holders for conventional details) we shall call the principle of justice in transfer.

* Source: *Anarchy, State and Utopia* (New York: Basic Books, 1974), pp. 149–54, 156–57, 159–63, 168, 174–75, 178–79, 182.

(And we shall suppose it also includes principles governing how a person may divest himself of a holding, passing it into an unheld state.)

If the world were wholly just, the following inductive definition would exhaustively cover the subject of justice in holdings.

1. A person who acquires a holding in accordance with the principle of justice in acquisition is entitled to that holding.
2. A person who acquires a holding in accordance with the principle of justice in transfer, from someone else entitled to the holding, is entitled to the holding.
3. No one is entitled to a holding except by (repeated) applications of 1 and 2.

The complete principle of distributive justice would say simply that a distribution is just if everyone is entitled to the holdings they possess under the distribution . . . .

Not all actual situations are generated in accordance with the two principles of justice in holdings: the principle of justice in acquisition and the principle of justice in transfer. Some people steal from others, or defraud them, or enslave them, seizing their product and preventing them from living as they choose, or forcibly exclude others from competing in exchanges. None of these are permissible modes of transition from one situation to another. And some persons acquire holdings by means not sanctioned by the principle of justice in acquisition. The existence of past injustice (previous violations of the first two principles of justice in holdings) raises the third major topic under justice in holdings: the rectification of injustice in holdings. If past injustice has shaped present holdings in various ways, some identifiable and some not, what now, if anything, ought to be done to rectify these injustices? . . .

Historical Principles and End-Result Principles

The general outlines of the entitlement theory illuminate the nature and defects of other conceptions of distributive justice. The entitlement theory of justice in distribution is *historical*; whether a distribution is just depends upon how it came about. In contrast, *current time-slice principles* of justice hold that the justice of a distribution is determined by how things are distributed (who has what) as judged by some *structural* principle(s) of just distribution. A utilitarian who judges between any two distributions by seeing which has the greater sum of utility and, if the sums tie, applies some fixed equality criterion to choose the more equal distribution, would hold a current time-slice principle of justice. As would someone who had a fixed schedule of trade-offs between the sum of happiness and equality. According to a current time-slice principle, all that needs to be looked at, in judging the justice of a distribution, is who ends up with what; in comparing any two distributions one need look only at the matrix presenting the distributions. No further information need be fed into a principle of justice. It is a consequence of such principles of justice that any two structurally identical distributions are equally just . . . .

Most persons do not accept current time-slice principles as constituting the whole story about distributive shares. They think it relevant in assessing the justice of a situation to consider not only the distribution it embodies, but also how that distribution came about. If some persons are in prison for murder or war crimes, we do not say that to assess the justice of the distribution in the society we must look only at what this person has, and that person has, and that person has…at the current time. We think it relevant to ask whether someone did something so that he *deserved* to be punished, deserved to have a lower share….

Patterning

…Almost every suggested principle of distributive justice is patterned: to each according to his moral merit, or needs, or marginal product, or how hard he tries, or the weighted sum of the foregoing, and so on. The principle of entitlement we have sketched is not patterned. There is no one natural dimension or weighted sum or combination of a small number of natural dimensions that yields the distributions generated in accordance with the principle of entitlement. The set of holdings that results when some persons receive their marginal products, others win at gambling, others receive a share of their mate's income, others receive gifts from foundations, others receive interest on loans, others receive gifts from admirers, others receive returns on investment, others make for themselves much of what they have, others find things, and so on, will not be patterned….

To think that the task of a theory of distributive justice is to fill in the blank in "to each according to his ____" is to be predisposed to search for a pattern; and the separate treatment of "from each according to his ____" treats production and distribution as two separate and independent issues. On an entitlement view these are *not* two separate questions. Whoever makes something, having bought or contracted for all other held resources used in the process (transferring some of his holdings for these cooperating factors), is entitled to it….

So entrenched are maxims of the usual form that perhaps we should present the entitlement conception as a competitor. Ignoring acquisition and rectification, we might say:

> From each according to what he chooses to do, to each according to what he makes for himself (perhaps with the contracted aid of others) and what others choose to do for him and choose to give him of what they've been given previously (under this maxim) and haven't yet expended or transferred.

This, the discerning reader will have noticed, has its defects as a slogan. So as a summary and great simplification (and not as a maxim with any independent meaning) we have:

> From each as they choose, to each as they are chosen.

How Liberty Upsets Patterns

It is not clear how those holding alternative conceptions of distributive justice can reject the entitlement conception of justice in holdings. For suppose a distribution favored by one of these non-entitlement conceptions is realized. Let us suppose it is your favorite one and let us call this distribution D1; perhaps everyone has an equal share, perhaps shares vary in accordance with some dimension you treasure. Now suppose that Wilt Chamberlain is greatly in demand by basketball teams, being a great gate attraction. (Also suppose contracts run only for a year, with players being free agents.) He signs the following sort of contract with a team: In each home game, twenty-five cents from the price of each ticket of admission goes to him. (We ignore the question of whether he is "gouging" the owners, letting them look out for themselves.) The season starts, and people cheerfully attend his team's games; they buy their tickets, each time dropping a separate twenty-five cents of their admission price into a special box with Chamberlain's name on it. They are excited about seeing him play; it is worth the total admission price to them. Let us suppose that in one season one million persons attend his home games, and Wilt Chamberlain winds up with $250,000, a much larger sum than the average income and larger even than anyone else has. Is he entitled to this income? Is this new distribution D2, unjust? If so, why? There is no question about whether each of the people was entitled to the control over the resources they held in D1; because that was the distribution (your favorite) that (for the purposes of argument) we assumed was acceptable. Each of these persons chose to give twenty-five cents of their money to Chamberlain. They could have spent it on going to the movies, or on candy bars, or on copies of *Dissent* magazine, or of *Monthly Review*. But they all, at least one million of them, converged on giving it to Wilt Chamberlain in exchange for watching him play basketball. If D1 was a just distribution, and people voluntarily moved from it to D2, transferring parts of their shares they were given under D1 (what was it for if not to do something with?), isn't D2 also just? If the people were entitled to dispose of the resources to which they were entitled (under D1), didn't this include their being entitled to give it to, or exchange it with, Wilt Chamberlain? Can anyone else complain on grounds of justice? Each other person already has his legitimate share under D1. Under D1, there is nothing that anyone has that anyone else has a claim of justice against. After someone transfers something to Wilt Chamberlain, third parties still have their legitimate shares; their shares are not changed. By what process could such a transfer among two persons give a rise to a legitimate claim of distributive justice on a portion of what was transferred, by a third party who had no claim of justice on any holding of the others before the transfer? To cut off objections irrelevant here, we might imagine the exchanges occurring in a socialist society, after hours. After playing whatever basketball he does in his daily work, or doing whatever other daily work he does, Wilt Chamberlain decides to put in overtime to earn additional money. (First his work quota is set; he works time over that.) Or imagine it is a skilled juggler people like to see, who puts on shows after hours....

The general point illustrated by the Wilt Chamberlain example is that no end-state principle or distributional patterned principle of justice can be continuously realized without continuous interference with people's lives. Any favored pattern would be transformed into one unfavored by the principle, by people choosing to act in various ways; for example, by people exchanging goods and services with other people, or giving things to other people, things the transferrers are entitled to under the favored distributional pattern. To maintain a pattern one must either continually interfere to stop people from transferring resources as they wish to, or continually (or periodically) interfere to take from some person's resources that others for some reason chose to transfer to them....

Patterned principles of distributive justice necessitate redistributive activities. The likelihood is small that any actual freely-arrived-at set of holdings fits a given pattern; and the likelihood is nil that it will continue to fit the pattern as people exchange and give. From the point of view of an entitlement theory, redistribution is a serious matter indeed, involving, as it does, the violation of people's rights. (An exception is those takings that fall under the principle of the rectification of injustices.)...

Locke's Theory of Acquisition

... [Let us] introduce an additional bit of complexity into the structure of the entitlement theory. This is best approached by considering Locke's attempt to specify a principle of justice in acquisition. Locke views property rights in an unowned object as originating through someone's mixing his labor with it. This gives rise to many questions. What are the boundaries of what labor is mixed with? If a private astronaut clears a place on Mars, has he mixed his labor with (so that he comes to own) the whole planet, the whole uninhabited universe, or just a particular plot? Which plot does an act bring under ownership?...

Locke's proviso that there be "enough and as good left in common for others" is meant to ensure that the situation of others is not worsened.... I assume that any adequate theory of justice in acquisition will contain a proviso similar to [Locke's]....

I believe that the free operation of a market system will not actually run afoul of the Lockean proviso.... If this is correct, the proviso will not...provide a significant opportunity for future state action.

4. The Right to Be Rich or Poor*

Peter Singer

When times are hard and governments are looking for ways to reduce expenditure, a book like *Anarchy, State, and Utopia* is about the last thing we need. That will be the reaction of some readers to this book. It is, of course, an unfair reaction, since a work of philosophy that consists of rigorous argument and needle-sharp analysis with absolutely none of the unsupported vague waffle that characterizes too many philosophy books must be welcomed whatever we think of its conclusions. The chances of Gerald Ford reasoning his way through Nozick's book to the conviction that he ought to cut back the activities of the state in fields like welfare, education, and health are not high. The book will probably do more good in raising the level of philosophical discussion than it will do harm in practical politics.

Robert Nozick's book is a major event in contemporary political philosophy. There has, in recent years, been no sustained and competently argued challenge to the prevailing conceptions of social justice and the role of the state. Political philosophers have tended to assume without argument that justice demands an extensive redistribution of wealth in the direction of equality; and that it is a legitimate function of the state to bring about this redistribution by coercive means like progressive taxation. These assumptions may be correct; but after *Anarchy, State, and Utopia* they will need to be defended and argued for instead of being taken for granted.

Anarchy, State, and Utopia falls into three sections, as its title indicates. Part I tries to show that a minimal type of state—the "nightwatchman" state of classical liberal theory, limited to protecting its citizens against force and fraud—can arise legitimately, without violating anyone's rights. In the second part Nozick argues that the minimal state is the most extensive state that can be justified and that any more extensive state does violate people's rights. The book ends with a section contending that the minimal state is, harsh appearances notwithstanding, an ideal worth fighting for.

---

* Source: Rev. of *Anarchy, State, and Utopia,* by Robert Nozick. *The New York Review of Books* 23.2 (March 1975), <http://www.nybooks.com/articles/9252>.

All three sections are well worth reading, although the third is the slightest. Here Nozick, finding incredible the supposition that there is one best form of society for everyone, proposes instead a "meta-utopia"—a framework for many diverse utopian experiments, all formed of voluntary communities, so that no one can impose his version of utopia on others. Within a community people may voluntarily adopt redistributive measures, and those refusing to participate may be excluded from the community; but within a nation, which would include many communities, there should be no compulsory redistribution. The idea is appealing because it enhances individual freedom. But there are serious objections that are not adequately considered. Could a community that wanted a lot of redistribution survive the departure of the wealthy members whose moral principles are weaker than their desire for wealth? Could it withstand the pressure of applications to join from the down-and-outs left to starve in neighboring communities run by ruthless capitalists?

Or, to take a different kind of objection, could a community maintain its dedication to an austere life of virtue if it were surrounded by the flashy temptations of American capitalism? Nozick would say that the choice between austere virtue and flashy temptation must be left to the individual; but doesn't this assume an ability to make free rational choices that most people simply do not possess? Is the free flow of information sufficient to wash away the encrusted muck of billions of dollars worth of advertising for a style of life devoted to the acquisition of consumer goods and the elimination of stains and odors? Nozick's vision of utopia fails to deal with the fundamental Marxist objection to classical liberalism: people may make choices, but they do so under given historical circumstances which influence their choices. We do not enable people to govern their lives by giving them a "free" choice within these limits while refusing to do anything about the contexts in which these choices are made.

To say this smacks of paternalism and has unpleasant totalitarian associations. But what if the choice lies not between paternalism and freedom, but between making a deliberate attempt to control the circumstances under which we live and allowing these circumstances to develop haphazardly, permitting only an illusory sense of individual liberty? I ask the question seriously, not rhetorically. Perhaps it can be answered, but Nozick passes it by with a fleeting reference to Tocqueville's idea that being free develops the capacity for freedom, and this reply does not touch the heart of the issue.

The arguments of Part I are directed mainly against the anarchist who objects to any state at all. Nozick does not say that a state is a good thing and we are all better off with a state than we would be without one. This obvious procedure for dealing with the anarchist would be foreign to Nozick's entire approach and would set a precedent subversive of his aim in the second part. Instead he maintains that we can get from a state of nature to a minimal state without violating anyone's rights, so that there is no point at which anyone can claim that the state has assumed authority illegitimately. Nozick begins his story in a state of nature modeled on that of John

Locke, but he leaves this natural condition by another route, avoiding the need for the agreement or social contract that has been a source of so much criticism for Locke and his followers.

Nozick's minimal state, or "state-like entity" as he sometimes calls it, is a kind of protection agency to which people in the state of nature pay a fee for protection from assault, robbery, and so on. Nozick argues plausibly that clients of the agency would give up to the agency their rights to punish violations of their rights, and that one protective association, or federation of protective associations, would become dominant in each geographical territory. So, without any express agreements or over-all intention on anyone's part, people in the state of nature would find themselves with a body that satisfies two fundamental conditions for being a state: it has a monopoly of force in its territory, and it protects the rights of everyone within the territory.

Together with the story of the development of the state in the first part there are many other interesting subsidiary discussions. There are sensible answers to such puzzling questions (for laissez-faire liberals) as why blackmail (payment for the service of silence about another's affairs) should be prohibited; and why, for that matter, we should ever prohibit anything, rather than allow violations of rights provided that the victims are adequately compensated. Although Nozick admits that the book contains no full-scale presentation of the moral basis for his views, there is some unorthodox moral philosophy, including a lengthy discussion of the place of nonhuman animals in morality. Nozick thereby becomes one of the small but growing number of contemporary philosophers who have given this neglected topic genuine consideration, and he joins those who urge radical changes in our treatment of nonhumans, including the recommendation that we stop eating them.[1]

Interesting as the first part is, for those of us who have little difficulty in accepting the moral legitimacy of some minimal kind of state, the excitement begins only when we enter the second part. A reader who is sympathetic to government policies designed to redistribute wealth and who has taken for granted the justice of such policies will be surprised at the strength of the arguments Nozick brings against this view.

One book cannot deal with all the reasons that have been urged in support of extending the functions of the state beyond the protection of its citizens against force and fraud. Therefore Nozick selects what he considers the strongest, and most widely accepted, case: the claim that a more extensive state is justified in order to achieve justice in the distribution of wealth. It is this claim that receives the brunt of his attack on the extended state.

Nozick uses the term "holdings" to describe the goods, money, and property of all kinds that people have. The issue, then, is what holdings people would have in a just society.

---

1 Some other philosophers who have written on this issue are included in *Animals, Men and Morals*, edited by S. and R. Godlovitch and J. Harris (Taplinger, 1973). See my review in *The New York Review*, April 5, 1973.

The position Nozick takes is a radical departure from the theories of distributive justice discussed by most philosophers, especially in recent years. Nozick characterizes the principles of justice usually advocated as "patterned." A patterned distribution is one which (to put the matter more loosely than Nozick does) can be summed up in some simple formula of the type: "To all according to his ———." The blank can be filled in by "need," "labor," "moral desert," "IQ," "noble blood," or whatever—the result will always be a patterned distribution. In any existing society, the distribution of wealth will presumably not correspond exactly to any preordained pattern, so that to achieve a just society we shall have to take a bit from here and give a bit there, until people's holdings correspond to what we think is the right pattern.

In contrast to all patterned theories, Nozick proposes the "entitlement theory": a distribution is just if it arises from a prior just distribution by legitimate means. Basically, you originally acquire something justly if you take something that belongs to nobody, without thereby making worse the position of others no longer able to use the thing. (For example, I can appropriate land for myself if it is unowned and there is enough good land left for others.) Here Nozick again follows Locke, although his account is more precise. Then there are legitimate ways of transferring things you own, especially voluntary exchange and gift. As a result there is no pattern to which a just distribution must conform. People may choose to retain what they start with, or give some of it, or all of it, away. They may make profitable investments, or unprofitable ones. They may live frugally and hoard what they have, or dissipate it in a wild spree. They may gamble. So long as their original holdings were justly acquired, and the decisions they made involved neither force nor fraud, the result will be just no matter how widely people's holdings vary. The entitlement theory of justice makes the justice of a given set of holdings depend on the history of those holdings, and not on the conformity of the outcome to a given pattern.

Both the strengths and the weaknesses of the entitlement theory are immediately apparent. On the one hand, can it really be just that one baby should come into the world with a multi-million-dollar trust fund, the best possible schooling, and family connections with the nation's leading politicians and financiers awaiting him, while another baby faces life in a dingy apartment with no money and nothing else to help him on his way in the world? Neither baby at the moment of birth can possibly deserve anything; an equal division would therefore seem the only just one.

On the other hand, if the father of the first baby acquired his holdings legitimately, violating no one's rights in the process, doesn't he have the liberty to give whatever is his to his son, if he should so choose? Isn't it implied in someone's owning something that he has the right to do with it what he will, provided he violates no one else's rights? And surely it is far-fetched to hold that the poorer baby has a *right* to some of the other baby's wealth, merely because his ancestors were less fortunate, less astute, or less frugal in their handling of their holdings.

Our intuitions lead us in both directions. One must be wrong. Nozick tries to convince us that it is the former set of intuitions—those relating to the injustice of inherited wealth and other inherited assets—that we should give up. He does not attempt the hopeless task of arguing that those born with large fortunes or valuable natural talents have done anything to deserve these assets. Nevertheless, he says, people are entitled to their inherited assets, whether or not they deserve them. In the case of wealth he points out that orthodox theories of justice overlook the right of the donor when they consider the worthiness of the recipient of the inheritance. As for natural talents, people do not violate anyone else's rights by having the natural talents they are born with. An artist has the right to keep a painting he has done even if his artistic talent was inherited and he did nothing to deserve it. So why shouldn't a born entrepreneur have a similar right to the fortune his talents have brought him through legitimate means?

The legitimacy of redistribution in the direction of equality is, as Nozick says, more often assumed than argued for. We discover that, say, the wealthiest 5 percent of the population hold 40 percent of the national wealth, and then we ask what can be done about it. On the entitlement view these facts do not in themselves suggest that we ought to do anything. It all depends on how the present distribution came about. It might have come about by unjust means, through force and fraud, or through an unjust original acquisition, in which case reparations should be paid to those who are now worse off because of this injustice (though Nozick is unable to explain how we decide whether a person's ancestor left sufficient good land for others when he appropriated his first field five hundred years ago). But the present distribution might also have come about entirely legitimately, in which case the compulsory redistribution of wealth would be a serious violation of people's rights.

Nozick's position sounds severe, and so it is. According to Nozick we have no obligation to help those worse off than we are. If a starving man drags himself to our house, where we are entertaining our friends with a sumptuous banquet, we are perfectly within our rights in sending him away without a crust. In mitigation, though, it is important to remember that Nozick has nothing against voluntary donations from the rich to the poor. The rich are within their rights to keep everything they have and throw what they cannot use down the sewer; but they also have the right to give everything away, and the generous and charitable will no doubt give some away.

Indeed, on the question of voluntary donations Nozick has some interesting points to make. He argues, I think conclusively, that those relatively wealthy people who advocate greater government redistribution (which would take from people like themselves and give to those poorer) can have no sound reason for not making, while they wait for the government to act, voluntary donations from their own pockets of the sum that would be taxed from them under the scheme they advocate. Presumably this argument applies to those who advocate greater government foreign aid, as well as to those who limit themselves to internal redistribution.

An ingenious illustration buttresses the entitlement theory. We start by supposing that holdings are distributed in accordance with some patterned conception of justice—let's say the conception of equality, so that everyone has exactly equal holdings. Now suppose that several basketball teams would like to have Wilt Chamberlain playing for them. He signs a special contract with one, stipulating that he gets twenty-five cents from the price of every home game ticket. The fans are happy to pay the surcharge; the excitement of seeing Chamberlain play is worth it to them. One million people attend during the season, so that Chamberlain winds up with $250,000, far more than anyone else in the society.

The transactions between Chamberlain and his fans have upset the original, hypothetically just, pattern of holdings; but, Nozick asks, is the new distribution unjust, and if so, why? Can it be a source of injustice that a million people chose to spend twenty-five cents on seeing Chamberlain play, rather than on candy bars or magazines? Since they chose to spend it in this way, knowing that it would go to Chamberlain, surely they can have no just claim against the man they have made rich. As for those citizens who did not attend the games, their holdings are entirely unaffected by the transactions between Chamberlain and his fans. If these third parties had no just claim against the holdings of the transacting parties before the payments took place, how can the transfer give them a just claim to part of what was transferred? Yet that is precisely what those who accept taxation for redistributive purposes must believe.

In general, Nozick says, no patterned principle of justice can prevail without continuous interference in people's lives. A socialist society would, as he puts it, have to "forbid capitalist acts between consenting adults."

I have been able to indicate only the main strand of Nozick's argument. There are many fascinating sidelines as well. For instance Nozick is able to show that if workers' control of factories is desirable, it will be possible to establish it within the framework of his theory, by voluntary action. Indeed, he points out, the larger trade unions already have sufficient financial reserves to set up worker-controlled enterprises; and even smaller groups, or a single wealthy radical, could do the same, especially since consumers who favor worker-controlled enterprises could band together and buy only from these companies. Why, Nozick asks pointedly, has this not happened?

Nozick also challenges the view that greater equality will produce an equality of self-esteem and the elimination of envy. Self-esteem, he claims, is based on criteria that differentiate; if these criteria are equalized it will need to be based on something else. Trotsky's vision of a communist society in which the ordinary man is able to fulfill his potential to such an extent that he becomes an Aristotle, a Goethe, or a Marx does not mean that the ordinary man will have greater self-esteem. New peaks will rise beyond the heights of Aristotle-Goethe-Marx, the ordinary man will think of himself as just another Aristotle-like commoner, and envy the new super-Aristotles.

There is also some hard-headed discussion of the Marxist idea of exploitation and the labor theory of value. On these side issues Nozick may not always be right, but he is always stimulating; an open-minded study of what he has to say could be a healthy tonic for romantic leftists.

On the main issue, what I have said should be enough to show that Nozick's case against compulsory redistribution is strong. Can it be met, and if so, how?

The first question here is whether to attempt to meet Nozick on the ground he has chosen—ground clearly indicated in the very first sentence of *Anarchy, State, and Utopia*: "Individuals have rights, and there are things no person or group may do to them (without violating their rights)."

So we must decide whether to try to show that a system of justice based on individual rights, including a right to property, can permit—or require—compulsory redistribution; or, on the other hand, to deny that individuals have the rights that Nozick says they have, in the strong sense of the term that he intends.

In raising this question we come back to the most basic division between moral and political philosophers of modern times. For centuries there have been two lines of thought about justice. According to utilitarian theory, espoused by David Hume, Jeremy Bentham, and later utilitarians, principles of justice are rules that work for the greater good of all. They are governed by the principles of utility. If we take from the rich and give to the poor we do so not because the poor are entitled to some of what the rich have but because the poor will benefit more from this redistribution than the rich will suffer. The utilitarian who is not trying to hedge will admit that his account of justice allows property to be confiscated from one person so that another, or several others, may benefit.

The alternative view of justice associated with John Locke and Immanuel Kant starts with individual rights and prohibits the use of one person as a means to another's end. The incorporation of Lockean rights into the Declaration of Independence and the Constitution of the United States ensured the dominance of this tradition in the political rhetoric and in the moral, legal, and political thinking of this country. There is a certain appropriateness in the fact that Nozick's chief opponent within this tradition is the American philosopher, his Harvard colleague, John Rawls.

In his recent and widely celebrated book, *A Theory of Justice*, Rawls tried to develop a conception of justice that would be an alternative to utilitarianism, taking seriously "the distinction between persons" (which he claims utilitarianism, in subordinating individual rights to the general good, does not do) and ruling out "even the tendency to regard men as means to one another's welfare." The problem Rawls faced, however, was how to square this with his intuitive conviction that justice requires us to improve the condition of the poorest members of our society, whose poverty is not really their own fault.

Rawls attempted to solve this problem by arguing that if people in what he calls "the original position"—a hypothetical state of nature in which, to ensure impartial decision-making, people are assumed to be ignorant of their own talents and socio-economic status—were to choose the fundamental principles of justice to be followed in a newly formed society, one of the principles they would choose would be that inequalities are allowable only in so far as they improve the position of the worst-off group in the society.

Rawls thinks that people in the original position would make this principle—which has been called the maximin rule, because it seeks to maximize the minimum level of welfare existing in the society—subordinate to another principle guaranteeing maximum equal liberty for all. Whether they would give this priority to liberty need not concern us here, since we are considering only economic redistribution.

Rawls's maximin principle is compatible with considerable inequality. If, as some economists argue, steeply progressive taxation reduces the incentive to work of the most talented members of society to the point where they contribute less to the society and everyone, including the worst-off, suffers, then it would be just, according to Rawls's principle, to allow these people to keep most of their wealth, although others may have much less. Doctors, for example, might be allowed to keep more than others. Nevertheless the maximin rule is difficult for egalitarians to argue against, because any attempt to approach closer to equality would necessarily, at the same time as it narrowed the gap between the worst-off and the better-off, make the worst-off still worse-off than they were before.

Though strongly protected against the attack from egalitarians that appeared most likely, the maximin principle was soon shown to be vulnerable at other spots. Since the appearance of *A Theory of Justice* a book and a number of critical reviews[2] have exposed fundamental weaknesses in its central arguments, including the argument for the maximin principle. The devastating critique of Rawls in *Anarchy, State, and Utopia*, directed especially at the case for redistribution in accordance with the maximin rule, must very nearly complete the demolition of Rawls's impressive structure.

In part, the force of Nozick's criticisms depends on Rawls's own desire that his theory account for and systematize the particular judgments about justice that we ordinarily make.[3] For Rawls, finding a plausible general theory that confirms most of our ordinary judgments of what is just is the aim of any theory of justice. But as Kenneth Arrow has noted in a discussion of Rawls's theory,[4] the most widely held intuition about distributive justice—which Arrow and most other teachers find it difficult to dissuade introductory students from thinking completely self-evident—is

---

2 The book-length study is *The Liberal Theory of Justice* by Brian Barry (Oxford UP, 1973). Among the more notable critical reviews have been those by Thomas Nagel in the *Philosophical Review* (April, 1973) and the two-part critique by R.M. Hare in *Philosophical Quarterly* (July and September, 1973).

3 This point was brought to my notice by Gregory Pence.

4 Kenneth J. Arrow, "Some Ordinalist-Utilitarian Notes on Rawls' Theory of Justice," *Journal of Philosophy* 70.9 (1973): 248.

the view that an individual is entitled to what he creates. This view is, of course, much closer to that of Nozick than to Rawls's.

I believe that Rawls is mistaken in thinking that the test of a moral theory is its ability to account for the particular moral judgments we already make. That approach comes too close to making the justification of what we already believe the sole task for moral philosophy. One of the strengths of Nozick's criticism, however, is that even if Rawls were to abandon his ideas about how moral theories are to be tested he would still be unable to defend his position. For Nozick has shown that Rawls's case for the maximin principle rests on an unjustifiable asymmetry between the worst-off and the best-off in a society. Rawls argues that the worst-off could accept the justice of, and cooperate in, a society governed in accordance with the maximin principle, but not one governed according to, say, the principle of utility. This is because in any society governed according to any principle other than the maximin principle there would always be a group of people at least as badly off as the worst-off in a maximin-ruled society.

Provided the maximin rule has been properly applied, this is necessarily true; but, Nozick insists, Rawls glosses over the equally important mirror-image question: why should the better-off accept the justice of and cooperate in the society? Under the maximin rule, after all, the better-off may have to make substantial sacrifices to help the worst-off, perhaps much greater sacrifices than they would have to make to satisfy the principle of utility. For instance, to put the matter in monetary terms, assume that a tax of 75 percent on all incomes over $15,000 would, after deducting administrative and other costs, allow welfare payments to the worst-off group to be increased by only $1 per person per year. The maximin rule would require that the tax be levied.

So Rawls is able to conclude that the maximin principle would be the one that people in the original position would agree to only because he considers the matter from the perspective of those who fear they will be among the worst-off, rather than from the perspective of those who hope to be among the better-off. For this reason he fails in his attempt to derive the maximin principle in a neutral manner from what reasonable people would agree upon under conditions requiring impartiality; and in addition Nozick is able to make the telling point that the fundamental flaw Rawls finds in utilitarianism—the failure to rule out "even the tendency to regard men as means to one another's welfare"—can be found in Rawls's own principle. The maximin rule treats the better-off as a means to the welfare of the worst-off. Indeed one could say (though Nozick does not) that the tendency to treat people as a means to another's end is greater under the maximin rule than under utilitarianism, since a utilitarian would give *equal* consideration to everyone's interests, whereas the maximin rule forbids giving *any* consideration to the interests of the better-off, allotting them goods *solely* in so far as doing so assists the worst-off.

There remain many interesting and illuminating points in Rawls's long book, but its foundations are now seriously undermined. The question we must face, then, is whether *any* conception of distributive justice that accepts individual rights, particularly the right to property, and prohibits absolutely treating one man as a means to the welfare of another can with-stand the arguments Nozick has directed primarily against Rawls. If the answer is negative we shall have to choose between a conception of justice such as Nozick's and our conviction that a society does not have to rely on the charity of its wealthy members for the relief of its poorest members.

The enthusiasm which greeted Rawls's theory of justice when it first appeared may in part be explained by the fact that it was the first fully worked-out alternative to utilitarianism since W.D. Ross's intuitionist theory lost favor in the 1930s.[5] If more careful consideration has found Rawls's theory wanting, opponents of utilitarianism lack, once again, a developed alternative theory—except, that is, for Nozick's entitlement view. Nonutilitarians not wishing to accept the conclusion that coercive redistribution of wealth is a serious violation of rights urgently require an alternative theory of rights.

What else is there? Not much. While, as Nozick points out, there is no lack of unsupported presumptions in favor of equality, there is a surprising dearth of *arguments* for equality. Nozick discusses one of the few arguments that have been widely discussed—generally with approval—by philosophers: that put forward by Bernard Williams in his article "The Idea of Equality."[6]

Williams argues that the proper ground of distribution of medical care is ill-health; and that, therefore, it is irrational for the distribution of medical care to be governed by the ability to pay. On first reading many of us will find this argument for some degree of equality convincing. But, Nozick asks, why should the internal goal of an activity take precedence over the particular purpose of the person performing the activity? By a parallel argument it could be said that the proper ground of distribution of barbering services is the need to get one's hair cut; but if we think a barber need cut the hair only of those able to pay, why should a doctor not do the same?

What Nozick's facetious counterexample indicates is that the plausibility of Williams's argument lies not in any supposed necessary truth about the proper ground of distribution of medical care but in the claim that a society should provide for the most important needs of its members. This is a plausible claim, but it is *only* a claim and Williams does not argue for it. So we still do not have an argument for equality.

Wisely, Nozick remarks that his readers will probably feel that the case for equality all hangs on some other argument, and says he would like to see *that* argument set out in detail. That, unfortunately, is where the attempt to refuse Nozick on the ground he has chosen—accepting a doctrine of individual rights that includes a right to property—rests at the present time. Which is not to say that it will rest there long. There is tremendous activity in moral and political philosophy nowadays and if a

---

5 See W.D. Ross, *The Right and the Good* (Oxford UP, 1930).
6 In *Philosophy, Politics and Society* (Second Series), Laslett and Runciman, eds. (Barnes and Noble, 1962).

response to Nozick's challenge is not already in preparation it soon will be.

What if we refuse to accept the ground Nozick has chosen? The natural alternative is then utilitarianism. There are other possibilities, but none that seems likely to be very attractive to those who reject Nozick's position because of its prohibition on coercive redistribution of wealth. In *A Theory of Justice*, for instance, Rawls considers as alternatives to his own theory only utilitarianism and what he calls "the Principle of Perfection." Perfectionism, which is the theory that we should maximize the achievement of excellence, was most strongly advocated by Nietzsche and is even further from concerning itself about the worst-off than Nozick's theory is; and when more plausible advocates of a perfectionist position talk about social justice, they tend to water down their perfectionism with a dose of something that looks like utilitarianism.[7]

Utilitarianism has no problem in justifying a substantial amount of compulsory redistribution from the rich to the poor. We all recognize that $1,000 means far less to people earning $100,000 than it does to people trying to support a family on $6,000. Therefore in normal circumstances we increase the total happiness when we take from those with a lot and give to those with little. Therefore that is what we ought to do. For the utilitarian it is as simple as that. The result will not be absolute equality of wealth. There may be some who need relatively little to be happy, and others whose expensive tastes require more to achieve the same level of happiness. If resources are adequate the utilitarian will give each enough to make him happy, and that will mean giving some more than others.

A more serious possibility is the one we discussed in connection with the maximin principle. If it is necessary to give more to those with talents useful to society, to encourage them to develop these talents in a way that will benefit others, then utilitarians would have to do this. Actually the evidence for this commonly accepted hypothesis is weak; financial incentives may not be as important as we think. So some inequality would result from the application of utilitarian principles to a society like ours, but far less than there is now, and the inequalities that remain would not (in my view) be objectionable.

Nozick describes Rawls's view as an "undeniably great advance over utilitarianism." From his standpoint that is a reasonable estimate. Rawls's theory is a half-way house between utilitarianism and Nozick's own position. But if having gone half-way with Rawls we are forced by the logic of our position to go all the way with Nozick, it could be that we went wrong when we started out. None of the arguments Nozick uses against Rawls is decisive when invoked against a utilitarian position. Utilitarianism gives a clear and plausible defense not merely of progressive taxation, welfare payments, and other methods of redistribution, but also of the general right of the

---

7 For example, Bertrand de Jouvenal, *The Ethics of Redistribution* (Cambridge UP, 1951).

state to perform useful functions beyond the protection of its citizens from force and fraud. Utilitarianism also provides an argument in defense of the claim behind Williams's argument for equality—that society should, so far as its resources allow, provide for the most important needs of its members.

Nor do we have to go all the way with the utilitarians to be in a position to advocate state-directed redistribution of income. The problem of whether we can accept a utilitarian account of noneconomic rights like the right to freedom of speech or freedom of worship need not be raised here, for Nozick's argument is mainly addressed to economic rights. We can deal with property in a utilitarian manner, rejecting the doctrine of an intrinsic right to property, without necessarily rejecting the idea that there are *some* intrinsic rights against the state. For the remainder of this discussion, though I shall talk simply of "utilitarianism," it will be this limited economic utilitarianism to which I am referring.

Nozick, aware that utilitarianism is a more fundamental rival to his position than other conceptions of justice, tries to get it out of the way in the first part of the book, when discussing the moral background of his theory. The discussion is sketchy, however, and falls below the level of the later sections. Nowhere is utilitarianism fully and systematically confronted. Nozick mentions some well-known objections but, with one exception, does not pursue the replies that utilitarians have made when these objections have been raised in the past.

The exception is interesting. In opposition to the view, which utilitarians have held, that the only things that are good or bad in themselves are states of consciousness, or conscious experiences (pleasant or happy ones being good, painful or miserable ones bad), Nozick asks us to imagine that we can build an "experience machine" which would give us the satisfactions of a wonderful life—any life we'd like—while we float in a tank with electrodes plugged into our brains.

If we had such a machine, Nozick says, we would choose not to use it—and this shows that things other than experience matter to us. In anticipation of the reply that we would not use the machine because, as good utilitarians, we would be concerned about other people's (and other animals') experiences as well as our own, Nozick makes the further assumption that *everyone* is able to plug into one of these machines. This means that we cannot give point to our lives by improving the experiences of other beings; the experience machine gives everyone who wants them the best possible experiences anyway. Nevertheless, Nozick says, we would not plug in, and this is because in addition to wanting to have certain experiences we want to do certain things and be a certain sort of person. We desire to live in contact with reality, and this no machine can do for us.

Perhaps. It is worth noting, though, that it is difficult to know what, in a world in which everyone could plug into an experience machine, there would be left to do, other than plug in; and how it would be possible to "be a certain sort of person." How could one be, for example, a kind or courageous person (Nozick's examples)?

What could I do to anyone else that showed kindness, if everyone else could have whatever experiences he wanted without my kindness? When would there ever be any point in being courageous? Maybe it would seem a pointless world, and plugging into the machine a pointless kind of existence, but that is because we are used to having the possibility of improving experiences, our own or those of another, to give point to our normal existence. Take away the point of trying to improve the experience of ourselves and others and perhaps we do take away the only thing beyond our own experience that gives point to our lives. Maybe life as a whole doesn't have any point beyond experience itself. Nozick's example is bizarre enough to have a bizarre answer, and the bizarreness of the answer that the orthodox form of utilitarianism gives is an insufficient reason for rejecting that theory.

Even if we find that Nozick's example does refute the idea that states of consciousness are the only things intrinsically good or bad, however, Nozick has refuted only one form of utilitarianism. Several recent utilitarian writers, including nearly all those writing in the field of welfare economics, have taken wants or desires, rather than states of consciousness, as the starting point for utilitarian calculations.[8] It is intrinsically good, on this view, if someone gets what he wants, and bad if he does not. This version of utilitarianism is not threatened by Nozick's experience machine; if there are things that we want other than experiences, well and good, utilitarianism will try to make it possible for us to get them.

So the utilitarian alternative to a theory of justice based on individual rights to property remains open; though other theories will no doubt be put forward, those wishing to avoid the conclusions of Nozick's book may find themselves reconsidering one or another version of utilitarianism, and questioning whether the right to property must be taken as seriously as American political thought has taken it for the last 200 years.

---

8 See, for example, Jan Narveson's *Morality and Utility* (Johns Hopkins, 1967). The upshot of R.M. Hare's ethical theory is also a utilitarianism of this type; see *Freedom and Reason* (Oxford UP, 1963) and "Wrongness and Harm" in *Essays on the Moral Concepts* (U of California P, 1972).

5. The Procedural Republic and the Unencumbered Self[*]

Michael J. Sandel

Political philosophy seems often to reside at a distance from the world. Principles are one thing, politics another, and even our best efforts to "live up" to our ideals typically founder on the gap between theory and practice.[1]

But if political philosophy is unrealizable in one sense, it is unavoidable in another. This is the sense in which philosophy inhabits the world from the start; our practices and institutions are embodiments of theory. To engage in a political practice is already to stand in relation to theory.[2] For all our uncertainties about ultimate questions of political philosophy—of justice and value and the nature of the good life—the one thing we know is that we live *some* answer all the time.

In this essay I will try to explore the answer we live now, in contemporary America. What is the political philosophy implicit in our practices and institutions? How does it stand, as philosophy? And how do tensions in the philosophy find expression in our present political condition?

It may be objected that it is a mistake to look for a single philosophy, that we live no "answer," only answers. But a plurality of answers is itself a kind of answer. And the political theory that affirms this plurality is the theory I propose to explore.

The Right and the Good

We might begin by considering a certain moral and political vision. It is a liberal vision, and like most liberal visions gives pride of place to justice, fairness, and individual rights. Its core thesis is this: a just society seeks not to promote any particular ends, but enables its citizens to pursue their own ends, consistent with a similar

---

* Source: *Political Theory* 12.1 (Feb. 1984): 81–96.

1 An excellent example of this view can be found in Samuel Huntington, *American Politics: The Promise of Disharmony* (Cambridge, MA: Harvard UP, 1981). See especially his discussion of the "ideals versus institutions" gap, pp. 10–12, 39–41, 61–84, 221–62.

2 See, for example, the conceptions of a "practice" advanced by Alasdair MacIntyre and Charles Taylor: MacIntyre, *After Virtue* (Notre Dame, IN: U of Notre Dame P, 1981), pp. 175–209; Taylor, "Interpretation and the Sciences of Man," *Review of Metaphysics* 25 (1971): 3–51.

liberty for all; it therefore must govern by principles that do not presuppose any particular conception of the good. What justifies these regulative principles above all is not that they maximize the general welfare, or cultivate virtue, or otherwise promote the good, but rather that they conform to the concept of *right*, a moral category given prior to the good, and independent of it.

This liberalism says, in other words, that what makes the just society just is not the *telos* or purpose or end at which it aims, but precisely its refusal to choose in advance among competing purposes and ends. In its constitution and its laws, the just society seeks to provide a framework within which its citizens can pursue their own values and ends, consistent with a similar liberty for others.

The ideal I've described might be summed up in the claim that the right is prior to the good, and in two senses: The priority of the right means first, that individual rights cannot be sacrificed for the sake of the general good (in this it opposes utilitarianism), and second, that the principles of justice that specify these rights cannot be premised on any particular vision of the good life. (In this it opposes teleological conceptions in general.)

This is the liberalism of much contemporary moral and political philosophy, most fully elaborated by Rawls, and indebted to Kant for its philosophical foundations.[3] But I am concerned here less with the lineage of this vision than with what seem to me three striking facts about it.

First, it has a deep and powerful philosophical appeal. Second, despite its philosophical force, the claim for the priority of the right over the good ultimately fails. And third, despite its philosophical failure, this liberal vision is the one by which we live. For us in late twentieth-century America, it is our vision, the theory most thoroughly embodied in the practices and institutions most central to our public life. And seeing how it goes wrong as philosophy may help us to diagnose our present political condition. So first, its philosophical power; second, its philosophical failure; and third, however briefly, its uneasy embodiment in the world.

But before taking up these three claims, it is worth pointing out a central theme that connects them. And that is a certain conception of the person, of what it is to be a moral agent. Like all political theories, the liberal theory I have described is something more than a set of regulative principles. It is also a view about the way the world is, and the way we move within it. At the heart of this ethic lies a vision of

---

3 John Rawls, *A Theory of Justice* (Oxford: Oxford UP, 1971); Immanuel Kant, *Groundwork of the Metaphysics of Morals*, trans. H.J. Paton (1785; New York: Harper and Row, 1956); Kant, *Critique of Pure Reason*, trans. Norman Kemp Smith (1781, 1787; London: Macmillan, 1929); Kant, *Critique of Practical Reason*, trans. L.W. Beck (1788; Indianapolis: Bobbs-Merrill, 1956); Kant, "On the Common Saying: 'This May Be True in Theory, But It Does Not Apply in Practice,'" in Hans Reiss, ed., *Kant's Political Writings* (1793; Cambridge: Cambridge UP, 1970). Other recent versions of the claim for the priority of the right over good can be found in Robert Nozick, *Anarchy, State, and Utopia* (New York: Basic Books, 1974); Ronald Dworkin, *Taking Rights Seriously* (London: Duckworth, 1977); Bruce Ackerman, *Social Justice in the Liberal State* (New Haven: Yale UP, 1980).

the person that both inspires and undoes it. As I will try to argue now, what make this ethic so compelling, but also, finally, vulnerable, are the promise and the failure of the unencumbered self.

Kantian Foundations

The liberal ethic asserts the priority of right, and seeks principles of justice that do not presuppose any particular conception of the good.[4] This is what Kant means by the supremacy of the moral law, and what Rawls means when he writes that "justice is the first virtue of social institutions."[5] Justice is more than just another value. It provides the framework that *regulates* the play of competing values and ends; it must therefore have a sanction independent of those ends. But it is not obvious where such a sanction could be found.

Theories of justice, and for that matter, ethics, have typically founded their claims on one or another conception of human purposes and ends. Thus Aristotle said the measure of a *polis* is the good at which it aims, and even J.S. Mill, who in the nineteenth century called "justice the chief part, and incomparably the most binding part of all morality," made justice an instrument of utilitarian ends.[6]

This is the solution Kant's ethic rejects. Different persons typically have different desires and ends, and so any principle derived from them can only be contingent. But the moral law needs a *categorical* foundation, not a contingent one. Even so universal a desire as happiness will not do. People still differ in what happiness consists of, and to install any particular conception as regulative would impose on some the conceptions of others, and so deny at least to some the freedom to choose their *own* conceptions. In any case, to govern ourselves in conformity with desires and inclinations, given as they are by nature or circumstance, is not really to be *self-*governing at all. It is rather a refusal of freedom, a capitulation to determinations given outside us.

According to Kant, the right is "derived entirely from the concept of freedom in the external relationships of human beings, and has nothing to do with the end which all men have by nature [i.e., the aim of achieving happiness] or with the recognized means of attaining this end."[7] As such, it must have a basis prior to all empirical ends. Only when I am governed by principles that do not presuppose any particular ends am I free to pursue my own ends consistent with a similar freedom for all.

But this still leaves the question of what the basis of the right could possibly be. If it must be a basis prior to all purposes and ends, unconditioned even by what

---

4 This section, and the two that follow, summarize arguments developed more fully in Michael Sandel, *Liberalism and the Limits of Justice* (Cambridge: Cambridge UP 1982).

5 Rawls (1971), p. 3.

6 John Stuart Mill, *Utilitarianism*, in *The Utilitarians* (1893; Garden City, NJ: Doubleday, 1973), p. 465; *On Liberty*, in *The Utilitarians*, p. 485 (originally published 1859).

7 Kant (1793), p. 73.

Kant calls "the special circumstances of human nature,"[8] where could such a basis conceivably be found? Given the stringent demands of the Kantian ethic, the moral law would seem almost to require a foundation in nothing, for any empirical precondition would undermine its priority. "Duty!" asks Kant at his most lyrical, "What origin is there worthy of thee, and where is to be found the root of thy noble descent which proudly rejects all kinship with the inclinations?"[9]

His answer is that the basis of the moral law is to be found in the *subject*, not the object of practical reason, a subject capable of an autonomous will. No empirical end, but rather "a subject of ends, namely a rational being himself, must be made the ground for all maxims of action."[10] Nothing other than what Kant calls "the subject of all possible ends himself" can give rise to the right, for only this subject is also the subject of an autonomous will. Only this subject could be that "something which elevates man above himself as part of the world of sense" and enables him to participate in an ideal, unconditioned realm wholly independent of our social and psychological inclinations. And only this thoroughgoing independence can afford us the detachment we need if we are ever freely to choose for ourselves, unconditioned by the vagaries of circumstance.[11]

Who or what exactly *is* this subject? It is, in a certain sense, *us*. The moral law, after all, is a law we give *ourselves*; we don't *find* it, we *will* it. That is how it (and we) escape the reign of nature and circumstance and merely empirical ends. But what is important to see is that the "we" who do the willing are not "we" qua particular persons, you and me, each for ourselves—the moral law is not up to us as individuals—but "we" qua participants in what Kant calls "pure practical reason," "we" qua participants in a transcendental subject.

Now what is to guarantee that I *am* a subject of this kind, capable of exercising pure practical reason? Well, strictly speaking, there *is* no guarantee; the transcendental subject is only a possibility. But it is a possibility I must *presuppose* if I am to think of myself as a free moral agent. Were I wholly an empirical being, I would not be capable of freedom, for every exercise of will would be conditioned by the desire for some object. All choice would be heteronomous choice, governed by the pursuit of some end. My will could never be a first cause, only the effect of some prior cause, the instrument of one or another impulse or inclination. "When we think of ourselves as free," writes Kant, "we transfer ourselves into the intelligible world as members and recognize the autonomy of the will."[12] And so the notion of a subject prior to and independent of experience, such as the Kantian ethic requires, appears not only possible but indispensable, a necessary presupposition of the possibility of freedom.

---

8 Kant (1785), p. 92.
9 Kant (1788), p. 89.
10 Kant (1785), p. 105.
11 Kant (1788), p. 89.
12 Kant (1785), p. 121.

How does all of this come back to politics? As the subject is prior to its ends, so the right is prior to the good. Society is best arranged when it is governed by principles that do not presuppose any particular conception of the good, for any other arrangement would fail to respect persons as being capable of choice; it would treat them as objects rather than subjects, as means rather than ends in themselves.

We can see in this way how Kant's notion of the subject is bound up with the claim for the priority of right. But for those in the Anglo-American tradition, the transcendental subject will seem a strange foundation for a familiar ethic. Surely, one may think, we can take rights seriously and affirm the primacy of justice without embracing the *Critique of Pure Reason*. This, in any case, is the project of Rawls.

He wants to save the priority of right from the obscurity of the transcendental subject. Kant's idealist metaphysic, for all its moral and political advantage, cedes too much to the transcendent, and wins for justice its primacy only by denying it its human situation. "To develop a viable Kantian conception of justice," Rawls writes, "the force and content of Kant's doctrine must be detached from its background in transcendental idealism" and recast within the "canons of a reasonable empiricism."[13] And so Rawls's project is to preserve Kant's moral and political teaching by replacing Germanic obscurities with a domesticated metaphysic more congenial to the Anglo-American temper. This is the role of the original position.

From Transcendental Subject to Unencumbered Self

The original position tries to provide what Kant's transcendental argument cannot—a foundation for the right that is prior to the good, but still situated in the world. Sparing all but essentials, the original position works like this: It invites us to imagine the principles we would choose to govern our society if we were to choose them in advance, before we knew the particular persons we would be—whether rich or poor, strong or weak, lucky or unlucky—before we knew even our interests or aims or conceptions of the good. These principles—the ones we would choose in that imaginary situation—are the principles of justice. What is more, if it works, they are principles that do not presuppose any particular ends.

What they *do* presuppose is a certain picture of the person, of the way we must be if we are beings for whom justice is the first virtue. This is the picture of the unencumbered self, a self understood as prior to and independent of purposes and ends.

Now the unencumbered self describes first of all the way we stand toward the things we have, or want, or seek. It means there is always a distinction between the values I *have* and the person I *am*. To identify any characteristics as *my* aims, ambitions, desires, and so on, is always to imply some subject "me" standing behind them, at a certain distance, and the shape of this "me" must be given prior to any

---

13 Rawls, "The Basic Structure as Subject," *American Philosophical Quarterly* 14.2 (1977): 165.

of the aims or attributes I bear. One consequence of this distance is to put the self *itself* beyond the reach of its experience, to secure its identity once and for all. Or to put the point another way, it rules out the possibility of what we might call *constitutive* ends. No role or commitment could define me so completely that I could not understand myself without it. No project could be so essential that turning away from it would call into question the person I am.

For the unencumbered self, what matters above all, what is most essential to our personhood, are not the ends we choose but our capacity to choose them. The original position sums up this central claim about us. "It is not our aims that primarily reveal our nature," writes Rawls, "but rather the principles that we would acknowledge to govern the background conditions under which these aims are to be formed.... We should therefore reverse the relation between the right and the good proposed by teleological doctrines and view the right as prior."[14]

Only if the self is prior to its ends can the right be prior to the good. Only if my identity is never tied to the aims and interests I may have at any moment can I think of myself as a free and independent agent, capable of choice.

This notion of independence carries consequences for the kind of community of which we are capable. Understood as unencumbered selves, we are of course free to join in voluntary association with others, and so are capable of community in the cooperative sense. What is denied to the unencumbered self is the possibility of membership in any community bound by moral ties antecedent to choice; he cannot belong to any community where the self *itself* could be at stake. Such a community—call it constitutive as against merely cooperative—would engage the identity as well as the interests of the participants, and so implicate its members in a citizenship more thoroughgoing than the unencumbered self can know.

For justice to be primary, then, we must be creatures of a certain kind, related to human circumstance in a certain way. We must stand to our circumstance always at a certain distance, whether as transcendental subject in the case of Kant, or as unencumbered selves in the case of Rawls. Only in this way can we view ourselves as subjects as well as objects of experience, as agents and not just instruments of the purposes we pursue.

The unencumbered self and the ethic it inspires, taken together, hold out a liberating vision. Freed from the dictates of nature and the sanction of social roles, the human subject is installed as sovereign, cast as the author of the only moral meanings there are. As participants in pure practical reason, or as parties to the original position, we are free to construct principles of justice unconstrained by an order of value antecedently given. And as actual, individual selves, we are free to choose our purposes and ends unbound by such an order, or by custom or tradition or

---

14 Rawls (1971), p. 560.

inherited status. So long as they are not unjust, our conceptions of the good carry weight, whatever they are, simply in virtue of our having chosen them. We are, in Rawls's words, "self-originating sources of valid claims."[15]

This is an exhilarating promise, and the liberalism it animates is perhaps the fullest expression of the Enlightenment's quest for the self-defining subject. But is it true? Can we make sense of our moral and political life by the light of the self-image it requires? I do not think we can, and I will try to show why not by arguing first within the liberal project, then beyond it.

Justice and Community

We have focused so far on the foundations of the liberal vision, on the way it derives the principles it defends. Let us turn briefly now to the substance of those principles, using Rawls as our example. Sparing all but essentials once again, Rawls's two principles of justice are these: first, equal basic liberties for all, and second, only those social and economic inequalities that benefit the least-advantaged members of society (the difference principle).

In arguing for these principles, Rawls argues against two familiar alternatives—utilitarianism and libertarianism. He argues against utilitarianism that it fails to take seriously the distinction between persons. In seeking to maximize the general welfare, the utilitarian treats society as whole as if it were a single person; it conflates our many, diverse desires into a single system of desires, and tries to maximize. It is indifferent to the distribution of satisfactions among persons, except insofar as this may affect the overall sum. But this fails to respect our plurality and distinctness. It uses some as means to the happiness of all, and so fails to respect each as an end in himself. While utilitarians may sometimes defend individual rights, their defense must rest on the calculation that respecting those rights will serve utility in the long run. But this calculation is contingent and uncertain. So long as utility is what Mill said it is, "the ultimate appeal on all ethical questions,"[16] individual rights can never be secure. To avoid the danger that their life prospects might one day be sacrificed for the greater good of others, the parties to the original position therefore insist on certain basic liberties for all, and make those liberties prior.

If utilitarians fail to take seriously the distinctness of persons, libertarians go wrong by failing to acknowledge the arbitrariness of fortune. They define as just whatever distribution results from an efficient market economy, and oppose all redistribution on the grounds that people are entitled to whatever they get, so long as they do not cheat or steal or otherwise violate someone's rights in getting it. Rawls opposes this principle on the ground that the distribution of talents and assets and even efforts by which some get more and others get less is arbitrary from a moral point of view, a matter of good luck. To distribute the good things in life on the

15 Rawls, "Kantian Constructivism in Moral Theory," *Journal of Philosophy* 77 (1980): 543.
16 Mill (1859), p. 485.

basis of these differences is not to do justice, but simply to carry over into human arrangements the arbitrariness of social and natural contingency. We deserve, as individuals, neither the talents our good fortune may have brought, nor the benefits that flow from them. We should therefore regard these talents as common assets, and regard one another as common beneficiaries of the rewards they bring. "Those who have been favored by nature, whoever they are, may gain from their good fortune only on terms that improve the situation of those who have lost out…. In justice as fairness, men agree to share one another's fate."[17]

This is the reasoning that leads to the difference principle. Notice how it reveals, in yet another guise, the logic of the unencumbered self. I cannot be said to deserve the benefits that flow from, say, my fine physique and good looks, because they are only accidental, not essential facts about me. They describe attributes I *have*, not the person I *am*, and so cannot give rise to a claim of desert. Being an unencumbered self, this is true of *everything* about me. And so I cannot, as an individual, deserve anything at all.

However jarring to our ordinary understandings this argument may be, the picture so far remains intact; the priority of right, the denial of desert, and the unencumbered self all hang impressively together.

But the difference principle requires more, and it is here that the argument comes undone. The difference principle begins with the thought, congenial to the unencumbered self, that the assets I have are only accidentally mine. But it ends by assuming that these assets are therefore *common* assets and that society has a prior claim on the fruits of their exercise. But this assumption is without warrant. Simply because I, as an individual, do not have a privileged claim on the assets accidentally residing "here," it does not follow that everyone in the world collectively does. For there is no reason to think that their location in society's province or, for that matter, within the province of humankind, is any *less* arbitrary from a moral point of view. And if their arbitrariness within *me* makes them ineligible to serve *my* ends, there seems no obvious reason why their arbitrariness within any particular society should not make them ineligible to serve that society's ends as well.

To put the point another way, the difference principle, like utilitarianism, is a principle of sharing. As such, it must presuppose some prior moral tie among those whose assets it would deploy and whose efforts it would enlist in a common endeavor. Otherwise, it is simply a formula for using some as means to others' ends, a formula this liberalism is committed to reject.

But on the cooperative vision of community alone, it is unclear what the moral basis for this sharing could be. Short of the constitutive conception, deploying an individual's assets for the sake of the common good would seem an offense against the "plurality and distinctness" of individuals this liberalism seeks above all to secure.

---

17 Rawls (1971), pp. 101–02.

If those whose fate I am required to share really are, morally speaking, *others*, rather than fellow participants in a way of life with which my identity is bound, the difference principle falls prey to the same objections as utilitarianism. Its claim on me is not the claim of a constitutive community whose attachments I acknowledge, but rather the claim of a concatenated collectivity whose entanglements I confront.

What the difference principle requires, but cannot provide, is some way of identifying those *among* whom the assets I bear are properly regarded as common, some way of seeing ourselves as mutually indebted and morally engaged to begin with. But as we have seen, the constitutive aims and attachments that would save and situate the difference principle are precisely the ones denied to the liberal self; the moral encumbrances and antecedent obligations they imply would undercut the priority of right.

What, then, of those encumbrances? The point so far is that we cannot be persons for whom justice is primary, and also be persons for whom the difference principle is a principle of justice. But which must give way? Can we view ourselves as independent selves, independent in the sense that our identity is never tied to our aims and attachments?

I do not think we can, at least not without cost to those loyalties and convictions whose moral force consists partly in the fact that living by them is inseparable from understanding ourselves as the particular persons we are—as members of this family or community or nation or people, as bearers of that history, as citizens of this republic. Allegiances such as these are more than values I happen to have, and to hold, at a certain distance. They go beyond the obligations I voluntarily incur and the "natural duties" I owe to human beings as such. They allow that to some I owe more than justice requires or even permits, not by reason of agreements I have made but instead in virtue of those more or less enduring attachments and commitments that, taken together, partly define the person I am.

To imagine a person incapable of constitutive attachments such as these is not to conceive an ideally free and rational agent, but to imagine a person wholly without character, without moral depth. For to have character is to know that I move in a history I neither summon nor command, which carries consequences nonetheless for my choices and conduct. It draws me closer to some and more distant from others; it makes some aims more appropriate, others less so. As a self-interpreting being, I am able to reflect on my history and in this sense to distance myself from it, but the distance is always precarious and provisional, the point of reflection never finally secured outside the history itself. But the liberal ethic puts the self beyond the reach of its experience, beyond deliberation and reflection. Denied the expansive self-understandings that could shape a common life, the liberal self is left to lurch between detachment on the one hand, and entanglement on the other. Such is the fate of the unencumbered self, and its liberating promise.

The Procedural Republic[18]

But before my case can be complete, I need to consider one powerful reply. While it comes from a liberal direction, its spirit is more practical than philosophical. It says, in short, that I am asking too much. It is one thing to seek constitutive attachments in our private lives; among families and friends, and certain tightly knit groups, there may be found a common good that makes justice and rights less pressing. But with public life—at least today, and probably always—it is different. So long as the nation-state is the primary form of political association, talk of constitutive community too easily suggests a darker politics rather than a brighter one; amid echoes of the moral majority, the priority of right, for all its philosophical faults, still seems the safer hope.

This is a challenging rejoinder, and no account of political community in the twentieth century can fail to take it seriously. It is challenging not least because it calls into question the status of political philosophy and its relation to the world. For if my argument is correct, if the liberal vision we have considered is not morally self-sufficient but parasitic on a notion of community it officially rejects, then we should expect to find that the political practice that embodies this vision is not *practically* self-sufficient either—that it must draw on a sense of community it cannot supply and may even undermine. But is that so far from the circumstance we face today? Could it be that through the original position darkly, on the far side of the veil of ignorance, we may glimpse an intimation of our predicament, a refracted vision of ourselves?

How does the liberal vision—and its failure—help us make sense of our public life and its predicament? Consider, to begin, the following paradox in the citizen's relation to the modern welfare state. In many ways, we in the 1980s stand near the completion of a liberal project that has run its course from the New Deal through the Great Society and into the present. But notwithstanding the extension of the franchise and the expansion on individual rights and entitlements in recent decades, there is a widespread sense that, individually and collectively, our control over the forces that govern our lives is receding rather than increasing. This sense is deepened by what appear simultaneously as the power and the powerlessness of the nation-state. On the one hand, increasing numbers of citizens view the state as an overly intrusive presence, more likely to frustrate their purposes than advance them. And yet, despite its unprecedented role in the economy and society, the modern state seems itself disempowered, unable effectively to control the domestic economy, to respond to persisting social ills, or to work America's will in the world.

This is a paradox that has fed the appeals of recent politicians (including Carter and Reagan), even as it has frustrated their attempts to govern. To sort it out, we need to identify the public philosophy implicit in our political practice, and to reconstruct

18 The account that follows is a tentative formulation of themes requiring more detailed elaboration and support.

its arrival. We need to trace the advent of the procedural republic, by which I mean a public life animated by the liberal vision and self-image we've considered.

The story of the procedural republic goes back in some ways to the founding of the republic, but its central drama begins to unfold around the turn of the century. As national markets and large-scale enterprise displaced a decentralized economy, the decentralized political forms of the early republic became outmoded as well. If democracy was to survive, the concentration of economic power would have to be met by a similar concentration of political power. But the Progressives understood, or some of them did, that the success of democracy required more than the central-ization of government; it also required the nationalization of politics. The primary form of political community had to be recast on a national scale. For Herbert Croly, writing in 1909, the "nationalizing of American political, economic, and social life" was "an essentially formative and enlightening political transformation." We would become more of a democracy only as we became "more of a nation...in ideas, in institutions, and in spirit."[19]

This nationalizing project would be consummated in the New Deal, but for the democratic tradition in America, the embrace of the nation was a decisive departure. From Jefferson to the populists, the party of democracy in American political debate had been, roughly speaking, the party of the provinces, of decentralized power, of small-town and small-scale America. And against them had stood the party of the nation—first Federalists, then Whigs, then the Republicans of Lincoln—a party that spoke for the consolidation of the union. It was thus the historic achievement of the New Deal to unite, in a single party and political program, what Samuel Beer has called "liberalism and the national idea."[20]

What matters for our purpose is that, in the twentieth century, liberalism made its peace with concentrated power. But it was understood at the start that the terms of this peace required a strong sense of national community, morally and politi-cally, to underwrite the extended involvements of a modern industrial order. If a virtuous republic of small-scale, democratic communities was no longer a pos-sibility, a national republic seemed democracy's next best hope. This was still, in principle at least, a politics of the common good. It looked to the nation, not as a neutral framework for the play of competing interests, but rather as a formative community, concerned to shape a common life suited to the scale of modern social and economic forms.

But this project failed. By the mid- or late-twentieth century, the national republic had run its course. Except for extraordinary moments, such as war, the nation proved too vast a scale across which to cultivate the shared self-understandings necessary to community in the formative, or constitutive sense. And so the gradual shift, in our practices and institutions, from a public philosophy of common purposes to one

19 Croly. *The Promise of American Life* (Indianapolis: Bobbs-Merrill, 1965), pp. 270–73.
20 Beer. "Liberalism and the National Idea," *The Public Interest* Fall (1966): 70–82.

of fair procedures, from a politics of good to a politics of right, from the national republic to the procedural republic.

Our Present Predicament

A full account of this transition would take a detailed look at the changing shape of political institutions, constitutional interpretation, and the terms of political discourse in the broadest sense. But I suspect we would find in the *practice* of the procedural republic two broad tendencies foreshadowed by its philosophy: first, a tendency to crowd out democratic possibilities; second, a tendency to undercut the kind of community on which it nonetheless depends.

Where liberty in the early republic was understood as a function of democratic institutions and dispersed power,[21] liberty in the procedural republic is defined in opposition to democracy, as an individual's guarantee against what the majority might will. I am free insofar as I am the bearer of rights, where rights are trumps.[22] Unlike the liberty of the early republic, the modern version permits—in fact even requires—concentrated power. This has to do with the universalizing logic of rights. Insofar as I have a right, whether to free speech or a minimum income, its provision cannot be left to the vagaries of local preferences but must be assured at the most comprehensive level of political association. It cannot be one thing in New York and another in Alabama. As rights and entitlements expand, politics is therefore displaced from smaller forms of association and relocated at the most universal form—in our case, the nation. And even as politics flows to the nation, power shifts away from democratic institutions (such as legislatures and political parties) and toward institutions designed to be insulated from democratic pressures, and hence better equipped to dispense and defend individual rights (notably the judiciary and bureaucracy).

These institutional developments may begin to account for the sense of power-lessness that the welfare state fails to address and in some ways doubtless deepens. But it seems to me a further clue to our condition recalls even more directly the predicament of the unencumbered self—lurching, as we left it, between detachment on the one hand, and entanglement on the other. For it is a striking feature of the welfare state that it offers a powerful promise of individual rights, and also demands of its citizens a high measure of mutual engagement. But the self-image that attends the rights cannot sustain the engagement.

As bearers of rights, where rights are trumps, we think of ourselves as freely choosing, individual selves, unbound by obligations antecedent to rights, or to the agreements we make. And yet, as citizens of the procedural republic that secures

---

21 See, for example, Laurence Tribe, *American Constitutional Law* (Mineola, NY: The Foundation, 1978), pp. 2–3.

22 See Ronald Dworkin, "Liberalism," in Stuart Hampshire, ed., *Public and Private Morality* (Cambridge: Cambridge UP, 1978), p. 136.

these rights, we find ourselves implicated willy-nilly in a formidable array of dependencies and expectations we did not choose and increasingly reject.

In our public life, we are more entangled, but less attached, than ever before. It is as though the unencumbered self presupposed by the liberal ethic had begun to come true—less liberated than disempowered, entangled in a network of obligations and involvements unassociated with any act of will, and yet unmediated by those common identifications or expansive self-definitions that would make them tolerable. As the scale of social and political organization has become more comprehensive, the terms of our collective identity have become more fragmented, and the forms of political life have outrun the common purpose needed to sustain them.

Something like this, it seems to me, has been unfolding in America for the past half-century or so. I hope I have said at least enough to suggest the shape a fuller story might take. And I hope in any case to have conveyed a certain view about politics and philosophy and the relation between them—that our practices and institutions are themselves embodiments of theory, and to unravel their predicament is, at least in part, to seek after the self-image of the age.[23]

23 An earlier version of this article was presented to the Political Philosophy Colloquium at Princeton University, and to the Legal Theory Workshop at Columbia Law School. I am grateful to the participants, and also to the Editor, William Connolly, for helpful comments and criticisms. I would also like to thank the Ford Foundation for support of a larger project of which this essay is a first installment.

6. Equality of What?*

The Tanner Lecture on Human Values. Delivered at Stanford University, May 22, 1979.

Amartya Sen

Discussions in moral philosophy have offered us a wide menu in answer to the question: equality of what? In this lecture I shall concentrate on three particular types of equality, viz., (i) utilitarian equality, (ii) total utility equality, and (iii) Rawlsian equality. I shall argue that all three have serious limitations, and that while they fail in rather different and contrasting ways, an adequate theory cannot be constructed even on the *combined* grounds of the three. Towards the end I shall try to present an alternative formulation of equality which seems to me to deserve a good deal more attention than it has received, and I shall not desist from doing some propaganda on its behalf.

First a methodological question. When it is claimed that a certain moral principle has shortcomings, what can be the basis of such an allegation? There seem to be at least two different ways of grounding such a criticism, aside from just checking its *direct* appeal to moral intuition. One is to check the *implications* of the principle by taking up particular cases in which the results of employing that principle can be seen in a rather stark way, and then to examine these implications against our intuition. I shall call such a critique a *case-implication critique*. The other is to move not from the general to the particular, but from the general to the *more* general. One can examine the consistency of the principle with another principle that is acknowledged to be more fundamental. Such prior principles are usually formulated at a rather abstract level, and frequently take the form of congruence with some very general procedures. For example, what could be reasonably assumed to have been chosen under the *as if* ignorance of the Rawlsian "original position," a hypothetical primordial state in which people decide on what rules to adopt without knowing

---

* Source: John Rawls and Sterling M. McMurrin, eds., *Liberty, Equality, and Law: Selected Tanner Lectures on Moral Philosophy* (Salt Lake City: U of Utah P, 1987).

who they are going to be—as if they could end up being any one of the persons in the community?[1] Or what rules would satisfy Richard Hare's requirement of "universalizability" and be consistent with "giving equal weights to the equal interests of the occupants of all the roles"?[2] I shall call a critique based on such an approach a *prior-principle critique*. Both approaches can be used in assessing the moral claims of each type of equality, and will indeed be used here.

1. Utilitarian Equality

Utilitarian equality is the equality that can be derived from the utilitarian concept of goodness applied to problems of distribution. Perhaps the simplest case is the "pure distribution problem": the problem of dividing a given homogeneous cake among a group of persons.[3] Each person gets more utility the larger his share of the cake, and gets utility *only* from his share of the cake; his utility increases at a diminishing rate as the amount of his share goes up. The utilitarian objective is to maximize the sum-total of utility irrespective of distribution, but that requires the *equality* of the *marginal* utility of everyone—marginal utility being the incremental utility each person would get from an additional unit of cake.[4] According to one interpretation, this equality of marginal utility embodies equal treatment of everyone's interests.[5]

The position is a bit more complicated when the total size of the cake is not independent of its distribution. But even then maximization of the total utility sum requires that transfers be carried to the point at which the marginal utility gain of the gainers equals the marginal utility loss of the losers, after taking into account the effect of the transfer on the size and distribution of the cake.[6] It is in this wider context that the special type of equality insisted upon by utilitarianism becomes

1 J. Rawls, *A Theory of Justice* (Cambridge, MA: Harvard UP, 1971), pp. 17–22. See also W. Vickrey, "Measuring Marginal Utility by Reactions to Risk," *Econometrica* 13 (1945), and J.C. Harsanyi, "Cardinal Welfare, Individualistic Ethics, and Interpersonal Comparisons of Utility," *Journal of Political Economy* 63 (1955).

2 R.M. Hare, *The Language of Morals* (Oxford: Clarendon, 1952); "Ethical Theory and Utilitarianism," in H.D. Lewis, ed., *Contemporary British Philosophy* (London: Allen and Unwin, 1976), pp. 116–17.

3 I have tried to use this format for an axiomatic contrast of the Rawlsian and utilitarian criteria in "Rawls versus Bentham: An Axiomatic Examination of the Pure Distribution Problem," in *Theory and Decision* 4 (1974); reprinted in N. Daniels, ed., *Reading Rawls* (Oxford: Blackwell, 1975). See also L. Kern, "Comparative Distributive Ethics: An Extension of Sen's Examination of the Pure Distribution Problem," in H.W. Gottinger and W. Leinfellner, eds., *Decision Theory and Social Ethics* (Dordrecht: Reidel, 1978), and J.P. Griffin, "Equality: On Sen's Equity Axiom," Keble College, Oxford, 1978, mimeographed.

4 The equality condition would have to be replaced by a corresponding combination of inequality requirements when the appropriate "continuity" properties do not hold. Deeper difficulties are raised by "non-convexities" (e.g., increasing marginal utility).

5 J. Harsanyi, "Can the Maximin Principle Serve as a Basis for Morality? A Critique of John Rawls' Theory," *American Political Science Review* 64 (1975).

6 As mentioned in footnote 4, the equality conditions would require modification in the absence of continuity of the appropriate type. Transfers must be carried to the point at which the marginal utility gain of the gainers from any further transfer is *no more than* the marginal utility loss of the losers.

assertively distinguished. Richard Hare has claimed that "giving equal weight to the equal interests of all the parties" would "lead to utilitarianism"—thus satisfying the prior-principle requirement of universalizability.[7] Similarly, John Harsanyi shoots down the non-utilitarians (including this lecturer, I hasten to add), by claiming for utilitarianism an exclusive ability to avoid "unfair discrimination" between "one person's and another person's equally urgent human needs."[8]

The moral importance of needs, on this interpretation, is based exclusively on the notion of utility. This is disputable, and having had several occasions to dispute it in the past,[9] I shall not shy away from disputing it in this particular context. But while I will get on to this issue later, I want first to examine the nature of utilitarian equality without—for the time being—questioning the grounding of moral importance entirely on utility. Even when utility is the sole basis of importance there is still the question as to whether the size of *marginal* utility, irrespective of *total* utility enjoyed by the person, is an adequate index of moral importance. It is, of course, possible to define a metric on utility characteristics such that each person's utility scale is coordinated with everyone else's in a way that equal social importance is simply "scaled" as equal marginal utility. If interpersonal comparisons of utility are taken to have no descriptive content, then this can indeed be thought to be a natural approach. No matter how the relative social importances are arrived at, the marginal utilities attributed to each person would then simply reflect these values. This can be done explicitly by appropriate interpersonal scaling,[10] or implicitly through making the utility numbering reflect choices in situations of *as if* uncertainty associated with the "original position" under the additional assumption that ignorance be interpreted as equal probability of being anyone.[11] This is not the occasion to go into the technical details of this type of exercise, but the essence of it consists in using a scaling procedure such that marginal utility measures are automatically identified as indicators of social importance.

This route to utilitarianism may meet with little resistance, but it is non-controversial mainly because it says so little. A problem arises the moment utilities and interpersonal comparisons thereof are taken to have some independent descriptive

7 Hare (1976), pp. 116–17.
8 John Harsanyi, "Non-linear Social Welfare Functions: A Rejoinder to Professor Sen," in R.E. Butts and J. Hintikka, eds., *Foundational Problems in the Social Sciences* (Dordrecht: Reidel, 1977), pp. 294–95.
9 *Collective Choice and Social Welfare* (San Francisco: Holden-Day, 1970), chapter 6 and section 11.4; "On Weights and Measures: Informational Constraints in Social Welfare Analysis," *Econometrica* 45 (1977). See also T.M. Scanlon's arguments against identifying utility with "urgency" in his "Preference and Urgency," *Journal of Philosophy* 72 (1975).
10 For two highly ingenious examples of such an exercise, see Peter Hammond, "Dual Interpersonal Comparisons of Utility and the Welfare Economics of Income Distribution," *Journal of Public Economics* 6 (1977): 51–57; and Menahem Yaari, "Rawls, Edgeworth, Shapley and Nash: Theories of Distributive Justice Re-examined," Research Memorandum No. 33, Center for Research in Mathematical Economics and Game Theory, Hebrew University, Jerusalem, 1978.
11 See Harsanyi (1955, 1975, 1977).

content, as utilitarians have traditionally insisted that they do. There could then be conflicts between these descriptive utilities and the appropriately scaled, essentially normative, utilities in terms of which one is "forced" to be a utilitarian. In what follows I shall have nothing more to say on utilitarianism through appropriate interpersonal scaling, and return to examining the traditional utilitarian position, which takes utilities to have interpersonally comparable descriptive content. How moral importance should relate to these descriptive features must, then, be explicitly faced.

The position can be examined from the prior-principle perspective as well as from the case-implication angle. John Rawls's criticism as a preliminary to presenting his own alternative conception of justice took mostly the prior-principle form. This was chiefly in terms of acceptability in the "original position," arguing that in the postulated situation of *as if* ignorance people would not choose to maximize the utility sum. But Rawls also discussed the violence that utilitarianism does to our notions of liberty and equality. Some replies to Rawls's arguments have reasserted the necessity to be a utilitarian by taking the "scaling" route, which was discussed earlier, and which—I think—is inappropriate in meeting Rawls's critique. But I must confess that I find the lure of the "original position" distinctly resistible since it seems very unclear what precisely would be chosen in such a situation. It is also far from obvious that prudential choice under *as if* uncertainty provides an adequate basis for moral judgment in *un*original, i.e., real-life, positions.[12] But I believe Rawls's more direct critiques in terms of liberty and equality do remain powerful.

Insofar as one is concerned with the *distribution* of utilities, it follows immediately that utilitarianism would in general give one little comfort. Even the minutest gain in total utility *sum* would be taken to outweigh distributional inequalities of the most blatant kind. This problem would be avoidable under certain assumptions, notably the case in which everyone has the *same* utility function. In the pure distribution problem, with this assumption the utilitarian best would require absolute equality of everyone's total utilities.[13] This is because when the marginal utilities are equated, so would be the total utilities if everyone has the same utility function. This is, however, egalitarianism by serendipity: just the accidental result of the marginal tail wagging the total dog. More importantly, the assumption would be very frequently violated, since there are obvious and well-discussed variations between human beings. John may be easy to please, but Jeremy not. If it is taken to be an acceptable prior-principle that the equality of the distribution of total utilities has some value, then the utilitarian conception of equality—marginal as it is—must stand condemned.

---

12 On this, see Thomas Nagel, "Rawls on Justice," *Philosophical Review* 83 (1973), and "Equality" in his *Mortal Questions* (Cambridge: Cambridge UP, 1979).

13 The problem is much more complex when the total cake is not fixed, and where the maximization of utility sum need not lead to the equality of total utilities unless some additional assumptions are made, e.g., the absence of incentive arguments for inequality.

The recognition of the fundamental diversity of human beings does, in fact, have very deep consequences, affecting not merely the utilitarian conception of social good, but others as well, including (as I shall argue presently) even the Rawlsian conception of equality. If human beings are identical, then the application of the prior-principle of universalizability in the form of "giving equal weight to the equal interest of all parties" simplifies enormously. Equal marginal utilities of all—reflecting one interpretation of the equal treatment of needs—coincides with equal total utilities—reflecting one interpretation of serving their overall interests equally well. With diversity, the two can pull in opposite directions, and it is far from clear that "giving equal weight to the equal interest of all parties" would require us to concentrate only on one of the two parameters—taking no note of the other.

The case-implication perspective can also be used to develop a related critique, and I have tried to present such a critique elsewhere.[14] For example, if person A as a cripple gets half the utility that the pleasure-wizard person B does from any given level of income, then in the pure distribution problem between A and B the utilitarian would end up giving the pleasure-wizard B more income than the cripple A. The cripple would then be doubly worse off: both since he gets less utility from the same level of income, *and* since he will also get less income. Utilitarianism must lead to this thanks to its single-minded concern with maximizing the utility sum. The pleasure-wizard's superior efficiency in producing utility would pull income away from the less efficient cripple.

Since this example has been discussed a certain amount,[15] I should perhaps explain what is being asserted and what is not. First, it is *not* being claimed that anyone who has lower total utility (e.g., the cripple) at any given level of income must of necessity have lower marginal utility also. This must be true for some levels of income, but need not be true everywhere. Indeed, the opposite could be the case when incomes are equally distributed. If that were so, then of course even utilitarianism would give the cripple more income than the non-cripple, since at that point the cripple would be the more efficient producer of utility. My point is that there is no guarantee that this will be the case, and more particularly, if it were the case that the cripple were not only worse off in terms of total utility but could convert income into utility less efficiently everywhere (or even just at the point of equal income division), then utilitarianism would compound his disadvantage by settling him with less income on top of lower efficiency in making utility out of income. The point, of course, is not about cripples in general, nor about all people with total utility disadvantage, but concerns people—including cripples—with disadvantage in terms of both total *and* marginal utility at the relevant points.

14 *On Economic Inequality* (Oxford: Clarendon, 1973), pp. 16–20.
15 See John Harsanyi, "Non-linear Social Welfare Functions," *Theory and Decision* 6 (1976): 311–12; Harsanyi (1977); Kern (1978); Griffin (1978); Richard B. Brandt, *A Theory of the Good and the Right* (Oxford: Clarendon, 1979), chapter 16.

Second, the descriptive content of utility is rather important in this context. Obviously, if utilities were scaled to reflect moral importance, then wishing to give priority to income for the cripple would simply amount to attributing a higher "marginal utility" to the cripple's income; but this—as we have already discussed—is a very special sense of utility—quite devoid of descriptive content. In terms of descriptive features, what is being assumed in our example is that the cripple can be helped by giving him income, but the increase in his utility as a consequence of a marginal increase in income is less—in terms of the accepted descriptive criteria—than giving that unit of income to the pleasure-wizard, when both have initially the same income.

Finally, the problem for utilitarianism in this case-implication argument is not dependent on an implicit assumption that the claim to more income arising from disadvantage must dominate over the claim arising from high marginal utility.[16] A system that gives some weight to both claims would still fail to meet the utilitarian formula of social good, which demands an exclusive concern with the latter claim. It is this narrowness that makes the utilitarian conception of equality such a limited one. Even when utility is accepted as the only basis of moral importance, utilitarianism fails to capture the relevance of overall advantage for the requirements of equality. The prior-principle critiques can be supplemented by case-implication critiques using this utilitarian lack of concern with distributional questions except at the entirely marginal level.

2. Total Utility Equality

Welfarism is the view that the goodness of a state of affairs can be judged entirely by the goodness of the utilities in that state.[17] This is a less demanding view than utilitarianism in that it does not demand—in addition—that the goodness of the utilities must be judged by their sum-total. Utilitarianism is, in this sense, a special case of welfarism, and provides one illustration of it. Another distinguished case is the criterion of judging the goodness of a state by the utility level of the worst-off person in that state—a criterion often attributed to John Rawls. (*Except* by John Rawls! He uses social primary goods rather than utility as the index of advantage, as we shall presently discuss.) One can also take some other function of the utilities—other than the sum-total or the minimal element.

Utilitarian equality is one type of welfarist equality. There are others, notably the equality of total utility. It is tempting to think of this as some kind of an analogue of utilitarianism shifting the focus from marginal utility to total utility. This correspondence is, however, rather less close than it might first appear. First of all, while we economists often tend to treat the marginal and the total as belonging to the

---

16 Such an assumption is made in my Weak Equity Axiom, proposed in Sen (1973), but it is unnecessarily demanding for rejecting utilitarianism. See Griffin (1978) for a telling critique of the Weak Equity Axiom, in this exacting form.

17 See Sen (1977), and also my "Welfarism and Utilitarianism," *Journal of Philosophy* 76 (1979).

same plane of discourse, there is an important difference between them. Marginal is an essentially *counter-factual* notion: marginal utility is the additional utility that *would be* generated if the person had one more unit of income. It contrasts what is observed with what allegedly would be observed if something else were different: in this case if the income had been one unit greater. Total is not, however, an inherently counter-factual concept; whether it is or is not would depend on the variable that is being totalled. In case of utilities, if they are taken to be observed facts, total utility will not be counter-factual. Thus total utility equality is a matter for direct observation, whereas utilitarian equality is not so, since the latter requires hypotheses as to what things would have been under different postulated circumstances. The contrast can be easily traced to the fact that utilitarian equality is essentially a consequence of sum *maximization*, which is itself a counter-factual notion, whereas total utility equality is an equality of some directly observed magnitudes.

Second, utilitarianism provides a complete ordering of all utility distributions—the ranking reflecting the order of the sums of individual utilities—but as specified so far, total utility equality does not do more than just point to the case of absolute equality. In dealing with two cases of non-equal distributions, something more has to be said so that they could be ranked. The ranking can be completed in many different ways.

One way to such a complete ranking is provided by the lexicographic version of the maximin rule, which is associated with the Rawlsian Difference Principle, but interpreted in terms of utilities as opposed to primary goods. Here the goodness of the state of affairs is judged by the level of utility of the worst-off person in that state; but if the worst-off persons in two states respectively have the same level of utility, then the states are ranked according to the utility levels of the second worst-off. If they too tie, then by the utility levels of the third worst-off, and so on. And if two utility distributions are matched at each rank all the way from the worst off to the best off, then the two distributions are equally good. Following a convention established in social choice theory, I shall call this *leximin*.

In what way does total utility equality lead to the leximin? It does this when combined with some other axioms, and in fact the analysis closely parallels the recent axiomatic derivations of the Difference Principle by several authors.[18] Consider four

18 See P.J. Hammond, "Equity, Arrow's Conditions and Rawls' Difference Principle," *Econometrica* 44 (1976); S. Strasnick, "Social Choice Theory and the Derivation of Rawls' Difference Principle," *Journal of Philosophy* 73 (1976); C. d'Aspremont and L. Gevers, "Equity and Informational Basis of Collective Choice," *Review of Economic Studies* 44 (1977); K.J. Arrow, "Extended Sympathy and the Possibility of Social Choice," *American Economic Review* 67 (1977); A.K. Sen, "On Weights and Measures: Informational Constraints in Social Welfare Analysis," *Econometrica* 45 (1977); R. Deschamps and L. Gevers, "Leximin and Utilitarian Rules: A Joint Characterization," *Journal of Economic Theory* 17 (1978); K.W.S. Roberts, "Possibility Theorems with Interpersonally Comparable Welfare Levels," *Review of Economic Studies* 47 (1980); P.J. Hammond, "Two Person Equity," *Econometrica* 47 (1979).

utility levels *a, b, c, d*, in decreasing order of magnitude. One can argue that in an obvious sense the pair of extreme points *(a, d)* displays greater inequality than the pair of intermediate points *(b, c)*. Note that this is a purely *ordinal* comparison based on ranking only, and the exact magnitudes of *a, b, c*, and *d* make no difference to the comparison in question. If one were *solely* concerned with equality, then it could be argued that *(b, c)* is superior—or at least non-inferior—to *(a, d)*. This requirement may be seen as a strong version of preferring equality of utility distributions, and may be called "utility equality preference." It is possible to combine this with an axiom due to Patrick Suppes which captures the notion of *dominance* of one utility distribution over another, in the sense of each element of one distribution being at least as large as the corresponding element in the other distribution.[19] In the two-person case this requires that state *x* must be regarded as at least as good as *y, either* if each person in state *x* has at least as much utility as himself in state y, *or* if each person in state *x* has at least as much utility as the *other* person in state *y. If*, in addition, at least one of them has strictly more, then of course *x* could be declared to be strictly better (and not merely at least as good). If this Suppes principle and the "utility equality preference" are combined, then we are pushed in the direction of leximin. Indeed, leximin can be fully derived from these two principles by requiring that the approach must provide a complete ordering of all possible states no matter what the interpersonally comparable individual utilities happen to be (called "unrestricted domain"), and that the ranking of any two states must depend on utility information concerning *those* states only (called "independence").

Insofar as the requirements other than utility equality preference (i.e., the Suppes principle, unrestricted domain, and independence) are regarded as acceptable—and they have indeed been widely used in the social choice literature—leximin can be seen as the natural concomitant of giving priority to the conception of equality focussing on total utility.

It should be obvious, however, that leximin can be fairly easily criticised from the prior-principle perspective as well as the case-implication perspective. Just as utilitarianism pays no attention to the force of one's claim arising from one's disadvantage, leximin ignores claims arising from the *intensity* of one's needs. The *ordinal* characteristic that was pointed out while presenting the axiom of utility equality preference makes the approach insensitive to the magnitudes of potential utility gains and losses. While in the critique of utilitarianism that was presented earlier I argued against treating these potential gains and losses as the only basis of moral judgment, it was *not* of course alleged that these have no moral relevance at all. Take the comparison of *(a, d)* vis-à-vis *(b, c)*, discussed earlier, and let *(b, c)* stand for *(3, 2)*. Utility equality preference would assert the superiority of *(3, 2)* over *(10, 1)* as well as *(4, 1)*. Indeed, it would not distinguish between the two cases at all. It is

---

19 P. Suppes, "Some Formal Models of Grading Principles," *Synthese* 6 (1966).

this lack of concern with "how much" questions that makes leximin rather easy to criticise *either* by showing its failure to comply with such prior-principles as "giving equal weight to the equal interest of all parties," *or* by spelling out its rather austere implications in specific cases.

Aside from its indifference to "how much" questions, leximin also has little interest in "how many" questions—paying no attention at all to the number of people whose interests are overridden in the pursuit of the interests of the worst off. The worst-off position rules the roost, and it does not matter whether this goes against the interests of one other person, or against those of a million or a billion other persons. It is sometimes claimed that leximin would not be such an extreme criterion if it could be modified so that this innumeracy were avoided, and if the interests of *one* worse-off position were given priority over the interests of exactly *one* better-off position, but not necessarily against the interests of *more than one* better-off position. In fact, one can define a less demanding version of leximin, which can be called leximin-2, which takes the form of applying the leximin principle *if* all persons other than two are indifferent between the alternatives, but not necessarily otherwise. Leximin-2, as a compromise, will be still unconcerned with "how much" questions on the magnitudes of utilities of the two non-indifferent persons, but need not be blinkered about "how many" questions dealing with numbers of people: the priority applies to one person over exactly one other.[20]

Interestingly enough, a consistency problem intervenes here. It can be proved that given the regularity conditions, viz., unrestricted domain and independence, leximin-2 logically entails leximin in general.[21] That is, given these regularity conditions, there is no way of retaining moral sensitivity to the number of people on each side by choosing the limited requirement of leximin-2 without going all the way to leximin itself. It appears that indifference to *how much* questions concerning utilities implies indifference to *how many* questions concerning the number of people on different sides. One innumeracy begets another.

Given the nature of these critiques of utilitarian equality and total utility equality respectively, it is natural to ask whether some *combination* of the two should not meet both sets of objections. If utilitarianism is attacked for its unconcern with inequalities of the utility distribution, and leximin is criticised for its lack of interest in the magnitudes of utility gains and losses, and even in the numbers involved, then isn't the right solution to choose some mixture of the two? It is at this point that the long-postponed question of the relation between utility and moral worth becomes crucial. While utilitarianism and leximin differ sharply from each other in the use that they

---

20 Leximin—and maximin—are concerned with conflicts between positional priorities, i.e., between ranks (such as the "worst-off position," "second worst-off position," etc.), and not with interpersonal priorities. When positions coincide with persons (e.g., the *same* person being the worst off in each state), then positional conflicts translate directly into personal conflicts.

21 Theorem 8, Sen (1977). See also Hammond (1979) for extensions of this result.

respectively make of the utility information, both share an exclusive concern with utility data. If non-utility considerations have any role in either approach, this arises from the part they play in the determination of utilities, or possibly as surrogates for utility information in the absence of adequate utility data. A combination of utilitarianism and leximin would still be confined to the box of welfarism, and it remains to be examined whether welfarism as a general approach is *itself* adequate.

One aspect of the obtuseness of welfarism was discussed clearly by John Rawls.

> In calculating the greatest balance of satisfaction it does not matter, except indirectly, what the desires are for. We are to arrange institutions so as to obtain the greatest sum of satisfactions; we ask no questions about their source or quality but only how their satisfaction would affect the total of well-being.... Thus if men take a certain pleasure in discriminating against one another, in subjecting others to a lesser liberty as a means of enhancing their self-respect, then the satisfaction of these desires must be weighed in our deliberations according to their intensity, or whatever, along with other desires.... In justice as fairness, on the other hand, persons accept in advance a principle of equal liberty and they do this without a knowledge of their more particular ends.... An individual who finds that he enjoys seeing others in positions of lesser liberty understands that he has no claim whatever to this enjoyment. The pleasure he takes in other's deprivation is wrong in itself: it is a satisfaction which requires the violation of a principle to which he would agree in the original position.[22]

It is easily seen that this is an argument not merely against utilitarianism, but against the adequacy of utility information for moral judgments of states of affairs, and is, thus, an attack on welfarism in general. Second, it is clear that as a criticism of welfarism—and *a fortiori* as a critique of utilitarianism—the argument uses a principle that is unnecessarily strong. If it were the case that pleasures taken "in other's deprivation" were not taken to be wrong in itself, but simply *disregarded*, even then the rejection of welfarism would stand. Furthermore, even if such pleasures were regarded as valuable, but *less* valuable than pleasures arising from other sources (e.g., enjoying food, work, or leisure), welfarism would still stand rejected. The issue—as John Stuart Mill had noted—is the lack of "parity" between one source of utility and another.[23] Welfarism requires the endorsement not merely of the widely shared intuition that any pleasure has some value—and one would have to be a bit of a kill-joy to dissent from this—but also the much more dubious proposition that pleasures must be relatively weighed *only* according to their respective intensities, irrespective of the source of the pleasure and the nature of the activity that goes with

---

22 Rawls (1971), pp. 30–31.
23 John Stuart Mill, *On Liberty* (1859), p. 140.

it. Finally, Rawls's argument takes the form of an appeal to the prior-principle of equating moral rightness with prudential acceptability in the original position. Even those who do not accept that prior principle could reject the welfarist no-nonsense counting of utility irrespective of all other information by reference to other prior principles, e.g., the irreducible value of liberty.

The relevance of non-utility information to moral judgments is the central issue involved in disputing welfarism. Libertarian considerations point towards a particular class of non-utility information, and I have argued elsewhere that this may require even the rejection of the so-called Pareto principle based on utility dominance.[24] But there are also other types of non-utility information which have been thought to be intrinsically important. Tim Scanlon has recently discussed the contrast between "urgency" and utility (or intensity of preference). He has also argued that "the criteria of well-being that we actually employ in making moral judgments are objective," and a person's level of well-being is taken to be "independent of that person's tastes and interests."[25] These moral judgments could thus conflict with utilitarian—and more generally (Scanlon could have argued) with welfarist—moralities, no matter whether utility is interpreted as pleasure, or—as is increasingly common recently—as desire-fulfilment.

However, acknowledging the relevance of objective factors does not require that well-being be taken to be independent of tastes, and Scanlon's categories are *too* pure. For example, a lack of "parity" between utility from self-regarding actions and that from other-regarding actions will go beyond utility as an index of well-being and will be fatal to welfarism, but the contrast is not, of course, independent of tastes and subjective features. "Objective" considerations can count along with a person's tastes. What is required is the denial that a person's well-being be judged *exclusively* in terms of his or her utilities. If such judgments take into account a person's pleasures and desire-fulfilments, but also certain objective factors, e.g., whether he or she is hungry, cold, or oppressed, the resulting calculus would still be non-welfarist. Welfarism is an extremist position, and its denial can take many different forms—pure and mixed—so long as totally ignoring non-utility information is avoided.

Second, it is also clear that the notion of urgency need not work only *through* the determinants of personal well-being—however broadly conceived. For example, the claim that one should not be *exploited* at work is not based on making exploitation an additional parameter in the specification of well-being on top of such factors as income and effort, but on the moral view that a person deserves to get what he—according to one way of characterizing production—has produced. Similarly, the urgency deriving from principles such as "equal pay for equal work" hits directly at discrimination without having to redefine the notion of personal well-being to take note of such discriminations. One could, for example, say: "She must be paid just as

24 Sen (1970), especially chapter 6. Also Sen (1979).
25 Scanlon (1975), pp. 658–59.

much as the men working in that job, not primarily because she would otherwise have a lower level of well-being than the others, but simply because she is doing the *same* work as the men there, and why should she be paid less?" These moral claims, based on non-welfarist conceptions of equality, have played important parts in social movements, and it seems difficult to sustain the hypothesis that they are purely "instrumental" claims—ultimately justified by their indirect impact on the fulfilment of welfarist, or other well-being-based, objectives.

Thus the dissociation of urgency from utility can arise from two different sources. One disentangles the notion of personal well-being from utility, and the other makes urgency not a function only of well-being. But, at the same time, the former does not require that well-being be independent of utility, and the latter does not necessitate a notion of urgency that is independent of personal well-being. Welfarism is a purist position and must avoid any contamination from either of these sources.

3. Rawlsian Equality

Rawls's "two principles of justice" characterize the need for equality in terms of— what he has called—"primary social goods."[26] These are "things that every rational man is presumed to want," including "rights, liberties and opportunities, income and wealth, and the social bases of self-respect." Basic liberties are separated out as having priority over other primary goods, and thus priority is given to the principle of liberty which demands that "each person is to have an equal right to the most extensive basic liberty compatible with a similar liberty for others." The second principle supplements this, demanding efficiency and equality, judging advantage in terms of an index of primary goods. Inequalities are condemned unless they work out to everyone's advantage. This incorporates the "Difference Principle" in which priority is given to furthering the interests of the worst-off. And that leads to maximin, or to leximin, defined not on individual utilities but on the index of primary goods. But given the priority of the liberty principle, no trade-offs are permitted between basic liberties and economic and social gain.

Herbert Hart has persuasively disputed Rawls's arguments for the priority of liberty,[27] but with that question I shall not be concerned in this lecture. What is crucial for the problem under discussion is the concentration on bundles of primary social goods. Some of the difficulties with welfarism that I tried to discuss will not apply to the pursuit of Rawlsian equality. Objective criteria of well-being can be directly accommodated within the index of primary goods. So can be Mill's denial of the parity between pleasures from different sources, since the sources can be discriminated on the basis of the nature of the goods. Furthermore, while the Difference Principle is egalitarian in a way similar to leximin, it avoids the much-

---

26 Rawls (1971), pp. 60–65.
27 H.L.A. Hart, "Rawls on Liberty and Its Priority," *University of Chicago Law Review* 40 (1973); reprinted in N. Daniels, ed., *Reading Rawls* (Oxford: Blackwell, 1975).

criticised feature of leximin of giving more income to people who are hard to please and who have to be deluged in champagne and buried in caviar to bring them to a normal level of utility, which you and I get from a sandwich and beer. Since advantage is judged not in terms of utilities at all, but through the index of primary goods, expensive tastes cease to provide a ground for getting more income. Rawls justifies this in terms of a person's responsibility for his own ends.

But what about the cripple with utility disadvantage, whom we discussed earlier? Leximin will give him more income in a pure distribution problem. Utilitarianism, I had complained, will give him *less*. The Difference Principle will give him neither more nor less on grounds of his being a cripple. His utility disadvantage will be irrelevant to the Difference Principle. This may seem hard, and I think it is. Rawls justifies this by pointing out that "hard cases" can "distract our moral perception by leading us to think of people distant from us whose fate arouses pity and anxiety."[28] This can be so, but hard cases do exist, and to take disabilities, or special health needs, or physical or mental defects, as morally irrelevant, or to leave them out for fear of making a mistake, may guarantee that the *opposite* mistake will be made.

And the problem does not end with hard cases. The primary goods approach seems to take little note of the diversity of human beings. In the context of assessing utilitarian equality, it was argued that if people were fundamentally similar in terms of utility functions, then the utilitarian concern with maximizing the sum-total of utilities would push us simultaneously also in the direction of equality of utility levels. Thus utilitarianism could be rendered vastly more attractive if people really were similar. A corresponding remark can be made about the Rawlsian Difference Principle. If people were basically very similar, then an index of primary goods might be quite a good way of judging advantage. But, in fact, people seem to have very different needs varying with health, longevity, climatic conditions, location, work conditions, temperament, and even body size (affecting food and clothing requirements). So what is involved is not merely ignoring a few hard cases, but overlooking very widespread and real differences. Judging advantage purely in terms of primary goods leads to a partially blind morality.

Indeed, it can be argued that there is, in fact, an element of "fetishism" in the Rawlsian framework. Rawls takes primary goods as the embodiment of advantage, rather than taking advantage to be a *relationship* between persons and goods. Utilitarianism, or leximin, or—more generally—welfarism does not have this fetishism, since utilities are reflections of one type of relation between persons and goods. For example, income and wealth are not valued under utilitarianism as physical units, but in terms of their capacity to create human happiness or to satisfy human desires. Even if utility is not thought to be the right focus for the person–good relationship, to have an entirely good-oriented framework provides a peculiar way of judging advantage.

---

28 John Rawls, "A Kantian Concept of Equality," *Cambridge Review* (February 1975): 96.

It can also be argued that while utility in the form of happiness or desire-fulfilment may be an *inadequate* guide to urgency, the Rawlsian framework asserts it to be *irrelevant* to urgency, which is, of course, a much stronger claim. The distinction was discussed earlier in the context of assessing welfarism, and it was pointed out that a rejection of welfarism need not take us to the point in which utility is given no role whatsoever. That a person's interest should have nothing directly to do with his happiness or desire-fulfilment seems difficult to justify. Even in terms of the prior-principle of prudential acceptability in the "original position," it is not at all clear why people in that primordial state should be taken to be so indifferent to the joys and sufferings in occupying particular positions, or if they are not, why their concern about these joys and sufferings should be taken to be morally irrelevant.

4. Basic Capability Equality

This leads to the further question: Can we not construct an adequate theory of equality on the *combined* grounds of Rawlsian equality and equality under the two welfarist conceptions, with some trade-offs among them? I would now like to argue briefly why I believe this too may prove to be informationally short. This can, of course, easily be asserted *if* claims arising from considerations other than well-being were acknowledged to be legitimate. Non-exploitation, or non-discrimination, requires the use of information not fully captured either by utility or by primary goods. Other conceptions of entitlements can also be brought in going beyond concern with personal well-being only. But in what follows I shall not introduce these concepts. My contention is that *even* the concept of *needs* does not get adequate coverage through the information on primary goods and utility.

I shall use a case-implication argument. Take the cripple again with marginal utility disadvantage. We saw that utilitarianism would do nothing for him; in fact it will give him *less* income than to the physically fit. Nor would the Difference Principle help him; it will leave his physical disadvantage severely alone. He did, however, get preferential treatment under leximin, and more generally, under criteria fostering total equality. His low level of total utility was the basis of his claim. But now suppose that he is no worse off than others in utility terms despite his physical handicap because of certain other utility features. This could be because he has a jolly disposition. Or because he has a low aspiration level and his heart leaps up whenever he sees a rainbow in the sky. Or because he is religious and feels that he will be rewarded in after-life, or cheerfully accepts what he takes to be just penalty for misdeeds in a past incarnation. The important point is that despite his marginal utility disadvantage, he has no longer a total utility deprivation. Now not even leximin—or any other notion of equality focussing on total utility—will do much for him. If we still think that he has needs as a cripple that should be catered to, then the basis of that claim clearly rests neither in high marginal utility, nor in low total utility, nor—of course—in deprivation in terms of primary goods.

It is arguable that what is missing in all this framework is some notion of "basic capabilities": a person being able to do certain basic things. The ability to move about is the relevant one here, but one can consider others, e.g., the ability to meet one's nutritional requirements, the wherewithal to be clothed and sheltered, the power to participate in the social life of the community. The notion of urgency related to this is not fully captured by either utility or primary goods, or any combination of the two. Primary goods suffers from fetishist handicap in being concerned with goods, and even though the list of goods is specified in a broad and inclusive way, encompassing rights, liberties, opportunities, income, wealth, and the social basis of self-respect, it still is concerned with good things rather than with what these good things *do* to human beings. Utility, on the other hand, *is* concerned with what these things do to human beings, but uses a metric that focusses not on the person's capabilities but on his mental reaction. There is something still missing in the combined list of primary goods and utilities. If it is argued that resources should be devoted to remove or substantially reduce the handicap of the cripple despite there being no marginal utility argument (because it is expensive), despite there being no total utility argument (because he is so contented), and despite there being no primary goods deprivation (because he has the goods that others have), the case must rest on something else. I believe what is at issue is the interpretation of needs in the form of basic capabilities. This interpretation of needs and interests is often implicit in the demand for equality. This type of equality I shall call "basic capability equality."

The focus on basic capabilities can be seen as a natural extension of Rawls's concern with primary goods, shifting attention from goods to what goods do to human beings. Rawls himself motivates judging advantage in terms of primary goods by referring to capabilities, even though his criteria end up focussing on goods as such: on income rather than on what income does, on the "social bases of self-respect" rather than on self-respect itself, and so on. If human beings were very like each other, this would not have mattered a great deal, but there is evidence that the conversion of goods to capabilities varies from person to person substantially, and the equality of the former may still be far from the equality of the latter.

There are, of course, many difficulties with the notion of "basic capability equality." In particular, the problem of indexing the basic capability bundles is a serious one. It is, in many ways, a problem comparable with the indexing of primary good bundles in the context of Rawlsian equality. This is not the occasion to go into the technical issues involved in such an indexing, but it is clear that whatever partial ordering can be done on the basis of broad uniformity of personal preferences must be supplemented by certain established conventions of relative importance.

The ideas of relative importance are, of course, conditional on the nature of the society. The notion of the equality of basic capabilities is a very general one, but any application of it must be rather culture-dependent, especially in the weighting of different capabilities. While Rawlsian equality has the characteristic of being both culture-dependent and fetishist, basic capability equality avoids fetishism, but remains culture-dependent. Indeed, basic capability equality can be seen as essentially an extension of the Rawlsian approach in a non-fetishist direction.

5. Concluding Remarks

I end with three final remarks. First, it is not my contention that basic capability equality can be the sole guide to the moral good. For one thing morality is not concerned only with equality. For another, while it is my contention that basic capability equality has certain clear advantages over other types of equality, I did not argue that the others were morally irrelevant. Basic capability equality is a partial guide to the part of moral goodness that is associated with the idea of equality. I have tried to argue that as a partial guide it has virtues that the other characterisations of equality do not possess.

Second, the index of basic capabilities, like utility, can be used in many different ways. Basic capability equality corresponds to total utility equality, and it can be extended in different directions, e.g., to leximin of basic capabilities. On the other hand, the index can be used also in a way similar to utilitarianism, judging the strength of a claim in terms of incremental contribution to *enhancing* the index value. The main departure is in focussing on a *magnitude* different from utility as well as the primary goods index. The new dimension can be utilised in different ways, of which basic capability equality is only one.

Last, the bulk of this lecture has been concerned with rejecting the claims of utilitarian equality, total utility equality, and Rawlsian equality to provide a sufficient basis for the equality-aspect of morality—indeed, even for that part of it which is concerned with needs rather than deserts. I have argued that none of these three is sufficient, nor is any combination of the three.

This is my main thesis. I have also made the constructive claim that this gap can be narrowed by the idea of basic capability equality, and more generally by the use of basic capability as a morally relevant dimension taking us beyond utility and primary goods. I should end by pointing out that the validity of the main thesis is not conditional on the acceptance of this constructive claim.[29]

---

29 For helpful comments I am most grateful to Derek Parfit, Jim Griffin, and John Perry.

Recommended Reading

Bell, D. (2009). "Communitarianism." *Stanford Encyclopedia of Philosophy.* <http://plato.stanford.edu/entries/communitarianism>.

Cohen, G.A. (1995). *Self-Ownership, Freedom, and Equality.* Cambridge: Cambridge UP.

Crisp, R. (2008). "Well-Being." Ed. E.N. Zalta. *Stanford Encyclopedia of Philosophy.* <http://plato.stanford.edu/entries/well-being>.

Griffin, J. (1986). *Well-Being.* Oxford: Clarendon.

Mill, J.S. (1978). *Utilitarianism.* Indianapolis: Hackett.

Nozick, R. (1974). *Anarchy, State and Utopia.* New York: Basic Books.

Parfit, D. (1984). *Reasons and Persons.* Oxford: Clarendon.

Pogge, T. (2007). *John Rawls: His Life and Theory of Justice.* Oxford: Oxford UP.

Rawls, J. (1971). *A Theory of Justice.* Cambridge, MA: Harvard UP.

Sandel, M. (1982). *Liberalism and the Limits of Justice.* Cambridge, MA: Harvard UP.

Sen, A., & Williams, B. (1982). *Utilitarianism and Beyond.* New York: Cambridge UP.

Singer, P. (2011). *Practical Ethics.* Cambridge: Cambridge UP.

Sumner, W. (1996). *Welfare, Happiness, and Ethics.* Oxford: Clarendon.

II

Poverty: Introduction

The most pressing ethical issue from a global perspective is perhaps the unequal, and arguably inequitable, distribution of wealth amongst nations and individuals, and the extent of extreme poverty.

Until the Industrial Revolution of the eighteenth century, all of us were, by contemporary standards, very poor. As late as 1820, Jeffrey Sachs tells us, the average income per person in Western Europe was around 90 per cent of the average income of Africa today.[1] The Industrial Revolution, which began in England roughly during the mid-eighteenth century and spread to Europe and beyond, made possible the mass production of goods and services on a scale previously unimaginable.

Since then all regions have experienced economic growth, but some regions, including Europe, North America, and Japan, have grown more rapidly. Today, as a consequence, there are vast inequalities in wealth between, on the one hand, the United States, Japan, and affluent European countries, and, on the other hand, the developing countries in the Global South. One-sixth of the world's population has achieved high-income status; an additional two-thirds have risen to middle-income status. A sixth of humanity, however, is stuck in extreme poverty.

The very poor are not like us. They do not live as we do but with fewer gadgets and less disposable income. In their detailed empirical study of the economic lives of the poor in 13 developing countries, Abhijit V. Banerjee and Esther Duflo describe the way in which the poor, those living on less than $2 per day, live—their domestic arrangements, patterns of consumption, occupations, and economic environment. The choices the poor make represent a rational response to poverty and, most

---

1 Jeffrey Sachs, *The End of Poverty: Economic Possibilities for Our Time* (New York: Penguin, 2005).

POVERTY

especially, Banerjee and Duflo suggest, to very limited access to efficient markets and infrastructure. These choices, however, lock in poverty and make it unfeasible for the poor to better themselves.

The poor, in both affluent countries and in low-income countries of the Global South, work harder than we do but have far less to show for their efforts. Like the Chicago ghetto-dwellers that sociologist Sudhir Vankatesh describes in his study of the underground economy, *Off the Books*,[2] and elsewhere, the poor in developing countries are "hustlers": individuals often operate a half-dozen or more informal microbusinesses, hustling customers who are usually equally poor. Without access to credit, without land titles, without the infrastructure to support their operations, and without adequate operating capital, they cannot build businesses that would lift them out of poverty. They can only hustle. The poor are not like us, in the lives they live or in the choices they make, because their circumstances are not like our circumstances.

The very rich, as F. Scott Fitzgerald remarked, are also not like us. "Dressing for Lula," which appeared in the *New Yorker*, spins off from a history of Daslu, a "heavily fortified boutique [where] São Paulo's richest women shop" to an account of the economic disparities in Brazil, which resulted in Luiz Inacio Lula da Silva's landslide victory in Brazil's presidential election. Author Rebecca Mead describes Daslu as a universe of luxury largely insulated from the outside world:

> The customers, who come from what are unflinchingly referred to as the best families, are attended by glossy-looking salesgirls from the same social class: Daslu functions as a kind of finishing school for the daughters of the rich.... Among the best customers of the store are the salesgirls...one of them, Carolina Nunes explained... "At least half the money we make we spend on clothes"...Nunes might wait an entire afternoon for a client lounging on the couch by the store's coffee counter with other underemployed Dasluzetes.[3]

Are these vast discrepancies of wealth morally acceptable? Are we morally obliged to do what we can to alleviate extreme poverty? And if we are, what should we do?

Peter Singer argues that ameliorating the distress of the global poor is a case of "easy rescue" comparable to rescuing a drowning child from a shallow pond: "[W]e can all save lives of people, both children and adults, who would otherwise die, and we can do so at a very small cost to us: the cost of a new CD, a shirt or a night out at a restaurant or concert, can mean the difference between life and death to more than one person somewhere in the world—and overseas aid agencies like Oxfam overcome the problem of acting at a distance."[4] Economists, however, suggest that

2 Sudhir Vankatesh, *Off the Books* (Cambridge, MA: Harvard UP, 2006).
3 Rebecca Mead, "Dressing for Lula," pp. 122–26 in this volume.
4 Peter Singer, "The Drowning Child and the Expanding Circle," p. 122 in this volume.

rescue may not be so easy. We can and, as Singer suggests, should contribute to aid agencies that provide food assistance and medical care to alleviate suffering, but promoting sustainable development in the Global South is problematic.

Amongst nations, patterns of poverty and prosperity are persistent, though not immutable. As Daron Acemoglu and James Robinson note, addressing the question of why nations fail, most current world equality emerged following the Industrial Revolution in the late eighteenth century. Earlier, not only were gaps in prosperity much smaller, but the rankings of nations were different. Why do nations fail? Acemoglu and Robinson, addressing this question, consider and dismiss three hypotheses. Nations on the first account fail because of physical geography—because they have insalubrious tropical climates, which sap energy or, according to the current revival of the hypothesis, because they lack large domesticable animals, land suitable for agriculture, access to sea routes, or other geographical disadvantages. Acemoglu and Robinson produce counterexamples. Is failure a consequence of culture? Or of ignorance by national decision makers? Acemoglu and Robinson argue that it is not. The immediate cause of failure, they argue, is political.

Nevertheless, even if the immediate cause of poverty in the Global South is political, we can still wonder why the political impediments to development figure disproportionately in the Global South. More importantly, we ask, what can be done to fix this?

Jeffrey Sachs, formerly director of the United Nations Millennium Project, an international future-research think-tank, and William Easterly offer competing analyses and remedies for global poverty. Sachs, founder of the Millennium Promise Alliance, devoted to achieving UN Millennium Goals,[5] argues that poor countries are stuck in "poverty traps" from which there is no escape except through the provision of massively scaled-up foreign aid. He holds that by substantially increasing aid to developing countries, extreme poverty can be eradicated within 20 years.

Easterly, Sachs's most prominent critic, is skeptical about this program. Noting that aid amounting to $2.3 trillion during the past five decades "has left the most aid-intensive regions . . . wallowing in continued stagnation," Easterly is skeptical of "the Big Plan" and recommends modest, piecemeal interventions in his current "Modest Proposal" critiquing Sachs.[6] Easterly argues that additional aid will be wasted and, in *The Illusive Quest for Growth*,[7] analyzes the reasons why foreign aid to many Third World countries since World War II has failed to produce sustainable development.

Paul Collier offers an alternative, nuanced analysis citing an entangled complex of factors including civil war, geographical disadvantage, bad governance, and the "resource curse" as impediments to development in sub-Saharan Africa. If the causes

---

5 <http://www.millenniumpromise.org/about/mdgs>.

6 William Easterly, "A Modest Proposal," pp. 147–50 in this volume.

7 William Easterly, *The Illusive Quest for Growth: Economists' Adventures in the Tropics* (Cambridge, MA: MIT, 2001).

of extreme poverty and stalled development are complex, the remedies are too. In addition to aid, Collier recommends protectionist policies in the short run to shield African manufacturers from Asian competition, more effective global policing to thwart corrupt kleptocrats, and, in a range of cases, military intervention.

It is easy enough to respond to famines, epidemics, and other emergencies with aid, and that is something we should most certainly do. But achieving sustainable development in poor countries of the Global South is fraught with complex, often intractable difficulties, and how they ought to be addressed is controversial. Sachs, Easterly, and Collier suggest radically different responses, but one thing that emerges from their analyses is that extricating the poor in developing countries from their predicament will not be a case of easy rescue.

7. The Economic Lives of the Poor[*]

Abhijit V. Banerjee and Esther Duflo

In what turned out to be a rhetorical master-move, the 1990 World Development Report from the World Bank defined the "extremely poor" people of the world as those who are currently living on no more than $1 per day per person, measured at the 1985 purchasing power parity (PPP) exchange rate.[1] Even though there have always been poverty lines—indeed one dollar per day was chosen in part because of its proximity to the poverty lines used by many poor countries[2]—this particular one has come to dominate the conversations about poverty in a particularly stark way.

But how actually does one live on less than one dollar per day? This essay is about the economic lives of the extremely poor: the choices they face, the constraints they grapple with, and the challenges they meet.

The available evidence on the economic lives of the extremely poor is incomplete in many important ways. However, a number of recent data sets and a body of new research have added a lot to what we know about their lives, and taken together there is probably enough to start building an image of the way they live their lives.

Our discussion of the economic lives of the extremely poor builds on household surveys conducted in 13 countries listed in Table 7.1: Cote d'Ivoire, Guatemala, India, Indonesia, Mexico, Nicaragua, Pakistan, Panama, Papua New Guinea, Peru, South Africa, Tanzania, and Timor Leste.

We mainly use the Living Standard Measurement Surveys (LSMS) conducted by the World Bank and the "Family Life Surveys" conducted by the Rand Corporation, all of which are publicly available. In addition, we also use two surveys that we conducted in India with our collaborators. The first was carried out in 2002 and 2003 in 100 hamlets of Udaipur District, Rajasthan (Banerjee, Deaton, and Duflo,

---

* Source: *Journal of Economic Perspectives* 21.1 (2007): 141–68.

1 In 1993, the poverty line was updated to $1.08 per person per day at the 1993 PPP exchange rate (this is the line we use in this paper).

2 For example, the "All India Rural" poverty line used by the Indian Planning Commission was Rs 328 per person per month, or $32 in PPP dollars in 1999/2000.

Table 7.1   Description of Data Sets

| | | | | Households (HHs) living on less than | | | |
| | | | | $1.08 per person per day | | $2.16 per person per day | |
Country	Source	Year	Avg. monthly consumption per capita (In PPP$)	Number surveyed	Percent of total surveyed HHs	Number surveyed	Percent of total surveyed HHs
Cote d'Ivoire	LSMS	1988	664.13	375	14%	1,411	49%
Guatemala	GFHS	1995	301.92	469	18%	910	34%
India-Hyderabad	Banerjee-Duflo-Glennerster	2005	71.61	106	7%	1,030	56%
India-Udaipur	Banerjee-Deaton-Duflo	2004	43.12	482	47%	883	86%
Indonesia	IFLS	2000	142.84	320	4%	2,106	26%
Mexico	MxFLS	2002	167.97	959	15%	2,698	39%
Nicaragua	LSMS	2001	117.34	333	6%	1,322	28%
Pakistan	LSMS	1991	48.01	1,573	40%	3,632	83%
Panama	LSMS	1997	359.73	123	2%	439	6%
Papua New Guinea	LSMS	1996	133.38	185	15%	485	38%
Peru	LSMS	1994	151.88	297	7%	821	20%
South Africa	LSMS	1993	291.33	413	5%	1,641	19%
Tanzania	LSMS	1993	50.85	1,184	35%	2,941	73%
Timor Leste	LSMS	2001	64.42	662	15%	2,426	51%

Sources: The Mexican Family Life Survey is documented in Rubalcava and Teruel (2004) and available at ⟨http://www.radix.uia.mx/ennvih/⟩. The LSMS are available from the World Bank LSMS project page. The IFLS and GFLS are available from the RAND FLS page ⟨http://www.rand.org/labor/FLS/⟩. The Udaipur data is available from ⟨www.povertyactionlab.org/data⟩. The Hyderabad data is forthcoming on the same page.

Notes: To compute the $1.08 and $2.16 poverty line for the countries in our sample, we use the 1993 consumption exchange rate provided by the World Bank (available at ⟨http://iresearch.worldbank.org/PovcalNet/jsp/index.jsp⟩) multiplied by the ratio of the country's Consumer Price Index to the US Consumer Price Index between 1993 and the year the survey was carried out. To compute average consumption per capita and the proportion of households in poverty, observations are weighted using ⟨survey weight * household size⟩.

2004). Udaipur is one of the poorer districts of India, with a large tribal population and an unusually high level of female illiteracy (at the time of the 1991 census, only 5 percent of women were literate in rural Udaipur). The second (Banerjee, Duflo, and Glennerster, 2005) surveyed 2,000 households in "slums" (or informal neighborhoods) of Hyderabad, the capital of the state of Andhra Pradesh and one of the boom-towns of post-liberalization India. We chose these countries and surveys because they provide detailed information on extremely poor households around the world, from Asia to Africa to Latin America, including information on what they consume, where they work, and how they save and borrow. To flesh out our main themes further, we also draw freely on the existing research literature.

From each of these surveys we identified the extremely poor as those living in households where the consumption per capita is less than $1.08 per person per day, as well as the merely "poor" defined as those who live under $2.16 a day using the PPP in year 1993 as benchmark.[3] The use of consumption, rather than income, is motivated by the better quality of the consumption data in these surveys (Deaton, 2004). Table 7.1 provides some background information on these surveys. It lists the countries, and the source of the survey data. It also lists the sample sizes: the numbers and the proportions of the extremely poor and the poor in each survey. The fraction of individuals living under $1 per day in the survey vary from 2 percent in Panama to 47 percent in Udaipur, and the fraction living under $2 per day varies from 6 percent in Panama to 86 percent in Udaipur....

There are many important issues with our identification of the poor. First, purchasing power parity exchange rates, which are essential to compute a "uniform" poverty line, have been criticized as inadequate, infrequently updated, and inapplicable to the consumption of the extremely poor (Deaton, 2004, 2006). Prices are typically higher in urban than in rural areas, and even in rural areas, the poor may pay different prices than everyone else. Also, reporting periods vary significantly from survey to survey and this, it has been shown, systematically affects what people report.

These problems may affect us less because we are not focused on counting the exact number of poor. In describing what their lives look like, misclassifying a number of households should not change anything very important about the averages we observe in the data, unless the number affected are very large, and those artificially moved into or out of poverty are very different than the other poor. It turns out that most of our conclusions do not change if we look at the poor rather than the extremely poor, which is of course reassuring. Nevertheless one cannot obviously entirely rule out the possibility that our results may have been very different had we used a different poverty line.

We will also assume that the people we are describing as the poor are the long-term poor in the sense that their permanent income is actually close to their observed consumption. If, instead, they were just transiting through poverty, some of the behaviors that we will observe (such as lack of savings) would be less puzzling, and others (like the lack of assets) would be much more so. We feel that this is a reasonable assumption in most of the countries, since the fraction of the population below $2.16 a day is actually sizeable (40 percent of the population or more in

---

3 In keeping with convention, we call these the $1 and $2 poverty lines, respectively.

the median country and more than 70 percent in quite a few) and it is unlikely that there are quite so many transients.[4] However, for this reason, the poor in Panama (where only 6 percent of the population is poor) or South Africa (where 19 percent are) may not be easily compared to the poor in some of the other countries, where they are much more numerous.

The Living Arrangements of the Poor

The typical extremely poor family tends to be rather large, at least by the standards of today's rich countries. The number of family members varies between about 6 and about 12, with a median value (across the different countries) of between 7 and 8, compared to 2.5 in the 2000 US census, for example.

Unfortunately not all surveys report fertility rates, which would have been the ideal way to check how much of these high numbers comes from the fact that there are a lot of children. The data does however give us some broad measures of the age structure in these families (the number of those below 13, between 13 and 18, above 51, etc.). The number of adults (i.e. those over 18) ranges from about 2.5 to about 5, with a median of about 3, which suggests a family structure where it is common for adults to live with people they are not conjugally related to (parents, siblings, uncles, cousins, etc.). This is a common finding in the literature on developing countries, and has often been related to the fact that when every penny counts, it helps to spread the fixed costs of living (like housing) over a larger number of people. Consistent with this view, we do see a fall in family size when we go from the extremely poor to the entire group below $2 a day, of the order of one half of one person or more, though at least some part of this comes from the fact that the extremely poor families have more children living with them.

The other fact is that there are a large number of children in these families. This does not necessarily imply high levels of fertility, as families often have multiple adult women. When we look at the number of children (ages 0 to 18) per woman in the child-bearing age (ages 21–50) we get numbers between 2 and 4 in both the rural and the urban sample, though the urban ratios tend to be slightly lower. These would not be especially high if they were actually fertility rates, but they are not—for example, a 51-year-old could have a child who is now 36, but we only include those who are below 18. A more useful exercise with this data is to compare the number of young people (those below 18) in these families with the number of older people (those above 51). The ratio varies between 3 and 9 in the rural sample with a median of 6, and between 2 and 11 in the urban sample, with a median once again of around 6. The corresponding number in the US is around 1. This is a very young population.

One reason the population is young is that there are a lot of younger people, which

---

4 The extremely poor are less numerous, but as we observed above, our conclusions are largely independent of the poor/extremely poor distinction.

reflects high fertility if not now, at least in the recent past. A second reason is that there are actually very few older people. The ratio of the number of older people (over age 51) to the number of people of "prime-age" (21–50) tends to be between 0.2 and 0.3 in both the rural and the urban sample. The corresponding number in the US, for example, is approximately 0.6. The difference probably owes a lot to the higher mortality rates among those who are older and poor in poor countries, though it is possible that older people are underrepresented in our sample because they tend to be richer. However in the latter case, we might have expected to find more of the older people among the poor (as compared to the extremely poor), whereas in the data there is no clear pattern.

How the Poor Spend Their Money

A common image of the extremely poor is that they do not get to make many real choices. Indeed there must be some people who work as hard as they can—which may not be particularly hard, because they are underfed and weak—and earn barely enough to cover their basic needs which they always try to fulfill in the least expensive way. Historically, poverty lines in many countries were originally set to capture exactly this definition of poverty—at the budget needed to buy a certain amount of calories, plus some other indispensable purchases (such as housing). A "poor" person was by definition someone without enough to eat.

Food and Other Consumption Purchases

Yet the average person living at under $1 per day does not seem to put every available penny into buying more calories. Among our 13 countries, food typically represents from 56 to 78 percent among rural households, and 56 to 74 percent in urban areas. For the rural poor in Mexico, slightly less than half the budget (49.6 percent) is allocated to purchase food.[5]

Of course they could be spending the rest of the money on other commodities which they also greatly need. Yet among the non-food items that the poor spend

5 The fact that the share spent on food, which is often seen as a physiological necessity, varies so much across countries is itself interesting. One possibility is that this represents the fact that the poor have more choice in some countries than in others, because consumption goods are cheaper relative to food in some countries. For example, India, a large economy with a long history of being relatively closed, has evolved a large menu of low-cost and lower-quality consumer goods that are produced almost exclusively for the domestic market; examples include toothpaste, cigarettes, and clothing. Other countries must buy these goods at higher prices on the global market. If the manufactured consumer goods that the average person buys in India tend to be inexpensive relative to their traded counterparts, the ratio between the consumption exchange rate at purchasing power parity and the official exchange rate ought to be relatively low in India. More generally: the lower this ratio, the lower the share of the consumption that should be made up of food. In our data, it turns out that the correlation between the ratio of the purchasing power parity exchange rate for consumption to the official exchange rate in 1993 and the share of expenditure spent on food is 0.33 among these 13 countries, although this sample is of course too small to support a definite conclusion.

significant amounts of money on, alcohol and tobacco show up prominently. The extremely poor in rural areas spent 4.1 percent of their budget on tobacco and alcohol in Papua New Guinea, 5.0 percent in Udaipur, India; 6.0 percent in Indonesia and 8.1 percent in Mexico; though in Guatemala, Nicaragua, and Peru, no more than 1 percent of the budget gets spent on these goods (possibly because they prefer other intoxicants).

Perhaps more surprisingly, it is apparent that spending on festivals is an important part of the budget for many extremely poor households. In Udaipur, over the course of the previous year, more than 99 percent of the extremely poor households spent money on a wedding, a funeral, or a religious festival. The median household spent 10 percent of its annual budget on festivals. In South Africa, 90 percent of the households living under $1 per day spent money on festivals. In Pakistan, Indonesia, and Cote d'Ivoire, more than 50 percent did likewise. Only in some Latin American countries in our sample—Panama, Guatemala, Nicaragua—are festivals not a notable part of the yearly expenditure for a significant fraction of the households. However in the LSMS surveys, unlike the Udaipur survey, people are not asked to account separately for the food that they bought because there was a festival. It is therefore probably no accident that the Udaipur number is the highest across the surveys, and there is reason to suspect that LSMS numbers would have been higher had the data been directly collected in those surveys.

On the other hand, the under $1 per day households spend very little on the forms of entertainment that are common in rich countries, such as movies, theater, or video shows. In all 13 of the countries in our sample, in the month preceding the survey the average extremely poor household spent less than 1 percent on any of these forms of entertainment. The comparable number for the United States is 5 percent. We can only speculate about the roots of this difference: Has the importance given to festivals and other indigenous forms of entertainment crowded out movie-going, or is it lack of access to movie theatres and such, that gives festivals the place that they occupy in their lives?

The propensity to own a radio or a television, a widespread form of entertainment for American households, varies considerably across countries. For example, among rural households living under $1 per day, ownership of a radio is 11 percent in the Udaipur survey, almost 60 percent in Nicaragua and Guatemala, and above 70 percent in South Africa and Peru. Similarly, no one owns a television in Udaipur, but in Guatemala nearly a quarter of households do, and in Nicaragua, the percentage is closer to a half.

These two phenomena appear to be related. In Udaipur, where the share spent on festivals is the highest, radio and television ownership is very low. In Pakistan, the fraction spent on festivals is 3.3 percent and only 30 percent have a radio. By contrast, in Nicaragua where 57 percent of the rural poor households, respectively, have a radio and 21 percent and 19 percent own a television, very few households report spending anything on festivals.[6] One wrinkle on this explanation is that the urban poor who are much more likely to own a television than the rural poor (60 versus 33 percent in Indonesia, 61 versus 10 percent in Peru, 38 versus 17 percent in South Africa), do not spend less on festivals than their rural counterparts. While this observation is based on only a few data points, it hints at the possibility of an unmet demand for entertainment among the rural poor—they would also like to buy a television, but perhaps the television signal does not reach their neighborhoods.

In either case, it is hard to escape the conclusion that the poor do see themselves as having a significant amount of choice, and choose not to exercise it in the direction of spending more on food—the typical poor household in Udaipur could spend up to 30 percent more on food than it actually does, just based on what it spends on alcohol, tobacco, and festivals. Indeed in most of the surveys the share spent on food is about the same for the poor and the extremely poor, suggesting that the extremely poor do not feel an extra compulsion to purchase more calories.

This conclusion echoes an old finding in the literature on nutrition: Even the extremely poor do not seem to be as hungry for additional calories as one might expect. Deaton and Subramanian (1996), using 1983 data from the Indian state of Maharashtra, found that even for the poorest, a 1 percent increase on overall expenditure translates into about a two-thirds of a percent increase in the total food expenditure of a poor family. Remarkably, the elasticity is not very different for the poorest individuals in the sample and the richest (although nobody is particularly rich in this sample). The Deaton and Subramanian estimate is one of the higher estimates. Thomas and Strauss (1997) found an elasticity of demand for food with respect to expenditure per capita of about a quarter for the poorest Brazilians.

Another way to make the same point is to look at what edibles the extremely poor are buying. Deaton and Subramanian (1996) note that among grains, in terms of calories per rupee, the millets (jowar and bajra) are clearly the best buy. Yet in their data, only about two-thirds of the total spending on grains is on these grains, while another 20 percent is on rice, which costs more than twice as much per calorie, and a further 10 percent or so is spent on wheat, which is a 70 percent more expensive way to get calories. In addition, the poor spend almost 7 percent of their total budget on sugar, which is both more expensive than grains as a source of calories and bereft of any other nutritional value. The same affinity for sugar also shows up in our Udaipur data: The poor spend almost 10 percent of their food budget on the

---

6 The ultimate source of variation here might be the relative prices of radios and televisions. There is a strong correlation between the ratio of the purchasing power exchange rate for consumption and the official exchange rate and the probability that a household owns a radio (the correlation is 0.36). The logic is probably quite similar to the argument presented earlier in the context of food consumption. Radios are tradable (they are all made in China). Since among manufactures, non-tradable goods are much less costly in some countries than others, while traded goods tend to be more similarly priced, people at the same expenditure levels at purchasing power parity can have widely differing levels of purchasing power in terms of traded goods.

category "sugar, salt and other processed foods" (this does not include cooking oil, which makes up another 6 percent of the expenditures on food). Even for the extremely poor, for every 1 percent increase in the food expenditure, about half goes into purchasing more calories, and half goes into purchasing more expensive (and presumably better tasting) calories.

Finally, to the extent that we can tell, the trend seems to be to spend even less money on food. In India, for example, it went from 70 percent in 1983 to 62 percent in 1999–2000, and the share of millet in the food budget dropped to virtually zero (Deaton, 2006). Not surprisingly, the poor are also consuming fewer calories over time (Meenakshi and Vishwanathan, 2003), though it is possible that this change reflects the fact their work involves less physical effort (Jha, 2004).

The Ownership of Assets
While all the surveys have some information about assets, the list of assets varies. To obtain a relatively coherent list across countries, we focus on radios, televisions, and bicycles. The share of people who own these particular assets varies significantly across countries.

As we already discussed, ownership of radio and television varies a lot from country to country, but is low in several of those countries. One reason may be the lack of signal. The other may be that it is not easy to buy a television if you are extremely poor: It is an expensive and lumpy transaction that one has to save up for if one is born poor. We do see a fairly steep income gradient in the ownership of radio and television: In all countries, the share of rural households owning a television is substantially larger for those who live on less than $2 a day than those living on less than $1 a day. For example, the share owning a television increases from 14 percent for those living on $1 a day to 45 percent for those living on less than $2 a day in Cote d'Ivoire; from 7 to 17 percent in South Africa; and from 10 to 21 percent in Peru. This pattern has been observed in other contexts (Filmer and Pritchett, 2001), and has been the basis for using the lack of durable goods as a marker for poverty. Our data suggests that this proxy can be appropriate within a country, but it could easily be misleading to use this measure in a cross-country comparison.

Among productive assets, land is the one that many people in the rural surveys seem to own though there is enormous country-to-country variation. Only 4 percent of those living under $1 a day own land in Mexico, 1.4 percent in South Africa, 30 percent in Pakistan, 37 percent in Guatemala, 50 percent in Nicaragua and Indonesia, 63 percent in Cote d'Ivoire, 65 percent in Peru; and 85 percent in Panama. In the Udaipur sample, 99 percent of the households below $1 a day own some land in addition to the land on which their house is built, although much of it is dry scrubland that cannot be cultivated for most of the year. However, when the extremely poor do own land, the plots tend to be quite small. The median landholding among the poor who own land is one hectare or less in Udaipur, Indonesia, Guatemala and

Timor, between 1 and 2 hectares in Peru, Tanzania, and Pakistan, and between 2 and 3 hectares in Nicaragua, Cote d'Ivoire, and Panama.

Apart from land, extremely poor households in rural areas tend to own very little by way of durable goods, including productive assets: 34 percent own a bicycle in Cote d'Ivoire, but less than 14 percent in Udaipur, Nicaragua, Panama, Papua New Guinea, Peru, and Timor Leste. In Udaipur, where we have detailed asset data, we find that most extremely poor households have a bed or a cot but only about 10 percent have a chair or a stool and 5 percent have a table. About half have a clock or a watch. Less than 1 percent have an electric fan, a sewing machine, a bullock cart, a motorized cycle of any kind, or a tractor. No one has a phone.

As we will see below, this is not because most of these households are employees and therefore have no use for such assets: On the contrary, many of the extremely poor households operate their own businesses, but do so with almost no productive assets.

The Pursuit of Health and Well-being

Should we worry about the fact that the poor are buying less food than they could? According to Deaton and Subramanian (1996), the poorest people—the ones in the bottom decile in terms of per capita expenditure—consume on average slightly less than 1400 calories a day. This is about half of what the Indian government recommends for a man with moderate activity, or a woman with heavy physical activity.[7] The shortfall seems enormous, though one could question whether the initial recommendation was appropriate. However, the Udaipur data, which has other health indicators, suggests that health is definitely reason for concern.

Among the extremely poor in Udaipur, only 57 percent report that the members of their household had enough to eat throughout the year. Among the poor adults in Udaipur, the average "body mass index" (that is, weight in kilograms divided by the square of the height in meters) is 17.8. Sixty-five percent of adult men and 40 percent of adult women have a body mass index below 18.5, the standard cutoff for being underweight (WHO expert consultation, 2004). Moreover, 55 percent of the poor adults in Udaipur are anemic, which means they have an insufficient number of red blood cells. The poor are frequently sick or weak. In Udaipur, 72 percent report at least one symptom of disease and 46 percent report an illness which has left them bedridden or necessitated a visit to the doctor over the last month. Forty-three percent of the adults and 34 percent of the adults aged under 50 report having difficulty with carrying out at least one of their "activities of daily living," such as working in the field, walking, or drawing water from a well. Diarrhea is extremely frequent among children. About one-seventh of the poor have vision problems, which may also be due to nutritional deficits (caused by either poor nutrition, or the diseases that afflict them, or a combination of the two).

---

7 See http://www.fao.org/documents/show_cdr.asp?url_file=/DOCREP/x0172e/x0172e02.htm.

Detailed information on health is not available in all the surveys we have, but most report health episodes that left a household member bedridden for a day or more, or required them to see a doctor. While this data is less than perfect, given that the poor may be less prone to recall and report such sicknesses than the rich, the general pattern is of a remarkably high level of morbidity. Among the rural poor living under $1 a day in Peru, South Africa, Timor Leste, Panama, and Tanzania, between 11 and 15 percent of households report having a member either being bedridden for at least a day or requiring a doctor. The number is between 21 and 28 percent in Pakistan, Indonesia, and Cote d'Ivoire, and between 35 and 46 percent in Nicaragua, Udaipur, and Mexico.

The poor generally do not complain about their health—but then they also do not complain about life in general either. While the poor certainly *feel* poor, their levels of self-reported happiness or self-reported health levels are not particularly low (Banerjee, Deaton, and Duflo, 2004). On the other hand, the poor do report that they are under a great deal of stress, both financial and psychological. In Udaipur, about 12 percent say that there has been a period of one month or more in the last year in which they were so "worried, tense, or anxious" that it interfered with normal activities like sleeping, working, and eating. Case and Deaton (2005) compare data from South Africa to the data from Udaipur and data from the United States. They find that the answers of poor South Africans and poor Indians about stress look very similar, while reported levels of stress are very much lower in the United States. The most frequently cited reason for such tensions is health problems (cited by 29 percent of respondents), with lack of food and death coming next (13 percent each). Over the last year, in 45 percent of the extremely poor households in Udiapur (and 35 percent of those living under $2 a day) adults had to cut the size of their meal at some point during the year and in 12 percent of them, children had to cut the size of their meals. In the extremely poor households under $1 per day, 37 percent report that, at some point in the past year, the adults in the household went without a meal for an entire day. Cutting meals is also strongly correlated with unhappiness.

Carrying enough savings to make sure that they never have to cut meals, should not be too hard for these households since, as noted above, they have substantial slack in their budgets and cutting meals is not that common. It would also make it easier for them to deal with healthcare emergencies. As such, saving a bit more would seem like a relatively inexpensive way to reduce stress.

Investment in Education
The extremely poor spend very little on education. The expenditure on education generally hovers around 2 percent of household budgets: higher in Pakistan (3 percent), Indonesia (6 percent) and Cote d'Ivoire (6 percent), but much lower in Guatemala (0.1 percent), and South Africa (0.8 percent). The fraction does not really

change very much when we go from the poor to the extremely poor, or from rural areas to urban areas, though in a few countries like Pakistan, urban families spend substantially more than rural families. This low level of expenditure on education is not because the children are out of school. In 12 of the 13 countries in our sample, with the exception of Cote d'Ivoire, at least 50 percent of both boys and girls aged 7 to 12 in extremely poor households are in school. In about half the countries, the proportion enrolled is greater than 75 percent among girls, and more than 80 percent among boys.

The reason spending is low is that children in poor households typically attend public schools or other schools that do not charge a fee. In countries where poor households spend more on education, it is typically because government schools have fees (as in Indonesia and Cote d'Ivoire). What they are doing might therefore be perfectly sensible, given that this is the reason why public education exists. The one concern comes from the mounting evidence, reported below, that public schools are often dysfunctional: This could be the reason why even very poor parents in Pakistan are pulling their children out of public schools and spending money to send them to private schools.

How the Poor Earn Their Money

Walking down the main street of the biggest slum in the medium sized Southern Indian city of Guntur at nine in the morning, the first thing one notices are the eateries: In front of every sixth house that directly faced the road, by our count, there was a woman sitting behind a little kerosene stove with a round cast-iron griddle roasting on it. Every few minutes someone would walk up to her and order a *dosa*, the rice and beans pancakes that almost everyone eats for breakfast in South India. She would throw a cupful of the batter on the griddle, swirl it around to cover almost the entire surface and drizzle some oil around the edges. A minute or two later, she would slide an off-white pock-marked pancake off the griddle, douse it in some sauce, fold it in a newspaper or a banana leaf and hand it to her client, in return for a rupee (roughly 15 cents, at PPP).

When we walked back down that same street an hour later, the women were gone. We found one inside her house, filling her daughter's plate with lunch that she had cooked while making the *dosas*. She told us that later that day, she was going out to vend her *saris*, the long piece of decorative cloth that Indian women drape around themselves. She gets plain nylon *saris* from the shop and stitches beads and small shiny pieces on them, and once a week, she takes them from house to house, hoping that women would buy them to wear on special occasions. And they do buy them, she said confidently. All the other *dosa* women we met that day had a similar story: once they are done frying *dosas*, they do something else. Some collect trash; others make pickles to sell; others work as laborers.

Entrepreneurship and Multiple Occupations Among the Poor

All over the world, a substantial fraction of the poor act as entrepreneurs in the sense of raising the capital, carrying out the investment, and being the full residual claimants for the earnings. In Peru, 69 percent of the households who live under $2 a day in urban areas operate a non-agricultural business. In Indonesia, Pakistan, and Nicaragua, the numbers are between 47 and 52 percent. A large fraction of the rural poor operate a farm (except in Mexico and South Africa, between 25 percent and 98 percent of the households who earn less than a dollar a day report being self employed in agriculture).[8] Moreover, many of the rural poor (from 7 percent in Udaipur up to 36 percent in Panama) also operate a nonagricultural business.

Many poor households have multiple occupations. Like the *dosa* women of Guntur, 21 percent of the households living under $2 a day in Hyderabad who have a business actually have more than one, while another 13 percent have both a business and a laborer's job. This multiplicity of occupations in urban areas is found in many other countries as well, though not everywhere. Among those earning less than $2 a day, 47 percent of the urban households in Cote d'Ivoire and Indonesia get their income from more than one source; 36 percent in Pakistan; 20.5 percent in Peru; and 24 percent in Mexico. However, in urban South Africa and Panama, almost no one has more than one occupation and only 9 percent do so in Nicaragua and Timor Leste.[9]

This pattern of multiple occupations is stronger in rural areas. In Udaipur district, as we discussed earlier, almost everybody owns some land and almost everybody does at least some agriculture. Yet only 19 percent of the households describe self-employment in agriculture as the *main* source of their income. Working on someone else's land is even rarer, with only 1 percent reporting this as their main source of income. In other words, the poor cultivate the land they own, no less and usually, no more. Yet, agriculture is not the mainstay of most of these households. The most common occupation for the poor in Udaipur is working as a daily laborer: 98 percent of households living under $1 per day in rural areas report doing this and 74 percent claim it is their main source of earnings.

This pattern is confirmed by data from a smaller survey of 27 villages randomly sampled from eight districts in West Bengal (Banerjee, 2006). In this survey, even households that claim to be the operators for a plot of land, spend only 40 percent of their time in agricultural activities on their own land. The fraction is not very different for men and women—women do less direct agricultural work but more

---

8   The low level of agriculture among the extremely poor in South Africa is easily explained. The black population, which contains almost all of the extremely poor people, were historically under the apartheid regime not allowed to own land outside the "homelands," and most of the land in the homelands was not worth cultivating.

9   This may however be a data problem: Anthropologists do claim that they observe multiple occupations in South African households (Francie Lund, verbal communication to Angus Deaton).

animal rearing, along with growing fruits and vegetables. Their other activities include teaching, sewing and embroidery, unpaid household work, and gathering fuel. Strikingly, almost 10 percent of the time of the average household is spent on gathering fuel, either for use at home or for sale. The median family in this survey has three working members and *seven* occupations.

In most of the Living Standard Measurement Surveys, households are not asked their main source of earnings, but the pattern of diversification among rural households is apparent nevertheless. In Guatemala, 65 percent of the rural extremely poor say they get some income from self-employment in agriculture, 86 percent work as laborers outside agriculture, and 24 percent are self-employed outside agriculture. In Indonesia, 34 percent of the rural extremely poor households work as laborers outside of agriculture, and 37 percent earn income from self employment outside of agriculture. In Pakistan, 51 percent of the rural extremely poor earn income from labor outside of agriculture, and 35 percent from a business outside of agriculture. Overall, the fraction of the rural extremely poor households who report that they conduct more than one type of activity to earn a living is 50 percent in Indonesia, 72 percent in Cote d'Ivoire, 84 percent in Guatemala, and 94 percent in Udaipur. It is smaller, but not negligible—between 10 and 20 percent—in Nicaragua, Panama, Timor Leste, and Mexico. Once again, an exception to this general pattern is South Africa, where less than 1 percent of the rural poor or extremely poor report multiple occupations.

Temporary Migration to Work

Where do rural households, which are often a walk of a half-hour or more from the nearest road, find all this non-agricultural work? The answer turns out to be the obvious one: they migrate.

Temporary migration is rarely documented in surveys, but in the Udaipur survey, which had questions about this activity, 60 percent of the poorest households report that someone from their family had lived outside for a part of the year in order to obtain work. For 58 percent of the families, the head of the household had migrated. The migrants typically complete multiple trips in a year. However, people do not leave for very long: The median length of a completed migration is one month, and only 10 percent of migration episodes exceed three months. Nor do most of the migrants travel very far: 28 percent stay in the district of Udaipur, and only 42 percent leave the state of Rajasthan.

In contrast, permanent migration for work reasons is rare, although many women move when they get married. Even if we look at households currently living in urban areas, where the inflow of immigrants is presumably higher than in rural areas, the share of extremely poor households who had one member that was born elsewhere and had migrated for work reasons was just 4 percent in Pakistan, 6 percent in Cote d'Ivoire, 6 percent in Nicaragua, and almost 10 percent in Peru. The 1991 Census of

India reports that only 14.7 percent of the male population lives somewhere other than where they were born. Indonesia is the only country in our data where the proportion is higher: 41 percent of the urban households came from elsewhere. Indonesia is also the only country in this sample where migration was explicitly subsidized.

Lack of Specialization

A pattern seems to emerge. Poor families do seek out economic opportunities, but they tend not to get too specialized. They do some agriculture, but not to the point where it would afford them a full living (for example by buying/renting/sharecropping more land). They also work outside, but only in short bursts—they do not move permanently to their place of occupation.

This lack of specialization has its costs. Many of these poor households receive most of their earnings from these outside jobs, despite only being away for 18 weeks of the year on average (in the case of Udaipur). As short-term migrants, they have little chance of learning their jobs better or ending up in a job that suits their specific talents or being promoted.

Even the non-agricultural businesses that the poor operate typically require relatively little specific skills. For example, the businesses in Hyderabad include 11 percent tailors, 8 percent fruit and vegetable sellers, 17 percent small general stores, 6.6 percent telephone booths, 4.3 percent auto owners, and 6.3 percent milk sellers. Except for tailoring, none of these jobs require the high levels of specialized competence that take a long time to acquire, and therefore are associated with higher earnings. In several ways, the poor are trading off opportunities to have higher incomes.

The Problem of Small Scale

The businesses of the poor typically operate at a remarkably small scale. As we saw, the average landholding for those who own land is usually quite tiny, and renting land is infrequent. Furthermore, most of this land is not irrigated and cannot be used all year round.

The scale of non-agricultural businesses run by the poor also tends to be pretty small. In the 13 countries in our sample, the median business operated by people living under $2 a day either in a rural or an urban location has no paid staff, and the average number of paid employees range between 0.14 in rural Nicaragua to 0.53 in urban Panama. Businesses are operated on average by 1.38 (in Peru) to 2.59 (in Cote d'Ivoire) people—most of them being family members. Most of these businesses have very few assets as well. In Hyderabad, only 20 percent of the businesses operate out of a separate room. In Pakistan, about 40 percent of the businesses of those living under $1 or $2 a day have a vehicle, but only 4 percent have a motorized vehicle and none have any machinery. In other countries, even non-motorized vehicles are rare. In Hyderabad, where we have an exhaustive list of business assets, the most common assets are tables, scales, and pushcarts.

Many of these businesses are probably operating at too small a scale for efficiency. The women making *dosas* spend a lot of time waiting: having fewer *dosa*-makers who do less waiting would be more efficient. In fact, it might make sense in efficiency terms for the *dosa*-makers to work in pairs: One to make the *dosas* and one to wrap them and make change.

Markets and the Economic Environment of the Poor

The economic choices of the poor are constrained by their market environment. The amount they save, for example, should vary with their access to a safe place to put their savings. Other constraints result from a lack of shared infrastructure. When the government builds a water line to your neighborhood, for example, you no longer need your own well. This section focuses on markets. The next takes up the issue of infrastructure.

The Market for Credit and the Poor

The data from our 13 countries suggests that the fraction of rural extremely poor households having an outstanding debt varies between countries, from 11 percent in rural Timor Leste to 93 percent in Pakistan. But what is consistent across the surveys is that very few of the poor households get loans from a formal lending source.

In the Udaipur sample, about two-thirds of the poor had a loan at the time of the interview. Of these, 23 percent are from a relative, 18 percent from a money lender, 37 percent from a shopkeeper, and only 6.4 percent from a formal source like a commercial bank or a cooperative. Lest one suspect that the low share of bank credit is due to the lack of physical access to banks, a similar pattern occurs in urban Hyderabad, where households living below $2 a day primarily borrow from moneylenders (52 percent), friends or neighbors (24 percent), and family members (13 percent), and only 5 percent of the loans are with commercial banks. The one country where a substantial share of the loans to the poor are formal in nature is Indonesia, where thanks to efforts by the Bank Rakyat Indonesia, one-third of the rural poor households borrow from a bank. In all the other countries, relatives, shopkeepers, and other villagers form, by far, the overwhelming source of borrowed funds.

Credit from informal sources tends to be expensive. In the Udaipur survey, where we have data on interest rates not available in other surveys, those living on less than $1 a day pay on average 3.84 percent per month for the credit they receive from informal sources. Those who consume between $1 and $2 a day per capita pay a little less: 3.13 percent per month. This is in part because they rely less on informal sources of credit and more on the formal sources than the extremely poor, and the formal sources are cheaper; and in part it reflects the fact that informal interest rates are lower for those with more land—the interest rate from informal sources drops by 0.40 percent per month for each additional hectare of land owned. The monthly interest rate we see in the Hyderabad sample is even higher: 3.94 percent per month for those living under $2 a day. This reflects the fact that few of these urban poor households have any land that they can use as collateral.

These high interest rates seem to occur not directly because of high rates of default, but as a result of the high costs of contract enforcement. While delay in repayment of informal loans is frequent, default is actually rare. For example, a "Summary Report on Informal Credit Markets in India" reports that across four case studies of moneylenders in rural India, default explains only 23 percent of the interest rate charged (Dasgupta, 1989). A well known study of rural moneylenders in Pakistan by Aleem (1990), finds that the median rate of default across money lenders is just 2 percent.

These low default rates are however anything but automatic: Contract enforcement in developing countries is often difficult, and in particular, it is not easy to get courts to punish recalcitrant borrowers. As a result, lenders often spend important resources making sure that their loans get repaid, which is what drives up the interest rates. The fact that lending depends so much on effective screening and monitoring also means that lending to the poor is especially difficult: The problem, at least in part, is that the poor have very little by way of collateral to secure the loan and therefore lenders hesitate to trust them with a lot of money. Given that the loan amount will in any case be small, it is not always clear that the profits from the transaction will be large enough to cover the cost of monitoring/screening. As a result, a lot of lenders are reluctant to lend to the poor. Moreover and for the same reason, informal lenders located close to the borrowers may be the only ones who are willing to lend to the poor—since monitoring/screening is relatively cheap for them. The trouble is that these informal lenders have to pay more for their deposits than the more formal institutions, since they are less capitalized and less regulated and do not have any government guarantees. This higher cost of deposits gets passed on to poorer borrowers. The gap can be considerable—in the study by Aleem, the cost of capital for the moneylenders was 32.5 percent in a year when banks were only paying 10 percent for their deposits.

The Market for Savings and the Poor

A main challenge for the poor who try to save is to find safety and a reasonable return. Stashing cash inside your pillow or elsewhere at home is neither safe nor particularly well-protected from inflation. In addition, recent research by Ashraf, Karlan, and Yin (2006) in the Philippines and Duflo, Kremer, and Robinson, (2006) in Kenya suggests that the poor, like everyone else, have problems resisting the temptation of spending money that they have at hand.

Few poor households have savings accounts. Except in Cote d'Ivoire, where 79 percent of the extremely poor households under $1 a day have a savings account, the fraction is below 14 percent in the other countries in our data. In Panama and Peru, less than 1 percent of such households have a savings account. In most countries, the share of households with a savings account is similar in rural and urban areas, and similar for those under $2 a day and those under $1 a day. Here India appears to be an exception, since only 6 percent of the extremely poor households in rural Udaipur have a savings account, while 25 percent of them do in the city of Hyderabad.

A lack of access to reliable savings accounts appears common to the poor everywhere, as documented in Stuart Rutherford's (2000) fascinating book, *The Poor and Their Money*. Rutherford describes the many strategies the poor use to deal with this problem: They form savings "clubs," where each person makes sure that the others do their savings. Self-help Groups (SHGs), popular in parts of India, and present in Indonesia as well, are saving clubs which also give loans to their members out of the accumulated savings (they are also sometimes linked to banks which offer them loans). In Africa, Rotating Savings and Credit Associations (ROSCAs) allow people to lend their savings to each other on a rotating basis. Others pay deposit collectors to collect their deposits and put them in a bank. Yet others deposit their savings with local moneylenders, with credit unions (which are essentially larger and much more formally organized Self-help Groups) or in an account at the local post office. And the reason why many of the poor respond so well to micro-credit is not necessarily because it offers them credit, but because once you take a loan and buy something with it, you have a disciplined way to save—namely, by paying down the loan.

However even participation in semi-formal savings institutions (such as Self-help Groups, ROSCAs and Microfinance Institutions) is not nearly as common among the poor as one might have expected. Even in India, despite the high visibility especially of SHGs, less than 10 percent of the poor in our Udaipur and Hyderabad surveys are part of an SHG or a ROSCA. The majority of the households who have any savings simply have it at the bank.

The Market for Insurance and the Poor

The poor have very little access to formal insurance. In many surveys, questions about insurance are not even asked. In six of the seven countries where there is data on this, less than 6 percent of the extremely poor are covered by health insurance of any kind. The exception is Mexico where about half of them have coverage. The numbers are not much higher in urban areas. Life insurance is a bit more common in India (and is, essentially, a form of savings). Four percent of the extremely poor in Udaipur and 10 percent in Hyderabad have life insurance.[10]

In principle, informal insurance can also be had through social networks. For example, Udry (1990) shows that poor villagers in Nigeria live a life that is shaped by a dense network of loan exchange: Over the course of one year, 75 percent of the households had made loans, 65 percent had borrowed money, and 50 percent had

---

10 Surprisingly, weather insurance is also essentially absent everywhere the world over (Morduch, 2006), although it would seem straightforward to provide insurance against observed weather patterns.

been both borrowers and lenders. Almost all of these loans took place between neighbors and relatives. Both the repayment schedule and the amount repaid were affected by both the lender's and the borrower's current economic conditions, underlining the role of these informal loans in providing insurance. Rosenzweig and Munshi (2005) argue that the same process happens in India through the *jati* or sub-caste networks.

Yet these informal networks have only a limited ability to protect the households against risk. The consumption of poor households is strongly affected by variations in their incomes, as has been shown by Deaton (1997) in Cote d'Ivoire, Munshi and Rosenzweig (2005) in India, Fafchamps and Lund (2003) in the Philippines, and Townsend (1995) in Thailand. Poor households also bear most health-care risks (both expenditures and foregone earnings) directly. For example, Gertler and Gruber (2002) find that in Indonesia a decline in the health index of the head of the household is associated with a decline in non-medical expenditures. In Udaipur, large expenditures on health ($70 and higher, at PPP) are covered by borrowing or dissaving. Only 2 percent of these expenses were paid for by someone else, and none came from the self-help groups. Twenty-four percent of the households in Hyderabad had to borrow to pay for health expenses in the last year.

When the poor come under economic stress, their form of "insurance" is often eating less or taking their children out of school. For example, Jacoby and Skoufias (1997) find that poor children leave school in bad years. Rose (1999) finds that the gap in mortality of girls relative to boys is much larger in drought years (but only for the landless households, who are not able to sell land or borrow to weather the crisis). They also are less likely to get medical treatment for themselves or their children: In the Udaipur sample, those who were sick in the last months and did not seek treatment (more than half) cite lack of money more often than any other reason (34 percent of the time). The lack of insurance also leads the poor to under-invest in risky, but profitable, technologies, such as new seeds (Morduch, 1995).

The weaknesses of informal insurance should not really be a surprise. Ultimately, informal insurance relies on the willingness of the fortunate to take care of those less favored, which limits the amount of insurance provided. Moreover, informal social networks are often not well-diversified. They tend to spread risk over households who live nearby and have similar incomes and occupations, as Fafchamps and Gubert (2005) show for the Philippines.

Unfortunately governments in these countries are not very effective at providing insurance either. For example, in most countries, the government is supposed to provide free health care to the poor. Yet, health care is rarely free. Government health-care providers often illegally charge for their own services and for medicines in reality. Also, as we will see, the quality of care in the public system is so low that the poor often end up visiting private providers.

A number of governments provide a form of income insurance through safety-net "food for work" programs. Under these programs, everyone is entitled to a certain number of days of government employment usually involving physical labor at a pre-announced (relatively low) wage. In Udaipur, where the years leading up to the survey had been particularly arid, 76 percent of the poor had at least one of the household members work on a public employment program of this kind. However, such schemes often offer only a limited number of jobs which might end up being doled out in a way that discriminates against the poor.

The Market for Land and the Poor

The land market is an issue for the poor because, for historical reasons, land is the one asset they tend to own. The one obvious problem with owning land is that land records in developing countries are often incomplete and many people do not have titles to their land. This, as many, including most famously, Hernando De Soto (2003), have emphasized, means that it is harder to sell the land or mortgage it.

From the point of view of the poor, this is especially troubling, because they tend to own a lot of the land that was either recently cleared or recently encroached upon, which is typically the land where tilling is incomplete. Field (2006) suggests that, in Peru, the poor, as a result, spend a lot of time protecting their claims to the land (since they have no title, they have no legal recourse).

The poor also suffer because where titles are missing or imperfectly enforced, political influence matters. In parts of Ghana, land belongs either to lineages or to the village, and cultivators have only rights of use. In this context, Goldstein and Udry (2005) show that the people who lack the political clout to protect them from having their land taken away from them by the village or their lineage (which typically includes the poor), do not leave their land fallow for long enough. Leaving land to fallow increases its productivity, but increases the risk that someone may seize it.

Finally there is a long tradition of research in agricultural economics that argues that the poor lack the incentives to make the best use of the land they are cultivating because they are agents rather than owners (Shaban, 1987). Banerjee, Gertler, and Ghatak (2002) found that a reform of tenancy that forced landlords to raise the share of output going to the sharecroppers (improving sharecroppers' incentives) and also gave them a secure right to the land, raised productivity by about 50 percent.

Infrastructure and the Economic Environment of the Poor

What we call infrastructure includes the entire spectrum from roads and power connections to schools, health facilities, and public health infrastructure (mostly water and sanitation). While there are different models of how such infrastructure gets supplied, with markets and the government playing differing roles, they are all usefully thought of as part of the environment in which people live, with some characteristics of a local public good, rather than something that can be purchased piecemeal by individuals.

The availability of physical infrastructure to the poor like electricity, tap water, and even basic sanitation (like access to a latrine) varies enormously across countries. In our sample of 13 countries, the number of rural poor households with access to tap water varies from none in Udaipur, to 36 percent in Guatemala. The availability of electricity varies from 1.3 percent in Tanzania to 99 percent in Mexico. The availability of a latrine varies from none in Udaipur, to 100 percent in Nicaragua. Different kinds of infrastructure do not always appear together. For example, in Indonesia, 97 percent of rural extremely poor households have electricity but only 6 percent have tap water. Some governments provide reasonable access to both electricity and tap water to the extremely poor: In Guatemala, 38 percent of the extremely poor rural households have tap water and 30 percent have electricity. Other governments do very little: In Udaipur, Papua New Guinea, Timor Leste, and South Africa, the share of the rural extremely poor with tap water or electricity is below 5 percent.

Generally, access to electricity and tap water is greater for the urban poor than the rural poor (which is probably fortunate since lack of sanitation in very dense surroundings can be disastrous for the disease environment). The only exception to this pattern in our 13 countries is Cote d'Ivoire, where rural households seem to have better access. Moreover, access to both tap water and electricity is typically higher for those under $2 a day than those under $1 a day.

In most low-income countries, there has been some attempt to make sure that poor households have access to primary schools and to basic health centers. For example, most Indian villages now have a school within a kilometer, and there is a health sub-center for every 10,000 people. However, the quality of the facilities that serve the poor tends to be low, even when they are available, and it is not clear how much they actually deliver. Chaudhury et al. (2005) report results on surveys they conducted to measure the absence of teachers and health workers in Bangladesh, Ecuador, India, Indonesia, Peru, and Uganda. They found that the average absence rate among teachers is 19 percent and the average absence rate among health workers is 35 percent. Moreover, because not all teachers and health workers are actually working when at their post, even this picture may be too favorable. Moreover, absence rates are generally higher in poor regions than in richer areas.

In an innovative study on health care quality, Das and Hammer (2004) collected data on the competence of doctors in Delhi, India, based on the kinds of questions they ask and the action they say they would take faced with a hypothetical patient, suffering from conditions they are likely to encounter in their practice. Every Delhi neighborhood, poor or rich, lives within 15 minutes of at least 70 health providers. However, the gap in competence of the average health practitioner between the poorest and richest neighborhoods is almost as large as the gap between the competence of a health provider with an MBBS degree (the equivalent of an MD in the United States) and a provider without such a qualification. In fact, an expert panel found that the treatments suggested by the average provider in their sample are slightly more likely to do harm rather than good, due to a combination of misdiagnosis and over-medication.

These differences in health care and basic sanitation infrastructure can directly affect mortality. Several surveys ask women about their pregnancies and the outcomes, including whether the child is still alive. We compute an infant mortality measure as the number of children who died before the age of 1 divided by the number of live births. The numbers are startling, especially when one takes into account the fact that they are likely to be underestimates (because not all children are remembered, especially if they died very early). Among the rural extremely poor, the lowest infant mortality that we observe is 3.4 percent in Indonesia. At the high end, infant mortality among the extremely poor is 8.7 percent in South Africa and Tanzania, 10 percent in Udaipur, and 16.7 percent in Pakistan. The rates are lower, but not much lower, in urban areas. The rates also remain high if the definition of poverty is expanded to include those who live under $2 a day. That child mortality is likely related at least in part to health infrastructure is suggested by Wagstaff (2003) who uses data from the demographic and health surveys to estimate prevalence of malnutrition and child mortality among those living under $1 a day in a number of countries. He finds very large difference between survival chances of poor children in different countries, and shows that they are correlated with health spending per capita in these countries.

The low quality of teaching in public schools has a clear effect on learning levels as well. In India, despite the fact that 93.4 percent of children ages 6–14 are enrolled in schools (75 percent of them in government schools), a recent nationwide survey found that 34.9 percent of the children age 7 to 14 cannot read a simple paragraph at second-grade level (Prathman, 2006). Moreover, 41.1 percent cannot do subtraction, and 65.5 percent cannot do division. Even among children in grades 6 to 8 in government schools, 22 percent cannot read a second-grade text.

In countries where the public provision of education and in health services is particularly low, private providers have stepped in. In the parts of India where public school absenteeism is the highest, the fraction of rural children attending private schools is also the highest (Chaudhury et al., 2005). However, these private schools are less than ideal: They do have lower teacher absenteeism than the public schools in the same village, but their teachers are significantly less qualified in the sense of having a formal teaching degree.

One sees a similar pattern in healthcare but in a more extreme version. Once again private providers who serve the poor are less likely to be absent and more likely to examine the patient with some care than their public counterparts, but they tend to be less well qualified (see for example, Das and Hammer (2004)). However unlike in education where most poor children are still in the public system even in countries and regions where public education is of extremely poor quality, where the public health care system has high levels of absence most people actually go to private providers. For example, in India, where absence of health care providers is 40 percent, 58 percent of the extremely poor households have visited a private health care provider in the last month. By contrast in Peru, where the absentee rate for health care providers is fairly low (25 percent) according to Chaudhury et al. (2005), only 9 percent of the rural extremely poor households have been to a private health provider in the last month. Within the Udaipur district, Banerjee, Deaton, and Duflo (2004) also found that the rate of usage of the public health facility is strongly correlated with the absence rate at the public health facilities in the areas.

Understanding the Economic Lives of the Poor

Many things about the lives of the poor start to make much more sense once we recognize that they have very limited access to efficient markets and quality infrastructure. The fact that they usually cultivate the land they own, no more and no less, for example, probably owes a lot to the agency problems associated with renting out land. In part, it must also reflect the fact that the poor, who typically own too little land relative to the amount of family labor and therefore are the obvious people to buy more land, suffer from lack of access to credit. This gets reinforced by the difficulties, discussed above, that the poor face in getting any kind of insurance against the many risks that a farmer needs to deal with: A second job outside agriculture secures you against much of that risk.

Why So Little Specialization?

More generally, risk spreading is clearly one reason why the poor, who might find risk especially hard to bear, tend not to be too specialized in any one occupation. They work part-time outside agriculture to reduce their exposure to farming risk, and keep a foot in agriculture to avoid being too dependent on their non-agricultural jobs.

Another reason for a second job is to occupy what would otherwise be wasted time. The reason people almost always give for why they diversify is because they have time on their hands. When we asked the *dosa*-sellers of Guntur why they did so many other things as well, they all said: "[We] can sell *dosas* in the morning. What do we do for the rest of the day?" Similarly, farmers who do not have irrigated land can only work the land when the land is not too dry, which depends on rainfall and/or irrigation. Finding some work outside agriculture is a way for them to make productive use of their time when the land is unusable. However this argument is incomplete. We also need to explain what made the women opt to sell *dosas*: After all they could have skipped the *dosas* and specialized in whatever they were doing for the rest of the day. Risk spreading remains a possible answer, but many of them seem to be in relatively safe occupations. And given the fact that almost everyone owns the cooking implement that one needs to make a *dosa* and entry [into the market] is free, it does not seem that *dosa*-making is an extraordinarily profitable activity.

A final, more compelling reason for doing multiple jobs is that the poor cannot raise the capital they would need to run a business that would fully occupy them. As we saw, most businesses operate with very few assets and little working capital. Likewise, some poor farmers might be able to irrigate their lands and make them usable for a larger part of the year, but they do not have the necessary access to funds. Of course, in agriculture, some down time will always remain, justifying a degree of multiple occupations. But this would be much more limited.

Why So Many Entrepreneurs?

Once we make this link between the tendency of the poor to be in multiple occupations and their access to financial markets, it is easy to see why so many of them are entrepreneurs. If you have few skills and little capital, and especially if you are a woman, being an entrepreneur is often easier than finding a job: You buy some fruits and vegetables (or some plastic toys) at the wholesalers and start selling them on the street; you make some extra *dosa* mix and sell the *dosas* in front of your house; you collect cow dung and dry it to sell it as a fuel; you attend to one cow and collect the milk. As we saw in Hyderabad, these are exactly the types of activity the poor are involved in.

It is important, however, not to romanticize the idea of these penniless entrepreneurs. Given that they have no money, borrowing is risky, and in any case no one wants to lend to them, the businesses they run are inevitably extremely small, to the point where there are clearly unrealized economies of scale. Moreover, given that so many of these firms have more family labor available to them than they can use, it is no surprise that they do very little to create jobs for others. This of course makes it harder for anyone to find a job and hence reinforces the proliferation of petty entrepreneurs.

Why Don't the Poor Eat More?

Another big puzzle is why the poor do not spend more on food both on average and especially out of the marginal dollar. Eating more and eating better (more grains and iron-rich foods, less sugar) would help them build up their BMI (which we noted tends to be very low).

One possibility is that eating more would not help them that much, or not for long, because they would become weak again at the first attack of disease, which will invariably occur. For example, Deaton, Cutler, and Lleras-Muney (2006) argue that nutrition is at best a very small part of what explains the tremendous gains in health around the world in the past few decades. However, some improvements in nutrition (reduction of anemia in particular) have been credibly linked to increased productivity (Thomas et al. 2004). Moreover, as we saw, not having enough to eat does, at a minimum, make the poor extremely unhappy.

Provided that eating more would increase their productivity, it is unlikely that the low levels of food consumption can be explained by a simple lack of self control (the poor cannot simply resist temptations to spend on other things, and don't have enough left to eat): As we noted above, they also spend surprisingly large amounts on entertainment—be it televisions, weddings, or festivals. All of these involve spending a large amount at one time, which implies some saving unless they happen to be especially credit-worthy. In other words, many poor people save money that they could have eaten today in order to spend more on entertainment in the future, which does not immediately fit the idea of their lacking self-control.

The need to spend more on entertainment rather than on food appears to be a strongly felt need, not something that would go away if the poor could plan better. One reason this might be the case is that the poor want to keep up with their neighbors. Fafchamps and Shilpi (2006) offer evidence from Nepal in which people were asked to assess whether their level of income as well as their levels of consumption of housing, food, clothing, health-care, and schooling were adequate. The answers to these questions were strongly negatively related to the average consumption of the other people living in the same village.

Why Don't the Poor Invest More in Education?

The children of the poor are, by and large, going to primary school. What parents are not doing is reacting to the low quality of these schools, either by sending their children to better and more expensive schools or by putting pressure on the government to do something about quality in government schools. Why not?

One reason is that poor parents, who may often be illiterate themselves, may have a hard time recognizing that their children are not learning much. One survey shows that poor parents in Eastern Uttar Pradesh in India have limited success in predicting whether their school-age children can read (Banerjee et al., 2005). Moreover, how can parents be confident that a private school would offer a better education, given that the teacher there is usually less qualified than the public school teachers? After all, researchers have only discovered this pattern in the last few years. As for putting pressure on the government, it is not clear that the average villager would know how to organize and do so.

Why Don't the Poor Save More?

The arguments based on lack of access to credit and insurance or labor market rigidities, by themselves, do not help very much in understanding why the poor are not more interested in accumulating wealth. As we saw above, they could easily save more without getting less nutrition, by spending less on alcohol, tobacco, festivals, and food items such as sugar, spice, and tea.

It is true that they typically have no bank accounts or other rewarding financial assets to put savings into, but many of them have their own businesses, and, as we argue above, these tend to be chronically under-funded: Why not save up to buy a new machine, or increase the stock in the shop? Moreover, as we saw above, a very substantial fraction of them have debt, and the interest rate on the debt often well exceeds 3 percent per month. Paying down debt is therefore a very attractive way to save. And even if you have no business to grow, and have no debt to repay, just holding some extra stocks for the proverbial rainy day (or more commonly "the drought") can save both worry and the misery of watching your children starve. In other words, precautionary motives for saving should be especially strong for the poor.

A part of the answer is probably that saving at home is hard: The money may be stolen (especially if you live in a house that cannot be locked) or simply grabbed by your spouse or your son. Perhaps equally importantly, if you have money at hand, you are constantly resisting temptation to spend: to buy something you want, to help someone who you find difficult to say no to, to let your child have the sweet he wants so badly. This is probably especially true of the poor, because many of the temptations you are being asked to resist are things that everyone else might take for granted.

The poor seem quite aware of their vulnerability to temptation. In the Hyderabad survey, the respondents were asked to name whether there are particular expenses that they would like to cut. 28 percent of the poor named at least one item they would like to cut. The top item that households would like to cut is alcohol and tobacco (mentioned by 44 percent of the households that want to cut out items). Then comes sugar, tea, and snacks (9 percent), festivals (7 percent), and entertainment (7 percent).

This is one place where self-knowledge does not help. Knowing that you face self-control problems makes you even less likely to try to save: You know that it would probably just end up feeding some future indefensible craving, and the machine that you so want to save for will never actually be acquired. Being naïve might actually help—you might just be lucky and save enough to buy the machine before the temptation gets to you.

Beyond Market Failures and Self-control Problems

An interesting example that spans many of the arguments we have used above is a study by Duflo, Kremer, and Robinson (2006) on investment in fertilizer in Kenya. According to surveys conducted over several years, just 40.3 percent of farmers had ever used fertilizer, and just 25 percent used fertilizer in any given year. Conservative estimates suggest that the average return to using fertilizer exceeds 100 percent, and the median return is above 75 percent. Duflo, Kremer, and Robinson conducted field trials of fertilizer on the farms of actual randomly selected farmers, which were meant to teach the farmers how to use fertilizer and the rewards of doing so. They found that the farmers who participated in the study are 10 percent more likely on average to use fertilizer in the very next season after the study, but only 10 percent more likely—and the effects fade after the first season.

When farmers were asked why they did not use fertilizer, most farmers replied that they did not have enough money. However, fertilizer can be purchased (and used) in small quantities, so this is another investment opportunity which seems easily accessible to farmers with even a small level of saving. This suggests that the issue, once again, is that farmers find it difficult to put away even small sums of money. The program in Kenya offered to sell farmers a voucher right after the harvest, which is when farmers have money in hand, which would entitle them to buy fertilizer later.

This program had a large effect: 39 percent of the farmers offered the voucher bought the fertilizer, and the effects are as large as a 50 percent subsidy on the cost of fertilizer. The voucher seemed to work as a commitment device to encourage saving. But what remains puzzling is that the farmers could have bought the fertilizer in advance on their own. Indeed, a huge majority of the farmers who bought the vouchers for future delivery of fertilizer requested immediate delivery, and then stored the fertilizer for later use. Moreover almost all of them used the fertilizer they bought. They apparently had no self-control problems in keeping the fertilizer, even though they could easily exchange the fertilizer for something more immediately consumable. Indeed, even if there were some transaction costs in selling, they would have to be very large indeed, given that these are people who appear to be willing to give up a 100 percent return in three to five months in order to consume now.

Why Don't the Poor Migrate for Longer?

A final puzzle is why the poor do not migrate for longer periods, given that they could easily earn much more by doing so. Munshi and Rosenzweig (2005) argue that the lack of long-term migration reflects the value of remaining close to one's social network, in a setting where the social network might be the only source of (informal) insurance available to people. However, those who migrate for short periods of up to a few months leave their entire family, who presumably can maintain their social links, behind. The ultimate reason seems to be that making more money is not a huge priority, or at least not a large enough priority to experience several months of living alone and often sleeping on the ground somewhere in or around the work premises.

In some ways this puzzle resembles the question of why the Kenyan farmers do not buy fertilizer right after the harvest even though they are happy to buy (and use it) if someone made the (small) effort to bring it to their farm. In both cases one senses a reluctance of poor people to commit themselves psychologically to a project of making more money. Perhaps at some level this avoidance is emotionally wise: Thinking about the economic problems of life must make it harder to avoid confronting the sheer inadequacy of the standard of living faced by the extremely poor.

Acknowledgements

We thank Andrei Shleifer for motivating us to undertake this exercise. We thank him and the editors of this journal for detailed suggestions on the previous draft of this paper. We thank Danielle Li, Marc Shotland, and Stefanie Stancheva for spectacular assistance in assembling the data, and Kudzai Takavarasha for carefully editing a previous draft. Special thanks to Angus Deaton for extremely useful advice and guidance, and extensive comments on the previous draft and to Gary Becker for helpful comments.

References:

Aleem, Irfan (1990). "Imperfect Information, Screening and the Costs of Informal Lending: A Study of a Rural Credit Market in Pakistan," *World Bank Economic Review* 3: 329–49.

Ashraf, Nava, Dean Karlan, and Wesley Yin (2006). "Tying Odysseus to the Mast: Evidence from a Commitment Savings Product in the Philippines." *Quarterly Journal of Economics*, forthcoming.

Banerjee, Abhijit, Rukmini Barnerji, Esther Duflo, Rachel Glennerster, Stuti Khemani, Sendhil Mullainathan, and Marc Shotland (2005). "The Impact of Information, Awareness and Participation on Learning Outcomes." Mimeo. MIT.

Banerjee, Abhijit, Angus Deaton, and Esther Duflo (2004). "Wealth, Health and Health Services in Rural Rajasthan." *American Economic Review* 94 (2): 326–30.

Banerjee, Abhijit, Esther Duflo, and Rachel Glennerster (2006). "A Snapshot of Micro enterprises in Hyderabad." Mimeo. MIT.

Banerjee, Abhijit, Paul Gertler, and Maitreesh Ghatak (2002). "Empowerment and Efficiency: Tenancy Reform in West Bengal." *Journal of Political Economy* 110 (2): 239–80.

Banerjee, Nirmala (2006). "A Survey of Occupations and Livelihoods of Households in West Bengal." Mimeo. Sachetana, Kolkata.

Case, Anne, and Angus Deaton (2005). "Health and Wealth among the Poor: India and South Africa Compared." *American Economic Review Papers and Proceedings* 95 (2): 229–33.

Chaudhury, Nazmul, Jeffrey Hammer, Michael Kremer, Karthik Muralidharan, and F. Halsey Rogers (2005). "Teacher Absence in India: A Snapshot." *Journal of the European Economic Association* 3 (2–3), April-May.

Das, Jishnu, and Jeffrey Hammer (2004). "Strained Mercy: The Quality of Medical Care in Delhi." *Economic and Political Weekly* 39 (9): 951–65.

Dasgupta, A. (1989). *Reports on Credit Markets in India: Summary*. Technical report. New Delhi: National Institute of Public Finance and Policy.

Dasgupta, P., and Debraj Ray (1986). "Inequality as a Determinant of Malnutrition and Unemployment: Policy." *Economic Journal* 96: 1011–34.

Deaton, Angus (2004). "Measuring Poverty." Abhijit Banerjee, Roland Benabou, and Dilip Mookherjee (eds.), *Understanding Poverty*. Oxford: Oxford UP.

Deaton, Angus (2006). "Purchasing Power Parity Exchange Rates for the Poor: Using Household Surveys to Construct PPPs." Mimeo. Princeton.

Deaton, Angus, David Cutler, and Adriana Lleras-Muney (2006). "The Determinants of Mortality." *Journal of Economic Perspectives.* Fall 2006.

Deaton, Angus, and Shankar Subramanian (1996). "The Demand for Food and Calories." *Journal of Political Economy* 104 (1): 133–62.

De Soto, Hernando (2003). *The Mystery of Capital: Why Capitalism Triumphs in the West and Fails Everywhere Else.* New York: Basic Books.

Duflo, Esther, Michael Kremer, and Jonathan Robinson (2006). "Why Don't Farmers Use Fertilizer: Evidence from Field Experiments." Mimeo, MIT.

Fafchamps, Marcel, and Flore Gubert (2005). "The Formation of Risk Sharing Networks." Working Papers DT/2005/13, DIAL (Développement, Institutions & Analyses de Long terme).

Fafchamps, Marcel, and Susan Lund (2003). "Risk-sharing Networks in Rural Philippines." *Journal of Development Economics* 71 (2): 261–87.

Field, Erica (2006). "Entitled to Work: Urban Property Rights and Labor Supply in Peru." Mimeo. Harvard.

Filmer, Deon, and Lant Pritchett (2001). "Estimating Wealth Effects without Expenditure Data—or Tears: An Application to Educational Enrollments in States of India." *Demography* 38 (1): 115–32.

Gertler, Paul, and Jonathan Gruber (2002). "Insuring Consumption against Illness." *American Economic Review* 92 (1): 50–70.

Goldstein, Markus, and Christopher Udry (2005). "The Profits of Power: Land Rights and Agricultural Investment in Ghana." Working Papers 929, Economic Growth Center, Yale University.

Jacoby, Hanan G., and Emmanuel Skoufias (1997). "Risk, Financial Markets, and Human Capital in a Developing Country." *Review of Economic Studies* 64 (3): 311–35.

Jha, Raghavendra (2004). "Calories Deficiency in Rural India in the Last Three Quinquennial Rounds of the NSS." Mimeo. Australian National University.

Meenakshi, J.V., and Brinda Vishwanathan (2003). "Calorie Deprivation in Rural India, 1983–1999/2000." *Economic and Political Weekly* January 25: 369–75.

Morduch, Jonathan (1995). "Income Smoothing and Consumption Smoothing." *Journal of Economic Perspectives* 9 (3): 103–14.

Morduch, Jonathan (2006). "Micro-Insurance: The Next Revolution?" In Abhijit Banerjee, Roland Benabou, and Dilip Mookherjee (eds.), *What Have We Learned About Poverty?* Oxford: Oxford UP.

Munshi, K., and M. Rosenzweig (2005). "Why Is Social Mobility in India So Low? Social Insurance, Inequality, and Growth." BREAD working paper no. 097.

Prathman (2006). Annual Status of Education Report. Mumbai: PRATHAM.

Rose, Elaina (1999). "Consumption Smoothing and Excess Female Mortality in Rural India." *Review of Economics and Statistics* 81 (1): 41–49.

Rutherford, Stuart (2000). *The Poor and Their Money.* New Delhi: Oxford UP.

Shaban, Radwan (1987). "Testing between Competing Models of Sharecropping." *Journal of Political Economy* 95 (5): 893–920.

Thomas, D., and J. Strauss (1997). "Health and Wages: Evidence on Men and Women in Urban Brazil." *Journal of Econometrics* 77: 159–85.

Thomas, Duncan, et al. (2004). "Causal Effect of Health on Labor Market Outcomes: Evidence from a Random Assignment Iron Supplementation Intervention." Mimeo. UCLA.

Townsend, Robert (1995). "Financial Systems in Northern Thai Villages." *Quarterly Journal of Economics* 110 (4): 1011–46.

Udry, Christopher (1990). "Credit Markets in Northern Nigeria: Credit as Insurance in a Rural Economy." *World Bank Economic Review* 4 (3): 251–69.

Wagstaff, Adam (2003). "Child Health on One Dollar a Day." *Social Science & Medicine* 57 (9): 1529–38.

World Health Organization Expert Consultation (2004). "Appropriate Body-Mass Index for Asian Populations and Its Implications for Policy and Intervention Strategies." *Lancet* 363 (9403): 157–63.

8. Dressing for Lula*

Rebecca Mead

It was hard, in the weeks before the landslide victory last October [2002] of Luiz Inácio Lula da Silva, the left-wing candidate in Brazil's recent presidential election, to find anyone who was very enthusiastic about his opponent, José Serra. Serra was a well-regarded economist and former health minister whose record of public service was accompanied by a deficit of charisma so severe that even his supporters noted his physical resemblance to Uncle Fester of the Addams Family. It was hard to find support for Serra, but not impossible, and a good place to look was within the cream-colored, heavily guarded walls of Daslu, a women's clothing store in a wealthy residential district of São Paulo. The store—which is windowless and has clusters of unsmiling security guards standing at its entrances, as if it were the embassy of a particularly beleaguered nation—caters to rich Brazilians, members of the ten per cent of the population who command nearly half the national income, and wear Chanel, Valentino, or Dolce & Gabbana. The Daslu customer does not speak in the voice of the man or woman on the street, not least because Daslu customers don't actually walk on the street but are driven around in Mercedeses that have been equipped with bulletproof windows and armored panels and, in some cases, gun-carrying chauffeurs. So, with the inevitable victory of Lula, as the new president is known, drawing near, the political chatter in the store ran to resigned humor at the dark days to come.

Six days before the election, a customer named Ruthinha Malzoni was at Daslu, making her selections from the designer collections that had just arrived from Europe. Malzoni is one of the city's better-known society figures, on account of her striking beauty, her startling agelessness, her personal charm, and her svelte aplomb when it comes to wearing the latest designer creations. She had arrived at the store wearing a white silk Dolce & Gabbana tailored suit and a vividly colored bustier by Dior, a massive crucifix of Brazilian gems resting on a cantilevered bosom, and had

---

* Source: *The New Yorker*, 17 March 2003.

settled into a curtained area with a rackful of clothes and a small gaggle of salesgirls, who rushed back and forth with armfuls of finery. Every so often, a maid in a black dress with a white lace collar and cuffs would appear with a tray, offering cups of espresso and glasses of water.

The real had slipped to its lowest point yet, almost four to the dollar; but the nation's financial crisis did not appear to be having any effect on Malzoni's lifestyle. She didn't need to try on any Chanel outfits, she said, because she'd been in Paris a month earlier, staying at the Plaza Athénée, and had been unable to resist popping across the street to the Chanel boutique. She was in the market for clothes for a New Year's trip to Hawaii, though she declared the gauzy four-and-a-half-thousand-real Blumarine dress she tried on for that purpose to be ugly. "I look like I could be taking care of children in this dress," she said. More to her liking was a fifteen-thousand-real beaver-fur bomber jacket by Dolce & Gabbana that could be worn only in the cold northern hemisphere, and a seven-thousand-real sequinned skirt by Blumarine that could be worn only after dark. Stripped to a thong and hopping in and out of outfits as swiftly as if she were playing a dozen characters in a one-woman show, she also purchased a black Valentino pants suit that tied in front, a bias-cut Prada skirt, a pair of velvet pants from Chloé, and a pair of high-heeled Dolce & Gabbana sandals that were adorned with enough dangling jewels to equip a chandelier.

Malzoni and her husband live in an apartment in a modern, high-security high-rise in São Paulo which has the atmosphere of a Parisian mansion from a more gracious era, with heavy swag curtains and antiqued mirror panels and gray-painted walls hung with twentieth-century Brazilian art. The Malzonis spend their weekends at the family "farm," an estate an hour outside São Paulo. Their large mansard-roofed house faces a lake and is surrounded by an eighteen-hole golf course, built to Paulo Malzoni's design. Paulo, who is Malzoni's third husband, develops shopping malls in São Paulo and Rio de Janeiro, but Ruthinha comes from a political family—her father was a senator, and her grandfather was the governor of a southern Brazilian state.

"I don't think we're going to have as many parties as we have clothes once Lula is elected," she said, trying on a pair of black-and-gold evening pants. "The husbands are all going to be too upset for parties." Either that or the parties would be ones she couldn't bring herself to go to—like the fund-raiser for Lula a week earlier, which the Malzonis had declined to attend. The host was an industrialist who appeared to nurture hopes of a position in the new government; his wife was thought to have her eye on an ambassadorship in Paris or Rome. "I heard that when Lula thanked the hostess at the end of the evening he addressed her as 'Compañero [comrade],'" Malzoni said, shuddering. One of the salesgirls brought out a dramatic Galliano dress with a daring gash across the front, exposing cleavage and the underside of one breast. The dress was deep red, the color that had been on the Socialist billboards and flags all over São Paulo that season, and Malzoni shrieked when she saw it. "This red one is the Lula dress!" she said. She wriggled into it, examined herself from all angles, and said, "Oh, we have to pray for the guy to be eliminated by an angel."

The Lula dress turned out not to be a good fit—"For this you need big boobs and a permissive husband," Malzoni said. Instead, she tried on a narrow black Galliano gown with a thick, low-slung belt in bright colors. "Now all I need are parties to go to, and a country happy enough for us to go dancing," she said.

Brazil is a country of huge economic disparities, in which the poorest forty per cent of the population command only eight per cent of the wealth, and those in the richest tier are as pampered as the nobility in pre-revolutionary France. The Malzonis employ, in their two homes, ten household workers, including a man who looks after the golf course and its enormous clubhouse. (The sitting room of the clubhouse is hung with photographs of golfing visitors to the Malzoni farm, such as Bill Clinton and Anthony Hopkins. Holding pride of place is a vintage photograph showing Fidel Castro, Raul Castro, and Che Guevara playing golf.) The rich make semi-annual shopping trips to Europe, timed to coincide with the arrival of the new fall and spring clothes. Wealthy Brazilians keep homes in Florida, and shuffle back and forth to New York as easily as a busy Brooklyn congressman—though the Malzonis have not been to New York since September 11, 2001, for fear of further terrorist attacks. They did visit Las Vegas last year, where they were obliged to submit to security checks. "They made me take off my Jimmy Choo shoes!" Ruthinha recalled. "The soles on those are so thin you couldn't fit a bomb in there!"

Within the precincts of the wealthy in São Paulo, Daslu is an institution, a provider of necessities to those who want for nothing. It was founded forty-five years ago by Lucia Piva de Albuquerque, the wife of a well-to-do lawyer, who started out by selling fashionable clothes to her friends in her home, donating part of the proceeds to charity. Lucia, an abbreviation of which provided the name for the store, died nineteen years ago, and was succeeded by her daughter Eliana Tranchesi, under whose direction the store has metastasized, engulfing an entire row of houses that have been joined together to form a warren of interconnected salons stuffed with merchandise, all hidden behind the bunker-like exterior wall.

For rich residents of São Paulo, all of life is conducted indoors, since it's only at private homes or in the right restaurants or stores that it is safe to wear a watch or jewelry; and Daslu—with its plushly furnished anteroom, where there are couches and book-piled coffee tables and sprays of orchids, and its racks of pretty clothes—is a universe of luxury largely insulated from the outside world. (Insulated, that is, except when the intrusion of that world is unavoidable, such as the time in 1990 when inflation rates of eighty per cent in one month rendered price tags on the clothes meaningless, because a gown would cost one amount in the morning and another by the end of the afternoon.) Daslu's Chanel shop has one of the highest turnovers per square foot of any Chanel store in the world; in the Prada department, shoes in all sizes and colors are piled on racks, as if they were in a very expensive branch of Payless.

Because the store consists of small rooms that once belonged to real houses, it feels intimate, but, at eleven thousand square feet, it is enormous. Part of that space is dedicated to international designers; the larger section is taken up with clothes sold under Daslu's own label: gauzy tops and low-cut jeans and fringed skirts and strappy beaded evening dresses. The Daslu collection is arranged by color—a khaki room, a pink room—so as to ease outfit coordination and more perfectly contrive the Daslu look, which is sexy and flirty and young, even when the women wearing the clothes sometimes share none of those characteristics.

The inside of Daslu has an even more rarefied character than most São Paulo environments, since not only the poor are excluded but also the men. Because there are no dressing rooms, men are not permitted beyond the coffee bar and the cash registers. On a busy day, the aisles are filled with women, from teen-agers to matrons, in various stages of undress and having undergone varying degrees of ingenious trussing, their undergarments ranging from what look like flesh-colored bike shorts to a pair of Nippits, a kind of disk-shaped Band-Aid that is plastered over the nipple, permitting its wearer to go braless without sacrificing the Barbie-doll-like regularity of form that is the Brazilian ideal.

The customers, who come from what are unflinchingly referred to as the best families, are attended by glossy-looking salesgirls from the same social class: Daslu functions as a kind of finishing school for the daughters of the rich and powerful in São Paulo; it is as if Bergdorf Goodman were staffed by the Hilton sisters and the Bush girls. Among the current Dasluzetes, as the salesgirls are called, are Sofia Alckmin, whose father has just been re-elected governor of the state of São Paulo, and who missed a day of work just before the election, after armed assailants attacked her brother's car and killed one of his bodyguards. The grunt work of the store is done by an army of maids, who commute each day from the poor, outlying districts of São Paulo to fold clothes and serve coffee.

Eight years ago, Tranchesi opened Daslu Homem, a men's store, across the street. It carries Zegna, Burberry, and many other European labels. The same building houses the Daslu Home collection; Daslu for kids, with tiny Tod's shoes and scaled-down Dolce & Gabbana leather jackets; and Daslu for pets, with coordinating leashes and canine sweaters. There's a bookstore of imported books, mostly concerned with international travel and design; several jewellers selling Brazilian gems; a wine store run by Tranchesi's brother, who is Brazil's largest importer of wine; a chocolate shop run by Tranchesi's sister-in-law; and a real-estate desk, where Daslu customers can find apartments to rent in Paris, London, and Rome.

Tranchesi has become one of the most prominent businesswomen in Brazil. (She and her three children are accompanied at all times by a pair of bodyguards apiece, so great is the fear of kidnapping.) Daslu has become a favorite destination for international fashion types, including Naomi Campbell and Mario Testino. Tranchesi, a divorcée, is forty-seven years old, with blond hair and a dewy complexion; she is admired in equal measure for her kindness and her shrewdness. Three days before Lula's Workers' Party, known as the P.T. party, swept the election, she sat in her cream-colored office, on the second floor of the store, and said, "We have always been expanding at Daslu. I have always been listening to my father, who says, 'This will be a year of crisis. Take care, this will be a hard year.' And instead we have always been increasing and increasing."

The poorest people of São Paulo live in the favelas, sprawling shantytowns, pitched into corners of cities. Many inhabitants make do without basic services, and the rule of law is that exercised by drug dealers. One of the consequences of the Third World condition of much of Brazil is that labor is cheap: the minimum wage is two hundred and ten reals (about sixty dollars) a month. Among the items available at Daslu is a tan leather vest punched with decorative holes that was made in one of the favelas in Rio de Janeiro, where dense villages perch precariously on the city's mountainsides. Daslu's own collection, which is created by a team of sixteen designers working to Eliana Tranchesi's specifications, is far cheaper than those from the international designers but is still beyond the reach of any but the wealthiest. A pair of velvet cargo pants costs 300 reals, which would be about a third of the monthly salary of the average Brazilian schoolteacher.

Among the best customers of the store are the salesgirls, who, for the most part, would not need their salaries to pay the rent even if they did not live in their parents' comfortable homes. "We go out a lot, and we see new clothes every day, and it's hard not to buy," one of them, Carolina Nunes, explained, while hanging out by the Chanel bags, checking her beeper occasionally to see whether a lawyer customer had shown up for her appointment yet. Nunes is a tall, slender, tan twenty-six-year-old whose father sells apartments in São Paulo, whose mother owns a chain of bistros, and whose boyfriend is an international sailing champion, a calling that requires Nunes to put in considerable time at the Rio de Janeiro yacht club. "We go to the beach every weekend, so we buy a new bikini every weekend," she said. "And we love sandals. At least half the money we make we spend on clothes." The previous day, she'd bought an eight-hundred-real suede jacket moments after it arrived in the store, as had a number of other salesgirls, and that afternoon the jacket kept parading by, accessorized in different ways—open over a skintight white tank top on one girl, tied modishly around the hips of another.

Like every Dasluzete, Nunes has a roster of personal clients; she earns a commission on every sale. Sometimes she is extremely busy, as when a customer from northern Brazil flies in for a day of shopping and orders the same Valentino sweater in four colors, or when the new Daslu collections arrive and the store is as crowded as Filene's Basement on sale day. At other times, Nunes might wait an entire afternoon for a client, lounging on the couch by the store's coffee counter with other underemployed Dasluzetes, as if they were high-end call girls killing time before a date.

The salesgirls also appear in the Daslu magazine, a catalogue that is sent to regular shoppers six times a year and that features photo spreads of the clothes, in addition to stories about the social lives of the Dasluzetes. A recent issue included an article about the trip Carolina Nunes and four other girls took to Turkey, where they were photographed in long white skirts and turquoise pendants outside Hagia Sophia. Four days after Lula's election, photographs for the Christmas edition of the magazine were shot at Eliana Tranchesi's home, a handsome Italianate mansion in an exclusive hilly district of São Paulo, which had been decked out with a massive Christmas tree surrounded by gifts, urns stuffed with roses, and tables laden with bowls of apples. Thousands of rose petals had been scattered over the swimming pool and were floating on the water's surface like a velvety coverlet.

By early evening, after many rolls of film and many bottles of champagne, some of the Dasluzetes had crashed on the white couches of a sitting room, where they huddled under silky blankets and chatted, while, on the large flat-screen TV, the evening news reported that the real had held steady and was even increasing in value against the dollar. A staff member of the magazine passed through and said to them, "You look like something from a favela!" The roses in the urns would be donated to a foundation begun by Mrs. Maria Lúcia Alckmin, the Governor's wife. Mrs. Alckmin had sought to find a way to make use of the leftover flowers from state functions, as well as from the private parties and weddings of her friends. She had established flower-arranging classes for residents of the favelas, so that they might be equipped to find work with one of São Paulo's florists.

A few days before the election, an e-mail began circulating in São Paulo which contained an image of Lula after a digital makeover. His grizzled beard and thatch of gray hair were tinted to a perfect blond, his weathered skin was smooth and tan, his eyes were sky blue, he wore a handsome blue suit and red tie, and the image was captioned "Daslula—O Candidato Perfeito."

The satire referred to the transformation that Lula, a metalworker turned trade-union leader, had undergone in terms of both appearance and politics in the run-up to the election, which was his fourth attempt at the presidency. He exchanged his work-ingman's shirtsleeves for tailored suits (which, it was rumored among the salesgirls at Daslu, he had bought at the Zegna store in Daslu Homem) and began promoting a notably less radical political program, forging alliances with Brazilian industrialists. Lula's victory was a cause for celebration on a par with Brazil's triumph in the World Cup earlier in the year, and on Election Day, a Sunday, the main commercial street in São Paulo, Avenida Paulista, was filled with cars cruising up and down, the drivers honking their horns while gleeful back-seat occupants brandished enormous P.T. flags from the car windows and Lula-supporting pedestrians danced by the roadside.

To the poor, Lula had promised improved health care, education, and unemployment benefits. The social system that generally prevails in Brazil, however, is one of noblesse oblige, in which the wealthy take care of the individuals in their personal employ. The rich consider this to be an absolute duty, though they tend not to see a similar obligation to submit to a fairer distribution of wealth on a national scale. Wealthy Brazilians often speak of their servants as being like members of the family. This does not mean, for example, that the houseboy at the Malzoni farm sits down to eat with the Malzonis, but it does mean that Ruthinha Malzoni continues to keep her son's former nanny on the payroll, complete with health benefits, even though her son is now twenty-five years old. For poor Brazilians, a steady job with an employer who will help pay for your children's education, help you find a job for a cousin or a sister, and step in should you have emergency medical bills has always been a more effective route to personal betterment than waiting for economic and political reform.

For this reason, the maids' positions at Daslu are as highly coveted as the salesgirls' positions, though by a notably different demographic; the head of staff of the maids, for example, is a woman of thirty-six whose first job, at the age of twelve, was as a nanny. There are a hundred and twenty maids at the store, and their role is to operate as support staff for the salesgirls—though it is generally acknowledged that the maids, who work full time rather than the six-hour shifts of the salesgirls, are far more familiar with the store's merchandise. (Their official title is "assistant," but they are known by the affectionate diminutive *aventalzinho*, or "little apron.") Unlike the salesgirls, the maids receive no commission; their salary is two thousand reals a month, and benefits include medical and dental care. Each month, they are also given a basket of staple goods, including rice, beans, and sugar.

Some years ago, after the fifteen-year-old son of one maid was shot to death by drug dealers, Eliana Tranchesi founded an educational program for the children of her employees, using money she received as a birthday gift. At a private school nearby, Tranchesi pays the fees of fifty or so Daslu children. She has also established her own day-care center, just around the corner from the store, where babies as young as four months can be installed. Some Dasluzetes volunteer their services at the center schooling a half-dozen four-year-olds in basic English or conducting a ballet class in which six or eight little girls totter around in pink tutus bought with funds donated by the salesgirls.

The maids are distinguished from the Dasluzetes not merely by skin color— lower income tends to correlate with darker complexions in Brazil—but by their outfits, which are a version of the uniform traditionally worn by domestic help: a black short-sleeved dress worn with white tights and flat white shoes. Within the store, the maids are always at work, folding sweaters or rehanging dresses; unlike the salesgirls, they are not permitted to sit on any of the chairs or sofas in the store. When a salesgirl is at work with a client, characterizing the chicness of this Gucci shoe or that Prada bag, the maids hover nearby, ready to procure a needed item, in the manner of nurses attending a surgeon performing a delicate operation.

The maids are not supposed to address the clients, and are not in the habit of socializing with the salesgirls, since they take their breaks in a building across the street, while the salesgirls have a private lounge inside the store. Still, fraternization of a sort does occur. "When something new comes into the store, the maids say to us, 'Please put it on, we want to see how it looks,'" Carolina Nunes said. Within Daslu, it is regarded as evidence of Eliana Tranchesi's lack of snobbishness that, at the Christmas party she gives for all the staff, she dances with the man in charge of the store's valet parking.

Nancy Tonello, one of Daslu's longest-serving maids, used to be a seamstress and speaks of working at Daslu as a privilege. "I got to know a whole world that is very different from the outside world, and I was enchanted," she said one day. "What is interesting about rich people is that they have a whole tradition—their families, and everything." Exposure to the customers has been an education for Tonello, who is fifty. "We can't go abroad every three months, but we can listen to them describing their trips," she said. "I have seen their behavior—small details, like how they take their coffee—and I have changed my own behavior because of that."

Tonello said that the maids did not resent the rich for having so much more than they did. "When we begin working here, we are taught to understand the differences between people—that some people have money, and that we shouldn't mind that, because that is the only way the store can exist," she said. After starting at Daslu eleven years ago, Tonello has worked her way up to assistant in the imported-lingerie department. There was, Tonello said, no higher position to which she could be promoted. At Daslu, no maid has ever become a salesgirl; though there is no house rule forbidding the possibility, it has never occurred to the management to propose such a promotion, and it has never occurred to any maid to ask for one.

What the coming political changes in Brazil mean for Daslu is still unclear, but so far, Tranchesi says, Brazil's economic problems have had no impact on the buying habits of her customers. "In Brazil, it is very hard to give up clothes," Tranchesi said a few days after the election. In fact, because the wealthy are not foolish enough to keep their money in reals, they have been able to take advantage of bargain prices, thanks to the exchange rate. "I think we are going to have a year of recession, and what happens to our client is that she doesn't feel the lack of money, but she feels the atmosphere," Tranchesi said.

Tranchesi's most immediate political problem is a more parochial one. The block on which Daslu sits is zoned for residential use only, and in recent years a neighborhood association has been protesting the expansion of the store. A week before the election, the *Folha de São Paulo* reported that it had been determined that Daslu was in violation of the zoning laws, and that, in spite of repeated efforts over the years by the store's powerful supporters to insure that it could continue business, Tranchesi had finally been given five days to close. That closure was postponed—Tranchesi said that it was never a serious proposition—but this spring a judge will rule on whether the São Paulo zoning laws are outdated, as Tranchesi and her supporters claim. Meanwhile, Tranchesi has been visiting with residents' groups, pointing out the benefits of having her establishment in the neighborhood; for instance, on the blocks immediately surrounding Daslu, crime has dropped to zero, an unheard-of figure in São Paulo, and one that, Tranchesi argues, more than compensates for the double-parked Mercedeses at her door.

The future of the store was one of the topics of conversation at a lunch that Ruthinha Malzoni shared, at her São Paulo apartment, with her longtime friend Kika Rivetti a few days after the election. Rivetti, too, runs a boutique, called Eclat, and she met Malzoni in the late sixties at a party, at which they found themselves wearing the same Zandra Rhodes dress. As lunch was served—champagne and pasta infused with bits of truffle, packets of which Malzoni had brought back from Paris—the two friends discussed the latest news in the gossip columns. A recent item described a dinner party given by a woman who suspected her husband of having an affair and had seated him opposite the woman in question, first sprinkling the floor under the table with talcum powder. "When he stood up, he had little white footprints all over his pants!" Malzoni said.

They talked about the report on Daslu in the *Folha de São Paulo*, and wondered whether the fact that the mayor of São Paulo, Marta Suplicy, was a Daslu customer would help Eliana Tranchesi in her bid to stay put, or whether Suplicy, a member of Lula's P.T. party, would not want to be seen doing anything to help the rich. Rivetti had gone to the fund-raising party for Lula that Malzoni had declined to attend. She had been impressed by Lula, in spite of herself. "If he does half of what he says he's going to do, it will be good," she said.

"If he does a third of what he says he's going to do," Malzoni said, skeptically.

"It's time for a change in Brazil," Rivetti replied. "But don't think I voted for him, my dear."

When the real started its descent against the dollar last year Tranchesi's established practice of buying designer clothes in France and Italy and New York suddenly became a lot more difficult. Fifty per cent of Daslu's revenues are generated from imported goods, and Tranchesi has been forced to strike deals with her European suppliers to stagger her payments for the fifty thousand pieces she imports every year. "They are understanding, and are giving us more days to pay," she said.

But she has also decided that she must start bringing dollars into the business; this spring, for the first time, a small selection of Daslu clothes will be available in high-end boutiques around the world. No New York store has picked them up, though they will be for sale at Saks, in Chevy Chase, Maryland; Browns, in London; and Villa Moda in Kuwait, among other locations. The decision to export was a last-minute one. "We decided to do it in August, when the dollar started going up," Tranchesi said.

One Saturday, Tranchesi was invited to a casual lunch for a few friends at the home of Nizan Guanaes, a well-known adman in São Paulo who had worked on the doomed campaign of José Serra. Guanaes lives not far from Daslu in an elegant house surrounded by high walls, at which guests must check in with a guard before passing through two heavy, clanking gates. In a month's time, Guanaes was to marry Tranchesi's right-hand woman at Daslu, Donata Meirelles, and Tranchesi was to be Meirelles's maid of honor. The wedding would be a big event on the São Paulo social calendar, and many of the choicest clothes at Daslu were hung with tags that read, "Don't sell to anyone for Donata's wedding," indicating that another customer had claimed the outfit. The planning for the wedding was still incomplete, and Meirelles wanted her guests to help her decide which chocolates would be offered at the reception; so after lunch had been served and everyone had retired to a table in the garden for coffee, a large box of fancy chocolates was added to the dessert offerings that had already been set out by a servant—a platter piled with slices of fresh fruit, and a large crystal bowl filled with scoops of mango, chocolate, and strawberry ice cream.

Guanaes, helping himself to dessert, said that Serra would have been a good president but was a terrible candidate. The country had been on the right economic track, and would have continued that way with Serra, and though public support for Lula was hardly surprising, it was misguided. "Look at me—I am fat," he said. "When I am on a diet, all my vital signs are better, but I feel miserable. That is what it has been like for the country."

The conversation turned to Daslu and the question of what would be the best marketing campaign for Tranchesi, now that she was attempting to make an international shopping public aware of her brand by selling Daslu clothes overseas. "What does the rest of the world think about when they think about Brazil?" Guanaes said. "Sex, the body, beautiful people, and soccer. You should show the Brazilian soccer team in your clothes, and Brazilian models." No less than Lula, Daslu needed a revamped image—not one that stressed the exclusiveness of the store, the inaccessibility of the world of Daslu to all but the élite, but one that reached out to ordinary people. "You should tell people that you have the best jeans in the world," Guanaes said, and a servant came around with more tiny cups of espresso, while the scoops of ice cream in the bowl melted into each other, resolving into a thick, liquid blur of yellow and brown and pink.

9. The Drowning Child and the Expanding Circle[*]

Peter Singer

To challenge my students to think about the ethics of what we owe to people in need, I ask them to imagine that their route to the university takes them past a shallow pond. One morning, I say to them, you notice a child has fallen in and appears to be drowning. To wade in and pull the child out would be easy but it will mean that you get your clothes wet and muddy, and by the time you go home and change you will have missed your first class.

I then ask the students: do you have any obligation to rescue the child? Unanimously, the students say they do. The importance of saving a child so far outweighs the cost of getting one's clothes muddy and missing a class, that they refuse to consider it any kind of excuse for not saving the child. Does it make a difference, I ask, that there are other people walking past the pond who would equally be able to rescue the child but are not doing so? No, the students reply, the fact that others are not doing what they ought to do is no reason why I should not do what I ought to do.

Once we are all clear about our obligations to rescue the drowning child in front of us, I ask: would it make any difference if the child were far away, in another country perhaps, but similarly in danger of death, and equally within your means to save, at no great cost—and absolutely no danger—to yourself? Virtually all agree that distance and nationality make no moral difference to the situation. I then point out that we are all in that situation of the person passing the shallow pond: we can all save lives of people, both children and adults, who would otherwise die, and we can do so at a very small cost to us: the cost of a new CD, a shirt or a night out at a restaurant or concert, can mean the difference between life and death to more than one person somewhere in the world—and overseas aid agencies like Oxfam overcome the problem of acting at a distance.

At this point the students raise various practical difficulties. Can we be sure that our donation will really get to the people who need it? Doesn't most aid get swal-

---

[*] Source: *New Internationalist* 289 (April 1997), <http://www.newint.org/issue289/drowning.htm>.

lowed up in administrative costs, or waste, or downright corruption? Isn't the real problem the growing world population, and is there any point in saving lives until the problem has been solved? These questions can all be answered: but I also point out that even if a substantial proportion of our donations were wasted, the cost to us of making the donation is so small, compared to the benefits that it provides when it, or some of it, does get through to those who need our help, that we would still be saving lives at a small cost to ourselves—even if aid organizations were much less efficient than they actually are.

I am always struck by how few students challenge the underlying ethics of the idea that we ought to save the lives of strangers when we can do so at relatively little cost to ourselves. At the end of the nineteenth century W.E.H. Lecky wrote of human concern as an expanding circle which begins with the individual, then embraces the family and "soon the circle ... includes first a class, then a nation, then a coalition of nations, then all humanity, and finally, its influence is felt in the dealings of man [sic] with the animal world."[1] On this basis the overwhelming majority of my students seem to be already in the penultimate stage—at least—of Lecky's expanding circle. There is, of course, for many students and for various reasons a gap between acknowledging what we ought to do, and doing it; but I shall come back to that issue shortly.

Our century is the first in which it has been possible to speak of global responsibility and a global community. For most of human history we could affect the people in our village, or perhaps in a large city, but even a powerful king could not conquer far beyond the borders of his kingdom. When Hadrian ruled the Roman Empire, his realm covered most of the "known" world, but today when I board a jet in London leaving what used to be one of the far-flung outposts of the Roman Empire, I pass over its opposite boundary before I am even halfway to Singapore, let alone to my home in Australia. Moreover no matter what the extent of the empire, the time required for communications and transport meant that there was simply no way in which people could make any difference to the victims of floods, wars, or massacres taking place on the other side of the globe. By the time anyone had heard of the events and responded, the victims were dead or had survived without assistance. "Charity begins at home" made sense, because it was only "at home"—or at least in your own town—that you could be confident that your charity would make any difference.

Instant communications and jet transport have changed all that. A television audience of two billion people can now watch hungry children beg for food in an area struck by famine, or they can see refugees streaming across the border in search of a safe place away from those they fear will kill them. Most of that huge audience also have the means to help people they are seeing on their screens. Each one of us

1 W.E.H. Lecky. *The History of European Morals* (Longman, 1892).

can pull out a credit card and phone in a donation to an aid organization which can, in a few days, fly in people who can begin distributing food and medical supplies. Collectively, it is also within the capacity of the United Nations—with the support of major powers—to put troops on the ground to protect those who are in danger of becoming victims of genocide.

Our capacity to affect what is happening, anywhere in the world, is one way in which we are living in an era of global responsibility. But there is also another way that offers an even more dramatic contrast with the past. The atmosphere and the oceans seemed, until recently, to be elements of nature totally unaffected by the puny activities of human beings. Now we know that our use of chlorofluorocarbons has damaged the ozone shield; our emission of carbon dioxide is changing the climate of the entire planet in unpredictable ways and raising the level of the sea; and fishing fleets are scouring the oceans, depleting fish populations that once seemed limitless to a point from which they may never recover. In these ways the actions of consumers in Los Angeles can cause skin cancer among Australians, inundate the lands of peasants in Bangladesh, and force Thai villagers who could once earn a living by fishing to work in the factories of Bangkok.

In these circumstances the need for a global ethic is inescapable. Is it nevertheless a vain hope? Here are some reasons why it may not be.

We live in a time when many people experience their lives as empty and lacking in fulfilment. The decline of religion and the collapse of communism have left but the ideology of the free market whose only message is: consume, and work hard so you can earn money to consume more. Yet even those who do reasonably well in this race for material goods do not find that they are satisfied with their way of life. We now have good scientific evidence for what philosophers have said throughout the ages: once we have enough to satisfy our basic needs, gaining more wealth does not bring us more happiness.

Consider the life of Ivan Boesky, the multimillionaire Wall Street dealer who in 1986 pleaded guilty to insider trading. Why did Boesky get involved in criminal activities when he already had more money than he could ever spend? Six years after the insider-trading scandal broke, Boesky's estranged wife Seema spoke about her husband's motives in an interview with Barbara Walters for the American ABC Network's *20/20* program. Walters asked whether Boesky was a man who craved luxury. Seema Boesky thought not, pointing out that he worked around the clock, seven days a week, and never took a day off to enjoy his money. She then recalled that when in 1982 *Forbes* magazine first listed Boesky among the wealthiest people in the US, he was upset. She assumed he disliked the publicity and made some remark to that effect. Boesky replied: "That's not what's upsetting me. We're no-one. We're nowhere. We're at the bottom of the list and I promise you I won't shame you like that again. We will not remain at the bottom of that list."

We must free ourselves from this absurd conception of success. Not only does it fail to bring happiness even to those who, like Boesky, do extraordinarily well in the competitive struggle; it also sets a social standard that is a recipe for global injustice and environmental disaster. We cannot continue to see our goal as acquiring more and more wealth, or as consuming more and more goodies, and leaving behind us an even larger heap of waste.

We tend to see ethics as opposed to self-interest; we assume that those who make fortunes from insider trading are successfully following self-interest—as long as they don't get caught—and ignoring ethics. We think that it is in our interest to take a more senior, better-paid position with another company, even though it means that we are helping to manufacture or promote a product that does no good at all, or is environmentally damaging. On the other hand, those who pass up opportunities to rise in their career because of ethical "scruples" about the nature of the work, or who give away their wealth to good causes, are thought to be sacrificing their own interest in order to obey the dictates of ethics.

Many will say that it is naive to believe that people could shift from a life based on consumption, or on getting on top of the corporate ladder, to one that is more ethical in its fundamental direction. But such a shift would answer a palpable need. Today the assertion that life is meaningless no longer comes from existentialist philosophers who treat it as a shocking discovery: it comes from bored adolescents for whom it is a truism. Perhaps it is the central place of self-interest, and the way in which we conceive of our own interest, that is to blame here. The pursuit of self-interest, as standardly conceived, is a life without any meaning beyond our own pleasure or individual satisfaction. Such a life is often a self-defeating enterprise. The ancients knew of the "paradox of hedonism," according to which the more explicitly we pursue our desire for pleasure, the more elusive we will find its satisfaction. There is no reason to believe that human nature has changed so dramatically as to render the ancient wisdom inapplicable.

Here ethics offer a solution. An ethical life is one in which we identify ourselves with other, larger, goals, thereby giving meaning to our lives. The view that there is harmony between ethics and enlightened self-interest is an ancient one, now often scorned. Cynicism is more fashionable than idealism. But such hopes are not groundless, and there are substantial elements of truth in the ancient view that an ethically reflective life is also a good life for the person leading it. Never has it been so urgent that the reasons for accepting this view should be widely understood.

In a society in which the narrow pursuit of material self-interest is the norm, the shift to an ethical stance is more radical than many people realize. In comparison with the needs of people going short of food in Rwanda, the desire to sample the wines of Australia's best vineyards pales into insignificance. An ethical approach to life does not forbid having fun or enjoying food and wine; but it changes our sense of priorities. The effort and expense put into fashion, the endless search for more and more refined gastronomic pleasures, the added expense that marks out the luxury-car market—all these become disproportionate to people who can shift perspective long enough to put themselves in the position of others affected by their actions. If the circle of ethics really does expand, and a higher ethical consciousness spreads, it will fundamentally change the society in which we live.

10. Toward a Theory of World Inequality[*]

Daron Acemoglu and James Robinson

We live in an unequal world.... In rich countries, individuals are healthier, live longer, and are much better educated. They also have access to a range of amenities and options in life, from vacations to career paths, that people in poor countries can only dream of. People in rich countries also drive on roads without potholes, and enjoy toilets, electricity, and running water in their houses. They also typically have governments that do not arbitrarily arrest or harass them; on the contrary, the governments provide services, including education, health care, roads, and law and order. Notable, too, is the fact that the citizens vote in elections and have some voice in the political direction their countries take....

The first country to experience sustained economic growth was England—or Great Britain, usually just Britain, as the union of England, Wales, and Scotland after 1707 is known. Growth emerged slowly in the second half of the eighteenth century as the Industrial Revolution, based on major technological breakthroughs and their application in industry, took root. Industrialization in England was soon followed by industrialization in most of Western Europe and the United States. English prosperity also spread rapidly to Britain's "settler colonies" of Canada, Australia, and New Zealand. A list of the thirty richest countries today would include them, plus Japan, Singapore, and South Korea. The prosperity of these latter three is in turn part of a broader pattern in which many East Asian nations, including Taiwan and subsequently China, have experienced recent rapid growth.

The bottom of the world income distribution paints as sharp and as distinctive a picture as the top. If you instead make a list of the poorest thirty countries in the world today, you will find almost all of them in sub-Saharan Africa. They are joined by countries such as Afghanistan, Haiti, and Nepal, which, though not in Africa, all share something critical with African nations, as we'll explain. If you went back

---

[*] Source: *Why Nations Fail: The Origins of Power, Prosperity, and Poverty* (New York: Crown, 2012).

fifty years, the countries in the top and bottom thirty wouldn't be greatly different. Singapore and South Korea would not be among the richest countries, and there would be several different countries in the bottom thirty, but the overall picture that emerged would be remarkably consistent with what we see today. Go back one hundred years, or a hundred and fifty, and you'd find nearly the same countries in the same groups....

While there is a lot of persistence in the patterns of prosperity we see around us today, these patterns are not unchanging or immutable. First,...most of current world inequality emerged since the late eighteenth century, following on the tails of the Industrial Revolution. Not only were gaps in prosperity much smaller as late as the middle of the eighteenth century, but the rankings which have been so stable since then are not the same when we go further back in history. In the Americas, for example, the ranking we see for the last hundred and fifty years was completely different five hundred years ago. Second, many nations have experienced several decades of rapid growth, such as much of East Asia since the Second World War and, more recently, China. Many of these subsequently saw that growth go into reverse. Argentina, for example, grew rapidly for five decades up until 1920, becoming one of the richest countries in the world, but then started a long slide. The Soviet Union is an even more noteworthy example, growing rapidly between 1930 and 1970, but subsequently experiencing a rapid collapse.

What explains these major differences in poverty and prosperity and the patterns of growth? Why did Western European nations and their colonial offshoots filled with European settlers start growing in the nineteenth century, scarcely looking back? What explains the persistent ranking of inequality within the Americas? Why have sub-Saharan African and Middle Eastern nations failed to achieve the type of economic growth seen in Western Europe, while much of East Asia has experienced breakneck rates of economic growth? One might think that the fact that world inequality is so huge and consequential and has such sharply drawn patterns would mean that it would have a well-accepted explanation. Not so. Most hypotheses that social scientists have proposed for the origins of poverty and prosperity just don't work and fail to convincingly explain the lay of the land.

The Geography Hypothesis

One widely accepted theory of the causes of world inequality is the geography hypothesis, which claims that the great divide between rich and poor countries is created by geographical differences. Many poor countries, such as those of Africa, Central America, and South Asia, are between the tropics of Cancer and Capricorn. Rich nations, in contrast, tend to be in temperate latitudes. This geographic concentration of poverty and prosperity gives a superficial appeal to the geography hypothesis, which is the starting point of the theories and views of many social scientists and pundits alike. But this doesn't make it any less wrong.

As early as the late eighteenth century, the great French political philosopher Montesquieu noted the geographic concentration of prosperity and poverty, and proposed an explanation for it. He argued that people in tropical climates tended to be lazy and to lack inquisitiveness. As a consequence, they didn't work hard and were not innovative, and this was the reason why they were poor. Montesquieu also speculated that lazy people tended to be ruled by despots, suggesting that a tropical location could explain not just poverty but also some of the political phenomena associated with economic failure, such as dictatorship. The theory that hot countries are intrinsically poor, though contradicted by the recent rapid economic advance of countries such as Singapore, Malaysia, and Botswana, is still forcefully advocated by some, such as the economist Jeffrey Sachs. The modern version of this view emphasizes not the direct effects of climate on work effort or thought processes, but two additional arguments: first, that tropical diseases, particularly malaria, have very adverse consequences for health and therefore labor productivity; and second, that tropical soils do not allow for productive agriculture. The conclusion, though, is the same: temperate climates have a relative advantage over tropical and semitropical areas. World inequality, however, cannot be explained by climate or diseases, or any version of the geography hypothesis. Just think of Nogales [a city that straddles the US-Mexico border, consisting of Nogales in the US state of Arizona, and Heroica Nogales in the Mexican state of Sonora]. What separates the two parts is not climate, geography, or disease environment, but the US-Mexico border. If the geography hypothesis cannot explain differences between the north and south of Nogales, or North and South Korea, or those between East and West Germany before the fall of the Berlin Wall, could it still be a useful theory for explaining differences between North and South America? Between Europe and Africa? Simply, no....

Another influential version of the geography hypothesis is advanced by the ecologist and evolutionary biologist Jared Diamond. He argues that the origins of intercontinental inequality at the start of the modern period, five hundred years ago, rested in different historical endowments of plant and animal species, which subsequently influenced agricultural productivity. In some places, such as the Fertile Crescent in the modern Middle East, there were a large number of species that could be domesticated by humans. Elsewhere, such as the Americas, there were not. Having many species capable of being domesticated made it very attractive for societies to make the transition from a hunter-gatherer to a farming lifestyle. As a consequence, farming developed earlier in the Fertile Crescent than in the Americas. Population density grew, allowing specialization of labor, trade, urbanization, and political development. Crucially, in places where farming dominated, technological innovation took place much more rapidly than in other parts of the world. Thus, according to Diamond, the differential availability of animal and plant species created differential intensities of farming, which led to different paths of technological change and prosperity across different continents.

Though Diamond's thesis is a powerful approach to the puzzle on which he focuses, it cannot be extended to explain modern world inequality. For example, Diamond argues that the Spanish were able to dominate the civilizations of the Americas because of their longer history of farming and consequent superior technology. But we now need to explain why the Mexicans and Peruvians inhabiting the former lands of the Aztecs and Incas are poor. While having access to wheat, barley, and horses might have made the Spanish richer than the Incas, the gap in incomes between the two was not very large. The average income of a Spaniard was probably less than double that of a citizen of the Inca Empire. Diamond's thesis implies that once the Incas had been exposed to all the species and resulting technologies that they had not been able to develop themselves, they ought quickly to have attained the living standards of the Spanish. Yet nothing of the sort happened. On the contrary, in the nineteenth and twentieth centuries, a much larger gap in incomes between Spain and Peru emerged. Today the average Spaniard is more than six times richer than the average Peruvian. This gap in incomes is closely connected to the uneven dissemination of modern industrial technologies, but this has little to do either with the potential for animal and plant domestication or with intrinsic agricultural productivity differences between Spain and Peru....

It should also be clear that Diamond's argument, which is about continental inequality, is not well equipped to explain variation within continents—an essential part of modern world inequality. For example, while the orientation of the Eurasian landmass might explain how England managed to benefit from the innovations of the Middle East without having to reinvent them, it doesn't explain why the Industrial Revolution happened in England rather than, say, Moldova. In addition, as Diamond himself points out, China and India benefited greatly from very rich suites of animals and plants, and from the orientation of Eurasia. But most of the poor people of the world today are in those two countries....

Geography is also unlikely to explain the poverty of the Middle East for similar reasons. After all, the Middle East led the world in the Neolithic Revolution, and the first towns developed in modern Iraq. Iron was first smelted in Turkey, and as late as the Middle Ages the Middle East was technologically dynamic. It was not the geography of the Middle East that made the Neolithic Revolution flourish in that part of the world, and it was, again, not geography that made the Middle East poor. Instead, it was the expansion and consolidation of the Ottoman Empire, and it is the institutional legacy of this empire that keeps the Middle East poor today....

The Culture Hypothesis
The second widely accepted theory, the culture hypothesis, relates prosperity to culture. The culture hypothesis, just like the geography hypothesis, has a distinguished lineage, going back at least to the great German sociologist Max Weber, who

argued that the Protestant Reformation and the Protestant ethic it spurred played a key role in facilitating the rise of modern industrial society in Western Europe. The culture hypothesis no longer relies solely on religion, but stresses other types of beliefs, values, and ethics as well.

Though it is not politically correct to articulate in public, many people still maintain that Africans are poor because they lack a good work ethic, still believe in witchcraft and magic, or resist new Western technologies. Many also believe that Latin America will never be rich because its people are intrinsically profligate and impecunious, and because they suffer from some "Iberian" or "mañana" culture. Of course, many once believed that the Chinese culture and Confucian values were inimical to economic growth, though now the importance of the Chinese work ethic as the engine of growth in China, Hong Kong, and Singapore is trumpeted.

Is the culture hypothesis useful for understanding world inequality? Yes and no. Yes, in the sense that social norms, which are related to culture, matter and can be hard to change, and they also sometimes support institutional differences, this book's explanation for world inequality. But mostly no, because those aspects of culture often emphasized—religion, national ethics, African or Latin values—are just not important for understanding how we got here and why the inequalities in the world persist. Other aspects, such as the extent to which people trust each other or are able to cooperate, are important but they are mostly an outcome of institutions, not an independent cause.

Let us go back to Nogales. As we noted earlier, many aspects of culture are the same north and south of the fence. Nevertheless, there may be some marked differences in practices, norms, and values, though these are not causes but outcomes of the two places' divergent development paths. For example, in surveys Mexicans typically say they trust other people less than the citizens of the United States say they trust others. But it is not a surprise that Mexicans lack trust when their government cannot eliminate drug cartels or provide a functioning unbiased legal system. The same is true with North and South Korea. The South is one of the richest countries in the world, while the North grapples with periodic famine and abject poverty. While "culture" is very different between the South and the North today, it played no role in causing the diverging economic fortunes of these two half nations. The Korean peninsula has a long period of common history. Before the Korean War and the division at the 38th parallel, it had an unprecedented homogeneity in terms of language, ethnicity, and culture. Just as in Nogales, what matters is the border. To the north is a different regime, imposing different institutions, creating different incentives. Any difference in culture between south and north of the border cutting through the two parts of Nogales or the two parts of Korea is thus not a cause of the differences in prosperity but, rather, a consequence....

What about Max Weber's Protestant ethic? Though it may be true that predominantly Protestant countries, such as the Netherlands and England, were the first economic successes of the modern era, there is little relationship between religion and economic success. France, a predominantly Catholic country, quickly mimicked the economic performance of the Dutch and English in the nineteenth century, and Italy is as prosperous as any of these nations today. Looking farther east, you'll see that none of the economic successes of East Asia have anything to do with any form of Christian religion, so there is not much support for a special relationship between Protestantism and economic success there, either....

But perhaps this is the wrong way to think about culture. Maybe the cultural factors that matter are not tied to religion but rather to particular "national cultures." Perhaps it is the influence of English culture that is important and explains why countries such as the United States, Canada, and Australia are so prosperous? Though this idea sounds initially appealing, it doesn't work, either. Yes, Canada and the United States were English colonies, but so were Sierra Leone and Nigeria. The variation in prosperity within former English colonies is as great as that in the entire world. The English legacy is not the reason for the success of North America.

There is yet one more version of the culture hypothesis: perhaps it is not English versus non-English that matters but, rather, European versus non-European. Could it be that Europeans are superior somehow because of their work ethic, outlook on life, Judeo-Christian values, or Roman heritage? It is true that Western Europe and North America, filled primarily by people of European descent, are the most prosperous parts of the world. Perhaps it is the superior European cultural legacy that is at the root of prosperity—and the last refuge of the culture hypothesis. Alas, this version of the culture hypothesis has as little explanatory potential as the others. A greater proportion of the population of Argentina and Uruguay, compared with the population of Canada and the United States, is of European descent, but Argentina's and Uruguay's economic performance leaves much to be desired. Japan and Singapore never had more than a sprinkling of inhabitants of European descent, yet they are as prosperous as many parts of Western Europe....

Just like the geography hypothesis, the culture hypothesis is also unhelpful for explaining other aspects of the lay of the land around us today....

The Ignorance Hypothesis

The final popular theory for why some nations are poor and some are rich is the ignorance hypothesis, which asserts that world inequality exists because we or our rulers do not know how to make poor countries rich. This idea is the one held by most economists, who take their cue from the famous definition proposed by the English economist Lionel Robbins in 1935 that "economics is a science which studies human behavior as a relationship between ends and scarce means which have alternative uses."

It is then a small step to conclude that the science of economics should focus on the best use of scarce means to satisfy social ends. Indeed, the most famous theoretical result in economics, the so-called First Welfare Theorem, identifies the circumstances under which the allocation of resources in a "market economy" is socially desirable from an economic point of view. A market economy is an abstraction that is meant to capture a situation in which all individuals and firms can freely produce, buy, and sell any products or services that they wish. When these circumstances are not present there is a "market failure." Such failures provide the basis for a theory of world inequality, since the more that market failures go unaddressed, the poorer a country is likely to be. The ignorance hypothesis maintains that poor countries are poor because they have a lot of market failures and because economists and policymakers do not know how to get rid of them and have heeded the wrong advice in the past. Rich countries are rich because they have figured out better policies and have successfully eliminated these failures. Could the ignorance hypothesis explain world inequality?

Could it be that African countries are poorer than the rest of the world because their leaders tend to have the same mistaken views of how to run their countries, leading to the poverty there, while Western European leaders are better informed or better advised, which explains their relative success? . . . .

The experience of Ghana's Prime Minister in 1971, Kofi Busia, illustrates how misleading the ignorance hypothesis can be. Busia faced a dangerous economic crisis. After coming to power in 1969, he, like Nkrumah before him, pursued unsustainable expansionary economic policies and maintained various price controls through marketing boards and an overvalued exchange rate. Though Busia had been an opponent of Nkrumah, and led a democratic government, he faced many of the same political constraints. As with Nkrumah, his economic policies were adopted not because he was "ignorant" and believed that these policies were good economics or an ideal way to develop the country. The policies were chosen because they were good politics, enabling Busia to transfer resources to politically powerful groups, for example in urban areas, who needed to be kept contented. Price controls squeezed agriculture, delivering cheap food to the urban constituencies and generating revenues to finance government spending. But these controls were unsustainable. Ghana was soon suffering from a series of balance-of-payment crises and foreign exchange shortages. Faced with these dilemmas, on December 27, 1971, Busia signed an agreement with the International Monetary Fund that included a massive devaluation of the currency.

The IMF, the World Bank, and the entire international community put pressure on Busia to implement the reforms contained in the agreement. Though the international institutions were blissfully unaware, Busia knew he was taking a huge political gamble. The immediate consequence of the currency's devaluation was rioting and discontent in Accra, Ghana's capital, that mounted uncontrollably until Busia was overthrown by the military, led by Lieutenant Colonel Acheampong, who immediately reversed the devaluation. The ignorance hypothesis differs from the geography and culture hypotheses in that it comes readily with a suggestion about how to "solve" the problem of poverty: if ignorance got us here, enlightened and informed rulers and policymakers can get us out and we should be able to "engineer" prosperity around the world by providing the right advice and by convincing politicians of what is good economics. Yet Busia's experience underscores the fact that the main obstacle to the adoption of policies that would reduce market failures and encourage economic growth is not the ignorance of politicians but the incentives and constraints they face from the political and economic institutions in their societies.

Although the ignorance hypothesis still rules supreme among most economists and in Western policymaking circles—which almost to the exclusion of anything else, focus on how to engineer prosperity—it is just another hypothesis that doesn't work. It explains neither the origins of prosperity around the world nor the lay of the land around us—for example, why some nations, such as Mexico and Peru, but not the United States or England, adopted institutions and policies that would impoverish the majority of their citizens, or why almost all sub-Saharan Africa and most of Central America are so much poorer than Western Europe or East Asia.

When nations break out of institutional patterns condemning them to poverty and manage to embark on a path to economic growth, this is not because their ignorant leaders suddenly have become better informed or less self-interested or because they've received advice from better economists....

[A]chieving prosperity depends on solving some basic political problems. It is precisely because economics has assumed that political problems are solved that it has not been able to come up with a convincing explanation for world inequality. Explaining world inequality still needs economics to understand how different types of policies and social arrangements affect economic incentives and behavior. But it also needs politics....

History, as we have seen, is littered with examples of reform movements that succumbed to the iron law of oligarchy and replaced one set of extractive institutions with even more pernicious ones. We have seen that England in 1688, France in 1789, and Japan during the Meiji Restoration of 1868 started the process of forging inclusive political institutions with a political revolution. But such political revolutions generally create much destruction and hardship, and their success is far from certain. The Bolshevik Revolution advertised its aim as replacing the exploitative economic system of tsarist Russia with a more just and efficient one that would bring freedom and prosperity to millions of Russians. Alas, the outcome was the opposite, and much more repressive and extractive institutions replaced those of the government the Bolsheviks overthrew.... Robert Mugabe was viewed by many as a freedom fighter ousting Ian Smith's racist and highly extractive Rhodesian regime. But Zimbabwe's institutions became no less extractive, and its economic performance has been even worse than before independence. What is common among the political revolutions that successfully paved the way for more inclusive institutions and the gradual institutional changes in North America, in England in the nineteenth century, and in Botswana after independence—which also led to significant strengthening of inclusive political institutions—is that they succeeded in empowering a fairly broad cross-section of society. Pluralism, the cornerstone of inclusive political institutions, requires political power to be widely held in society, and starting from extractive institutions that vest power in a narrow elite, this requires a process of empowerment....

What can be done to kick-start or perhaps just facilitate the process of empowerment and thus the development of inclusive political institutions? The honest answer of course is that there is no recipe for building such institutions. Naturally there are some obvious factors that would make the process of empowerment more likely to get off the ground. These would include the presence of some degree of centralized order so that social movements challenging existing regimes do not immediately descend into lawlessness; some preexisting political institutions that introduce a modicum of pluralism, such as the traditional political institutions in Botswana, so that broad coalitions can form and endure; and the presence of civil society institutions that can coordinate the demands of the population so that opposition movements can neither be easily crushed by the current elites nor inevitably turn into a vehicle for another group to take control of existing extractive institutions. But many of these factors are historically predetermined and change only slowly. The Brazilian case illustrates how civil society institutions and associated party organizations can be built from the ground up, but this process is slow, and how successful it can be under different circumstances is not well understood....

Pamphlets and books informing and galvanizing people played an important role during the Glorious Revolution in England, the French Revolution, and the march toward democracy in nineteenth-century Britain. Similarly, media, particularly new forms based on advances in information and communication technology, such as Web blogs, anonymous chats, Facebook, and Twitter, played a central role in Iranian opposition against Ahmadinejad's fraudulent election in 2009 and subsequent repression, and they seem to be playing a similarly central role in the Arab Spring protests that are ongoing as this manuscript is being completed.

Authoritarian regimes are often aware of the importance of a free media, and do their best to fight it.... But of course a free media and new communication technologies can help only at the margins, by providing information and coordinating the demands and actions of those vying for more inclusive institutions. Their help will translate into meaningful change only when a broad segment of society mobilizes and organizes in order to effect political change, and does so not for sectarian reasons or to take control of extractive institutions, but to transform extractive institutions into more inclusive ones. Whether such a process will get under way and open the door to further empowerment, and ultimately to durable political reform, will depend, as we have seen in many different instances, on the history of economic and political institutions, on many small differences that matter and on the very contingent path of history.

11. Investing in Development: A Practical Plan to Achieve the Millennium Development Goals[*]

The UN Millennium Project

> The UN Millennium Project has been a unique undertaking. Its 10 task forces, Secretariat, and broad array of participants from academia, government, UN agencies, international financial institutions, nongovernmental organizations, donor agencies, and the private sector created a worldwide network of development practitioners and experts across an enormous range of countries, disciplines, and organizations. The Project was made possible by the unique commitment, skills, and convictions of the task force coordinators, who led their groups to take on some of the most challenging development questions of our generation, and by the task force members, who gave remarkably of their time. This has been a global effort, in the service of a great global cause—the Millennium Development Goals (MDGs). Our Project has been a microcosm of a larger truth: achieving the Millennium Development Goals will require a global partnership suitable for an interconnected world. The world truly shares a common fate....

> This triumph of the human spirit gives us the hope and confidence that extreme poverty can be cut by half by the year 2015, and indeed ended altogether within the coming years. The world community has at its disposal the proven technologies, policies, financial resources, and most importantly, the human courage and compassion to make it happen.
> —Jeffrey D. Sachs, January 2005

---

[*] Source: UN Millennium Project (2005), <http://www.unmillenniumproject.org/reports/index_overview.htm>.

Millennium Development Goals

Goal 1: Eradicate extreme poverty and hunger
Target 1. Halve, between 1990 and 2015, the proportion of people whose income is less than $1 a day
Target 2. Halve, between 1990 and 2015, the proportion of people who suffer from hunger

Goal 2: Achieve universal primary education
Target 3. Ensure that, by 2015, children everywhere, boys and girls alike, will be able to complete a full course of primary schooling

Goal 3: Promote gender equality and empower women
Target 4. Eliminate gender disparity in primary and secondary education, preferably by 2005, and in all levels of education no later than 2015

Goal 4: Reduce child mortality
Target 5. Reduce by two-thirds, between 1990 and 2015, the under-five mortality rate

Goal 5: Improve maternal health
Target 6. Reduce by three-quarters, between 1990 and 2015, the maternal mortality ratio

Goal 6: Combat HIV/AIDS, malaria, and other diseases
Target 7. Have halted by 2015 and begun to reverse the spread of HIV/AIDS
Target 8. Have halted by 2015 and begun to reverse the incidence of malaria and other major diseases

Goal 7: Ensure environmental sustainability
Target 9. Integrate the principles of sustainable development into country policies and programs and reverse the loss of environmental resources
Target 10. Halve, by 2015, the proportion of people without sustainable access to safe drinking water and basic sanitation
Target 11. Have achieved by 2020 a significant improvement in the lives of at least 100 million slum dwellers

Goal 8: Develop a global partnership for development
Target 12. Develop further an open, rule-based, predictable, nondiscriminatory trading and financial system (includes a commitment to good governance, development, and poverty reduction—both nationally and internationally)

Target 13. Address the special needs of the Least Developed Countries (includes tariff- and quota-free access for Least Developed Countries' exports, enhanced program of debt relief for heavily indebted poor countries [HIPCs] and cancellation of official bilateral debt, and more generous official development assistance for countries committed to poverty reduction)

Target 14. Address the special needs of landlocked developing countries and small island developing states (through the Program of Action for the Sustainable Development of Small Island Developing States and 22nd General Assembly provisions)

Target 15. Deal comprehensively with the debt problems of developing countries through national and international measures in order to make debt sustainable in the long term

Some of the indicators listed below are monitored separately for the least developed countries, Africa, landlocked developing countries, and small island developing states

Target 16. In cooperation with developing countries, develop and implement strategies for decent and productive work for youth

Target 17. In cooperation with pharmaceutical companies, provide access to affordable essential drugs in developing countries

Target 18. In cooperation with the private sector, make available the benefits of new technologies, especially information and communications technologies

Ten Key Recommendations

Recommendation 1

Developing country governments should adopt development strategies bold enough to meet the Millennium Development Goal (MDG) targets for 2015. We term them MDG-based poverty reduction strategies. To meet the 2015 deadline, we recommend that all countries have these strategies in place by 2006. Where Poverty Reduction Strategy Papers (PRSPs) already exist, those should be aligned with the MDGs.

Recommendation 2

The MDG-based poverty reduction strategies should anchor the scaling up of public investments, capacity building, domestic resource mobilization, and official development assistance. They should also provide a framework for strengthening governance, promoting human rights, engaging civil society, and promoting the private sector. The MDG-based poverty reduction strategies should:

- Be based on an assessment of investments and policies needed to reach the goals by 2015.
- Spell out the detailed national investments, policies, and budgets for the coming three to five years.

- Focus on rural productivity, urban productivity, health, education, gender equality, water and sanitation, environmental sustainability, and science, technology, and innovation.
- Focus on women's and girls' health (including reproductive health) and education outcomes, access to economic and political opportunities, right to control assets, and freedom from violence.
- Promote mechanisms for transparent and decentralized governance.
- Include operational strategies for scale-up, such as training and retaining skilled workers.
- Involve civil society organizations in decisionmaking and service delivery, and provide resources for monitoring and evaluation.
- Outline a private sector promotion strategy and an income generation strategy for poor people.
- Be tailored, as appropriate, to the special needs of landlocked, small island developing, least developed, and fragile states.
- Mobilize increased domestic resources by up to four percentage points of GNP by 2015.
- Calculate the need for official development assistance.
- Describe an "exit strategy" to end aid dependency, appropriate to the country's situation.

Note: Recommendations for sector-specific policies and investments are summarized in this report and described at length in the individual reports of the UN Millennium Project task forces.

Recommendation 3

Developing country governments should craft and implement the MDG-based poverty reduction strategies in transparent and inclusive processes, working closely with civil society organizations, the domestic private sector, and international partners.

- Civil society organizations should contribute actively to designing policies, delivering services, and monitoring progress.
- Private sector firms and organizations should contribute actively to policy design, transparency initiatives and, where appropriate, public-private partnerships.

Recommendation 4

International donors should identify at least a dozen MDG "fast-track" countries for a rapid scale-up of official development assistance (ODA) in 2005, recognizing that many countries are already in a position for a massive scale-up on the basis of their good governance and absorptive capacity.

Recommendation 5

Developed and developing countries should jointly launch, in 2005, a group of Quick Win actions to save and improve millions of lives and to promote economic growth. They should also launch a massive effort to build expertise at the community level. The Quick Wins include but are not limited to:

- Free mass distribution of malaria bed-nets and effective antimalaria medicines for all children in regions of malaria transmission by the end of 2007.
- Ending user fees for primary schools and essential health services, compensated by increased donor aid as necessary, no later than the end of 2006.
- Successful completion of the 3 by 5 campaign to bring 3 million AIDS patients in developing countries onto antiretroviral treatment by the end of 2005.
- Expansion of school meals programs to cover all children in hunger hotspots using locally produced foods by no later than the end of 2006.
- A massive replenishment of soil nutrients for smallholder farmers on lands with nutrient-depleted soils, through free or subsidized distribution of chemical fertilizers and agroforestry, by no later than the end of 2006.

The massive training program of community-based workers should aim to ensure, by 2015, that each local community has:

- Expertise in health, education, agriculture, nutrition, infrastructure, water supply and sanitation, and environmental management.
- Expertise in public sector management.
- Appropriate training to promote gender equality and participation.

Recommendation 6

Developing country governments should align national strategies with such regional initiatives as the New Partnership for Africa's Development and the Caribbean Community (and Common Market), and regional groups should receive increased direct donor support for regional projects. Regional development groups should:

- Be supported to identify, plan, and implement high-priority cross-border infrastructure projects (roads, railways, watershed management).
- Receive direct donor support to implement cross-border projects.
- Be encouraged to introduce and implement peer-review mechanisms to promote best practices and good governance.

Recommendation 7

High-income countries should increase official development assistance (ODA) from 0.25 percent of donor GNP in 2003 to around 0.44 percent in 2006 and 0.54 percent in 2015 to support the Millennium Development Goals, particularly in low-income countries, with improved ODA quality (including aid that is harmonized, predictable, and largely in the form of grants-based budget support). Each donor should reach 0.7 percent no later than 2015 to support the Goals and other development assistance priorities. Debt relief should be more extensive and generous.

- ODA should be based on actual needs to meet the Millennium Development Goals and on countries' readiness to use the ODA effectively.
- Criteria for evaluating the sustainability of a country's debt burden must be consistent with the achievement of the Goals.
- Aid should be oriented to support the MDG-based poverty reduction strategy, rather than to support donor-driven projects.
- Donors should measure and report the share of their ODA that supports the actual scale-up of MDG-related investments.
- Middle-income countries should also seek opportunities to become providers of ODA and give technical support to low-income countries.

Recommendation 8
High-income countries should open their markets to developing country exports through the Doha trade round and help Least Developed Countries raise export competitiveness through investments in critical trade-related infrastructure, including electricity, roads, and ports. The Doha Development Agenda should be fulfilled and the Doha Round completed no later than 2006.

Recommendation 9
International donors should mobilize support for global scientific research and development to address special needs of the poor in areas of health, agriculture, natural resource and environmental management, energy, and climate. We estimate the total needs to rise to approximately $7 billion a year by 2015.

Recommendation 10
The UN Secretary-General and the UN Development Group should strengthen the coordination of UN agencies, funds, and programs to support the MDGs, at headquarters and country level. The UN Country Teams should be strengthened and should work closely with the international financial institutions to support the Goals.

- The UN Country Teams should be properly trained, staffed, and funded to support program countries to achieve the Goals.
- The UN Country Teams and the international financial institutions (World Bank, International Monetary Fund, regional development banks) should work closely at country level to improve the quality of technical advice.

Poverty Traps
Many well governed countries are too poor to help themselves. Many well intentioned governments lack the fiscal resources to invest in infrastructure, social services, environmental management, and even the public administration necessary to

improve governance. Further, dozens of heavily indebted poor and middle-income countries are forced by creditor governments to spend large proportions of their limited tax receipts on debt service, undermining their ability to finance vital investments in human capital and infrastructure. In a pointless and debilitating churning of resources, the creditors provide development assistance with one hand and then withdraw it in debt servicing with the other.

In an important recent policy initiative, the US government established a set of transparent indicators that identifies poor but reasonably well governed countries that can qualify for funding from its new Millennium Challenge Account. The list of 30 countries includes Bolivia, Ghana, Mali, and Mozambique. Despite significant efforts and real progress, these countries, and many like them, pass the governance test but still fail to make adequate progress toward the Goals.

The reasons are clear. They lack the basic infrastructure, human capital, and public administration—the foundations for economic development and private sector–led growth. Without roads, soil nutrients, electricity, safe cooking fuels, clinics, schools, and adequate and affordable shelter, people are chronically hungry, burdened by disease, and unable to save. Without adequate public sector salaries and information technologies, public management is chronically weak. These countries are unable to attract private investment flows or retain their skilled workers.

The Goals create a solid framework for identifying investments that need to be made. They point to targets of public investment—water, sanitation, slum upgrading, education, health, environmental management, and basic infrastructure—that reduce income poverty and gender inequalities, improve human capital, and protect the environment. By achieving the Goals, poor countries can establish an adequate base of infrastructure and human capital that will enable them to escape from the poverty trap.

Escaping the poverty trap. When a country's capital stock (including physical, natural, and human capital) is too low, the economy is unproductive. Households are impoverished, and the environment is degraded. This leads to several problems:

- *Low saving rates.* Poor households use all their income to stay alive, and so cannot save for the future. The few who can afford to save often have no access to formal banking.
- *Low tax revenues.* Governments lack the budgetary resources for public investments and public administrations using qualified managers and modern information systems.
- *Low foreign investment.* Foreign investors stay away from economies without basic infrastructure—those with costly and unreliable roads, ports, communication systems, and electricity.
- *Violent conflict.* Resource scarcity can often fuel latent tensions among competing groups.

- *Brain drain.* Skilled workers leave the country because of low salaries and little hope for the future.
- *Unplanned or ill-timed births and rapid population growth.* Impoverished people living in rural areas have the highest fertility rates and the largest families. Rapid population growth and shrinking farm sizes make rural poverty worse. Poor people (in rural and urban areas) have less access to information and services to space or limit their pregnancies in accord with their preferences.
- *Environmental degradation.* People in poverty lack the means to invest in the environment and the political power to limit damage to local resources, resulting in soil nutrient depletion, deforestation, overfishing, and other environmental damage. These degraded conditions undermine rural incomes, and contribute to poor health and rural-urban migration, leading to new settlement in environmentally fragile periurban areas.

All these adverse results reinforce and amplify poverty. Without private saving, public investment, and foreign investment, there is no improvement in productivity. With brain drain, population growth, environmental degradation, and ongoing risk of violence, the situation continues to degenerate.

The key to escaping the poverty trap is to raise the economy's capital stock to the point where the downward spiral ends and self-sustaining economic growth takes over. This requires a big push of basic investments between now and 2015 in public administration, human capital (nutrition, health, education), and key infrastructure (roads, electricity, ports, water and sanitation, accessible land for affordable housing, environmental management)....

The Key Elements for Rapid Scale-up

The core challenge of the Goals lies in financing and implementing the interventions at scale—for two reasons. One is the sheer range of interventions that should be implemented simultaneously to reach the Goals. The second is the need to reach large proportions of the population. National scale-up is the process of bringing essential MDG-based investments and services to most or all of the population, on an equitable basis, by 2015.

Scale-up needs to be carefully planned and overseen to ensure successful and sustainable implementation. The level of planning is much more complex than for any single project. Scaling up for the Goals requires a working partnership within and between government, the private sector, NGOs, and civil society....

Getting Started in 2005—Launching a Decade of Bold Ambition

There is still enough time to meet the Millennium Development Goals—though barely. With a systematic approach and decade-long horizon, many countries now dismissed as too poor or too far off track could still achieve the Goals. The UN Millennium Project argues strongly for introducing a longer term horizon into international development policy, one that focuses on overcoming short-term constraints by scaling up approaches to meet basic needs. But the need for longer term horizons should not be confused with, or detract attention from, the need for urgent action. Without a bold breakthrough in the coming year, a large number of countries that could still achieve the Goals will be consigned to failure....

The world also needs to move urgently with specific actions of scale-up toward the Goals. Only by acting now can sufficient numbers of doctors or engineers be trained, service delivery capacity strengthened, and infrastructure improved to meet the Goals. To start the decade of bold ambition toward 2015, we recommend a series of worldwide initiatives to kickstart progress, translating the Goals quickly from ambition to action....

The Benefits: The Case for a Decade of Bold Ambition

The Millennium Development Goals lay out a challenging and achievable vision for dramatically reducing poverty in all its forms, with tremendous benefits for the entire world....

But the Millennium Development Goals are only a mid-station to ending absolute poverty. Even if the Goals are achieved in every country, extreme poverty will remain a major issue requiring ongoing attention. Although a scale-up in high-quality development assistance will allow many countries to graduate from the need for large-scale external budget support, the poorest countries will still require ongoing support equal to 10–20 percent of their GDP to graduate from external assistance sometime after 2015—likely by 2025... Until then, and to eventually make development assistance obsolete, sustained aid will be crucial. To that end, high-income countries will need to maintain support at close to 0.7 percent of their GNI for some period beyond 2015... By 2015 extreme poverty can be cut by half. By 2025 extreme poverty can be substantially eliminated....

Fortunately, the costs of achieving the Goals are entirely affordable and well within the promises of 0.7 percent made at Monterrey and Johannesburg. The required doubling of annual official development assistance to $135 billion in 2006, rising to $195 billion by 2015, pales beside the wealth of high-income countries— and the world's military budget of $900 billion a year. Indeed, the increased development assistance will make up only half a percent of rich countries' combined income....

To ensure success, in 2005 the world must start building capacity, improving policies, and delivering the investments needed to meet the Millennium Development Goals. This effort will need to be sustained at the global, national, and local level over the next 10 years. And only by acting now can long-term environmental challenges, such as climate change and fisheries depletion, be contained before they inflict irreparable harm on the poor countries able to protect themselves the least.

Urgent action is needed if we are to usher in a decade of bold ambition to achieve the Millennium Development Goals. Developing countries need to make every effort to mobilize around the Goals. Rich countries need to ask themselves if they should be more concerned, as many of them are today, with pointing fingers at the responsibilities of poor countries than with meeting their own commitments. In 2005 the world needs desperately to follow through on its commitments, taking quick practical steps at scale before the Goals become impossible to achieve. If we fail to invest now, it will be a very long way to the next Millennium Summit in the year 3000.

12. A Modest Proposal*

William Easterly

Jeffrey D. Sachs's guided tour to the poorest regions of the Earth is enthralling and maddening at the same time—enthralling, because his eloquence and compassion make you care about some very desperate people; maddening, because he offers solutions that range all the way from practical to absurd. It's a shame that Sachs's prescriptions are unconvincing because he is resoundingly right about the tragedy of world poverty. As he puts it, newspapers should (but don't) report every morning, "More than 20,000 people perished yesterday of extreme poverty."

That appalling toll has given Sachs his life's mission. Two themes recur in his long career of advising heads of state in poor nations, which he chronicles in fascinating detail in this book. First is his favored approach of "shock therapy" (a term he dislikes but has found impossible to shake): a comprehensive package of economic reforms that attempts to fix all problems simultaneously and quickly. Second is his conviction that the West should always give a lot of money to support these packages. These two themes unify a book that sometimes seems like a disparate collection of Sachs's adventures in Bolivia, Poland, Russia and Africa on issues ranging from stopping high inflation, leaping from communism to capitalism, canceling Third World debt, curing malaria and AIDS, and now eliminating poverty in Africa and everywhere else.

Over the past two decades, Sachs has simply been the world's greatest economic reformer. It's perhaps fitting that he has enlisted Bono, the lead singer of U2 and development activist, to pen an introduction: the rock star as economist meets the economist as rock star. Perhaps someone so gifted and hardworking can be forgiven if his narrative is a little self-serving—for instance, when he portrays his plans as responsible for early successes in Bolivia and Poland. At the same time, he prefers a more complicated analysis for the failures in which he was involved, like the chaos

---

* Source: Rev. of *The End of Poverty: Economic Possibilities for Our Time*, by Jeffrey D. Sachs. *Washington Post* March 13, 2005: BW03, <http://www.washingtonpost.com>.

in Russia, later stagnation in Bolivia and Africa's perpetual crisis (their geography was bad, they didn't follow his advice, the West didn't give them enough aid, etc.).

The climax of *The End of Poverty* is Sachs's far-reaching plan to end world poverty—a sort of Great Leap Forward. His characteristically comprehensive approach to eliminating world poverty derives from his conviction that everything depends on everything else—that, for instance, you cannot cure poverty in Africa without beating AIDS, which requires infrastructure, which requires stable government, and so forth.

Social reformers have found two ways to respond to this complexity; Karl Popper summed them up best a half-century ago as "utopian social engineering" versus "piecemeal democratic reform." Sachs is the intellectual leader of the utopian camp. To end world poverty once and for all, he offers a detailed Big Plan that covers just about everything, in mind-numbing technical jargon, from planting nitrogen-fixing leguminous trees to replenish soil fertility, to antiretroviral therapy for AIDS, to specially programmed cell phones to provide real-time data to health planners, to rainwater harvesting, to battery-charging stations and so on. Sachs proposes that the UN secretary general personally run the overall plan, coordinating the actions of thousands of officials in six UN agencies, UN country teams, the World Bank and the International Monetary Fund. Sachs's Big Plan would launch poor countries out of a "poverty trap" and end world poverty by 2025, as the book's title advertises. The world's rich countries would pay for a large share of the Big Plan—somehow doing an exact financial "Needs Assessment," seeing how much poor country governments can pay and then having rich donors pay the rest. The donors will fill what he calls the "financing gap" by doubling donor-nation foreign aid in 2006, then nearly doubling it again by 2015.

What's the alternative? The piecemeal reform approach (which his book opposes) would humbly acknowledge that nobody can fully grasp the complexity of the political, social, technological, ecological and economic systems that underlie poverty. It would eschew the arrogance that "we" know exactly how to fix "them." It would shy away from the hubris of what he labels the "breathtaking opportunity" that "we" have to spread democracy, technology, prosperity and perpetual peace to the entire planet. Large-scale crash programs, especially by outsiders, often produce unintended consequences. The simple dreams at the top run afoul of insufficient knowledge of the complex realities at the bottom. The Big Plans are impossible to evaluate scientifically afterward. Nor can you hold any specific agency accountable for their success or failure. Piecemeal reform, by contrast, motivates specific actors to take small steps, one at a time, then tests whether that small step made poor people better off, holds accountable the agency that implemented the small step, and considers the next small step.

What's the evidence on how well the two approaches work? Sachs pays surprisingly little attention to the history of aid approaches and results. He seems unaware that his Big Plan is strikingly similar to the early ideas that inspired foreign aid in the 1950s and '60s. Just like Sachs, development planners then identified countries caught in a "poverty trap," did an assessment of how much they would need to make a "big push" out of poverty and into growth, and called upon foreign aid to fill the "financing gap" between countries' own resources and needs. This legacy has influenced the bureaucratic approach to economic development that's been followed ever since—albeit with some lip service to free markets—by the World Bank, regional development banks, national aid agencies like USAID and the UN development agencies. Spending $2.3 trillion (measured in today's dollars) in aid over the past five decades has left the most aid-intensive regions, like Africa, wallowing in continued stagnation; it's fair to say this approach has not been a great success. (By the way, utopian social engineering does not just fail for the left; in Iraq, it's not working too well now for the right either.)

Meanwhile, some piecemeal interventions have brought success. Vaccination campaigns, oral rehydration therapy to prevent diarrhea and other aid-financed health programs have likely contributed to a fall in infant mortality in every region, including Africa. Aid projects have probably helped increase access to primary and secondary education, clean water and sanitation. Perhaps it is also easier to hold aid agencies accountable for results in these tangible areas. (Many of Sachs's specific recommendations might make sense as piecemeal reforms—i.e., if done one at a time in small steps, with subsequent evaluation and accountability.)

Indeed, the broader development successes of recent decades, most of them in Asia, happened without the Big Plan—and without significant foreign aid as a proportion of the recipient country's income. Gradual free market reforms in China and India in the 1980s and '90s (which Sachs implausibly argues were shock therapy in disguise) have brought rapid growth. Moreover, the West itself achieved gradual success through piecemeal democratic and market reforms over many centuries, not through top-down Big Plans offered by outsiders. Do we try out shock therapy only on the powerless poor?

"Success in ending the poverty trap," Sachs writes, "will be much easier than it appears." Really? If it's so easy, why haven't five decades of effort gotten the job done? Sachs should redirect some of his outrage at the question of why the previous $2.3 trillion didn't reach the poor so that the next $2.3 trillion does. In fact, ending poverty is not easy at all. In those five decades, poverty researchers have learned a great deal about the complexity of toxic politics, bad history (including exploitative or inept colonialism), ethnic and regional conflicts, elites' manipulation of politics and institutions, official corruption, dysfunctional public services, malevolent police forces and armies, the difficulty of honoring contracts and property rights, unaccountable and excessively bureaucratic donors and many other issues. Sachs, however, sees these factors as relatively unimportant. Indeed, he seems deaf to the babble and bungling of the UN agencies he calls upon to run the Big Plan, not to mention other unaccountable and ineffectual aid agencies.

So, in Sachs's eyes, what does matter in producing poverty? His book blames the perception of bad government in Africa on racial prejudice in the West, an insult to the many courageous Africans who have protested against their often appalling rulers. To Sachs, poverty reduction is mostly a scientific and technological issue (hence the technical jargon above), in which aid dollars can buy cheap interventions to fix development problems.

But that's too neat. What about the World Bank studies in Guinea, Cameroon, Uganda and Tanzania, which estimated that 30 to 70 percent of government drugs disappeared into the black market rather than reaching the patients? Sachs calls for huge increases in aid to his favorite countries, like Malawi and Ethiopia, overlooking inconvenient factors such as the worsening of Malawi's famine because corrupt officials sold off its strategic grain reserves and because autocratic Ethiopian rulers have favored their own minority Tigrean ethnic group. Sachs is right that bad government is not disproportionately an African problem; democracy has been making progress in Africa, while rulers in Azerbaijan, Cambodia and Turkmenistan make some African autocrats look like Thomas Jefferson. But Sachs's anti-poverty prescriptions rest heavily on the kindness of some pretty dysfunctional regimes, not to mention the famously inefficient international aid bureaucracy.

Perhaps we can excuse these allegedly easy-to-achieve dreams as the tactics of a fundraiser for the poor—someone who's out to galvanize public opinion to back dramatically higher aid abroad. Sachs was born to play the role of fundraiser. And it's easier to feel good about his sometimes simplistic sales pitch for foreign aid if it leads to spending more dollars on desperately poor people, as opposed to, say, wasteful weapons systems.

The danger is that when the utopian dreams fail (as they will again), the rich-country public will get even more disillusioned about foreign aid. Sachs rightly notes that we need not worry whether the pathetic amount of current US foreign aid—little more than a 10th of a penny for every dollar of US income—is wasted. Foreign aid's prospects will brighten only if aid agencies become more accountable for results, and demonstrate to the public that some piecemeal interventions improve the lives of desperate people. So yes, do read Sachs's eloquent descriptions of poverty and his compelling ethical case for the rich to help the poor. Just say no to the Big Plan.

13. Poverty Reduction in Africa[*]

Paul Collier

Globally, the number of people in absolute poverty has been in decline for ≈25 years, yet in Africa it is still increasing. The challenge of poverty reduction in Africa is of a different order from that elsewhere and will require different strategies. Other low-income regions are growing rapidly, and there the issue is how to diffuse growth. In the middle-income regions, redistribution could radically reduce absolute poverty. Africa has not been growing, and its income level is too low for redistribution to resolve poverty.[1] Hence, Africa's problem is to break out of an economic stagnation that has persisted for three decades. This article deploys existing primary research into an integrated argument that accounts for Africa's economic distinctiveness and derives implications for international policies for poverty reduction.[2]

During the present decade, African growth has accelerated, although not sufficiently rapidly to prevent continuing divergence. This may mark a decisive turn-around in the region's economic performance, but much of it is accounted for by the boom in the world prices of Africa's commodity exports, the scramble to extract its raw materials, and recent peace settlements. Each of these is a fragile basis for sustained growth. Hence, Africa's longer economic experience remains pertinent. On average, over the period 1960–2000, Africa's population-weighted per capita annual growth of gross domestic product (GDP) was a mere 0.1%. It stagnated, whereas other regions experienced accelerating growth. Indeed, between 1980 and 2000 the annual rate of divergence was an astounding 5%.

Africa's growth failure has attracted competing explanations. During the 1980s the World Bank diagnosed the problem as inappropriate economic policies, with Berg (1) offering the first clear statement of this position. Bates (2) was the first to explain these dysfunctional policy choices in terms of the interests of powerful

* Source: *Proceedings of the National Academy of Sciences* 104.43 (2007): 16763–68.

1 Indeed, although income inequality in Africa has been rising, this may be necessary to retain skilled labor in the face of its increasing international mobility, given the stagnation of average income.

2 For a fuller version see ref. 8.

groups, notably the taxation of export agriculture. During the 1990s, the limited response to reform induced a broader search for explanations (3, 4). Recently, three further explanations have gained currency: institutions (5), leadership (6), and geography (7). In this article I emphasize geography, although not on the health aspects that have been the main recent concern of Sachs (7). I suggest that the role for institutions, and indeed for leadership, varies according to Africa's distinctive physical and human geography.

In the next section, I consider physical geography, showing how strategies will need to differ radically among Africa's countries. Then, I turn to human geography and the political problems that this has created. To an extent these problems have been surmounted: Africa's human geography may explain delayed take-off rather than predict persistent stagnation. Then, I consider three interactions between physical geography and human geography that generate intractable problems, and I conclude with implications for international strategies.

Physical Geography: Three Opportunity Groups

Africa's defining physical geography is of a massive land area divided into 44 countries, with a low population density. Because Africa is land-abundant, yet low-income, natural resource endowments loom large. However, they are unevenly distributed. Parts of Africa are abundant in natural resources, but others are resource-scarce. Further, because Africa is enormous and divided into many countries, many of them are landlocked. Potentially, these two distinctions create four possible categories. However, in growth regressions, the resource-rich coastal countries and the resource-rich landlocked countries are not significantly different. If the resources are sufficiently valuable, being landlocked is not a significant disadvantage to their extraction. Conversely, the coastal countries are generally not in a position to take advantage of nonresource exports because of the effects of Dutch disease on their export competitiveness. We thus have three categories: resource-rich, resource-scarce but coastal, and resource-scarce and landlocked. In growth regressions these three categories have had sharply distinct performances globally, and this has been mirrored in Africa. The best-performing category globally has been the coastal, resource-scarce countries of which there are many Asian examples. The worst-performing category globally has been the landlocked and resource-scarce. In between, the resource-rich countries have on average grown moderately but with large differences both between countries and time periods. Table 13.1 shows the growth rates for each category.

Africa broadly followed the global pattern, with three differences. The largest difference was in the category of countries that are resource-scarce and coastal: since around 1980 the non-African economies in this category have been outperforming their African counterparts by ≈5% per year. Nor is this confined to China and India.

Even when these two are excluded, there is a severe divergence. The second difference was in the resource-rich category, although here the difference has persisted since the 1960s. Only in the category of landlocked and resource-scarce countries, which globally have been slow-growing, is the difference modest. The cumulative implications of these differences in growth rates for the path of GDP per capita have been dramatic. Essentially, outside Africa countries have on average decisively broken out of poverty, rising above $5,000 per capita, as long as they are not landlocked and resource-scarce. Indeed, thanks to their fast growth they are converging on the developed countries. By contrast, in Africa on average countries in all three categories have stayed resolutely stuck below $2,000 per capita. As a result, Africa has been diverging from the rest of mankind. The third difference between Africa and the other developing regions is in the distribution of population between the three categories. In the developing world other than Africa some 88% of the population lives in coastal, resource-scarce countries, 11% in resource-rich countries, and a mere 1% in landlocked resource-scarce countries. In Africa the population is approximately evenly spread between the three groups. Thus, the African population is heavily skewed toward the globally slow-growing category of landlocked, resource-scarce, and away from the globally fast-growing category of coastal, resource-scarce. This unfortunate distribution accounts for around one percentage point of growth: even if African countries grew at the mean of their category, the distinctive distribution of the population would imply slower overall growth. However, the key importance of distinguishing between the three geographic categories is that their opportunities are sufficiently different that strategies for accelerated growth are likely to differ. I now turn to the opportunities and constraints characteristic of each category.

Table 13.1   Growth per capita, by opportunity category and decade

Decade	Overall 43 SSA	Overall 56 Other	Overall Difference	Coastal 43 SSA	Coastal 56 Other	Coastal Difference	Landlocked 43 SSA	Landlocked 56 Other	Landlocked Difference	Resource-rich 43 SSA	Resource-rich 56 Other	Resource-rich Difference
1960s	1.04	2.29	1.25	1.36	2.25	0.89	0.16	0.74	0.58	2.08	3.85	1.77
1970s	0.86	3.23	2.37	1.32	3.18	1.86	−0.31	1.26	1.57	1.42	3.89	2.47
1980s	−0.79	4.32	5.11	−0.85	4.68	5.53	0.14	1.56	1.42	−1.67	1.50	3.17
1990–2000	−0.46	4.46	4.91	0.27	4.74	4.47	−1.30	1.91	3.21	−0.42	2.47	2.89
Total	0.13	3.63	3.50	0.50	3.79	3.29	−0.36	1.40	1.76	0.29	2.89	2.60

The sample includes all developing countries with full availability of data. Growth rates are population-weighted. The annual growth rates are population-weighted. Note that the country composition of the group averages changes as the group composition evolves. SSA: Sub-Saharan Africa.

Landlocked and Resource-Scarce. The most striking difference between Africa and other developing regions is in the proportion of the population in landlocked, resource-scarce countries. Outside of Africa areas with these poor endowments seldom became independent countries: they became the hinterlands of countries that are more fortunately endowed. Nevertheless, being landlocked and resource-scarce does not necessarily lock a country into poverty: there are some obvious examples of success such as Switzerland. However, Switzerland has benefited from its neighborhood. In effect, being landlocked has not cut it off from international markets but rather placed it at the heart of a regional market. More generally, the most promising strategy for such countries has been to orient their economies toward trade with their neighbors. As the barriers to international trade have come down this has become easier, and indeed outside of Africa the growth of landlocked, resource-scarce countries have accelerated. Collier and O'Connell (9) estimate growth spillovers from neighbors, attempting to control for the coincidence of growth rates in a neighborhood caused by common shocks. Globally, on average if neighbors grow at an additional one percentage point that raises the growth of the country itself by 0.4%. Outside of Africa the landlocked, resource-scarce economies on average gain larger spillovers, at 0.7%: they orient their economies toward making the most of these spillovers. By contrast, in Africa the growth spillover for the landlocked, resource-scarce economies is a mere 0.2%. Paradoxically, to date this failure of regional integration has not really mattered. Until recently even the more fortunately located African countries have largely failed to grow. Hence, there has been very little growth to spill over, which suggests that the critical path for the landlocked, resource-scarce countries to succeed is first that their more fortunate neighbors need to harness their opportunities, and only then that the subregional economies need to become radically more integrated.

Overall, the landlocked, resource-scarce countries triply depend on their neighbors. Most obviously, they depend on their coastal neighbors for access to the sea. This is an unreciprocated dependence: Uganda depends on Kenya for access, but Kenya does not depend on Uganda. Coastal countries differ in how seriously they prioritize the interests of their landlocked neighbors. Nuno and Venables (10) investigated the international transport costs faced by landlocked countries in importing a standard container from the United States. They found that while the average landlocked country indeed faced radically higher transport costs than coastal countries, the costs differed enormously. They were able to trace these differences to expenditures on transport infrastructure in the coastal neighbors: where the neighbor had prioritized investment in transport infrastructure the landlocked country faced substantially lower transport costs.

The second dependence is less obvious. The landlocked have an interest in the economic governance of neighboring countries because if their neighbors continue to forego opportunities this closes off their own opportunities. Again, this is not a reciprocated dependence: the prospects for Niger critically depend on whether Nigeria harnesses its opportunities: a buoyant Nigerian economy would provide the natural market for livestock reared in Niger. By contrast, economic governance in Niger is of virtually no consequence for Nigeria. The third dependence is that it takes two to integrate: the landlocked cannot integrate unless their neighbors implement policies that enable it to happen. The integration agenda is partly a matter of practical policy such as the removal of road blocks and harassment by customs officials. To continue with the Nigerian example, there are more official road blocks per kilometer of transport arteries to neighbors in Nigeria than anywhere else in West Africa (11). It is partly a matter of trade policies: until 2005 Nigeria refused to implement the Economic Community of West African States free-trade area agreement, and in the mid-1990s Kenya, without warning, banned the import of maize from Uganda. Finally, it is a matter of infrastructure: more roads need to be built and maintained, not just for access to the coast but for access to the regional market. Again, this dependence is not fully reciprocal. The potential for integration into the regional market matters more for the landlocked than for their neighbors.

Between them, these three unreciprocated dependencies create a question mark over national sovereignty. If the viability of the landlocked, resource-scarce nations depends on the decisions of their more fortunate neighbors, they need to have some right of voice in those decisions. This suggests that Africa has a much greater need for political architecture above the level of the nation than do other regions.

It is possible that developments such as e-trade and air freight that do not disadvantage landlocked countries might offer a new route to global integration. Clearly, the landlocked countries should push these opportunities to the hilt. Being landlocked is not a choice, but being airlocked is largely a matter of airline regulation and competition policy. The policies that produced high-cost monopolies such as Air Afrique were mistaken. Similarly, the twin pillars of e-trade are telecoms and education. Policies that raise the cost of international telecoms, or make access unreliable, and the neglect of tertiary education that was an unfortunate by-product of the education for all policies pursued during the 1990s, are thus costly for landlocked, resource-scarce countries. Although these countries are the core of Africa's poverty problem, I am going to focus on the other two opportunity categories. It is the inability of the African countries in these categories to harness opportunities that has been decisive.

Resource-Rich. Now consider the resource-rich countries. These are increasingly important in Africa, partly as a result of higher commodity prices and partly as a result of resource discoveries. Globally, high commodity prices are a mixed blessing for resource-exporting countries. Consider the consequences for growth in a country where commodity exports are 35% of GDP if the prices of its exports double. Collier and Goderis (12) find that for the first 5 years growth is significantly higher. By the fifth year this faster growth has cumulatively raised constant-price GDP by ≈4% compared with what would have happened with lower prices. This increase in the quantity of output is additional to the direct income effect of the improvement in the terms of trade: with exports initially 35% of GDP, the doubling of price directly raises income by 35%. Thus, by the fifth year the economy is in the midst of a bonanza in which real income has risen by ≈39%. However, from then on things typically go badly wrong. The full effects take a long time to work their way through: only ≈7% of the initial disequilibrium is eliminated each year. However, after 25 years, the doubling of export prices has actually reduced constant-price GDP relative to its counterfactual. The effect is substantial, with constant-price GDP lowered by 26%. The effect on income is much smaller because the decline in output is mitigated by the fact that the terms of trade improvement are still directly raising income by 35%. Hence, the net effect on income is modest. The massive decline in output is, however, astonishing. The sustained windfall obviously creates the potential for radically higher investment and so, cumulatively over 25 years there should be large increases in output. What goes wrong?

Three processes generate this long-term adverse effect. One is Dutch disease, which makes nonresource exports uncompetitive: in Nigeria oil exports led to the rapid collapse of agricultural exports. Dutch disease can indeed foreclose other export opportunities. In a study that focuses on growth rates industry-by-industry, Rajan and Subramanian (13) show that exchange rate appreciation reduces the growth rates of labor-intensive industries. However, Collier and Goderis (12) control for Dutch disease and find that although it has an effect it is only a minor part of the explanation. They find that a more important factor is macroeconomic volatility. For example, as Addison (14) shows, since the discovery of oil Nigeria has been among the 10 most volatile economies in the world. Volatility can be detrimental to growth in several respects. It makes investment more risky and so tends to discourage it. Further, public-spending decisions tend to become compromised, with extravagant commitments being made during booms that then force drastic cuts in vital expenditures during troughs. However, between them, Dutch disease and volatility account for less than half of the overall adverse long-term effects. The remaining process is caused by misgovernance. Countries in which governance is initially poor face a substantial risk of turning resource windfalls into catastrophe.

There is also evidence that governance is likely to deteriorate as a result of the windfalls. Resource-rich societies will inevitably have large public sectors: the resource rents are taxed for them to accrue to the nation, and the revenues from these taxes will then be spent by the government. Effective public spending is thus critical for both living standards and private activity, and, because the public sector is a large part of the economy, its own productivity growth is a key component of overall growth. In turn, this requires either that government should aspire to national goals or that it is accountable to citizens and so required to achieve national goals regardless of its aspirations. Until recently, Africa was ruled by narrow ethnic autocracies that lacked national aspirations. Since the 1990s the spread of democracy across much of resource-rich Africa might potentially provide accountability to citizens. Unfortunately, the statistical evidence suggests that instead of democracy improving the way in which resource revenues are used, resource revenues undermine how democracy works. Collier and Hoeffler (15) find that globally over the period 1970–2002 in the absence of natural resource rents democracies tend to grow significantly faster than autocracies but that the opposite holds when resource rents are large. They suggest that in resource-rich countries democracy tends to get corrupted into patronage politics as resource rents substitute for taxation. With low taxation citizens are not "provoked" into scrutinizing government, which weakens the checks and balances upon the use of power. This produces an unbalanced form of democracy in which electoral competition, which constrains how power is achieved, is not matched by checks and balances that constrain how power is used. Without strong checks and balances electoral competition drives political parties to resort to patronage: votes are bought instead of won. They introduce a quantitative measure of checks and balances developed by Beck et al. (16) and find that distinctively in the resource-rich societies these checks and balances are significantly beneficial for growth, whereas electoral competition is highly detrimental. Further, they find that over time checks and balances are gradually eroded by resource rents. An implication appears to be that those resource-rich countries that are democratic need a distinctive democracy with strong checks and balances rather than fierce electoral competition. Africa has such a country, namely Botswana. The government of Botswana has not faced severe electoral competition: despite continuous democracy it has never lost power. It does, however, have impressively strong checks and balances, notably rules for public spending. Unfortunately, Botswana is exceptional. Other resource-rich African countries are now democratic, but they are "instant democracies." As demonstrated by Afghanistan and Iraq, it is possible to establish electoral competition in any conditions, but it is harder to establish effective checks and balances. Nigeria under President Shehu Shagari (1979–1983) displayed the classic patronage politics of resource rents in the context of intense electoral competition without effective checks and balances. Although democratic, it failed to harness the Nigerian oil bonanza for sustained growth. In summary, resource-rich countries need a form of democracy with unusually strong checks and balances, but typically get a form in which they are unusually weak. Here leadership can make a difference and did so in Botswana.

Resource-Scarce and Coastal. I now turn to the resource-scarce, coastal economies. These are in the category that globally has had the fastest growth, but in which African performance has been least encouraging. It might be argued that none of Africa's economies are truly resource-scarce because even those without valuable natural resources have large endowments of land relative to population and so have a comparative advantage in agriculture (17). However, Africa's exceptionally rapid population growth is changing even this advantage. Countries such as Kenya and Senegal face sufficient pressure on land that continuation in their traditional specialization will condemn them to slow growth, with agricultural technical progress offset by diminishing returns to labor. The only African country to succeed in this category has been Mauritius, which followed the Asian pattern in transforming itself through exports of manufactures from an impoverished sugar economy into an upper-middle income country and by far Africa's richest economy.

Whereas in resource-rich countries the state has to be large, in the coastal, resource-scarce economies the state need not be central to development. The core growth process in these economies is to break into global markets for some labor-intensive product. This is fundamentally a matter for the private sector. The state may, as in parts of East Asia, actively help in this process, but it is by no means necessary. Indeed, the essential aspect of government behavior is that it should not actively inhibit the emergence of a new export sector by burdensome regulation, taxation, or predation. Before 1980 manufacturing and services were concentrated in the Organization for Economic Cooperation and Development (OECD) economies, locked in partly by trade restrictions but mainly by economies of agglomeration. The concept of economies of agglomeration is that when many firms in the same activity are clustered in the same city their costs of production are lower. For example, because there is a large pool of skilled labor and suppliers of inputs, individual firms do not need to hoard skilled labor or carry high inventories. Around 1980 a combination of trade liberalization and the widening gap in labor costs between the OECD and developing countries began to make it profitable for industry to relocate to low-income countries. This process is explosive: as firms relocate agglomeration economies build up in the new location and make it progressively more competitive. The chosen locations where these new agglomerations became established were in Asia. The factors that determined this choice need only have been temporary and need not have been massive. However, once Asia got ahead of Africa, the forces of agglomeration made it progressively harder for Africa to break in. Currently, Africa has no significant advantage over Asia in terms of labor costs while having large disadvantages in terms of agglomeration economies.

Human Geography

I now turn to the other important distinctive aspect of Africa's geography: human geography, both political and social. Africa's political geography is unmistakably striking: it is divided into far more countries that any other region, despite being less populous than either South or East Asia. As a result, the average population of its countries is radically smaller than that of other regions. Africa's social geography is also unmistakable: despite the division into tiny countries the typical country is ethnically more diverse. Small population and ethnic diversity are the two distinctive socio-political features of African geography: each creates problems.

Globally, being small is no impediment to being rich: Luxembourg is as rich as the United States. But in the context of development being small poses problems. After independence, Africa, like other developing regions, plunged into a range of bad economic policies and governance. The process of achieving a sustained and decisive turnaround from such configurations is difficult: despite being economically dysfunctional they were politically rather stable. Chauvet and Collier (18) investigate such turnarounds on global data for 1974–2004 and find that having a small population makes change less likely. They suggest that the process of critiquing past failure and implementing a strategy for change is helped by scale. For example, scale enables a society to have a specialist press that can conduct economic discussion. Chinese and Indian society were each able to diagnose failure and implement radical change purely through internal debates, whereas a small society such as the Central African Republic has a dearth of skills. Thus, Africa's political geography has made economic reform more difficult and helps to account for the greater persistence of poor policies in Africa than in other regions. In the past decade many African societies have succeeded in designing and implementing a measure of economic reform. Hence, the greater difficulty of reform in small countries may account for why reform was slower in Africa, rather than be a prognosis.

Not only is reform more difficult if population is small, but the risk of state collapse into violence is greater.[3] The typical civil war is enormously costly for both the economy and its neighbors and lasts a long time. Even once the war is over, the society has a high risk of reversion to conflict. Although the risk that a country has a civil war increases with population size, the elasticity is far less than unity. Thus, a territory divided into two countries faces a higher risk of civil war in at least one of its countries than if it is unified. The likely explanation is that the provision of security is subject to scale economies: the typical African nation is too small for its government to provide effective internal security unless other conditions are benign. This is a major reason Africa has a higher incidence of civil war than South Asia. Further, the costs of civil war are not confined to the country at war: around half the economic costs accrue to neighbors. Regional and international actors thus have a role in enhancing African security.

The other socio-political aspect of African geography is the high ethnic diversity of the typical country. Ethnic diversity need not be a decisive impediment to development, but it does have implications for political architecture. Specifically, the more diverse is the society the more beneficial is democracy for growth.[4] A possible explanation for this statistical relationship is that in an ethnically diverse

---

3 The following discussion is based on Collier and Hoeffler (19); Collier, Hoeffler, and Rohner (20); and Collier, Hoeffler, and Soderbom (21).
4 The following discussion is based on Collier (22) and Alesina and La Ferrara (23).

society an autocracy usually rests on the military power of a single ethnic group. The more diverse is the society the smaller is likely to be the share of the population constituted by the ethnic group in power. A minority in power has an incentive to redistribute to itself at the expense of the public good of national growth. Ethnically diverse democracies may be messy, but they force the coalition in power to be large. This increases the attraction of broad-based growth relative to redistribution to the groups in power. However, an alternative explanation is that those diverse societies that manage to maintain democracy have exceptional characteristics such as tolerance, and it is these rather than democracy that is decisive. To date, attempts to address this ambiguity in causation point to the former explanation. A second aspect of ethnic diversity is that it makes collective action for public-service provision more difficult: intergroup trust is limited. A corollary is that the boundaries between public and private provision should be drawn more in favor of private provision in societies that are more diverse. Another corollary is that public spending may be more effective if it is decentralized: at the local level Africa is much less ethnically diverse than at the national level. A third aspect of diversity is that it makes a society more prone to violent conflict.

Physical and Human Geography Interacted: Africa's Dilemma

Finally, I bring together physical geography with human geography. The interaction of the two creates three acutely difficult problems for African economic development.

Resource-Rich and Ethnically Diverse Societies. Africa's current economic opportunity is its natural resource rents. A disproportionate share of Africa's population lives in resource-rich countries, and for the foreseeable future commodity prices are going to be high with discoveries skewed toward the region. As set out in [the section] *Physical Geography: Three Opportunity Groups* [above], large resource rents imply a large state and hence the central importance of effective public spending, but also make democracy detrimental to the growth process. It seems that the typical resource-rich country might grow faster under autocracy. However, as set out in [the section] *Human Geography*, Africa's high ethnic diversity makes autocracy damaging: Africa's resource-rich countries may not have the option of growth through autocracy. Further, ethnic diversity weakens the ability of the society to hold public services accountable. Because such collective action is more difficult, an ethnically diverse society is best suited to a relatively small domain of the state. However, resource-rich Africa does not have the option of a small public sector: resource rents inevitably accrue to the government and will largely be spent by it.

So what sort of political system would best serve a resource-rich and ethnically diverse country such as is commonly found in Africa? Autocracy may be irredeemably dysfunctional in the context of ethnic diversity, but democracy is not irredeemably dysfunctional in the context of resource rents. The form of polity that appears to be best suited to ethnically diverse societies with resource rents is a democracy with unusually strong checks and balances and decentralized public spending. How the government can use power needs to be constrained, rather than simply how it attains power. Botswana demonstrates both that this combination is possible in Africa and that it is effective in delivering development in resource-rich societies. For many years Botswana was the fastest growing economy in the world. Yet currently Botswana is exceptional: most resource-rich states have unusually weak checks and balances. The key challenge currently facing Africa's resource-rich societies is to build such polities.

International actors have a role to play in supporting the struggle to build effective checks and balances. To date, the clearest example of such assistance is the Extractive Industries Transparency Initiative (EITI), launched by the British government in 2002 and promptly adopted by the Nigerian reform team that entered government in 2003. Although the EITI demonstrates how useful international "templates" can be in the management of resource rents, in its present form it covers only a small part of the vital issues. Unfortunately, there is a danger that far from the EITI constituting a modest first step, even the present version will be eroded by the reluctance of the Chinese authorities to adopt the new international standards of conduct.

Resource-rich societies face a further difficulty during export booms. Globally, during these booms the pace of policy reform slows (18). Hence, societies that have painfully realized that rapid reform is necessary, such as has been the case in Nigeria since 2003, may find that boom conditions remove the sense of urgency from the reform agenda and divert political attention to the contest for spending. Thus, the very conditions in which good policies have their highest pay-off tend to undermine the political process of achieving them.

Resource-Scarce Societies with Small, Diverse Populations. The second problem caused by the interaction of physical geography and human geography is that coastal, resource-scarce Africa has missed its opportunity to break into global markets for labor-intensive goods and services. What were the critical factors that decided firms against an African location in the 1980s? In Francophone Africa the overvaluation of the Communauté Financière d'Afrique franc precluded export diversification. Lusophone Africa was beset by civil war. South Africa was in the late stages of the apartheid regime. Among the other coastal, resource-scarce countries, Ghana, Tanzania, and Madagascar were in crises as a result of experiments with socialism, and Kenya was beset by the ethnic politics of redistribution. Mauritius was the only coastal, resource-scarce country not precluded from manufactured exports by such misfortunes. However, as discussed above, Africa was prone to these disparate syndromes because of the problems generated by its distinctive human geography. Its societies were too small and diverse to provide the public goods of security and good economic policy. Africa has substantially succeeded in surmounting these problems: its human geography inflicted prolonged but not permanent disadvantages. Although on average African economic governance remains significantly weaker than other regions, there are now several coastal, resource-scarce countries where governance has improved, notably Ghana, Kenya, Tanzania, Senegal, and Madagascar. Yet even these countries have still not decisively broken into global markets.

The most probable explanation for the slow pace of export penetration is that Africa missed the boat. The policy mistakes happened to occur at precisely the critical time when Africa could otherwise have broken in on level terms with Asia. Now, Asia has huge agglomeration advantages and so reasonable policies are not enough. The logic of the new economic geography is that Africa will have to wait until the wage gap between Africa and Asia is approximately as wide as that between the OECD and Asia at the time when Asia broke into OECD markets, a process that would take decades.

What Africa needs is temporary protection from Asia in OECD markets. It was critical to the success of Mauritius that benefited from the now-expired MultiFiber Agreement. Currently, the United States gives Africa such preferences through the Africa Growth and Opportunity Act (AGOA) and the European Union through Everything but Arms (EBA). Indeed, a variant of this special protection was part of the failed Hong Kong offer for least-developed countries. The principle has thus already been conceded. However, as with all trade policy the devil is in the detail. All these schemes fail because, for different reasons, the details of the schemes limit their effectiveness. Until extended in December 2006, AGOA offered too short a period of committed market access; EBA applies to the wrong African countries and its rules of origin are too restrictive; and the Hong Kong offer compounded the weaknesses of EBA with limitations on product coverage. The most successful of the three is AGOA: Collier and Venables (24) show that its "special rule" relaxing rules of origin for apparel imports has increased Africa's apparel exports to the American market 7-fold in 5 years, whereas EBA has been completely ineffective. Just as the economies of scale generated by clusters have shut Africa out of manufacturing markets, any breakthrough is likely to be concentrated in a few countries. However, this concentration of success might itself be advantageous. Were Kenya, Ghana, and Senegal to start growing at Asian rates there would be competitive pressure on other governments to reform.

Slow-Growing Economies with Small, Diverse Populations. The final problem generated by the interaction of human and physical geography is a heightened risk of violent internal conflict. African countries have characteristics that globally make a country prone to such conflict. As discussed above, the key consequence of Africa's distinctive geography has been slow growth and hence the perpetuation of low income. Yet globally, slow growth and low income are both important risk factors making violent conflict more likely. This is compounded by dependence on natural resource exports, which again globally makes violent conflict more likely. The core social characteristics of the typical African country, a small but ethnically diverse population, are also globally important risk factors. Finally, globally civil war tends to be recurrent: postconflict situations are fragile. Africa's tendency toward these risk factors accounts for why the region has had so much civil war.

There is evidence that international security interventions can be effective in these environments. Collier, Hoeffler, and Soderbom (25) analyze 66 postconflict situations and find that international peacekeeping substantially and significantly brings down the risks of reversion to conflict. Similarly, Doyle and Sambanis (26) find that while United Nations operations are not able to end wars, they are effective at maintaining postconflict peace. Yet postconflict situations in Africa have typically attracted far fewer international peacekeepers than those of other regions for obvious reasons of geo-political interest. Collier, Hoeffler, and Rohner (20) analyze globally the characteristics that make a country prone to the initial onset of conflict. They find that for the 30 years 1965–1995 during which France provided informal security guarantees to Francophone Africa, these countries had an incidence of civil war onset only one-third of that which would otherwise have been predicted. After the Rwandan atrocities of 1994, France abandoned this policy of guarantees. Hence, neither peacekeeping nor guarantees are currently being deployed to a degree that seem commensurate with their effectiveness.

Conclusion: Four Implications for Policies to Reduce African Poverty

Primarily, although not exclusively, African poverty reduction depends on raising African growth. Africa currently faces its best opportunity for growth since the commodity boom of the mid-1970s. In the intervening period, African economic performance has been worse than that of any other region. The explanation for this is not that African economic behavior is fundamentally different from elsewhere, but rather that African geographic endowments are distinctive.

In respect of physical geography Africa is not only distinctive but its countries are differentiated. The greater share of Africa's population in landlocked, resource-scarce countries as opposed to coastal, resource-scarce countries alone accounts for one percentage point off Africa's growth rate compared with other regions. Further, because opportunities differ across the region, strategies need to be differentiated. This applies both to what African governments should see as critical priorities and to what external actors can do to assist. In respect of human geography Africa is distinctive but not so differentiated. Most African countries have small populations and yet are ethnically diverse. A corollary of small countries is that Africa has found both policy reform and the internal security more difficult than other regions. Fortunately, Africa has made progress on both of these problems: hopefully, the small-country problem merely helps to account for Africa's troubled recent past, not its future. A corollary of ethnic diversity is that democracy is more important for economic performance, and that the domain of the public sector should be kept small and decentralized. Again, these may be problems of the past: the region has partially democratized, reduced the size of the state and decentralized spending. Hence, recent developments are hopeful: in some respects Africa's distinctive geography may be more important in explaining its past than in predicting its future. However, the interactions of physical and human geography have created intractable and important problems that have yet to be addressed and that probably need both regional and international action.

One is how to manage resource rents in the context of ethnic diversity. The most appropriate polity is a design that such countries tend not to have: strong checks and balances on how governments can use power and decentralized public spending. This is a political challenge for the resource-rich African states. The international community can also do much to assist African societies to build the necessary checks and balances by setting out templates such as the Extractive Industries Transparency Initiative and reforming banking secrecy to make the embezzlement of resource rents more difficult. In these resource-rich states the international community may have more scope for poverty reduction through such governance policies than through its traditional reliance on aid.

The second problem is how to compete with Asia despite having let Asia get decisively ahead. International action will be needed to give coastal, resource-scarce Africa a second chance by temporary preferential market access that offsets Asian economies of agglomeration. For these countries international trade policies may be more important for poverty reduction than additional aid, or at least be a useful complement to aid.

The third problem is proneness to violent internal conflict. Because of the large regional economic spillovers, this is a regional issue. However, there may be scope for expanding international peacekeeping and security guarantees, a recent model being the military support for Sierra Leone provided by Britain. Such security interventions may need to become integral to international strategy for African poverty reduction.

The fourth, and perhaps least tractable problem, is that so much of Africa's population lives in landlocked, resource-scarce states. I have discussed how, because these states have multiple forms of dependency on neighbors, Africa needs a strong regional political architecture that can internalize these externalities. Despite a plethora of regional and subregional institutions, African states have to date been unwilling to cede sufficient sovereignty to make them effective (27). In the absence of a regional political solution, the international community will need to rethink its aid strategy. These countries currently lack realistic opportunities to reach middle-income levels of development. They are thus the epicenter of the future poverty problem. Hence, poverty reduction in these societies is likely to need large and sustained aid inflows, not so much for investment in economic development, but rather for the direct raising of consumption levels. At present there is no such category of aid, nor a mechanism for sustained delivery to poor people. Humanitarian aid, which indeed is intended directly to raise consumption, is designed only to meet short-term emergencies. Long-term aid, while targeted toward low-income countries, is currently intended to raise income. The international community has not yet faced the prospect that even with our best efforts these societies are likely to remain low income for a long time.

References

1. Berg E (1981) *Accelerated Development in Sub-Saharan Africa* (World Bank, Washington, DC).
2. Bates R (1981) *Markets and States in Tropical Africa* (California UP, Berkeley, CA).
3. Collier P, Gunning JW (1999) *J Econ Literature* 37:64–111.
4. Collier P, Gunning JW (1999) *J Econ Perspect* 13:3–22.
5. Acemoglu D, Johnson S, Robinson J (2001) *Am Econ Rev* 91:1369–1401.
6. Jones BF, Olken BA (2005) *Q J Econ* 120:835–864.
7. Sachs JF (2003) *Institutions Don't Rule: The Direct Effects of Geography on Per Capita Income* (National Bureau of Economic Research, Cambridge, UK).
8. Collier P (2007) *The Bottom Billion* (Oxford Univ Press, New York).
9. Collier P, O'Connell S (2007) in *The Political Economy of Economic Growth in Africa: 1960–2000*. Ed. Ndulu BJ, O'Connell SA, Bates R, Collier P, Soludo CC (Cambridge UP, Cambridge, UK), pp 76–136.
10. Nuno L, Venables A (2001) *World Bank Econ Rev* 15:451–479.
11. Alaba O, Adenikinju A, Collier P (2007) in *Economic Policy Options for a Prosperous Nigeria*. Ed. Collier P, Soludo C, Pattillo C (Palgrave MacMillan, Basingstoke, UK), in press.
12. Collier P, Goderis B (2007) *World Econ* 8:1–15.
13. Rajan RG, Subramanian A (2005) *What Undermines Aid's Impact on Growth?* (International Monetary Fund, Washington, DC), IMF Working Paper 05/126.
14. Addison D (2007) in *Economic Policy Options for a Prosperous Nigeria*, eds Collier P, Soludo C, Pattillo C (Palgrave MacMillan, Basingstoke, UK), in press.
15. Collier P, Hoeffler A (2006) *Testing the Neocon Agenda: Democracy and Resource Rents* (Centre for the Study of African Economies, Oxford, UK).
16. Beck T, Clarke G, Groff A, Keefer P, Walsh P (2001) *World Bank Econ Rev* 15:165–176.
17. Wood A, Mayer J (2001) *Cambridge J Econ* 25:369–394.
18. Chauvet L, Collier P (2006) *Helping Hand?* (Centre for the Study of African Economies, Oxford, UK).
19. Collier P, Hoeffler A (2004) in *Global Crises: Global Solutions*, ed Lomberg B (Cambridge UP, Cambridge, UK), pp 129–156.
20. Collier P, Hoeffler A, Rohner D (2006) *Beyond Greed and Grievance: Feasibility and Civil War* (Centre for the Study of African Economies, Oxford, UK).

21. Collier P, Hoeffler A, Soderbom M (2007) *J Peace Res*, in press.
22. Collier P (2001) *Econ Policy* 32:127–166.
23. Alesina A, La Ferrara E (2005) *J Econ Literature* 63:762–800.
24. Collier P, Venables A (2007) *World Econ* 30:1467–1497.
26. Collier P, Hoeffler A, Soderbom M (2007) *J Peace Res*, in press.
27. Doyle MW, Sambanis N (2006) *Making War and Building Peace: United Nations Peacekeeping Operations* (Princeton UP, Princeton).
28. Collier P (2007) *J Afr Econ*, in press.

Recommended Reading

Banerjee, A.D. (2011). "Poor Economics." *Poor Economics: A Radical Rethinking of the Way to Fight Poverty.* <http://www.pooreconomics.com>.

Banerjee, A., & Duflo, E. (2011). *Poor Economics: A Radical Rethinking of the Way to Fight Global Poverty.* New York: PublicAffairs.

Cohen, G.A. (2000). *If You're an Egalitarian, How Come You're So Rich?* Cambridge, MA: Harvard UP.

Collier, P. (2008). *The Bottom Billion.* New York: Oxford UP.

Dworkin, R. (2000). *Sovereign Virtue: The Theory and Practice of Equality.* Cambridge, MA: Harvard UP.

Easterly, W. (2001). *The Elusive Quest for Growth: Economists' Adventures in the Tropics.* Cambridge, MA: MIT Press.

Miller, R.W. (2010). *Globalizing Justice: The Ethics of Poverty and Power.* Oxford: Oxford UP.

Roemer, J.E. (1996). *Theories of Distributive Justice.* Cambridge, MA: Harvard UP.

Sachs, J. (2006). *The End of Poverty: Economic Possibilities for Our Time.* New York: Penguin.

Yunus, M. (2008). *Creating a World Without Poverty.* New York: PublicAffairs.

III

Globalization: Introduction

The Anti-globalization Movement and the Battle of Seattle

According to the British essayist William Hazlitt, "[T]here were a hundred thousand country fellows in ... [Henry VIII's] time ready to fight to the death against popery, without knowing whether popery was a man or a horse."[1] And in November 1999, over 40,000 demonstrators converged on the Washington State Convention and Trade Center in Seattle, the site of the World Trade Organization (WTO) Ministerial Conference, to voice their opposition to globalization—whatever it was.

Protesters represented a rainbow coalition of NGOs, religious groups, labor unions, student organizations, environmentalists, and political groups from the anti-capitalist left to the anarchist right, with a variety of complaints. What was wrong with the WTO? According to the anti-globalization movement's literature it was undemocratic, trampled labor and human rights, destroyed the environment, increased hunger, hurt poor little countries by privileging rich powerful nations, and undermined national sovereignty;[2] it gave multinational corporations unlimited power, enslaved the peoples of the Global South and imposed white, Western, and in particular American hegemony of the world order.

But was it a man or a horse?

---

1 <http://quotationsbook.com/quote/4247/>.
2 <http://www.globalexchange.org/campaigns/wto/OpposeWTO.html>. This site is a fair example of popular objections to the WTO.

Bretton Woods Institutions and the Washington Consensus

Economic globalization is the increasing integration of economies around the world, through trade and financial flows, but also through the movement of labor and technology across international borders.

The WTO is an international organization that deals with the rules of trade between nations: administering trade agreements, providing a forum for trade negotiations, handling trade disputes, and providing technical assistence and training for developing countries.[3] Established in 1995, it is the successor to the General Agreement on Tariffs and Trade (GATT), which was created at the 1944 Bretton Woods Conference along with the International Bank for Reconstruction and Development (subsequently part of the World Bank) and the International Monetary Fund (IMF), to manage the international economic system. The "Bretton Woods system" in which these institutions figured was a response to the international Great Depression of the 1930s and the two world wars that were driven in part by economic pressures. In light of these events, there was a consensus that the international economic system required government intervention.

During the period from the end of World War II through the 1970s, it was widely accepted that state power should be freely deployed alongside of, or intervening in or even substituting for, market processes to achieve the welfare of its citizens and economic growth. While the three decades following the end of the war, when this policy was implemented, were a period of economic growth and prosperity, by the 1970s it appeared that this system was no longer working. The collapse of the Communist bloc and chronic economic crises during the 1980s promoted further worries about state interventionism and a push for free market reform.

In the 1980s, *neoliberalism*, a market-driven approach to economic and social policy that stressed the efficiency of private enterprise, liberalized trade, and open markets gained approval among Washington-based international economic organizations, including the IMF and World Bank. Advocates argued that the integration of national economies through liberalized trade and open markets promoted efficiency through competition and specialization.

But, as critics note, markets do not necessarily ensure that the benefits of increased efficiency are shared by all, and, during the twentieth century, while global GDP increased almost five-fold, the gaps between rich and poor countries, and between rich and poor people within countries, grew. The 2008 IMF report, which heads this section, describes the course of globalization and poses the hard questions addressed in subsequent readings. Does globalization increase poverty and inequality? Does globalization harm workers in developing countries? Does it set back the interests of workers in affluent countries, which face competition from low-wage economies? How can the poorest countries, which are increasingly falling behind more affluent countries economically, catch up?

---

3 <http://www.wto.org/english/thewto_e/whatis_e/whatis_e.htm>.

Globalization and the Global South

Does globalization work for the poor? Kevin Watkins, Senior Policy Advisor with Oxfam, argues that it can, but that so far it has not. During the last decades of the twentieth century, economic inequality among nations and people grew, while the incidence of global poverty was hardly diminished. Watkins argues that "openness"—the removal of trade barriers along with associated domestic free-market reforms—is not in and of itself an effective poverty-reduction strategy. Indeed, he concludes, the current rules of the multilateral trading system are designed to concentrate advantage in the rich world.

David Dollar and Aart Kraay, in response, disagree. Challenging Watkins's data and analysis, they claim that personal income inequality did not in fact increase during the period in question and that extreme poverty declined. They note further that when countries in the developing world that they identify as globalizers are compared with other poor countries which were not globalizers, the former have made more significant progress in reducing poverty as they have integrated with the global economy.

Joseph Stiglitz, formerly chief economist of the World Bank, notes that affluent countries, which seek to impose free-market policies on developing countries, have not adopted these policies themselves. "I have always been struck by the divergence between the policies that America pushes on developing countries and those practiced in the US itself," writes Stiglitz. "Nor is America alone: most other successful developing and developed countries pursue similar 'heretical' policies."[4]

Matthew Zwolinski, addressing anti-globalization activists' concerns about workers' rights, argues that well-meaning campaigns to shut down sweatshops in developing countries are misguided from the moral point of view. Zwolinski's essay poses the difficult ethical question of exploitation, perhaps the fundamental question raised by economic globalization. Intuitively, the wider the scope of our choices, the better off we are. Exploitative offers expand the range of options available to individuals in desperate circumstances and give them the chance to extricate themselves. We have a nagging sense that exploitative offers are morally wrong—not merely because we could or should have done better but because it seems inherently bad to take advantage of other's bad luck. Are they?

In the last essay in this section, political scientist Benjamin Barber considers the social and political consequences of economic globalization. Barber imagines "two possible political futures—both bleak, neither democratic. The first is a retribalization of large swaths of humankind by war and bloodshed.... [The second] one commercially homogenous global network: one McWorld"[5] dominated by multinational corporations operating under the auspices of global free-market capitalism.

---

4 Joseph Stiglitz, "Do What We Did, Not What We Say," pp. 184–86 in this volume.
5 Barber, "Jihad vs. McWorld," p. 208 in this volume.

14. Globalization: Threat or Opportunity?*

IMF Staff

I. Introduction

The term "globalization" has acquired considerable emotive force. Some view it as a process that is beneficial—a key to future world economic development—and also inevitable and irreversible. Others regard it with hostility, even fear, believing that it increases inequality within and between nations, threatens employment and living standards and thwarts social progress. This brief offers an overview of some aspects of globalization and aims to identify ways in which countries can tap the gains of this process, while remaining realistic about its potential and its risks.

Globalization offers extensive opportunities for truly worldwide development but it is not progressing evenly. Some countries are becoming integrated into the global economy more quickly than others. Countries that have been able to integrate are seeing faster growth and reduced poverty. Outward-oriented policies brought dynamism and greater prosperity to much of East Asia, transforming it from one of the poorest areas of the world 40 years ago. And as living standards rose, it became possible to make progress on democracy and economic issues such as the environment and work standards.

By contrast, in the 1970s and 1980s when many countries in Latin America and Africa pursued inward-oriented policies, their economies stagnated or declined, poverty increased and high inflation became the norm. In many cases, especially Africa, adverse external developments made the problems worse. As these regions changed their policies, their incomes have begun to rise. An important transformation is underway. Encouraging this trend, not reversing it, is the best course for promoting growth, development and poverty reduction.

The crises in the emerging markets in the 1990s have made it quite evident that the opportunities of globalization do not come without risks—risks arising from volatile capital movements and the risks of social, economic, and environmental degradation

* Source: International Monetary Fund, 12 April 2000 <http://www.imf.org/external/np/exr/ ib/2000/041200to.htm>.

created by poverty. This is not a reason to reverse direction, but for all concerned—in developing countries, in the advanced countries, and of course investors—to embrace policy changes to build strong economies and a stronger world financial system that will produce more rapid growth and ensure that poverty is reduced.

How can the developing countries, especially the poorest, be helped to catch up? Does globalization exacerbate inequality or can it help to reduce poverty? And are countries that integrate with the global economy inevitably vulnerable to instability? These are some of the questions covered in the following sections.

II. What is Globalization?

Economic "globalization" is a historical process, the result of human innovation and technological progress. It refers to the increasing integration of economies around the world, particularly through trade and financial flows. The term sometimes also refers to the movement of people (labor) and knowledge (technology) across international borders. There are also broader cultural, political and environmental dimensions of globalization that are not covered here.

At its most basic, there is nothing mysterious about globalization. The term has come into common usage since the 1980s, reflecting technological advances that have made it easier and quicker to complete international transactions—both trade and financial flows. It refers to an extension beyond national borders of the same market forces that have operated for centuries at all levels of human economic activity—village markets, urban industries, or financial centers.

Markets promote efficiency through competition and the division of labor—the specialization that allows people and economies to focus on what they do best. Global markets offer greater opportunity for people to tap into more and larger markets around the world. It means that they can have access to more capital flows, technology, cheaper imports, and larger export markets. But markets do not necessarily ensure that the benefits of increased efficiency are shared by all. Countries must be prepared to embrace the policies needed, and in the case of the poorest countries may need the support of the international community as they do so.

III. Unparalleled Growth, Increased Inequality: 20th Century Income Trends

Globalization is not just a recent phenomenon. Some analysts have argued that the world economy was just as globalized 100 years ago as it is today. But today commerce and financial services are far more developed and deeply integrated than they were at that time. The most striking aspect of this has been the integration of financial markets made possible by modern electronic communication.

The 20th century saw unparalleled economic growth, with global per capita GDP increasing almost five-fold. But this growth was not steady—the strongest expansion came during the second half of the century, a period of rapid trade expansion accompanied by trade—and typically somewhat later, financial—liberalization.

Figure 14.1

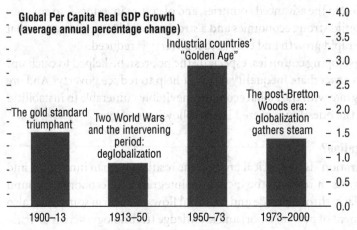

**Global Per Capita Real GDP Growth
(average annual percentage change)**

Industrial countries'
"Golden Age"

The gold standard
triumphant

Two World Wars
and the intervening
period:
deglobalization

The post-Bretton
Woods era:
globalization
gathers steam

1900–13   1913–50   1950–73   1973–2000

Figure 14.2

In the twentieth century, per capita income has risen faster in the rich than in the poor
countries and at different speeds in different subperiods.

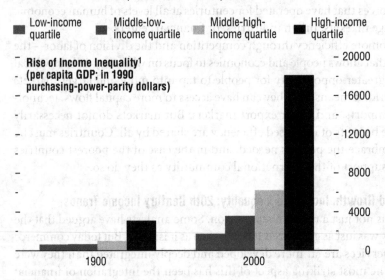

■ Low-income
quartile

■ Middle-low-
income quartile

■ Middle-high-
income quartile

■ High-income
quartile

**Rise of Income Inequality[1]
(per capita GDP; in 1990
purchasing-power-parity dollars)**

1900   2000

Sources: Angus Maddison, *Monitoring the World Economy 1820–1992* (Paris:
Organization for Economic Cooperation and Development, 1995); and IMF staff estimates.

[1]Countries' populations have been assigned to income quartiles according to GDP per
capita in each country; each quartile contains 25 percent of world population.

Figure 14.1 breaks the century into four periods.[1] In the inter-war era, the world turned its back on internationalism—or globalization as we now call it—and countries retreated into closed economies, protectionism and pervasive capital controls. This was a major factor in the devastation of this period, when per capita income growth fell to less than 1 percent during 1913–50. For the rest of the century, even though population grew at an unprecedented pace, per capita income growth was over 2 percent, the fastest pace of all coming during the post-World War boom in the industrial countries.

The story of the 20th century was of remarkable average income growth, but it is also quite obvious that the progress was not evenly dispersed. The gaps between rich and poor countries, and rich and poor people within countries, have grown. The richest quarter of the world's population saw its per capita GDP increase nearly six-fold during the century, while the poorest quarter experienced less than a three-fold increase (Figure 14.2). Income inequality has clearly increased. But, as noted below, per capita GDP does not tell the whole story (see section IV).

IV. Developing Countries: How Deeply Integrated?

Globalization means that world trade and financial markets are becoming more integrated. But just how far have developing countries been involved in this integration? Their experience in catching up with the advanced economies has been mixed. Figure 14.3 shows that in some countries, especially in Asia, per capita incomes have been moving quickly toward levels in the industrial countries since 1970. A larger number of developing countries have made only slow progress or have lost ground. In particular, per capita incomes in Africa have declined relative to the industrial countries and in some countries have declined in absolute terms. Figure 14.4 illustrates part of the explanation: the countries catching up are those where trade has grown strongly.

Consider four aspects of globalization:

- **Trade:** Developing countries as a whole have increased their share of world trade—from 19 percent in 1971 to 29 percent in 1999. But Figure 14.3 shows great variation among the major regions. For instance, the newly industrialized economies (NIEs) of Asia have done well, while Africa as a whole has fared poorly. The composition of what countries export is also important. The strongest rise by far has been in the export of manufactured goods. The share of primary commodities in world exports—such as food and raw materials—that are often produced by the poorest countries, has declined.

- **Capital movements:** Figure 14.5 depicts what many people associate with globalization, sharply increased private capital flows to developing countries during much of the 1990s. It also shows that (a) the increase followed a particularly "dry"

---

1 The discussion in this section is elaborated in the *World Economic Outlook*, International Monetary Fund, Washington DC, May 2000.

Figure 14.3 Output Performance and Trade Shares: Developing Countries and Newly Industrialized Asian Economies [1]

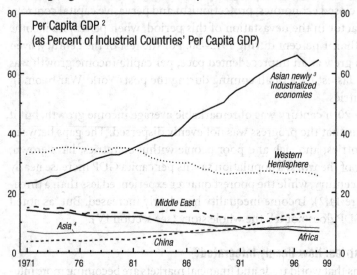

Per Capita GDP [2]
(as Percent of Industrial Countries' Per Capita GDP)

- Asian newly [3] industrialized economies
- Western Hemisphere
- Middle East
- Asia [4]
- China
- Africa

Figure 14.4

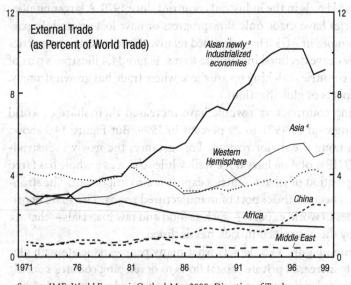

External Trade
(as Percent of World Trade)

- Asian newly [3] industrialized economies
- Asia [4]
- Western Hemisphere
- China
- Africa
- Middle East

Source: IMF, *World Economic Outlook* May 2000; Direction of Trade.
[1] Excludes oil exporting countries.
[2] Purchasing power parity terms.
[3] Hong Kong SAR, Korea, Singapore, Tiawan Province of China.
[4] Excludes China.

period in the 1980s; (b) net official flows of "aid" or development assistance have fallen significantly since the early 1980s; and (c) the composition of private flows has changed dramatically. Direct foreign investment has become the most important category. Both portfolio investment and bank credit rose but they have been more volatile, falling sharply in the wake of the financial crises of the late 1990s.

• **Movement of people**: Workers move from one country to another partly to find better employment opportunities. The numbers involved are still quite small, but in the period 1965-90, the proportion of labor forces round the world that was foreign born increased by about one-half. Most migration occurs between developing countries. But the flow of migrants to advanced economies is likely to provide a means through which global wages converge. There is also the potential for skills to be transferred back to the developing countries and for wages in those countries to rise.

Fig. 14.5   Developing Countries: Net Capital Flows[1]

(In percent of developing countries' GDP)

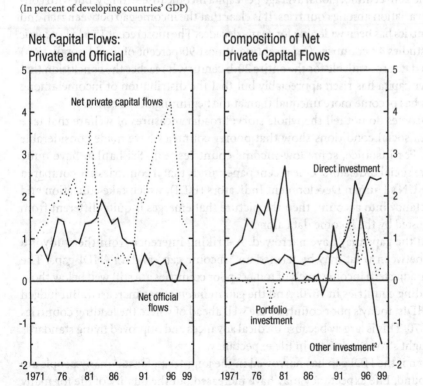

Source: *IMF World Economic Outlook Databases*: (May 2000), Direction of Trade
[1] Excludes oil exporting countries.
[2] Consists largely of bank lending.

- **Spread of knowledge (and technology)**: Information exchange is an integral, often overlooked, aspect of globalization. For instance, direct foreign investment brings not only an expansion of the physical capital stock, but also technical innovation. More generally, knowledge about production methods, management techniques, export markets and economic policies is available at very low cost, and it represents a highly valuable resource for the developing countries.

The special case of the economies in transition from planned to market economies—they too are becoming more integrated with the global economy—is not explored in much depth here. In fact, the term "transition economy" is losing its usefulness. Some countries (e.g., Poland, Hungary) are converging quite rapidly toward the structure and performance of advanced economies. Others (such as most countries of the former Soviet Union) face long-term structural and institutional issues similar to those faced by developing countries.

V. Does Globalization Increase Poverty and Inequality?

During the 20th century, global average per capita income rose strongly, but with considerable variation among countries. It is clear that the income gap between rich and poor countries has been widening for many decades. The most recent *World Economic Outlook* studies 42 countries (representing almost 90 percent of world population) for which data are available for the entire 20th century. It reaches the conclusion that output per capita has risen appreciably but that the distribution of income among countries has become more unequal than at the beginning of the century.

But incomes do not tell the whole story; broader measures of welfare that take account of social conditions show that poorer countries have made considerable progress. For instance, some low-income countries, e.g., Sri Lanka, have quite impressive social indicators. One recent paper[2] finds that if countries are compared using the UN's Human Development Indicators (HDI), which take education and life expectancy into account, then the picture that emerges is quite different from that suggested by the income data alone.

Indeed the gaps may have narrowed. A striking inference from the study is a contrast between what may be termed an "income gap" and an "HDI gap." The (inflation-adjusted) income levels of today's poor countries are still well below those of the leading countries in 1870. And the gap in *incomes* has increased. But judged by their HDIs, today's poor countries are well ahead of where the leading countries were in 1870. This is largely because medical advances and improved living standards have brought strong increases in life expectancy.

But even if the HDI gap has narrowed in the long-term, far too many people are losing ground. Life expectancy may have increased but the quality of life for many

---

2 Nicholas Crafts, *Globalization and Growth in the Twentieth Century*, IMF Working Paper, WP/00/44, Washington, DC, April 2000.

has not improved, with many still in abject poverty. And the spread of AIDS through Africa in the past decade is reducing life expectancy in many countries.

This has brought new urgency to policies specifically designed to alleviate poverty. Countries with a strong growth record, pursuing the right policies, can expect to see a sustained reduction in poverty, since recent evidence suggests that there exists at least a one-to-one correspondence between growth and poverty reduction. And if strongly pro-poor policies—for instance in well-targeted social expenditure—are pursued then there is a better chance that growth will be amplified into more rapid poverty reduction. This is one compelling reason for all economic policy makers, including the IMF, to pay heed more explicitly to the objective of poverty reduction.

VI. How Can the Poorest Countries Catch Up More Quickly?

Growth in living standards springs from the accumulation of physical capital (investment) and human capital (labor), and through advances in technology (what economists call total factor productivity).[3] Many factors can help or hinder these processes. The experience of the countries that have increased output most rapidly shows the importance of creating conditions that are conducive to long-run per capita income growth. Economic stability, institution building, and structural reform are at least as important for long-term development as financial transfers, important as they are. What matters is the whole package of policies, financial and technical assistance, and debt relief if necessary.

Components of such a package might include:
- Macroeconomic stability to create the right conditions for investment and saving;
- Outward oriented policies to promote efficiency through increased trade and investment;
- Structural reform to encourage domestic competition;
- Strong institutions and an effective government to foster good governance;
- Education, training, and research and development to promote productivity;
- External debt management to ensure adequate resources for sustainable development.

All these policies should be focussed on country-owned strategies to reduce poverty by promoting pro-poor policies that are properly budgeted—including health, education, and strong social safety nets. A participatory approach, including consultation with civil society, will add greatly to their chances of success.

Advanced economies can make a vital contribution to the low-income countries' efforts to integrate into the global economy:
- By promoting trade. One proposal on the table is to provide unrestricted market access for all exports from the poorest countries. This should help them move

---

3 These issues are explored in greater depth in IMF, *World Economic Outlook*, May 2000, Chapter IV.

beyond specialization on primary commodities to producing processed goods for export.

- By encouraging flows of private capital to the lower-income countries, particularly foreign direct investment, with its twin benefits of steady financial flows and technology transfer.

- By supplementing more rapid debt relief with an increased level of new financial support. Official development assistance (ODA) has fallen to 0.24 percent of GDP (1998) in advanced countries (compared with a UN target of 0.7 percent). As Michel Camdessus, the former Managing Director of the IMF put it: "The excuse of aid fatigue is not credible—indeed it approaches the level of downright cynicism—at a time when, for the last decade, the advanced countries have had the opportunity to enjoy the benefits of the peace dividend."

The IMF supports reform in the poorest countries through its new Poverty Reduction and Growth Facility. It is contributing to debt relief through the initiative for the heavily indebted poor countries.[4]

VII. An Advanced Country Perspective: Does Globalization Harm Workers' Interests?

Anxiety about globalization also exists in advanced economies. How real is the perceived threat that competition from "low-wage economies" displaces workers from high-wage jobs and decreases the demand for less skilled workers? Are the changes taking place in these economies and societies a direct result of globalization?

Economies are continually evolving and globalization is one among several other continuing trends. One such trend is that as industrial economies mature, they are becoming more service-oriented to meet the changing demands of their population. Another trend is the shift toward more highly skilled jobs. But all the evidence is that these changes would be taking place—not necessarily at the same pace—with or without globalization. In fact, globalization is actually making this process easier and less costly to the economy as a whole by bringing the benefits of capital flows, technological innovations, and lower import prices. Economic growth, employment and living standards are all higher than they would be in a closed economy.

But the gains are typically distributed unevenly among groups within countries, and some groups may lose out. For instance, workers in declining older industries may not be able to make an easy transition to new industries.

What is the appropriate policy response? Should governments try to protect particular groups, like low-paid workers or old industries, by restricting trade or capital flows? Such an approach might help some in the short-term, but ultimately it is at the expense of the living standards of the population at large. Rather, governments

---

4 These are described in the factsheets "The Poverty Reduction and Growth Facility (PRGF)—Operational Issues," and "Overview: Transforming the Enhanced Structural Adjustment Facility (ESAF) and the Debt Initiative for the Heavily Indebted Poor Countries (HIPCs)," which may be viewed at <www.imf.org>.

should pursue policies that encourage integration into the global economy while putting in place measures to help those adversely affected by the changes. The economy as a whole will prosper more from policies that embrace globalization by promoting an open economy, and, at the same time, squarely address the need to ensure the benefits are widely shared. Government policy should focus on two important areas:
- education and vocational training, to make sure that workers have the opportunity to acquire the right skills in dynamic changing economies; and
- well-targeted social safety nets to assist people who are displaced.

VIII. Are Periodic Crises an Inevitable Consequence of Globalization?

The succession of crises in the 1990s—Mexico, Thailand, Indonesia, Korea, Russia, and Brazil—suggested to some that financial crises are a direct and inevitable result of globalization. Indeed one question that arises in both advanced and emerging market economies is whether globalization makes economic management more difficult (Box 14.1).

Box 14.1 Does globalization reduce national sovereignty in economic policy-making?

Does increased integration, particularly in the financial sphere make it more difficult for governments to manage economic activity, for instance by limiting governments' choices of tax rates and tax systems, or their freedom of action on monetary or exchange rate policies? If it is assumed that countries aim to achieve sustainable growth, low inflation and social progress, then the evidence of the past 50 years is that globalization contributes to these objectives in the long term.

In the short-term, as we have seen in the past few years, volatile short-term capital flows can threaten macroeconomic stability. Thus in a world of integrated financial markets, countries will find it increasingly risky to follow policies that do not promote financial stability. This discipline also applies to the private sector, which will find it more difficult to implement wage increases and price markups that would make the country concerned become uncompetitive.

But there is another kind of risk. Sometimes investors—particularly short-term investors—take too sanguine a view of a country's prospects and capital inflows may continue even when economic policies have become too relaxed. This exposes the country to the risk that when perceptions change, there may be a sudden brutal withdrawal of capital from the country.

In short, globalization does not reduce national sovereignty. It does create a strong incentive for governments to pursue sound economic policies. It should create incentives for the private sector to undertake careful analysis of risk. However, short-term investment flows may be excessively volatile.

Efforts to increase the stability of international capital flows are central to the ongoing work on strengthening the international financial architecture. In this regard, some are concerned that globalization leads to the abolition of rules or constraints on business activities. To the contrary—one of the key goals of the work on the international financial architecture is to develop standards and codes that are based on internationally accepted principles that can be implemented in many different national settings.

Clearly the crises would not have developed as they did without exposure to global capital markets. But nor could these countries have achieved their impressive growth records without those financial flows.

These were complex crises, resulting from an interaction of shortcomings in national policy and the international financial system. Individual governments and the international community as a whole are taking steps to reduce the risk of such crises in future.

At the national level, even though several of the countries had impressive records of economic performance, they were not fully prepared to withstand the potential shocks that could come through the international markets. Macroeconomic stability, financial soundness, open economies, transparency, and good governance are all essential for countries participating in the global markets. Each of the countries came up short in one or more respects.

At the international level, several important lines of defense against crisis were breached. Investors did not appraise risks adequately. Regulators and supervisors in the major financial centers did not monitor developments sufficiently closely. And not enough information was available about some international investors, notably offshore financial institutions. The result was that markets were prone to "herd behavior"—sudden shifts of investor sentiment and the rapid movement of capital, especially short-term finance, into and out of countries.

The international community is responding to the global dimensions of the crisis through a continuing effort to strengthen the architecture of the international monetary and financial system. The broad aim is for markets to operate with more transparency, equity, and efficiency. The IMF has a central role in this process, which is explored further in separate fact sheets.[5]

---

5 See "Progress in Strengthening the Architecture of the International Monetary System," <http://www.imf.org/external/np/exr/facts/arcguide.htm> and "Guide to Progress in Strengthening of the International Financial System," <http://www.imf.org/external/np/exr/facts/arcguide.htm>.

IX. The Role of Institutions and Organizations

National and international institutions, inevitably influenced by differences in culture, play an important role in the process of globalization. It may be best to leave an outside commentator to reflect on the role of institutions:

> ...That the advent of highly integrated commodity and financial markets has been accompanied by trade tensions and problems of financial instability should not come as a surprise,...The surprise is that these problems are not even more severe today, given that the extent of commodity and financial market integration is so much greater.
>
> One possibility in accounting [for this surprise] is the stabilizing role of the institutions built in the interim. At the national level this means social and financial safety nets. At the international level it means the WTO, the IMF, the Basle Committee of Banking Supervisors. These institutions may be far from perfect, but they are better than nothing, judging from the historical correlation between the level of integration on one hand and the level of trade conflict and financial instability on the other.[6]

X. Conclusion

As globalization has progressed, living conditions (particularly when measured by broader indicators of well-being) have improved significantly in virtually all countries. However, the strongest gains have been made by the advanced countries and only some of the developing countries.

That the income gap between high-income and low-income countries has grown wider is a matter for concern. And the number of the world's citizens in abject poverty is deeply disturbing. But it is wrong to jump to the conclusion that globalization has caused the divergence, or that nothing can be done to improve the situation. To the contrary: low-income countries have not been able to integrate with the global economy as quickly as others, partly because of their chosen policies and partly because of factors outside their control. No country, least of all the poorest, can afford to remain isolated from the world economy. Every country should seek to reduce poverty. The international community should endeavor—by strengthening the international financial system, through trade, and through aid—to help the poorest countries integrate into the world economy, grow more rapidly, and reduce poverty. That is the way to ensure all people in all countries have access to the benefits of globalization.

---

6 Michael D. Bordo, Barry Eichengreen, and Douglas A. Irwin, "Is Globalization Today Really Different than Globalization a Hundred Years Ago?" Working Paper 7195, National Bureau of Economic Research, Cambridge, MA, June 1999.

15. Do What We Did, Not What We Say[*]

Joseph E. Stiglitz

Today, many emerging markets, from Indonesia to Mexico, are told that there is a certain code of conduct to which they must conform if they are to be successful. The message is clear: here is what advanced industrial countries do, and have done. If you wish to join the club, you must do the same. The reforms will be painful, vested interests will resist, but with enough political will, you will reap the benefits.

Each country draws up a list of what is to be done, and each government is held accountable in terms of its performance. In all countries, balancing the budget and controlling inflation are high on the list, but so are structural reforms. In the case of Mexico, for example, opening up the electricity industry, which Mexico's constitution reserves to the government, has become the structural reform of the day demanded by the West. So analysts—mindlessly one is tempted to say—praise Mexico for its progress in controlling its budget and inflation, but criticize it for lack of progress in electricity reform.

As someone who was intimately involved in economic policy making in the US, I have always been struck by the divergence between the policies that America pushes on developing countries and those practiced in the US itself. Nor is America alone: most other successful developing and developed countries pursue similar "heretical" policies.

For example, both political parties in the US now accept the notion that when a country is in a recession, it is not only permissible, but even *desirable*, to run deficits. Yet all over the world, developing countries are told that central banks should focus exclusively on price stability. America's central bank, the Federal Reserve Board, has a mandate to balance growth, employment, and inflation—and it is a mandate that brings it popular support.

---

[*] Source: Project Syndicate, October 6, 2003, <http://www.project-syndicate.org/commentary/stiglitz31/English>.

While free marketers rail against industrial policy, in the US the government actively supports new technologies, and has done so for a long time. The first telegraph line was built by the US Federal Government between Baltimore and Washington in 1842; the Internet, which is so changing today's economy, was developed by the US military. Much of modern American technological progress is based on government-funded research in biotechnology or defense.

Similarly, while many countries are told to privatize social security, America's public social security system is efficient (with transactions costs a fraction of private annuities), and customers are responsive to it. It has been pivotal in almost eliminating poverty among America's elderly.

While the US Social Security System now faces a problem with under-funding, so do a large fraction of America's private pension programs. And the public pension system has provided the elderly with a kind of security—both against inflation and the vagaries of the stock market—that the private market to date simply has not.

Correspondingly, many aspects of American economic policy contribute significantly to America's success, but are hardly mentioned in discussions of development strategies. For more than a hundred years, America has had strong anti-trust laws, which broke up private monopolies in many areas, such as oil. In some emerging markets, telecom monopolies are stifling development of the Internet, and hence economic growth. In others, monopolies in trade deprive countries of the advantages of international competition, while monopolies in cement significantly raise the price of construction.

The American government also played an important role in developing the country's financial markets—by providing credit directly or through government-sponsored enterprises, and by partially guaranteeing a quarter or more of all loans. Fannie Mae, the government-created entity responsible for providing mortgages for middle-class Americans, helped lower mortgage costs and played a significant role in making America one of the countries with the largest proportion of private home ownership.

The Small Business Administration provided the capital to help small businesses—some of which, like Federal Express, have grown into major businesses creating thousands of jobs. Today, US Federal Government student loans are central to ensuring that all Americans have access to a college education, just as in earlier years, government finance helped bring electricity to all Americans.

Occasionally, America has experimented with free-market ideology and deregulation—sometimes with disastrous effects. President Ronald Reagan's deregulation of the Savings and Loan Associations led to an infamous wave of bank failures that cost American taxpayers several hundred billion dollars and contributed to the economic recession of 1991.

Those in Mexico, Indonesia, Brazil, India and other emerging markets should be told a quite different message: do not strive for a mythical free-market economy, which has never existed. Do not follow the encomiums of US special interests, whether in the corporate or financial arena, because, although they preach free markets, back home they rely on the US government to advance their aims.

Instead, developing economies should look carefully, not at what America says, but at what it did in the years when America emerged as an industrial power, and what it does today. There is a remarkable similarity between those policies and the activist measures pursued by the highly successful East Asian economies over the past two decades.

16. Making Globalization Work for the Poor[*]

Kevin Watkins

Economists are sometimes chastised for their inability to reach a consensus view. George Bernard Shaw, the Irish playwright, captured the mood rather neatly when he wrote: "If all economists were laid end to end, they wouldn't reach a conclusion." If he were writing today, he would be forced to concede the rider "unless they were discussing the benefits for the poor of openness to trade."

"Openness" has become the great religion of the globalization era. No meeting of international financial institutions is complete without a homily to its benign effects. In the view of the IMF, the World Bank, and most northern governments, removing barriers to trade is one of the most powerful things that governments can do to give the poor a bigger stake in global prosperity. As a World Bank research report published in 2001 concluded, openness explains why "globalization leads to faster growth and poverty reduction in poor countries." Expressed differently, openness—along with associated free market reforms—holds the key to making globalization work for the poor.

Some critics respond by asserting that globalization can never work for the poor and that integration into global markets will inevitably cause more poverty and inequality. Widespread as it is, such "globaphobia" is unjustified. International trade has the potential to act as a powerful catalyst for poverty reduction, as the experience of East Asia demonstrates. It can provide poor countries and people with access to the markets, technologies, and ideas needed to sustain higher and more equitable patterns of growth.

But if globaphobia is unjustified, so too is "globaphilia"—an affliction, widespread on Nineteenth Street in Washington, that holds that increased integration through trade and openness is an almost automatic passport to more rapid growth and poverty reduction.

---

* Source: *Finance & Development* 39.1 (March 2002), <http://www.imf.org/external/pubs/ft/fandd/2002/03/watkins.htm>.

Growing Income Inequalities

Bluntly stated, the argument that globalization is working for the poor does not deserve to be taken seriously. Between 1988 and 1998, the incidence of global poverty fell by the derisory rate of 0.2 percent a year. Already obscene global income inequalities are widening. At the end of the 1990s, high-income countries representing 14 percent of the world's population accounted for over three-fourths of world income—roughly the same as at the start of the decade. The world economy ended the 1980s more unequal than any national economy, and since then it has become even more unequal (the global Gini coefficient rose by 3 points between 1988 and 1993 alone). These figures come from a 1999 World Bank report, "True World Income Distribution, 1988 and 1993," authored by Branko Milanovic of the World Bank Development Research Group. Of course, they can be disputed. Some economists, on the basis of no credible evidence, assert that the incomes of rich and poor countries are starting to converge. Surely, the real issue is that current patterns of global inequality are inconsistent not just with civilized values but also with the international commitment to halve poverty by 2015.

International trade is reinforcing income inequalities. Because exports are growing faster than global GDP, they have an increasingly important bearing on income distribution. And world trade shares mirror income distribution patterns. Thus, for every $1 generated through export activity, $0.75 goes to the world's richest countries. Low-income countries receive around $0.03. Unless developing countries capture a far larger share of exports, trade will continue to fuel widening gaps in absolute income.

Within many developing countries, globalization is exacerbating inequalities at various levels. Income gaps based on access to markets, productive assets, and education are widening, acting as a brake on poverty-reduction efforts. At the same time, integration into global markets is reinforcing other forms of deprivation, notably in relation to gender. Globalization has drawn millions of women into employment, but increased income has gone hand in hand with extreme forms of exploitation, the erosion of workers' rights, and increased vulnerability to global markets. "Flexibility" in labor markets has become a euphemism for stark violations of basic rights. As one Colombian flower worker recently interviewed by Oxfam put it: "Yes, I have more money, but I have lost my health. I have a job—but I have no rights and no security." One of the problems with the current debate on globalization is that the non-income dimensions of poverty—such as self-respect, security, and health—have been ignored.

The Problem with Openness

The champions of openness claim that a renewed commitment to liberalization holds the key to making globalization work for the poor. Econometric survey results have been cited as evidence of the scientific veracity of this claim. Confidence in that evidence is reflected in policy conditions on trade liberalization attached to IMF-World Bank loans and in the advice of northern governments to their southern counterparts. One recent IMF review of seven Poverty Reduction and Growth Facility programs found that each loan came with seven trade policy conditions attached. Following the 1997 financial collapse in East Asia, the IMF's rescue loans again came heavily laden with import-liberalization requirements. Most northern governments fully support this approach. For example, the UK Department for International Development's white paper on globalization provided a ringing endorsement of trade openness—as ever, citing World Bank "evidence." Unfortunately, the evidence in question is based on dubious economics and a highly selective interpretation of data and does not justify the confidence in policy prescription.

The most widely cited case for openness has been set out by David Dollar and Aart Kraay of the World Bank. Briefly summarized, their case rests on two core arguments. The first is that openness is associated with higher growth. Dollar and Kraay identify 24 developing countries that have seen large increases in openness, defined as a rising share of trade in GDP. These "globalizers"—a group that includes Brazil, China, India, Mexico, and Thailand—achieved per capita growth rates that were 4 percent higher than those of non-globalizers in the 1990s, a huge difference. The second argument is that increased trade is not associated, on average, with a systematic tendency to increased inequality: the poor share in growth in proportion to their existing share of national income. Other things being equal, the combination of higher growth and no change in income distribution translates into more rapid poverty reduction.

Some of the problems with this approach stem from the use of large samples to derive weighted averages. Using an unweighted average, the per capita growth rate for the "globalizers" falls to 1.5 percent (roughly the same as the non-globalizers)—and 10 of the 24 countries in the group record growth rates for the 1990s of 1 percent or less. Hardly an impressive foundation for sustained poverty reduction.

The more serious problem concerns what is being measured. Essentially, Dollar and Kraay are capturing an economic outcome in the form of a trade-to-GDP ratio. They then proceed to use changes in this ratio as a proxy for changes in trade policy. The implicit assumption is that trade liberalization is responsible for successful integration, with success in this case being defined as faster growth and poverty reduction.

In reality, this is little more than a speculative leap of faith. Countries such as China, Thailand, and Vietnam may be premier globalizers. They also have a strong record on economic growth and poverty reduction. Yet they have liberalized imports very slowly and still have relatively restrictive trade barriers. Conversely, countries such as Brazil, Haiti, Mexico, Peru, and Zambia have been world-beaters when it comes to import liberalization, but have a weak record on growth and poverty reduction. In short, many first-rate globalizers have fifth-rate records on poverty reduction.

The point here is not to replace an openness blueprint with a protectionist one. But surely we need to look more closely at such issues as the sequencing, pace, and structure of import liberalization. To the extent that any broad lessons emerge from East Asia, one of the most important appears to be that export liberalization and promotion were pursued both in advance of, and far more aggressively than, import liberalization.

The position of Latin America is striking. Governments in the region have liberalized imports far more rapidly than in any other region, turning their countries into models of trade openness. The returns in terms of poverty reduction have been abysmal. At the end of the 1990s, some 15 million more people were living below the $1 a day poverty line than in 1987, despite economic recovery. In much of Latin America, rapid import liberalization has been associated with further concentration of already extreme inequalities. For example, in Peru, the livelihoods of the rural poor have been adversely affected by surges of cheap—often subsidized—food imports, while large-scale commercial farms have the resources to take advantage of export opportunities. On the balance sheet of winners and losers from trade liberalization, the poor are all too frequently to be found on the wrong side of the ledger.

What Latin America demonstrates is that distribution does matter. To assert that, on average, the incomes of the poor rise on a one-to-one basis with economic growth is to miss the point. Countries with low levels of income inequality can expect to register far higher rates of poverty reduction than highly unequal countries. The reasons are obvious. If the poor account for only a small share of national income, the rate of poverty reduction will be far slower. A highly unequal country like Brazil has to grow at three times the rate of Vietnam to achieve the same average income increase among the poorest one-fifth of its population. In Uganda, the ratio of economic growth to poverty reduction was 1:1 in the first half of the 1990s, compared with 1:0.2 in Peru. While it is true that rising inequality can be counteracted by rapid growth—as in China—it also reduces the rate of poverty reduction.

What really matters for the debate on globalization is why some countries have been more successful than others in combining export growth with poverty reduction. Increasing the share of the poor in market-based growth requires strategies that range from land redistribution to investment in marketing infrastructure, improved access to education and health care, and measures to tackle corruption. It may also require policies that have become anathema in the "openness" era, including border protection for smallholder farmers and (on a selective and temporary basis) for infant industries, the restoration of basic labor rights, and minimum-wage protection.

The critical point is that openness in and of itself is not a poverty-reduction strategy. Poverty Reduction Strategy Papers (PRSPs), the documents prepared by governments entering IMF-World Bank programs, provide a real opportunity to develop a genuinely poverty-focused approach to trade policy. Unfortunately, that opportunity is being lost. Most PRSPs do little more than restate the familiar mantras on the benefits of openness, often with grave implications for poverty reduction. For instance, Cambodia's interim PRSP envisages rapid across-the-board import liberalization, with tariffs being lowered to an average of 5 percent even for sensitive agricultural products, such as rice. Yet, in a country where one-third of the population lives below the poverty line, it offers no assessment of the implications for rural poverty and income distribution, notwithstanding the fact that rice is the mainstay of the rural economy.

Selective Openness

In one respect, openness is a curious economic doctrine. Northern trade and finance ministries are among its most ardent exponents, especially when directing policy advice to poor countries. Yet when it comes to their home economies, the principles of free trade are honored more in the breach than in the observance. The underlying ethos is "do as we say, not as we do," which is not a constructive basis for more inclusive globalization.

The costs of northern protectionism to developing countries have been well documented. On a conservative estimate, they are losing $50 billion annually. When poor countries enter global markets, they face tariffs some four times higher, on average, in industrial countries than those faced by other industrial countries. The most punitive tariffs are to be found in precisely those areas—such as labor-intensive manufacturing and agriculture—where developing countries enjoy the strongest potential advantage. Nowhere are the double standards more staggering than in agriculture. While developing countries liberalize, industrial countries spend $1 billion a day subsidizing overproduction and export dumping, destroying on an epic scale the livelihoods of vulnerable smallholder farmers in the process. The beneficiaries of this jamboree are a handful of politically influential large-scale farmers, such as the grain barons of the Paris Basin and the peanut magnates of Georgia.

One analytical tool that throws some light on the extent of northern hypocrisy is the IMF's Trade Restrictiveness Index (TRI)—a scale of openness that ranks countries from 1 (completely open) to 10 (completely closed). The countries of the European Union and the United States and Japan measure 4 on the TRI. Meanwhile, countries as poor as Uganda, Peru, and Bolivia measure between 1 and 2.

Uneven liberalization is one of the reasons that industrial countries continue to capture the lion's share of the benefits from globalization. Developing countries are absorbing the costs of adjusting to more open trade regimes, while northern protectionism excludes them from market opportunities. Current approaches to IMF-World Bank loan conditionality are reinforcing this unequal trade bargain. It is certainly hard to imagine the governments of France or the United States accepting liberalization conditions in agriculture routinely applied in poor countries.

Toward a New Consensus

If we are to meet the challenge of poverty reduction, the sterile debate between "globaphobes" and "globaphiles" needs to be consigned to its proper place in the dustbin of the last decade of the old millennium. Governments, international financial institutions, and civil society need to engage in a real dialogue over how to make globalization work as a more powerful force for poverty reduction and social justice. At a national level, trade policy has to be brought into the mainstream of national strategies for poverty reduction and redistribution.

At the global level, northern governments need to do far more to create the conditions under which developing countries can capture a larger share of the benefits from trade. They could usefully start with a bonfire of tariff and nontariff measures applied to developing country exporters. But this is only a first requirement. At present, the rules of the multilateral trading system are designed to concentrate advantage in the rich world. The major beneficiaries of World Trade Organization agreements on intellectual property rights will be northern transnational companies, not the world's poor. Meanwhile, issues of vital concern to developing countries, such as the protracted crisis in commodity markets, do not even register on the global agenda. Making trade work for the poor requires rules that do something more than reflect the self-interest of the rich.

Response
David Dollar and Aart Kraay

Kevin Watkins's article, "Making Globalization Work for the Poor," contains much that is consistent with our article in *Finance & Development* (September 2001), which was based on our working paper, "Trade, Growth, and Poverty." We agree with Watkins that globaphobia is unjustified and that international trade, rather than causing more poverty and inequality, can be a powerful catalyst for poverty reduction by providing poor countries with access to the markets, technologies, and ideas they need for faster and more equitable growth. And, although it is not the subject of our paper, we do agree with Watkins's emphasis on the costs for poor countries of rich country protectionism—a view also expressed in the World Bank's *World Development Report 2000/2001: Attacking Poverty.*

Although there is much that we agree on, naturally we do not agree with Watkins's claim that our work is based on "dubious economics and a highly selective interpretation of data." Our research on the links between trade, growth, and poverty reduction was partly stimulated by the globaphobes' claims that increased flows of foreign trade and investment were making poor countries and the poor people in them worse off. We took these popular claims—as well as academic critiques of the evidence on trade and growth—seriously. Contrary to what some critics have been saying, we found that integration of poor countries with the global economy is associated with faster growth and poverty reduction. This does not mean that we subscribe to the simplistic view that "a renewed commitment to liberalization holds the key to making globalization work for the poor," as Watkins suggests. Rather, our finding is that increased participation in world trade, *together with good economic and social policies*, has worked well for a diverse group of poor countries. To quote from our paper,

> It would be naïve to assert that all of this improvement in growth should be attributed to the greater openness of these globalizing economies: all of them have been engaged in wide-ranging economic reforms....China, Hungary, India, and Vietnam...strengthened property rights and carried out other reforms....Virtually all of the Latin American countries included in the grouping stabilized high inflation and adjusted fiscally....(pp. 9–10)

Watkins criticizes our work on the grounds that our "implicit assumption is that trade liberalization is responsible for successful integration, with success in this case being defined as faster growth and poverty reduction." This is somewhat puzzling. To be clear, we define increased integration as a rise in the ratio of constant-price exports and imports to constant-price GDP, and we show that increased integration is associated with faster growth and poverty reduction. We also recognize explicitly, in our paper and in our *Finance & Development* article, that these changes in trade shares are only an imperfect proxy for measures of trade policy. Our only claim is that *changes* in trade shares are likely to be better proxies for *changes* in trade policy than *levels* of trade volumes are for *levels* of trade policy. It is also undeniable that some of the countries that have lowered trade barriers have not seen increases in trade and growth or a reduction of poverty; we recognize this in our paper. But this brings us back to another point on which we do agree with Watkins: "openness in and of itself is not a poverty-reduction strategy." We do not claim that it is. The evidence suggests that a more liberal trade regime is one part of a policy package for successful growth and poverty reduction.

Finally, Watkins argues that personal income inequality is widening worldwide and points to globalization as the main culprit. We disagree on both points. First, Watkins selectively cites just one estimate of an increase in the global Gini coefficient of 3 points between 1988 and 1993. But other estimates, including our own, which are cited in the *Finance & Development* article, show either little change in inequality between the 1980s and 1990s or even a modest decline. And, as discussed in our article, given the vast measurement problems one encounters in constructing such estimates, none of these small changes in either direction over relatively short periods is likely to be statistically robust. In our view, what can be said robustly about global inequality is that it clearly rose between 1820 and 1980 and then stabilized, with perhaps a modest decline, afterwards. Similarly, concerning extreme poverty —the term used to characterize those living on less than $1 a day—the number of poor people continued to climb historically, until about 1980. Since 1980, the number of poor people has declined by an estimated 200 million.

Second, the experience of the countries we identify as globalizers has in fact been a force for reduced global inequality since 1980. The vast majority of the world's poor in 1980 lived in China, India, and a few other poor Asian countries, such as Bangladesh and Vietnam. Rapid growth in these countries has narrowed the gap in living standards relative to the developed world for a large fraction of the world's population, and all of these countries have reduced poverty significantly as they have integrated with the global economy. Their success makes a mockery of the extreme claims of the antiglobalization movement.

17. Sweatshops, Choice, and Exploitation[*]

Matthew Zwolinski

1. Introduction

For the most part, individuals who work in sweatshops choose to do so.[1] They might not *like* working in sweatshops, and they might strongly desire that their circumstances were such that they did not have to do so. Nevertheless, the fact that they choose to work in sweatshops is morally significant. Taken seriously, workers' consent to the conditions of their labor should lead us to abandon certain moral objections to sweatshops, and perhaps even to view them as, on net, a good thing.

---

[*] Source: *Business Ethics Quarterly* 17.4 (2007): 689–727. Note: This reading is not identical to the original published version. It was edited by the volume editor, after publication in the *Business Ethics Quarterly*, because of space limitations in the current volume. The author's argument and conclusion have not been altered. The full article can be located at DOI: 10.5840/beq20071745.

[1] Definitions of "sweatshop" vary. Arnold and Hartman (2006) define a sweatshop as "any workplace in which workers are typically subject to two or more of the following conditions: income for a 48 hour workweek less than the overall poverty rate for that country; systematic forced overtime; systematic health and safety risks due to negligence or the willful disregard of employee welfare; coercion; systematic deception that places workers at risk; and underpayment of earnings." Similarly, the US General Accounting Office defines a sweatshop as a business that "regularly violates both wage or child labor and safety or health laws" (US General Accounting Office, 1988). Both of these definitions have merit insofar as they detail the specific kinds of offenses for which sweatshops are generally criticized. But both are, I think, parasitic on a more fundamental *moral* judgment—that a sweatshop is a business that is doing something *wrong*. The boundaries of this moral judgment are fuzzy—sometimes it might take two types of offense to qualify as a sweatshop, sometimes fewer or more. But when we label something a sweatshop, I believe we are making at least a *prima facie* moral judgment about that entity—that it is behaving in a way that it ought not to behave. See Zwolinski, 2006. The drawback of this approach is that it runs the risk of skirting the substantive debate over the morality of sweatshops by definition. To avoid this, I propose that we define them as industries which violate labor standards (either host-country legal standards or standards defined by international norms) in some of the ways described above in a way which makes their actions *prima facie* wrong. Low wages and psychological coercion appear to be wrongful business practices, but our definition of sweatshop should be open to the possibility that they will be proven not to be so, at least in some cases. For purposes of this essay, I will be interested exclusively in sweatshops in the developing world, and will draw a distinction between sweatshops—which tend to be legally recognized, above-ground businesses, even if some of their specific practices may be illegal or immoral—and the informal sector of the economy,

This argument, or something like it, is the core of a number of popular and academic defenses of the moral legitimacy of sweatshops. It has been especially influential among economists, who point to the voluntary nature of sweatshop employment as evidence for the claim that Western governments ought not to restrict the importation of goods made by sweatshops (Anderson, 1996, p. 694), or that labor-rights organizations ought not to seek to change the law in countries which host sweatshops in order to establish higher minimum wages or better working conditions (Krugman, 1997; Maitland, 1996), or, finally, that consumer boycotts of sweatshop-produced goods are misguided (Kristof & Wudunn, 2000).

This paper seeks to defend a version of the argument above, while at the same time clarifying its structure and content.... My position ... is that there is a strong moral reason for third parties such as consumers and host- and home-country governments to refrain from acting in ways which are likely to deprive sweatshop workers of their jobs, and that both the policies traditionally promoted by anti-sweatshop activists (e.g., increasing the legal regulation of sweatshops, legally prohibiting the sale of sweatshop-produced goods, or subjecting such goods to economic boycott), and some more recent proposals by anti-sweatshop academics (i.e., voluntary self-regulation via industry-wide standards or universal moral norms) are subject to criticism on these grounds.[2] ...

2. The Argument

1. Most sweatshop workers choose to accept the conditions of their employment, even if their choice is made from among a severely constrained set of options.[3]
2. The fact that they choose the conditions of their employment from within a constrained set of options is strong evidence that they view it as their most-preferred option (within that set).

---

where many of the same practices which occur in sweatshops may occur, but in which enterprises lack the official legal standing that sweatshops have. There are moral debates to be had over the treatment of workers in the informal sector, but the debate over sweatshops has tended to view this sector as an *alternative* to sweatshop labor, and one which does not share the direct connection to questions regarding the responsibilities of MNEs (multi-national enterprises). I therefore limit my discussion in this paper to sweatshops as an aspect of the formal economy.

2 For a clearer statement of the sorts of interference my argument seeks to criticize, see the next section of this paper.

3 Many philosophers, myself included, find this severely constrained set of options objectionable. For the purposes of this paper, however, I am treating sweatshops as a somewhat isolated moral phenomenon. That is, I am asking what we should do about sweatshops, while holding most of the other conditions of the world (large inequalities of wealth among nations, severe poverty in the developing world, and a growing system of global capitalism) constant. I hold them constant not because I think they are good things, nor because I think that we ought to do nothing about them, but because this seems to me the only way to make any progress on an issue that is pressing and cannot wait for the resolution of these other problems. Poverty, inequality, and economic development all need to be addressed. My paper seeks to tell us what we should do about sweatshops in the meantime.

3. The fact that they view it as their most-preferred option is strong evidence that we will harm them by taking that option away.
4. It is also plausible that sweatshop workers' choice to accept the conditions of their employment is sufficiently autonomous that taking the option of sweatshop labor away from them would be a violation of their autonomy.
5. All else being equal, it is wrong to harm people or to violate their autonomy.
6. Therefore, all else being equal, it is wrong to take away the option of sweatshop labor from workers who would otherwise choose to engage in it.

I believe this argument (hereafter, "The Argument") captures and clarifies what lies behind many popular defenses of sweatshops. There are three things to note about it. The first is that, unlike popular defenses, The Argument clearly distinguishes two different ways in which workers' choices can serve to establish a claim of non-interference against those who act in ways that make sweatshop labor a non-option—one based in respect for workers' autonomy (1, 4, 5, and 6) and another based in an obligation not to harm (1, 2, 3, 5, and 6). Unlike the standard economic defense of sweatshops, then, The Argument is not purely consequentialist in nature. Appeals to consequences are relevant in The Argument's appeal to the preference-evincing power of choice, which cautions us to avoid harming workers by frustrating their revealed preferences.[4] But The Argument has a deontological foundation as well, which is brought out in its notion of autonomy-exercising choice. Here, The Argument counsels us to refrain from interfering in sweatshop workers' choices, not because that interference would frustrate preference-satisfaction, but because doing so would violate workers' autonomy in their choice of employment.

The second thing to note about The Argument is that, again unlike popular defenses, it is clear regarding the nature of the moral transformation that sweatshop workers' choices effect. Their choice establishes a claim of non-interference against those who might wish to prevent them from engaging in sweatshop labor, or make that labor more difficult to obtain. That is all that is claimed by The Argument. It does not attempt to show that workers' choices render the treatment bestowed on them by their employers morally praiseworthy. It does not even attempt to show

---

4 Note that while this argument relies on considerations that are consequentialist in nature, it does not necessarily rely on a classically utilitarian formulation of consequentialism. My own view, in fact, is that to the extent consequentialist considerations are relevant, they are probably more prioritarian in form than strictly aggregationalist. In other words, we have a duty to promote good consequences, but that duty is especially weighty with regards to the worst-off. This makes the issue of sweatshops especially pressing. Minimum wage laws in a country like the United States might have some of the same unemployment effects as regulations on sweatshops in the developing world. But the people put out of work by regulations in the developing world are in a much worse position both antecedently and subsequent to regulation, and so our moral duty to protect them from harm is both more urgent, and more significant relative to other moral obligations that we might have.

that their choice renders such treatment morally *permissible*.[5] And, finally, it does not establish an *insuperable* claim against interference. The Argument shows that harming sweatshop workers or violating their autonomy is wrong, but leaves open the possibility that these wrongs could be justifiable in certain circumstances. The Argument simply shifts the burden of proof onto those who wish to prohibit sweatshop labor to provide such justification.

The final thing to note about The Argument is that its success is extremely sensitive to a wide range of empirical facts. The truth of premise 1, for instance, hinges on whether people *do* in fact choose to work in sweatshops, and fails in cases of genuinely forced labor. The claim that we harm sweatshop workers by removing what they see as their best option (premise 3) depends on particular facts about the nature of an individual's preferences and their relation to her well-being, and the claim that workers' choices are autonomous (premise 4) depends on the particular conditions under which the choice to accept sweatshop labor is made. This sensitivity to empirical facts means that we cannot determine *a priori* whether The Argument is successful. But this is as it should be. Sweatshops are a complicated phenomenon, and while philosophers have an important contribution to make to the conversation about their moral justifiability, it is only a partial contribution. For the complete picture, we need to supplement our moral theorizing with data from (at least) economists, psychologists, and social scientists. In this paper, I will draw on empirical data to support my argument where it is available. Since I am not well positioned to evaluate the soundness of such data, however, I will attempt to clearly signal when I appeal to it, and to indicate the way in which The Argument's success is or is not reliant on its veracity.

3. What Policies Does The Argument Oppose?

The Argument's conclusion is that it is wrong to "take away" the option of sweatshop labor from those who would otherwise choose to engage in it. But what exactly does it mean to take away the option of sweatshop labor? What sort of policies is The Argument meant to oppose?

a. Bans and Boycotts

The most obvious way in which the option of sweatshop labor can be "taken away" is a legal ban on sweatshops or, more commonly, on the sale or importation of sweatshop-produced goods. The mechanism by which the former sort of ban removes the option of sweatshop labor is fairly obvious. But bans on the sale or importation of sweatshop goods can, if effective and large enough in scale, achieve the same results. If goods made in sweatshops cannot be sold, then it seems likely that sweatshops will

---

5 The ways in which sweatshops treat their employees might be morally repugnant and absolutely impermissible. But this is not enough to establish that it is morally permissible for third parties to interfere.

stop producing such goods, and those who were employed in their production will be out of work.[6] Economists and others have therefore criticized such bans as counterproductive in the quest to aid the working poor.[7] As a result, neither sort of ban is defended by many anti-sweatshop scholars writing today, but many activists and politicians persist in their support of such measures.[8] The Argument condemns them.

b. Legal Regulation

Bans on the importation or sale of sweatshop-produced goods take sweatshop jobs away from their workers by making their continued employment no longer economically viable for their employers. The increased legal regulation of sweatshops can accomplish the same effect for the same reason. Legal attempts to ameliorate working conditions in sweatshops by regulating the use of and pay for overtime, minimum wage laws, or workplace safety, for instance, raise the cost which sweatshops must incur to employ their workers. This cost is passed on to the MNE which, in turn, might decide once costs have passed a certain level, to move their operations to another country where labor is more productive or less heavily regulated.[9]

---

6   This is, of course, an empirical claim. It is at least logically possible that sweatshops will respond to boycotts by ceasing to engage in immoral behavior without negatively affecting employment. My argument against boycotts proceeds on the assumption, which I cannot defend here, that the outcome described in the main body of the paper is a significantly likely (though not certain) one.

7   Ian Maitland, for instance, argues in his seminal paper on sweatshops that "attempts to improve on market outcomes" with regard to sweatshop wages, such as boycotts or legal regulation, can yield "unforeseen tragic consequences" (Maitland, 1996, p. 604). Similarly, Powell (2006) argues that "many of the means chosen by [anti-sweatshop] activists will not promote the ends of more ethical treatment of workers."

8   The National Labor Committee, for instance, promotes on the main page of its website a bill pending in the US Congress (S. 3485 and H.5635) which would ban the import, export, or sale of sweatshop goods in the United States (National Labor Committee, 2006). See also in this vein Bernstein (2002), which discusses the launching of the Campaign for the Abolition of Sweatshops and Child Labor and quotes Georgetown law professor Robert Stumberg as noting that "measures against sweatshops being considered include bans on such imports, forced disclosure of factories where imported goods are made, and bans on government purchases of sweatshop goods." Finally, see the statement of the organization "Scholars Against Sweatshops" (SASL, 2001). This 2001 document signed by over 350 economists and other academics, calls both for the adoption of codes of conduct by universities which would restrict the sorts of apparel companies with which they could do business, and for stricter legal and economic regulations in countries that host sweatshops. In response to those who worry that such restrictive measures might harm the very sweatshop workers they seek to benefit, the authors reassure us "the *aim* of the anti-sweatshop movement is obviously not to induce negative *unintended* consequences such as higher overall unemployment in developing countries" (page 3, emphasis added). For obvious reasons, this seems to miss the point.

9   Again, these are empirical speculations which, though reasonably supported by economic theory, cannot be defended in this paper. If my empirical assumptions turn out to be false, then the consequentialist case against the legal regulation of sweatshops is significantly weakened, though one could still argue that the regulations impermissibly interfere in workers' freedom to enter into what they believe to be mutually beneficial contractual arrangements.

Calls for the increased legal regulation of sweatshops are more common among both activists and academics alike.[10] It is worth noting, though, that calls for the increased enforcement of existing regulations are likely to be indistinguishable in their effects. Many laws in the developing world which ostensibly regulate sweatshop activity are either poorly enforced or completely ignored.[11] Sometimes the lack of enforcement is simply due to insufficient resources on the part of the enforcement agency. But sometimes it is a deliberate choice, since government officials want the tax revenue that MNEs bring to the country and worry that increasing the cost of doing business could lead those MNEs to stay away or leave. Calls for the enforcement of existing regulations do have the advantage over calls for new regulation in that such enforcement will help to promote the rule of law—a key value in both economic development and a healthy democracy.[12] But in terms of their effect on workers' jobs, they are equally bad, and equally opposed by The Argument.

c. Voluntary Self-Regulation

Today, many of the most prominent academic critics of sweatshops focus their energy on calls for voluntary self-regulation on the part of sweatshops. Their hope is that self-regulation can correct the moral failings of sweatshops while at the same time avoiding the unintended harms caused by the more heavy-handed attempts described above.

Nothing in The Argument is opposed to voluntary self-regulation as such. If, as The Argument was specifically formulated to allow, many of the activities of sweatshops are immoral, then they ought to change, and voluntary self-regulation will often be the best way to accomplish this change.

Furthermore, by providing concrete examples of "positive deviancy"—cases where multinational enterprises have made changes to improve conditions for workers in their supply chain above and beyond those required by market pressures or

---

10 See, for instance, the references in footnote 8. Additionally, Hartman et al. claim that "because market transactions cannot be relied upon as a basis of avoiding rights violations, the protection of rights must come from the imposition of governmental controls or an effective realignment of consumer choice criteria" (Hartman, Shaw, & Stevenson, 2003, p. 214). Along similar lines, Jan Murray claims that while many anti-sweatshop academics have begun to focus on voluntary corporate self-regulation, it would be "counterproductive to suggest that firms can be seen as the *sole* implementers of the core labor standards, so from both a theoretical and practical perspective it is necessary to see corporate efforts as part of a regulatory continuum" involving both legal regulation, industry-wide standards, and self-regulation by individual firms (Murray, 2003, p. 38, emphasis added).

11 See D. Arnold & Hartman (2006, section IV.A) for a discussion of this phenomenon with specific examples.

12 See, for instance, D.G. Arnold & Bowie (2003, section III), which does not explicitly call for governments to increase their enforcement of existing laws, but does call for MNEs to ensure that their contractors are complying with those laws regardless of enforcement.

the law—much of the recent scholarship on self-regulation has provided a valuable model for firms who wish to begin making changes in the right direction.[13]

There are, however, two significant causes for concern over the precise way in which the case for self-regulation has been made in the recent literature. First, to the extent that "voluntary" self-regulation is to be accomplished by industry-wide standards, the regulation is really only voluntary for the industry as a whole.[14] For any individual firm, compliance is essentially mandatory. Individual firms, then, are in much the same position as they would be under legal regulation, insofar as those who cannot afford to comply with the mandated standard would be forced to cut costs or alter their production in a way that could negatively affect the employment of sweatshop workers. Additionally, industry-wide standards serve as an impediment to the market's discovery process. By establishing *one* standard with which all firms must comply, this sort of approach discourages (and in some cases, prohibits) individual firms from experimenting with their own standards which might be better suited to the particular context in which they are operating.[15]

The second and less well-recognized problem is that by making the case for self-regulation in terms of the *rights* workers have to certain forms of treatment and the *obligations* that MNEs have to ensure such treatment, supporters of "voluntary" self-regulation end up putting too strong a demand on MNEs for the kind of reform they desire, while paying insufficient attention to ways of helping workers that fall short of their desired goal.

...Labor which falls short of a living wage can still help a worker feed their family, educate their children, and generally make their lives better than they would have been without it. This is a morally significant benefit, and one our system of moral norms should at the very least *permit*, if not encourage.

Thus, while The Argument does not condemn voluntary self-regulation as such, it *does* condemn the claim that outsourcing labor to the developing world is only permissible if certain minimum standards are met. For we cannot simply assume that MNEs will continue to outsource labor to the developing world if the only conditions under which they may permissibly do so are ones in which the costs of outsourced labor are significantly higher than they are now.[16] And without this assumption,

---

13 See, for instance, D. Arnold & Hartman (2006) and D. Arnold, Hartman, & Wokutch (2003).

14 Such industry-wide standards are often preferred by anti-sweatshop academics for a variety of reasons having to do with compliance and cost-sharing. See, generally, D. Arnold, Hartman, & Wokutch (2003) and, specifically, D. Arnold & Hartman (2006, p. 696)

15 See Powell (2006, section iv). His point, as I take it, is based on the logic of incentives rather than an inductive survey of empirical data. In Hayekian terms, industry-wide standards have the potential to stifle the market's ability to serve as a "discovery process," finding new ways to utilize scarce resources and scattered knowledge to improve human well-being. See Hayek (1968).

16 Sometimes the advocates of voluntary reform write as though this could be assumed. Bowie and Arnold, for instance, write that "our contention is that it is economically feasible for MNEs

our system of moral norms ought not to prohibit MNEs from outsourcing labor in a way which falls short of meeting Arnold's standards, for to do so would be to deprive workers of the ability to engage in labor they would freely choose to accept, and thereby frustrate workers' choices and harm the very people we intended to help.

4. [A Challenge] to The Argument

[...]

c. Exploitation

One of the more common charges against sweatshops is that they exploit their workers. Such a charge, if true, might undermine our confidence in The Argument's conclusion by drawing our attention to a moral consideration ignored by the argument. But much depends on how we understand the concept of exploitation. Sometimes we use the term to refer to certain cases where *A* harms *B* and *A* benefits as a result.... [But] a proper understanding of exploitation will make room for mutually advantageous, as well as harmful, exploitative transactions.[17]

In what ways might mutually beneficial transactions be wrongfully exploitative? There are various ways in which such a claim might be spelled out. One way is to say that [a mutually beneficial transaction] is exploitative insofar as [its] benefits are unfairly distributed in some way.[18] Any mutually beneficial exchange will be a positive-sum game, due to the differences in the values each party assigns to the objects of the exchange. In other words, mutually beneficial exchanges will create a *social surplus*—an amount of utility greater than that which existed prior to the exchange. But the way in which this social surplus is divided depends largely on the bargaining skill and position of the parties. One way of framing the claim that exchanges are exploitative, even if mutually beneficial, is thus to say that even though they benefit both parties, they do not benefit one of them *enough*.[19] ... To

to voluntarily raise wages in factories in developing economies without causing increases in unemployment. MNEs may choose to raise wages while maintaining existing employment levels. Increased labor costs that are not offset by greater productivity may be passed on to consumers, or, if necessary, absorbed through internal cost cutting measures such as reductions in executive compensation" (D.G. Arnold & Bowie, 2003, p. 239). For a thorough economic critique of this assumption, see Powell (2006, especially section iii). As a point of mere logic, however, the fact that some MNEs have managed to raise benefits without (visibly) reducing employment is hardly a good indicator that employment will not be reduced if *all* MNEs are placed under a moral obligation to raise benefits.

17 On this point, see Wertheimer (1996, chapter one).

18 This is essentially the approach taken by Chris Meyers (2004, p. 320). Meyers argues that A's act toward B can be exploitative even if it benefits B, if it involves A's unfairly taking advantage of B, A's benefiting from B's misfortune, and A's benefiting disproportionately relative to A's contribution.

19 Chris Meyers denies that his account can be characterized in this way (Meyers, 2004, pp. 326-27). On his account, the wrong of exploitation derives not from a failure to benefit the exploitee enough, but from the taking advantage of their desperate situation and from benefiting disproportionately from their contribution. I agree that failure to benefit enough is not the *only* condition necessary

determine whether a mutually beneficial exchange is exploitative, we must compare the gains made by the parties not (necessarily) to the baseline of no-exchange-at-all, but rather to the baseline in which each party acts within their rights with respect to the other, and ensure that parties are left at least as well off as they would be under *those* circumstances.[20]

There are several ways in which concerns about exploitation might be relevant to an assessment of The Argument. The first has to do with the wages paid to sweatshop laborers.…

If sweatshops have an obligation to pay a living wage to sweatshop workers, or if they have an obligation to pay a wage which fairly divides the social surplus derived from the labor arrangement, then those who pay a wage below this level might be guilty of exploitation even if the worker benefits from the job relative to a baseline of no job at all. They might be guilty of exploitation because they are taking advantage of workers' vulnerability (their lack of better available options) in order to obtain agreement to an unjust wage contract.…

Part of what we would need to do, then, in order to resolve the question of whether sweatshop wages are exploitative, is to develop a theory of just wages. I am not convinced that such a task is possible, and it is certainly not one I can hope to engage in here. For the sake of argument, however, let us assume that some such principle can be specified, and see what conclusions this supposition leads us to in the case of sweatshop labor.

It is important to begin this discussion by noting that the bulk of the empirical data suggest that wages paid by sweatshops are significantly higher than those paid by potential workers' other possible sources of employment. Aitken et al., for instance, show that wages paid by multinational firms are generally higher than wages paid by domestic firms in developing nations,[21] a fact which was cited by the Academic Consortium on International Trade (ACIT) in support of their claim that universities should exercise caution before signing on to Codes of Conduct that might have the effect of reducing American clothing firms use of labor in developing countries.[22] Furthermore, recent research has shown that sweatshop wages are higher regardless of whether they are paid by multinational firms or by domestic subcontractors—3 to 7 times as high as the national income in the Dominican Republic, Haiti, Honduras, and

---

for an act to be exploitative. But insofar as Meyers' account relies on the notion of "disproportionate benefit," he seems committed to saying that *part* of what is wrong with exploitation is that it fails to benefit the exploitee enough. After all, it is presumably not merely A's benefiting a lot from his interaction with B to which Meyers objects, but the fact that A does not share enough of that benefit with B—*i.e.*, that A does not benefit B enough.

20 Thus, unlike Meyers (2004, p. 321), I do not think that we can analyze the unfairness of exploitation without an appeal to rights. A full theory of exploitation, then, would require a full theory of rights, which I obviously cannot hope to provide here. I have thus crafted The Argument in such a way as to remain as neutral as possible between competing conceptions of rights.

21 Aitken, Harrison, & Lipsey (1996).

22 ACIT (2000). Brown, Deardorff, & Stern (2004) reach similar conclusions.

Nicaragua, for example.[23] And if anything, these data probably tend to understate the extent to which sweatshop laborers out-earn other individuals in the developing world, as many of those other individuals work in either agriculture or the "informal economy," where wages (and other benefits) tend to be much lower, but numbers for which are not accounted for in the standard economic statistics.[24] Of course, these facts, by themselves, do not refute the charge of exploitation, since it is possible that while sweatshop wages are higher than wages earned by non-sweatshop laborers, the wages still represent an unfair division of the cooperative surplus generated by the employment arrangement. Perhaps sweatshops are taking advantage of the low wages paid by domestic industries in the developing world to reap exploitative profits by paying wages that are high enough to attract workers, but much lower than the firm could afford if they were willing to settle for a more reasonable level of profit. Resolving this question would require, in addition to a moral theory of just wages, an examination of the rate of profit made by MNEs who outsource the manufacture of products to third world sweatshops, compared with the profit-rates of non-outsourcing firms in the same industry, and firms in relevantly similar industries. If the profit rates of sweatshop-employing MNEs are significantly higher than other firms in the relevant comparison class, this would be some evidence for the claim that they are unfairly exploiting their workers.[25]

For now, however, I want to leave the full resolution of these empirical questions to the economists, and return to an analysis of the concept of "exploitation."[26] Suppose it turns out to be true that MNEs are earning an unusually high rate of profit from their use of sweatshop labor—high enough that they could afford to pay significantly higher wages without putting the firm at risk.[27] Such firms could be said to be taking advantage of workers' vulnerability to benefit disproportionately from their labor agreements. Are they guilty of an objectionable form of exploitation? Are they acting in a blameworthy manner?

23 Powell & Skarbek (2006).

24 Maitland (1996).

25 Whether the absence of unusually high profit margins would constitute evidence *against* the exploitation thesis depends on the precise content of the correct theory of just wages/profits. Even if profits in sweatshop-employing MNEs are not any higher than profits in any other industry, it might still be the case that sweatshop wages are exploitative, if we define an exploitative wage/profit relationship in terms independent of and more demanding than market competitiveness.

26 My purpose in doing so is not to dismiss the importance of these empirical questions. Indeed, as I note in section 3, the soundness of The Argument cannot be fully assessed without settling precisely these sorts of questions. As a philosopher, however, I can do no more here than report the most recent relevant data and analyses provided by others better suited to that task.

27 This argument seems to presuppose that there is considerable slack in the market for international labor. I have not seen any evidence to indicate that this is actually the case, and it strikes me as a rather implausible claim when made about the market for such labor *generally*. See Powell (2006) for a more thorough examination of this issue. Nevertheless, I am interested in seeing what follows morally, if the claim turns out to be true.

There is something rather odd about saying that they are. Recall that the form of exploitation with which we are concerned here is mutually advantageous exploitation. The charge against firms is not that they are *harming* workers, but that the benefit they gain from the transaction is disproportionate to that gained by the workers. But the firms are doing *something* to help. The wages they pay to workers make those workers better off than they used to be—even if it is not as well-off as we think they ought to be made.

Do they have an obligation to do more? Consider the fact that most individuals do *nothing* to make Third-World workers better off. Are *they* blameworthy? As blameworthy as sweatshops? We need not suppose that such individuals do *nothing* charitable. Perhaps they spend their resources helping local causes, or global causes other than poverty-relief. My point is that it would be odd to blame MNEs for helping *some* when we blame individuals less (or not at all) for helping *none*.[28]

The same point can be made comparing MNEs that outsource to Third-World sweatshops with businesses that do not. Take, for example, a US firm which could outsource production to the Third World, but chooses to produce domestically instead. Let us suppose that the firm, *qua* firm, does not donate any of its profits to the cause of Third-World poverty relief. Is such a firm blameworthy? Again, it would be odd to say that it was innocent, or *less* guilty than MNEs that outsource to sweatshops, when the latter does *something* to make workers in the Third World better off, while the former does *nothing*. Yet firms which do nothing in this way draw nothing like the ire drawn by firms which contract with sweatshops. This seems to suggest an incoherence between our understanding of the wrongfulness of exploitative wage agreements and our other moral judgments about duties to aid.

This same incoherence can be gotten at from a different direction. Sweatshops make the people who work for them better off.[29] But there are a lot of people who are *not* made better off by sweatshops. They are not necessarily *harmed* by them; their position is simply unaffected one way or the other. Anyone who works in agriculture, for instance, or in the informal sector of the economy, will not benefit (directly) from the wages paid by sweatshops. Such individuals lack the skill or the opportunity to take advantage of the benefits that sweatshop labor offers. As a result, they tend to be much worse off in monetary terms than sweatshop workers. To illustrate: Ian Maitland notes that in 1996, workers in Nike's Indonesian plant in Serang earned the legal minimum wage of 5,200 rupiahs per day. By contrast, the

---

28 Sollars & Englander (2007, p. 119) make a similar point. Actually, individual persons are probably the wrong comparison class. After all, for all we know, the individual persons who compose the MNEs under consideration do quite a bit, *qua* individuals, to help relieve poverty in the Third World. Perhaps they send a substantial portion of the dividend checks they receive from their stock holdings in the firm to OXFAM.

29 At least, those which we are considering in the context of arguments regarding mutually beneficial exploitation do.

typical agricultural worker earned only 2,000 rupiahs per day.[30] Yet, most people do not fault Nike for doing *nothing* to improve the position of agricultural workers. Why, then, should they be faulted for doing *something* to improve the position of (some) urban workers?

The problem, then, is this. We criticize a firm for failing to benefit a certain group of individuals sufficiently, even though it benefits that group a little. But we do not fault other firms for failing to benefit that group at all, and we do not fault the firm in question for failing to benefit other, possibly much worse-off groups, at all. What could justify this seeming disparity in our moral judgments?[31] ...

Bibliography

ACIT. 2000. ACIT Letter to University Presidents. Available at http://www.ford-school.unuch.eclu/rsie/acit/Documents/July29SweatshopLetter.pdf.

Aitken, B., Harrison, A., & Lipsey, R. 1996. Wages and foreign ownership: A comparative study of Mexico, Venezuela, and the United States. *Journal of International Economics*, 40: 345-71.

Anderson, W. 1996. Kathie Lee's children. *The Free Market*, 14. http://www.niises.org/freemarket_detail.asp?control=45&sortorder=articledate.

Arnold, D.G., & Bowie, N.E. 2003. Sweatshops and respect for persons. *Business Ethics Quarterly* 13: 221-42.

Arnold, D.G., & Hartman, L. 2006. Worker rights and low wage industrialization: How to avoid sweatshops. *Human Rights Quarterly* 28: 676-700.

Arnold, D.G., Hartman, L., & Wokutch, R.E. 2003. *Rising above sweatshops: Innovative approaches to global labor challenges*. Westport, CT: Praeger.

Bernstein, A. 2002. Remember sweatshops? *Business Week*, September 30. http://www.businessweek.com/magazine/content/02_39/c3801015.htm#B3801017.

Hartman, L., Shaw, B., & Stevenson, R. 2003. Exploring the ethics and economics of global labor standards: A challenge to integrated social contract theory. *Business Ethics Quarterly* 13: 193-220.

Kristof, N.D., & Wudunn, S. 2000. Two cheers for sweatshops. *The New York Times*, September 24. http://www.nytimes.com/library/magazine/home/20000924mag-sweatshops.html.

---

30 Maitland (1996, p. 599).

31 The argument above is, of course, a kind of incoherence argument, and as such it leaves its target with an option regarding how to respond. One might respond, as I am inclined to do, by denying that sweatshops are acting wrongly in failing to pay higher wages to their workers. Or one might respond that *everyone else* is acting wrongly by not benefiting workers in the developing world at all. Actually, I'm inclined to believe that there is something to this latter response as well. My point here is merely that it seems wrong to say that sweatshops are acting *especially* wrong by failing to provide their workers with a (greater) benefit. If there is a moral duty to aid the world's poor, it is one which binds all of us, not just MNEs and the sweatshops with which they contract.

Krugman, P. 1997. In praise of cheap labor. *Slate*, March 21. http://www.slate.com/id/1918.

Maitland, I. 1996. The great non-debate over international sweatshops. In T.L. Beauchamp & N.E. Bowie (Eds.), *Ethical Theory and Business* (6th ed.): 593-605. Englewood Cliffs, NJ: Prentice Hall.

Meyers, C. 2004. Wrongful beneficence: Exploitation and third world sweatshops. *Journal of Social Philosophy*, 35: 319-33.

Murray, J. 2003. The global context: Multinational enterprises, labor standards, and regulation. In Arnold, Hartman, & Wokutch 2003: 27-48.

National Labor Committee. 2006. Support grows for anti-sweatshop legislation. Available at http://www.nlcnet.org/live/article.php?id=120. Accessed September 19, 2006.

Powell, B. 2006. In reply to sweatshop sophistries. *Human Rights Quarterly* 28: 1031-42.

Powell, B., & Skarbek, D. 2006. Sweatshops and third world living standards: Are the jobs worth the sweat? *Journal of Labor Research* 27: 263-74.

SASL. 2001. Scholars Against Sweatshop Labor Statement. Available at http://www.peri.umass.edu/SASL-Statement.253.0.html. Accessed September 12, 2006.

US General Accounting Office, H.R.D. 1988. Sweatshops in the US: Opinions on their extent and possible enforcement options. Washington, DC.

Wertheimer, A. 1996. *Exploitation*. Princeton, NJ: Princeton UP.

Zwolinski, M. 2006. Sweatshops. In J. Ciment (Ed.), *Social issues encyclopedia*. New York: M.E. Sharpe.

18. Jihad vs. McWorld*

Benjamin R. Barber

Just beyond the horizon of current events lie two possible political futures—both bleak, neither democratic. The first is a retribalization of large swaths of humankind by war and bloodshed: a threatened Lebanonization of national states in which culture is pitted against culture, people against people, tribe against tribe—a Jihad in the name of a hundred narrowly conceived faiths against every kind of inter-dependence, every kind of artificial social cooperation and civic mutuality. The second is being borne in on us by the onrush of economic and ecological forces that demand integration and uniformity and that mesmerize the world with fast music, fast computers, and fast food—with MTV, Macintosh, and McDonald's, pressing nations into one commercially homogenous global network: one McWorld tied together by technology, ecology, communications, and commerce. The planet is fall-ing precipitantly apart *AND* coming reluctantly together at the very same moment.

These two tendencies are sometimes visible in the same countries at the same instant: thus Yugoslavia, clamoring just recently to join the New Europe, is explod-ing into fragments; India is trying to live up to its reputation as the world's larg-est integral democracy while powerful new fundamentalist parties like the Hindu nationalist Bharatiya Janata Party, along with nationalist assassins, are imperiling its hard-won unity. States are breaking up or joining up: the Soviet Union has dis-appeared almost overnight, its parts forming new unions with one another or with like-minded nationalities in neighboring states. The old interwar national state based on territory and political sovereignty looks to be a mere transitional development.

The tendencies of what I am here calling the forces of Jihad and the forces of McWorld operate with equal strength in opposite directions, the one driven by parochial hatreds, the other by universalizing markets, the one re-creating ancient subnational and ethnic borders from within, the other making national borders

---

* Source: *The Atlantic*, March 1992, <http://www.theatlantic.com/magazine/archive/1992/03/jihad-vs-mcworld/3882/>.

porous from without. They have one thing in common: neither offers much hope to citizens looking for practical ways to govern themselves democratically. If the global future is to pit Jihad's centrifugal whirlwind against McWorld's centripetal black hole, the outcome is unlikely to be democratic—or so I will argue.

McWorld, or the Globalization of Politics

Four imperatives make up the dynamic of McWorld: a market imperative, a resource imperative, an information-technology imperative, and an ecological imperative. By shrinking the world and diminishing the salience of national borders, these imperatives have in combination achieved a considerable victory over factiousness and particularism, and not least of all over their most virulent traditional form—nationalism. It is the realists who are now Europeans, the utopians who dream nostalgically of a resurgent England or Germany, perhaps even a resurgent Wales or Saxony. Yesterday's wishful cry for one world has yielded to the reality of McWorld.

THE MARKET IMPERATIVE. Marxist and Leninist theories of imperialism assumed that the quest for ever-expanding markets would in time compel nation-based capitalist economies to push against national boundaries in search of an international economic imperium. Whatever else has happened to the scientistic predictions of Marxism, in this domain they have proved farsighted. All national economies are now vulnerable to the inroads of larger, transnational markets within which trade is free, currencies are convertible, access to banking is open, and contracts are enforceable under law. In Europe, Asia, Africa, the South Pacific, and the Americas such markets are eroding national sovereignty and giving rise to entities—international banks, trade associations, transnational lobbies like OPEC and Greenpeace, world news services like CNN and the BBC, and multinational corporations that increasingly lack a meaningful national identity—that neither reflect nor respect nationhood as an organizing or regulative principle.

The market imperative has also reinforced the quest for international peace and stability, requisites of an efficient international economy. Markets are enemies of parochialism, isolation, fractiousness, war. Market psychology attenuates the psychology of ideological and religious cleavages and assumes a concord among producers and consumers—categories that ill fit narrowly conceived national or religious cultures. Shopping has little tolerance for blue laws, whether dictated by pub-closing British paternalism, Sabbath-observing Jewish Orthodox fundamentalism, or no-Sunday-liquor-sales Massachusetts puritanism. In the context of common markets, international law ceases to be a vision of justice and becomes a workaday framework for getting things done—enforcing contracts, ensuring that governments abide by deals, regulating trade and currency relations, and so forth.

Common markets demand a common language, as well as a common currency, and they produce common behaviors of the kind bred by cosmopolitan city life everywhere. Commercial pilots, computer programmers, international bankers, media specialists, oil riggers, entertainment celebrities, ecology experts, demographers, accountants, professors, athletes—these compose a new breed of men and women for whom religion, culture, and nationality can seem only marginal elements in a working identity. Although sociologists of everyday life will no doubt continue to distinguish a Japanese from an American mode, shopping has a common signature throughout the world. Cynics might even say that some of the recent revolutions in Eastern Europe have had as their true goal not liberty and the right to vote but well-paying jobs and the right to shop (although the vote is proving easier to acquire than consumer goods). The market imperative is, then, plenty powerful; but, notwithstanding some of the claims made for "democratic capitalism," it is not identical with the democratic imperative.

THE RESOURCE IMPERATIVE. Democrats once dreamed of societies whose political autonomy rested firmly on economic independence. The Athenians idealized what they called autarky, and tried for a while to create a way of life simple and austere enough to make the polis genuinely self-sufficient. To be free meant to be independent of any other community or polis. Not even the Athenians were able to achieve autarky, however: human nature, it turns out, is dependency. By the time of Pericles, Athenian politics was inextricably bound up with a flowering empire held together by naval power and commerce—an empire that, even as it appeared to enhance Athenian might, ate away at Athenian independence and autarky. Master and slave, it turned out, were bound together by mutual insufficiency.

The dream of autarky briefly engrossed nineteenth-century America as well, for the underpopulated, endlessly bountiful land, the cornucopia of natural resources, and the natural barriers of a continent walled in by two great seas led many to believe that America could be a world unto itself. Given this past, it has been harder for Americans than for most to accept the inevitability of interdependence. But the rapid depletion of resources even in a country like ours, where they once seemed inexhaustible, and the maldistribution of arable soil and mineral resources on the planet, leave even the wealthiest societies ever more resource-dependent and many other nations in permanently desperate straits.

Every nation, it turns out, needs something another nation has; some nations have almost nothing they need.

THE INFORMATION-TECHNOLOGY IMPERATIVE. Enlightenment science and the technologies derived from it are inherently universalizing. They entail a quest for descriptive principles of general application, a search for universal solutions to particular problems, and an unswerving embrace of objectivity and impartiality.

Scientific progress embodies and depends on open communication, a common discourse rooted in rationality, collaboration, and an easy and regular flow and exchange of information. Such ideals can be hypocritical covers for power-mongering by elites, and they may be shown to be wanting in many other ways, but they are entailed by the very idea of science and they make science and globalization practical allies.

Business, banking, and commerce all depend on information flow and are facilitated by new communication technologies. The hardware of these technologies tends to be systemic and integrated—computer, television, cable, satellite, laser, fiber-optic, and microchip technologies combining to create a vast interactive communications and information network that can potentially give every person on earth access to every other person, and make every datum, every byte, available to every set of eyes. If the automobile was, as George Ball once said (when he gave his blessing to a Fiat factory in the Soviet Union during the Cold War), "an ideology on four wheels," then electronic telecommunication and information systems are an ideology at 186,000 miles per second—which makes for a very small planet in a very big hurry. Individual cultures speak particular languages; commerce and science increasingly speak English; the whole world speaks logarithms and binary mathematics.

Moreover, the pursuit of science and technology asks for, even compels, open societies. Satellite footprints do not respect national borders; telephone wires penetrate the most closed societies. With photocopying and then fax machines having infiltrated Soviet universities and *samizdat* literary circles in the eighties, and computer modems having multiplied like rabbits in communism's bureaucratic warrens thereafter, *glasnost* could not be far behind. In their social requisites, secrecy and science are enemies.

The new technology's software is perhaps even more globalizing than its hardware. The information arm of international commerce's sprawling body reaches out and touches distinct nations and parochial cultures, and gives them a common face chiseled in Hollywood, on Madison Avenue, and in Silicon Valley. Throughout the 1980s one of the most-watched television programs in South Africa was *The Cosby Show*. The demise of apartheid was already in production. Exhibitors at the 1991 Cannes film festival expressed growing anxiety over the "homogenization" and "Americanization" of the global film industry when, for the third year running, American films dominated the awards ceremonies. America has dominated the world's popular culture for much longer, and much more decisively. In November of 1991 Switzerland's once insular culture boasted best-seller lists featuring *Terminator 2* as the No. 1 movie, *Scarlett* as the No. 1 book, and Prince's *Diamonds and Pearls* as the No. 1 record album. No wonder the Japanese are buying Hollywood film studios even faster than Americans are buying Japanese television sets. This kind of software supremacy may in the long term be far more important than hardware superiority, because culture has become more potent than armaments. What is the power of the Pentagon compared with Disneyland? Can the Sixth Fleet keep up with CNN? McDonald's in Moscow and Coke in China will do more to create a global culture than military colonization ever could. It is less the goods than the brand names that do the work, for they convey life-style images that alter perception and challenge behavior. They make up the seductive software of McWorld's common (at times much too common) soul.

Yet in all this high-tech commercial world there is nothing that looks particularly democratic. It lends itself to surveillance as well as liberty, to new forms of manipulation and covert control as well as new kinds of participation, to skewed, unjust market outcomes as well as greater productivity. The consumer society and the open society are not quite synonymous. Capitalism and democracy have a relationship, but it is something less than a marriage. An efficient free market after all requires that consumers be free to vote their dollars on competing goods, not that citizens be free to vote their values and beliefs on competing political candidates and programs. The free market flourished in junta-run Chile, in military-governed Taiwan and Korea, and, earlier, in a variety of autocratic European empires as well as their colonial possessions.

THE ECOLOGICAL IMPERATIVE. The impact of globalization on ecology is a cliché even to world leaders who ignore it. We know well enough that the German forests can be destroyed by Swiss and Italians driving gas-guzzlers fueled by leaded gas. We also know that the planet can be asphyxiated by greenhouse gases because Brazilian farmers want to be part of the twentieth century and are burning down tropical rain forests to clear a little land to plough, and because Indonesians make a living out of converting their lush jungle into toothpicks for fastidious Japanese diners, upsetting the delicate oxygen balance and in effect puncturing our global lungs. Yet this ecological consciousness has meant not only greater awareness but also greater inequality, as modernized nations try to slam the door behind them, saying to developing nations, "The world cannot afford your modernization; ours has wrung it dry!"

Each of the four imperatives just cited is transnational, transideological, and transcultural. Each applies impartially to Catholics, Jews, Muslims, Hindus, and Buddhists; to democrats and totalitarians; to capitalists and socialists. The Enlightenment dream of a universal rational society has to a remarkable degree been realized—but in a form that is commercialized, homogenized, depoliticized, bureaucratized, and, of course, radically incomplete, for the movement toward McWorld is in competition with forces of global breakdown, national dissolution, and centrifugal corruption. These forces, working in the opposite direction, are the essence of what I call Jihad.

Jihad, or the Lebanonization of the World

OPEC, the World Bank, the United Nations, the International Red Cross, the multinational corporation...there are scores of institutions that reflect globalization. But they often appear as ineffective reactors to the world's real actors: national states and, to an ever greater degree, subnational factions in permanent rebellion against uniformity and integration—even the kind represented by universal law and justice. The headlines feature these players regularly: they are cultures, not countries; parts, not wholes; sects, not religions; rebellious factions and dissenting minorities at war not just with globalism but with the traditional nation-state. Kurds, Basques, Puerto Ricans, Ossetians, East Timoreans, Québécois, the Catholics of Northern Ireland, Abkhasians, Kurile Islander Japanese, the Zulus of Inkatha, Catalonians, Tamils, and, of course, Palestinians—people without countries, inhabiting nations not their own, seeking smaller worlds within borders that will seal them off from modernity.

A powerful irony is at work here. Nationalism was once a force of integration and unification, a movement aimed at bringing together disparate clans, tribes, and cultural fragments under new, assimilationist flags. But as Ortega y Gasset noted more than sixty years ago, having won its victories, nationalism changed its strategy. In the 1920s, and again today, it is more often a reactionary and divisive force, pulverizing the very nations it once helped cement together. The force that creates nations is "inclusive," Ortega wrote in *The Revolt of the Masses*. "In periods of consolidation, nationalism has a positive value, and is a lofty standard. But in Europe everything is more than consolidated, and nationalism is nothing but a mania...."

This mania has left the post-Cold War world smoldering with hot wars; the international scene is little more unified than it was at the end of the Great War, in Ortega's own time. There were more than thirty wars in progress last year, most of them ethnic, racial, tribal, or religious in character, and the list of unsafe regions doesn't seem to be getting any shorter. Some new world order!

The aim of many of these small-scale wars is to redraw boundaries, to implode states and resecure parochial identities: to escape McWorld's dully insistent imperatives. The mood is that of Jihad: war not as an instrument of policy but as an emblem of identity, an expression of community, an end in itself. Even where there is no shooting war, there is fractiousness, secession, and the quest for ever smaller communities. Add to the list of dangerous countries those at risk: In Switzerland and Spain, Jurassian and Basque separatists still argue the virtues of ancient identities, sometimes in the language of bombs. Hyperdisintegration in the former Soviet Union may well continue unabated—not just a Ukraine independent from the Soviet Union but a Bessarabian Ukraine independent from the Ukrainian republic; not just Russia severed from the defunct union but Tatarstan severed from Russia. Yugoslavia makes even the disunited, ex-Soviet, nonsocialist republics that were once the Soviet Union look integrated, its sectarian fatherlands springing up within factional motherlands like weeds within weeds within weeds. Kurdish independence would threaten the territorial integrity of four Middle Eastern nations. Well before the current cataclysm Soviet Georgia made a claim for autonomy from the Soviet Union, only to be faced with its Ossetians (164,000 in a republic of 5.5 million) demanding their own self-determination within Georgia. The Abkhasian minority in Georgia has followed suit. Even the good will established by Canada's once promising Meech Lake protocols is in danger, with Francophone Quebec again threatening the dissolution of the federation. In South Africa the emergence from apartheid was hardly achieved when friction between Inkatha's Zulus and the African National Congress's tribally identified members threatened to replace Europeans' racism with an indigenous tribal war. After thirty years of attempted integration using the colonial language (English) as a unifier, Nigeria is now playing with the idea of linguistic multiculturalism—which could mean the cultural breakup of the nation into hundreds of tribal fragments. Even Saddam Hussein has benefited from the threat of internal Jihad, having used renewed tribal and religious warfare to turn last season's mortal enemies into reluctant allies of an Iraqi nationhood that he nearly destroyed.

The passing of communism has torn away the thin veneer of internationalism (workers of the world unite!) to reveal ethnic prejudices that are not only ugly and deep-seated but increasingly murderous. Europe's old scourge, anti-Semitism, is back with a vengeance, but it is only one of many antagonisms. It appears all too easy to throw the historical gears into reverse and pass from a Communist dictatorship back into a tribal state.

Among the tribes, religion is also a battlefield. ("Jihad" is a rich word whose generic meaning is "struggle"—usually the struggle of the soul to avert evil. Strictly applied to religious war, it is used only in reference to battles where the faith is under assault, or battles against a government that denies the practice of Islam. My use here is rhetorical, but does follow both journalistic practice and history.) Remember the Thirty Years War? Whatever forms of Enlightenment universalism might once have come to grace such historically related forms of monotheism as Judaism, Christianity, and Islam, in many of their modern incarnations they are parochial rather than cosmopolitan, angry rather than loving, proselytizing rather than ecumenical, zealous rather than rationalist, sectarian rather than deistic, ethnocentric rather than universalizing. As a result, like the new forms of hypernationalism, the new expressions of religious fundamentalism are fractious and pulverizing, never integrating. This is religion as the Crusaders knew it: a battle to the death for souls that if not saved will be forever lost.

The atmospherics of Jihad have resulted in a breakdown of civility in the name of identity, of comity in the name of community. International relations have sometimes taken on the aspect of gang war—cultural turf battles featuring tribal factions that were supposed to be sublimated as integral parts of large national, economic, postcolonial, and constitutional entities.

The Darkening Future of Democracy
These rather melodramatic tableaux vivants do not tell the whole story, however. For all their defects, Jihad and McWorld have their attractions. Yet, to repeat and insist, the attractions are unrelated to democracy. Neither McWorld nor Jihad is remotely

democratic in impulse. Neither needs democracy; neither promotes democracy. McWorld does manage to look pretty seductive in a world obsessed with Jihad. It delivers peace, prosperity, and relative unity—if at the cost of independence, community, and identity (which is generally based on difference). The primary political values required by the global market are order and tranquillity, and freedom—as in the phrases "free trade," "free press," and "free love." Human rights are needed to a degree, but not citizenship or participation—and no more social justice and equality than are necessary to promote efficient economic production and consumption. Multinational corporations sometimes seem to prefer doing business with local oligarchs, inasmuch as they can take confidence from dealing with the boss on all crucial matters. Despots who slaughter their own populations are no problem, so long as they leave markets in place and refrain from making war on their neighbors (Saddam Hussein's fatal mistake). In trading partners, predictability is of more value than justice.

The Eastern European revolutions that seemed to arise out of concern for global democratic values quickly deteriorated into a stampede in the general direction of free markets and their ubiquitous, television-promoted shopping malls. East Germany's Neues Forum, that courageous gathering of intellectuals, students, and workers which overturned the Stalinist regime in Berlin in 1989, lasted only six months in Germany's mini-version of McWorld. Then it gave way to money and markets and monopolies from the West. By the time of the first all-German elections, it could scarcely manage to secure three percent of the vote. Elsewhere there is growing evidence that glasnost will go and perestroika—defined as privatization and an opening of markets to Western bidders—will stay. So understandably anxious are the new rulers of Eastern Europe and whatever entities are forged from the residues of the Soviet Union to gain access to credit and markets and technology—McWorld's flourishing new currencies—that they have shown themselves willing to trade away democratic prospects in pursuit of them: not just old totalitarian ideologies and command-economy production models but some possible indigenous experiments with a third way between capitalism and socialism, such as economic cooperatives and employee stock-ownership plans, both of which have their ardent supporters in the East.

Jihad delivers a different set of virtues: a vibrant local identity, a sense of community, solidarity among kinsmen, neighbors, and countrymen, narrowly conceived. But it also guarantees parochialism and is grounded in exclusion. Solidarity is secured through war against outsiders. And solidarity often means obedience to a hierarchy in governance, fanaticism in beliefs, and the obliteration of individual selves in the name of the group. Deference to leaders and intolerance toward outsiders (and toward "enemies within") are hallmarks of tribalism—hardly the attitudes required for the cultivation of new democratic women and men capable of governing themselves. Where new democratic experiments have been conducted in retribalizing societies, in both Europe and the Third World, the result has often been anarchy, repression, persecution, and the coming of new, noncommunist forms of very old kinds of despotism. During the past year, Havel's velvet revolution in Czechoslovakia was imperiled by partisans of "Czechland" and of Slovakia as independent entities. India seemed little less rent by Sikh, Hindu, Muslim, and Tamil infighting than it was immediately after the British pulled out, more than forty years ago.

To the extent that either McWorld or Jihad has a *NATURAL* politics, it has turned out to be more of an antipolitics. For McWorld, it is the antipolitics of globalism: bureaucratic, technocratic, and meritocratic, focused (as Marx predicted it would be) on the administration of things—with people, however, among the chief things to be administered. In its politico-economic imperatives McWorld has been guided by laissez-faire market principles that privilege efficiency, productivity, and beneficence at the expense of civic liberty and self-government.

For Jihad, the antipolitics of tribalization has been explicitly antidemocratic: one-party dictatorship, government by military junta, theocratic fundamentalism—often associated with a version of the *Fuhrerprinzip* that empowers an individual to rule on behalf of a people. Even the government of India, struggling for decades to model democracy for a people who will soon number a billion, longs for great leaders; and for every Mahatma Gandhi, Indira Gandhi, or Rajiv Gandhi taken from them by zealous assassins, the Indians appear to seek a replacement who will deliver them from the lengthy travail of their freedom.

The Confederal Option

How can democracy be secured and spread in a world whose primary tendencies are at best indifferent to it (McWorld) and at worst deeply antithetical to it (Jihad)? My guess is that globalization will eventually vanquish retribalization. The ethos of material "civilization" has not yet encountered an obstacle it has been unable to thrust aside. Ortega may have grasped in the 1920s a clue to our own future in the coming millennium:

> Everyone sees the need of a new principle of life. But as always happens in similar crises—some people attempt to save the situation by an artificial intensification of the very principle which has led to decay. This is the meaning of the "nationalist" outburst of recent years...things have always gone that way. The last flare, the longest; the last sigh, the deepest. On the very eve of their disappearance there is an intensification of frontiers—military and economic.

Jihad may be a last deep sigh before the eternal yawn of McWorld. On the other hand, Ortega was not exactly prescient; his prophecy of peace and internationalism came just before blitzkrieg, world war, and the Holocaust tore the old order to bits. Yet democracy is how we remonstrate with reality, the rebuke our aspirations offer to history. And if retribalization is inhospitable to democracy, there is nonetheless a form of democratic government that can accommodate parochialism and communitarianism, one that can even save them from their defects and make them more tolerant and participatory: decentralized participatory democracy. And if McWorld is indifferent to democracy, there is nonetheless a form of democratic government that suits global markets passably well—representative government in its federal or, better still, confederal variation.

With its concern for accountability, the protection of minorities, and the universal rule of law, a confederalized representative system would serve the political needs of McWorld as well as oligarchic bureaucratism or meritocratic elitism is currently doing. As we are already beginning to see, many nations may survive in the long term only as confederations that afford local regions smaller than "nations" extensive jurisdiction. Recommended reading for democrats of the twenty-first century is not the US Constitution or the French Declaration of Rights of Man and Citizen but the Articles of Confederation, that suddenly pertinent document that stitched together the thirteen American colonies into what then seemed a too loose confederation of independent states but now appears a new form of political realism, as veterans of Yeltsin's new Russia and the new Europe created at Maastricht will attest.

By the same token, the participatory and direct form of democracy that engages citizens in civic activity and civic judgment and goes well beyond just voting and accountability—the system I have called "strong democracy"—suits the political needs of decentralized communities as well as theocratic and nationalist party dictatorships have done. Local neighborhoods need not be democratic, but they can be. Real democracy has flourished in diminutive settings: the spirit of liberty, Tocqueville said, is local. Participatory democracy, if not naturally apposite to tribalism, has an undeniable attractiveness under conditions of parochialism.

Democracy in any of these variations will, however, continue to be obstructed by the undemocratic and antidemocratic trends toward uniformitarian globalism and intolerant retribalization which I have portrayed here. For democracy to persist in our brave new McWorld, we will have to commit acts of conscious political will—a possibility, but hardly a probability, under these conditions. Political will requires much more than the quick fix of the transfer of institutions. Like technology transfer, institution transfer rests on foolish assumptions about a uniform world of the kind that once fired the imagination of colonial administrators. Spread English justice to the colonies by exporting wigs. Let an East Indian trading company act as the vanguard to Britain's free parliamentary institutions. Today's well-intentioned quick-fixers in the National Endowment for Democracy and the Kennedy School of Government, in the unions and foundations and universities zealously nurturing contacts in Eastern Europe and the Third World, are hoping to democratize by long distance. Post Bulgaria a parliament by first-class mail. Fed Ex the Bill of Rights to Sri Lanka. Cable Cambodia some common law.

Yet Eastern Europe has already demonstrated that importing free political parties, parliaments, and presses cannot establish a democratic civil society; imposing a free market may even have the opposite effect. Democracy grows from the bottom up and cannot be imposed from the top down. Civil society has to be built from the inside out. The institutional superstructure comes last. Poland may become democratic, but then again it may heed the Pope, and prefer to found its politics on its Catholicism, with uncertain consequences for democracy. Bulgaria may become democratic, but it may prefer tribal war. The former Soviet Union may become a democratic confederation, or it may just grow into an anarchic and weak conglomeration of markets for other nations' goods and services.

Democrats need to seek out indigenous democratic impulses. There is always a desire for self-government, always some expression of participation, accountability, consent, and representation, even in traditional hierarchical societies. These need to be identified, tapped, modified, and incorporated into new democratic practices with an indigenous flavor. The tortoises among the democratizers may ultimately outlive or outpace the hares, for they will have the time and patience to explore conditions along the way, and to adapt their gait to changing circumstances. Tragically, democracy in a hurry often looks something like France in 1794 or China in 1989.

It certainly seems possible that the most attractive democratic ideal in the face of the brutal realities of Jihad and the dull realities of McWorld will be a confederal union of semi-autonomous communities smaller than nation-states, tied together into regional economic associations and markets larger than nation-states—participatory and self-determining in local matters at the bottom, representative and accountable at the top. The nation-state would play a diminished role, and sovereignty would lose some of its political potency. The Green movement adage "Think globally, act locally" would actually come to describe the conduct of politics.

This vision reflects only an ideal, however—one that is not terribly likely to be realized. Freedom, Jean-Jacques Rousseau once wrote, is a food easy to eat but hard to digest. Still, democracy has always played itself out against the odds. And democracy remains both a form of coherence as binding as McWorld and a secular faith potentially as inspiriting as Jihad.

Recommended Reading

Appiah, K.A. (2006). *Cosmopolitanism: Ethics in a World of Strangers.* Princeton, NJ: Princeton UP.

Klien, N. (2008). *The Shock Doctrine: The Rise of Disaster Capitalism.* Picador.

Krugman, P. (21 May 1997). "In Praise of Cheap Labor." Retrieved 3 August 2011 from *The Slate.*

Nissanke, Machiko, and Eric Thorbecke, eds. (2010). *The Poor under Globalization in Asia, Latin America and Africa.* Oxford: Oxford UP.

Preble, John F. (2010). "Toward a Framework for Achieving a Sustainable Globalization." *Business & Society Review* 115 (3): 329–66.

Scott, Linda, et al. (2011). "Beyond Poverty: Social Justice in a Global Marketplace. Journal of Public Policy & Marketing" 30 (1): 39–46.

Sodhi, J.S. (2011). "Beyond GDP: The Debate on Globalization & Development." *Indian Journal of Industrial Relations* 46 (4): 562–70.

Soleymani, Mohammad. (2010). "The Heavy Price of Globalization and Sustainable Development." *Perspectives on Global Development & Technology* 9 (1/2): 101–18.

Spence, Michael. (2011). "The Impact of Globalization on Income and Employment." *Foreign Affairs* 90 (4): 28–41.

Zoellick, Robert G. (2010). "The End of the Third World." *International Economy* 24 (2): 40–43.

Colonialism, Neo-Colonialism, and Aid: Introduction

Nations and States

It is traditional to distinguish nations from states. *Nations* are understood as ethnic or cultural communities while *states* are understood to be sovereign political entities. From the perspective of the twenty-first century, from the Western perspective in particular, no social unit other than the nuclear family seems more natural than the *nation-state*, the cultural community, which enjoys political sovereignty. Indeed, the nation-state can be seen as an extended family of sorts, consisting of a community bound together by language, culture, and (real or fictional) kinship, living in the same place, which is economically and politically integrated and enjoys a high degree of self-determination or sovereignty.

But the nation-state is a parochial novelty. Historically, the human groups taken to be "natural" have often been either smaller or larger than typical modern nation-states—from clans, tribes, and city-states to empires. More importantly, not all states—sovereign political entities that typically occupy more or less contiguous territory—are coextensive with nations; and not all nations, understood as ethnic or cultural communities, occupy states. Some nations have no states or, like the Kurds, are spread over multiple sovereign states. Others have been colonized or incorporated into empires—from the territories absorbed into Hellenistic empires after Alexander's conquests to former British colonies in Africa, which achieved independence only as recently as the mid-twentieth century.

Nationalism, the quest by peoples for political self-determination, has been a global force for over two centuries. Self-determination, the principle according to which nations have the right to choose their sovereignty and international political status without external compulsion or interference, is recognized by international law and embodied in the United Nations *International Covenant on Economic, Social and Cultural Rights*, which states:

> All peoples have the right of self-determination. By virtue of that right they freely determine their political status and freely pursue their economic, social and cultural development...The States Parties to the present Covenant, including those having responsibility for the administration of Non-Self-Governing and Trust Territories, shall promote the realization of the right of self-determination, and shall respect that right, in conformity with the provisions of the Charter of the United Nations.[1]

Here the UN affirmed its support for nationalism and bound member states to promote the progress of any colonized peoples whose territories it administered to sovereign statehood.

National self-determination, however, has proved to be a mixed blessing. All other things being equal, we are better off getting what we want and determining our own destinies and so individual self-determination is a good thing. But national self-determination is *collective* self-determination—the right of groups to determine their corporate destinies. And collective self-determination can undermine individual self-determination—particularly for low-status individuals, including women, and members of minority groups. Christian and Jewish minorities, although relegated to second-class citizenship, fared better under the auspices of the Ottoman Empire than in former Ottoman territories after Turkey and its provincial colonies achieved national self-determination as conventional nation-states.

Colonial powers have, at least occasionally, promoted the interests of women, members of ethnic minorities, and other individuals who occupy the least desirable positions within indigenous cultures. As discussed in the General Introduction, when Hindu priests complained about the British ban on *sati*—the practice of burning widows alive on their husbands' funeral pyres—Sir Charles Napier, a British colonial administrator, is said to have responded:

> Be it so. This burning of widows is your custom; prepare the funeral pile. But my nation has also a custom. When men burn women alive we hang them, and confiscate all their property. My carpenters shall therefore erect gibbets on which to hang all concerned when the widow is consumed. Let us all act according to national customs.[2]

---

1 <http://www2.ohchr.org/english/law/cescr.htm>.
2 William Napier, *History of General Sir Charles Napier's Administration of Scinde* (London: Chapman and Hall, 1851), p. 35.

Indian widows did better under the British colonial regime than they did when high-caste, indigenous males were free to practice their native customs. National "self-determination" quite often cashes out as domination by indigenous elites. Does national self-determination benefit the bulk of the population? Are they—in particular women, ethnic minorities, and low-status individuals—better off with local warlords than with relatively benign colonial administrators?

Colonialism

National self-determination is not an unmixed blessing and, arguably, colonialism may not be an unmitigated curse. Dinesh D'Souza can muster two cheers for it. Writing of his native India, he argues that "against their intentions the colonialists brought things to India that have immeasurably enriched the lives of the descendants of colonialism.... Colonialism was the transmission belt that brought to Asia, Africa, and South America the blessings of Western civilization."[3] Ironically, it is another native of the Indian subcontinent and defender of the British Raj, Rudyard Kipling, whose short story "Lispeth" embodies the most powerful and emotionally compelling argument against colonialism.

The sting of colonialism is racism. In Kipling's story Lispeth, a child of indigenous people adopted as an infant by missionaries left home to return to her ancestral tribe when she learnt that her adoptive family regarded her as an outsider and a heathen. "She took to her own unclean people savagely," Kipling writes, "as if to make up the arrears of the life she had stepped out of; and, in a little time, she married a wood-cutter who beat her, after the manner of paharis, and her beauty faded soon." Although her adoptive parents, the Chaplain and his wife, put her defection down to race, Kipling is skeptical:

> "There is no law whereby you can account for the vagaries of the heathen," said the Chaplain's wife, "and I believe that Lispeth was always at heart an infidel." Seeing she had been taken into the Church of England at the mature age of five weeks, this statement does not do credit to the Chaplain's wife.[4]

The story is familiar. No matter how educated or acculturated indigenous people are, white settlers in the colonies regard them as infidels at heart who cannot be assimilated and exclude them. And that provides some support for national self-determination—understood as an arrangement in which individuals are ruled by members of their own "nation" or ethnic group. It may be that all other things being equal, members of our own ethnic group are more likely to treat us decently—though it is rare that all other things are equal.

---

3 Dinesh D'Souza, "Two Cheers for Colonialism," pp. 273–76 in this volume.
4 Rudyard Kipling, "Lispeth," pp. 279–82 in this volume.

Ideally, we should not be bound by race or ethnic origin. We should not have to count on ties of race and blood to secure fairness and decent treatment. In the US, ethnicity has become insignificant and race is becoming increasingly less important for political purposes. During the earlier part of the last century, ethnic bloc voting, particularly in big cities run by political machines, was significant. Nowadays "white ethnic" bloc voting has virtually disappeared, as most Americans have come to the conclusion that they do not need to elect members of their ancestral ethnic group, or others who have cut deals with its representatives, to benefit politically. In 2008 Americans elected Barack Obama to the nation's highest political office: black and white Americans, and Americans of every ethnic origin, recognized that an African American could support their interests.

Things are different in other ethnically diverse regions, where people believe, with justification, that their well-being depends on maintaining members of their ethnic group in positions of authority. This provides some rationale for national-ism. In these regions, individuals recognize that they are likely to do better living in states dominated by members of their ethnic group, or by others who are prepared to negotiate with their ethnic group's representatives. Nationalism may therefore be a necessary evil: necessary because of the pervasiveness of racism, and the refusal of dominant groups to allow minorities to assimilate; but evil because national sover-eignty can license indigenous high-status males to oppress women, ethnic minori-ties, and other low-status groups, and to block external agencies from interfering.

Humanitarian Intervention

Sometimes interference seems warranted. However, humanitarian intervention—the armed interference in one state by another with the stated objective of reducing suffering or ending human rights violations—poses serious difficulties, which J.L. Holzgrefe considers in his account of the humanitarian intervention debate. When does our duty to stop human rights violations or to alleviate suffering override our commitment to respect national sovereignty and self-determination?

Current attitudes in support of humanitarian intervention have been formed in response to the Allied discovery of the Holocaust at the end of World War II and, more recently, by the genocide in Rwanda and ongoing ethnic cleansing in Darfur. Historically, however, humanitarian intervention has been a pretext for colonialist and neo-colonialist projects. In his classic essay, Mill defends humanitarian inter-vention in support of British imperialism:

> [T]here assuredly are cases in which it is allowable to go to war, without hav-
> ing been ourselves attacked, or threatened with attack.... To suppose that
> the same international customs, and the same rules of international morality,
> can obtain between one civilized nation and another, and between civilized
> nations and barbarians, is a grave error.... [B]arbarians have no rights as a

nation, except a right to such treatment as may, at the earliest possible period, fit them for becoming one.[5]

Currently there is little sympathy for imperialistic projects and Mill's remarks about "barbarians" would not now be acceptable in polite company. His discussion, however, raises vexed questions about the limits of state sovereignty.

Aid

While military intervention and imperialist projects raise red flags, Western observers typically assume that aid, provided by donor nations and NGOs, is beneficial or, at the very least, innocuous. Aid, however, is rarely unconditional or untainted and, critics argue, in a range of cases it is *de facto* a neo-colonialist enterprise. Clifford Bob argues that "where marketing trumps justice, local challengers—whether environmental groups, labor rights activists, or independence-minded separatists...jostle for attention among dozens of equally worthy competitors... [and] contend against well-heeled opponents.... Under pressure to sell their causes to the rest of the world, local leaders may end up undermining their original goals or alienating the domestic constituencies they ostensibly represent."[6]

Is self-help a viable alternative to aid? Muhammad Yunus tells how and why he founded the Grameen Bank in his native Bangladesh, the first of many microcredit schemes directed chiefly toward women in developing countries, which have been instrumental in lifting some families out of poverty.

Critics, however, note that the benefits of microcredit are limited. Aneel Karnani argues that employment, not microcredit, is the solution. "Why is microcredit not more effective?" Karnani asks.

> The problem lies not with microcredit but rather with microenterprises.... Some clients of microcredit are certainly true entrepreneurs, and have created thriving businesses—these are the heart-warming anecdotes. But the vast majority of microcredit clients are caught in subsistence activities with no prospect of competitive advantage.... With low skills, little capital and no scale economies, these businesses operate in arenas with low entry barriers and too much competition; they have low productivity and lead to meager earnings that cannot lift their owners out of poverty.
>
> This should not be too surprising. Most people do not have the skills, vision, creativity, and persistence to be true entrepreneurs. Even in developed countries with high levels of education and infrastructure, about 90% of the labor force are employees rather than entrepreneurs.[7]

---

5 John Stuart Mill, "A Few Words on Non-Intervention," pp. 260–72 in this volume.
6 Clifford Bob, "Merchants of Morality," pp. 283–93 in this volume.
7 Aneel Karnani, "Employment, not Microcredit, Is the Solution," pp. 300–03 in this volume.

More than ever the world is divided between the rich and the poor, between affluent countries with vast resources and poor countries where poverty breeds corruption and violence, which in turn lock in poverty. We who have the resources would like to improve conditions in these countries for self-interested as well as humanitarian reasons: poverty, corruption, and violence spill over. But it is not clear what kinds of intervention would be most effective, and it is controversial whether some interventions in the business of sovereign states, even with the best of intentions, are morally acceptable.

19. The Humanitarian Intervention Debate*

J.L. Holzgrefe

On 6 April 1994, President Habyarimana of Rwanda and several top government officials were killed when their plane was shot down by a surface-to-air missile on its approach to Kigali airport. Within hours, members of the Hutu-dominated government, presidential guard, police, and military started rounding up and executing opposition politicians. The army set up roadblocks at 50 to 100 meter intervals throughout Kigali. The airport was surrounded and sealed. Telephone lines were cut. Military intelligence distributed lists of the government's political opponents to death squads: "every journalist, every lawyer, every professor, every teacher, every civil servant, every priest, every doctor, every clerk, every student, every civil rights activist were hunted down in a house-to-house operation. The first targets were members of the never-to-be-constituted broad-based transitional government."[1]

Once the Tutsi leadership and intelligentsia were killed, the army, presidential guard, and the Interahamwe militia, the youth wing of the ruling Hutu party, began executing anyone whose identity cards identified them as Tutsis. When checking identity cards became too time-consuming, they executed anyone with stereotypical Tutsi features. On 9 April, the Interahamwe militia directed by presidential guards hacked to death 500 men, women, and children who had taken shelter in the Catholic mission in Kigali. In another incident, the Interahamwe shot 120 men and boys who had taken refuge in St. Famille Church in Kigali. Soldiers killed any wounded Tutsis who made it to hospital. One killer went so far as to thank hospital staff for providing a "Tutsi collection point."[2] The Hutu radio station Radio Télévision Libre Milles Collines coordinated the killing. "You have missed some of the enemies [in such and such a place]," it told its listeners, "Some are still alive. You must go back there and finish them off…. The graves are not yet quite full. Who is going to do the good

---

* Source: J.L. Holzgrefe and Robert O. Koehane (eds.), *Humanitarian Intervention: Ethical, Legal, and Political Dilemmas* (Cambridge: Cambridge UP, 2003), 15–52.
1 Linda Melvern, *A People Betrayed: The Role of the West in Rwanda's Genocide* (Zed Books, London, 2000), p. 127.
2 Ibid., p. 142.

work and help us fill them completely?"[3] In Taba, the Interahamwe killed all male Tutsis, forced the women to dig graves to bury the men, and then threw the children in the graves. "I will never forget the sight of my son pleading with me not to bury him alive," one survivor recalled. "[H]e kept trying to come out and was beaten back. And we had to keep covering the pit with earth until there was no movement left."[4]

Massacres such as these became commonplace throughout Rwanda. An estimated 43,000 Tutsis were killed in Karama Gikongoro, a further 100,000 massacred in Butare. Over 16,000 people were killed around Cyangugu; 4,000 in Kibeho; 5,500 in Cyahinda; 2,500 in Kibungo.[5] Other examples are not hard to find.[6] By early May, one journalist observed that one bloated and mutilated body plunged over the Rusomo Falls on the Kagera River every minute. "Hundreds and hundreds must have passed down the river in the past week and they are still coming.... A terrible genocidal madness has taken over Rwanda. It is now completely out of control."[7] So many bodies littered the streets of Kigali that prisoners were detailed to load them into dump trucks. As one eyewitness recounted: "Some one flagged [the dump truck] down and dragged [a] body from under the tree and threw it into the...truck which was almost full and people were moaning and crying, you could see that some were not dead."[8] The sub-prefect of Kigali prefecture later admitted that 67,000 bodies were disposed of in this way. In three short months, as many as 1 million Tutsis were shot, burned, starved, tortured, stabbed, or hacked to death.[9]

The international community did nothing to stop the Rwandan genocide.[10] A complete holocaust was only prevented by the military victory of the Rwandan Patriotic Front—a Tutsi guerrilla army based in the north of the country. *But what, if anything, should the international community have done to stop the carnage? Did it have a moral duty to intervene? Did it have a legal right to do so? What should it*

---

3 Quoted in G. Prunier, *The Rwanda Crisis: History of a Genocide* (Hurst & Co., London, 1995), p. 224.

4 UN Commission on Human Rights, *Report of the Special Rapporteur on Violence against Women, Its Causes and Consequences*, Ms. Radhika Coomaraswamy (E/CN.4/1998/54/Add. 1), 4 February 1998, p. 10. Quoted in Melvern, *A People Betrayed*, p. 158.

5 Alison L. Des Forges, *"Leave None to Tell the Story": Genocide in Rwanda* (Human Rights Watch, New York, c. 1999), pp. 303–594; quoted in Melvern, *A People Betrayed*, p. 200.

6 Ibid.

7 Richard Dowden, "Sweet Sour Stench of Death Fills Rwanda," *Independent*, 7 May 1994. Quoted in Melvern, *A People Betrayed*, p. 189.

8 Interview with Colonel Quist, transcript, tape 28. *Twenty-Twenty Television*, July 1994. Quoted in Melvern, *A People Betrayed*, p. 133.

9 Boutros Boutros-Ghali, "Introduction," *The United Nations and Rwanda 1993–1996* (Department of Public Information, United Nations, New York, 1996), p. 4.

10 "We must all recognise that...we have failed in our response to the agony of Rwanda, and thus have acquiesced in the continued loss of human life. Our readiness and capacity for action has been demonstrated to be inadequate at best, and deplorable at worst, owing to the absence of the collective political will." "Report of the Secretary-General on the Situation in Rwanda [S/1994/640, 31 May 1994]," *UN and Rwanda 1993–1996*, p. 291. See also Nicholas J. Wheeler, *Saving Strangers: Humanitarian Intervention in International Society* (Oxford UP, Oxford, 2000), pp. 219–30; Melvern, *A People Betrayed*, pp. 186–206.

have done if the United Nations Security Council had refused to authorize a military intervention? If it had a duty to intervene, how could it have overcome the political barriers to intervention? And, most importantly, what measures should be taken to prevent similar catastrophes in the future?

It is the aim of this chapter to examine some of the answers commonly given to these and other questions. The first section very briefly defines humanitarian intervention. The second section discusses the ethics of humanitarian intervention, distinguishing various theories according to the source, objects, weight, and breadth of moral concern. The discussion focuses on the following ethical theories: utilitarianism; natural law; social contractarianism; communitarianism; and legal positivism. The third section surveys classicist and legal realist readings of the sources of international law with a view to determining the present legality of humanitarian intervention. The literature on the ethics and legality of humanitarian intervention is riven with disagreement. This chapter seeks to identify and critically assess the (often unexamined) moral and empirical assumptions behind these disagreements.

Definition of Humanitarian Intervention

What is humanitarian intervention? For the purposes of this volume, it is the threat or use of force across state borders by a state (or group of states) aimed at preventing or ending widespread and grave violations of the fundamental human rights of individuals other than its own citizens, without the permission of the state within whose territory force is applied.[11]

In defining humanitarian intervention in this way, I deliberately exclude two types of behavior occasionally associated with the term. They are: non-forcible interventions such as the threat or use of economic, diplomatic, or other sanctions;[12] and forcible interventions aimed at protecting or rescuing the intervening state's own nationals.[13] I do this, not because the legality or morality of these types of

---

11 I am indebted to Allen Buchanan for his help in formulating this definition of humanitarian intervention.

12 "Humanitarian intervention should be understood to encompass...non-forcible methods, namely intervention undertaken without military force to alleviate mass human suffering within sovereign borders." David J. Scheffer, "Towards a Modern Doctrine of Humanitarian Intervention," 23 *University of Toledo Law Review* (1992), 266; Fernando R. Tesón, *Humanitarian Intervention: An Inquiry into Law and Morality* (2nd ed., Transnational Publishers, Irvington-on-Hudson, 1997), p. 135; Fernando R. Tesón, "Collective Humanitarian Intervention," 17 *University of Michigan Law School Journal* (1996), 325–27.

13 "I assume that humanitarian intervention...is a short-term use of armed force by a government...for the protection from death or grave injury of nationals of the acting State...by their removal from the territory of the foreign State." R. Baxter in Richard B. Lillich ed., *Humanitarian Intervention and the United Nations* (UP of Virginia, Charlottesville, 1973), p. 53; Ulrich Beyerlin, "Humanitarian Intervention," in Rudolf Bernhardt ed., 3 *Encyclopedia of Public International Law* (North-Holland Publishing Co., Amsterdam, 1982), pp. 213–14; Natolino Ronzitti, *Rescuing Nationals Abroad Through Military Coercion and Intervention on Grounds of Humanity* (Martinus Nijhoff, Dordrecht, 1985), pp. 89–113.

interventions is uninteresting or unimportant, but because the question of whether states may use *force* to protect the human rights of individuals other than their own citizens is more urgent and controversial.

The Ethics of Humanitarian Intervention

Does the international community have a moral duty to intervene to end massive human rights violations like the Rwandan genocide? The arguments for or against the justice of humanitarian intervention are classified in a wide variety of ways. Michael J. Smith distinguishes political realist and liberal views.[14] J. Bryan Hehir differentiates moral and legal arguments, whereas Mark R. Wicclair contrasts rule-oriented and consequence-oriented ones.[15] Other scholars categorize the subject in still different ways.[16] All these taxonomies have much to recommend them. Nevertheless, no single dichotomy adequately captures all the important differences between the principal views on the justice of humanitarian intervention. It is for this reason that I shall classify these views according to which side of not one, but four ethical divides they fall.

The first ethical divide concerns the proper *source* of moral concern. *Naturalist* theories of international justice contend that morally binding international norms are an inherent feature of the world; a feature that is discovered through reason or experience. These theories maintain that particular facts about the world possess an intrinsic moral significance which human beings are powerless to alter. In contrast, *consensualist* theories of international justice claim that the moral authority of any given international norm derives from the explicit or tacit consent of the agents subject to that norm. On this view, just norms are made, not discovered. They are the product of consent and so only binding on the parties to the agreement.

The second ethical divide concerns the appropriate *objects* of moral concern. *Individualist* theories of international justice are concerned ultimately only with the welfare of individual human beings. In contrast, *collectivist* theories of international justice maintain that groups—typically ethnic groups, races, nations, or states—are

---

14 Michael J. Smith, "Humanitarian Intervention: An Overview of the Ethical Issues," 12 *Ethics and International Affairs* (1998), 63–79.

15 J. Bryan Hehir, "The Ethics of Non-intervention: Two Traditions," in Peter G. Brown and Douglas Maclean eds., *Human Rights and US Foreign Policy: Principles and Applications* (Lexington Books, Lexington, 1979), pp. 121–39; J. Bryan Hehir, "Intervention: From Theories to Cases," 9 *Ethics and International Affairs* (1995), 1–13; Mark R. Wicclair, "Human Rights and Intervention," in Brown and Maclean, *Human Rights and US Foreign Policy*, pp. 141–57. See also David R. Mapel and Terry Nardin, "Convergence and Divergence in International Ethics," in Terry Nardin and David R. Mapel eds., *Traditions of International Ethics* (Cambridge UP, Cambridge, 1992), pp. 299–318.

16 See Jeff McMahan, "The Ethics of International Intervention," in Anthony Ellis ed., *Ethics and International Affairs* (Manchester UP, Manchester, 1986), pp. 24–51; Howard Adelman, "The Ethics of Humanitarian Intervention: The Case of the Kurdish Refugees," 6 *Public Affairs Quarterly* (1992), 62–87; Pierre Laberge, "Humanitarian Intervention: Three Ethical Positions," 9 *Ethics and International Affairs* (1995), 15–35.

proper objects of moral concern. It is crucial to note, however, that collectivists view groups entirely "in non-aggregative terms, that is, without reference to the rights, interests or preferences of the individuals" that compose them.[17] In other words, collectivists hold that groups can have interests independent of, and potentially in conflict with, those of their members.

The third ethical divide concerns the appropriate *weight* of moral concern. *Egalitarian* theories of international justice claim that the objects of moral concern must be treated equally. By this they mean that no object of moral concern should count for more than any other object of moral concern. *Inegalitarian* theories, in contrast, require or permit them to be treated unequally.

The final ethical divide concerns the proper *breadth* of moral concern. *Universalist* theories assert that *all* relevant agents—wherever they exist—are the proper objects of moral concern. *Particularist* theories, in contrast, hold that only *certain* agents—some human beings, but not others; some races, nations, states, but not others—are the proper objects of moral concern.

Readers should bear these distinctions in mind as I survey the principal theories of the justice of humanitarian intervention: utilitarianism; natural law; social contractarianism; communitarianism; and legal positivism.

Utilitarianism

Utilitarianism is the naturalist doctrine that an action is just if its consequences are more favorable than unfavorable to all concerned. For utilitarians, an action's consequences are everything. Conduct is never good or bad in itself. Only its effects on human well-being make it good or bad. Utilitarianism is naturalist because it holds that human well-being is an intrinsic good. It is individualist, egalitarian, and universalist because, in Jeremy Bentham's famous phrase, "each is to count for one and no one for more than one."[18]

Most versions of utilitarianism are more precisely formulated than the general principle stated above. First, the nature of well-being must be specified. Most nineteenth-century utilitarians held that acts are good to the extent they satisfy individuals' preferences. However, some utilitarians, noting people's propensity to want only what is realistically attainable rather than their actual desires, argue that it is individuals' objective "interests" or "welfare" rather than their subjective preferences that should be maximized. Second, the object of moral evaluation must be specified. "Act-utilitarians" contend that *each human action* is the proper object of moral evaluation. By this, they mean that a specific act is just if its immediate and direct consequences are more favorable than unfavorable to all concerned. In

---

17 Fernando R. Tesón, *A Philosophy of International Law* (Westview, Boulder, 1998), p. 41. See also Tesón, *Humanitarian Intervention*, pp. 55–61.
18 Quoted in R.M. Hare, "Rules of War and Moral Reasoning," 1 *Philosophy and Public Affairs* (1972), 170.

contrast, "rule-utilitarians" hold that a *specific class of actions* (rules, norms, and maxims) is the proper object of moral evaluation. By this, they mean that an act is just if it conforms to a set of rules whose general adoption increases aggregate well-being more than the general adoption of any other set of rules.

A simple example will illustrate the difference between act-and rule-utilitarianism. Take the question: "Should individuals keep their promises?" Act-utilitarians contend that the morality of keeping a promise depends solely upon whether keeping it would maximize human well-being. Rule-utilitarians, in contrast, argue that individuals should keep their promises if general adherence to the rule "individuals should keep their promises" best promotes human well-being.

As with promise-keeping, act-utilitarians argue that the justice of any humanitarian intervention depends entirely on its consequences. If its effect is to increase aggregate well-being, then it is just; if its immediate and direct effect is to decrease aggregate well-being, then it is unjust. Crudely put, act-utilitarians argue that a humanitarian intervention is just if it saves more lives than it costs, and unjust if it costs more lives than it saves. An act-utilitarian could argue that Tanzania's intervention in Uganda was just because, by overthrowing the Amin dictatorship, it saved more lives than it cost. For the same reason, an act-utilitarian could argue that India's intervention in Bangladesh was unjust because "more people died in Bangladesh during the two or three weeks when the Indian army was liberating the country than had been killed previously."[19]

Act-utilitarianism is commonly criticized for asking both too much and too little of people. It asks too much because it obliges us to aid anyone who would gain more from our assistance than we would lose by giving it. Put slightly differently, it obliges us to help others to the point at which our own well-being is reduced to the same level as those whose well-being we are attempting to improve.[20] Jeremy Bentham thus writes that it is unjust if a

> nation should refuse to render positive services to a foreign nation, when the rendering of them would produce more good to the last-mentioned nation, than would produce evil to itself. For example if the given nation, without having reason to fear for its own preservation ... should obstinately prohibit commerce with them and a foreign nation:—or if when a foreign nation should be visited with misfortune, and require assistance, it should neglect to furnish it.[21]

Act-utilitarianism's extreme altruism is the logical consequence of its individualist, egalitarian, and universalist premises. Such demanding moral obligations, however,

---

19 Thomas M. Franck in Lillich, *Humanitarian Intervention and the UN*, p. 65.
20 Peter Singer, "Famine, Affluence and Morality," 1 *Philosophy and Public Affairs* (1972), 231.
21 Jeremy Bentham, "Principles of International Law," in John Bowring ed., *The Works of Jeremy Bentham* (Russell & Russell, New York, 1962), vol. II, pp. 538–89.

are widely considered far beyond the moral capacities of ordinary men and women.

Act-utilitarianism also asks too little because it does not prohibit some actions that seem intuitively quite wrong. Supporters claim that any sort of military action is permissible if it saves more lives than it loses.[22] Thus, for example, NATO's killing of ten civilian employees of Radio Television Serbia (RTS) in Belgrade during Operation Allied Force could be justified on act-utilitarian grounds if destroying "a source of propaganda that's prolonging this war and causing untold new suffering to the people of Kosovo" saved more lives than it cost.[23] Act-utilitarianism is thus sharply at odds with the natural law view that some harms (e.g., the torture or execution of prisoners of war, terror bombing, attacks on neutrals, and the like) are forbidden without exception or qualification.

Unlike act-utilitarianism, rule-utilitarianism claims that rules are the proper objects of moral evaluation because, as Robert E. Goodin points out, a significant portion of human well-being comes from coordinating the actions of a great many individual agents.

> Often the only way to maximize the utility that arises from my act is by knowing (or guessing) what others are likely to do. But knowing with any certainty is...impossible (or impossibly costly) in a world populated by act-utilitarian agents. The best way to coordinate our actions with those of others, and thereby to maximize the utility from each of our actions as individuals as well as from each of our actions collectively, is to promulgate rules (themselves chosen with an eye to maximizing utility, of course) and to adhere to them.[24]

If people do not observe the same moral rules, trust will erode and aggregate well-being decrease. Thus, for instance, if the rule "individuals must keep their promises" is not generally observed, economic activity will decline and with it aggregate well-being. At its deepest level, then, act-utilitarianism is inimical to the rule of law. As Michael J. Glennon points out:

> While the law may sometimes incorporate cost-benefit analysis in various "balancing tests," cost-benefit analysis is, at a fundamental level, not law. Indeed, one can question whether a legal system does not admit failure when it adopts case-bound balancing tests, which in their subjectivity and non-universality

---

22 "[A] military action (e.g., a bombing raid) is permissible only if the utility... of victory to all concerned, multiplied by the increase in its probability if the action is executed, on the evidence (when the evidence is reasonably solid, considering the stakes), is greater than the possible disutility of the action to both sides multiplied by its probability." R.B. Brandt, "Utilitarianism and War," 1 *Philosophy and Public Affairs* (1972), 157.

23 Clare Short, United Kingdom International Development Secretary. Quoted in Derek Brown, "Killing the Messengers," *Guardian*, London, 23 April 1999.

24 Robert E. Goodin, *Utilitarianism as a Public Philosophy* (Cambridge UP, Cambridge, 1995), p. 18.

rob law of its predictability. The case-by-case approach is, *juridically*, a cop-out, and an acknowledgement that no reasonable rule can be fashioned to govern all circumstances that can foreseeably arise.[25]

Act-utilitarians reply that if the consequences of a specific act (including damage to social trust and therefore future human well-being) are still more favorable than unfavorable to all concerned, then it should be performed. Anything else is "rule fetishism"—the unutilitarian adherence to rules for their own sake. Act-utilitarians thus feel perfectly justified in lying to Hutu death squads about the Tutsis hiding in their basements—even though observing the rule "tell the truth" maximizes utility in all other circumstances.[26]

For rule-utilitarians, the justice of a humanitarian intervention depends, not on its consequences, but on whether it is permitted or required by a rule that, if followed by everyone, produces the best consequences for all concerned. Unfortunately, though not unsurprisingly, there is considerable disagreement between rule-utilitarians as to which rule satisfies this criterion. Some rule-utilitarians—or, more accurately, some writers who use rule-utilitarian arguments—claim that humanitarian interventions fail, on balance, to secure the best consequences for all concerned. H. Scott Fairley, for instance, asserts that "the use of force for humanitarian ends more often than not has become self-defeating, increasing the human misery and loss of life it was intended originally to relieve."[27] Ian Brownlie and Caroline Thomas likewise doubt that the positive consequences of the United States intervention in the Dominican Republic and the Tanzanian intervention in Uganda exceeded their negative ones.[28] Other authors make the case that humanitarian interventions reduce well-being by increasing the likelihood of international society "collapsing into a state of war."[29] "Violations of human rights are indeed all too common," writes Louis

---

25 Michael J. Glennon, *Limits of Law, Prerogatives and Power: Interventionism after Kosovo* (Palgrave, New York, 2001), pp. 6–7.

26 Rule-utilitarians can respond to this criticism by limiting the application of rules. For example, they may qualify the rule "Always tell the truth" with the phrase "except where doing so will cause the death of innocents." Act-utilitarians, however, counter that, if such a rule applies to only one act, rule-utilitarianism collapses into act-utilitarianism and, if it applies to a class of actions, it remains susceptible to the criticism outlined above. J.J.C. Smart, "An Outline of a System of Utilitarian Ethics," in J.J.C. Smart and Bernard Williams eds., *Utilitarianism: For and Against* (Cambridge UP, Cambridge, 1973), pp. 1–73.

27 H. Scott Fairley, "State Actors, Humanitarian Intervention and International Law: Reopening Pandora's Box," 10 *Georgia Journal of International and Comparative Law* (1980), 63. See also R. George Wright, "A Contemporary Theory of Humanitarian Intervention," 4 *Florida International Law Journal* (1989), 440.

28 Ian Brownlie, "Humanitarian Intervention," in John Norton Moore ed., *Law and Civil War in the Modern World* (Johns Hopkins UP, Baltimore, 1974), p. 224; Caroline Thomas, "The Pragmatic Case against Intervention," in Ian Forbes and Mark Hoffman eds., *Political Theory, International Relations and the Ethics of Intervention* (St. Martin's Press, New York, 1993), pp. 93–94.

29 Michael Walzer, *Just and Unjust Wars: A Moral Argument with Historical Illustrations* (3rd ed., Basic Books, New York, 2000), p. 59.

Henkin, "and if it were permissible to remedy them by external use of force, there would be no law to forbid the use of force by almost any state against almost any other."[30] If humanitarian intervention were legal, powerful states would receive "an almost unlimited right to overthrow governments alleged to be unresponsive to the popular will or the goal of self-determination."[31]

Other rule-utilitarians disagree. Andrew Mason and Nicholas J. Wheeler, to cite only one example, conclude that non-interventionists "are unable to show that a properly regulated and suitably constrained practice of humanitarian intervention would be morally impermissible, or create a worse world than the one we currently live in.... [A]llowing humanitarian intervention in some cases...would promote overall well-being. So far from forbidding humanitarian intervention, consequentialist reasoning will support it...."[32]

An exasperating feature of the debate within and between act- and rule-utilitarianism is that neither side supports their claims with anything more than anecdotal evidence. A systematic analysis of the welfare consequences of humanitarian interventions and non-interventions is sadly lacking. Until such a study is completed, our ability to judge the merits of the competing utilitarian claims is gravely handicapped.

Natural law
Natural law is the naturalist doctrine that human beings have certain moral duties by virtue of their common humanity. Its basic precepts are discovered through reason and therefore available to anyone capable of rational thought. Like human nature, they are also universal and immutable.[33]

---

30 Louis Henkin, *How Nations Behave: Law and Foreign Policy* (2nd ed., Columbia UP, New York, 1979), p. 145.
31 Oscar Schachter, "The Legality of Pro-democratic Invasion," 78 *American Journal of International Law* (1984), 649. See also Ian Brownlie, *International Law and the Use of Force by States* (Clarendon Press, Oxford, 1991), pp. 340–41; Ian Brownlie, "Thoughts on Kindhearted Gunmen," in Lillich, *Humanitarian Intervention and the UN*, pp. 139–48; Farooq Hassan, "*Realpolitik* in International Law: After Tanzanian–Ugandan Conflict 'Humanitarian Intervention' Reexamined," 17 *Willamette Law Review* (1981), 862; Jack Donnelly, "Human Rights, Humanitarian Intervention, and American Foreign Policy: Law, Morality, and Politics," 37 *Journal of International Affairs* (1984), 321–22; Oscar Schachter, "The Lawful Resort to Unilateral Force," 10 *Yale Journal of International Law* (1985), 294; Ved P. Nanda, "Tragedies in Northern Iraq, Liberia, Yugoslavia, and Haiti—Revisiting the Validity of Humanitarian Intervention under International Law—Part I," 20 *Denver Journal of International Law and Policy* (1992), 309; Peter Malanczuk, *Humanitarian Intervention and the Legitimacy of the Use of Force* (Het Spinhuis, Amsterdam, 1993), pp. 30–31.
32 Andrew Mason and Nick Wheeler, "Realist Objections to Humanitarian Intervention," in Barry Holden ed., *The Ethical Dimensions of Global Change* (Macmillan, Basingstoke, 1996), p. 106.
33 Natural law is "right reason in harmony with nature; it is of universal application, unchanging and everlasting; it summons to duty by its commands, and averts from wrongdoing by its prohibitions...we cannot be freed from its obligations by senate or people, and we need not look outside ourselves for an expounder or interpreter of it." Marcus Tullius Cicero, "De Re Publica," III, xxii, 3: in Marcus Tullius Cicero, *De Re Publica and De Legibus* (Harvard UP, Cambridge, Mass., 1928), p. 211.

For natural law theorists, our common human nature generates common moral duties—including, in some versions, a right of humanitarian intervention.[34] Our moral obligations to others, writes Joseph Boyle,

> are not limited to people with whom we are bound in community by contract, political ties, or common locale. We are obliged to help whoever [sic] we can...and to be ready to form and promote decent relations with them...This general duty to help others is the most basic ground within this common morality for interference in the internal affairs of one nation by outsiders, including other nations and international bodies. The specific implications of the general duty to provide help depend on a number of highly contingent factors, including respect for a nation's sovereignty and awareness of the limits of outside aid. But the normative ground is there, and...in extreme circumstances it can justify the use of force.[35]

The Dutch jurist Hugo Grotius is a famous proponent of this view. In *De Jure Belli ac Pacis* [On the Law of War and Peace], he argues that, where a tyrant "should inflict upon his subjects such treatment as no one is warranted in inflicting," other states may exercise a right of humanitarian intervention.[36] Grotius bases this right on the natural law notion of *societas humana*—the universal community of humankind.[37] "The fact must also be recognized," he writes, "that kings, and those who possess rights equal to those kings, have the right of demanding punishments not only on account of injuries committed against themselves or their subjects, but also on account of injuries which do not directly affect them but excessively violate the law of nature or of nations in regard of any person whatsoever."[38]

Note that Grotius talks of the right—not the duty—of humanitarian intervention. States have a discretionary right to intervene on behalf of the oppressed. But they do not have to exercise the right if their own citizens are unduly burdened in doing so.[39] Natural law theorists who defend a duty of humanitarian intervention conceive it as an imperfect duty, like the duties of charity and beneficence.[40] States

---

34 Terry Nardin, "The Moral Basis of Humanitarian Intervention," 16 *Ethics and International Affairs* (2002), 57–70. See also Alan Donagan, *The Theory of Morality* (U of Chicago P, Chicago, 1977); John Finnis, *Natural Law and Natural Rights* (Oxford UP, Oxford, 1980); Robert P. George, "Natural Law and International Order," in David R. Mapel and Terry Nardin eds., *International Society: Diverse Ethical Perspectives* (Princeton UP, Princeton, 1998), pp. 54–69.

35 Joseph Boyle, "Natural Law and International Ethics," in Nardin and Mapel, *Traditions of International Ethics*, p. 123.

36 Hugo Grotius, *De Jure Belli ac Pacis* (Oxford UP, Oxford, 1925), Book II, ch. 25, sec. 8, vol. II, p. 584.

37 Ibid., Book II, ch. 20, sec. 8, vol. II, pp. 472–73.

38 Ibid., Book II, ch. 20, sec. 40, vol. II, p. 503.

39 Ibid., Book II, ch. 25, sec. 7, vol. II, pp. 582–83.

40 Moral duties are often classified as perfect or imperfect. A perfect duty is one for which there is a corresponding right. For example, if I have a duty not to execute prisoners of war, you, as a

may discharge it at their own discretion and in the manner of their own choosing. The victims of genocide, mass murder, and slavery possess no "right of humanitarian rescue"—no moral claim to the help of any specific state.

Although an imperfect duty of humanitarian intervention comports easily with the belief that states should privilege the well-being of their own citizens over the well-being of foreigners, it can have terrible consequences. "The general problem," writes Michael Walzer,

> is that intervention, even when it is justified, even when it is necessary to prevent terrible crimes—even when it poses no threat to regional or global stability, is an imperfect duty—a duty that doesn't belong to any particular agent. Somebody ought to intervene, but no specific state or society is morally bound to do so. And in many of these cases, no one does. People are indeed capable of watching and listening and doing nothing. The massacres go on, and every country that is able to stop them decides that it has more urgent tasks and conflicting priorities; the likely costs of intervention are too high.[41]

If one is concerned about preventing or stopping genocide, mass murder, and slavery, an imperfect duty of humanitarian intervention will not do. If "persons as such have certain rights," writes Allen Buchanan, "then surely one ought not only to respect persons' rights by not violating them. *One ought also to contribute to creating arrangements that will ensure that persons' rights are not violated.* To put the same point somewhat differently, respect for persons requires doing something to ensure that they are treated respectfully."[42] It is not enough for a state to refrain from violating human rights itself. It also must create and participate in international institutions that prevent or stop gross human rights violations wherever they occur. A perfect duty of humanitarian intervention is, in principle, wholly compatible with the precepts of natural law. But in practice no natural law theorists advocate it.

By contrast, many natural law theorists maintain that, far from possessing an imperfect duty of humanitarian intervention, states have a perfect duty of non-intervention. Christian Wolff, Emer de Vattel, and Immanuel Kant, for example, contend that states have a duty to refrain from interfering in each other's affairs for

---

prisoner of war, have a right not to be executed. An imperfect duty is one for which there is no corresponding right. "Duties of charity, for example, require us to contribute to one or another of a large number of eligible recipients, no one of whom can claim our contribution from us as his due. Charitable contributions are more like gratuitous services, favours, and gifts than like repayments of debts or reparations; and yet we do have duties to be charitable." Joel Feinberg, *Rights, Justice and the Bounds of Liberty: Essays in Social Philosophy* (Princeton UP, Princeton, 1980), p. 144. See also David Lyons, "The Correlativity of Rights and Duties," 4 *Noûs* (1970), 45–55; John Rawls, *A Theory of Justice* (Belknap, Cambridge, MA., 1971), pp. 108–17.

41 Walzer, *Just and Unjust Wars*, p. xiii.

42 Allen Buchanan, "The Internal Legitimacy of Humanitarian Intervention," 7 *Journal of Political Philosophy* (1999), 84; emphasis added.

the same reason that individuals have a duty to respect each other's autonomy.[43] "To interfere in the government of another…," writes Christian Wolff, "is opposed to the natural liberty of nations, by virtue of which one nation is altogether independent of the will of other nations in its actions…. If any such things are done, they are done altogether without right."[44] This argument rests on an analogy between persons and states. "Just as persons are autonomous agents, and are entitled to determine their own action free from interference as long as the exercise of their autonomy does not involve the transgression of certain moral constraints, so, it is claimed, states are also autonomous agents, whose autonomy is similarly deserving of respect."[45] The collectivist analogy, however, is a poor one. As Charles R. Beitz, Fernando R. Tesón, and many others argue, states are simply not unified agents with unified wills.[46] Indeed, at no time is this clearer than when a government commits gross human rights abuses against its own citizens.

Social contractarianism

Social contractarianism is the naturalist doctrine that moral norms derive their binding force from the mutual consent of the people subject to them. This mutual consent, however, is not between real people in real choice situations. Rather, it is between ideal agents in ideal choice situations. For social contractarians, norms are morally obligatory only *if* free, equal, and rational agents would consent to them. By defining justice in this way, they avoid the criticism that actual norms are rarely, if ever, chosen freely. It is by idealizing the choice situation that social contractarians ensure that mutual consent is genuine; that it is not the product of force or fraud.

Although social contractarian arguments possess a similar structure, they are far from identical. One area of disagreement concerns the identity of the contracting parties. Some social contractarians contend that norms are just if the *citizens of a state* would consent to them.[47] Others claim that they are just if the *states* themselves

---

43 Christian Wolff, *Jus Gentium Methodo Scientifica Pertractatum* (Carnegie Classics of International Law, New York, 1934), ch. I, secs. 256–57, p. 131; Emer de Vattel, *The Law of Nations or the Principles of Natural Law* (Carnegie Institution, Washington, DC, 1916), Book I, ch. III, sec. 37; Book II, ch. IV, sec. 54, pp. 19, 131; Immanuel Kant, "Perpetual Peace: A Philosophical Sketch," in Hans Reiss ed., *Kant: Political Writings* (2nd enlarged ed., Cambridge UP, Cambridge, 1991), p. 96; Immanuel Kant, *The Metaphysical Elements of Justice: Part I of the Metaphysics of Morals* (Macmillan, New York, 1965), part II, sec. 2, subsection 60, p. 123. See also Alan H. Goldman, "The Moral Significance of National Boundaries," 7 *Midwest Studies in Philosophy* (1982), 438–41; Gerald Elfstrom, "On Dilemmas of Intervention," 93 *Ethics* (1983), 713.

44 Wolff, *Jus Gentium Methodo Scientifica Pertractatum*, ch. I, secs. 256–57, p. 131.

45 McMahan, "Ethics of International Intervention," pp. 28–29.

46 Charles R. Beitz, *Political Theory and International Relations* (Princeton UP, Princeton, 1979), pp. 71–83; Tesón, *Humanitarian Intervention*, pp. 55–100; Tesón, *Philosophy of International Law*, pp. 39–47.

47 Richard Cox, *Locke on War and Peace* (Clarendon Press, Oxford, 1960); David Gauthier, "Hobbes on International Relations," in David Gauthier ed., *The Logic of Leviathan* (Oxford UP, Oxford, 1969), pp. 206–12; Murray Forsyth, "Thomas Hobbes and the External Relations of States," 5 *Brit-*

would consent to them.[48] Still others argue that they are just if all *human beings* would consent to them.[49] The identity of the contracting parties is important because it affects which norms would be chosen—and hence which are morally binding. For example, if the citizens of a state were the contracting parties, then a duty to maximize the "national interest" would be selected. As Allen Buchanan explains:

> The state is understood as the creation of a hypothetical contract among those who are to be its citizens, and the terms of the contract they agree on are justified by showing how observance of those terms serves their interests. No one else's interests are represented, so legitimate political authority is naturally defined as authority exercised for the good of the parties to the contract, the citizens of this state…. The justifying function of the state—what justifies the interference with liberty that it entails—is the well-being and freedom of its members. There is no suggestion that the state must do anything to serve the cause of justice in the world at large. What makes the government legitimate is that it acts as the faithful agent of its own citizens. And to that extent, government acts legitimately only when it occupies itself exclusively with the interests of the citizens of the state of which it is the government.[50]

The justice of any given intervention thus hinges on whether it benefits or harms the "national interest." For writers who define this term narrowly (i.e., as the sum of security and material interests), interventions aimed at ending gross human rights abuses in foreign countries are almost always unjust.[51] Samuel P. Huntington's assertion that "it is morally unjustifiable and politically indefensible that members of the [United States] Armed Forces should be killed to prevent Somalis from killing

ish Journal of International Studies (1979), 196–209; Hedley Bull, "Hobbes and the International Anarchy," 48 *Social Research* (1981), 717–38; H. Williams, *International Relations and the Limits of Political Theory* (Macmillan, Basingstoke, 1996), pp. 90–109. See also Thomas L. Pangle, "The Moral Basis of National Security: Four Historical Perspectives," in Klaus Knorr ed., *Historical Dimensions of National Security Studies* (UP of Kansas, Lawrence, 1976), pp. 307–72.

48 Rawls, *Theory of Justice*, p. 378; John Charvet, "International Society from a Contractarian Perspective," in Mapel and Nardin, *International Society*, pp. 114–31; John Rawls, *The Law of Peoples* (Harvard UP, Cambridge, MA, 1999).

49 Beitz, *Political Theory*; Charles R. Beitz, "Justice and International Relations," in H. Gene Blocker and Elizabeth H. Smith eds., *John Rawls' Theory of Social Justice* (Ohio UP, Athens, 1980), pp. 211–38; Charles R. Beitz, "Nonintervention and Communal Integrity," 9 *Philosophy and Public Affairs* (1980), 385–91; Thomas W. Pogge, *Realizing Rawls* (Cornell University Press, Ithaca, 1989); Thomas W. Pogge, "Cosmopolitanism and Sovereignty," 103 *Ethics* (1992), 48–75; Charles R. Beitz, "Cosmopolitanism, Liberalism, and the States System," in Chris Brown ed., *Political Restructuring in Europe: Ethical Perspectives* (Routledge, London, 1994), pp. 123–36.

50 Buchanan, "Internal Legitimacy," pp. 74–75.

51 Hans J. Morgenthau, *In Defense of the National Interest: A Critical Examination of American Foreign Policy* (Knopf, New York, 1951).

one another" is a recent example of this view.[52] For authors who define "national interest" more expansively (i.e., as the sum of security, material, and what Joseph S. Nye, Jr. calls "humanitarian interests"), interventions aimed at ending genocide, mass murder, or slavery can be morally obligatory in certain circumstances.[53] In either case, the interests of the intervening state count for *everything* in assessing an intervention's legitimacy; the interests of the target state count for *nothing*.

The particularist conclusions of this argument are also inconsistent with its universalist premises. As Allen Buchanan makes clear, this variety of social contractarianism

> justifies the state as a coercive apparatus by appeal to the need to protect *universal* interests, while at the same time limiting the right of the state to use its coercive power to the protection of a *particular* group of persons, identified by the purely contingent characteristic of happening to be members of the same political society.... If the interests whose protection justifies the state are human interests, common to all persons, then surely a way of thinking about the nature of states and the role of government that provides no basis for obligations to help ensure that the interests of all persons are protected is fundamentally flawed.[54]

The widespread appeal of the "national interest" argument rests in large measure on the inegalitarian, particularist view that states should privilege the well-being of their own citizens over the well-being of nameless persons in distant lands. This claim, however, needs to be justified....

Other social contractarians claim that international norms are morally binding if *states* would consent to them. The early John Rawls (the Rawls of *A Theory of Justice*), for example, contends that international norms are morally binding if the rational representatives of states deciding behind a "veil of ignorance"—deciding without "knowing anything about the particular circumstances of their own society, its power and strength in comparison to other nations"—would consent to them.[55] In this "original position,"

> the contracting parties, in this case representatives of states, are allowed only enough knowledge to make a rational choice to protect their interests but not so much that the more fortunate among them can take advantage of their

---

52 Samuel P. Huntington, "New Contingencies, Old Roles," 2 *Joint Forces Quarterly* (1992), 338. See also Robert H. Jackson, "The Political Theory of International Society," in K. Booth and S. Smith eds., *International Relations Theory Today* (Polity, Cambridge, 1995), p. 123.

53 Joseph S. Nye, Jr., "Redefining the National Interest," 78 *Foreign Affairs* (1999), 22–35.

54 Buchanan, "Internal Legitimacy," p. 79; emphasis added.

55 Rawls, *Theory of Justice*, p. 378.

special situation. This original position is fair between nations; it nullifies the contingencies and biases of historical fate. Justice between states is determined by the principles that would be chosen in the original position so interpreted.[56]

Rawls concludes that "the right of a people to settle their own affairs without the intervention of foreign powers" is an international norm that state representatives would consent to if deprived of this information.[57]

Other social contractarians disagree.[58] They reject the collectivist assumptions of Rawls's argument in *A Theory of Justice*, claiming instead that international norms are just only to the extent that they would be assented to by *human beings* deciding behind a "veil of ignorance." These scholars argue that a duty of humanitarian intervention is just because human beings deciding behind a "veil of ignorance" (i.e., deciding in ignorance of the type of state in which they lived) would consent to it. As Fernando R. Tesón explains:

> If the parties [deciding behind the veil of ignorance] believed that some societies were likely to be grossly unjust then it is plausible to conclude that … they would prefer a principle of limited intervention on behalf of human rights. And this is so because the first aim of the parties in the original position is to see that the fundamental rights of *individuals* within every state are recognized and observed. The purpose of the state organization is to protect the rights of individuals. Because the parties in the original position [would] agree to terms of cooperation that are mutually acceptable and fair, the aim of the international community thus created … should also be the protection of the rights of individuals, and not the prerogatives of princes. Therefore it is doubtful that the parties in the original position would agree to the unqualified rule of non-intervention that would jeopardize the very rights the original position is primarily supposed to secure.[59]

In recent years, John Rawls has added a lot of communitarian water to his social contractarian wine. He now argues that international norms are just to the extent that the rational representatives of "decent" peoples deciding behind a "veil of ignorance" would assent to them. In *The Law of Peoples*, he maintains that states owe a duty of humanitarian rescue to the citizens of "outlaw" states; that is, to peoples whose governments fail to protect such basic human rights "as freedom from slavery and

---

56 Ibid., p. 378.
57 Ibid., p. 378.
58 Beitz, *Political Theory*; Wicclair, "Human Rights and Intervention," pp. 141–57; Mark R. Wicclair, "Rawls and the Principle of Non-intervention," in Blocker and Smith, *John Rawls' Theory of Social Justice*, pp. 289–308; Beitz, "Justice and International Relations," pp. 211–38; Beitz, "Nonintervention and Communal Integrity," pp. 385–91; Tesón, *Humanitarian Intervention*, pp. 61–74.
59 Tesón, *Humanitarian Intervention*, pp. 65–66.

serfdom, liberty (but not equal liberty) of conscience, and security of ethnic groups from mass murder and genocide."[60] But, significantly, he also contends that states do not owe a duty of humanitarian intervention to the citizens of so-called "decent" states; that is, to peoples whose governments guarantee basic human rights, but fail to protect so-called "rights of liberal democratic citizenship," i.e., rights of civic equality, democratic governance, free speech, free association, free movement, and the like. Violations of these liberal-democratic rights are not a *casus belli*, he reasons, because a duty of humanitarian intervention on these grounds would not be assented to by the rational representatives of "decent" peoples (i.e., peoples who respect human, though not necessarily liberal-democratic, rights) deciding behind a "veil of ignorance."[61] This raises the crucial question why "decent" peoples rather than rational individuals should be parties to the original contract. As Rawls simply stipulates that they should, his argument is at best incomplete—at worst arbitrary.[62]

Communitarianism

Communitarianism is the consensualist, particularist doctrine that norms are morally binding insofar as they "fit" the cultural beliefs and practices of specific communities.[63] "Justice is relative to social meanings," writes a leading communitarian, Michael Walzer.[64] "There are an infinite number of possible lives, shaped by an infinite number of possible cultures, religions, political arrangements, geographical conditions, and so on. A given society is just if its substantive life is lived in a certain way—that is, in a way faithful to the shared understandings of its members."[65] In the hands of communitarians, moral philosophy thus becomes moral anthropology—the discovery and

---

60 Rawls, *Law of Peoples*, p. 79.
61 Ibid., pp. 32–33. See also Fernando R. Tesón, "The Rawlsian Theory of International Law," 9 *Ethics and International Affairs* (1995), 83–99.
62 "This account of decency...is developed by setting out various criteria and explaining their meaning. The reader has to judge whether a decent people...is to be tolerated and accepted as a member in good standing of the Society of Peoples. It is my conjecture that most reasonable citizens of a liberal society will find peoples who meet these two criteria acceptable as peoples in good standing. Not all reasonable persons will, certainly, yet most will." Rawls, *Law of Peoples*, p. 67.
63 Melvyn Frost, *Towards a Normative Theory of International Relations* (Cambridge UP, Cambridge, 1986); David Miller, "The Ethical Significance of Nationality," 98 *Ethics* (1988), 647–62; NJ Rengger, "A City which Sustains All Things? Communitarianism and International Society," 21 *Millennium: Journal of International Studies* (1992), 353–69; Anthony Black, "Nation and Community in the International Order," 19 *Review of International Studies* (1993), 81–89; Robert H. Jackson, "Armed Humanitarianism," 48 *International Journal* (1993), 579–606; David Miller, *On Nationality* (Oxford UP, Oxford, 1995); David Morrice, "The Liberal–Communitarian Debate in Contemporary Political Philosophy and Its Significance for International Relations," 26 *Review of International Studies* (2000), 233–51; Robert H. Jackson, *The Global Covenant: Human Conduct in a World of States* (Oxford UP, Oxford, 2000), pp. 249–93.
64 Michael Walzer, *Spheres of Justice: A Defense of Pluralism and Equality* (Basil Blackwell, Oxford, 1983), p. 312.
65 Ibid., p. 313.

description of the "inherited cultures" that rule people's lives.[66] These "inherited cultures" are morally binding because they are the product of long processes of "association and mutuality," "shared experience," "cooperative activity"—in short, they are binding because they are the product of consent.[67]

A duty of humanitarian intervention is just, according to Walzer, because it "fits" the "inherited cultures" of political communities everywhere.[68] It is justified, he writes,

> when it is a response... to acts "that shock the moral conscience of mankind."
> The old-fashioned language seems to me exactly right. It is not the conscience
> of political leaders that one refers to in such cases. They have other things to
> worry about and may well be required to repress their feelings of indignation
> and outrage. The reference is to the moral convictions of ordinary men and
> women, acquired in the course of everyday activities.[69]

This global culture of human solidarity demands that states intervene whenever one of their number massacres, enslaves, or forcibly expels large numbers of its citizens or collapses into a frenzied, murderous anarchy.[70] Other communitarians, however, are not so sure. Hedley Bull, for instance, observes that "there is no present tendency for states to claim, or for the international community to recognize, any such right."[71]

The principal flaws of communitarianism—its moral relativism and conservatism—are well known and need not be rehearsed here.[72] A less well-known, though equally important, failing is that "consent," as communitarians conceive it, cannot generate morally binding norms. The communitarian conception of consent, writes Gerald Doppelt,

---

66 Michael Walzer, "The Moral Standing of States: A Response to Four Critics," 9 *Philosophy and Public Affairs* (1980), 211. See also Walzer, *Spheres of Justice*, pp. 28–29; Walzer, *Just and Unjust Wars*, p. 45.
67 Walzer, *Spheres of Justice*, p. 313; Walzer, *Just and Unjust Wars*, p. 54.
68 Walzer, "Moral Standing of States," pp. 211–12; Michael Walzer, *Thick and Thin: Moral Argument at Home and Abroad* (U of Notre Dame P, Notre Dame, 1994), pp. 15–19; Michael Walzer, "The Politics of Rescue," 62 *Social Research* (1995), 53–66.
69 Walzer, *Just and Unjust Wars*, p. 107.
70 Walzer, "Moral Standing of States," pp. 217–18.
71 Hedley Bull, "Conclusion," in Hedley Bull ed., *Intervention in World Politics* (Clarendon, Oxford, 1984), p. 193.
72 Richard A. Wasserstrom, "Review of *Just and Unjust Wars*," 92 *Harvard Law Review* (1978), 536–45; David Luban, "Just War and Human Rights," 9 *Philosophy and Public Affairs* (1980), 160–81; David Luban, "The Romance of the Nation-State," 9 *Philosophy and Public Affairs* (1980), 392–97; Beitz, "Nonintervention and Communal Integrity," pp. 385–91; Gerald Doppelt, "Statism without Foundations," 9 *Philosophy and Public Affairs* (1980), 398–403; Jerome Slater and Terry Nardin, "Nonintervention and Human Rights," 48 *Journal of Politics* (1986), 86–96; Tesón, *Humanitarian Intervention*, pp. 92–99; Richard Bellamy, "Justice in the Community: Walzer on Pluralism, Equality and Democracy," in David Boucher and Paul Kelly eds., *Social Justice: From Hume to Walzer* (Routledge, London, 1998), pp. 157–80; Tom J. Farer, "Does Walzer Still Work?" 41 *Public Affairs* (2000), 12–13.

is supposed to refer to a social process in which the activity of individuals "makes" or "shapes" a common life and independent community. But this picture is inherently vague and blurs important distinctions between the radically different terms on which individuals and groups are able to participate in, or influence, the life of a particular society.... [Wherever societies are divided] into racial, economic, or religious groups with radically unequal political freedoms, civil rights, economic opportunities, living conditions, literacy or health...the oppressed group has little, if any, real choice or control concerning the harsh terms of its social participation. At the very least, all reflective people (and nations) distinguish between the social participation of a group or individual based on force, coercion, bare material survival, ignorance, or blind habit and another kind which is "free" and approximates a meaningful sense of consent.[73]

Simply put, naturalists claim that communitarianism ignores the warping effects that asymmetries of wealth, power, and status have on expressions of consent. If individuals were truly free to construct their communities as they saw fit, they would choose norms quite different from those thrust on them by the dead hand of tradition.

Legal positivism

Legal positivism, as a normative doctrine, is the consensualist, collectivist view that norms are just if they are lawful; that is, if they are enacted according to accepted procedures.[74] The content of the norm is irrelevant to its binding force. One has a moral obligation to obey the law *qua* law. As Kenneth Einar Himma explains:

To claim that there is a moral obligation to obey law qua law is to claim that a legal standard is morally obligatory...*because* that standard is a law; in other words, it is to claim that a proposition of law is morally obligatory *in virtue of* being legally valid. Thus, someone who violates the law commits a moral wrong *in virtue of* performing an act that is inconsistent with the law.[75]

This view is known within legal positivism as the "separability thesis"—the claim that binding laws have absolutely no need to "reproduce or satisfy certain demands of morality, though in fact they have often done so."[76]

---

73 Gerald Doppelt, "Walzer's Theory of Morality in International Relations," 8 *Philosophy and Public Affairs* (1978), 20–21. See also Beitz, *Political Theory*, pp. 67–105; Charles R. Beitz, "Bounded Morality: Justice and the State in World Politics," 33 *International Organization* (1979), 412–14.

74 Legal positivism is also an analytic doctrine that seeks to distinguish legal norms from non-legal ones.

75 Kenneth Einar Himma, "Positivism, Naturalism, and the Obligation to Obey Law," 36 *Southern Journal of Philosophy* (1998), 151.

76 H.L.A. Hart, "Positivism and the Separation of Law and Morals," 71 *Harvard Law Review* (1958), 593–629; H.L.A. Hart, *The Concept of Law* (2nd ed., Oxford UP, Oxford, 1994), pp. 181–82. See

The separability thesis is vigorously contested by naturalists of all stripes. Joel Feinberg, to give only one example, asks: "Why should I have any respect or duty of fidelity toward a statute with a wicked or stupid content just because it was passed into law by a bunch of men (possibly very wicked men like the Nazi legislators) according to the accepted recipes for making law?"[77] A small number of legal positivists concede Feinberg's point—arguing instead that one has a moral obligation to obey the law *qua* law only if it is enacted according to just legislative procedures.[78] But what is a just legislative procedure? In international law, "state consent"—expressed in the form of treaties and international custom—is the accepted procedure for enacting legal norms. But is "state consent" a just legislative procedure? Legal positivists could argue that "state consent" is the legally valid (and hence morally binding) legislative procedure because it is the legislative procedure that states recognize as legally valid (and hence morally binding). Such a claim, however, would be self-referential at best—tautological at worst. One could argue with equal consistency that "Nazi Party consent" was the legally valid (and hence morally binding) legislative procedure in Nazi Germany because it was the legislative procedure that the Nazi Party recognized as legally valid (and hence morally binding). To have a plausible normative theory, legal positivists need to justify (i) their collectivist assumption that states are the *proper agents* to enact binding norms, and (ii) their consensualist assumption that actual consent—whose problems we have briefly noted above—is the *proper means* for enacting such norms. To do this, however, they must employ the sorts of naturalist arguments that the separability thesis expressly forbids.[79]

The legality of Humanitarian Intervention

Legal positivists argue that there is a moral duty to obey the law. But what is the law? According to Article 38(I) of the Statute of the International Court of Justice, international norms are legally binding if they are incorporated in "a. international conventions, whether general or particular, establishing rules expressly recognized by the contesting states; b. international custom, as evidence of a general practice accepted as law...." Although this Statute is technically only binding on the International

---

also Joseph Raz, *The Authority of Law: Essays on Law and Morality* (Clarendon, Oxford, 1979); Joseph Raz, *The Concept of a Legal System: An Introduction to the Theory of Legal Systems* (2nd ed., Clarendon, Oxford, 1980).

77 Joel Feinberg, "Civil Disobedience in the Modern World," 2 *Humanities in Society* (1979), 43–44. See also Lon L. Fuller, "Positivism and Fidelity to Law: A Reply to Professor Hart," 71 *Harvard Law Review* (1958), 630; Jules Coleman, "On the Relationship between Law and Morality," 2 *Ratio Juris* (1989), 66–78; Tesón, *Philosophy of International Law*, pp. 92–97.

78 Himma, "Positivism, Naturalism," pp. 145–61.

79 John Rawls, "Legal Obligation and the Duty of Fair Play," in Sidney Hook ed., *Law and Philosophy* (New York UP, New York, 1964), pp. 3–18; M.B.E. Smith, "Do We Have a Prima Facie Obligation to Obey the Law?" 82 *Yale Law Journal* (1973), 950–76; Klaus Füsser, "Farewell to 'Legal Positivism': The Separation Thesis Unravelling," in Robert George ed., *The Autonomy of Law: Essays on Legal Positivism* (Clarendon, Oxford, 1996), pp. 119–62.

Court of Justice, it is widely accepted as the authoritative statement of the sources of international law.

International conventions

The Charter of the United Nations

The paramount international convention governing the exercise of armed force in the international community is the Charter of the United Nations. Opponents of humanitarian intervention point to Article 2(4)'s injunction that "[a]ll states...refrain in their international relations from the threat or use of force against the territorial integrity and political independence of any state, or in any other manner inconsistent with the purpose of the United Nations." They also note Article 2(7)'s declaration that "[n]othing in the present Charter shall authorize the United Nations to intervene in matters which are essentially within the domestic jurisdiction of any state."

For most international lawyers, this is the end of the matter. The meaning of the UN Charter is clear. A small, but growing, number of international legal scholars, however, beg to disagree. They advance three arguments aimed at reconciling humanitarian intervention with the UN's *jus ad bellum* regime.

First, they argue that "Article 2(4) does not forbid the threat or use of force *simpliciter*; it forbids it only when directed against the territorial integrity or political independence of any State."[80] Thus, if a "genuine humanitarian intervention does not result in territorial conquest or political subjugation...it is a distortion to argue that [it] is prohibited by article 2(4)."[81]

Most international lawyers dispute this argument on the ground that the drafters of the Charter clearly intended the phrase "territorial integrity or political independence of any State" to reinforce, rather than restrict, the ban on the use of force in international relations. "If it is asserted," writes Ian Brownlie, "that the phrase may have a qualifying effect then the writers making this assertion face the difficulty that it involves an admission that there is an ambiguity, and in such a case recourse may be had to the *travaux préparatoires*, which reveal a meaning contrary to that asserted."[82] Oscar Schachter is blunter: "The idea that wars waged in a good cause such

---

80 Julius Stone, *Aggression and World Order: A Critique of United Nations' Theories of Aggression* (Stevens, London, 1958), p. 95.

81 Tesón, *Humanitarian Intervention*, p. 151. "Since a humanitarian intervention seeks neither a territorial change nor a challenge to the political independence of the State involved and is not only not inconsistent with the purposes of the United Nations but is rather in conformity with the most fundamental peremptory norms of the Charter, it is a distortion to argue that it is precluded by Article 2(4)." W. Michael Reisman with the collaboration of Myres S. McDougal, "Humanitarian Intervention to Protect the Ibos," in Lillich, *Humanitarian Intervention and the UN*, p. 177.

82 Brownlie, *International Law and the Use of Force*, p. 267. See also Michael Akehurst, "Humanitarian Intervention," in Bull, *Intervention in World Politics*, p. 105; Rosalyn Higgins, *The Development of International Law through the Political Organs of the United Nations* (Oxford UP, Oxford, 1963), p. 183.

as democracy and human rights would not involve a violation of territorial integrity or political independence demands an Orwellian construction of those terms."[83]

This debate, like so many in international law, turns on how to interpret the relevant international conventions. There are, broadly speaking, two approaches to the question. The advocates of what Tom J. Farer calls the "classicist view" presume that the parties to a treaty "had an original intention which can be discovered primarily through textual analysis and which, in the absence of some unforeseen change in circumstances, must be respected until the agreement has expired or has been replaced by mutual consent."[84] In contrast, champions of the rival approach, "legal realism," see

> explicit and implicit agreements, formal texts, and state behavior as being in a condition of effervescent interaction, unceasingly creating, modifying, and replacing norms. Texts themselves are but one among a large number of means for ascertaining original intention. Moreover, realists postulate an accelerating contraction in the capacity and the authority of original intention to govern state behavior. Indeed, original intention does not govern at any point in time. For original intention has no intrinsic authority. The past is relevant only to the extent that it helps us to identify currently prevailing attitudes about the propriety of a government's acts and omissions.[85]

If one accepts the classicist view, the illegality of unauthorized humanitarian intervention is patent. If one adopts the legal realist view, however, its legal status depends in large measure on the attitude of the contemporary international community towards it.

The second way many legal realists have sought to reconcile humanitarian intervention with the UN's *jus ad bellum* regime is to claim the phrase "or in any other manner inconsistent with the purposes of the United Nations" permits unauthorized humanitarian intervention where the Security Council fails to realize one of its chief purposes—the protection of human rights.[86] According to W. Michael Reisman, if the Security Council had functioned as originally designed,

---

83 Schachter, "Legality of Pro-democratic Invasion," p. 649.

84 Tom J. Farer, "An Inquiry into the Legitimacy of Humanitarian Intervention," in Lori Fisler Damrosch and David J. Scheffer eds., *Law and Force in the New International Order* (Westview Press, Boulder, 1991), p. 186.

85 Ibid., p. 186.

86 "The purposes of the United Nations are … [t]o achieve international co-operation in … encouraging respect for human rights and for fundamental freedoms for all without distinction as to race, sex, language or religion" (Article 1(3)). "[T]he United Nations shall promote … universal respect for, and observance of, human rights and fundamental freedoms for all" (Article 55). "All members shall pledge themselves to take joint and separate action in cooperation with the Organisation for the achievement of the purposes set forth in Article 55" (Article 56).

it would have obviated the need for the [unauthorized] use of force. States with a grievance could have repaired to the Security Council, which could then apply the appropriate quantum and form of authoritative coercion and thereby vindicate the rights it found had been violated.... But the security system of the United Nations was premised on a consensus between the permanent members of the Security Council.[87] Lamentably, that consensus dissolved early in the history of the organisation. Thereafter ... [p]art of the systematic justification for the theory of Article 2(4) disappeared.[88]

On this view, if the Security Council fails to end massive human rights violations, states may do so without authorization.[89]

Classicists respond by noting that the negotiating history of the Charter supports the contention that the conjunction "or" in the phrase "or in any other manner inconsistent with the purposes of the United Nations" was meant to supplement, rather than qualify, the prohibition on the unauthorized use of armed force. In other words, the drafters of Article 2(4) intended to ban states from using force *against both the territorial integrity and political independence* of other states *and* in any other manner inconsistent with the promotion of human rights.[90] They also

87 Reisman's assumption that the UN security system presupposed a continuation of the wartime alliance between the United States, the United Kingdom, the Soviet Union, France, and China is not without its critics. "During the formation of the United Nations," writes Judy A. Gallant, "numerous states initially hoped to eliminate the veto but quickly understood that it was a precondition to ensuring the very existence of the United Nations. The veto power was the cost that the less influential nations paid for the inclusion of the five major powers in the new collective security system." Judy A. Gallant, "Humanitarian Intervention and Security Council Resolution 688: A Reappraisal in Light of a Changing World Order," 7 *American University Journal of International Law and Policy* (1992), 898–99.

88 W. Michael Reisman, "Criteria for the Lawful Use of Force in International Law," 10 *Yale Journal of International Law* (1985), 279–80. See also Stone, *Aggression and World Order*, pp. 43, 95–96; W. Friedmann, *The Changing Structure of International Law* (Columbia University Press, New York, 1964), p. 259; Richard B. Lillich, "Humanitarian Intervention: A Reply to Ian Brownlie and a Plea for Constructive Alternatives," in Moore, *Law and Civil War*, p. 230; W. Michael Reisman, "Coercion and Self-determination: Construing Charter Article 2(4)," 78 *American Journal of International Law* (1984), 642–45; Daniel Wolf, "Humanitarian Intervention," 9 *Michigan Year Book of International Legal Studies* (1988), 368.

89 "The deterioration of the Charter security regime has stimulated a partial revival of a type of [unauthorized] *jus ad bellum*.... Nine basic categories appear to have emerged in which one finds varying support for [unauthorized] uses of force. They [include] ... humanitarian intervention." Reisman, "Criteria for the Lawful Use of Force," p. 281. See also Tesón, *Humanitarian Intervention*, pp. 157–62; David M. Kresock, "'Ethnic Cleansing' in the Balkans: The Legal Foundations of Foreign Intervention," 27 *Cornell International Law Journal* (1994), 234–37.

90 "The delegate of Brazil adverted to the possibility of a restricted interpretation of the phrase. The United States delegate 'made it clear that the intention of the authors of the original text was to state in the broadest terms an absolute all-inclusive prohibition; the phrase "or in any other manner" was designed to insure that there should be no loop-holes.'" Brownlie, *International Law and the Use of Force*, p. 268, n. 6; Sean Murphy, *Humanitarian Intervention: The United Nations in an Evolving World Order* (U of Pennsylvania P, Philadelphia, 1996), p. 73. Even as notable a propo-

note that the contrary interpretation has twice been rejected by the International Court of Justice.[91]

Once again, if one accepts the classicist view, the illegality of unauthorized humanitarian intervention is clear. If one adopts the legal realist view, however, its legal status depends in large measure on the international community's current attitude towards such interventions. This is examined below....

The third way legal realists seek to legitimate humanitarian intervention is through an expansive interpretation of Article 39 of the UN Charter. This article states that the Security Council may authorize the use of force in response to "any threat to the peace, breach of the peace or act of aggression." Legal realists argue that this article, by giving the Security Council jurisdiction over any "threat to *the* peace," rather than over any threat to *international* peace, permits it to intervene to end human rights violations that lack transboundary effects.[92]

Once again, classicists beg to differ. Massive and pervasive human rights violations, writes Lori Fisler Damrosch,

> do not necessarily entail threats to peace and security.... Economic sanctions and other nonforcible measures are quite acceptable methods for enforcement of the full range of international human rights law, whether or not the human rights violations in question endanger international security. States may adopt such nonforcible measures of their own or through collective mechanisms, including those sponsored by the United Nations as well as by regional organizations. But there is no clear authority to be found in the UN Charter for transboundary *uses of force* against violations that do not themselves pose a transboundary threat to peace and security.[93]

This view, as Damrosch herself acknowledges, is difficult to defend on purely legal grounds.[94] First, the records of both the Dumbarton Oaks and San Francisco Conferences plainly show the drafters of the UN Charter wanted the Security Council

---

nent of humanitarian intervention as Anthony A. D'Amato concedes the drafters of the Charter intended to ban forcible self-help in defense of human rights. Anthony A. D'Amato, *International Law: Process and Prospect* (Transnational Publishers, Dobbs Ferry, 1987), p. 54.

91 *Corfu Channel Case (Merits), ICJ Reports, 1949*, p. 35; *Nicaragua* v. *US (Merits), ICJ Reports, 1986*, p. 97.

92 "[T]he decision of the Security Council on what constitutes a threat to international peace and security is a political one and subject to its political discretion." Malanczuk, *Humanitarian Intervention*, p. 26; Jost Delbrück, "A Fresh Look at Humanitarian Intervention under the Authority of the United Nations," 67 *Indiana Law Journal* (1992), 898–99.

93 Lori Fisler Damrosch, "Commentary on Collective Military Intervention to Enforce Human Rights," in Damrosch and Scheffer, *Law and Force*, p. 219.

94 "My concern about using the Security Council or the General Assembly in the kinds of situations under discussion relates not so much to the constitutional law of the UN Charter as to the wisdom of starting down this road." Ibid., p. 220.

to have wide discretion in determining the existence of any threat to the peace.[95] Second, and more importantly, the Security Council itself rejects it. The UN's interventions in Somalia (1992), Rwanda (1994), and Haiti (1994) all support the contention that the Security Council presently believes it is empowered under Chapter VII of the UN Charter to authorize the use of military force to end massive human rights abuses.[96]

In Somalia, for example, the Security Council determined that the civil war was "a threat to international peace and security."[97] To be sure, the collapse of the Somali state produced refugee flows that affected neighboring countries. But, as Sean D. Murphy notes,

> the Security Council's resolution made no mention of refugees, and the subsequent intervention was not designed simply to repatriate those refugees. The primary focus of the intervention under UNITAF was, rather, to open food relief lines into Somalia so as to prevent widespread starvation and disease among Somalis *in Somalia.*... [O]ne benefit of these actions was the creation of conditions for the repatriation of Somali refugees, but to cast the intervention as designed wholly or predominantly to address that issue would be incorrect.[98]

In Rwanda, the Security Council likewise determined that the massacre of up to a million Tutsis constituted "a threat to peace."[99] And while it parenthetically noted the "massive exodus of refugees to neighbouring countries," the Security Council's preoccupation was with ending the "acts of genocide...*in Rwanda*"; "the ongoing violence *in Rwanda*"; "the continuation of systematic and widespread killings of the civilian population *in Rwanda*"; and the "*internal* displacement of some 1.5 million

---

95 "[A]n overwhelming majority of the participating governments were of the opinion that the circumstances in which threats to the peace or aggression might occur are so varied that [Article 39] should be left as broad and as flexible as possible." US Department of State, *Charter of the United Nations: Report to the President on the Result of the San Francisco Conference (1945)* (Greenwood Press, New York, 1969), p. 91. See also Jochen A. Frowein, "Article 39," in Simma et al., *Charter of the UN*, pp. 607–08.

96 Humanitarian interventions in Liberia (1990), northern Iraq (1991), southern Iraq (1992), and Sierra Leone (1998) neither support nor undermine the proposition that the UN has a right to use military force to end massive human rights abuses. In all four cases, the Security Council acquiesced in, rather than formally authorized, the use of armed force to protect human rights. Security Council Resolution 688, UNSCOR, 2982nd mtg., 5 April 1991; Security Council Resolution 788, UNSCOR, 3138th mtg., 19 November 1992; Security Council Resolution 813, UNSCOR, 3187th mtg., 26 March 1993; Security Council Resolution 1156, UNSCOR, 3861st mtg., 16 March 1998; Security Council Resolution 1162, UNSCOR, 3872nd mtg., 17 April 1998; Security Council Resolution 1181, UNSCOR, 3902nd mtg., 13 July 1998.

97 Security Council Resolution 688, UNSCOR, 2982nd mtg., 3 December 1992.

98 Murphy, *Humanitarian Intervention*, pp. 286–87.

99 Security Council Resolution 929, UNSCOR, 3392nd mtg., 22 June 1994.

Rwandans."[100] Again, no impartial observer could conclude that the Security Council thought that it was only the transboundary effects of the Rwandan genocide, rather than the genocide itself, that permitted it to intervene.

Finally, in Haiti, the Security Council determined that the "deterioration of the humanitarian situation in Haiti, in particular the continuing escalation . . . of systematic violations of *civil* liberties"[101] constituted a "threat to peace" in the region.[102] In addition, although it expressed grave concern for the "desperate plight of Haitian refugees,"[103] there is little evidence that it thought that these transboundary effects alone, and not the "climate of fear" created by the "illegal de facto regime," gave it the right to intervene.[104]

The Charter's drafting history and recent Security Council practice thus strongly support the legal realist contention that UN-sanctioned humanitarian interventions are lawful exceptions to the Charter's general prohibition of forcible self-help in international relations.[105]

Human Rights Conventions

The UN Charter's apparent ban on unauthorized humanitarian intervention does not mean that states are free to treat their own citizens as they wish. To the contrary, most states are signatories to conventions that legally oblige them to respect the

---

100 Security Council Resolution 925, UNSCOR, 3388th mtg., 8 June 1994; Security Council Resolution 929, UNSCOR, 3392nd mtg., 22 June 1994, para. 3; emphases added.

101 Security Council Resolution 940, UNSCOR, 3413th mtg., 31 July 1994; emphasis added.

102 Fernando R. Tesón contends that "the Security Council did *not* determine that the situation in Haiti constituted a threat to international peace and security while asserting that it was acting under Chapter VII." Tesón, "Collective Humanitarian Intervention," p. 358. This claim is mistaken, as the relevant sections of Security Council Resolutions 841 and 940 plainly show: "*The Security Council . . .* [*d*]*etermining* that . . . the continuation of this situation threatens international peace and security in the region . . . [and *a*]*cting*, therefore, under Chapter VII of the Charter of the United Nations . . . [*d*]*ecides* . . . ." "*The Security Council . . .* [*d*]*etermining* that the situation in Haiti continues to constitute a threat to peace and security in the region . . . [and *a*]*cting* under Chapter VII of the Charter of the United Nations authorises Member States to form a multinational force under unified command and control and, in this framework, to use all necessary means to facilitate the departure from Haiti of the military leadership . . . [and] the prompt return of the legitimately elected President . . . ." Security Council Resolution 841, UNSCOR, 3238th mtg., 16 June 1993; Security Council Resolution 940, UNSCOR, 3413th mtg., 31 July 1994.

103 Security Council Resolution 940, UNSCOR, 3413th mtg., 31 July 1994.

104 Security Council Resolution 841, UNSCOR, 3238th mtg., 16 June 1993.

105 While it is widely accepted that the UN Security Council can authorize humanitarian interventions, there is considerable disagreement about whether a state or group of states claiming to be acting pursuant to *implied* or *ambiguous* Security Council authorizations is acting lawfully. See Thomas M. Franck, "Interpretation and Change in the Law of Humanitarian Intervention," ch. 6 in this volume [i.e., Holzgrefe and Keohane (eds.), *Humanitarian Intervention*]; Jules Lobel and Michael Ratner, "Bypassing the Security Council: Ambiguous Authorizations to Use Force, Cease-fires and the Iraqi Inspection Regime," 93 *American Journal of International Law* (1999), 124–54.

human rights of their citizens.[106] Nevertheless, the mere existence of these obligations, as Jack Donnelly observes,

> does not imply that any international actor is authorized to implement or
> enforce those obligations. Just as in domestic politics, governments are free to
> adopt legislation with extremely weak, or even non-existent, implementation
> measures, states are free to create and accept international legal obligations
> that are to be implemented entirely through national action. And this is in fact
> what states have done with international human rights. None of the obligations
> to be found in multilateral human rights treaties may be coercively enforced
> by any external actor.[107]

It has been suggested that the Genocide Convention (1948), by enjoining its signatories to "prevent and punish" the "crime of genocide," may be the exception that
proves this rule.[108] But, as the text of that convention makes clear, the only way in
which the contracting parties may legally prevent acts of genocide is by calling upon
"the competent organs of the United Nations to take such action as they consider
appropriate."[109] Such an "enforcement" mechanism clearly does not establish a right
of unauthorized humanitarian intervention.

In sum, the most important source of international law, international conventions, seems to permit the UN Security Council to authorize humanitarian interventions by its members. More controversial, however, is the claim that it also allows
unauthorized humanitarian interventions.

---

106 These include: Covenant to Suppress the Slave Trade and Slavery (1926); Convention on the
Prevention and Punishment of the Crime of Genocide (1948); European Convention for the
Protection of Human Rights and Fundamental Freedoms (1950); International Covenant on
Economic, Social and Cultural Rights (1966); International Convention on the Elimination of
All Forms of Racial Discrimination (1965); International Covenant on Civil and Political Rights
(1966); Optional Protocol to the International Covenant on Civil and Political Rights (1966);
American Convention on Human Rights (1969); Convention on the Elimination of All Forms of
Discrimination against Women (1979); African Charter on Human and Peoples' Rights (1981);
United Nations Convention against Torture and Other Cruel, Inhuman or Degrading Treatment
(1984); United Nations Convention on the Rights of the Child (1989). For texts see Ian Brownlie,
Basic Documents on Human Rights (3rd ed., Oxford UP, New York, 1992).

107 Jack Donnelly, "Human Rights, Humanitarian Crisis, and Humanitarian Intervention," 48
International Journal (1993), 623. See also Jack Donnelly, *International Human Rights* (Westview
Press, Boulder, 1993), pp. 57–97.

108 Scheffer, "Towards a Modern Doctrine," p. 289; United Nations Convention on the Prevention
and Punishment of the Crime of Genocide (1948), Article I. Julie Mertus goes further: "If the
target state is party to any of the relevant human rights conventions, or if the human right can
be said to be customary international law applicable to all states, humanitarian intervention can
be grounded or categorized as a means of enforcing these obligations on behalf of victims." Julie
Mertus, "The Legality of Humanitarian Intervention: Lessons from Kosovo," 41 *William and
Mary Law Review* (2000), 1773.

109 United Nations Convention on the Prevention and Punishment of the Crime of Genocide (1948),
Article VIII.

Customary International Law

Some scholars argue for the continued existence of a customary right of unauthorized humanitarian intervention.[110] According to them, state practice in the nineteenth and early twentieth centuries established such a right; a right that was "neither terminated nor weakened" by the creation of the United Nations.[111] This right remains so secure, they argue, that "only its limits and not its existence is subject to debate."[112]

Classicists contest this view on two grounds. First, they contend that the handful of pre-Charter humanitarian interventions (Britain, France, and Russia in Greece [1827–30]; France in Syria [1860–61]; Russia in Bosnia-Herzegovina and Bulgaria [1877–78]; United States in Cuba [1898]; and Greece, Bulgaria, and Serbia in Macedonia [1903–08, 1912–13]) were insufficient to establish a customary right of humanitarian intervention.[113] Indeed, such a right was not even invoked, let alone exercised, in the face of the greatest humanitarian catastrophes of the pre-Charter era, including the massacre of 1 million Armenians by the Turks (1914–19), the forced starvation of 4 million Ukrainians by the Soviets (1930s); the massacre of hundreds of thousands of Chinese by the Japanese (1931–45); and the extermination of 6 million Jews by the Nazis (1939–45). It may also be noted that there is little or no evidence that the international community considered such a right legally binding (*opinio juris sive necessitatis*), a *sine qua non* of customary international law.[114]

---

110 Richard B. Lillich, "Forcible Self-help by States to Protect Human Rights," 53 *Iowa Law Review* (1967), 334; Jean-Pierre L. Fonteyne, "The Customary International Law Doctrine of Humanitarian Intervention: Its Current Validity under the UN Charter," 4 *California Western International Law Journal* (1974), 203–70; Lillich, "Reply to Ian Brownlie," pp. 229–51; Michael J. Bazyler, "Re-examining the Doctrine of Humanitarian Intervention in Light of the Atrocities in Kampuchea and Ethiopia," 23 *Stanford Journal of International Law* (1987), 547–619.

111 Reisman, "Humanitarian Intervention to Protect the Ibos," p. 171.

112 International Law Association, *The International Protection of Human Rights by General International Law* (Interim Report of the Sub-Committee, International Committee on Human Rights, The Hague, 1970), p. 11, quoted in Fonteyne, "Customary International Law Doctrine," pp. 235–36. See also M. Ganji, *International Protection of Human Rights* (Librairie E. Droz, Geneva, 1962); Nanda, "Tragedies in Northern Iraq, Liberia, Yugoslavia and Haiti," p. 310; Bazyler, "Re-examining the Doctrine," p. 573; M. Trachtenberg, "Intervention in Historical Perspective," in Laura W. Reed and Carl Kaysen eds., *Emerging Norms of Justified Intervention* (Committee on International Security Studies, American Academy of Arts and Sciences, Cambridge, MA, 1993), pp. 15–36; Barry M. Benjamin, "Unilateral Humanitarian Intervention: Legalizing the Use of Force to Prevent Human Rights Atrocities," 16 *Fordham International Law Journal* (1992–93), 126.

113 Brownlie, *International Law and the Use of Force*, pp. 339–41; Thomas M. Franck and Nigel S. Rodley, "After Bangladesh: The Law of Humanitarian Intervention by Military Force," 67 *American Journal of International Law* (1973), 279–85; Brownlie, "Humanitarian Intervention," pp. 220–21; Beyerlin, "Humanitarian Intervention," p. 212; Ronzitti, *Rescuing Nationals Abroad*, pp. 89–93; Malanczuk, *Humanitarian Intervention*, pp. 7–11.

114 J. Charney, "The Persistent Objector Rule and the Development of Customary International Law," 56 *British Yearbook of International Law* (1985), 1–24; R. Bernhardt, "Customary International Law," in Bernhardt, 1 *Encyclopedia of Public International Law*, pp. 898–905; G. Danilenko, *Law-making in the International Community* (Martinus Nijhoff, Dordrecht, 1993), pp. 81–109; Ian Brownlie, *Principles of Public International Law* (5th ed., Clarendon, Oxford, 1998), pp. 4–11; Michael Byers, *Custom, Power and the Power of Rules: International Relations and Customary International Law* (Cambridge UP, Cambridge, 1999), pp. 129–203.

Second, classicists contend that, even if one concedes that a customary right of humanitarian intervention existed in the pre-Charter era, it did not legally survive the creation of the UN's *jus ad bellum* regime. If one accepts the strictures of classicism, the only way such a right could have endured was if it were a peremptory international norm (*jus cogens*), i.e., a norm that was "accepted and recognised by the international community...as a norm from which no derogation is permitted."[115] Yet, as noted above, there is considerable doubt as to whether such a right even existed, let alone possessed the status of a peremptory international norm. Indeed, the very establishment of the United Nations, with its ostensible ban on unauthorized humanitarian intervention, is strong prima facie evidence to the contrary.

Of course, the burden of proving the continued existence of a customary right of unauthorized humanitarian intervention is lightened considerably if one accepts a legal realist interpretation of the UN Charter. In addition to avoiding the need to show that the doctrine of humanitarian intervention was a peremptory international norm in the pre-Charter period, one may point to a number of post-Charter interventions—the United States in the Dominican Republic (1965); India in East Pakistan (1971); Vietnam in Kampuchea (1978–93); Tanzania in Uganda (1979); ECOWAS in Liberia (1990–95); Britain, France, and the United States in Iraq (since 1991); ECOWAS in Sierra Leone (since 1998); and NATO in Kosovo (since 1999)—as evidence of its continued existence.

Yet having to meet a lighter burden of proof is not identical to actually doing so. Classicists still note that this alleged right lacks the two recognized attributes of a binding international norm: general observance and widespread acceptance that it is lawful (*opinio juris sive necessitatis*).[116] In support of this contention, they point to the highly selective exercise of the right of unauthorized humanitarian intervention in recent history. No state or regional organization, for example, intervened to prevent or end the massacre of several hundred thousand ethnic Chinese in Indonesia (mid-1960s); the killing and forced starvation of almost half a million Ibos in Nigeria (1966–70); the slaughter and forced starvation of well over a million black Christians by the Sudanese government (since the late 1960s); the killing of tens of thousands of Tutsis in Rwanda (early 1970s); the murder of tens of thousands of Hutus in Burundi (1972); the slaying of 100,000 East Timorese by the Indonesian government (1975–99); the forced starvation of up to 1 million Ethiopians by their government (mid-1980s); the murder of 100,000 Kurds in Iraq (1988–89); and the

---

115 Vienna Convention on the Law of Treaties (1969), Article 53. See also Jochen A. Frowein, "*Jus Cogens*," in Bernhardt, 7 *Encyclopedia of Public International Law*, pp. 327–30; L. Hannikainen, *Peremptory Norms (Jus Cogens) in International Law: Historical Development, Criteria, Present Status* (Lakimiesliiton Kustannus, Helsinki, 1988); G. Danilenko, "International *Jus Cogens*: Issues of Law-making," 2 *European Journal of International Law* (1991), 42–65.

116 Franck and Rodley, "After Bangladesh," p. 296; Ian Brownlie, "Non-use of Force in Contemporary International Law," in William E. Butler ed., *Non-use of Force in International Law* (Martinus Nijhoff, Dordrecht, 1989), pp. 25–26; Farer, "An Inquiry into the Legitimacy," pp. 192–95.

killing of tens of thousands of Hutus in Burundi (since 1993). But while the classicists are correct to highlight the selective exercise of this putative right, their argument, as Dino Kritsiotis notes,

> misconceives the theoretical and traditional understanding of humanitarian intervention in international law, which has been framed as a *right* of states and not as an *obligation* requiring action. Inherent in the very conception of a right is an element of selectivity in the exercise of that right. This is in keeping with the right-holder's sovereign discretion to decide whether or not to exercise the right in question and commit its armed forces to foreign territories and explains why it is the right *of*—rather than the right *to*—humanitarian intervention that has taken hold in practice as well as legal scholarship.[117]

Because the doctrine of unauthorized humanitarian intervention is a permissive rather than a mandatory norm, the selectivity of its exercise is no barrier to its being a customary international law.

The task of showing that a right of unauthorized humanitarian intervention possesses the second attribute of a customary international norm (widespread acceptance that it is lawful [*opinio juris sive necessitatis*]) is more difficult. The long list of UN General Assembly resolutions rejecting such a right argues strongly against this claim.[118] In 1999, for example, that august body passed, by a vote of 107 to 7 (with 48 abstentions), the following denunciation of NATO's intervention in Kosovo:

> *The General Assembly … Reaffirming …* that no State may use or encourage the use of economic, political or any other type of measures to coerce another State in order to obtain from it the subordination of the exercise of its sovereign rights … [and] *Deeply concerned* that, despite the recommendations adopted on this question by the General Assembly … [unauthorized] coercive measures

---

117 Dino Kritsiotis, "Reappraising Policy Objections to Humanitarian Intervention," 19 *Michigan Journal of International Law* (1998), 1027.

118 "No state has the right to intervene, directly or indirectly, for any reason whatever, in the internal or external affairs of any other State." Declaration on the Inadmissibility of Intervention in the Domestic Affairs of States (1965), GA Res. 2131, UNGAOR, 20th sess., UN Doc. A/6220 (1965).
    "Armed intervention and all other forms of interference or attempted threats against the personality of the State or against its political, economic and cultural elements, are in violation of international law." Declaration on Principles of International Law concerning Friendly Relations and Cooperation among States (1970), GA Res. 2625, UNGAOR, 25th sess., UN Doc. A/8028 (1970).
    "The sovereignty, territorial integrity and national unity of States must be fully respected in accordance with the Charter of the United Nations. In this context, humanitarian assistance *should be provided with the consent of the affected country* and in principle on the basis of an appeal by the affected country." Declaration on Strengthening of the Coordination of Humanitarian Emergency Assistance of the United Nations (1991), GA Res. 46/182, UNGAOR, 46th sess., UN Doc. A/RES/46/182 (1991).

continue to be promulgated and implemented with all their extraterritorial effects...*Rejects* [unauthorized] coercive measures with all their extraterritorial effects as tools for political or economic pressure against any country.[119]

More significantly, even states that have intervened to end heinous human rights abuses have been loath to invoke a customary right of unauthorized humanitarian intervention to defend their actions. India's ostensible justification of its invasion of East Pakistan was self-defense.[120] Vietnam claimed that it was responding to a "large-scale aggressive war" being waged by Cambodia.[121] Tanzania defended its overthrow of the Amin regime as an appropriate response to Uganda's invasion, occupation, and annexation of the Kagera salient the preceding year.[122] ECOWAS's justification of its invasions of Liberia and Sierra Leone was that it was invited to intervene by the legitimate governments of those states.[123] NATO defended Operation Allied Force on the grounds that it was "consistent with" Security Council Resolutions 1160, 1199, and 1203.[124] It is irrelevant that these justifications are specious if not false. What is noteworthy is the fact that the states concerned felt they could not appeal to a right of unauthorized humanitarian intervention to legitimate their actions. If there is presently a right of unauthorized humanitarian intervention, it is a right that dares not speak its name.[125]

---

119 GA Res. 54/172, UNGAOR, 54th sess., UN Doc. A/RES/54/172 (1999).

120 Akehurst, "Humanitarian Intervention," p. 96; Franck and Rodley, "After Bangladesh," pp. 276–77; Ronzitti, *Rescuing Nationals Abroad*, pp. 96, 108–09; Wil D. Verwey, "Humanitarian Intervention under International Law," 32 *Netherlands International Law Review* (1985), 401–02.

121 Foreign Ministry Statement (6 January 1979), quoted in Murphy, *Humanitarian Intervention*, p. 104. See also Gary Klintworth, *Vietnam's Intervention in Cambodia in International Law* (Australian Government Publishing Service, Canberra, 1989), pp. 15–33.

122 Ronzitti, *Rescuing Nationals Abroad*, pp. 102–06; Hassan, "Realpolitik," pp. 859–912.

123 Murphy, *Humanitarian Intervention*, pp. 146–58; Karsten Nowrot and Emily W. Schabacker, "The Use of Force to Restore Democracy: International Legal Implications of the ECOWAS Intervention in Sierra Leone," 14 *American University International Law Review* (1998), 321–412; J. Levitt, "Humanitarian Intervention by Regional Actors in Internal Conflicts: The Cases of ECOWAS in Liberia and Sierra Leone," 12 *Temple International and Comparative Law Journal* (1998), 333–75.

124 Wheeler, *Saving Strangers*, pp. 275–81.

125 Belgium was the lone NATO member to claim that Operation Allied Force was a legitimate exercise of a customary right of humanitarian intervention. "NATO, and the Kingdom of Belgium in particular, felt obliged to intervene to forestall an ongoing humanitarian catastrophe, acknowledged in Security Council resolutions. To safeguard what? To safeguard, Mr. President, essential values which also rank as *jus cogens*. Are the right to life, physical integrity, the prohibition of torture, are these not norms with the status of *jus cogens*? They undeniably have this status, so much so that international instruments on human rights (the European Human Rights Convention, the agreements mentioned above) protect them in a waiver clause (the power of suspension in case of war of all human rights except right to life and integrity of the individual): thus they are absolute rights, from which we may conclude that they belong to the *jus cogens*. Thus, NATO intervened to protect fundamental values enshrined in the *jus cogens* and to prevent an impending catastrophe recognized as such by the Security Council." "Public sitting held on Monday 10 May 1999, at the Peace Palace, Vice-President Weeramantry, Acting President, presiding in the case concerning *Legality of Use of Force* (*Yugoslavia v. Belgium*)." Available at http://www.icj-cij.org/icjwww/idocket/iybe/iybeframe.htm (5 March 2002).

In sum, even if one accepts legal realism's relaxed attitude to the sources of international law, it still takes a highly selective reading of those sources to conclude that a right of unauthorized humanitarian intervention is presently legal. One must bear in mind, however, that demonstrating that unauthorized humanitarian intervention is illegal is not, unless you are a legal positivist, the same as proving that it is immoral.

Conclusion

Having surveyed the principal arguments about the morality and legality of humanitarian intervention, let me conclude by offering the following three observations.

First, any attempt to separate legal questions from moral ones is doomed to failure. Take, for example, the debate between classicists and legal realists. This debate is ostensibly about how best to identify state intent. Classicists aver that it is best found in the plain meaning of international conventions. Legal realists claim that it is best distilled from the widest range of relevant sources. Still one cannot help feeling that the debate is, at a deeper level, about quite different issues. Classicists claim that international law is the lone, best, hope of stopping powerful states from running amok, and view legal realist attempts to weaken its already all-too-feeble restraining effects with barely concealed horror. Legal realists, for their part, fear that international law, in the hands of classicists, risks becoming an irrelevance at best, and a hindrance at worst. They worry that, in a rapidly changing world with precious few resources for legal reform, past expressions of state intent will become obstacles to new expressions of state intent. The relative merits of these two views, however, cannot be decided *a priori*. They depend instead on the character of the system's powerful states and the types of international reform those states are trying to pursue. Legal realism is unquestionably more appealing when the international system is dominated by liberal democracies pursuing a human rights agenda. By the same token, classicism is more appealing when the international system is dominated by totalitarian and authoritarian states pursuing imperialist policies. My point here is that, even in the selection of interpretive methods, legal positivists cannot avoid making moral judgments.

Second, much theorizing about the justice of humanitarian intervention takes place in a state of vincible ignorance. All too often, the empirical claims upon which different ethical theories rest are little more than guesswork. To be sure, the task of testing a claim that this or that humanitarian intervention will (or would) affect human well-being in this or that way is fraught with methodological and practical difficulties. To begin with, there is the problem of identifying a humanitarian intervention's direct and immediate consequences—let alone its peripheral and remote ones. Next, there is the problem of determining how these consequences affect human well-being. While these problems are formidable, they are not insurmountable. One can crudely measure how a humanitarian intervention will affect human well-being by comparing the number of people who actually died in a similar intervention in the past with the number of people *who would have died had that intervention not occurred*.[126] One way of testing this counterfactual proposition is to (i) find out how mortality rates changed in the course of the humanitarian catastrophe; (ii) discover where in the catastrophe's "natural" course the intervention occurred; and (iii) compare the actual post-intervention mortality rates with the projected ones. If the latter exceed the former, then one can reasonably conclude that the humanitarian intervention (and any others like it) is, on utilitarian terms, just; if the former exceed the latter, then one can assume that the reverse is true. Given the importance of various factual claims to both defenders and critics of humanitarian intervention, empirical studies of this kind are absolutely essential if these disagreements are ever to be resolved.

Finally, most disagreements about the justice of humanitarian intervention are caused less by differing conceptions of the *source* of moral concern than by differing conceptions of the proper *breadth* and *weight* of that concern. As we have just seen, some naturalists support a duty of humanitarian intervention—others do not. Some consensualists support a duty of humanitarian intervention—others do not. Identical meta-ethical premises simply do not generate identical, or even broadly similar, ethical conclusions. But, as we have also just seen, similar views about the proper weight and breadth of moral concern *do* produce similar ethical conclusions. Most egalitarians and universalists, for instance, strongly favor a duty of humanitarian intervention, while most inegalitarians and particularists strongly oppose it. The justice of humanitarian intervention thus seems to turn on how one answers the following questions:

What should the breadth and weight of one's moral concern be?
Should it extend beyond one's family, friends, and fellow citizens?
Should it extend to those nameless strangers in distant lands facing genocide, massacre, or enslavement?
Should the needs of these strangers weigh as much as the needs of family, friends, and fellow citizens?

Inegalitarian-particularists reply that we owe a greater duty of care to our family, friends, and fellow citizens than we owe to nameless strangers in distant lands. This view is intuitively appealing—within limits. Egalitarian-universalists respond that all human beings have a right to life and liberty. Duties to family, friends, and fellow citizens are owed once this moral minimum is secured. This is intuitively appealing—again within limits. Is there any way to reconcile these conflicting moral feelings?

---

126 James D. Fearon, "Counterfactuals and Hypothesis Testing in Political Science," 43 *World Politics* (1991), 169–95; Philip E. Tetlock and Aaron Barkin eds., *Counterfactual Thought Experiments in World Politics: Logical, Methodological and Psychological Perspectives* (Princeton UP, Princeton, 1997).

THE HUMANITARIAN INTERVENTION DEBATE

One possible solution is offered by Robert E. Goodin who argues that the inegal-itarian-particularist—or "special"—duties we owe our families, friends, and fellow citizens are simply the ways in which the egalitarian-universalist—or "general"—duties we owe humanity are assigned to particular people.[127]

A great many general duties point to tasks that, for one reason or another, are pursued more effectively if they are subdivided and particular people are assigned special responsibility for particular portions of the task. Sometimes the reason this is so has to do with the advantages of specialization and divi-sion of labor. Other times it has to do with [irregularity in the distribution of] the information required to do a good job, and the limits on people's capacity for processing requisite quantities of information about a great many cases at once.... Whatever the reason, however, it is simply the case that our general duties toward people are sometimes more effectively discharged by assigning special responsibility for that matter to some particular agents.... The duties that states (or, more precisely, their officials) have vis-à-vis their own citizens [therefore] are not in any deep sense special. At root, they are merely the general duties that everyone has toward everyone else worldwide. National boundaries simply visit upon those particular state agents special responsibil-ity for discharging those general obligations vis-à-vis those individuals who happen to be their own citizens.[128]

But Goodin also recognizes that if states are unwilling or unable to protect the lives and liberties of their citizens—if they degenerate into anarchy or tyranny—then the duty to safeguard these rights reverts to the international community.[129] In other words, if the duties we owe to families, friends, and fellow citizens derive their moral force from the duties we owe to human beings in general, "then they are susceptible to being overridden (at least at the margins, or in exceptional circum-stances) by those more general considerations."[130] A very strong case can be made that humanitarian catastrophes such as the Rwandan genocide are just these sorts of "exceptional circumstances."[131]

---

127 Goodin, *Utilitarianism*, p. 280.
128 Ibid., pp. 282, 283.
129 Ibid., pp. 284–87.
130 Ibid., p. 280.
131 I would like to thank Elizabeth Kiss, Bob Keohane, and Allen Buchanan for their extraordinarily valuable comments on earlier drafts of this chapter.

20. A Few Words on Non-Intervention*

John Stuart Mill

There is a country in Europe, equal to the greatest in extent of dominion, far exceeding any other in wealth, and in the power that wealth bestows, the declared principle of whose foreign policy is, to let other nations alone. No country apprehends or affects to apprehend from it any aggressive designs. Power, from of old, is wont to encroach upon the weak, and to quarrel for ascendancy with those who are as strong as itself. Not so this nation. It will hold its own, it will not submit to encroachment, but if other nations do not meddle with it, it will not meddle with them. Any attempt it makes to exert influence over them, even by persuasion, is rather in the service of others, than of itself: to mediate in the quarrels which break out between foreign States, to arrest obstinate civil wars, to reconcile belligerents, to intercede for mild treatment of the vanquished, or finally, to procure the abandonment of some national crime and scandal to humanity, such as the slave-trade. Not only does this nation desire no benefit to itself at the expense of others, it desires none in which all others do not as freely participate. It makes no treaties stipulating for separate commercial advantages. If the aggressions of barbarians force it to a successful war, and its victorious arms put it in a position to command liberty of trade, whatever it demands for itself it demands for all mankind. The cost of the war is its own; the fruits it shares in fraternal equality with the whole human race. Its own ports and commerce are free as the air and the sky: all its neighbours have full liberty to resort to it, paying either no duties, or, if any, generally a mere equivalent for what is paid by its own citizens, nor does it concern itself though they, on their part, keep all to themselves, and persist in the most jealous and narrow-minded exclusion of its merchants and goods.

A nation adopting this policy is a novelty in the world; so much so, it would appear, that many are unable to believe it when they see it. By one of the practical

---

* Source: *Libertarian Alliance*, Foreign Policy Perspectives No. 8, <http://www.libertarian.co.uk/lapubs/forep/forep008.pdf>.

paradoxes which often meet us in human affairs, it is this nation which finds itself, in respect of its foreign policy, held up to obloquy as the type of egoism and selfishness; as a nation which thinks of nothing but of out-witting and out-generalling its neighbours. An enemy, or a self-fancied rival who had been distanced in the race, might be conceived to give vent to such an accusation in a moment of ill-temper. But that it should be accepted by lookers-on, and should pass into a popular doctrine, is enough to surprise even those who have best sounded the depths of human prejudice. Such, however, is the estimate of the foreign policy of England most widely current on the Continent. Let us not flatter ourselves that it is merely the dishonest pretence of enemies, or of those who have their own purposes to serve by exciting odium against us, a class including all the Protectionist writers, and the mouthpieces of all the despots and of the Papacy. The more blameless and laudable our policy might be, the more certainly we might count on its being misrepresented and railed at by these worthies. Unfortunately the belief is not confined to those whom they can influence, but is held with all the tenacity of a prejudice, by innumerable persons free from interested bias. So strong a hold has it on their minds, that when an Englishman attempts to remove it, all their habitual politeness does not enable them to disguise their utter unbelief in his disclaimer. They are firmly persuaded that no word is said, nor act done, by English statesmen in reference to foreign affairs, which has not for its motive principle some peculiarly English interest. Any profession of the contrary appears to them too ludicrously transparent an attempt to impose upon them. Those most friendly to us think they make a great concession in admitting that the fault may possibly be less with the English people, than with the English Government and aristocracy. We do not even receive credit from them for following our own interest with a straightforward recognition of honesty as the best policy. They believe that we have always other objects than those we avow; and the most far-fetched and unplausible suggestion of a selfish purpose appears to them better entitled to credence than anything so utterly incredible as our disinterestedness. Thus, to give one instance among many, when we taxed ourselves twenty millions (a prodigious sum in their estimation) to get rid of negro slavery, and, for the same object, perilled, as everybody thought, destroyed as many thought, the very existence of our West Indian colonies, it was, and still is, believed, that our fine professions were but to delude the world, and that by this self-sacrificing behaviour we were endeavouring to gain some hidden object, which could neither be conceived nor described, in the way of pulling down other nations. The fox who had lost his tail had an intelligible interest in persuading his neighbours to rid themselves of theirs: but we, it is thought by *our* neighbours, cut off our own magnificent brush, the largest and finest of all, in hopes of reaping some inexplicable advantage from inducing others to do the same.

It is foolish attempting to despise all this—persuading ourselves that it is not our fault, and that those who disbelieve *us* would not believe though one should rise from the dead. Nations, like individuals, ought to suspect some fault in themselves when they find they are generally worse thought of than they think they deserve, and they may well know that they are somehow in fault when almost everybody but themselves thinks them crafty and hypocritical. It is not solely because England has been more successful than other nations in gaining what they are all aiming at, that they think she must be following after it with a more ceaseless and a more undivided chase. This indeed is a powerful predisposing cause, inclining and preparing them for the belief. It is a natural supposition that those who win the prize have striven for it; that superior success must be the fruit of more unremitting endeavour; and where there is an obvious abstinence from the ordinary arts employed for distancing competitors, and they are distanced nevertheless, people are fond of believing that the means employed must have been arts still more subtle and profound. This preconception makes them look out in all quarters for indications to prop up the selfish explanation of our conduct. If our ordinary course of action does not favour this interpretation, they watch for exceptions to our ordinary course, and regard these as the real index to the purposes within. They moreover accept literally all the habitual expressions by which we represent ourselves as worse than we are; expressions often heard from English statesmen, next to never from those of any other country—partly because Englishmen, beyond all the rest of the human race, are so shy of professing virtues that they will even profess vices instead; and partly because almost all English statesmen, while careless to a degree which no foreigner can credit, respecting the impression they produce on foreigners, commit the obtuse blunder of supposing that low objects are the only ones to which the minds of their non-aristocratic fellow-countrymen are amenable, and that it is always expedient, if not necessary, to place those objects in the foremost rank.

All, therefore, who either speak or act in the name of England, are bound by the strongest obligations, both of prudence and of duty, to avoid giving either of these handles for misconstruction: to put a severe restraint upon the mania of professing to act from meaner motives than those by which we are really actuated, and to beware of perversely or capriciously singling out some particular instance in which to act on a worse principle than that by which we are ordinarily guided. Both these salutary cautions our practical statesmen are, at the present time, flagrantly disregarding.

We are now in one of those critical moments, which do not occur once in a generation, when the whole turn of European events, and the course of European history for a long time to come, may depend on the conduct and on the estimation of England. At such a moment, it is difficult to say whether by their sins of speech or of action our statesmen are most effectually playing into the hands of our enemies, and giving most colour of justice to injurious misconception of our character and policy as a people.

To take the sins of speech first: What is the sort of language held in every oration which, during the present European crisis, any English minister, or almost any considerable public man, addresses to parliament or to his constituents? The eternal repetition of this shabby *refrain*—"We did not interfere, because no English interest was involved;" "We ought not to interfere where no English interest is concerned." England is thus exhibited as a country whose most distinguished men are not ashamed to profess, as politicians, a rule of action which no one, not utterly base, could endure to be accused of as the maxim by which he guides his private life; not to move a finger for others unless he sees his private advantage in it. There is much to be said for the doctrine that a nation should be willing to assist its neighbours in throwing off oppression and gaining free institutions. Much also may be said by those who maintain that one nation is incompetent to judge and act for another, and that each should be left to help itself, and seek advantage or submit to disadvantage as it can and will. But of all attitudes which a nation can take up on the subject of intervention, the meanest and worst is to profess that it interferes only when it can serve its own objects by it. Every other nation is entitled to say, "It seems, then, that non-interference is not a matter of principle with you. When you abstain from interference, it is not because you think it wrong. You have no objection to interfere, only it must not be for the sake of those you interfere with; they must not suppose that you have any regard for their good. The good of others is not one of the things you care for; but you are willing to meddle, if by meddling you can gain anything for yourselves." Such is the obvious interpretation of the language used.

There is scarcely any necessity to say, writing to Englishmen, that this is not what our rulers and politicians really mean. Their language is not a correct exponent of their thoughts. They mean a part only of what they seem to say. They do mean to disclaim interference for the sake of doing good to foreign nations. They are quite sincere and in earnest in repudiating this. But the other half of what their *words* express, a willingness to meddle if by doing so they can promote any interest of England, they do not mean. The thought they have in their minds, is not the interest of England, but her security. What they would say, is, that they are ready to act when England's safety is threatened, or any of her interests hostilely or unfairly endangered. This is no more than what all nations, sufficiently powerful for their own protection, do, and no one questions their right to do. It is the common right of self-defence. But if we mean this, why, in Heaven's name, do we take every possible opportunity of saying, instead of this, something exceedingly different? Not self-defence, but aggrandizement, is the sense which foreign listeners put upon our *words*. Not simply to protect what we have, and that merely against unfair arts, not against fair rivalry; but to add to it more and more without limit, is the purpose for which foreigners think we claim the liberty of intermeddling with them and their affairs. If our actions make it impossible for the most prejudiced observer to believe that we aim at or would accept any sort of mercantile monopolies, this has no effect on their minds but to make them think that we have chosen a more cunning way to the same end. It is a generally accredited opinion among Continental politicians, especially those who think themselves particularly knowing, that the very existence of England depends upon the incessant acquisition of new markets for our manufactures; that the chase after these is an affair of life and death to us; and that we are at all times ready to trample on every obligation of public or international morality, when the alternative would be, pausing for a moment in that race. It would be superfluous to point out what profound ignorance and misconception of all the laws of national wealth, and all the facts of England's commercial condition, this opinion presupposes: but such ignorance and misconception are unhappily very general on the Continent; they are but slowly, if perceptibly, giving way before the advance of reason; and for generations, perhaps, to come, we shall be judged under their influence. Is it requiring too much from our practical politicians to wish that they would sometimes bear these things in mind? Does it answer any good purpose to express ourselves as if we did not scruple to profess that which we not merely scruple to do, but the bare idea of doing which never crosses our minds? Why should we abnegate the character we might with truth lay claim to, of being incomparably the most conscientious of all nations in our national acts? Of all countries which are sufficiently powerful to be capable of being dangerous to their neighbours, we are perhaps the only one whom mere scruples of conscience would suffice to deter from it. We are the only people among whom, by no class whatever of society, is the interest or glory of the nation considered to be any sufficient excuse for an unjust act; the only one which regards with jealousy and suspicion, and a proneness to hostile criticism, precisely those acts of its Government which in other countries are sure to be hailed with applause, those by which territory has been acquired, or political influence extended. Being in reality better than other nations, in at least the negative part of international morality, let us cease, by the language we use, to give ourselves out as worse.

But if we ought to be careful of our language, a thousand times more obligatory is it upon us to be careful of our deeds, and not suffer ourselves to be betrayed by any of our leading men into a line of conduct on some isolated point, utterly opposed to our habitual principles of action—conduct such that if it were a fair specimen of us, it would verify the calumnies of our worst enemies, and justify them in representing not only that we have no regard for the good of other nations, but that we actually think their good and our own incompatible, and will go all lengths to prevent others from realizing even an advantage in which we ourselves are to share. This pernicious, and, one can scarcely help calling it, almost insane blunder, we seem to be committing on the subject of the Suez Canal.

It is the universal belief in France that English influence at Constantinople, strenuously exerted to defeat this project, is the real and only invincible obstacle to its being carried into effect. And unhappily the public declarations of our present Prime Minister not only bear out this persuasion, but warrant the assertion that we oppose the work because, in the opinion of our Government, it would be injurious to the interest of England. If such be the course we are pursuing, and such the motive of it, and if nations have duties, even negative ones, towards the weal of the human race, it is hard to say whether the folly or the immorality of our conduct is the most painfully conspicuous.

Here is a project, the practicability of which is indeed a matter in dispute, but of which no one has attempted to deny that, supposing it realized, it would give a facility to commerce, and consequently a stimulus to production, an encouragement to intercourse, and therefore to civilization, which would entitle it to a high rank among the great industrial improvements of modern times. The contriving of new means of abridging labour and economizing outlay in the operations of industry, is the object to which the larger half of all the inventive ingenuity of mankind is at present given up; and this scheme, if realized, will save, on one of the great highways of the world's traffic, the circumnavigation of a continent. An easy access of commerce is the main source of that material civilization, which, in the more backward regions of the earth, is the necessary condition and indispensable machinery of the moral; and this scheme reduces practically by one half, the distance, commercially speaking, between the self-improving nations of the world and the most important and valuable of the unimproving. The Atlantic Telegraph is esteemed an enterprise of world-wide importance because it abridges the transit of mercantile intelligence merely. What the Suez Canal would shorten is the transport of the goods themselves, and this to such an extent as probably to augment it manifold.

Let us suppose, then—for in the present day the hypothesis is too un-English to be spoken of as anything more than a supposition—let us suppose that the English nation saw in this great benefit to the civilized and uncivilized world a danger or damage to some peculiar interest of England. Suppose, for example, that it feared, by shortening the road, to facilitate the access of foreign navies to its Oriental possessions. The supposition imputes no ordinary degree of cowardice and imbecility to the national mind; otherwise it could not but reflect that the same thing which would facilitate the arrival of an enemy, would facilitate also that of succour; that we have had French fleets in the Eastern seas before now, and have fought naval battles with them there, nearly a century ago; that if we ever became unable to defend India against them, we should assuredly have them there without the aid of any canal; and that our power of resisting an enemy does not depend upon putting a little more or less of an obstacle in the way of his coming, but upon the amount of force which we are able to oppose to him when come. Let us assume, however, that the success of the project would do more harm to England in some separate capacity, than the good which, as the chief commercial nation, she would reap from the great increase of commercial intercourse. Let us grant this: and I now ask, what then? Is there any morality, Christian or secular, which bears out a nation in keeping all the rest of mankind out of some great advantage, because the consequences of their obtaining it may be to itself, in some imaginable contingency, a cause of inconvenience? Is a nation at liberty to adopt as a practical maxim, that what is good for the human race is bad for itself, and to withstand it accordingly? What is this but to declare that its interest and that of mankind are incompatible—that, thus far at least, it is the enemy of the human race? And what ground has it of complaint if, in return, the human race determine to be *its* enemies? So wicked a principle, avowed and acted on by a nation, would entitle the rest of the world to unite in a league against it, and never to make peace until they had, if not reduced it to insignificance, at least sufficiently broken its power to disable it from ever again placing its own self-interest before the general prosperity of mankind.

There is no such base feeling in the British people. They are accustomed to see their advantage in forwarding, not in keeping back, the growth in wealth and civilization of the world. The opposition to the Suez Canal has never been a national opposition. With their usual indifference to foreign affairs, the public in general have not thought about it, but have left it, as (unless when particularly excited) they leave all the management of their foreign policy, to those who, from causes and reasons connected only with internal politics, happen for the time to be in office. Whatever has been done in the name of England in the Suez affair has been the act of individuals, mainly, it is probable, of one individual; scarcely any of his countrymen either prompting or sharing his purpose, and most of those who have paid any attention to the subject (unfortunately a very small number) being, to all appearance, opposed to him.

But (it is said) the scheme cannot be executed. If so, why concern ourselves about it? If the project can come to nothing, why profess gratuitous immorality and incur gratuitous odium to prevent it from being tried? Whether it will succeed or fail is a consideration totally irrelevant; except thus far, that if it is sure to fail, there is in our resistance to it the same immorality, and an additional amount of folly; since, on that supposition, we are parading to the world a belief that our interest is inconsistent with its good, while if the failure of the project would really be any benefit to us, we are certain of obtaining that benefit by merely holding our peace.

As a matter of private opinion, the present writer, so far as he has looked into the evidence, inclines to agree with those who think that the scheme cannot be executed, at least by the means and with the funds proposed. But this is a consideration for the shareholders. The British Government does not deem it any part of its business to prevent individuals, even British citizens, from wasting their own money in unsuccessful speculations, though holding out no prospect of great public usefulness in the event of success. And if, though at the cost of their own property, they acted as pioneers to others, and the scheme, though a losing one to those who first undertook it, should, in the same or in other hands, realize the full expected amount of ultimate benefit to the world at large, it would not be the first nor the hundredth time that an unprofitable enterprise has had this for its final result.

There seems to be no little need that the whole doctrine of non-interference with foreign nations should be reconsidered, if it can be said to have as yet been considered as a really moral question at all. We have heard something lately about being willing to go to war for an idea. To go to war for an idea, if the war is aggressive, not defensive, is as criminal as to go to war for territory or revenue; for it is as little justifiable to force our ideas on other people, as to compel them to submit to our will in any other respect. But there assuredly are cases in which it is allowable to go to war, without having been ourselves attacked, or threatened with attack; and it is very important that nations should make up their minds in time, as to what these cases are. There are *few* questions which more require to be taken in hand by ethical and political philosophers, with a view to establish some rule or criterion whereby the justifiableness of intervening in the affairs of other countries, and (what is sometimes fully as questionable) the justifiableness of refraining from intervention, may be brought to a definite and rational test. Whoever attempts this, will be led to recognise more than one fundamental distinction, not yet by any means familiar to the public mind, and in general quite lost sight of by those who write in strains of indignant morality on the subject. There is a great difference (for example) between the case in which the nations concerned are of the same, or something like the same, degree of civilization, and that in which one of the parties to the situation is of a high, and the other of a very low, grade of social improvement. To suppose that the same international customs, and the same rules of international morality, can obtain between one civilized nation and another, and between civilized nations and barbarians, is a grave error, and one which no statesman can fall into, however it may be with those who, from a safe and unresponsible position, criticise statesmen. Among many reasons why the same rules cannot be applicable to situations so different, the two following are among the most important. In the first place, the rules of ordinary international morality imply reciprocity. But barbarians will not reciprocate. They cannot be depended on for observing any rules. Their minds are not capable of so great an effort, nor their will sufficiently under the influence of distant motives. In the next place, nations which are still barbarous have not got beyond the period during which it is likely to be for their benefit that they should be conquered and held in subjection by foreigners. Independence and nationality, so essential to the due growth and development of a people further advanced in improvement, are generally impediments to theirs. The sacred duties which civilized nations owe to the independence and nationality of each other, are not binding towards those to whom nationality and independence are either a certain evil, or at best a questionable good. The Romans were not the most clean-handed of conquerors, yet would it have been better for Gaul and Spain, Numidia and Dacia, never to have formed part of the Roman Empire? To characterize any conduct whatever towards a barbarous people as a violation of the law of nations, only shows that he who so speaks has never considered the subject. A violation of great principles of morality it may easily be; but barbarians have no rights as a *nation*, except a right to such treatment as may, at the earliest possible period, fit them for becoming one. The only moral laws for the relation between a civilized and a barbarous government, are the universal rules of morality between man and man.

The criticisms, therefore, which are so often made upon the conduct of the French in Algeria, or of the English in India, proceed, it would seem, mostly on a wrong principle. The true standard by which to judge their proceedings never having been laid down, they escape such comment and censure as might really have an improving effect, while they are tried by a standard which can have no influence on those practically engaged in such transactions, knowing as they do that it cannot, and if it could, ought not to be observed, because no human being would be the better, and many much the worse, for its observance. A civilized government cannot help having barbarous neighbours: when it has, it cannot always content itself with a defensive position, one of mere resistance to aggression. After a longer or shorter interval of forbearance, it either finds itself obliged to conquer them, or to assert so much authority over them, and so break their spirit, that they gradually sink into a state of dependence upon itself, and when that time arrives, they are indeed no longer formidable to it, but it has had so much to do with setting up and pulling down their governments, and they have grown so accustomed to lean on it, that it has become morally responsible for all evil it allows them to do. This is the history of the relations of the British Government with the native States of India. It never was secure in its own Indian possessions until it had reduced the military power of those States to a nullity. But a despotic government only exists by its military power. When we had taken away theirs, we were forced, by the necessity of the case, to offer them ours instead of it. To enable them to dispense with large armies of their own, we bound ourselves to place at their disposal, and they bound themselves to receive, such an amount of military force as made us in fact masters of the country. We engaged that this force should fulfil the purposes of a force, by defending the prince against all foreign and internal enemies. But being thus assured of the protection of a civilized power, and freed from the fear of internal rebellion or foreign conquest, the only checks which either restrain the passions or keep any vigour in the character of an Asiatic despot, the native Governments either became so oppressive and extortionate as to desolate the country, or fell into such a state of nerveless imbecility, that every one, subject to their will, who had not the means of defending himself by his own armed followers, was the prey of anybody who had a band of ruffians in his pay. The British Government felt this deplorable state of things to be its own work; being the direct consequence of the position in which, for its own security, it had placed itself towards the native governments. Had it permitted this to go on indefinitely, it would have deserved to be accounted among the worst political malefactors. In some cases (unhappily not in all) it had endeavoured to take precaution against these mischiefs by a special article in the treaty, binding the prince to reform his administration, and in future to govern in conformity to the advice of the British Government. Among the treaties in which a provision of this sort had been inserted, was that with Oude.

For fifty years and more did the British Government allow this engagement to be treated with entire disregard; not without frequent remonstrances, and occasionally threats, but without ever carrying into effect what it threatened. During this period of half a century, England was morally accountable for a mixture of tyranny and anarchy, the picture of which, by men who knew it well, is appalling to all who read it. The act by which the Government of British India at last set aside treaties which had been so pertinaciously violated, and assumed the power of fulfilling the obligation it had so long before incurred, of giving to the people of Oude a tolerable government, far from being the political crime it is so often ignorantly called, was a criminally tardy discharge of an imperative duty. And the fact, that nothing which had been done in all this century by the East India Company's Government made it so unpopular in England, is one of the most striking instances of what was noticed in a former part of this article—the predisposition of English public opinion to look unfavourably upon every act by which territory or revenue are acquired from foreign States, and to take part with any government, however unworthy, which can make out the merest semblance of a case of injustice against our own country.

But among civilized peoples, members of an equal community of nations, like Christian Europe, the question assumes another aspect, and must be decided on totally different principles. It would be an affront to the reader to discuss the immorality of wars of conquest, or of conquest even as the consequence of lawful war; the annexation of any civilized people to the dominion of another, unless by their own spontaneous election. Up to this point, there is no difference of opinion among honest people; nor on the wickedness of commencing an aggressive war for any interest of our own, except when necessary to avert from ourselves an obviously impending wrong. The disputed question is that of interfering in the regulation of another country's internal concerns; the question whether a nation is justified in taking part, on either side, in the civil wars or party contests of another: and chiefly, whether it may justifiably aid the people of another country in struggling for liberty; or may impose on a country any particular government or institutions, either as being best for the country itself, or as necessary for the security of its neighbours.

Of these cases, that of a people in arms for liberty is the only one of any nicety, or which, theoretically at least, is likely to present conflicting moral considerations. The other cases which have been mentioned hardly admit of discussion. Assistance to the government of a country in keeping down the people, unhappily by far the most frequent case of foreign intervention, no one writing in a free country needs take the trouble of stigmatizing. A government which needs foreign support to enforce obedience from its own citizens, is one which ought not to exist; and the assistance given to it by foreigners is hardly ever anything but the sympathy of one despotism with another. A case requiring consideration is that of a protracted civil war, in which the contending parties are so equally balanced that there is no probability of a speedy issue; or if there is, the victorious side cannot hope to keep down the vanquished but by severities repugnant to humanity, and injurious to the permanent welfare of the country. In this exceptional case it seems now to be an admitted doctrine, that the neighbouring nations, or one powerful neighbour with the acquiescence of the rest, are warranted in demanding that the contest shall cease, and a reconciliation take place on equitable terms of compromise. Intervention of this description has been repeatedly practised during the present generation, with such general approval, that its legitimacy may be considered to have passed into a maxim of what is called international law. The interference of the European Powers between Greece and Turkey, and between Turkey and Egypt, were cases in point. That between Holland and Belgium was still more so. The intervention of England in Portugal, a *few* years ago, which is probably less remembered than the others, because it took effect without the employment of actual force, belongs to the same category. At the time, this interposition had the appearance of a bad and dishonest backing of the government against the people, being so timed as to hit the exact moment when the popular party had obtained a marked advantage, and seemed on the eve of overthrowing the government, or reducing it to terms. But if ever a political act which looked ill in the commencement could be justified by the event, this was, for, as the fact turned out, instead of giving ascendancy to a party, it proved a really healing measure; and the chiefs of the so-called rebellion were, within a *few* years, the honoured and successful ministers of the throne against which they had so lately fought.

With respect to the question, whether one country is justified in helping the people of another in a struggle against their government for free institutions, the answer will be different, according as the yoke which the people are attempting to throw off is that of a purely native government, or of foreigners; considering as one of foreigners, every government which maintains itself by foreign support. When the contest is only with native rulers, and with such native strength as those rulers can enlist in their defence, the answer I should give to the question of the legitimacy of intervention is, as a general rule, No. The reason is, that there can seldom be anything approaching to assurance that intervention, even if successful, would be for the good of the people themselves. The only test possessing any real value, of a people's having become fit for popular institutions, is that they, or a sufficient portion of them to prevail in the contest, are willing to brave labour and danger for their liberation. I know all that may be said, I know it may be urged that the virtues of freemen cannot be learnt in the school of slavery, and that if a people are not fit for freedom, to have any chance of becoming so they must first be free. And this would be conclusive, if the intervention recommended would really give them freedom. But the evil is, that if they have not sufficient love of liberty to be able to wrest it from merely domestic oppressors, the liberty which is bestowed on them by other hands than their own, will have nothing real, nothing permanent. No people ever was and remained free, but because it was determined to be so; because neither its rulers nor any other party in the nation could compel it to be otherwise. If a people—especially one whose freedom has not yet become prescriptive—does not value it sufficiently to fight for it, and maintain it against any force which can be mustered *within* the country, even by those who have the command of the public revenue, it is only a question in how *few* years or months that people will be enslaved. Either the government which it has given to itself, or some military leader or knot of conspirators who contrive to subvert the government, will speedily put an end to all popular institutions: unless indeed it suits their convenience better to leave them standing, and be content with reducing them to mere forms; for, unless the spirit of liberty is strong in a people, those who have the executive in their hands easily work any institutions to the purposes of despotism. There is no sure guarantee against this deplorable issue, even in a country which has achieved its own freedom; as may be seen in the present day by striking examples both in the Old and New Worlds: but when freedom has been achieved *for* them, they have little prospect indeed of escaping this fate. When a people has had the misfortune to be ruled by a government under which the feelings and the virtues needful for maintaining freedom could not develop themselves, it is during an arduous struggle to become free by their own efforts that these feelings and virtues have the best chance of springing up. Men become attached to that which they have long fought for and made sacrifices for, they learn to appreciate that on which their thoughts have been much engaged; and a contest in which many have been called on to devote themselves for their country, is a school in which they learn to value their country's interest above their own.

It can seldom, therefore—I will not go so far as to say never—be either judicious or right, in a country which has a free government, to assist, otherwise than by the moral support of its opinion, the endeavours of another to extort the same blessing from its native rulers. We must except, of course, any case in which such assistance is a measure of legitimate self-defence. If (a contingency by no means unlikely to occur) this country, on account of its freedom, which is a standing reproach to despotism everywhere, and an encouragement to throw it off, should find itself menaced with attack by a coalition of Continental despots, it ought to consider the popular party in every nation of the Continent as its natural ally, the Liberals should be to it, what the Protestants of Europe were to the Government of Queen Elizabeth. So, again, when a nation, in her own defence, has gone to war with a despot, and has had the rare good fortune not only to succeed in her resistance, but to hold the conditions of peace in her own hands, she is entitled to say that she will make no treaty, unless with some other ruler than the one whose existence as such may be a perpetual menace to her safety and freedom. These exceptions do but set in a clearer light the reasons of the rule; because they do not depend on any failure of those reasons, but on considerations paramount to them, and coming under a different principle.

But the case of a people struggling against a foreign yoke, or against a native tyranny upheld by foreign arms, illustrates the reasons for *non-intervention* in an opposite way; for in this case the reasons themselves do not exist. A people the most attached to freedom, the most capable of defending and of making a good use of free institutions, may be unable to contend successfully for them against the military strength of another nation much more powerful. To assist a people thus kept down, is not to disturb the balance of forces on which the permanent maintenance of freedom in a country depends, but to redress that balance when it is already unfairly and violently disturbed. The doctrine of *non-intervention*, to be a legitimate principle of morality, must be accepted by all governments. The despots must consent to be bound by it as well as the free States. Unless they do, the profession of it by free countries comes but to this miserable issue, that the wrong side may help the wrong, but the right must not help the right. Intervention to enforce *non-intervention* is always rightful, always moral, if not always prudent. Though it be a mistake to *give* freedom to a people who do not value the boon, it cannot but be right to insist that if they do value it, they shall not be hindered from the pursuit of it by foreign coercion. It might not have been right for England (even apart from the question of prudence) to have taken part with Hungary in its noble struggle against Austria; although the Austrian Government in Hungary was in some sense a foreign yoke. But when, the Hungarians having shown themselves likely to prevail in this struggle, the Russian despot interposed, and joining his force to that of Austria, delivered back the Hungarians, bound hand and foot, to their exasperated oppressors, it would have been an honourable and virtuous act on the part of England to have declared that this should not be, and that if Russia gave assistance to the wrong side, England would aid the right. It might not have been consistent with the regard which every nation is bound to pay to its own safety, for England to have taken up this position single-handed. But England and France together could have done it; and if they had, the Russian armed intervention would never have taken place, or would have been disastrous to Russia alone: while all that those Powers gained by not doing it, was that they had to fight Russia five years afterwards, under more difficult circumstances, and without Hungary for an ally. The first nation which, being powerful enough to make its voice effectual, has the spirit and courage to say that not a gun shall be fired in Europe by the soldiers of one Power against the revolted subjects of another, will be the idol of the friends of freedom throughout Europe. That declaration alone will ensure the almost immediate emancipation of every people which desires liberty sufficiently to be capable of maintaining it: and the nation which gives the word will soon find itself at the head of an alliance of free peoples, so strong as to defy the efforts of any number of confederated despots to bring it down. The prize is too glorious not to be snatched sooner or later by some free country; and the time may not be distant when England, if she does not take this heroic part because of its heroism, will be compelled to take it from consideration for her own safety.

21. Two Cheers for Colonialism*

Dinesh D'Souza

Colonialism has gotten a bad name in recent decades. Anti-colonialism was one of the dominant political currents of the twentieth century, as dozens of European colonies in Asia and Africa became free. Today we are still living with the aftermath of colonialism. Apologists for terrorism, including Osama Bin Laden, argue that terrorist acts are an understandable attempt on the part of subjugated non-Western peoples to lash out against their longtime Western oppressors. Activists at the World Conference on Racism, including the Reverend Jesse Jackson, have called for the West to pay reparations for slavery and colonialism to minorities and natives of the Third World.

These justifications of violence, and calls for monetary compensation, rely on a large body of scholarship that has been produced in the Western academy. This scholarship, which goes by the names of "anti-colonial studies," "postcolonial studies," or "subaltern studies," is now an intellectual school in itself, and it exercises a powerful influence on the humanities and social sciences. The leading Western figures include Edward Said, Gayatri Spivak, Walter Rodney, and Samir Amin. The arguments of these Western scholars are supported by Third World intellectuals like Wole Soyinka, Chinweizu, Ashis Nandy, and (perhaps most influential of all) Frantz Fanon.

The assault against colonialism and its legacy has many dimensions, but at its core it is a theory of oppression that relies on three premises. First, colonialism and imperialism are distinctively Western evils that were inflicted on the non-Western world. Second, as a consequence of colonialism, the West became rich and the colonies became impoverished; in short, the West succeeded at the expense of the colonies. Third, the descendants of colonialism are worse off than they would have been had colonialism never occurred.

In a widely-used text, *How Europe Underdeveloped Africa*, the Marxist scholar Walter Rodney blames European colonialism for "draining African wealth and

---

* Source: *The Chronicle of Higher Education* 48.35 (10 May 2002).

making it impossible to develop more rapidly the resources of the continent." A similar note is struck by the African writer Chinweizu in his influential book *The West and the Rest of Us*. Chinweizu offers the following explanation for African poverty: "White hordes have sallied forth from their western homelands to assault, loot, occupy, rule, and exploit the world. Even now the fury of their expansionist assault upon the rest of us has not abated." In his classic work *The Wretched of the Earth* Frantz Fanon writes, "European opulence has been founded on slavery. The well being and progress of Europe have been built up with the sweat and the dead bodies of Negroes, Arabs, Indians, and the yellow races."

These notions are pervasive and emotionally appealing. By suggesting that the West became dominant because it is oppressive, they provide an explanation for Western global dominance without encouraging white racial arrogance. They relieve the Third World of blame for its wretchedness. Moreover, they imply politically egalitarian policy solutions: the West is in possession of the "stolen goods" of other cultures, and it has a moral and legal obligation to make some form of repayment. I was raised to believe in such things, and among most Third World intellectuals they are articles of faith. The only problem is that they are not true.

There is nothing uniquely Western about colonialism. My native country of India, for example, was ruled by the British for more than two centuries, and many of my fellow Indians are still smarting about that. What they often forget, however, is that before the British came, the Indians were invaded and conquered by the Persians, by the Mongols, by the Turks, by Alexander the Great, by the Afghans, and by the Arabs. Depending on how you count, the British were the eighth or ninth foreign power to invade India since ancient times. Indeed ancient India was itself settled by the Aryan people who came from the north and subjugated the dark-skinned indigenous people.

Those who identify colonialism and empire only with the West either have no sense of history, or they have forgotten about the Egyptian empire, the Persian empire, the Macedonian empire, the Islamic empire, the Mongol empire, the Chinese empire, and the Aztec and Inca empires in the Americas. Shouldn't the Arabs be paying reparations for their destruction of the Byzantine and Persian empires? Come to think of it, shouldn't the Byzantine and Persian people also pay reparations to the descendants of the people they subjugated? And while we're at it, shouldn't the Muslims reimburse the Spaniards for their seven-hundred-year rule?

As the example of Islamic Spain suggests, the people of the West have participated in the game of conquest not only as the perpetrators, but also as the victims. Ancient Greece, for example, was conquered by Rome, and the Roman Empire itself was destroyed by invasions of Huns, Vandals, Lombards, and Visigoths from northern Europe. America, as we all know, was itself a colony of England before its war of independence; England, before that, was subdued and ruled by the Norman kings from France. Those of us living today are taking on a large project if we are going to settle upon a rule of social justice based upon figuring out whose ancestors did what to whom.

The West did not become rich and powerful through colonial oppression. It makes no sense to claim that the West grew rich and strong by conquering other countries and taking their stuff. How did the West manage to do this? In the late Middle Ages, say the year 1500 A.D., the West was by no means the most affluent or most powerful civilization. Indeed the civilizations of China and of the Arab-Islamic world exceeded the West in wealth, in knowledge, in exploration, in learning, and in military power. So how did the West gain so rapidly in economic, political, and military power that, by the nineteenth century, it was able to conquer virtually all the civilizations in the world? This question demands to be answered, and the oppression theorists have never provided an adequate explanation.

Moreover, the West could not have reached its current stage of wealth and influence by stealing from other cultures for the simple reason that there wasn't very much to take. "Oh yes there was," the retort often comes. "The Europeans stole the raw material to build their civilization. They took rubber from Malaya, and cocoa from West Africa, and tea from India." But as economic historian P.T. Bauer points out, before British rule, there were no rubber trees in Malaya, nor cocoa trees in West Africa, nor tea in India. The British brought the rubber tree to Malaya from South America. They brought tea to India from China. And they taught the Africans to grow cocoa, a crop the native people had previously never heard of. None of this is to deny that when the colonialists could exploit native resources, they did. But this larceny cannot possibly account for the enormous gap in economic, political, and military power that opened up between the West and the rest of the world.

What, then, is the source of that power? The reason the West became so affluent and dominant in the modern era is that it invented three institutions: science, democracy, and capitalism. All these institutions are based on universal impulses and aspirations, but those aspirations were given a unique expression in Western civilization.

Consider science. It is based on a shared human trait: the desire to know. People in every culture have tried to learn about the world. Thus the Chinese recorded the eclipses, the Mayans developed a calendar, the Hindus discovered the number zero, and so on. But science—which requires experiments, and laboratories, and induction, and verification, and what one scholar has termed "the invention of invention," the scientific method—this is a Western institution. Similarly tribal participation is universal, but democracy—which involves free elections, and peaceful transitions of power, and separation of powers—is a Western idea. Finally, the impulse to trade is universal, and there is nothing Western about the use of money, but capitalism—which requires property rights, and contracts, and courts to enforce them, and ultimately limited-liability corporations, stock exchanges, patents, insurance, double-entry book keeping—this ensemble of practices that defines modern capitalism was developed in the West.

It is the dynamic interaction between these three Western institutions—science, democracy, and capitalism—that has produced the great wealth, strength, and success of Western civilization. An example of this interaction is technology, which arises out of the marriage between science and capitalism. Science provides the knowledge that leads to invention, and capitalism supplies the mechanism by which the invention is transmitted to the larger society, as well as the economic incentive for inventors to continue to make new things.

Now we can understand better why the West was able, between the sixteenth and the nineteenth century, to subdue the rest of the world and bend it to its will. Indian elephants and Zulu spears were no match for British jeeps and rifles. Colonialism and imperialism are not the cause of the West's success; they are the result of that success. The wealth and power of European nations made them arrogant and stimulated their appetite for global conquest. Colonial possessions added to the prestige, and to a much lesser degree to the wealth, of Europe. But the primary cause of Western affluence and power is internal—the institutions of science, democracy, and capitalism acting in concert. Consequently it is simply wrong to maintain that the rest of the world is poor because the West is rich, or that the West grew rich off "stolen goods" from Asia, Africa, and Latin America, because the West created its own wealth, and still does.

The descendants of colonialism are better off than they would have been had colonialism never happened. I would like to illustrate this point through a personal example. While I was a young boy, growing up in India, I noticed that my grandfather, who had lived under British colonialism, was instinctively and habitually anti-white. He wasn't just against the English, he was generally against the white man. I realized that he had an anti-white animus that I did not share. This puzzled me: why did he and I feel so differently?

Only years later, after a great deal of reflection and a fair amount of study, did the answer finally hit me. The reason for our difference of perception was that colonialism had been pretty bad for him, but pretty good for me. Another way to put it was that colonialism had injured those who lived under it, but paradoxically it proved beneficial to their descendants. Much as it chagrins me to admit it—and much as it will outrage many Third World intellectuals for me to say it—my life would have been much worse had the British never ruled India.

How is this possible? Virtually everything that I am, what I do, and my deepest beliefs, all are the product of a worldview that was brought to India by colonialism. I am a writer, and I write in English. My ability to do this, and to reach a broad market, is entirely thanks to the British. My understanding of technology, which allows me, like so many Indians, to function successfully in the modern world, was entirely the product of a Western education that came to India as a result of the British. So also my beliefs in freedom of expression, in self-government, in equality of rights under the law, and in the universal principle of human dignity—they are all the product of Western civilization.

I am not suggesting that it was the intention of the colonialists to give all these wonderful gifts to the Indians. Colonialism was not based on philanthropy: it was a form of conquest and rule. The English came to India to govern, and they were not primarily interested in the development of the natives, whom they viewed as picturesque savages. It is impossible to measure, or overlook, the pain and humiliation that was inflicted by the rulers over their long period of occupation. Understandably the Indians chafed under this yoke. Toward the end of the British reign in India Mahatma Gandhi was asked, "What do you think of Western civilization?" He replied, "I think it would be a good idea."

Despite their suspect motives and bad behavior, however, the British needed a certain amount of infrastructure in order to effectively govern India. So they built roads, and shipping docks, and railway tracks, and irrigation systems, and government buildings. Then the British realized that they needed courts of law to adjudicate disputes that went beyond local systems of dispensing justice. And so the English legal system was introduced, with all its procedural novelties, such as "innocent until proven guilty." The English also had to educate the Indians, in order to communicate with them and to train them to be civil servants in the empire. Thus Indian children were exposed to Shakespeare, and Dickens, and Hobbes, and Locke. In this way the Indians began to encounter new words and new ideas that were unmentioned in their ancestral culture: "liberty," "sovereignty," "rights," and so on.

This brings me to the greatest benefit that the British provided to the Indians: they taught them the language of freedom. Once again, it was not the objective of the English to encourage rebellion. But by exposing Indians to the ideas of the West, they did. The Indian leaders were the product of Western civilization. Gandhi studied in England and South Africa, Nehru was a product of Harrow and Cambridge. This exposure was not entirely to the good; Nehru, for example, who became India's first prime minister after independence, was highly influenced by Fabian socialism through the teachings of Harold Laski. The result was that India had a mismanaged socialist economy for a generation. But my broader point is that the champions of Indian independence acquired the principles and the language and even the strategies of liberation from the civilization of their oppressors. This was true not just of India but also of other Asian and African countries that broke free of the European yoke.

My conclusion is that against their intentions the colonialists brought things to India that have immeasurably enriched the lives of the descendants of colonialism. It is doubtful that non-Western countries would have acquired these good things by themselves. It was the British who, applying a universal notion of human rights, in the early nineteenth century abolished the ancient Indian institution of *sati*—the custom of tossing widows on the funeral pyre of their dead husbands. There is no reason to believe that the Indians, who had practiced *sati* for centuries, would have reached such a conclusion on their own. Imagine an African or Indian king encountering the works of Locke or Madison and saying, "You know, I think those fellows have a good point. I should relinquish my power and let my people decide whether they want me or someone else to rule." Somehow, I don't see this as likely.

Colonialism was the transmission belt that brought to Asia, Africa, and South America the blessings of Western civilization. Many of those cultures continue to have serious problems of tyranny, tribal and religious conflict, poverty, and under-development, but this is not due to an excess of Western influence but due to the fact that those countries are insufficiently Westernized. Sub-Saharan Africa, which is probably in the worst position, has been described by UN Secretary General Kofi Annan as "a cocktail of disasters." But this is not because colonialism in Africa lasted so long but because it lasted a mere half-century. It was too short to permit Western institutions to take firm root. Consequently after their independence most African nations have retreated into a kind of tribal barbarism that can only be remedied with more Western influence, not less. Africa needs more Western capital, more technology, more rule-of-law, and more individual freedom.

None of this is to say that colonialism by itself was a good thing, only that bad institutions sometimes produce good results. Colonialism, I freely acknowledge, was a harsh regime for those who lived under it. My grandfather would have a hard time giving even one cheer for colonialism. As for me, I cannot manage three, but I am quite willing to grant two. So here it is: two cheers for colonialism! Maybe you will now see why I am not going to be sending an invoice for reparations to Tony Blair.

22. Lispeth*

Rudyard Kipling

> *Look, you have cast out Love! What Gods are these*
> *You bid me please?*
> *The Three in One, the One in Three? Not so!*
> *To my own Gods I go.*
> *It may be they shall give me greater ease*
> *Than your cold Christ and tangled Trinities.*
> *—The Convert*

She was the daughter of Sonoo, a Hill-man, and Jadeh his wife. One year their maize failed, and two bears spent the night in their only poppy-field just above the Sutlej Valley on the Kotgarth side; so, next season, they turned Christian, and brought their baby to the Mission to be baptized. The Kotgarth Chaplain christened her Elizabeth, and "Lispeth" is the Hill or pahari pronunciation.

Later, cholera came into the Kotgarth Valley and carried off Sonoo and Jadeh, and Lispeth became half-servant, half-companion to the wife of the then Chaplain of Kotgarth. This was after the reign of the Moravian missionaries, but before Kotgarth had quite forgotten her title of "Mistress of the Northern Hills."

Whether Christianity improved Lispeth, or whether the gods of her own people would have done as much for her under any circumstances, I do not know; but she grew very lovely. When a Hill girl grows lovely, she is worth traveling fifty miles over bad ground to look upon. Lispeth had a Greek face—one of those faces people paint so often, and see so seldom. She was of a pale, ivory color and, for her race, extremely tall. Also, she possessed eyes that were wonderful; and, had she not been dressed in the abominable print-cloths affected by Missions, you would, meeting her on the hill-side unexpectedly, have thought her the original Diana of the Romans going out to slay.

---

* Source: <http://ebooks.adelaide.edu.au/k/kipling/rudyard/plain/chapter1.html>.

Lispeth took to Christianity readily, and did not abandon it when she reached womanhood, as do some Hill girls. Her own people hated her because she had, they said, become a memsahib and washed herself daily; and the Chaplain's wife did not know what to do with her. Somehow, one cannot ask a stately goddess, five foot ten in her shoes, to clean plates and dishes. So she played with the Chaplain's children and took classes in the Sunday School, and read all the books in the house, and grew more and more beautiful, like the Princesses in fairy tales. The Chaplain's wife said that the girl ought to take service in Simla as a nurse or something "genteel." But Lispeth did not want to take service. She was very happy where she was.

When travellers—there were not many in those years—came to Kotgarth, Lispeth used to lock herself into her own room for fear they might take her away to Simla, or somewhere out into the unknown world.

One day, a few months after she was seventeen years old, Lispeth went out for a walk. She did not walk in the manner of English ladies—a mile and a half out, and a ride back again. She covered between twenty and thirty miles in her little constitutionals, all about and about, between Kotgarth and Narkunda. This time she came back at full dusk, stepping down the breakneck descent into Kotgarth with something heavy in her arms. The Chaplain's wife was dozing in the drawing-room when Lispeth came in breathing hard and very exhausted with her burden. Lispeth put it down on the sofa, and said simply:

"This is my husband. I found him on the Bagi Road. He has hurt himself. We will nurse him, and when he is well, your husband shall marry him to me."

This was the first mention Lispeth had ever made of her matrimonial views, and the Chaplain's wife shrieked with horror. However, the man on the sofa needed attention first. He was a young Englishman, and his head had been cut to the bone by something jagged. Lispeth said she had found him down the khud, so she had brought him in. He was breathing queerly and was unconscious.

He was put to bed and tended by the Chaplain, who knew something of medicine; and Lispeth waited outside the door in case she could be useful. She explained to the Chaplain that this was the man she meant to marry; and the Chaplain and his wife lectured her severely on the impropriety of her conduct. Lispeth listened quietly, and repeated her first proposition. It takes a great deal of Christianity to wipe out uncivilized Eastern instincts, such as falling in love at first sight. Lispeth, having found the man she worshipped, did not see why she should keep silent as to her choice. She had no intention of being sent away, either. She was going to nurse that Englishman until he was well enough to marry her. This was her little programme.

After a fortnight of slight fever and inflammation, the Englishman recovered coherence and thanked the Chaplain and his wife, and Lispeth—especially Lispeth—for their kindness. He was a traveller in the East, he said—they never talked about "globe-trotters" in those days, when the P. & O. fleet was young and small— and had come from Dehra Dun to hunt for plants and butterflies among the Simla hills. No one at Simla, therefore, knew anything about him. He fancied he must have fallen over the cliff while stalking a fern on a rotten tree-trunk, and that his coolies must have stolen his baggage and fled. He thought he would go back to Simla when he was a little stronger. He desired no more mountaineering.

He made small haste to go away, and recovered his strength slowly. Lispeth objected to being advised either by the Chaplain or his wife; so the latter spoke to the Englishman, and told him how matters stood in Lispeth's heart. He laughed a good deal, and said it was very pretty and romantic, a perfect idyl of the Himalayas; but, as he was engaged to a girl at Home, he fancied that nothing would happen. Certainly he would behave with discretion. He did that. Still he found it very pleasant to talk to Lispeth, and walk with Lispeth, and say nice things to her, and call her pet names while he was getting strong enough to go away. It meant nothing at all to him, and everything in the world to Lispeth. She was very happy while the fortnight lasted, because she had found a man to love.

Being a savage by birth, she took no trouble to hide her feelings, and the Englishman was amused. When he went away, Lispeth walked with him, up the Hill as far as Narkunda, very troubled and very miserable. The Chaplain's wife, being a good Christian and disliking anything in the shape of fuss or scandal—Lispeth was beyond her management entirely—had told the Englishman to tell Lispeth that he was coming back to marry her. "She is but a child, you know, and, I fear, at heart a heathen," said the Chaplain's wife. So all the twelve miles up the hill the Englishman, with his arm around Lispeth's waist, was assuring the girl that he would come back and marry her; and Lispeth made him promise over and over again. She wept on the Narkunda Ridge till he had passed out of sight along the Muttiani path.

Then she dried her tears and went in to Kotgarth again, and said to the Chaplain's wife: "He will come back and marry me. He has gone to his own people to tell them so." And the Chaplain's wife soothed Lispeth and said: "He will come back." At the end of two months, Lispeth grew impatient, and was told that the Englishman had gone over the seas to England. She knew where England was, because she had read little geography primers; but, of course, she had no conception of the nature of the sea, being a Hill girl. There was an old puzzle-map of the World in the House. Lispeth had played with it when she was a child. She unearthed it again, and put it together of evenings, and cried to herself, and tried to imagine where her Englishman was. As she had no ideas of distance or steamboats, her notions were somewhat erroneous. It would not have made the least difference had she been perfectly correct; for the Englishman had no intention of coming back to marry a Hill girl. He forgot all about her by the time he was butterfly-hunting in Assam. He wrote a book on the East afterwards. Lispeth's name did not appear.

At the end of three months, Lispeth made daily pilgrimage to Narkunda to see if her Englishman was coming along the road. It gave her comfort, and the Chaplain's wife, finding her happier, thought that she was getting over her "barbarous and most indelicate folly." A little later the walks ceased to help Lispeth and her temper grew very bad. The Chaplain's wife thought this a profitable time to let her know the real state of affairs—that the Englishman had only promised his love to keep her quiet—that he had never meant anything, and that it was "wrong and improper" of Lispeth to think of marriage with an Englishman, who was of a superior clay, besides being promised in marriage to a girl of his own people. Lispeth said that all this was clearly impossible, because he had said he loved her, and the Chaplain's wife had, with her own lips, asserted that the Englishman was coming back.

"How can what he and you said be untrue?" asked Lispeth.

"We said it as an excuse to keep you quiet, child," said the Chaplain's wife.

"Then you have lied to me," said Lispeth, "you and he?"

The Chaplain's wife bowed her head, and said nothing. Lispeth was silent, too for a little time; then she went out down the valley, and returned in the dress of a Hill girl—infamously dirty, but without the nose and ear rings. She had her hair braided into the long pig-tail, helped out with black thread, that Hill women wear.

"I am going back to my own people," said she. "You have killed Lispeth. There is only left old Jadeh's daughter—the daughter of a pahari and the servant of Tarka Devi. You are all liars, you English."

By the time that the Chaplain's wife had recovered from the shock of the announcement that Lispeth had 'verted to her mother's gods, the girl had gone; and she never came back.

She took to her own unclean people savagely, as if to make up the arrears of the life she had stepped out of; and, in a little time, she married a wood-cutter who beat her, after the manner of paharis, and her beauty faded soon.

"There is no law whereby you can account for the vagaries of the heathen," said the Chaplain's wife, "and I believe that Lispeth was always at heart an infidel." Seeing she had been taken into the Church of England at the mature age of five weeks, this statement does not do credit to the Chaplain's wife.

Lispeth was a very old woman when she died. She always had a perfect command of English, and when she was sufficiently drunk, could sometimes be induced to tell the story of her first love-affair.

It was hard then to realize that the bleared, wrinkled creature, so like a wisp of charred rag, could ever have been "Lispeth of the Kotgarth Mission."

23. Merchants of Morality*

Clifford Bob

For decades, Tibet's quest for self-determination has roused people around the world. Inspired by appeals to human rights, cultural preservation, and spiritual awakening, tens of thousands of individuals and organizations lend moral, material, and financial support to the Tibetan cause. As a result, greater autonomy for Tibet's 5.2 million inhabitants remains a popular international campaign despite the Chinese government's 50-year effort to suppress it.

However, while Tibet's light shines brightly abroad, few outsiders know that China's borders hold other restive minorities: Mongols, Zhuang, Yi, and Hui, to name only a few. Notable are the Uighurs, a group of more than 7 million located northwest of Tibet. Like the Tibetans, the Uighurs have fought Chinese domination for centuries. Like the Tibetans, the Uighurs face threats from Han Chinese in-migration, communist development policies, and newly strengthened antiterror measures. And like the Tibetans, the Uighurs resist Chinese domination with domestic and international protest that, in Beijing's eyes, makes them dangerous separatists. Yet the Uighurs have failed to inspire the broad-based foreign networks that generously support and bankroll the Tibetans. International celebrities—including actors Richard Gere and Goldie Hawn, as well as British rock star Annie Lennox—speak out on Tibet's behalf. But no one is planning an Uighur Freedom Concert in Washington, DC. Why?

Optimistic observers posit a global meritocracy of suffering in which all deserving causes attract international support. Howard H. Frederick, founder of the online activist network Peacenet, has argued that new communications technologies help create global movements in which individuals rise above personal, even national self-interest and aspire to common-good solutions to problems that plague the entire planet. And Allen L. Hammond of the World Resources Institute recently wrote that the combination of global media, new technologies, and altruistic nongovernmental

* Source: *Foreign Policy* 129 (March/April 2002).

organizations (NGOs) may soon empower the have-nots of the world, bringing them simple justice by creating a radical transparency in which no contentious action would go unnoticed and unpublicized.

But even while a handful of groups such as the Tibetans have capitalized on the globalization of NGOs and media to promote their causes, thousands of equally deserving challengers, such as the Uighurs, have not found their place in the sun. While the world now knows about East Timor, similar insurrections in Indonesian Aceh and Irian Jaya remain largely off the international radar screen. Among environmental conflicts, a small number of cases such as the Brazilian rubber tappers' struggle to save the Amazon, the conflict over China's Three Gorges Dam, and the recent fight over the Chad-Cameroon pipeline have gained global acclaim. But many similar environmental battles, like the construction of India's Tehri Dam, the destruction of the Guyanese rain forests, and the construction of the Trans Thai-Malaysia gas pipeline are waged in anonymity. Whole categories of other conflicts—such as landlessness in Latin America and caste discrimination in South Asia—go likewise little noticed. To groups challenging powerful opponents in these conflicts, global civil society is not an open forum marked by altruism, but a harsh, Darwinian marketplace where legions of desperate groups vie for scarce attention, sympathy, and money.

In a context where marketing trumps justice, local challengers—whether environmental groups, labor rights activists, or independence-minded separatists—face long odds. Not only do they jostle for attention among dozens of equally worthy competitors, but they also confront the pervasive indifference of international audiences. In addition, they contend against well-heeled opponents (including repressive governments, multinational corporations, and international financial institutions) backed by the world's top public relations machines. Under pressure to sell their causes to the rest of the world, local leaders may end up undermining their original goals or alienating the domestic constituencies they ostensibly represent. Moreover, the most democratic and participatory local movements may garner the least assistance, since Western NGOs are less likely to support groups showing internal strife and more inclined to help a group led by a strong, charismatic leader. Perhaps most troubling of all, the perpetuation of the myth of an equitable and beneficent global civil society breeds apathy and self-satisfaction among the industrialized nations, resulting in the neglect of worthy causes around the globe.

Pitching the Product

The ubiquity of conflict worldwide creates fierce competition for international support. In a 2001 survey, researchers at Leiden University in the Netherlands and the Institute for International Mediation and Conflict Resolution in Washington, DC, identified 126 high-intensity conflicts worldwide (defined as large-scale armed conflicts causing more than 1,000 deaths from mid-1999 to mid-2000), 78 low-intensity conflicts (100 to 1,000 deaths from mid-1999 to mid-2000), and 178 violent political conflicts (less than 100 deaths from mid-1999 to mid-2000). In these and many other simmering disputes, weak challengers hope to improve their prospects by attracting international assistance.

Local movements usually follow two broad marketing strategies: First, they pitch their causes internationally to raise awareness about their conflicts, their opponents, and sometimes their very existence. Second, challengers universalize their narrow demands and particularistic identities to enhance their appeal to global audiences.

Critical to the success of local challengers is access to major Western NGOs. Many groups from low-profile countries are ignored in the developed world's key media centers and therefore have difficulty gaining visibility among even the most transnational of NGOs. Moreover, despite the Internet and the much-ballyhooed "CNN effect," repressive regimes can still obstruct international media coverage of local conflicts. In the 1990s, for example, the government of Papua New Guinea did just that on Bougainville island, site of a bloody separatist struggle that cost 15,000 lives, or roughly 10 percent of the island's population. During an eight-year blockade (1989–97), foreign journalists could enter the island only under government guard, while the rebels could dispatch emissaries abroad only at great risk. India has used similar tactics in Kashmir, prohibiting independent human rights monitors from entering the territory and seizing passports of activists seeking to plead the Kashmiri case before the UN General Assembly and other bodies. Less effectively, Sudan has tried to keep foreigners from entering the country's vast southern region to report on the country's 19-year civil war.

Even for causes from "important" countries, media access—and therefore global attention—remains highly uneven. Money makes a major difference, allowing wealthier movements to pay for media events, foreign lobbying trips, and overseas offices, while others can barely afford places to meet. For example, long-term support from Portugal helped the East Timorese eventually catch the world's attention; other Indonesian separatist movements have not had such steady friends. And international prizes such as the Goldman Environmental Prize, the Robert F. Kennedy Human Rights Award, and the Nobel Peace Prize have become important vehicles of internationalization. In addition to augmenting a leader's resources, these awards raise a cause's visibility, facilitate invaluable contacts with key transnational NGOs and media, and result in wider support. For instance, Mexican "farmer ecologist" Rodolfo Montiel Flores's receipt of the $125,000 Goldman Prize in 2000 boosted the campaign to release him from prison on false charges stemming from his opposition to local logging practices. Not surprisingly, such prizes have become the object of intense salesmanship by local groups and their international champions.

Local challengers who have knowledge of global NGOs also have clear advantages. Today's transnational NGO community displays clear hierarchies of influence and reputation. Large and powerful organizations such as Human Rights Watch,

Amnesty International, Greenpeace, and Friends of the Earth have the resources and expertise to investigate claims of local groups from distant places and grant them legitimacy. Knowledge of these key "gatekeeper" NGOs—their identities, goals, evidentiary standards, and openness to particular pitches—is crucial for a local movement struggling to gain support. If homegrown knowledge is scarce, local movements may try to link themselves to a sympathetic and savvy outsider, such as a visiting journalist, missionary, or academic. Some Latin American indigenous groups, including Ecuador's Huaoroni and Cofán, Brazil's Kayapó, and others, have benefited from the kindness of such strangers, who open doors and guide their way among international networks.

Small local groups with few connections or resources have more limited options for raising international awareness and thus may turn to protest. Yet domestic demonstrations often go unseen abroad. Only spectacular episodes—usually violent ones—draw international media coverage. And since violence is anathema to powerful international NGOs, local groups who use force as an attention-grabbing tactic must carefully limit, justify, and frame it. For example, the poverty and oppression that underlay the 1994 uprising by Mexico's Zapatista National Liberation Army went largely unnoticed at home and abroad for decades. In the face of such indifference, the previously unknown Zapatistas resorted to arms and briefly seized the city of San Cristóbal on January 1, 1994. Immediately tarred by the Mexican government as "terrorists," the Zapatistas in fact carefully calibrated their use of force, avoiding civilian casualties and courting the press. Other tactics also contributed to the Zapatistas' international support, but without these initial dramatic attacks, few people beyond Mexico's borders would now know or care about the struggles of Mexico's indigenous populations.

The NGO Is Always Right

To improve their chances of gaining support, local movements also conform themselves to the needs and expectations of potential backers in Western nations. They simplify and universalize their claims, making them relevant to the broader missions and interests of key global players. In particular, local groups try to match themselves to the substantive concerns and organizational imperatives of large transnational NGOs.

Consider Nigeria's Ogoni ethnic group, numbering perhaps 300,000 to 500,000 people. Like other minorities in the country's southeastern Niger delta, the Ogoni have long been at odds with colonial authorities and national governments over political representation. In the late 1950s, as Royal Dutch/Shell and other multinationals began producing petroleum in the region, the Ogoni claimed that the Nigerian federal government was siphoning off vast oil revenues yet returning little to the minorities who bore the brunt of the drilling's impact. In the early 1990s, an Ogoni movement previously unknown outside Nigeria sought support from Greenpeace, Amnesty International, and other major international NGOs. Initially, these appeals were rejected as unsubstantiated, overly complex, and too political. Ogoni leaders responded by downplaying their contentious claims about minority rights in a poor, multiethnic developing state and instead highlighting their environmental grievances, particularly Shell's "ecological warfare" against the indigenous Ogoni. Critical to this new emphasis was Ogoni leader Ken Saro-Wiwa's recognition of "what could be done by an environment group [in the developed world] to press demands on government and companies."

The Ogoni's strategic shift quickly led to support from Greenpeace, Friends of the Earth, and the Sierra Club. These and other organizations provided funds and equipment, confirmed and legitimated Ogoni claims, denounced the Nigerian dictatorship, boycotted Shell, and eased Ogoni access to governments and media in Europe and North America. In the summer of 1993, as the Ogoni's domestic mobilizations brought harsh government repression, human rights NGOs also took notice. The 1994 arrest and 1995 execution of Saro-Wiwa ultimately made the Ogoni an international symbol of multinational depredation in the developing world, but it was their initial repositioning as an environmental movement that first put them on the global radar screen. (For its part, Shell countered with its own spin, attacking Saro-Wiwa's credibility as a spokesman for his people and denying his allegations against the company.)

Similar transformations have helped other local causes make global headway. In drumming up worldwide support for Guatemala's Marxist insurgency in the 1980s, activist Rigoberta Menchú projected an indigenous identity that resonated strongly with left-leaning audiences in Western Europe and North America. Her book *I, Rigoberta Menchú* made her an international symbol of indigenous oppression, helping her win the Nobel Peace Prize in 1992, year of the Columbus quincentenary, despite her association with a violent rebel movement. As anthropologist David Stoll later showed, however, Menchú and the guerrillas may have enjoyed more backing among international solidarity organizations than among their country's poor and indigenous peoples. According to Stoll, external support may have actually delayed the guerrillas' entry into domestic negotiations by several years, prolonging the war and costing lives.

Mexico's Zapatistas have also benefited abroad from their indigenous identity. At the beginning of their 1994 rebellion, the Zapatistas issued a hodgepodge of demands. Their initial call for socialism was quickly jettisoned when it failed to catch on with domestic or international audiences, and their ongoing demands for Mexican democratization had mainly domestic rather than international appeal. But it was the Zapatistas' "Indianness" and their attacks first on the North American Free Trade Agreement (NAFTA) and then on globalization that found pay dirt in the international arena. (Little coincidence that the day they chose to launch the movement—January 1, 1994—was also the day NAFTA went into effect.) Once the appeal of these issues had become clear, they took center stage in the Zapatistas' contacts with external supporters. Indeed, the Zapatistas and their masked (non-Indian) leader Subcomandante Marcos became potent symbols for antiglobalization activists worldwide. In February and March 2001, when a Zapatista bus caravan traversed southern Mexico and culminated in a triumphant reception in the capital's central square, dozens of Italian *tute bianche* ("White Overalls"), activists prominent in antiglobalization protests in Europe, accompanied the Zapatistas as bodyguards. Even the French farmer and anti-McDonald's campaigner José Bové was present to greet Marcos.

Focusing on an internationally known and notorious enemy (such as globalization or NAFTA) is a particularly effective way of garnering support. In recent years, multinational corporations and international financial institutions have repeatedly served as stand-ins for obscure or recalcitrant local enemies. Even when a movement itself is little known, it can project an effective (if sometimes misleading) snapshot of its claims by identifying itself as the anti-McDonald's movement, the anti-Nike movement, or the anti-Unocal movement. Blaming a villain accessible in the developed world also forges strong links between distant social movements and the "service station on the block," thus inspiring international solidarity.

Such strategies are not aimed only at potential supporters on the political left. The recent growth of a well-funded Christian human rights movement in the United States and Europe has helped many local groups around the world. One major beneficiary is John Garang's Sudan People's Liberation Army, made up mostly of Christians from southern Sudan fighting against the country's Muslim-dominated north. Rooted in ethnic, cultural, and religious differences, the conflict has been aggravated by disputes over control of natural resources. Since fighting broke out in 1983, the war has attracted little attention, despite the deaths of an estimated 2 million people. As late as September 1999, then Secretary of State Madeleine Albright reportedly stated that "the human rights situation in Sudan is not marketable to the American people." However, in the mid-1990s, "slave redemptions" (in which organizations like Christian Solidarity International buy back Christians from their Muslim captors) as well as international activism by Christian human rights organizations began to raise the conflict's profile. The start of oil extraction by multinationals provided another hook to attract concern from mainstream human rights and environmental organizations. Joined by powerful African-American politicians in the United States angered over the slave trade, conservative NGOs have thrown their support behind Garang's group, thereby feeding perceptions of the conflict as a simple Christian-versus-Muslim clash. These NGOs have also found a receptive audience in the administration of US President George W. Bush, thus boosting Garang's chances of reaching a favorable settlement.

By contrast, failure to reframe obscure local issues (or reframing them around an issue whose time has passed) can produce international isolation for a struggling insurgent group. Two years after the Zapatista attacks, another movement sprang from the poverty and oppression of southern Mexico, this time in the state of Guerrero. The Popular Revolutionary Army attacked several Mexican cities and demanded an old-style communist revolution. But these rebels drew little support or attention, particularly in contrast to the Zapatistas and their fashionable antiglobalization rhetoric. Meanwhile, Brazil's Landless Peasants Movement and smaller movements of the rural poor in Paraguay and Venezuela have suffered similar fates both because their goals seem out of step with the times and because their key tactic—land invasions—is too controversial for many mainstream international NGOs. In the Niger delta, radical movements that have resorted to threats, sabotage, and kidnappings have also scared off international support despite the similarity of their grievances to those of the Ogoni.

Leaders for Sale

If marketing is central to a local movement's gaining international support, a gifted salesman, one who identifies himself completely with his "product," is especially valuable. Many individual leaders have come to embody their movements: Myanmar's (Burma) Aung San Suu Kyi, South Africa's Nelson Mandela, as well as the Dalai Lama, Menchú, and Marcos. Even when known abroad only through media images, such leaders can make a host of abstract issues seem personal and concrete, thus multiplying a movement's potential support. For this reason, international tours have long been a central strategy for domestic activists. In the late-19th and early-20th centuries, for example, Sun Yat-sen crisscrossed the world seeking support for a nationalist revolution in China. Attracting international notice when he was briefly kidnapped by the Manchus in London, Sun found himself in Denver, Colorado, on another lobbying trip when the revolution finally came in 1911. Today, for well-supported insurgents, such roadshows are highly choreographed, with hard-charging promoters; tight schedules in government, media, and NGO offices; and a string of appearances in churches, college lecture halls, and community centers. In November 2001, for example, Oronto Douglas, a leader of Nigeria's Ijaw minority, embarked on a six-city, seven-day tour throughout Canada, where he promoted the Ijaw cause along with his new Sierra Club book *Where Vultures Feast: Shell, Human Rights, and Oil in the Niger Delta*.

What transforms insurgent leaders into international icons? Eloquence, energy, courage, and single-mindedness can undeniably create a charismatic mystique. But transnational charisma also hinges on a host of pedestrian factors that are nonetheless unusual among oppressed groups. Fluency in a key foreign language, especially English; an understanding of Western protest traditions; familiarity with the international political vogue; and expertise in media and NGO relations—all these factors are essential to giving leaders the chance to display their more ineffable qualities. Would the Dalai Lama appear as charismatic through a translator? For his part, Subcomandante Marcos has long insisted that he is but an ordinary man, whose way with words just happened to strike a responsive chord at an opportune moment.

Most of these prosaic characteristics are learned, not innate. Indeed, many NGOs now offer training programs to build advocacy capacity, establish contacts, and develop media smarts. The Unrepresented Nations and Peoples Organization in the Hague regularly holds intensive, week-long media and diplomacy training sessions for its member "nations," replete with role plays and mock interviews, helping them put their best foot forward in crucial venues. (Among others, Ken Saro-Wiwa praised the program for teaching him nonviolent direct action skills.) One of the most elaborate programs is the Washington, DC-based International Human Rights Law Group's two-year Advocacy Bridge Program, which aims to "increase the skills of local activists to amplify their issues of concern globally" and to "facilitate their access to international agenda-setting venues." Under the program, dozens of participants from around the world, chosen to ensure equal participation by women, travel to Washington for one week of initial training and then to Geneva for three weeks of on-site work at the UN Human Rights Commission. In their second year, "graduates" help train a new crop of participants.

Successful insurgent leaders therefore often look surprisingly like the audiences they seek to capture, and quite different from their downtrodden domestic constituencies. Major international NGOs often look for a figure who neatly embodies their own ideals, meets the pragmatic requirements of a "test case," or fulfills romantic Western notions of rebellion—in short, a leader who seems to mirror their own central values. Other leaders, deaf to the international zeitgeist or simply unwilling to adapt, remain friendless and underfunded.

The High Price of Success
Many observers have trumpeted global civil society as the great last hope of the world's have-nots. Yet from the standpoint of local challengers seeking international support, the reality is bleak. The international media is often myopic: Conflicts attract meager reporting unless they have clear relevance, major importance, or huge death tolls. Technology's promise also remains unfulfilled. Video cameras, Web access, and cellular phones are still beyond the reach of impoverished local challengers. Even if the vision of "radical transparency" were realized—and if contenders involved in messy political wrangles in fact desired complete openness—international audiences, flooded with images and appeals, would have to make painful choices. Which groups deserve support? Which causes are more "worthy" than others?

Powerful transnational NGOs, emblematic of global civil society, also display serious limitations. While altruism plays some role in their decision making, NGOs are strategic actors who seek first and foremost their own organizational survival. At times this priority jibes nicely with the interests of local clients in far-flung locations, but often it does not. When selecting clients from a multitude of deserving applicants, NGOs must be hard-nosed, avoiding commitments that will harm their reputations or absorb excessive resources. Their own goals, tactics, constituencies, and bottom lines constantly shape their approaches. Inevitably, many deserving causes go unsupported.

Unfortunately, the least participatory local movements may experience the greatest ease in winning foreign backing. Charismatic leadership is not necessarily democratic, for instance, yet external support will often strengthen a local leader's position, reshaping the movement's internal dynamics as well as its relations with opponents. Among some Tibetan communities today, there are rumblings of discontent over the Dalai Lama's religiously legitimated leadership, but his stature has been so bolstered by international support that dissident elements are effectively powerless. Indeed, any internal dissent—if visible to outsiders—will often reduce international interest. NGOs want their scarce resources to be used effectively. If they see discord instead of unity, they may take their money and clout elsewhere rather than risk wasting them on internal disputes.

The Internet sometimes exacerbates this problem: Internecine feuds played out on public listservs and chat rooms may alienate foreign supporters, as has happened with some members of the pro-Ogoni networks. And although much has been made about how deftly the Zapatistas used the Internet to get their message out, dozens of other insurgents, from Ethiopia's Oromo Liberation Front to the Western Sahara's Polisario Front have Web sites and use e-mail. Yet they have failed to spark widespread international enthusiasm. As the Web site for Indonesia's Papua Freedom Organization laments, "We have struggled for more than 30 years, and the world has ignored our cause." Crucial in the Zapatistas' case was the appeal of their message (and masked messenger) to international solidarity activists, who used new technologies to promote the cause to broader audiences. In fact, for most of their conflict with the Mexican government, the Zapatistas have not had direct access to the Internet. Instead, they have sent communiqués by hand to sympathetic journalists and activists who then publish them and put them on the Web. Thus the Zapatistas' seemingly sophisticated use of the Internet has been more a result of their appeal to a core group of supporters than a cause of their international backing.

Perhaps most worrisome, the pressure to conform to the needs of international NGOs can undermine the original goals of local movements. By the time the Ogoni had gained worldwide exposure, some of their backers in the indigenous rights community were shaking their heads at how the movement's original demands for political autonomy had gone understated abroad compared to environmental and human rights issues. The need for local groups to click with trendy international issues fosters a homogeneity of humanitarianism: Unfashionable, complex, or intractable conflicts fester in isolation, while those that match or—thanks to savvy marketing—appear to match international issues of the moment attract disproportionate support. Moreover, the effort to please international patrons can estrange a movement's jet-setting elite from its mass base or leave it unprepared for domestic responsibilities. As one East Timorese leader stated after international pressure moved the territory close to independence, "We have been so focused on raising public awareness about our cause that we didn't seriously think about the structure of a government."

The quest for international support may also be dangerous domestically. To gain attention may require risky confrontations with opponents. Yet few international NGOs can guarantee a local movement's security, leaving it vulnerable to the attacks of enraged authorities. If a movement's opponent is receptive to rhetorical pressure, the group may be saved, as the Zapatistas were. If not, it will likely face its enemies alone. The NATO intervention in Kosovo provides a rare exception. But few challengers have opponents as notorious and strategically inconvenient as Slobodan Milošević. Even in that case, Albanian leader Ibrahim Rugova's nonviolent strategies met years of international inaction and neglect; only when the Kosovo Liberation Army brought the wrath of Yugoslavia down on Kosovo and after Milošević thumbed his nose at NATO did the intervention begin.

Historically, desperate local groups have often sought support from allies abroad. Given geographical distance as well as political and cultural divides, they have been forced to market themselves. This was true not only in the Chinese Revolution but also in the Spanish Civil War, the Indian nationalist movement, and countless Cold War struggles. But the much-vaunted emergence of a global civil society was supposed to change all that, as the power of technologies meshed seamlessly with the good intentions of NGOs to offset the callous self-interest of states and the blithe indifference of faraway publics.

But for all the progress in this direction, an open and democratic global civil society remains a myth, and a potentially deadly one. Lost in a self-congratulatory haze, international audiences in the developed world all too readily believe in this myth and in the power and infallibility of their own good intentions. Meanwhile, the grim realities of the global morality market leave many local aspirants helpless and neglected, painfully aware of international opportunities but lacking the resources, connections, or know-how needed to tap them.

24. The Grameen Bank*

Muhammad Yunus

Over many years, Amena Begum had become resigned to a life of grinding poverty and physical abuse. Her family was among the poorest in Bangladesh—one of thousands that own virtually nothing, surviving as squatters on desolate tracts of land and earning a living as day laborers.

In early 1993 Amena convinced her husband to move to the village of Kholshi, 112 kilometers (70 miles) west of Dhaka. She hoped the presence of a nearby relative would reduce the number and severity of the beatings that her husband inflicted on her. The abuse continued, however—until she joined the Grameen Bank. Oloka Ghosh, a neighbor, told Amena that Grameen was forming a new group in Kholshi and encouraged her to join. Amena doubted that anyone would want her in their group. But Oloka persisted with words of encouragement. "We're all poor—or at least we all were when we joined. I'll stick up for you because I know you'll succeed in business."

Amena's group joined a Grameen Bank Center in April 1993. When she received her first loan of $60, she used it to start her own business raising chickens and ducks. When she repaid her initial loan and began preparing a proposal for a second loan of $110, her friend Oloka gave her some sage advice: "Tell your husband that Grameen does not allow borrowers who are beaten by their spouses to remain members and take loans." From that day on, Amena suffered significantly less physical abuse at the hands of her husband. Today her business continues to grow and provide for the basic needs of her family.

Unlike Amena, the majority of people in Asia, Africa and Latin America have few opportunities to escape from poverty. According to the World Bank, more than 1.3 billion people live on less than a dollar a day. Poverty has not been eradicated in the 50 years since the Universal Declaration on Human Rights asserted that each individual has a right to

---

* Source: *Scientific American*, November 1999, pp. 114-19.

A standard of living adequate for the health and well-being of himself and of his family, including food, clothing, housing and medical care and necessary social services, and the right to security in the event of unemployment, sickness, disability, widowhood, old age or other lack of livelihood in circumstances beyond his control.

Will poverty still be with us 50 years from now? My own experience suggests that it need not.

After completing my Ph.D. at Vanderbilt University, I returned to Bangladesh in 1972 to teach economics at Chittagong University. I was excited about the possibilities for my newly independent country. But in 1974 we were hit with a terrible famine. Faced with death and starvation outside my classroom, I began to question the very economic theories I was teaching. I started feeling there was a great distance between the actual life of poor and hungry people and the abstract world of economic theory.

I wanted to learn the real economics of the poor. Because Chittagong University is located in a rural area, it was easy for me to visit impoverished households in the neighboring village of Jobra. Over the course of many visits, I learned all about the lives of my struggling neighbors and much about economics that is never taught in the classroom. I was dismayed to see how the indigent in Jobra suffered because they could not come up with small amounts of working capital. Frequently they needed less than a dollar a person but could get that money only on extremely unfair terms. In most cases, people were required to sell their goods to moneylenders at prices fixed by the latter.

This daily tragedy moved me to action. With the help of my graduate students, I made a list of those who needed small amounts of money. We came up with 42 people. The total amount they needed was $27.

I was shocked. It was nothing for us to talk about millions of dollars in the classroom, but we were ignoring the minuscule capital needs of 42 hardworking, skilled people next door. From my own pocket, I lent $27 to those on my list.

Still, there were many others who could benefit from access to credit. I decided to approach the university's bank and try to persuade it to lend to the local poor. The branch manager said, however, that the bank could not give loans to the needy: the villagers, he argued, were not creditworthy.

I could not convince him otherwise. I met with higher officials in the banking hierarchy with similar results. Finally, I offered myself as a guarantor to get the loans.

In 1976 I took a loan from the local bank and distributed the money to poverty-stricken individuals in Jobra. Without exception, the villagers paid back their loans. Confronted with this evidence, the bank still refused to grant them loans directly. And so I tried my experiment in another village, and again it was successful. I kept expanding my work, from two to five, to 20, to 50, to 100 villages, all to convince the bankers that they should be lending to the poor. Although each time we expanded to a new village the loans were repaid, the bankers still would not change their view of those who had no collateral.

Because I could not change the banks, I decided to create a separate bank for the impoverished. After a great deal of work and negotiation with the government, the Grameen Bank ("village bank" in Bengali) was established in 1983.

From the outset, Grameen was built on principles that ran counter to the conventional wisdom of banking. We sought out the very poorest borrowers, and we required no collateral. The bank rests on the strength of its borrowers. They are required to join the bank in self-formed groups of five. The group members provide one another with peer support in the form of mutual assistance and advice. In addition, they allow for peer discipline by evaluating business viability and ensuring repayment. If one member fails to repay a loan, all members risk having their line of credit suspended or reduced.

Chart 1

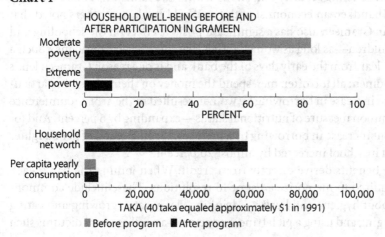

HOUSEHOLD WELL-BEING BEFORE AND AFTER PARTICIPATION IN GRAMEEN

The Power of Peers

Typically a new group submits loan proposals from two members, each requiring between $25 and $100. After these two borrowers successfully repay their first five weekly installments, the next two group members become eligible to apply for their own loans. Once they make five repayments, the final member of the group may apply. After 50 installments have been repaid, a borrower pays her interest, which is slightly above the commercial rate. The borrower is now eligible to apply for a larger loan.

The bank does not wait for borrowers to come to the bank; it brings the bank to the people. Loan payments are made in weekly meetings consisting of six to eight groups, held in the villages where the members live. Grameen staff attend these meetings and

often visit individual borrowers' homes to see how the business—whether it be raising goats or growing vegetables or hawking utensils—is faring.

Today Grameen is established in nearly 39,000 villages in Bangladesh. It lends
to approximately 2.4 million borrowers, 94 percent of whom are women. Grameen
reached its first $1 billion in cumulative loans in March 1995, 18 years after it began
in Jobra. It took only two more years to reach the $2-billion mark. After 20 years of
work, Grameen's average loan size now stands at $180. The repayment rate hovers
between 96 and 100 percent.

A year after joining the bank, a borrower becomes eligible to buy shares in Grameen. At present, 94 percent of the bank is owned by its borrowers. Of the 13 members of the board of directors, nine are elected from among the borrowers; the rest
are government representatives, academics, myself and others.

A study carried out by Sydney R. Schuler of John Snow, Inc., a private research
group, and her colleagues concluded that a Grameen loan empowers a woman by
increasing her economic security and status within the family. In 1998 a study by
Shahidur R. Khandker, an economist with the World Bank, and others noted that
participation in Grameen also has a significant positive effect on the schooling and
nutrition of children—as long as women rather than men receive the loans. (Such a
tendency was clear from the early days of the bank and is one reason Grameen lends
primarily to women: all too often men spend the money on themselves.) In particular, a 10 percent increase in borrowing by women resulted in the arm circumference
of girls—a common measure of nutritional status—expanding by 6 percent. And for
every 10 percent increase in borrowing by a member, the likelihood of her daughter
being enrolled in school increased by almost 20 percent.

Not all the benefits derive directly from credit. When joining the bank, each
member is required to memorize a list of 16 resolutions. These include common-
sense items about hygiene and health—drinking clean water, growing and eating
vegetables, digging and using a pit latrine, and so on—as well as social dictums such

Chart 2

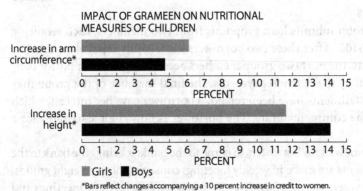

IMPACT OF GRAMEEN ON NUTRITIONAL MEASURES OF CHILDREN

Increase in arm circumference*

Increase in height*

■ Girls ■ Boys

*Bars reflect changes accompanying a 10 percent increase in credit to women.

as refusing dowry and managing family size. The women usually recite the entire list at the weekly branch meetings, but the resolutions are not otherwise enforced.

Even so, Schuler's study revealed that women use contraception more consistently after joining the bank. Curiously, it appears that women who live in villages where Grameen operates, but who are not themselves members, are also more likely to adopt contraception. The population growth rate in Bangladesh has fallen dramatically in the past two decades, and it is possible that Grameen's influence has accelerated the trend.

In a typical year 5 percent of Grameen borrowers—representing 125,000 families—rise above the poverty level. Khandker concluded that among these borrowers extreme poverty (defined by consumption of less than 80 percent of the minimum requirement stipulated by the Food and Agriculture Organization of the United Nations) declined by more than 70 percent within five years of their joining the bank.

To be sure, making a microcredit program work well—so that it meets its social goals and also stays economically sound—is not easy. We try to ensure that the bank serves the poorest: only those living at less than half the poverty line are eligible for loans. Mixing poor participants with those who are better off would lead to the latter dominating the groups. In practice, however, it can be hard to include the most abjectly poor, who might be excluded by their peers when the borrowing groups are being formed. And despite our best efforts, it does sometimes happen that the money lent to a woman is appropriated by her husband.

Given its size and spread, the Grameen Bank has had to evolve ways to monitor the performance of its branch managers and to guarantee honesty and transparency. A manager is not allowed to remain in the same village for long, for fear that he may develop local connections that impede his performance. Moreover, a manager is never posted near his home. Because of such constraints—and because managers are required to have university degrees—very few of them are women. As a result, Grameen has been accused of adhering to a paternalistic pattern. We are sensitive to this argument and are trying to change the situation by finding new ways to recruit women.

Grameen has also often been criticized for being not a charity but a profit-making institution. Yet that status, I am convinced, is essential to its viability. Last year a disastrous flood washed away the homes, cattle and most other belongings of hundreds of thousands of Grameen borrowers. We did not forgive the loans, although we did issue new ones and give borrowers more time to repay. Writing off loans would banish accountability, a key factor in the bank's success.

Liberating Their Potential

The Grameen model has now been applied in 40 countries. The first replication, begun in Malaysia in 1986, currently serves 40,000 poor families; their repayment rate has consistently stayed near 100 percent. In Bolivia, micro-credit has allowed women to make the transition from "food for work" programs to managing their own businesses. Within two years the majority of women in the program acquire enough credit history and financial skills to qualify for loans from mainstream banks. Similar success stories are coming in from programs in poor countries everywhere. These banks all target the most impoverished, lend to groups and usually lend primarily to women.

The Grameen Bank in Bangladesh has been economically self-sufficient since 1995. Similar institutions in other countries are slowly making their way toward self-reliance. A few small programs are also running in the US, such as in inner-city Chicago. Unfortunately, because labor costs are much higher in the US than in developing countries—which often have a large pool of educated unemployed who can serve as managers or accountants—the operations are more expensive there. As a result, the US programs have had to be heavily subsidized.

In all, about 22 million poor people around the world now have access to small loans. Microcredit Summit, an institution based in Washington, DC, serves as a resource center for the various regional microcredit institutions and organizes yearly conferences. Last year the attendees pledged to provide 100 million of the world's poorest families, especially their women, with credit by the year 2005. The campaign has grown to include more than 2,000 organizations, ranging from banks to religious institutions to nongovernmental organizations to United Nations agencies.

The standard scenario for economic development in a poor country calls for industrialization via investment. In this "top-down" view, creating opportunities for employment is the only way to end poverty. But for much of the developing world, increased employment exacerbates migration from the countryside to the cities and creates low-paying jobs in miserable conditions. I firmly believe that, instead, the eradication of poverty starts with people being able to control their own fates. It is not by creating jobs that we will save the poor but rather by providing them with the opportunity to realize their potential. Time and time again I have seen that the poor are poor not because they are lazy or untrained or illiterate but because they cannot keep the genuine returns on their labor.

Self-employment may be the only solution for such people, whom our economies refuse to hire and our taxpayers will not support. Microcredit views each person as a potential entrepreneur and turns on the tiny economic engines of a rejected portion of society. Once a large number of these engines start working, the stage can be set for enormous socioeconomic change.

Applying this philosophy, Grameen has established more than a dozen enterprises, often in partnership with other entrepreneurs. By assisting microborrowers and microsavers to take ownership of large enterprises and even infrastructure companies, we are trying to speed the process of overcoming poverty. Grameen Phone, for instance, is a cellular telephone company that aims to serve urban and rural Bangladesh. After a pilot study in 65 villages, Grameen Phone has taken a loan to extend its activities to all villages in which the bank is active. Some 50,000 women, many of whom have never seen a telephone or even an electric light, will become the providers of telephone service in their villages. Ultimately, they will become the owners of the company itself by buying its shares. Our latest innovation, Grameen Investments, allows US individuals to support companies such as Grameen Phone while receiving interest on their investment. This is a significant step toward putting commercial funds to work to end poverty.

I believe it is the responsibility of any civilized society to ensure human dignity to all members and to offer each individual the best opportunity to reveal his or her creativity. Let us remember that poverty is not created by the poor but by the institutions and policies that we, the better off, have established. We can solve the problem not by means of the old concepts but by adopting radically new ones.

25. Employment, Not Microcredit, Is the Solution[*]

Aneel Karnani

The Nobel Peace Prize for 2006 was awarded to the Grameen Bank in Bangladesh and its founder Muhammad Yunus, a pioneer of the microcredit movement. The Nobel Committee affirmed that microcredit must play "a major part" in eliminating poverty. The United Nations, having designated 2005 as the International year of Microcredit, declares on its website, "currently microentrepreneurs use loans as small as $100 to grow thriving businesses and, in turn, provided for their families, leading to strong and flourishing local economies."[1] The Indian bank ICICI plans to make loans of as little as $100 to 25 million rural clients in five years. Finance Minister P. Chidambaram too is a supporter of microcredit.

Given this intensity of interest in microcredit, it is reasonable to ask whether it is really an effective tool for eradicating poverty. Microcredit often yields non-economic benefits such as increasing self-esteem and social cohesion, and empowering women. It also helps the poor smooth consumption over periods of cyclical or unexpected crisis. But, that is not enough; the key issue is whether microcredit helps eradicate poverty. *The Economist* magazine concluded that while "heart-warming case studies abound, rigorous empirical analyses are rare." A few studies have even found that microcredit has a negative impact on poverty; poor households simply become poorer through the additional burden of debt. However, most studies suggest that microcredit is beneficial but only to a limited extent. The reality is less attractive than the promise.

Why is microcredit not more effective? The problem lies not with microcredit but rather with microenterprises. The United Nations' declaration that microentrepreneurs use loans to grow thriving businesses leading to flourishing economies is hype. A client of microcredit is an entrepreneur in the literal sense: she raises

---

[*] Source: Ross School of Business Paper No. 1065, <http://papers.ssrn.com/sol3/papers.cfm?abstract_id=962941>.

1 <http://www.yearofmicrocredit.org/>.

the capital, manages the business and is the residual claimant of the earnings. But, the current usage of the word "entrepreneur" requires more than the literal definition. Entrepreneurship is the engine of Joseph Schumpeter's dynamism of "creative destruction." An entrepreneur is a person of vision and creativity who converts a new idea into a successful innovation, into a new business model. Some clients of microcredit are certainly true entrepreneurs, and have created thriving businesses— these are the heart-warming anecdotes. But the vast majority of microcredit clients are caught in subsistence activities with no prospect of competitive advantage. In an insightful survey on the economic lives of the poor, Abhijit Banerjee writes that the self-employed poor usually have no specialized skills and often practice multiple occupations. Many of these businesses operate at too small a scale. Banerjee points out that the median business operated by the poor has no paid staff; most of these businesses have very few assets as well. With low skills, little capital and no scale economies, these businesses operate in arenas with low entry barriers and too much competition; they have low productivity and lead to meager earnings that cannot lift their owners out of poverty.

This should not be too surprising. Most people do not have the skills, vision, creativity, and persistence to be true entrepreneurs. Even in developed countries with high levels of education and infrastructure, about 90% of the labor force are employees rather than entrepreneurs. Even with greater availability of financial services in developed countries, only a small fraction have used credit for entrepreneurial purposes. Most clients of microcredit are not microentrepreneurs by choice and would gladly take a factory job at reasonable wages if possible. We should not romanticize the idea of the "poor as entrepreneurs." The International Labor Organization (ILO) uses a more appropriate term: "own account workers."

Employment

Creating opportunities for steady employment at reasonable wages is the best way to take people out of poverty. The ILO states that "nothing is more fundamental to poverty reduction than employment." In development economics there is much theoretical and empirical support for the increasing preponderance of wage labor in a developing economy. It is instructive to look at the pattern of poverty and employment over time in China, India and Africa (which together account for about three-quarters of the poor in the world), using World Bank and ILO data.

In China, where the incidence of poverty has declined significantly, a large and growing fraction of the population is employed. In Africa, where the incidence of poverty has remained unchanged, a small and shrinking fraction of the population is employed. India's performance lies somewhere in between. India's efforts at poverty reduction have been hampered by its poor performance in job creation. A recent IMF Working Paper attributes India's jobless growth to a distorted emphasis on capital intensive and skill intensive development path. Capital intensive sectors, such as heavy manufacturing, and skill intensive sectors, such as information technology, will not solve India's poverty problem. The trickle-down effects of general economic growth are too little and too slow. India needs to emphasize growth in labor-intensive, low-skill sectors such as light manufacturing, garments and tourism. Seven IITs do not compensate for 40% illiteracy rate. Bangalore does not compensate for the pervasive poverty in Bihar.

	People below $2/day Late 1980s	People below $2/day Late 1990s
China	67.4%	50.1%
India	83.2%	78.8%
Africa	76.1%	76.1%

	Employment/Population Late 1980s	Employment/Population Late 1990s
China	51.0%	58.7%
India	29.5%	35.8%
Africa	33.4%	30.1%

Scale Economies

Many people who have jobs are still stuck below the poverty line—the working poor. Whether an employee is "poor" or not depends on her wages, size of the household, and the income of other household members. It is not enough to create jobs; we also have to increase productivity such that the wages are high enough to enable the employees to rise above poverty.

	Working poor/Employment Late 1980s	Working poor/Employment Late 1990s
China	79.6%	35.2%
India	75.0%	62.0%
Africa	63.4%	65.4%

On this dimension too, India's performance is mediocre. One cause of this poor growth in productivity in India is inadequate scale economies in its enterprises. The IMF study cited earlier found that the average firm size in India is less then one-tenth the comparable size in other emerging economies. The emphasis on microcredit will only make this problem worse.

Rather than lending $200 to 500 women so that each can buy a sewing machine and set up a microenterprise manufacturing garments, it is much better to lend $100,000 to an entrepreneur with managerial capabilities and business acumen and help her to set up a garment-manufacturing business employing 500 people. Now the business can exploit economies of scale, deploy specialized assets, and use modern business processes to generate value for both its owners and employees.

Recommended Reading

Buruma, I. (2005). *Occidentalism*. London: Atlantic Books.

Easterly, W. (2006). *The White Man's Burden: Why the West's Efforts to Aid the Rest Have Done So Much Ill and So Little Good*. New York: Penguin.

Irwin, R. (2008). *Dangerous Knowledge: Orientalism and its Discontents*. New York: Overlook.

Lewis, B. (2001). *What Went Wrong?* Oxford: Oxford UP.

Miscevid, N. (2010). "Nationalism." *The Stanford Encyclopedia of Philosophy* (Summer 2010 ed.). <http://plato.stanford.edu/archives/sum2010/entries/nationalism/>

Moyo, D. (2010). *Dead Aid: Why Aid Is Not Working and How There Is a Better Way for Africa*. New York: Farrar, Straus and Giroux.

Said, E. (1979). *Orientalism*. New York: Vintage.

UN Millennium Project. (2005). UN Millennium Development Library: Overview (UN Millennium Project). EarthScan.

V

War, Revolution, and Terrorism: Introduction

The Nature of War

War is an "actual, intentional and widespread armed conflict between political communities."[1] Typically wars have been international, occurring between states. But hostilities between communities within states, who wish to achieve independence or to assume power, are also counted as wars, albeit civil wars, revolutions, or wars of independence. Thus the Algerian struggle for independence from France of 1954 to 1962 set non-state actors against both the colonial regime and one another.

Frantz Fanon, a psychiatrist from Martinique, became the leading political theorist of the National Liberation Front (FLN), which fought for independence against the French colonial regime. In *The Wretched of the Earth*, written during the Algerian war, Fanon addresses the question of whether, and if so when, violence is legitimate in the interests of securing independence from colonial rule. Fanon explores the psychological effect of colonialism as well as the broader implications for building movements against colonialism and imperialism.

Deepak Lal writes in defense of empires, which, he notes, maintain peace, promote trade, and put a lid on ethnic conflict. Nevertheless empires have, as Lal notes, gotten a bad name: "imperialism" is assumed to be uncontroversially undesirable and, for almost a century, nationalism has been unstoppable. Nineteenth-century racialist doctrines, twentieth-century genocides, and socio-biology have persuaded people of good will that we do best if we live in nation-states, or at best autonomous

---

1 *Stanford Encyclopedia of Philosophy*, <http://plato.stanford.edu/entries/war/>.

political units, dominated by our kin. Frantz Fanon, born and raised in an overseas department of France, discovered to his dismay when he got to European France that he was regarded as an alien because of his color. Fanon's experience has been regarded as inevitable: humans are, according to the received view, wired to care for kin at the expense of outsiders and so, in the interests of promoting well-being, it is widely held that every ethnic group should enjoy political "self-determination."

But the boundaries of nation-states rarely cut along the joints, and virtually every country includes ethnic minorities. Armed conflict among ethnic groups seeking hegemony or political independence has been a feature of twentieth-century history and is ongoing.

At the time of this writing virtually all the armed conflicts around the globe, like the Algerian conflict, involve violent non-state actors—from al-Qaeda and Hamas to drug cartels operating along the US–Mexican border, companies of Somali pirates, and the Mafia. But even though—at least according to Tony Soprano—Mafiosi regard themselves as "soldiers," not all armed conflict is war. War, as distinct from other varieties of violent conflict, is ultimately about governance: it is aimed at determining who gets power, wealth, and resources in a given territory, who is a citizen, which values are supported, which laws are adopted, and how territorial borders are defined.

When conflict concerning these issues cannot be evaded and cannot be resolved by negotiation or other non-violent means, people make war. War should be, we believe, at best a last resort.

When to Make War

War is bad. It inevitably leads to the premature death of combatants and, almost always, non-combatants, as well as wounding, maiming, and the destruction of property. It depletes resources, impoverishes populations, stymies progress, and undermines social stability. In addition to the immediate human costs of war—the death, pain, and disruption of people's lives—war is also among the most wasteful human activities. As Einstein famously remarked, "I know not with what weapons World War III will be fought, but World War IV will be fought with sticks and stones."[2]

Is war ever justified? Traditionally, there have been two answers to this question—and a non-answer. Pacifists hold that war is never justified; advocates of just-war theories hold that it is sometimes justified. Realists, however, hold that the question of when, if ever, war is just cannot be sensibly asked. States, on this last account, are not moral agents and indeed, applying moral concepts to the conduct of international affairs is generally inappropriate. States seek to maximize expected self-interest. It is important to note, however, that realists may nevertheless endorse many of the same restrictions on the conduct of war that just-war theorists favor on self-interested,

---

2 <http://www.quotationspage.com/quote/329.html>.

pragmatic grounds. In order to limit the destructiveness of war for all concerned, prudent states, acting out of self-interest, might promote compliance with conventions according to which wars should be fought only in response to aggression and non-combatants are not targeted. Realism *per se* is neither more hawkish nor more dovish than just-war theories. It simply provides a different rationale for policy.

Leaving aside the realist non-answer, the most popular answers to the question of whether, and if so when, war is justified take the form of just-war theories. The just-war tradition addresses not only the question of when war is justified (*jus ad bellum*), but also that of how war may legitimately be conducted (*jus in bello*) and how war ought to be terminated (*jus post bellum*).

According to the just-war theory, a state or political community is justified in going to war only if the following six conditions are met:

1. **Just cause.** War is legitimate only when undertaken for the right reasons, which include but are not limited to self-defense, defense of others from external attack, the protection of innocents, and the punishment of grievous wrong-doing.
2. **Right intention.** A state that goes to war must be *motivated* by a just cause—not merely use such a cause as an excuse for pursuing ulterior ends.
3. **Proper authority and public declaration.** The decision to go to war must be made by appropriate authorities according to proper procedures.
4. **Last resort.** War is legitimate only when diplomatic negotiation and other peaceful alternatives have failed.
5. **Probability of success.** A state may not go to war if doing so has no chance of achieving legitimate ends.
6. **Proportionality.** A just war must be cost-effective: the ends to be achieved must offset the evils, in particular, the human costs of war.

While these conditions seem eminently reasonable, exactly when they are met is a controversial issue. Perhaps the most vexed cases concern those involving the protection of innocents in circumstances where authoritarian regimes engage in serious human-rights violations. At the time of this writing, people throughout the Arab world are revolting against dictatorial governments, some of which are waging war against their citizens. When is humanitarian intervention justified?

Philosopher David Luban canvasses the classic "just war" theory and considers hard cases. According to the UN definition and doctrine of national sovereignty, the crime of aggressive war is a crime of state against state, which violates state sovereignty through illegitimate intervention. Luban notes, however, that the doctrine of non-intervention does not explain why the duty of non-intervention is a moral one. Luban argues that a state must be legitimate in order for a moral duty of non-intervention in its affairs to exist, and violations of basic human rights undermine legitimacy. A just war, Luban argues, is a war in defense of socially basic human rights.

Are there any other circumstances in which war is morally permissible? There is a long tradition that holds that war is never just. Soran Reader, writing within that tradition, defends pacifism, arguing that we must dismantle our war-machines. Can pacifism, as Reader suggests, be made plausible?

How to Make War

Leaving aside the question of whether, and if so when, war is just, there is a further moral issue. If we wage war, for whatever reason, we must address the question of how war should be conducted. *Jus in bello*, justice in war, refers to rules for right conduct in war. The law of war, considered to be an aspect of public international law, includes the Geneva Conventions and rules established by the Hague Convention for justice in war.

Thomas Nagel, in "War and Massacre," argues that certain restrictions in the conduct of warfare are neither arbitrary nor merely conventional, and that their validity does not depend simply on their usefulness. The rules of war, Nagel argues, have a moral basis even though conventions now officially in force are far from giving it perfect expression.

There is something disconcerting, and even ghoulish, about establishing rules for warfare. We agree that chemical and biological weapons may not be used—but that the use of guns and bombs is legitimate: we implicitly agree that killing is acceptable so long as it is done by an approved mechanism. We ban rape and pillage, and the killing of non-combatants, but we countenance the killing of conscripts and volunteers below the age of majority. Nevertheless, War happens, and given that it does, we are surely better off agreeing on rules and restrictions.

26. Concerning Violence*

Frantz Fanon

National liberation, national renaissance, the restoration of nationhood to the people, commonwealth: whatever may be the headings used or the new formulas introduced, decolonization is always a violent phenomenon. At whatever level we study it—relationships between individuals, new names for sports clubs, the human admixture at cocktail parties, in the police, on the directing boards of national or private banks—decolonization is quite simply the replacing of a certain "species" of men by another "species" of men. Without any period of transition, there is a total, complete, and absolute substitution. It is true that we could equally well stress the rise of a new nation, the setting up of a new state, its diplomatic relations, and its economic and political trends. But we have precisely chosen to speak of that kind of tabula rasa which characterizes at the outset all decolonization. Its unusual importance is that it constitutes, from the very first day, the minimum demands of the colonized. To tell the truth, the proof of success lies in a whole social structure being changed from the bottom up. The extraordinary importance of this change is that it is willed, called for, demanded. The need for this change exists in its crude state, impetuous and compelling, in the consciousness and in the lives of the men and women who are colonized. But the possibility of this change is equally experienced in the form of a terrifying future in the consciousness of another "species" of men and women: the colonizers.

Decolonization, which sets out to change the order of the world, is, obviously, a program of complete disorder. But it cannot come as a result of magical practices, nor of a natural shock, nor of a friendly understanding. Decolonization, as we know, is a historical process: that is to say that it cannot be understood, it cannot become intelligible nor clear to itself except in the exact measure that we can discern the movements which give it historical form and content. Decolonization is the meeting

---

* Source: *The Wretched of the Earth* (New York: Grove Press, 1968: Constance Farrington, 1963), pp. 35–95.

of two forces, opposed to each other by their very nature, which in fact owe their originality to that sort of substantification which results from and is nourished by the situation in the colonies. Their first encounter was marked by violence and their existence together—that is to say the exploitation of the native by the settler—was carried on by dint of a great array of bayonets and cannons. The settler and the native are old acquaintances. In fact, the settler is right when he speaks of knowing "them" well. For it is the settler who has brought the native into existence and who perpetuates his existence. The settler owes the fact of his very existence, that is to say, his property, to the colonial system.

Decolonization never takes place unnoticed, for it influences individuals and modifies them fundamentally. It transforms spectators crushed with their inessentiality into privileged actors, with the grandiose glare of history's floodlights upon them. It brings a natural rhythm into existence, introduced by new men, and with it a new language and a new humanity. Decolonization is the veritable creation of new men. But this creation owes nothing of its legitimacy to any supernatural power; the "thing" which has been colonized becomes man during the same process by which it frees itself.

In decolonization, there is therefore the need of a complete calling in question of the colonial situation. If we wish to describe it precisely, we might find it in the well-known words: "The last shall be first and the first last." Decolonization is the putting into practice of this sentence. That is why, if we try to describe it, all decolonization is successful.

The naked truth of decolonization evokes for us the searing bullets and blood-stained knives which emanate from it. For if the last shall be first, this will only come to pass after a murderous and decisive struggle between the two protagonists. That affirmed intention to place the last at the head of things, and to make them climb at a pace (too quickly, some say) the well-known steps which characterize an organized society, can only triumph if we use all means to turn the scale, including, of course, that of violence.

You do not turn any society, however primitive it may be, upside down with such a program if you have not decided from the very beginning, that is to say from the actual formulation of that program, to overcome all the obstacles that you will come across in so doing. The native who decides to put the program into practice, and to become its moving force, is ready for violence at all times. From birth it is clear to him that this narrow world, strewn with prohibitions, can only be called in question by absolute violence.

The colonial world is a world divided into compartments. It is probably unnecessary to recall the existence of native quarters and European quarters, of schools for natives and schools for Europeans; in the same way we need not recall apartheid in South Africa. Yet, if we examine closely this system of compartments, we will at least be able to reveal the lines of force it implies. This approach to the colonial world, its ordering and its geographical layout will allow us to mark out the lines on which a decolonized society will be reorganized.

The colonial world is a world cut in two. The dividing line, the frontiers are shown by barracks and police stations. In the colonies it is the policeman and the soldier who are the official, instituted go-betweens, the spokesmen of the settler and his rule of oppression. In capitalist societies the educational system, whether lay or clerical, the structure of moral reflexes handed down from father to son, the exemplary honesty of workers who are given a medal after fifty years of good and loyal service, and the affection which springs from harmonious relations and good behavior—all these aesthetic expressions of respect for the established order serve to create around the exploited person an atmosphere of submission and of inhibition which lightens the task of policing considerably. In the capitalist countries a multitude of moral teachers, counselors and "bewilderers" separate the exploited from those in power. In the colonial countries, on the contrary, the policeman and the soldier, by their immediate presence and their frequent and direct action maintain contact with the native and advise him by means of rifle butts and napalm not to budge. It is obvious here that the agents of government speak the language of pure force. The intermediary does not lighten the oppression, nor seek to hide the domination; he shows them up and puts them into practice with the clear conscience of an upholder of the peace; yet he is the bringer of violence into the home and into the mind of the native.

The zone where the natives live is not complementary to the zone inhabited by the settlers. The two zones are opposed, but not in the service of a higher unity. Obedient to the rules of pure Aristotelian logic, they both follow the principle of reciprocal exclusivity. No conciliation is possible, for of the two terms, one is superfluous. The settlers' town is a strongly built town, all made of stone and steel. It is a brightly lit town; the streets are covered with asphalt, and the garbage cans swallow all the leavings, unseen, unknown and hardly thought about. The settler's feet are never visible, except perhaps in the sea; but there you're never close enough to see them. His feet are protected by strong shoes although the streets of his town are clean and even, with no holes or stones. The settler's town is a well-fed town, an easygoing town; its belly is always full of good things. The settlers' town is a town of white people, of foreigners.

The town belonging to the colonized people, or at least the native town, the Negro village, the medina, the reservation, is a place of ill fame, peopled by men of evil repute. They are born there, it matters little where or how; they die there, it matters not where, nor how. It is a world without spaciousness; men live there on top of each other, and their huts are built one on top of the other. The native town is a hungry town, starved of bread, of meat, of shoes, of coal, of light. The native town is a crouching village, a town on its knees, a town wallowing in the mire. It is a town of niggers and dirty Arabs. The look that the native turns on the settler's town is a look of lust, a look of envy; it expresses his dreams of possession—all manner of possession: to sit at the settler's table, to sleep in the settler's bed, with his wife if possible. The colonized man is an envious man. And this the settler knows very well; when their glances meet he ascertains bitterly, always on the defensive, "They want to take our place." It is true, for there is no native who does not dream at least once a day of setting himself up in the settler's place....

As soon as the native begins to pull on his moorings, and to cause anxiety to the settler, he is handed over to well-meaning souls who in cultural congresses point out to him the specificity and wealth of Western values. But every time Western values are mentioned they produce in the native a sort of stiffening or muscular lockjaw. During the period of decolonization, the native's reason is appealed to. He is offered definite values, he is told frequently that decolonization need not mean regression, and that he must put his trust in qualities which are well-tried, solid, and highly esteemed. But it so happens that when the native hears a speech about Western culture he pulls out his knife—or at least he makes sure it is within reach. The violence with which the supremacy of white values is affirmed and the aggressiveness which has permeated the victory of these values over the ways of life and of thought of the native mean that, in revenge, the native laughs in mockery when Western values are mentioned in front of him. In the colonial context the settler only ends his work of breaking in the native when the latter admits loudly and intelligibly the supremacy of the white man's values. In the period of decolonization, the colonized masses mock at these very values, insult them, and vomit them up.

This phenomenon is ordinarily masked because, during the period of decolonization, certain colonized intellectuals have begun a dialogue with the bourgeoisie of the colonialist country. During this phase, the indigenous population is discerned only as an indistinct mass. The few native personalities whom the colonialist bourgeois have come to know here and there have not sufficient influence on that immediate discernment to give rise to nuances. On the other hand, during the period of liberation, the colonialist bourgeoisie looks feverishly for contacts with the elite and it is with these elite that the familiar dialogue concerning values is carried on. The colonialist bourgeoisie, when it realizes that it is impossible for it to maintain its domination over the colonial countries, decides to carry out a rearguard action with regard to culture, values, techniques, and so on. Now what we must never forget is that the immense majority of colonized peoples is oblivious to these problems. For a colonized people the most essential value, because the most concrete, is first and foremost the land: the land which will bring them bread and, above all, dignity. But this dignity has nothing to do with the dignity of the human individual: for that human individual has never heard tell of it. All that the native has seen in his country is that they can freely arrest him, beat him, starve him: and no professor of ethics, no priest has ever come to be beaten in his place, nor to share their bread with him. As far as the native is concerned, morality is very concrete; it is to silence the settler's defiance, to break his flaunting violence—in a word, to put him out of the picture. The well-known principle that all men are equal will be illustrated in the colonies from the moment that the native claims that he is the equal of the settler. One step more, and he is ready to fight to be more than the settler. In fact, he has already decided to eject him and to take his place; as we see it, it is a whole material and moral universe which is breaking up. The intellectual who for his part has followed the colonialist with regard to the universal abstract will fight in order that the settler and the native may live together in peace in a new world. But the thing he does not see, precisely because he is permeated by colonialism and all its ways of thinking, is that the settler, from the moment that the colonial context disappears, has no longer any interest in remaining or in co-existing....

The settler makes history and is conscious of making it. And because he constantly refers to the history of his mother country, he clearly indicates that he himself is the extension of that mother country. Thus the history which he writes is not the history of the country which he plunders but the history of his own nation in regard to all that she skims off, all that she violates and starves.

The immobility to which the native is condemned can only be called in question if the native decides to put an end to the history of colonization—the history of pillage, and to bring into existence the history of the nation—the history of decolonization.

A world divided into compartments, a motionless, Manicheistic world, a world of statues: the statue of the general who carried out the conquest, the statue of the engineer who built the bridge; a world which is sure of itself, which crushes with its stones the backs flayed by whips: this is the colonial world. The native is a being hemmed in; apartheid is simply one form of the division into compartments of the colonial world. The first thing which the native learns is to stay in his place, and not to go beyond certain limits. This is why the dreams of the native are always of muscular prowess; his dreams are of action and of aggression. I dream I am jumping, swimming, running, climbing; I dream that I burst out laughing, that I span a river in one stride, or that I am followed by a flood of motorcars which never catch up with me. During the period of colonization, the native never stops achieving his freedom from nine in the evening until six in the morning.

The colonized man will first manifest this aggressiveness which has been deposited in his bones against his own people. This is the period when the niggers beat each other up, and the police and magistrates do not know which way to turn when faced with the astonishing waves of crime in North Africa. We shall see later how this phenomenon should be judged. When the native is confronted with the colonial order of things, he finds he is in a state of permanent tension. The settler's world is a hostile world, which spurns the native, but at the same time it is a world of which he is envious. We have seen that the native never ceases to dream of putting himself in the place of the settler—not of becoming the settler but of substituting himself for the settler. This hostile world, ponderous and aggressive because it fends off the colonized masses with all the harshness it is capable of, represents not merely a hell from which the swiftest flight possible is desirable, but also a paradise close at hand which is guarded by terrible watchdogs....

What are the forces which in the colonial period open up new outlets and engender new aims for the violence of colonized peoples? In the first place there are the political parties and the intellectual or commercial elites. Now, the characteristic feature of certain political structures is that they proclaim abstract principles but refrain from issuing definite commands. The entire action of these nationalist political parties during the colonial period is action of the electoral type: a string of philosophicopolitical dissertations on the themes of the rights of peoples to self-determination, the rights of man to freedom from hunger and human dignity, and the unceasing affirmation of the principle: "One man, one vote." The national political parties never lay stress upon the necessity of a trial of armed strength, for the good reason that their objective is not the radical overthrowing of the system. Pacifists and legalists, they are in fact partisans of order, the new order—but to the colonialist bourgeoisie they put bluntly enough the demand which to them is the main one: "Give us more power." On the specific question of violence, the elite are ambiguous. They are violent in their words and reformist in their attitudes. When the nationalist political leaders say something, they make quite clear that they do not really think it.

This characteristic on the part of the nationalist political parties should be interpreted in the light both of the make-up of their leaders and the nature of their followings. The rank-and-file of a nationalist party is urban. The workers, primary schoolteachers, artisans, and small shopkeepers who have begun to profit—at a discount, to be sure—from the colonial setup, have special interests at heart. What this sort of following demands is the betterment of their particular lot: increased salaries, for example. The dialogue between these political parties and colonialism is never broken off. Improvements are discussed, such as full electoral representation, the liberty of the press, and liberty of association. Reforms are debated. Thus it need not astonish anyone to notice that a large number of natives are militant members of the branches of political parties which stem from the mother country. These natives fight under an abstract watchword: "Government by the workers," and they forget that in their country it should be nationalist watchwords which are first in the field. The native intellectual has clothed his aggressiveness in his barely veiled desire to assimilate himself to the colonial world. He has used his aggressiveness to serve his own individual interests.

Thus there is very easily brought into being a kind of class of affranchised slaves, or slaves who are individually free. What the intellectual demands is the right to multiply the emancipated, and the opportunity to organize a genuine class of emancipated citizens. On the other hand, the mass of the people have no intention of standing by and watching individuals increase their chances of success. What they demand is not the settler's position of status, but the settler's place. The immense majority of natives want the settler's farm. For them, there is no question of entering into competition with the settler. They want to take his place.

The peasantry is systematically disregarded for the most part by the propaganda put out by the nationalist parties. And it is clear that in the colonial countries the peasants alone are revolutionary, for they have nothing to lose and everything to gain. The starving peasant, outside the class system, is the first among the exploited to discover that only violence pays. For him there is no compromise, no possible coming to terms; colonization and decolonization are simply a question of relative strength. The exploited man sees that his liberation implies the use of all means, and that of force first and foremost. When in 1956, after the capitulation of Monsieur Guy Mollet to the settlers in Algeria, the Front de Libération Nationale, in a famous leaflet, stated that colonialism only loosens its hold when the knife is at its throat, no Algerian really found these terms too violent. The leaflet only expressed what every Algerian felt at heart: colonialism is not a thinking machine, nor a body endowed with reasoning faculties. It is violence in its natural state, and it will only yield when confronted with greater violence.

At the decisive moment, the colonialist bourgeoisie, which up till then has remained inactive, comes into the field. It introduces that new idea which is in proper parlance a creation of the colonial situation: non-violence. In its simplest form this non-violence signifies to the intellectual and economic elite of the colonized country that the bourgeoisie has the same interests as they and that it is therefore urgent and indispensable to come to terms for the public good. Non-violence is an attempt to settle the colonial problem around a green baize table, before any regrettable act has been performed or irreparable gesture made, before any blood has been shed. But if the masses, without, waiting for the chairs to be arranged around the baize table, listen to their own voice and begin committing outrages and setting fire to buildings, the elite and the nationalist bourgeois parties will be seen rushing to the colonialists to exclaim, "This is very serious! We do not know how it will end; we must find a solution—some sort of compromise."

This idea of compromise is very important in the phenomenon of decolonization, for it is very far from being a simple one. Compromise involves the colonial system and the young nationalist bourgeoisie at one and the same time. The partisans of the colonial system discover that the masses may destroy everything. Blown-up bridges, ravaged farms, repressions, and fighting harshly disrupt the economy. Compromise is equally attractive to the nationalist bourgeoisie, who since they are not clearly aware of the possible consequences of the rising storm, are genuinely afraid of being swept away by this huge hurricane and never stop saying to the settlers: "We are still capable of stopping the slaughter; the masses still have confidence in us; act quickly if you do not want to put everything in jeopardy." One step more, and the leader of the nationalist party keeps his distance with regard to that violence. He loudly proclaims that he has nothing to do with these Mau-Mau, these terrorists, these throat-slitters. At best, he shuts himself off in a no man's land between the terrorists and the settlers and willingly offers his services as go-between; that is to say, that as the settlers cannot discuss terms with these Mau-Mau, he himself will be quite willing to begin negotiations. Thus it is that the rear guard of the national struggle, that very party of people who have never ceased to be on the other side in the fight, find themselves somersaulted into the van of negotiations and compromise—precisely because that party has taken very good care never to break contact with colonialism.

Before negotiations have been set afoot, the majority of nationalist parties confine themselves for the most part to explaining and excusing this "savagery." They do not assert that the people have to use physical force, and it sometimes even happens that they go so far as to condemn, in private, the spectacular deeds which are declared to be hateful by the press and public opinion in the mother country. The legitimate excuse for this ultra-conservative policy is the desire to see things in an objective light; but this traditional attitude of the native intellectual and of the leaders of the nationalist parties is not, in reality, in the least objective. For in fact they are not at all convinced that this impatient violence of the masses is the most efficient means of defending their own interests. Moreover, there are some individuals who are convinced of the ineffectiveness of violent methods; for them, there is no doubt about it, every attempt to break colonial oppression by force is a hopeless effort, an attempt at suicide, because in the innermost recesses of their brains the settler's tanks and airplanes occupy a huge place. When they are told "Action must be taken," they see bombs raining down on them, armored cars coming at them on every path, machine-gunning and police action…and they sit quiet. They are beaten from the start. There is no need to demonstrate their incapacity to triumph by violent methods; they take it for granted in their everyday life and in their political maneuvers….

Yet in spite of the metamorphoses which the colonial regime imposes upon it in the way of tribal or regional quarrels, that violence makes its way forward, and the native identifies his enemy and recognizes all his misfortunes, throwing all the exacerbated might of his hate and anger into this new channel. But how do we pass from the atmosphere of violence to violence in action? What makes the lid blow off? There is first of all the fact that this development does not leave the settler's blissful existence intact. The settler who "understands" the natives is made aware by several straws in the wind showing that something is afoot. "Good" natives become scarce; silence falls when the oppressor approaches; sometimes looks are black, and attitudes and remarks openly aggressive. The nationalist parties are astir, they hold a great many meetings, the police are increased and reinforcements of soldiers are brought in. The settlers, above all the farmers isolated on their land, are the first to become alarmed. They call for energetic measures.

The authorities do in fact take some spectacular measures. They arrest one or two leaders, they organize military parades and maneuvers, and air force displays. But the demonstrations and warlike exercises, the smell of gunpowder which now fills the atmosphere, these things do not make the people draw back. Those bayonets and cannonades only serve to reinforce their aggressiveness. The atmosphere becomes dramatic, and everyone wishes to show that he is ready for anything. And it is in these circumstances that the guns go off by themselves, for nerves are jangled, fear reigns and everyone is trigger-happy....

Let us return to considering the single combat between native and settler. We have seen that it takes the form of an armed and open struggle. There is no lack of historical examples: Indo-China, Indonesia, and of course North Africa. But what we must not lose sight of is that this struggle could have broken out anywhere, in Guinea as well as Somaliland, and moreover today it could break out in every place where colonialism means to stay on, in Angola, for example. The existence of an armed struggle shows that the people are decided to trust to violent methods only. He of whom they have never stopped saying that the only language he understands is that of force, decides to give utterance by force. In fact, as always, the settler has shown him the way he should take if he is to become free. The argument the native chooses has been furnished by the settler, and by an ironic turning of the tables it is the native who now affirms that the colonialist understands nothing but force. The colonial regime owes its legitimacy to force and at no time tries to hide this aspect of things. Every statue, whether of Faidherbe or of Lyautey, of Bugeaud or of Sergeant Blandan—all these conquistadors perched on colonial soil do not cease from proclaiming one and the same thing: "We are here by the force of bayonets."...

In all armed straggles, there exists what we might call the point of no return. Almost always it is marked off by a huge and all-inclusive repression which engulfs all sectors of the colonized people. This point was reached in Algeria in 1955 with the 12,000 victims of Phillippeville, and in 1956 with Lacoste's instituting of urban and rural militias.[1]

---

1 We must go back to this period in order to judge the importance of this decision on the part of the French government in Algeria. Thus we may read in "Résistance Algérienne," No. 4, dated 28 March 1957, the following: "In reply to the wish expressed by the General Assembly of the United Nations, the French Government has now decided to create urban militias in Algeria. 'Enough blood has been spilled' was what the United Nations said; Lacoste replies 'Let us form militias.' 'Cease fire,' advised UNO; Lacoste vociferates, 'We must arm the civilians.' Whereas the two parties face-to-face with each other were on the recommendation of the United Nations invited to contact each other with a view to coming to an agreement and finding a peaceful and democratic solution, Lacoste decrees that henceforward every European will be armed and should open fire on any person who seems to him suspect. It was then agreed (in the Assembly) that savage and iniquitous repression verging on genocide ought at all costs to be opposed by the authorities: but Lacoste replies 'Let us systematize the repression and organize the Algerian manhunt.' And, symbolically, he entrusts the military with civil powers, and gives military powers to civilians. The ring is closed. In the middle, the Algerian, disarmed, famished, tracked down, jostled, struck, lynched, will soon be slaughtered as a suspect. Today, in Algeria, there is not a single Frenchman who is not authorized and even invited to use his weapons. There is not a single Frenchman, in Algeria, one month after the appeal for calm made by UNO, who is not permitted, and obliged to search out, investigate and pursue suspects.

Then it became clear to everybody, including even the settlers, that "things couldn't go on as before." Yet the colonized people do not chalk up the reckoning. They record the huge gaps made in their ranks as a sort of necessary evil. Since they have decided to reply by violence, they therefore are ready to take all its consequences. They only insist in return that no reckoning should be kept, either, for the others.

"One month after the vote on the final motion of the General Assembly of the United Nations, there is not one European in Algeria who is not party to the most frightful work of extermination of modern times. A democratic solution? Right, Lacoste concedes; let's begin by exterminating the Algerians, and to do that, let's arm the civilians and give them carte blanche. The Paris press, on the whole, has welcomed the creation of these armed groups with reserve. Fascist militias, they've been called. Yes; but on the individual level, on the plane of human rights, what is fascism if not colonialism when rooted in a traditionally colonialist country? The opinion has been advanced that they are systematically legalized and commended; but does not the body of Algeria bear for the last one hundred and thirty years wounds which gape still wider, more numerous and more deep-seated than ever? 'Take care,' advises Monsieur Kenne-Vignes..., 'do we not by the creation of these militias risk seeing the gap widen between the two communities in Algeria?' Yes; but is not colonial status simply the organized reduction to slavery of a whole people? The Algerian revolution is precisely the affirmed contestation of that slavery and that abyss. The Algerian revolution speaks to the occupying nation and says: 'Take your fangs out of the bleeding flesh of Algeria! Let the people of Algeria speak!'

"The creation of militias, they say, will lighten the tasks of the Army. It will free certain units whose mission will be to protect the Moroccan and Tunisian borders. In Algeria, the Army is six hundred thousand strong. Almost all the Navy and the Air Force are based there. There is an enormous, speedy police force with a horribly good record since it has absorbed the ex-torturers from Morocco and Tunisia. The territorial units are one hundred thousand strong. The task of the Army, all the same, must be lightened. So let us create urban militias. The fact remains that the hysterical and criminal frenzy of Lacoste imposes them even on clear-sighted French people. The truth is that the creation of militias carries its contradiction even in its justification. The task of the French Army is never-ending. Consequently, when it is given as an objective the gagging of the Algerian people, the door is closed on the future forever. Above all, it is forbidden to analyze, to understand, or to measure the depth and the density of the Algerian revolution: departmental leaders, housing-estate leaders, street leaders, house leaders, leaders who control each landing.... Today, to the surface checker-board is added an underground network.

"In 48 hours two thousand volunteers were enrolled. The Europeans of Algeria responded immediately to Lacoste's call to kill. From now on, each European must check up on all surviving Algerians in his sector; and in addition he will be responsible for information, for a 'quick response' to acts of terrorism, for the detection of suspects, for the liquidation of runaways and for the reinforcement of police services. Certainly, the tasks of the Army must be lightened. Today, to the surface mopping-up is added a deeper harrowing. Today, to the killing which is all in the day's work is added planified murder. 'Stop the bloodshed,' was the advice given by UNO. 'The best way of doing this,' replied Lacoste, 'is to make sure there remains no blood to shed.' The Algerian people, after having been delivered up to Massu's hordes, is put under the protection of the urban militias. By his decision to create these militias, Lacoste shows quite plainly that he will brook no interference with HIS war. It is a proof that there are no limits once the rot has set in. True, he is at the moment a prisoner of the situation; but what a consolation to drag everyone down in one's fall!

"After each of these decisions, the Algerian people tense their muscles still more and fight still harder. After each of these organized, deliberately sought after assassinations, the Algerian people builds up its awareness of self, and consolidates its resistance. Yes; the tasks of the French Army are infinite: for oh, how infinite is the unity of the people of Algeria!"

To the saying "All natives are the same" the colonized person replies, "All settlers are the same."[2]

When the native is tortured, when his wife is killed or raped, he complains to no one. The oppressor's government can set up commissions of inquiry and of information daily if it wants to; in the eyes of the native, these commissions do not exist. The fact is that soon we shall have had seven years of crimes in Algeria and there has not yet been a single Frenchman indicted before a French court of justice for the murder of an Algerian. In Indo-China, in Madagascar, or in the colonies the native has always known that he need expect nothing from the other side. The settler's work is to make even dreams of liberty impossible for the native. The native's work is to imagine all possible methods for destroying the settler. On the logical plane, the Manicheism of the settler produces a Manicheism of the native. To the theory of the "absolute evil of the native" the theory of the "absolute evil of the settler" replies.

The appearance of the settler has meant in the terms of syncretism the death of the aboriginal society, cultural lethargy, and the petrification of individuals. For the native, life can only spring up again out of the rotting corpse of the settler. This then is the correspondence, term by term, between the two trains of reasoning.

But it so happens that for the colonized people this violence, because it constitutes their only work, invests their characters with positive and creative qualities. The practice of violence binds them together as a whole, since each individual forms a violent link in the great chain, a part of the great organism of violence which has surged upward in reaction to the settler's violence in the beginning. The groups recognize each other and the future nation is already indivisible. The armed struggle mobilizes the people, that is to say, it throws them in one way and in one direction.

The mobilization of the masses, when it arises out of the war of liberation, introduces into each man's consciousness the ideas of a common cause, of a national destiny, and of a collective history. In the same way the second phase, that of the building-up of the nation, is helped on by the existence of this cement which has been mixed with blood and anger. Thus we come to a fuller appreciation of the originality of the words used in these underdeveloped countries. During the colonial period the people are called upon to fight against oppression; after national liberation, they are called upon to fight against poverty, illiteracy, and underdevelopment. The struggle, they say, goes on. The people realize that life is an unending contest.

---

2 This is why there are no prisoners when the fighting first starts. It is only through educating the local leaders politically that those at the head of the movement can make the masses accept 1) that people coming from the mother country do not always act of their own free will and are sometimes even disgusted by the war; 2) that it is of immediate advantage to the movement that its supporters should show by their actions that they respect certain international conventions; 3) that an army which takes prisoners is an army, and ceases to be considered as a group of wayside bandits; 4) that whatever the circumstances, the possession of prisoners constitutes a means of exerting pressure which must not be overlooked in order to protect our men who are in enemy hands.

We have said that the native's violence unifies the people. By its very structure, colonialism is separatist and regionalist. Colonialism does not simply state the existence of tribes; it also reinforces it and separates them. The colonial system encourages chieftaincies and keeps alive the old Marabout confraternities. Violence is in action all-inclusive and national. It follows that it is closely involved in the liquidation of regionalism and of tribalism. Thus the national parties show no pity at all toward the caids and the customary chiefs. Their destruction is the preliminary to the unification of the people.

At the level of individuals, violence is a cleansing force. It frees the native from his inferiority complex and from his despair and inaction; it makes him fearless and restores his self-respect. Even if the armed struggle has been symbolic and the nation is demobilized through a rapid movement of decolonization, the people have the time to see that the liberation has been the business of each and all and that the leader has no special merit. From thence comes that type of aggressive reticence with regard to the machinery of protocol which young governments quickly show. When the people have taken violent part in the national liberation they will allow no one to set themselves up as "liberators." They show themselves to be jealous of the results of their action and take good care not to place their future, their destiny, or the fate of their country in the hands of a living god. Yesterday they were completely irresponsible; today they mean to understand everything and make all decisions. Illuminated by violence, the consciousness of the people rebels against any pacification. From now on the demagogues, the opportunists, and the magicians have a difficult task. The action which has thrown them into a hand-to-hand struggle confers upon the masses a voracious taste for the concrete. The attempt at mystification becomes, in the long run, practically impossible.

27. Just War and Human Rights[*]

David Luban

Doctrines of just war have been formulated mainly by theologians and jurists in order to provide a canon applicable to a variety of practical situations. No doubt these doctrines originate in a moral understanding of violent conflict. The danger exists, however, that when the concepts of the theory are adopted into the usage of politics and diplomacy their moral content is replaced by definitions which are merely convenient. If that is so, the concepts of the traditional theory of just war could be exactly the wrong starting point for an attempt to come to grips with the relevant moral issues.

[...]

I

[...]

The UN Definition and the Doctrine of Sovereignty: A Critique

As it is formulated in the UN definition, the crime of aggressive war is a crime of state against state. Each state, according to international law, has a duty of non-intervention into the affairs of other states: indeed, this includes not just military intervention, but, in Lauterpacht's widely accepted definition, any "dictatorial interference in the sense of action amounting to the denial of the independence of the State."[1] At the basis of this duty lies the concept of state sovereignty, of which in fact the duty of non-intervention is considered a "corollary."[2] Now the concept of sovereignty has been interpreted in a multitude of ways, and has at different times covered a multitude of sins (in such forms as the notorious doctrine that sovereign states are above the law and entitled to do anything); but in its original use by Bodin, it meant that there can be only one ultimate source of law in a nation,

---

* Source: *Philosophy and Public Affairs* 9.2 (Winter 1980): 160–81.

1 Hersch Lauterpacht, *International Law and Human Rights* (London: Stevens, 1950), p. 167.

2 The term is used in Ian Brownlie, *Principles of Public International Law*, 2nd ed. (Oxford: Clarendon, 1973), p. 280.

namely the sovereign.[3] This doctrine suffices to explain why intervention is a crime, for "dictatorial interference" of one state in another's affairs in effect establishes a second legislator.

The doctrine does not, however, explain why the duty of non-intervention is a moral duty. For the recognition of a state as sovereign means in international law only that it in fact exercises sovereign power,[4] and it is hard to see how that fact could confer moral rights on it. Might, or so we are told, does not make right. Rather, one should distinguish mere *de facto* exercise of sovereign power from legitimate exercise of it. The natural argument would then be that the duty of non-intervention exists only toward states which are legitimate (in the sense of the term employed in normative political theory).

Before accepting this argument, however, we must consider another possibility, namely that the duty of non-intervention in a state's affairs is not a duty owed to that state, but to the community of nations as a whole. This, in fact, seems to be one idea behind the United Nations Charter. The experience of World War II showed the disastrous nature of escalating international violence, and an absolute ban on the initiation of warfare is justified on what we would now call rule-utilitarian grounds: regardless of the moral stature of a state, or the empirical likelihood of escalation in a given case, military intervention in the state's affairs is forbidden for the sake of international security.

I want to reject this argument as the basis for a theory of just war, however. For by giving absolute primacy to the world community's interest in peace, it does not really answer the question of when a war is or can be just; rather, it simply refuses to consider it. Obviously, the dangers posed by a war in the volatile political configuration of the nuclear era must weigh heavily into the question of *jus ad bellum*. But to make this the only factor is to refuse a priori to consider the merits of particular issues, and this is simply to beg the question of *jus ad bellum*.

Thus, I return to the claim that a state must be legitimate in order for a moral duty of non-intervention in its affairs to exist. If this is so, it pulls the rug out from under the UN definition, which is simply indifferent to the question of legitimacy, and thus to the whole moral dimension of the issue. We may put this in more graphic terms. When State *A* recognizes State *B*'s sovereignty it accepts a duty of non-intervention in *B*'s internal affairs. In other words, it commits itself to pass over what *B* actually does to its own people unless *B* has entered into international agreements regulating its domestic behavior; and even in this case *A* cannot intervene militarily to enforce these agreements.[5] No matter if *B* is repulsively tyrannical; no matter if it consists of

3 J.L. Brierly, *The Law of the Nations*, 6th ed., ed. Humphrey Waldock (Oxford: Oxford UP, 1963), pp. 7–16. See Bodin, *République* (n.p.: Scientia Aalen, 1961), Book One, Chap. 8.
4 This is discussed in Brownlie, *Public International Law*, chap. 5, pp. 89–108.
5 On the relation of international agreements with the duty of non-intervention, particularly in the case of human rights, see Louis Henkin, "Human Rights and 'Domestic Jurisdiction,'" in Thomas Buergenthal, ed., *Human Rights, International Law and the Helsinki Accords* (New York: Universe

the most brutal torturers or sinister secret police; no matter if its ruling generals make its primary export bullion shipped to Swiss banks. If *A* recognizes *B*'s sovereignty it recognizes *B*'s right to enjoy its excesses without "dictatorial interference" from outside.

Really, however, the point retains its force no matter what the character of *B*. The concept of sovereignty is morally flaccid, not because it applies to illegitimate regimes, but because it is insensitive to the entire dimension of legitimacy.

Can the UN definition be repaired, then, by restricting the concepts of sovereignty and aggression to legitimate states? This would certainly be a step in the right direction; but the attempt underlines a puzzle about the whole strategy of defining *jus ad bellum* as a crime against states. Wars are not fought by states, but by men and women. There is, therefore, a conceptual lacuna in such a definition. It can be bridged only by explaining how a crime against a state is also a crime against its citizens, that is, by relating men and women to their states in a morally cogent fashion. This, I take it, is what the concept of legitimacy is supposed to do. A legitimate state has a right against aggression because people have a right to their legitimate state. But if so we should be able to define *jus ad bellum* directly in terms of human rights, without the needless detour of talk about states. Nor is this simply a question of which terms are logically more basic. If the rights of states are derived from the rights of humans, and are thus in a sense one kind of human rights, it will be important to consider their possible conflicts with other human rights. Thus, a doctrine of *jus ad bellum* formulated in terms of human rights may turn out not to consider aggression the sole crime of war. Indeed, this is what I shall argue in Section III.

First, however, it will be helpful to consider more closely the connection between a state's rights and those of its citizens. For I have criticized the UN definition (and the doctrine of sovereignty) by suggesting that its focus on the former shows indifference to the latter.

II

Contract, Nation, and State

This argument may be clarified by examining social contract theory, the canonical modern account of legitimacy. The key feature of contract theory for our present

Books, 1977), pp. 21–40, and Thomas Buergenthal, "Domestic Jurisdiction, Intervention, and Human Rights: The International Law Perspective," in Peter G. Brown and Douglas Maclean, eds., *Human Rights and U.S. Foreign Policy* (Lexington, MA: Lexington Books, 1979), pp. 111–20. Both agree that even when the right of domestic jurisdiction over human rights has been "signed away" by a state, military intervention against it is proscribed. This doctrine, a product of the United Nations era, has replaced the nineteenth-century doctrine which permitted humanitarian intervention on behalf of oppressed peoples. The legal issues are discussed in the readings collected in Richard B. Lillich and Frank C. Newman, eds., *International Human Rights: Problems of Law and Policy* (Boston: Little, Brown and Company, 1979), pp. 484–544. The case analyzed there is India's 1971 intervention into Bangladesh; on this see also Oriana Fallaci's interview with Zulfikar Ali Bhutto, in *Interview With History* (Boston: Houghton Mifflin Co., 1976), pp. 182–209.

discussion is its conception of the rights of political communities, particularly their right against aggression. According to contract theory, a political community is made legitimate by the consent (tacit or explicit) of its members; it thereby acquires rights which derive from the rights of its members. Thus the rights of political communities are explained by two rather harmless assumptions: that people have rights, and that those rights may be transferred through freely given consent. Contract theory, then, appears to offer a particularly clear account of how aggression against a political community is a crime against its members.

However, it is important to note that the term "political community" has two radically distinct meanings, corresponding to two very different conceptions of the social contract. The seventeenth-century theorists distinguished between a contract by which people bind themselves into a community prior to any state—Locke's version—and a contract by which people set a sovereign over them—Hobbes' version. Let us call the former a "horizontal" and the latter a "vertical" contract.[6]

A horizontal contract may be explicit: Arendt, in introducing the terms, suggests the Mayflower Compact as a paradigm case of a horizontal contract to which consent was explicitly rendered. More often, however, the consent is given tacitly through the process of everyday living itself. In Walzer's words:

> Over a long period of time, shared experiences and cooperative activity of many different kinds shape a common life. "Contract" is a metaphor for a process of association and mutuality....[7]

Such a contract gives rise to a *people* or, as I shall say in order to emphasize the people's existence as a political community, to a *nation*. But only the vertical contract can legitimate a *state*. A state is an ongoing institution of rule over, or government of, its nation. It is a drastic error to confuse the two; for while every government loudly asserts, "Le peuple, c'est moi!" it is clear that this is never literally true and seldom plausible even as a figure of speech. And it is equally obvious what ulterior motives and interests lie behind the assertion.

A state's rights can be established only through a vertical contract, which according to social-contract theory means nothing more or less than that the state is legitimate. This, too, requires consent, and this will be consent over and above that which establishes the horizontal contract. For the nation is prior to the state. Political communities, not sets of atomic individuals, consent to be governed. Of course it is the typical argument of totalitarianism, with its idolatry of the state, to deny this. For example, Giovanni Gentile, the "philosopher of fascism," says:

---

6 I adopt this terminology from Hannah Arendt, "Civil Disobedience," in *Crises of the Republic* (New York: Harcourt, Brace, Jovanovich, 1972), pp. 85–87. See also her *On Revolution* (New York: Viking, 1965), pp. 169–71. It appears also in Michael Walzer, "The Problem of Citizenship," *Obligations* (New York: Simon and Schuster, 1970), p. 207.

7 Walzer, *Just and Unjust Wars* (New York: Basic Books, 1977), p. 54.

For it is not nationality that creates the State, but the State which creates nationality, by setting the seal of actual existence on it. It is through the *conquest* of unity and independence that the nation gives proof of its political will, and establishes its existence as a State.[8]

Gentile had in mind Italy's struggle for unity in the Risorgimento; evidently, he believed that until the Italian state was established the nation as such did not exist. But what, then, gave "proof of its political will"? Gentile calls it the nation, and he is right, although this is inconsistent with his original contention that before the state the nation did not exist. A national liberation movement comes about when a people acts as a political community, that is, as a nation; its state comes later if it comes at all. The nation is the more-or-less permanent social basis of any state that governs it.

The relevance of these distinctions for just-war theory is this: clearly, aggression violates a state's rights only when the state possesses these rights. According to contract theory this entails that the state has been legitimated by the consent of its citizens. An illegitimate state, that is, one governing without the consent of the governed is, therefore, morally if not legally estopped from asserting a right against aggression. The *nation* possesses such a right, to be sure, but the state does not. Thus we have returned to the argument of the preceding section, which in our present terminology amounts to the claim that the concept of sovereignty systematically and fallaciously confuses a nation and its state, granting illegitimate states a right to which they are not entitled.

Curiously, Walzer himself falls prey to this confusion in his theory of just war. He attempts to give a contractarian justification of the UN definition, grounding the rights of states in a social contract based on tacit consent as characterized above ("shared experiences and cooperative activity of many kinds shape a common life"). This form of consent, however, can only refer to the horizontal contract, and can thus ground only the rights of nations, not of states. As Gerald Doppelt points out, "Walzer's theory seems to operate on two levels: on the *first* level, he implicitly identifies the state with the established government...; on the *second* level, he identifies the state with the people, nation, or political community—not its *de facto* government...."[9] This is precisely a confusion of vertical with horizontal contracts. Doppelt goes on to criticize Walzer on grounds quite similar to those suggested by my argument: an illegitimate and tyrannical state cannot derive sovereign rights against aggression from the rights of its own oppressed citizens, when it itself is denying them those same rights.

The question which we are facing is this: what sort of evidence shows that consent to a state has indeed been rendered? I shall not attempt to give a general answer

---

8 Giovanni Gentile, *Genesis and Structure of Society*, trans. H.S. Harris (Urbana: U of Illinois P, 1966), pp. 121–22.

9 Gerald Doppelt, "Walzer's Theory of Morality in International Relations," *Philosophy & Public Affairs* 8.1 (Fall 1978): 9.

here, since the issue is quite complex. Two things, however, are clear. The first is that the mere existence of the nation cannot be sufficient evidence of the required sort: it would then legitimate any pretender. This is why Walzer's contract in no way establishes a state's rights, contrary to his claim. The second is that clear evidence can exist that a state is *not* based on consent and hence *not* legitimate.

An example drawn from the recent Nicaraguan revolution will illustrate this. On 22 August 1978 a band of Sandinista guerrillas took over the National Palace in Nicaragua, holding virtually the entire parliament hostage. They demanded and received the release of political prisoners, a large ransom, and free passage to Panama. Newspapers reported that as the guerrillas drove to the airport the streets were lined with cheering Nicaraguans. Within two days a general strike against the government of Anastasio Somoza Debayle had shut down the country; it was unusual in that it had the support of Nicaragua's largest business association, and thus seemed to voice a virtually unanimous rejection of the Somoza regime. Soon armed insurrection began. In the city of Matagalpa the barricades were manned mainly by high school students and other youths. Somoza responded by ordering the air force to bomb Matagalpa; the Matagalpans sent delegates to the bishopric to ask the church to intervene on their behalf with the government. The rebellion spread; at this point American newspapers were routinely referring to the Nicaraguan events as a struggle between the Nicaraguan people and the National Guard (the army). In a press statement strongly reminiscent of Woody Allen's *Bananas*, Somoza stated that his was the cause of Nicaraguan freedom, since he enjoyed the support of virtually the entire National Guard. By October the uprising was crushed—albeit temporarily—by sheer force of arms.

I do not pretend to possess a detailed understanding of Nicaraguan politics. However, it does not take a detailed understanding to realize that when the populace of a capital city cheers the guerrillas who have taken their own parliament hostage, when labor unions and business associations are able to unite in a general strike, and when a large city's residents must ask for third-party intervention to prevent their own government from bombing them to rubble, the government in question enjoys neither consent nor legitimacy. The evidence, I submit, is more than sufficient to back this claim.

It might be objected that this example shows only that the Somoza regime was illegitimate, not the Nicaraguan state as such. The distinction between regime and state, however, is simply this: the regime is a particular distribution of men and women over the leadership posts which the state institutionalizes. (I shall ignore the complication that replacements can be made in some posts without the regime changing.) If this is so, then the objection amounts to the claim that the Nicaraguan people might consent to an institutional structure involving a leadership position with Somoza's powers—that is, that they might consent to a dictatorial structure which they could change only through armed struggle. It is clear that this claim possesses vanishingly small plausibility; ultimately, I believe it rests on the question-begging assumption that a nation always consents to some state or other.

This example underlines the moral impotence of the concept of sovereignty. For other states continued to recognize the sovereignty of the Somoza regime and thus committed themselves to a policy of non-intervention in the state's war against its nation. No doubt such decisions were discreet; they were certainly not moral.[10]

Other examples are—unfortunately—not hard to find. One thinks of the Organization of African Unity's frosty reception of Tanzania's "aggression" in Uganda, despite the notorious illegitimacy of Idi Amin's regime.[11] The point is graphically illustrated as well by the United States government's response to the conquest of Cambodia by Vietnam in January 1979. The Carter administration had frequently pinpointed the regime of Pol Pot and Ieng Sary as the worst human rights violator in the world, and some reports suggested that the "auto-genocide" in Cambodia was the most awful since the Holocaust.[12] Nevertheless, the State Department denounced Vietnam for aggression and violation of Cambodia's territorial integrity and sovereignty; and this despite the fact that the Vietnamese-installed regime's first announcement concerned the restoration of human rights in Cambodia.[13] [...]

The Modern Moral Reality of War

Modern international law is coeval with the rise of the European nation-state in the seventeenth and eighteenth centuries. As the term suggests, it is within the historical context of nation-states that a theory will work whose tendency is to equate the rights of nations with the rights of states. It is plausible to suggest that an attack on the French state amounts to an attack on the French nation (although even here some doubts are possible: a Paris Communard in 1871 would hardly have agreed). But when nations and states do not characteristically coincide, a theory of *jus ad bellum* which equates unjust war with aggression, and aggression with violations of state sovereignty, removes itself from the historical reality of war.

---

10 Walzer would, it seems, agree; see *Just and Unjust Wars*, p. 98.

11 See *Amnesty International Report 1978* (London: Amnesty International Publications, 1979), pp. 89–92, and Amnesty's *Human Rights in Uganda* (London: Amnesty International Publications, 1978).

12 See *Amnesty International Report 1978*, pp. 167–70, for detailed instances.

13 "...A profound moral and political issue is at stake. Which is the greater evil: the continuation of a tyrannical and murderous regime, or a flagrant violation of national sovereignty?...the Carter Administration...decided without hesitation...that the violation of Cambodia's sovereignty was a greater enormity than the Cambodian regime's violations of human rights...." Henry Kamm, "The Cambodian Dilemma," *The New York Times Magazine*, 4 February 1979, pp. 54–55. Evidently, this view was shared by the United Nations, which voted recently to seat a delegation from the deposed Pol Pot government rather than the Vietnam-supported Heng Samrin regime, on the grounds that no matter how unappetizing the behavior of the former, it would be wrong to condone aggression by recognizing the latter.

In citing these examples I am not entering any large moral claims on behalf of Vietnam or Tanzania, both of which are accountable for their share of human rights violations. Here I am in agreement with Walzer (*Just and Unjust Wars*, p. 105) that pure motives and clean hands are not necessary to morally justify an intervention. The present essay was written in early 1979, before the current Cambodian famine, in which it appears that the policies of Vietnam may be just as horrifying as those of the Khmer Rouge.

World politics in our era is marked by two phenomena: a breakup of European hegemony in the Third World which is the heritage of nineteenth-century imperialism; and maneuvering for hegemony by the (neo-imperialist) superpowers, perhaps including China. The result of this process is a political configuration in the Third World in which states and state boundaries are to an unprecedented extent the result of historical accident (how the European colonial powers parceled up their holdings) and political convenience (how the contending superpowers come to terms with each other). In the Third World the nation-state is the exception rather than the rule. Moreover, a large number of governments possess little or no claim to legitimacy. As a result of these phenomena, war in our time seems most often to be revolutionary war, war of liberation, civil war, border war between newly established states, or even tribal war, which is in fact a war of nations provoked largely by the noncongruence of nation and state.

In such circumstances a conception of *jus ad bellum* like the one embodied in the UN definition fails to address the moral reality of war. It reflects a theory that speaks to the realities of a bygone era. The result is predictable. United Nations debates—mostly ineffectual in resolving conflicts—and discussions couched in terms of aggression and defense, have deteriorated into cynical and hypocritical rhetoric and are widely recognized as such. Nor is this simply one more instance of the well-known fact that politicians lie in order to dress up their crimes in sanctimonious language. For frequently these wars are fought for reasons which are recognizably moral. It is just that their morality cannot be assessed in terms of the categories of the UN definition; it must be twisted and distorted to fit a conceptual Procrustes' bed.

III

Human Rights and the New Definition

What, then, are the terms according to which the morality of war is to be assessed? In order to answer this question, let me return to my criticism of the contractarian derivation of the rights of states from the rights of individuals. States—patriots and Rousseau to the contrary—are not to be loved, and seldom to be trusted. They are, by and large, composed of men and women enamored of the exercise of power, men and women whose interests are consequently at least slightly at variance with those of the rest of us. When we talk of the rights of a state, we are talking of rights—"privileges" is a more accurate word—which those men and women possess over and above the general rights of man; and this is why they demand a special justification.

I have not, however, questioned the framework of individual rights as an adequate language for moral discourse. It is from this framework that we may hope to discover the answer to our question. Although I accept the vocabulary of individual rights for the purpose of the present discussion, I do not mean to suggest that its propriety cannot be questioned. Nevertheless, talk of individual rights does capture much of the moral reality of contemporary politics, as talk of sovereignty and states' rights does not. This is a powerful pragmatic reason for adopting the framework.

To begin, let me draw a few elementary distinctions. Although rights do not necessarily derive from social relations, we do not have rights apart from them, for rights are always claims on other people. If I catch pneumonia and die, my right to life has not been violated unless other humans were directly or indirectly responsible for my infection or death. To put this point in syntactic terms, a right is not to be thought of as a one-place predicate, but rather a two-place predicate whose arguments range over the class of beneficiaries and the class of obligors. A human right, then, will be a right whose beneficiaries are all humans and whose obligors are all humans in a position to effect the right. (The extension of this latter class will vary depending on the particular beneficiary.)[14] Human rights are the demands of all of humanity on all of humanity. This distinguishes human rights from, for example, civil rights, where the beneficiaries and obligors are specified by law.

By a *socially basic human right* I mean a right whose satisfaction is necessary to the enjoyment of any other rights.[15] Such rights deserve to be called "basic" because, while they are neither intrinsically more valuable nor more enjoyable than other human rights, they are means to the satisfaction of all rights, and thus they must be satisfied even at the expense of socially non-basic human rights if that is necessary. In Shue's words, "Socially basic human rights are everyone's minimum reasonable demands upon the rest of humanity." He goes on to argue that socially basic human rights include security rights—the right not to be subject to killing, torture, assault, and so on—and subsistence rights, which include the rights to healthy air and water, and adequate food, clothing, and shelter.[16]

Such rights are worth fighting for. They are worth fighting for not only by those to whom they are denied but, if we take seriously the obligation which is indicated when we speak of human rights, by the rest of us as well (although how strictly this obligation is binding on "neutrals" is open to dispute). This does not mean that any infringement of socially basic human rights is a *casus belli*: here as elsewhere in the theory of just war the doctrine of proportionality applies. But keeping this reservation in mind we may formulate the following, to be referred to henceforth as the "new definition":

---

14 Other analyses of the concept of "human right" are possible. Walzer, for example, makes the interesting suggestion that the beneficiary of human rights is not a person but humanity itself (*Just and Unjust Wars*, p. 158). Such an analysis has much to recommend it, but it does not concern us here, for humanity will still enjoy its rights through particular men and women.

15 I take this concept from Henry Shue, "Foundations for a Balanced US Policy on Human Rights: The Significance of Subsistence Rights" (College Park, MD: Center for Philosophy and Public Policy Working Paper HRFP-1, 1977), pp. 3–4. Shue discusses it in detail in *Basic Rights: Subsistence, Affluence, and U.S. Foreign Policy* (Princeton: Princeton UP, in press), chap. 1.

16 Ibid., pp. 3, 6–12.

(3) A just war is (i) a war in defense of socially basic human rights (subject to proportionality); or (ii) a war of self-defense against an unjust war.

(4) An unjust war is (i) a war subversive of human rights, whether socially basic or not, which is also (ii) not a war in defense of socially basic human rights.

I shall explain. The intuition here is that any proportional struggle for socially basic human rights is justified, even one which attacks the non-basic rights of others. An attack on human rights is an unjust war *unless* it is such a struggle. This is why clause (4) (ii) is necessary: without it a war could be both just and unjust. Clause (3) (ii) is meant to capture the moral core of the principle of self-defense,... And it is worth noting that clause (4) (i) is an attempt to reformulate the concept of aggression as a crime against people rather than states; an aggressive war is a war against human rights. Since the rights of nations may be human rights (I shall not argue the pros or cons of this here), this notion of aggression may cover ordinary cases of aggression against nations.

Let me emphasize that (3) and (4) refer to *jus ad bellum*, not *jus in bello*. When we consider the *manner* in which wars are fought, of course, we shall always find violations of socially basic human rights. One might well wonder, in that case, whether a war can ever be justified. Nor is this wonder misplaced, for it addresses the fundamental horror of war. The answer, if there is to be one, must emerge from the doctrine of proportionality; and here I wish to suggest that the new definition is able to make sense of this doctrine in a way which the UN definition is not.[17] For the UN definition would have us measure the rights of states against socially basic human rights, and this may well be a comparison of incommensurables. Under the new definition, on the other hand, we are asked only to compare the violations of socially basic human rights likely to result from the fighting of a war with those which it intends to rectify. Now this comparison, like the calculus of utilities, might be Benthamite pie-in-the-sky; but if it is nonsense, then proportionality under the UN definition is what Bentham once called the theory of human rights: "nonsense on stilts."

---

17 The new definition also allows us to make sense of an interesting and plausible suggestion by Melzer, namely that a just war (in the sense of *jus ad bellum*) conducted in an unjust way (*jus in bello*) becomes unjust (*jus ad bellum*), in other words, that the *jus ad bellum* is "anchored" in the *jus in bello*. On the new definition this would follow from the fact that a war conducted in a sufficiently unjust way would violate proportionality. See Yehuda Melzer, *Concepts of Just War* (Leiden: A.W. Sijthoff, 1975), pp. 87–93.

28. In Defense of Empires[*]

Deepak Lal

Empires have undeservedly gotten a bad name, particularly in America, ever since President Woodrow Wilson proclaimed the end of the Age of Empires and ushered in the Age of Nations. But this was not always so. In an 1881 letter to British Prime Minister William Gladstone, King Bell and King Acqua of the Cameroons River, West Africa, wrote:

> We want to be under Her Majesty's control. We want our country to be governed by British Government. We are tired of governing this country ourselves, every dispute leads to war, and often to great loss of lives, so we think it is best thing to give up the country to you British men who no doubt will bring peace, civilization, and Christianity in the country.... We are quite willing to abolish all our heathen customs.... No doubt God will bless you for putting a light in our country.[1]

Gladstone demurred, and Germany snapped up the offer instead.

This example provides the major justifications for and against empires. The major argument in favor of empires is that, through their pax, they provide the most basic of public goods—order—in an anarchical international society of states. This is akin to maintaining order in social life. In *The Anarchical Society*, the late Hedley Bull cogently summarized the three basic values of all social life, which any international order should seek to protect: first, that life is secured against violence leading to death or bodily harm; second, that promises once made are kept; and third, that "the possession of things will remain stable to some degree and will not be subject to challenges that are constant and without limit."[2]

---

* Source: Deepak Lal, *In Defense of Empires* (Washington, DC: AEI Press, 2004).
1 Kings Bell and Acqua to William Gladstone, November 6, 1881, Foreign Office 403/18, Public Record Office, Kew, in M.W. Doyle, *Empires* (Ithaca: Cornell UP, 1986), 162.
2 H. Bull, *The Anarchical Society* (New York: Columbia UP, 1977), 4.

Empires—which we can define as "multi-ethnic conglomerates held together by transnational organizational and cultural ties"[3]— have historically both maintained peace and promoted prosperity for a simple reason. The centers of the ancient civilizations in Eurasia, which practiced sedentary agriculture and yielded a surplus to feed the towns, were bordered in the north and south by areas of nomadic pastoralism: the steppes of the north and the semidesert of the Arabian Peninsula to the south. In these regions, the inhabitants had kept up many of the warlike traditions of our hunter-gatherer ancestors and were prone to prey upon the inhabitants of the sedentary plains, at times attempting to convert them into their chattel like cattle.[4] This meant that the provision of one of the classical public goods—protection of citizens from invaders—required the extension of territory to some natural barriers that could keep the barbarians at bay. The Roman, Chinese, and various Indian empires were partly created to provide this pax, which was vital to keeping their labor-intensive and sedentary forms of making a living intact. The pax of various imperia has thus been essential in providing one of the basic public goods required for prosperity.

These empires can be distinguished as either multicultural or homogenizing. The former included the Abbasid, the Ottoman, the Austro-Hungarian, the British, and the various Indian empires, where little attempt was made to change "the habits of the heart" of the constituent groups—or if it was, as in the early British Raj, an ensuing backlash led to a reversal of policy.

The homogenizing empires, by contrast, sought to create a "national" identity out of the multifarious groups in their territory. The best example is China, where the ethnic mix was unified as Hans through the bureaucratic device of writing their names in characters in a Chinese form and suppressing any subsequent discontent through the subtle repression of a bureaucratic authoritarian state.[5] The Han were an ethnic group whose leaders created the Chin dynasty. They created a unified Han identity by making other ethnic groups adopt their language, Mandarin Chinese, which forced them to adopt their Chinese characters for even something as intimate as writing their own names. In our own time, the American "melting pot"—creating Americans out of a multitude of ethnicities by adherence to a shared civic culture and a common language—has resulted in a similar homogenized imperial state. Likewise, the supposedly ancient "nations" of Britain and France were created through a state-led homogenizing process.[6] India, by contrast, is another imperial state whose political unity is a legacy of the British Raj, but whose multiethnic character is underwritten by an ancient hierarchical structure which accommodates these different groups as different castes.

---

3 P.J. Cain and A.G. Hopkins, *British Imperialism, 1699–2000* (Harlow, UK: Longman, 2002), 664.
4 W.H. McNeill, *A History of the World*, 3rd ed. (New York: Oxford UP, 1979).
5 W.J.F. Jenner, *The Tryanny of History: The Roots of China's Crisis* (London: Penguin, 1992).
6 See L. Colley, *Britons* (New Haven: Yale UP, 1992).

Despite nationalist rhetoric, an imperial pax has usually succeeded in providing this essential public good—order—in the past. Consider an ordinary citizen (of any ethnic and religious origin) of either of the two nineteenth-century empires extinguished by President Wilson at Versailles (the Austro-Hungarian and the Ottoman) who is contemplating the likelihood of his grandchildren living, surviving, and passing on property to their children. Compare him to a citizen of a postimperial successor state pondering the same prospect. There can be no doubt of the great deterioration of opportunities that has befallen the average citizen of the successor states. The situation in many ways is worse in Africa, with its millions of refugees and ethnic slaughter—even if we consider the inhuman and brutal regime of Leopold's Belgian Empire in the Congo. In many parts of the postimperial world, the main beneficiaries of the Age of Nations have been the "nationalist" predatory elites who have failed to provide even the most elemental of public goods—law and order.

The imperial pax has also historically been associated with globalization—which is not a new phenomenon—and the prosperity it breeds, for two important reasons. First, in the language of institutional economics, transaction costs are reduced by these transnational organizations, through their extension of metropolitan property rights to other countries. Second, by integrating loosely linked or even autarkic countries and regions—through free flows of goods, capital, and people—into a common economic space, empires promote those gains from trade and specialization emphasized by Adam Smith, leading to what I label Smithian intensive growth. Thus the Graeco-Roman empires linked the areas around the Mediterranean; the Abbasid Empire of the Arabs linked the worlds of the Mediterranean and the Indian Ocean; the Mongol Empire linked China with the Near East; the various Indian empires created a common economic space in the subcontinent; and the expanding Chinese Empire linked the economic spaces of the Yellow River with those of the Yangtze. The British were the first to knit the whole world together through their empire. But most of these empires ultimately declined.

Given the existing technology and the inevitable predatoriness of the state, most empires overextended themselves.[7] Though as table 1 (from the late Sam Finer's masterful *History of Government*) shows, most lasted for longer than this ex-colony has existed as an independent state. The decline of empires was followed by a disintegration of the enlarged economic spaces they had created. As Finer notes about the disintegration of the Roman Empire:

> If a peasant family in Gaul, or Spain, or northern Italy had been able to foresee the misery and exploitation that was to befall his grandchildren and their grandchildren, on and on and on for the next 500 years, he would have been singularly spiritless—and witless too—if he had not rushed to the aid of the

---

7 For a model of the predatory state which explains this rise and fall of empires, see Deepak Lal, *The Hindu Equilibrium*, vol. 1, chap. 13.2 (Oxford: Clarendon, 1988).

empire. And even then the kingdoms that did finally emerge after the year 1000 were poverty stricken dung heaps compared with Rome. Not till the full Renaissance in the sixteenth century did Europeans begin to think of themselves as in any ways comparable to Rome, and not till the "Augustan Age" of the eighteenth century did they regard their civilization as its equal.[8]

TABLE 1
LIFE SPAN OF EMPIRES

Egypt	2580 BC–30 BC	2,820 years
China	212 BC–1912 AD	2,133 years
Rome	509 BC–476 AD	985 years
Assyria	1356 BC–612 BC	744 years
Byzantine	330 AD–1204 AD	874 years
Venice	687 AD–1799 AD	1,112 years
Caliphate	632 AD–943 AD	312 years
Ottoman	c.1350 AD–1918 AD	568 years
Achemenian Persian Empire	550 BC–330 BC	220 years
Sassanian Persian Empire	224 AD–651 AD	427 years
British Empire in India	1757 AD–1947	190 years

SOURCE: S.E. Finer, *The History of Government*, vol. 1 (Oxford: Oxford University Press, 1997), 31–32.

In our own times, the death of the nineteenth-century liberal international economic order (LIEO) built by Pax Britannia on the fields of Flanders led to nearly a century of economic disintegration and disorder, which has only been repaired in the last decade, with the undisputed emergence of the United States as the world leader. But is the United States willing and able to maintain its pax, which will underwrite the resurrection of another LIEO (like the British in the nineteenth century), and if not, what are the likely consequences? These are the central questions to consider.

Gladstone's reasons for not acceding to the request of Kings Bell and Acqua of the Cameroons River are still resonant today, not least in the hearts of many classical liberals. For, though Adam Smith did not have much to say about empires per se,[9]

---

8 S.E. Finer, *The History of Government*, vol. 1 (Oxford: Oxford UP, 1997), 34.

9 Smith did have a lot to say about the costs and benefits of colonies, particularly in North America. But colonization is only one form of direct imperialism. India, for example, was not a colony (with white settlers), but was a central part of the British Empire. Nor was all of it ruled directly. The

his followers Cobden and Bright—the leaders of the anti-imperial party, along with Gladstone, the Liberals' leader—argued that the imperialists' belief that empire was in England's economic interests was false. Even today, economic historians are unable to agree whether or not the benefits of retaining and expanding the formal British Empire after 1850 exceeded its costs.[10] The nineteenth-century classical liberals rightly maintained that, as foreign trade and investment were mutually advantageous (a nonzero sum game), no empire was needed to obtain these gains from trade. All that was required was free trade and laissez-faire....

The Liberals, however, did not altogether eschew empire, for as Angell states:

Where the condition of a territory is such that the social and economic cooperation of other countries with it is impossible, we may expect the intervention of military force, not as the result of the "annexationist illusion," but as the outcome of real social forces pushing to the maintenance of order. That is the story of England in Egypt, or, for that matter, in India. And if America has any justification in the Philippines at all, it is not that she has "captured" these populations by force of conquest, as in the old days a raiding tribe might capture a band of cattle, but that she is doing there a work of police and administration which the natives cannot do for themselves.[11]

This is the "white man's burden" argument for empire, which meant that even Liberals were in favor of an empire to maintain a pax.

It was Woodrow Wilson who questioned this "policing" justification for empire. He was a utopian whose world view was a strange mixture of classical liberalism, Burkean conservatism, Presbyterianism, and socialism.[12] He referred to himself as an imperialist on two occasions, but meaning only a form of economic imperialism, in line with his former student Frederick Jackson Turner, whose frontier thesis "implied that the US required greater foreign markets in order to sustain its prosperity."[13] But "for every sentence he uttered on commerce, he spoke two on the moral responsibility of the United States to sustain its historic idealism and render the service of its democracy."[14] During his campaign for the Democratic presidential nomination

---

princely states that formed a large part of the British Raj were ruled indirectly through British Political Agents assigned to the "native" rulers.

10 See P.J. Cain, "Was It Worth Having? The British Empire, 1850–1950," *Revista de Historia Economica* 16 (1998), 351–76.

11 Ibid., 139.

12 In an essay written in 1886 (buried in his papers till 1968), Wilson reconciles his Burkean belief in democracy by stating, "For it is very clear that in fundamental theory socialism and democracy are almost if not quite the one and the same. They both rest at bottom on the absolute right of the community to determine its own destiny and that of its members." Cited in T.J. Knock, *To End All Wars* (Princeton, NJ: Princeton UP, 1992), 7.

13 Ibid., 10.

14 Ibid., 10.

in 1912, Wilson said, "I believe that God planted in us visions of liberty…that we are chosen…to show the way to the nations of the world how they shall walk in the paths of liberty."[15] The instrument for achieving this Utopia was to be the League of Nations, maintaining collective security and bringing transgressors into line through sanctions. The traditional notion of "national interest," which had governed the European balance-of-power system, was eschewed, to be replaced by a community of nation-states in which the weak and the strong would have equal rights. In his new world order, said Wilson, the only questions would be: "Is it right? Is it just? Is it in the interest of mankind?"[16]…

After the Second World War, the United Nations resurrected this Wilsonian universal moralism. Once again, the anthropomorphic identification of states as persons and the presumption of an essential harmony of interests among these equal world "citizens" was proclaimed. Collective economic sanctions brought into line those that broke international norms. As a detailed study by Gary Huffbauer and his associates shows, these sanctions have been ineffective and inefficient in serving their foreign policy goals.[17] By contrast, the nineteenth-century British pax was not maintained through economic sanctions to change states' behavior; instead, direct or indirect imperialism was used. The contrasting lessons from the last two centuries are of obvious relevance to the current confrontation with the "Axis of Evil" and the global "War on Terror."

II

A second important aspect of an empire's pax is the transnational legal system created for the protection of property rights, particularly those of foreigners. As Lipson shows in his brilliant study *Standing Guard*, this was due to the commercial treaties signed by European states in the mid-nineteenth century. The treaties provided rules for protecting international property rights, which "hardened into general principles of international law."[18] These international standards built upon the system of commercial law that had been established as a result of Pope Gregory VII's eleventh-century papal revolution.[19] The treaties of Westphalia (1648) and Paris (1763) further strengthened the economic rights of foreigners and their property

---

15 Ibid., 11.

16 Ibid., 10.

17 G. Huffbauer, J. Schott, and K. Elliot, *Economic Sanctions Reconsidered* (Washington, DC: Institute of International Economics, 1990); Lal, "Development and Spread."

18 Lipson notes that according to these principles, "foreigners were deemed subject to local laws, as they had been since the Middle Ages, but national jurisdiction over aliens and their property had to comply with a variety of international standards." C. Lipson, *Standing Guard* (Berkeley: U of California P, 1985), 8.

19 See H. Berman, *Law and Revolution* (Cambridge, MA: Harvard UP, 1983); Deepak Lal, *Unintended Consequences* (Cambridge, MA: MIT P, 1998).

abroad. The nineteenth century saw a culmination of this process, with the security of foreign persons and their property guaranteed by every European state, the United States (soon after its independence at the end of the eighteen century), and the new Latin American states (after their wars of independence). This extension of the international rule of law covered what was previously Christendom in Europe and the New World, and the role of the medieval Catholic Church in providing the first "international" legal system which covered the Christian States in Europe.

Since legal systems are in part derived from people's cosmological beliefs (as I denoted them in *Unintended Consequences*), it is not surprising that this common international standard was readily adopted in lands where people had a shared cosmological heritage. Matters differed greatly when it came to areas with dissimilar cosmological beliefs in the Middle East, Asia, and Africa. Even there, the principle of reciprocity—which had partly led the European states of the Middle Ages to accede to various international standards—was also behind the Ottoman Empire's acceptance of various "capitulation" treaties dating back to the 1500s. Under these treaties, the Ottomans granted commercial privileges to the states of Christendom; in return, Muslim merchants and other subjects of the Ottomans received protection for their goods and persons abroad. The principle of reciprocal protection was directly written into the Ottoman Treaty of 1540.

With its growing economic strength and increased concern about Russian expansion in the Eastern Mediterranean, Britain signed the Anglo-Turkish convention in 1838, which effectively opened up the Ottoman Empire to European trade and investment. In time, with the growing enfeeblement of the Ottomans, new arrangements arose concerning disputes with foreigners, whereby "international property rights were effectively guaranteed by the extra territorial application of European and American laws."[20]

The European powers under British leadership found that in parts of the world where European cosmological beliefs were alien, to expand trade and investment, they had to create systems of foreign concessions and extraterritorial laws—as in the treaty ports of the Far East. Where political arrangements were fragile—as in Africa—the creation of political and legal structures to serve commercial expansion led to difficult choices for the Victorians in integrating the agricultural periphery with the dynamic industrialism of Europe and the United States.[21] "Their policies naturally aimed at a vast, global extension of commerce. At the same time, they tried to limit the direct imposition of political and military controls, which were expensive and difficult to manage."[22]

---

20 Lipson, *Standing Guard*, 14.
21 See A.G. Hopkins, "Property Rights and Empire Building: Britain's Annexation of Lagos, 1861," *Journal of Economic History* 40 (1980): 777–98.
22 Lipson, *Standing Guard*, 15.

This global network of laws protecting foreign capital allowed the worldwide expansion of the "gentlemanly capitalism" of London, which Cain and Hopkins have persuasively argued was the hallmark and real motivating force behind the British Empire. This legal framework was an essential element of Pax Britannia. Together with the economic integration through free trade and an international payments system based in London, it allowed the empire to fulfill a wider mission—the world's first comprehensive development program. After 1815, Britain aimed to establish a set of like-minded allies that would cooperate in keeping the world safe from what George Canning called the "youthful and stirring nations" (such as the United States), which proclaimed the virtues of republican democracy, and from a "league of worn out governments" in Europe, whose future lay too obviously in the past. Britain offered an alternative vision of a liberal international order bound together by mutual interest in commercial progress and underpinned by a respect for property, credit, and responsible government, preferably of the kind found at home.[23]

TABLE 2

A TURNING POINT CHRONOLOGY

1840	Chile	1900	Cuba
1850	Brazil	1910	Korea
1850	Malaysia	1920	Morocco
1850	Thailand	1925	Venezuela
1860	Argentina	1925	Zambia
1870	Burma	1947	India
1876	Mexico	1947	Pakistan
1880	Algeria	1949	China
1880	Japan	1950	Iran
1880	Peru	1950	Iraq
1880	Sri Lanka	1950	Turkey
1885	Colombia	1952	Egypt
1895	Taiwan	1965	Indonesia
1895	Ghana	1965	Afghanistan
1895	Ivory Coast	1965	Bangladesh
1895	Nigeria	1965	Ethiopia
1895	Kenya	1965	Mozambique
1900	Uganda	1965	Nepal
1900	Zimbabwe	1965	Sudan
1900	Tanzania	1965	Zaire
1900	Phillippines		

SOURCE: Lloyd Reynolds, *Economic Growth in the Third World* (New Haven: Yale University Press, 1983), 958.

---

23 Cain and Hopkins, *British Imperialism*, 650.

Compared with the previous millennia, the results were stupendous. From 1850 to 1914—the height of this nineteenth century LIEO—many parts of the third world for the first time experienced intensive growth for a sustained period. In his survey of the economic histories of forty-one developing countries, Lloyd Reynolds dated the turning points when developing countries entered the era of intensive growth. This era was accompanied by a sustained rise in per-capita incomes, as compared with the ubiquitous extensive growth of the past, when output growth just kept up with population growth (table 2).

GDP FOR MAJOR COUNTRIES, 1500–1998, RUSSIA = 100

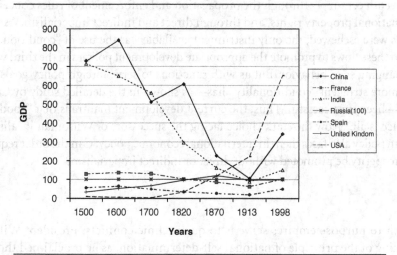

Source: Angus Maddison, *The World Economy: A Millennial Perspective* (OECD, 2001), table B-18.

The First World War marked the beginning of the end of this nineteenth-century LIEO. As shown in figure 1—which charts the relative economic strength of various potential (and actual) imperial contenders from the nineteenth century to the 1950s—it is clear that by 1914 the United States was by far the dominant economic power. But after the First World War it retreated into isolationism, and during the Great Depression (in part caused by its faulty monetary policy), the United States failed to do what Britain in the depression of the 1870s had done as the economic world leader—maintain open markets for trade and finance....

But the United States did try during the Second World War (at Bretton Woods) to resurrect the three pillars on which the nineteenth-century LIEO had been built— free trade, the gold standard, and free capital mobility. But while the British Empire had fostered these pillars by example, treaties, and direct and indirect imperialism, the United States instead created transnational institutions—the General Agreement on Tariffs and Trade (GATT), followed by the World Trade Organization (WTO), the International Monetary Fund (IMF), and the World Bank....

The World Bank was the instrument chosen to resurrect the international capital market which had been closed in particular to developing countries, due to their defaults in the 1930s. Laws were passed that forbade US financial intermediaries from holding foreign government bonds.[24] But the financial intermediation role of the Bank was soon overtaken by its role as a multilateral foreign aid agency, in part to participate in the Cold War—both by tying the "non-aligned" to the free world and by promoting economic development. The World Bank was to be used to create another international development program, analogous to the one the British had promoted in the nineteenth century—through the propagation and enforcement of rules concerning international property rights, and through direct and indirect imperialism. As these routes were eschewed, the only instrument available was the use of "conditionality" tied to these flows to promote the appropriate development policies in the third world, by changing state behavior. But as with sanctions to serve foreign policy goals, this ever more stringent "conditionality" has—as shown in the detailed study by Collier et al.—been unsuccessful. Thus, the current development mantra is that "good governance is all." Now the stark choice facing the successors of Wilsonian idealism in foreign policy also faces them in international economic policy: Can the order required for prosperity be promoted without direct or indirect imperialism?

III

The third purpose empires serve is to quell ethnic conflicts. President Wilson's invoking of the principle of national self-determination, as he proclaimed the new moral Age of Nations to replace the immoral Age of Empires, let the ethnic genie out of the bottle. As Dean Acheson noted in a speech at Amherst College on December 9, 1964, this lofty principle

> has a doubtful moral history. [Woodrow Wilson] used it against our enemies in the First World War to dismember the Austro-Hungarian and Ottoman Empires, with results which hardly inspire enthusiasm today. After the Second World War the doctrine was invoked against our friends in the dissolution of their colonial connections.... On the one occasion when the right of self-determination—then called secession—was invoked against our own government by the Confederate States of America, it was rejected with a good deal of bloodshed and moral fervor. Probably you will agree it was rightly rejected.[25]

---

24 W.A. Lewis, *Growth and Fluctuations*, 1870–1913 (London: Allen and Unwin, 1978), 49.
25 Dean Acheson, "Ethics in International Relations Today," in *The Puritan Ethic in United States Foreign Policy*, ed. D.L. Larson (Princeton, NJ: Van Nostrand, 1966), 134–35.

From the viewpoint of global order, the most common form of deadly conflict today is civil war in the name of cultural self-determination. Recent research by Oxford's Paul Collier and his associates on the causes of civil wars finds that the relationship of ethno-linguistic fragmentation in a state and the risk of a civil war forms an inverted U in shape.[26] The most homogenous as well as the most fragmented states are least at risk of civil war. There is thus likely to be bipolarity in the institutions best able to deal with ethnic diversity. One (complete fragmentation) is found in empires. The other (homogeneity) is surprisingly a course Keynes advocated during the Second World War when speculating about the ideal political postwar order in Europe. Skidelsky reports on one of Keynes's fancies:

> A view of the post-war world which I find sympathetic and attractive ... is that we should encourage small political and cultural units, combined into larger, and more or less closely knit, economic units. It would be a fine thing to have thirty or forty capital cities in Europe, each the center of a self-governing country entirely free from national minorities (who would be dealt with by migrations where necessary) and the seat of government and parliament and university center, each with their own pride and glory and their own characteristics and excellent gifts. But it would be ruinous to have thirty or forty entirely independent economic and currency unions.[27]

But as Skidelsky notes, "this pleasing picture of a re-medievalised Europe did not survive in later drafts."[28] This homogenized solution, which as Keynes recognized could involve "ethnic cleansing," has clearly been eschewed by the West—as witnessed by its actions in Bosnia and Kosovo. This reflects the hopes of much progressive thought over the last two centuries—stemming from the Enlightenment—that transnational and "modern" forms of association, such as class, would transcend primordial forms of association, such as ethnicity and culture (of which nationalism is an offshoot). But contemporary history continues to show the power of these primordial forces....

At least in principle, the Keynes solution seems to be in keeping with human nature. As in a globalized economy, size does not matter for prosperity—demonstrated by the shining examples of the city-states of Hong Kong and Singapore. Prosperity is feasible, as long as someone maintains a global pax.

However, the events in Bosnia and Kosovo show that the United States and its allies have (rightly in my view) chosen to impose a regional pax by reconstructing parts of the Balkan Austro-Hungarian Empire. The High Representative of the

---

26 See P. Collier and A. Hoeffler, "On Economic Causes of Civil War," *Oxford Economic Papers* 50 (1998): 563–73.

27 See R. Skidelsky, *John Maynard Keynes*, vol. 3, chap. 5 (London: Macmillan, 2000), 38.

28 Ibid.

UN in Bosnia, and the Chief Administrator of Kosovo are the equivalent of British viceroys in areas of direct imperialism, and political agents in those of indirect imperialism. Similarly, the recent Afghan peace is underwritten by an allied police force—another form of indirect imperialism—much as the British sought to do through their Residents in Afghanistan during their imperium.

IV

Even if there is a case for Pax Americana to maintain global peace and protect property rights, Paul Kennedy has argued that it would lead to "imperial overstretch" and the nationalist backlash that has undermined past empires. American foreign policy has tolerated such resistance in the past, but it seems unlikely that it will pose a serious challenge to the Pax Americana....

From the experience of the British Empire, we have some idea of the administrative cost of running an empire—based on both direct and indirect imperialism. At the end of the Second World War, the elite administrative division of the colonial service in Africa— including district officers and central secretariats, but not railway, agriculture, or other specialist departments—numbered slightly more than 1,200 men, spread over more than a dozen colonies covering nearly 2 million square miles, with an estimated population of 43 million. The Sudan Political Service, which reported to the Foreign Office, had 125 senior officials for a territory twice the size of Texas. For a population of 353 million, the Indian Civil Service had a maximum strength of 1,250 covenanted members, whereas the relatively well-manned Malayan Civil Service possessed some 220 elite administrators for a mere 3.2 million people.[29] In total, less than 3,000 civil servants from the metropolis ran the empire. This can be compared with the huge numbers of nonclerical officials in the transnational organizations—the UN, the World Bank, the IMF, and the WTO—currently seeking to run the postwar Wilsonian international political and economic order.

These small number of metropolitan civil servants were supplemented by a large army of English-speaking "Creoles." In India, in his famous "Minute on Education," Lord Macaulay stated that the English wished to create an English-educated native middle class "who may be interpreters between us and the millions whom we govern; a class of persons, Indian in blood and colour, but English in taste, in opinions, in morals, and in intellect."[30] He also foresaw that this could in time lead to the creation of the class which would contest and replace British rule. Thus in the 1833 Charter Debate in the British Parliament, Macaulay said: "It may be that the public mind of

---

29 J.W. Cole, "Colonial Rule," in *The Oxford History of the British Empire*, vol. 4, ed. J.M. Brown and W.M. Roger Louis (Oxford: Oxford UP, 1999), 232.
30 See T.B. Macaulay, *The Complete Works of Lord Macaulay*, 12 vols. (London: Longmans, Green and Co, 1898); and Lal, *Hindu Equilibrium*, chap. 5.

Major Powers, 1988–2000

	1988	1989	1990	1991	1992	1993
China	2.7	2.7	2.7	2.5	2.7	2.1
France	3.7	3.6	3.5	3.5	3.4	3.3
India	3.1	2.9	2.7	2.5	2.3	2.4
Russia	15.8	14.2	12.3	0.0	5.5	5.3
UK	4.1	4.1	3.9	4.2	3.8	3.5
USA	5.7	5.5	5.3	4.7	4.8	4.5
EU	1.7	1.7	1.7	1.7	1.7	1.7

	1994	1995	1996	1997	1998	1999	2000
China	1.9	1.8	1.8	1.9	2.0	2.1	2.1
France	3.3	3.1	3.0	2.9	2.8	2.7	2.6
India	2.3	2.2	2.1	2.2	2.2	2.4	2.4
Russia	5.9	4.1	3.8	4.2	3.2	3.6	4.0
UK	3.3	3.0	2.9	2.7	2.6	2.5	2.5
USA	4.1	3.8	3.5	3.3	3.1	3.0	3.1
EU	1.7	1.7	1.7	1.7	1.7	1.7	1.7

SOURCE: Stockholm International Peace Research Institute, sipri.org/contents/milap/milex/mex_database.

India may expand under our system till it has outgrown that system, that by good government we may educate our subjects into a capacity for better government; that, having become instructed in European knowledge, they may, in some future age demand European institutions. Whether such a day will ever come I know not. But never will I attempt to avert or retard it. Whenever it comes, it will be the proudest day in English history."[31]

These "Macaulay's children," as we may call them, were to overthrow the empire. Their nationalist revolts were part of that "Creole nationalism" which, as Benedict Anderson argued, overthrew colonial rule in the Americas. The major complaint of the "Creoles" against the Peninsulares (descendents of the conquistadores of the Iberian peninsula) was that, even though in almost every respect—language, descent, customs—they were indistinguishable, they had an inferior status because

31 Macaulay, *Complete Works*, vol. 11, 585–86.

of the accident of their birth. In India, Macaulay's children also had an inferior status, despite being English in every respect except "blood and colour." This racism ultimately unraveled the British Empire, by fueling "Creole nationalism." But in its early phase, the British Raj had behaved like a traditional Indian power. The notions of racial exclusiveness which came to characterize its late imperial phase were alien to India's early British rulers, who exhibited a more robust delight in both the country's mores and its women. The shock of the Mutiny of 1857 and the arrival of English women turned the British in India from "nabobs" to "sahibs."

But there was another route to prevent the rise of "Creole nationalism," and this was the example of Rome, where in 212 AD, Caracalla declared all free men citizens of Rome. This meant that the Romanized elites in the provinces could and did form part of a common Roman political and social elite, and some of these non-Romans also became emperors. This Caracallan threshold, as it has been called, was never crossed by the British Empire, because of its racial exclusiveness.

One of the strengths of the United States is that, in its public and increasingly private philosophy, racism no longer plays a part—as witnessed by the fact that two of its major foreign policy leaders are African Americans. Moreover, the United States has now moved to recognizing dual citizenship, as have many other countries—with even the most nationalist like India planning to follow. With the growth of a cosmopolitan class of primarily American-trained technicians and executives (culturally and often personally linked) at work in many different countries, there already exists the core of a global "Roman" political and economic elite—open to the talents—which could run this new US imperium.

V

Nevertheless, will not a US imperium cause a coalition to form against it, as Christopher Layne from the Cato Institute argued recently?[32] He claims the historical record shows that hegemonic powers are likely to be challenged by a coalition of other states, for "when one state becomes more powerful—becomes a hegemon—the imbalance of power in its favor is a menace to the security of all other states."[33] Envy, jealousy, and even hatred are the inevitable and unenviable consequences of disparities in economic and military power. But should the dominant power then actively seek to become poorer and weaker so it may be loved, or to prevent other powers from "ganging up" against it in the future? Or should it instead try to use its hegemony to bring other great powers into a concert maintaining the global pax (as the British did in the nineteenth century), recognizing that its dominance will lead to emulation by many—the "soft power" idealists so often talk about—but also fear and loathing among others. Preventing the latter from spilling over into global

32 C. Layne, "The Power Paradox," *Los Angeles Times*, October 6, 2002.
33 Ibid.

disorder has been one of the essential tasks of imperial statesmanship. To undertake it sensibly, however, a country must recognize that it is an imperial power. Empires come before imperialism. Like other economically and militarily dominant powers in the past, the United States has acquired an empire, but it is reluctant to face the resulting imperial responsibilities because it refuses to face up to the reality in its domestic discourse. This would require the development of a theory for the beneficent exercise of its power. Wishing the empire would just go away or could be managed by global love and compassion is to bury one's head in the sand and promote global disorder.

If we look at the current threats to global or regional political and economic order, there would seem to be a convergence—rather than a divergence—in the interests of the United States and other potential great powers. There are clearly two major regions of the world where disorder rules: the vast region spanning the Islamic world in the Middle East and Central Asia, and the continent of Africa....

At the end of the first millennium, the dominant world civilization was that of Islam. The Syrian geographer Al-Muqaddasi described the Islamic world at the turn of the millenium: "The strict political unity which had once characterized Islam had been shattered in the tenth century...yet a sense of comity survived, and travelers could feel at home throughout the Dar al-Islam—or to use an image popular with poets—in a garden of Islam, cultivated, walled against the world, yielding for its privileged occupation, shades and tastes of paradise."[34]

This paradise was shattered by the rise of the West. When the Ottomans were turned back after the siege of Vienna in 1683, the Islamic world went into relative decline, and by the end of the First World War and the dismemberment of the Ottoman Empire, it was clear that Islam was a defeated civilization. This had also been true of the other great Eurasian civilizations—the Indian, the Chinese, the Japanese—when they encountered the West. These civilizations had two responses to the Western onslaught in the nineteenth century. The first was that of the oyster, which closes its shell. The other was to modernize, to try to master foreign technology and way of life, and to fight the alien culture with its own weapons. Japan is the prime example of a country which chose the latter route. India and China seesawed between the two responses and took nearly a century truly to come to terms with modernization. Some Islamic countries, in particular Attaturk's Turkey and Mehmet Ali's Egypt, also took the second route, but only partially. The other remedy, the oyster—whereby Muslims sought to regain Allah's favor by purifying Islam from the corruptions that had crept into Muslim lives over the centuries—has had much greater resonance. For deep cultural reasons I cannot go into on this occasion, the other non-Muslim civilizations have come to realize that modernization does not entail westernization, and hence ancient cosmological beliefs can be maintained,

---

34 F. Fernandez-Armesto, *Millennium* (New York: Scribner, 1995), 35.

even when material beliefs have to change to modernize.[35] Yet as William McNeill notes, it was Islam's misfortune (unlike the Japanese) that despite many voices—for example, Sir Sayed Ahmad in nineteenth-century India—stating that modernity could be reconciled with Islam, "the two remedies seemed always diametrically opposed to one another. Reformers' efforts therefore tended to cancel out, leaving the mass of Muslim society more confused and frustrated than ever."[36]

Until the Muslim world wholeheartedly embraces modernization, recognizing that it does not involve westernization and the giving up of its soul, there is little hope the Islamist threat will be eliminated. But how is such a change to come about?

Consider the Middle East world created with the dismemberment of the Ottoman Empire. Apart from Egypt, Turkey, Saudi Arabia, and Iran, the rest of the states in the Middle East today are the artificial creations of the victorious powers which dismembered the Ottoman Empire. Thus Iraq, instead of being—as Saddam Hussein has claimed—the successor state of Nebuchadnezzar, was actually put together by Britain as a unit containing Kurdish, Sunni, and Shia tribes in the region. This artificial tribal confederation has always been brittle, and its unity has been maintained not by any national feeling but by tribal deals and most recently by terror.

The Kingdom of Saudi Arabia is also not the descendant of any ancient Arab state, but the result of a religious movement—the Wahabi's (an extreme version of Islam) creating a state in central Arabia in the eighteenth century.[37] This state, along with Yemen, maintained its independence through the turbulent period when the British and the French held mandates over most of Palestine and the Arabian Peninsula. But, "without known resources, with few links with the outside world, and surrounded on all sides by British power, [they] ... could be independent only within limits."[38] The discovery of small amounts of oil in the 1930s changed Saudi fortunes.

This oil was discovered, extracted, and exported by Western companies, and by 1960, the total Middle Eastern oil reserves were estimated to be about 60 percent of known world reserves. Given the erosion of international rules concerning property

---

35 But see Lal, *Unintended Consequences*, chap. 4.

36 McNeill, *History*, 390.

37 Religious reformer Muhammad ibn Abdul Wahhab (1703–92) began to preach the need for Muslims to return to the teaching of Islam as understood by the followers of Ibn Hanbal: strict obedience to the Quran and Hadith, as they were interpreted by responsible scholars in each generation, and rejection of all that could be regarded as illegitimate innovations. The reformer made an alliance with Muhammad ibn Sau'd, ruler of a small market town, Diriyya, and this led to the formation of a state which claimed to live under the guidance of the sharia and tried to bring the pastoral tribes all around it under its guidance too. The state rejected the claims of the Ottomans to be the protectors of the authentic Islam. By the first years of the nineteenth century, the armies of the new state had expanded; they had sacked the Shia shrines in southwestern Iraq and occupied the holy cities of Hejaj. A. Hourani, *A History of the Arab Peoples* (Cambridge, MA: Harvard UP, 1991), 257–58.

38 Ibid., 319.

rights, and the growth of statism, the Saudi oil fields—along with others in Iraq and Iran—were nationalized. The Saudis were, moreover, protected by the United States.

In 1945, Franklin Delano Roosevelt flew from Yalta to Suez, where he met King Ibn Saud aboard the US navy ship Quincy. They struck the deal that would eventually "fuel" the cold war. Saudi Arabian oil flowed to the west, matching the Soviet's reserves. In return, the US promised security to the dynasty.... But there was always a tension at the heart of the arrangement. On the Quincy, the King was adamant that he could not compromise on his opposition to a future state for the Jews in the Muslim land of Palestine. The US dilemma ever since has been to reconcile its backing of Israel with its protection of Saudi Arabia.[39]

September 11 finally showed the dangers in this Faustian pact. The pact concerns both money and ideology. The Saudis have maintained a tightrope act for half a century. They have balanced their alliance with the infidels and the untold riches they provide the dynasty by maintaining probably the most virulent and medieval form of Islam in their own country and using their newfound wealth to propagate it through financing mosques and Wahabi preachers around the world. The madrasas (Islamic religious schools) in Pakistan—which produced the Taliban—were all run by Wahabis. The charitable donations required of all believers have often—perhaps innocently—ended up in charities which funded Al Qaeda. The Saudis have directly and indirectly funded the mosques and madrasas which preach hatred against the infidels—the Jews, Christians, and above all, the Hindus—to young minds, who learn little if anything about the modern world. But for the Saudis to eschew or put a stop to this funding would undoubtedly create a Wahabi backlash in Saudi Arabia and end the dynasty.

For the rest of the world, the poison spread by Wahabi evangelism is becoming intolerable. Imagine if German schools only taught anti-Semitism, or those in America were just teaching the young to hate blacks. But this is what the large number of madrasas—funded by the Saudis, in Pakistan and many other countries around the world—are teaching. If there is to be an end to the "war on terror," this poisoning of the Muslim mind clearly must stop.

Numerous commentators have argued that this poison continues to spread successfully because of ongoing Arab-Israeli confrontation and the anger it arouses in the Arab street, which provides the Islamists with an unlimited supply of jehadis. Without going into the historical rights and wrongs of the issue—on which I have always believed the Arabs have a rightful grievance—there are two reasons this issue (despite Arab rhetoric) is merely another symptom of the Islamic world's failure to

---

39 Giles Keppel, "The Jihad in Search of a Cause," *Financial Times*, 2 September 2002.

come to terms with modernity and of the common tactic used by the third world to externalize its domestic problems.

First, the Camp David accord brokered by President Clinton in 2000–2001 gave the Palestinians virtually everything they had requested, except the so-called "right of return." Yet Arafat turned it down and instead launched the intifada. He and every Arab government knew no Israeli government could agree to the "right of return," which in effect would involve the extinction of Israel. Apart from that, Barak had accepted almost every other Palestinian demand.

Amazingly, the "right of return" after fifty years is still a controversial issue, being kept alive by the large number of Palestinians still in refugee camps. Why do they remain there after fifty years? My family and I—along with millions of others—lost our land and property as a result of the Partition of India in 1947. We were refugees. Both the Indian and Pakistani governments provided some help, but most importantly, the refugees, after a little while, made new lives for themselves. Consequently, there are no refugee camps on both sides of the Indo-Pak border with millions demanding the "right of return."

History is never just, and economists have been right to maintain that "bygones are bygones." This is particularly important in the highly contested territory of Palestine, and it became clear to me in the late 1970s when a colleague from University College London was carrying out a dig near the Wailing Wall. He took me down and showed me layer upon layer of corpses. The ones in each layer had been killed by those above, who were in turn killed by those above them. Deciding who has the original rights to this fiercely contested territory, where might has been right for millennia would defeat even the wisdom of Solomon. Sensibly, throughout history, losers in these continual shifts in fortune have come to terms with their losses and continued with their lives.

The Palestinians could have done the same. There was plenty of land in neighboring Arab countries to provide them housing, and given the untold oil wealth that accrued in nearby Arab states, there should have been no financial impediment to their rehabilitation. Yet fifty years later, two generations have lived in the misery of these camps, waiting for the Israeli state to be destroyed. There can be no peace on those terms with Israel. Under the circumstances, what should any Prime Minister of Israel—even an Arab—do in the face of the current intifada? I have never received an answer to this question from any Arab leader with whom I have discussed the issue.

The only solution to the Arab-Israeli problem, therefore, lies in the Muslim world's coming to terms with modernity and the other Arab states' providing both land (if needed) and resources from their oil wealth to resettle the refugees. This requires that Saudi, Syrian and Iranian direct and indirect support for the intifada must end. The current status quo in the Middle East is untenable. The primary task of a Pax Americana must be to find ways to create a new order in the Middle East, where cosmological beliefs are preserved, but the prosperity resulting from modernity leads to the end of jihad, thus easing the confusion that has plagued the Islamic soul for over a century.

A few points can be made regarding how this is to be accomplished. Many accusingly say that any such rearrangement of the status quo would be an act of imperialism[40] and would largely be motivated by the desire to control Middle Eastern oil. I argue that, far from being objectionable, imperialism is precisely what is needed to restore order in the Middle East....

VI

There are those who still believe that moral suasion will be enough to solve the Arab-Israeli dispute, and together with the use of sanctions, bring order to the Middle East. The Europeans in particular are vociferous adherents of the Wilsonian order, with their demand for multilateral action through the UN. But this is just the usual tactic of the weak: to tie Gulliver down with a million strings so that he cannot move. In terms of military and economic power, increasingly, the Europeans are becoming second-order powers; it is unlikely that any lack of support on their part will endanger an American pax. But as they have done for fifty years, they will no doubt continue to be free riders on whatever pax is created. The fears that an assertive America will provoke an aggressive countercoalition are exaggerated.

After September 11, despite much continuing ambivalence, the United States at long last seems to be awakening from the Wilsonian dream and realizing its unique responsibility—like the British in the nineteenth century—to maintain global order. As I have emphasized, this involves the promotion of modernization—particularly in the Muslim world—but not westernization. The continuing domestic resonance of Wilsonian idealism in US foreign policy, however, has the potential to undermine this emerging pax by creating a backlash, if the required modernization is mistaken for westernization.

Given its domestic homogenizing tendencies, the United States (along with various other Western countries) is attempting to legislate its habits of the heart around the world—human rights, democracy, egalitarianism, labor, environmental

---

40 Thus Joseph Nye stated on a possible war with Iraq: "If the US is perceived as an imperialist power, in the region, we shall encounter an antiimperial reaction that could breed a new generation of terrorists." Joseph Nye, "Owls Are Wiser about Iraq than Hawks," *Financial Times*, 21 October 2002. Two points need to be made. First, the region has been ruled by empires for millenia, some long lasting like the Roman and the Ottoman. To think that the mere existence of an empire will in itself breed terrorism—even if it brings peace and prosperity—seems to fly against history. Second, the title of his piece seems to suggest that an imperial power has to be a hawk. The effective exercise of imperial power depends upon the circumstances, requiring behavior sometimes like a hawk, sometimes like a dove, and quite often like an owl. The failure of Nye—along with so many international-relations experts in the United States—to recognize and accept that, for good or ill, the United States is already an imperial power, leads to the confusions displayed in this and other similar articles.

standards, and so on. But its claim that it is thereby promoting universal values is unjustified.

There is an important difference between the cosmological beliefs of what became the Christian West and those of the other ancient agrarian civilizations of Eurasia.[41] Christianity has a number of distinctive features that it shares with its Semitic cousin Islam, but not entirely with its parent Judaism, and that are not to be found in any of the other great Eurasian religions. The most important is its universality. Neither the Jews, nor the Hindu or Chinese civilizations had religions claiming to be universal. One could not choose to be a Hindu, Chinese, or Jew; he was born as one. This also meant that, unlike Christianity and Islam, these religions did not proselytize. Third, only the Semitic religions, being monotheistic, have also been egalitarian. Nearly all other Eurasian religions (apart from Buddhism) believed in some form of hierarchical social order. By contrast, alone among the Eurasian civilizations, the Semitic ones (though least so the Jewish) emphasized the equality of men's souls in the eyes of their monotheistic deities. Dumont has rightly characterized the resulting profound divide between the societies of Homo Aequalis, which believe all men are born equal (as the philosophes and the American Constitution proclaim), and those of Homo Hierarchicus, which believe no such thing.[42] The so-called universal values promoted by the West are no more than the culture-specific, proselytizing ethic of what remains at heart Western Christendom. Nor is there a necessary connection—as the West claims—between democracy and development.[43] If democracy is to be preferred as a form of government, it is not because of its instrumental value in promoting prosperity (at times it may well not), but because it promotes a different Western value—liberty. Again, many civilizations have placed social order above this value, and it would be imperialistic for the West to ask them to change their ways.

If no universal claims for cherished Western cosmological beliefs are valid, it is unlikely that they will be found acceptable by the rest of the world. If the West ties its moral crusade too closely to the emerging processes of globalization and modernization, there is a danger that there will also be a backlash against globalization. This potential cultural imperialism poses a greater threat to the acceptance of a new Pax Americana in developing countries—particularly the Muslim countries—than

---

41 In *Unintended Consequences*, I make an important distinction between the *material* and *cosmological* beliefs of different cultures. The former relate to beliefs about the material world, including how to make a living. The latter involve how man relates to his fellow human beings and his place in the world—in Plato's words, "how one should live." There is considerable cross-cultural evidence that while material beliefs are highly malleable, cosmological beliefs are not and are, moreover, derived from the common linguistic parent of the given culture. That is why the modernization promoted by globalization, which requires changing material beliefs, need not require westernization, which implies a change in cosmological beliefs.

42 L. Dumont, *Homo Hierarchicus* (London: Weidenfeld and Nicolson, 1970).

43 See Deepak Lal and H. Myint, *The Political Economy of Poverty, Equity and Growth* (Oxford: Clarendon, 1996).

the unfounded fears of their cultural nationalists that the modernization promoted by globalization will lead to the erosion of cherished national cultures.[44]

Conclusions

Empires have unfairly gotten a bad name, not least in US domestic politics. This is particularly unfortunate, as the world needs an American pax to provide both global peace and prosperity. The arguments that this is too costly are not convincing. If instead of this pax, however, the United States seeks to create an international moral order by attempting to legislate its "habits of the heart" through ethical imperialism, it is likely to breed disorder. The most urgent task in the new imperium is to bring the world of Islam into the modern world, without seeking to alter its soul. I have given reasons to believe the United States should be able to fulfill this imperial task. But is it willing? Given the continuing resonance of Wilsonian moralism in public discourse, I am doubtful. There must first be an acceptance in domestic politics that the United States is an imperial power. The real debate about how best to use that power could then sensibly ensue.

---

44 See Lal, *Unintended Consequences*; Lal, "Cultural Self-Determination"; and Lal, "Globalisation."

29. Making Pacifism Plausible*

Soran Reader

Introduction

First, some terminology. By "war" I mean the violent action of one state upon another for the sake of a political end; by "violence," action which causes physical harm to its victims, who are irreducibly physically individual persons. "Pacifism" is the view that war is always morally wrong; and, for want of any other word, I use "war-ism" to denote the position it opposes, that war may sometimes be morally justified.[1] I use the term "war-machine" to refer to the institutions necessary for it to be possible to make war—systems of military expertise, armies of trained soldiers, systems for the research and development of weapons.

These definitions immediately limit my brief. Because my concern is with war as a state-state relation, I do not consider the moral status of other "armed conflicts," whether these be guerrilla wars, tribal conflicts or conflicts between neighbouring groups individuated in some other way. Because my concern is with the morality of war insofar as it is *violent*, rather than lethal (see the discussion of Cochran and Norman, below) or merely coercive, I do not argue for pacifism from the wrongness of *killing* in particular; and nor do my arguments have any direct implications for the moral status of wars conducted in other, non-violent ways. Because I take it

---

* Source: *Journal of Applied Philosophy* 17.2 (2000): 169–80.

1 Note that the war-ist here is not yet someone who thinks that war is ever a positive good—he is just someone who thinks that in some contexts it can be justified. Martin Ceadel (1987) *Thinking About Peace and War* (Oxford, Oxford UP) distinguishes five positions within the ethics of war, from militarism (war is a positive human good), to absolutist pacifism (no violence whatsoever can be justified). I am here interested in a simpler two-way distinction, between those who think war is sometimes defensible—"war-ists"—and those who think it never is—pacifists. Duane L. Cady (1989) *From Warism to Pacifism: A Moral Continuum* (Philadelphia, Temple UP) and elsewhere, has coined the same term (without the hyphen), for much the same purpose. Some have suggested that the term "bellicist" would be more apt. But it has a current use which picks out a distinct position of its own—a fatalistic acceptance of war, prior to the distinction between defence and offence within the institution. See Ceadel, op. cit., p. 12.

that violence is a phenomenon which depends on the reality of individual persons, I neither exploit nor directly criticise those strategies in the ethics of war which claim an analogy between individual violent action and collective violent action. I simply assume that where the state violence of war is to be justified, it is justification for harms to particular persons that is required. The plausibility of this assumption must be measured against the plausibility of any alternative. And because my concern is with the *moral* status of war, my arguments have no effect on so-called "realist" claims, that war is justified or simply required by considerations other than moral ones—political, economic or even biological. In common with most parties, I assume that it is *moral* justification we seek for war, so as to defend it to our electorates and our children.

War-ism is very firmly institutionalised. Intuition in favour of (at least) defence against tyranny is entrenched and widespread, and intuition in favour of humanitarian intervention is strong and growing. In a context like this, pacifism is on the back foot. We might call this set-up, following Flew, "the presumption of war-ism."[2] Very few contemporary Anglo-American philosophers challenge it. Duane Cady is almost unique in the effort he has made to develop a nuanced attack on war-ism.[3] He explores the continuity between just-war thinking and pacifist thinking, and argues that there is no sharp distinction to be drawn; he also develops a rich notion of the "positive peace" of pacifism, as more than mere absence of conflict, and uses this to argue war-ism is problematic in its proposal that we should (or even can) use violence to achieve peace thus understood. Other writers who sympathise with pacifism include Richard Norman, John Rawls, Jonathan Glover, Jenny Teichman and Nicholas Denyer.[4] But all fall short of an argued endorsement of the position. Norman prefers to think of himself as a "pacificist"—someone who morally disapproves of war, but believes that in some contexts it is a morally defensible course of action. Rawls, Glover and Teichman are most sympathetic with a position they call "contingent" pacifism, which holds that although a just war is in principle possible, facts about modern weaponry etc. make it a matter of practical—thus, contingent—impossibility that such a war could ever take place. In contrast, the pacifism which may follow from a basic moral intuition about persons, MSP, is not *contingent*—it depends on essential features of state-state war, such as its reliance on a war-machine, its use of soldiers, and its violence.

---

2 Antony Flew (1976) *The Presumption of Atheism* (London, Elek/Pemberton).
3 Cady, op. cit.
4 Richard Norman (1988) "The case for pacifism," *Journal of Applied Philosophy*, 5, pp. 197–210; John Rawls (1971) *A Theory of Justice* (Harvard), §58; Jonathan Glover (1977) *Causing Death and Saving Lives* (London, Pelican); Jenny Teichman (1986) *Pacifism and the Just War* (Oxford, Blackwell); Nicholas Denyer (2000) "Just War," in Roger Teichman (ed.) *Logic, Cause and Action* (London/Cambridge, Cambridge UP), pp. 137–51.

1. A Familiar Intuition about the Moral Status of Persons

The homely intuition with which my arguments begin is this: persons have a certain moral status, and they have it because they are persons. Wherever they go, whoever they are with, persons matter morally as much, and in the same way, as each other.[5] I shall not argue for this intuition (hereafter MSP). Rather, I shall explore what follows for the ethics of war if we take it to be true, and require ourselves to act in accordance with it. I think it makes the moral justification of war impossible. Thus, in the jargon of traditional debate, it excludes the possibility of a just war, and establishes the truth of pacifism.[6]

What is the status of MSP? When I set out to explore the possibility that the truth of MSP implies the truth of pacifism, I rely on the thought that we—readers of this paper, policy-makers and ordinary people—find MSP more plausible and important, than we do any claim which conflicts with it. It is only our unreflective habitual commitment to war-ist politics, which prevents us from seeing just how and to what extent war-ism is in tension with our commitment to MSP. My suggestion in this paper is that, once we begin to make this faultline in our moral thinking explicit, pacifist claims will come to seem much more compelling to us.

It might be asked how MSP is related to views about the moral status of persons enshrined in the major moral theories. We could say that MSP combines the separate thoughts about persons which utilitarianism and Kantianism make central. But it would better reflect the priorities of this approach to put it thus: utilitarianism and Kantianism pull apart thoughts which naturally arise together in our ordinary and evolving folk-conception of the way in which persons matter. The utilitarian emphasises that all persons matter as much as each other; the Kantian that certain things may not be done to persons. The utilitarian introduces a problematic idea, which does not follow from the basic thought captured in MSP, that one person's well-being can be traded for the well-being of another; the Kantian disagrees, insisting that this may absolutely never be done. Neither the tradeability idea in utilitarianism, nor its absolutist denial in Kantianism, is intuitive. Accordingly, in what follows I

---

5 This intuition does not say that we cannot rationally make any moral distinctions based on considerations that don't affect personhood—community membership, say. We justly make a distinction between refugees and citizens, for example, to enable us to meet the special needs of refugees. But such distinctions between persons as are morally acceptable to us today, all rest on the bedrock of the basic intuition about their moral status as persons. This contrasts with historic discriminations, such as enslavement and patriarchy, where it was precisely the personhood of those who are discriminated against that was denied, and this denial used to justify discrimination.

6 Denyer, op. cit., gestures in the direction of a similar thought about how pacifism follows from basic moral convictions, but the idea is not developed. At the end of his paper Denyer concludes that our basic moral intuitions about "the immunity of the innocent" and the "munity of the nocent" (i.e., who may justly be harmed), clash with any workable law of war which could be used to decide who may be harmed in a conflict, and notes that it is far from obvious that we should give up these moral intuitions. I argue for the pacifist conclusion directly, and rely on a simpler moral intuition than those he describes, which are not basic, I suggest, but can be shown to follow from MSP.

shall assume that the tradeability question is an open one, and endeavour to ensure that my arguments do not rely on presupposing a conclusion either way. I want to rest the weight of argument here not on any utilitarian or Kantian credentials which MSP might share in, but on the familiarity and plausibility of MSP in our moral community, and the moral repugnance of rejecting it.

2. The Presumption of War-ism

How does the presumption of war-ism look in the light of MSP? War is supposed to offer the only answer to a problem—the problem of international injustice, which may be expansionist (the war will be defensive), or simply powerful within its own community (the war will be interventionist and humanitarian).[7] This situation is commonly thought to present a decisive challenge to the pacifist. It is first supposed that we have here a single question. We have the means to make war—our war-machine—and Hitler (or similar) is threatening us. The question is: "Now shall we use our war-machine?"; the pacifist is anyone who answers "No." But this question—and not just the war-machine!—is loaded in favour of war-ism. As it is posed, it relies on presuppositions about the nature of communities (they have war-machines) and their relations (they may justly ignore each other unless extraordinarily provoked) which a consistent thinker who is committed to MSP will need to consider and revise. Far from being the defining question in the ethics of war, the "Hitler's coming!" type of question can arise only at the end of a long series of questions, to which war-ist answers have already been given.

For his solution to be plausible, the war-ist must suppose that the problem of international injustice is an external problem. This thought emerges from a certain kind of communitarianism: it holds that membership of community makes a difference to moral status. Given this assumption, it seems natural that moral requirements for action by states not yet affected by the problem should be initially extremely lax; and that once the problem begins to threaten the security of our home state, moral requirements should be extremely permissive. Initially, in the war-ist scheme, we are not required to do anything at all in response to the presence of a tyrant in another community. It seems obvious, to this way of thinking, that the emergence of a Hitler or a Saddam Hussein imposes no moral requirements on "us," the members of another, separate political and moral community, and that

---

7 There are other causes for war which have been taken to be just, of course. At the most extreme, the *militarist*—Ceadel's term—is someone who takes war to be a good and necessary manifestation of an aspect of human nature; the idea that war is somehow "glorious," and is for those involved in fighting "what childbirth is for women—an initiation into the power of life and death" (John Mueller (1991) "War: Natural But Not Necessary," in Robert Hinde (ed.) *The Institution of War* (London, Macmillan), pp. 13–29, at p. 18) is familiar, but generally discredited. For a magisterial list, addressed to a political leader, of the kinds of justification that might be offered for making war, and strategies for making those justifications convincing, see Aristotle, *Rhetoric to Alexander*, 1425a7–b19.

we should allow our interactions with such communities to be guided by political or economic rather than moral considerations. On this communitarian view, *our* tyrants are our problem, and *their* tyrants are their problem. Initially, we need do nothing about "their" political problems; later, if we are threatened, we may do just about anything to eliminate the threat.

But seen in the light of MSP, this model of relations between communities looks quite wrong. First it requires too little from members of the community of nations, and then it permits them too much. It follows simply from MSP, that if tyranny affects persons, it is the concern of persons everywhere. The *location* of the tyrant, and *which people* he tyrannises, make no moral difference to what may or should be done to him; to what may or should be done to members of the afflicted community. Whether we have Saddam Hussein accumulating power in the Gulf, or John Smith accumulating power in Grimsby, we have a moral duty grounded in MSP to take political and legal steps to deal with the (international) problem of injustice as soon as it arises, wherever it arises and whoever it affects. Notice that this isn't just pious talk of universal human rights—MSP reflects the way that our *actual moral connections* cross community boundaries in the way described. For example, I might be a travelling salesman, with family and friends living in the Gulf. In that case, the sense in which tyranny in the Gulf *matters* will be much more readily cognitively and emotionally accessible to me, than the sense in which tyranny in Grimsby should matter because it is happening within the boundaries of the state in which I am a voting citizen.[8]

Nothing is claimed here about how strong the requirement to deal with tyranny is—whether, for example, it is as important for the British government to respond to the crisis of the collapse of political sovereignty in Zaire as it is for them to respond to the state-injustice that afflicts Burma; or whether Britain is more responsible than Albania in these contexts. These are questions for which there are no ready answers—policy has to be made, rather than discovered. The point is that MSP deprives us of an option we continue to presume: we cannot make a moral distinction between internal and external problems; a boundary cannot of itself reduce moral responsibility, and so can no longer be given on its own either as a reason for the neglect of a moral problem, or as a justification for a response to a moral problem which would not be permissible in the internal case.

That war-ism latterly permits "too much," in the form of the unjustifiable violence against the community in which a tyrant is dominant, is, from a pacifist point of view, a direct consequence of its initially requiring too little. If we are morally required from the outset to deal with tyranny as, when and wherever it arises, we

---

8 See Mary Kaldor (1991) "Do Modern Economies Require War or Preparations for Warfare?" in Robert Hinde (ed.) *The Institution of War* (London, Macmillan), pp. 178–91, at p. 190, for an optimistic account of how the rise of international community may obviate the need for war as a means to focusing political power.

should never be in the position in which the "Hitler's coming!" question arises. It is not just that pacifism would deprive us of the option of war; it is that as pacifists we will not need it, just as we do not think that we need a war-machine and its deployment to deal with the "internal" problem of political injustice when that arises. So we see that MSP deprives us of one resource we might have called upon to support the presumption of war-ism, the internal/external distinction. What effect will it have on something else which covertly buttresses the presumption, the war-machine?

Can we be committed to MSP and justifiably develop and maintain *the means* to fight wars? There is no analogy to this question in other applied-ethical contexts where the rights and wrongs of violence or killing are debated. We cannot, for euthanasia, separate the question of whether we should have *the capacity* to perform euthanasia, from the question of whether or not we should perform it. The capacity is given. But war-machines are not given. Soldierly expertise and weapons technology, from battering-rams to guns to nuclear missiles and fighter jets, are made, and so moral questions arise, about whether we should make them. Commitment to MSP implies that we cannot set up a war-machine if it involves us in failing to value all persons fully and equally as persons. If we are concerned about the well-being of the community whose support we fund, and aim to maximise well-being, would we do best to house, educate and heal our citizens, or should we rather acquire the capacity to defend them or crusade for them against external Hitlers? This was the way Costa Rica made the decision to abolish their war-machine in 1948, and Haiti is making it now. If we consider the function of the proposed war-machine, we might doubt whether it is morally permissible to imagine, create and plan to use skills and devices destructive of human life. Or we might focus on the community and its elected leaders, and ask whether a community can justly use persons to produce the mechanisms of war. We might think tactically, and consider whether, on balance, we think we can in fact make the world safer by institutionalising the power to inflict massive harm through our war-machine, when the distinction between defensive and offensive arming is a matter of trust in each other's intentions, and trust is evidently so fragile.

So MSP obliges us to be doubtful even about the moral acceptability of developing and maintaining the inanimate machinery for making war: it diverts resources, involves the imagination of wicked deeds and the creation of dangerous objects, and it threatens others. What are the implications of MSP for that other essential part of the war-machine, the army of soldiers?

Soldiers, of course, are persons—they come directly within the class of things to which MSP refers. There are two aspects to this: what MSP permits or requires persons to do or be; and what MSP permits us to expect from or do to other persons. On both counts, seen in the light of MSP the position of the soldier faces profound moral problems. A soldier is traditionally conceived as an unquestioning defender unto death of his community. But our commitment to MSP involves something like the thought that as persons, we bear inalienable *responsibility* for our moral agency. Now, this means that a person cannot morally consent to do things for which they will not be morally responsible. But is this not precisely what the soldier attempts to do? The soldier, by volunteering his unquestioning loyalty and obedience, can be seen to seek to displace responsibility for his actions onto anybody else—his commander, his government, the people of his community. But to be a moral person in the sense of MSP, he must take moral responsibility for his every action. This means he has to know what he is doing and why he is doing it, such that he is satisfied that justifications are available. So MSP means that no-one can any longer consent to *be* a soldier as traditionally conceived. *Either* the consent fails, and the soldier, contrary to appearances (and to the moral pretence of the community!) retains moral responsibility and is culpable to the extent that they act in ways that they may not judge to be justified; *or* the consent succeeds, and they cease thereby to be moral persons. The inalienability of moral responsibility entailed by MSP may not matter for actions which are not especially morally significant—blind obedience to the state in guiding traffic, for example, might count as an innocuous example of this failing. But in cases where the attempt to alienate responsibility involves the agent in activities with uncontentiously considerable moral significance, like killing, harming and coercing, their moral failing is anything but innocuous; and their culture's failure to make the moral problem explicit is anything but a forgivable oversight.

What about those who employ soldiers—is what they do permissible from the standpoint of MSP? MSP constrains what we—the commander, the government or fellow-citizens—can morally require a person to do for us. We cannot morally *require* anybody to do anything for us that is not morally permissible for them. If the above argument is right, a person morally cannot alienate their responsibility for morally significant actions. It follows that we cannot ask them to do so, either. So, employing soldiers is morally wrong. Recruiting soldiers is morally wrong, and paying taxes to be used for either of the above purposes is wrong too. In conclusion, we have made explicit what contemporary defenders of the just war appear not to see: that commitment to MSP deprives us of justification for several features of the institution of war—we cannot use an internal/external distinction to limit our moral responsibilities for persons; we cannot go ahead and install or maintain our war-machine without asking whether it is wasteful, corrupting or threatening, and we cannot justifiably *ourselves consent* to be soldiers, and nor can we justifiably *require others* to be soldiers for us. So, our commitment to MSP may oblige us to dismantle our war-machine and send our soldiers home. But even if ways can be found of making the maintenance of a war-machine consistent with MSP, I think MSP still makes it morally impossible for us ever to use one. This is because MSP implies that, as persons, "enemies"—even soldiers—matter as much and in the same way as any other persons. It follows that moral justifications for our treatment of them will have to meet the same requirements as justifications for the ways we treat "our own" people. I argue in the next section that facts about war make this impossible.

3. Harming the Enemy: Justifying Violence against Persons

MSP implies that the same kinds of considerations will be required to justify actions on political enemies, as are required to justify actions on any other persons. In war, the action we are morally concerned with is violent. What does moral justification of violence require? There are two stages to the justification of violence which need to be distinguished, and which have important implications for the ethics of war. First, there are the *formal* requirements for the justification of violence. These describe what has to be in place for it to be even in principle *possible* to justify a violent action. The formal requirement can be expressed roughly in the following schema for a justification sentence (JS):

JS It will be justifiable to harm x, iff it is true of x that {p \/ q \/ r \/ . . .}
(In this notation, "iff" means "if and only if" and "\/" means "or".)

Notice that JS has so far imposed no constraints at all on how p or q or r or . . . need to be filled in to yield a true JS. For all we know so far, it might be possible to justify harming x, provided it is true of them that they pick their nose, love pigeons or have blue eyes. When we add MSP to JS, we put ourselves in a position to begin to spell out what a morally acceptable content for p or q or r now might be. Roughly, facts about what a person *has done*, or what they *intend to do*, are the kinds of facts that MSP enables us to use to justify harms against persons. (It is this distinguishes the moral requirements of MSP from, say, those of ideologies like racism, which characteristically claim that features which have nothing to do with what a person has done or intends, like colour or ethnicity, may justify harms.) MSP, then, implies that violence against a person can only be justifiable either when they are guilty of some transgression (this expresses our intuition about the justifiability of punitive violence), or when they are actively threatening some transgression (this expresses our intuition about the justifiability of violence in self-defence). But notice that these constraints on p or q or r, are still pretty much *formal* conditions—they have said nothing yet about *what kind of action* is to be counted as a transgression or intention grave enough to justify a violent act. So far, we have claimed that we think it will only be *possible* in principle to justify violence against a person, if they are known to have done or to threaten a transgression which, in the view of the consensus of the moral community, is sufficiently grave.

It is often assumed in writing about the ethics of war that the pacifist must be committed to some actual specific claim, about what a transgressor must have done or must intend for violence against them to be justifiable. Thus, "absolutist pacifists" are identified as those who stipulate that violence against persons can never be justified (i.e., no possible p or q or r, could yield a true JS); Richard Norman argues that the most plausible form of pacifism will be one that stipulates that killing can only be justified when a life is taken or threatened;[9] and David Cochran, drawing on others' work, argues similarly that only threats to life can justify the taking of life (which in addition must never be directly intended and always be a last resort): that a JS justifying killing in war would have to look something like the following:

JS(1) It will be justifiable to kill x iff {p: we do not intend to kill x & q: we have tried everything else to stop x & r: x intends our death}[10]

He then argues for pacifism on the grounds that this JS is never satisfied in war. But the conclusion against war can be established more simply at the formal level, I think. If we can argue from the requirements for the justification of violence *per se*—the formal features of JS—to the wrong of war, we will establish its immorality more decisively that way. We do not need to make specific claims about the content of the justifiers in JS—we do not need to say precisely *which* transgressions must have been done or be threatened, for a justification sentence to work. We are then in a position to see the non-formal specification of transgressions in its proper light—as an essentially contestable matter for the moral community to decide. Although the moral community may *aspire* to agreement about which wrongs can justify violent responses, agreement about this is still far from being attained. And it is equally important to appreciate that this lack of consensus does not put any obstacles in the way of our developing effective arguments against war.

In a morally significant number of cases in war, I suggest, no JS can be filled in. If this is right, the process of moral justification cannot even begin, and the pacifist can rest her case. I would make this claim in particular about the indiscriminate violence of war, for which the term "bombings" may serve. Most of the "bombing" violence that goes on in war is in principle incapable of justification. It is not that a particular JS cannot be filled in (as in Cochran's argument); it is that no JS at all can be given for such contexts, because *nothing* which could reasonably be used to fill in p or q or r, is known to the agent who is doing the harm. Soldiers who drop bombs and spray ammunition commonly do not know *anything* about the persons they harm; not even what uniform they are wearing. In bombing, then, the moral problem is that we cannot meet even the minimal formal requirements for moral justification.

It might be objected that this argument illicitly relies on a Kantian answer to the tradeability question mentioned in Section 1—that in supposing that to justify

---

9 Norman, op. cit.
10 Cochran [op. cit.]. Note how Cochran's argument excludes from possible justification all punitive violence; at the same time as it leaves open the possibility of justification for any or all non-lethal harm.

violence against a person you need to know facts about what they have done or intend, I have excluded the real (utilitarian) possibility that we might know that good consequences will emerge from bombing a group of people (say, their government will give up, shortening the conflict), and that this is sufficient to justify the bombing. I don't think that my argument relies on a Kantian thought here. What is sought, is a moral justification for the violent acts constituting war—specifically, here, indiscriminate violent acts. These acts are individuated, and identified as violent, by the damage they do to particular bodily persons. So, we need *moral* answers to the question, "Why was *she* harmed?" My point is that, in bombing cases, no *moral* answer to that question is available. The utilitarian answer at best provides us with an explanation of her death—she died because she was in the wrong place at the wrong time. It does not, and *cannot*, tell us how and why it was *right* to harm *her*.

But what of the other cases in war, where it seems that we do know enough about those who are harming and those who are harmed, to offer a viable JS? Any filling will have to satisfy the additional formal constraints supplied by MSP—that is, it will have to refer to the *actions and intentions* of proposed victims. This immediately protects from possibly justifiable harm the vast majority of victims in war: those wearing certain clothes; those who say certain things; those who happen to live near military installations; those who are conscripted against their will; those who are forced into aggression by hunger, other deprivation or ignorance. Plenty of authors have noted just how widely the notion of "innocence" extends in war, and just how tightly it constrains who may justifiably be harmed (Nick Denyer, again, is notable here). It is commonly thought that facts about the inevitability of harming the innocent furnish the most decisive grounds for the rejection of war. But I think we can go further than this. We can say, not only that war is bad because it involves harming the innocent, but also that even in cases where the "guilty" (or "nocent," in Denyer's phrase)—those implicated in the enemy state's unjust projects in the right way—are harmed, the relation between the agents and victims of violence is usually not of the right kind to justify the violence under the description required, if it is as part of a *war between states*, rather than as a harm to an individual, that we need to justify the act. The moral problem here, in contrast with the bombing case above, is not so much that we cannot meet the formal requirements for justification, as that any true JS we can come up with will not be apt to justify the violent act as part of the political process of a particular war.

It is natural to think that violence between soldiers offers a paradigm of violence in war which can be justified, if any can be. Even in the light of MSP, it looks as if harms to enemy soldiers as they attack will be morally justifiable; and it seems to follow that if war-making can be refined so that only soldiers are ever attacked, then war as such will be justifiable. But this thought does not survive scrutiny. Consider the individual soldiers of two armies engaged in direct violent conflict on a battlefield. All are armed, all directly threatening, all can see each other. Is there here a relation between each soldier and the soldiers he kills, such that a true JS can be produced, which meets the constraints of MSP, so that the violence may be justified? Does our soldier know that the enemy he faces is either guilty of a transgression, or threatens one? It seems clear that he does: while he does not know anything about the soldier's past, about his connections with the intentions of the community he defends—that is, he knows nothing about the enemy soldier's involvement with the state he represents—he certainly does know what he threatens, namely, our soldier's life itself. His violent act of self-defence against the enemy soldier, then, is justifiable: a true JS can be given, that satisfies the requirements of MSP.

But if we look at this relation more closely, we see that it does not yet give us what we need to justify the violence as a part of the *war*—the collective activity of the whole army for the political ends of the state it represents. The violence that the soldier's knowledge here makes justifiable is only that of individual self-defence. Our soldier in the decisive moment knows that he will be killed if he does not kill. But our soldier cannot know that his opponent deserves violence for his part in the enemy state's projects. So if he kills justifiably, as an irreducibly responsible human agent, he can do so only in self-defence (or perhaps to punish the harms he has seen the soldier inflict on others). His act of violence, then, is not and cannot be justified by a JS of the form:

JS(2) It is justifiable to harm x because it is true of x that {x has done or threatens to do something as a responsible member of the enemy state}

The only justification we can get, will be one that goes:

JS(3) It is justifiable to harm x because it is true of x that {x has harmed or intends to harm other persons}

So, what we see on the battlefield, far from being the most justifiable violence of all in war, is the most unjustifiable, from the point of view of the political aims of the states involved: it amounts to a mass of chaotic self-defensive killing in ignorance, which has as little necessary connection with the rational intentions of the communities these soldiers represent, as any riot or bar-room brawl.

David Cochran also thinks that no satisfactory JS can be produced for soldier-soldier harms. But this is because of the content he stipulates that p and q and r must have. His argument at once permits too much—when it fails to exclude non-lethal violence—and too little—when it denies that soldier-soldier violence is morally justified *at all*. We need not follow Cochran in making the implausible claim that the soldier, threatened with death, is not justified in killing. Instead, we can allow that a justification-sentence can be produced for soldier-soldier harms, but note that it is simply not apt to serve as part of the justification of a *war*, conceived as a relation between states rather than between individual persons. Facts about the state do not need to feature—and because of the heavy epistemic constraints of the battlefield context, never can feature—in the statements used to justify soldier-soldier harms.

There are three responses the war-ist might make. First, he might deny that the only available justifiers refer to personal threat. He might say that the battlefield context itself supplies the further level of information required to yield justifiers apt to justify a war: the soldier who threatens our soldier's life is an *enemy* soldier; the enemy is engaged in an attempt to destroy our community. To this I can only repeat the opposing intuition: in a battlefield context, with its characteristic threat of death, it is impossible to know of the enemy one faces that he is responsible and implicated in the state's projects. This whole argument is a roundabout way of making a simple point: the battlefield is not just a poor context for arrest, proof of guilt, trial and imposition of just penalty; it is a context that makes a mockery of all those ideas.

Second the war-ist might draw on the individual/state analogy to develop a satisfactory justification-sentence.[11] He might argue that we do not need information about every individual victim to make violence against them justifiable. Rather, we can establish the guilt of the enemy collective community prior to battle. We then infer guilt from community membership, which we establish for every individual from facts like the wearing of a certain uniform, or being present in a certain location. This, it is hoped, will enable us to justify our harms indirectly. But, of course, MSP places these strategies beyond our moral reach: such features as membership of a collective, clothing, equipment and location make no difference to the moral status of a person; they do nothing to reduce the particular demand for moral consideration which is made by each individual. It follows that such justifiers as "he is a member of the enemy state (and we know this because he wears enemy uniform)" cannot be used in any true JS which meets the constraints of MSP. In fact, any attempt to justify harms in this way manifests a grave failure in moral sensibility. If our victim only looks like a member of a bad collective, then when we harm her we make her a scapegoat, and this is simply wicked.

Third, the war-ist might try to justify harms to soldiers by saying that although our individual soldier does not know that the enemies he faces are guilty or threatening in the relevant political sense, the officers, strategists and politicians who are the responsible agents in war *do* know about the distribution of guilt, and this makes soldier-soldier harms justifiable. Although the soldier knows not what he

---

11 Much discussion in the ethics of war revolves around aspects of the individual/state analogy, which I do not discuss, because it is simply inconsistent with MSP. Norman (op. cit.) makes a particularly good job, I think, of arguing that the analogy between individual self-defence, and defence of a community's integrity, on which Michael Walzer (1980) *Just and Unjust Wars* (London, Penguin), relies in defending the idea of a just war, makes no sense unless one thinks of it as a response to the threat of actual extermination of (individual living members of) the group; in which case the analogy gives us no special right of self-defence for communities over and above the right of self-defence enjoyed by individuals; and so no means for justifying the practice of war.

does, the authorities whom he obeys do know, and take full moral responsibility for his actions; and accordingly, it is facts about them which make justification possible. My response, as to the previous argument, will be obvious: it violates the moral requirements of irreducible responsibility for individual agents entailed by MSP above. The soldier is inalienably a moral person, not a machine. If what he does is not justifiable as the act of an individual moral person, it is not justifiable at all, any more than the acts of a psychopath or a machine could be. And any attempt to use him to undertake actions not justifiable in the requisite way, represents a violation of his autonomy of a very serious kind, as I argued earlier. We might also add another thought that is obvious: authorities in war, necessarily removed as they are from the realities of the battlefield, are unlikely to know very much that is morally salient about the enemy soldiers it is proposed we should harm. They will not know of any particular soldier whether he has been coerced, say. So even if we accepted justification-sentences which went up a level, we would have to throw most of them out for the same reason: no information, or no morally relevant information, or no politically salient information of the kind apt to justify a war (and not just any old self-defensive harm).

4. Conclusion: Pacifism ... with Hit-Squads?

So, someone committed to MSP will be inclined to think it impermissible to set up a war-machine, for a range of reasons, including those outlined above. She will think that we are morally required to attend to tyranny before it threatens to invade; and that we cannot justifiably use or agree to be used as soldiers. She will also think that killing the innocent in war is wrong, that indiscriminate violence in war is chaotic and so in principle unjustifiable; and, further, that even the discriminate violence between soldiers in war is usually not justifiable in the way required to justify war. In short, she will be a pacifist, pending the presentation of more persuasive arguments for war-ism. But she will also recognise that, even in wars as presently conducted, there will be a small category of violent actions, amid all the evil and chaos, which might be morally justifiable. These will be targeted acts of violent punishment or prevention against members of an enemy state who are known to be responsible for grave wrongs. So, we should notice that the MSP-pacifist need not exclude as a moral option for a good state, the setting up of some kind of coercive machinery for dealing with this kind of international injustice when and where it arises. The only moral constraints are that such a system—analogous, of course, to a police system, as anti-war pacifists have long argued—should not use persons to perform violent acts which they, as responsible individual agents, know *a priori* to be unjustifiable; and it may only use mechanisms of violence which are fully discriminate. So, it is thus far conceivable that a defender of MSP should support a pacifist system of international relations which permits targeted disabling violent interventions into tyrannical power-systems wherever they arise. Richard Norman hints at something similar, when he notes that all attempts to justify war seem to end up failing to justify *that*, but perhaps making justifiable something more modest and targeted, like a campaign of assassination. I add to this the thought that what we have here is not so much a recommendation for a new kind of *war*, but the adoption of a consistent anti-war pacifism. Developing a plausible pacifism here has involved taking MSP to be true, and seeing what it permits and what it prescribes. It does not permit war, nor yet even the development and maintenance of the means for threatening war (the "war-machine"). It prescribes inter- and intra-national political engagement to deal with international injustice wherever it arises. But there is no moral reason why it cannot permit the use of perfectly discriminate, targeted violence for which the agents can be held morally responsible, in dealing with international injustice. A plausible pacifism, then, might well be one that condones the use of hit-squads. And maybe this is just what we need to make pacifism more popular—a show of strength; a few public executions....

30. War and Massacre[*][1]

Thomas Nagel

From the apathetic reaction to atrocities committed in Vietnam by the United States and its allies, one may conclude that moral restrictions on the conduct of war command almost as little sympathy among the general public as they do among those charged with the formation of US military policy. Even when restrictions on the conduct of warfare are defended, it is usually on legal grounds alone: their moral basis is often poorly understood. I wish to argue that certain restrictions are neither arbitrary nor merely conventional, and that their validity does not depend simply on their usefulness. There is, in other words, a moral basis for the rules of war, even though the conventions now officially in force are far from giving it perfect expression.

I

No elaborate moral theory is required to account for what is wrong in cases like the Mylai massacre, since it did not serve, and was not intended to serve, any strategic purpose. Moreover, if the participation of the United States in the Indo-Chinese war is entirely wrong to begin with, then that engagement is incapable of providing a justification for *any* measures taken in its pursuit—not only for the measures which are atrocities in every war, however just its aims.

But this war has revealed attitudes of a more general kind, that influenced the conduct of earlier wars as well. After it has ended, we shall still be faced with the problem of how warfare may be conducted, and the attitudes that have resulted in the specific conduct of this war will not have disappeared. Moreover, similar problems can arise in wars or rebellions fought for very different reasons, and against very different opponents. It is not easy to keep a firm grip on the idea of what is not permissible in warfare, because while some military actions are obvious atrocities, other cases are more difficult to assess, and the general principles underlying these judgments

---

* Source: *Philosophy and Public Affairs* 1.2 (Winter 1972): 123–44.
1 This paper grew out of discussions at the Society for Ethical and Legal Philosophy, and I am indebted to my fellow members for their help.

remain obscure. Such obscurity can lead to the abandonment of sound intuitions in favor of criteria whose rationale may be more obvious. If such a tendency is to be resisted, it will require a better understanding of the restrictions than we now have.

I propose to discuss the most general moral problem raised by the conduct of warfare: the problem of means and ends. In one view, there are limits on what may be done even in the service of an end worth pursuing—and even when adherence to the restriction may be very costly. A person who acknowledges the force of such restrictions can find himself in acute moral dilemmas. He may believe, for example, that by torturing a prisoner he can obtain information necessary to prevent a disaster, or that by obliterating one village with bombs he can halt a campaign of terrorism. If he believes that the gains from a certain measure will clearly outweigh its costs, yet still suspects that he ought not to adopt it, then he is in a dilemma produced by the conflict between two disparate categories of moral reason: categories that may be called *utilitarian* and *absolutist*.

Utilitarianism gives primacy to a concern with what will *happen*. Absolutism gives primacy to a concern with what one is *doing*. The conflict between them arises because the alternatives we face are rarely just choices between *total outcomes*: they are also choices between alternative pathways or measures to be taken. When one of the choices is to do terrible things to another person, the problem is altered fundamentally; it is no longer merely a question of which outcome would be worse.

Few of us are completely immune to either of these types of moral intuition, though in some people, either naturally or for doctrinal reasons, one type will be dominant and the other suppressed or weak. But it is perfectly possible to feel the force of both types of reason very strongly; in that case the moral dilemma in certain situations of crisis will be acute, and it may appear that every possible course of action or inaction is unacceptable for one reason or another.

II

Although it is this dilemma that I propose to explore, most of the discussion will be devoted to its absolutist component. The utilitarian component is straightforward by comparison, and has a natural appeal to anyone who is not a complete skeptic about ethics. Utilitarianism says that one should try, either individually or through institutions, to maximize good and minimize evil (the definition of these categories need not enter into the schematic formulation of the view), and that if faced with the possibility of preventing a great evil by producing a lesser, one should choose the lesser evil. There are certainly problems about the formulation of utilitarianism, and much has been written about it, but its intent is morally transparent. Nevertheless, despite the addition of various refinements, it continues to leave large portions of ethics unaccounted for. I do not suggest that some form of absolutism can account for them all, only that an examination of absolutism will lead us to see the complexity, and perhaps the incoherence, of our moral ideas.

Utilitarianism certainly justifies *some* restrictions on the conduct of warfare. There are strong utilitarian reasons for adhering to any limitation which seems natural to most people—particularly if the limitation is widely accepted already. An exceptional measure which seems to be justified by its results in a particular conflict may create a precedent with disastrous long-term effects.[2] It may even be argued that war involves violence on such a scale that it is never justified on utilitarian grounds—the consequences of refusing to go to war will never be as bad as the war itself would be, even if atrocities were not committed. Or in a more sophisticated vein it might be claimed that a uniform policy of never resorting to military force would do less harm in the long run, if followed consistently, than a policy of deciding each case on utilitarian grounds (even though on occasion particular applications of the pacifist policy might have worse results than a specific utilitarian decision). But I shall not consider these arguments, for my concern is with reasons of a different kind, which may remain when reasons of utility and interest fail.[3]

In the final analysis, I believe that the dilemma cannot always be resolved. While not every conflict between absolutism and utilitarianism creates an insoluble dilemma, and while it is certainly right to adhere to absolutist restrictions unless the utilitarian considerations favoring violation are overpoweringly weighty and extremely certain—nevertheless, when that special condition is met, it may become impossible to adhere to an absolutist position. What I shall offer, therefore, is a somewhat qualified defense of absolutism. I believe it underlies a valid and fundamental type of moral judgment—which cannot be reduced to or overridden by other principles. And while there may be other principles just as fundamental, it is particularly important not to lose confidence in our absolutist intuitions, for they are often the only barrier before the abyss of utilitarian apologetics for large-scale murder.

III

One absolutist position that creates no problems of interpretation is pacifism: the view that one may not kill another person under any circumstances, no matter what good would be achieved or evil averted thereby. The type of absolutist position that I am going to discuss is different. Pacifism draws the conflict with utilitarian considerations very starkly. But there are other views according to which violence may be undertaken, even on a large scale, in a clearly just cause, so long as certain absolute restrictions on the character and direction of that violence are observed. The line is drawn somewhat closer to the bone, but it exists.

2 Straightforward considerations of national interest often tend in the same direction: the inadvisability of using nuclear weapons seems to be overdetermined in this way.

3 These reasons, moreover, have special importance in that they are available even to one who denies the appropriateness of utilitarian considerations in international matters. He may acknowledge limitations on what may be done to the soldiers and civilians of other countries in pursuit of his nation's military objectives, while denying that one country should in general consider the interests of nationals of other countries in determining its policies.

The philosopher who has done most to advance contemporary philosophical discussion of such a view, and to explain it to those unfamiliar with its extensive treatment in Roman Catholic moral theology, is G.E.M. Anscombe. In 1958 Miss Anscombe published a pamphlet entitled *Mr. Truman's Degree*,[4] on the occasion of the award by Oxford University of an honorary doctorate to Harry Truman. The pamphlet explained why she had opposed the decision to award that degree, recounted the story of her unsuccessful opposition, and offered some reflections on the history of Truman's decision to drop atom bombs on Hiroshima and Naga-saki, and on the difference between murder and allowable killing in warfare. She pointed out that the policy of deliberately killing large numbers of civilians either as a means or as an end in itself did not originate with Truman, and was common practice among all parties during World War II for some time before Hiroshima. The Allied area bombings of German cities by conventional explosives included raids which killed more civilians than did the atomic attacks; the same is true of certain fire-bomb raids on Japan.

The policy of attacking the civilian population in order to induce an enemy to surrender, or to damage his morale, seems to have been widely accepted in the civilized world, and seems to be accepted still, at least if the stakes are high enough. It gives evidence of a moral conviction that the deliberate killing of noncombatants—women, children, old people—is permissible if enough can be gained by it. This follows from the more general position that any means can in principle be justified if it leads to a sufficiently worthy end. Such an attitude is evident not only in the more spectacular current weapons systems but also in the day-to-day conduct of the nonglobal war in Indochina: the indiscriminate destructiveness of antipersonnel weapons, napalm, and aerial bombardment; cruelty to prisoners; massive relocation of civilians; destruction of crops; and so forth. An absolutist position opposes to this the view that certain acts cannot be justified no matter what the consequences. Among those acts is murder—the deliberate killing of the harmless: civilians, prisoners of war, and medical personnel.

In the present war such measures are sometimes said to be regrettable, but they are generally defended by reference to military necessity and the importance of the long-term consequences of success or failure in the war. I shall pass over the inadequacy of this consequentialist defense in its own terms. (That is the dominant form of moral criticism of the war, for it is part of what people mean when they ask, "Is it

---

4 (Privately printed.) See also her essay "War and Murder," in *Nuclear Weapons and Christian Conscience*, ed. Walter Stein (London, 1963). The present paper is much indebted to these two essays throughout. These and related subjects are extensively treated by Paul Ramsey in *The Just War* (New York, 1968). Among recent writings that bear on the moral problem are Jonathan Bennett, "Whatever the Consequences," *Analysis* 26.3 (1966): 83–102; and Philippa Foot, "The Problem of Abortion and the Doctrine of the Double Effect," *The Oxford Review* 5 (1967): 5–15. Miss Anscombe's replies are "A Note on Mr. Bennett," *Analysis* 26.3 (1966): 208, and "Who is Wronged?" *The Oxford Review* 5 (1967): 16–17.

worth it?") I am concerned rather to account for the inappropriateness of offering any defense of that kind for such actions.

Many people feel, without being able to say much more about it, that something has gone seriously wrong when certain measures are admitted into consideration in the first place. The fundamental mistake is made there, rather than at the point where the overall benefit of some monstrous measure is judged to outweigh its disadvantages, and it is adopted. An account of absolutism might help us to understand this. If it is not allowable to *do* certain things, such as killing unarmed prisoners or civilians, then no argument about what will happen if one doesn't do them can show that doing them would be all right.

Absolutism does not, of course, require one to ignore the consequences of one's acts. It operates as a limitation on utilitarian reasoning, not as a substitute for it. An absolutist can be expected to try to maximize good and minimize evil, so long as this does not require him to transgress an absolute prohibition like that against murder. But when such a conflict occurs, the prohibition takes complete precedence over any consideration of consequences. Some of the results of this view are clear enough. It requires us to forgo certain potentially useful military measures, such as the slaughter of hostages and prisoners or indiscriminate attempts to reduce the enemy civilian population by starvation, epidemic infectious diseases like anthrax and bubonic plague, or mass incineration. It means that we cannot deliberate on whether such measures are justified by the fact that they will avert still greater evils, for as intentional measures they cannot be justified in terms of any consequences whatever.

Someone unfamiliar with the events of this century might imagine that utilitarian arguments, or arguments of national interest, would suffice to deter measures of this sort. But it has become evident that such considerations are insufficient to prevent the adoption and employment of enormous antipopulation weapons once their use is considered a serious moral possibility. The same is true of the piecemeal wiping out of rural civilian populations in airborne antiguerrilla warfare. Once the door is opened to calculations of utility and national interest, the usual speculations about the future of freedom, peace, and economic prosperity can be brought to bear to ease the consciences of those responsible for a certain number of charred babies.

For this reason alone it is important to decide what is wrong with the frame of mind which allows such arguments to begin. But it is also important to understand absolutism in the cases where it genuinely conflicts with utility. Despite its appeal, it is a paradoxical position, for it can require that one refrain from choosing the lesser of two evils when that is the only choice one has. And it is additionally paradoxical because, unlike pacifism, it permits one to do horrible things to people in some circumstances but not in others.

IV

Before going on to say what, if anything, lies behind the position, there remain a few relatively technical matters which are best discussed at this point.

First, it is important to specify as clearly as possible the kind of thing to which absolutist prohibitions can apply. We must take seriously the proviso that they concern what we deliberately do to people. There could not, for example, without incoherence, be an absolute prohibition against *bringing about* the death of an innocent person. For one may find oneself in a situation in which, no matter what one does, some innocent people will die as a result. I do not mean just that there are cases in which someone will die no matter what one does, because one is not in a position to affect the outcome one way or the other. That, it is to be hoped, is one's relation to the deaths of most innocent people. I have in mind, rather, a case in which someone is bound to die, but who it is will depend on what one does. Sometimes these situations have natural causes, as when too few resources (medicine, lifeboats) are available to rescue everyone threatened with a certain catastrophe. Sometimes the situations are manmade, as when the only way to control a campaign of terrorism is to employ terrorist tactics against the community from which it has arisen. Whatever one does in cases such as these, some innocent people will die as a result. If the absolutist prohibition forbade doing what would result in the deaths of innocent people, it would have the consequence that in such cases nothing one could do would be morally permissible.

This problem is avoided, however, because what absolutism forbids is *doing* certain things to people, rather than bringing about certain *results*. Not everything that happens to others as a result of what one does is something that one has *done* to them. Catholic moral theology seeks to make this distinction precise in a doctrine known as the law of double effect, which asserts that there is a morally relevant distinction between bringing about the death of an innocent person deliberately, either as an end in itself or as a means, and bringing it about as a side effect of something else one does deliberately. In the latter case, even if the outcome is foreseen, it is not murder, and does not fall under the absolute prohibition, though of course it may still be wrong for other reasons (reasons of utility, for example). Briefly, the principle states that one is sometimes permitted knowingly to bring about as a side effect of one's actions something which it would be absolutely impermissible to bring about deliberately as an end or as a means. In application to war or revolution, the law of double effect permits a certain amount of civilian carnage as a side effect of bombing munitions plants or attacking enemy soldiers. And even this is permissible only if the cost is not too great to be justified by one's objectives.

However, despite its importance and its usefulness in accounting for certain plausible moral judgments, I do not believe that the law of double effect is a generally applicable test for the consequences of an absolutist position. Its own application is not always clear, so that it introduces uncertainty where there need not be uncertainty.

In Indochina, for example, there is a great deal of aerial bombardment, strafing, spraying of napalm, and employment of pellet- or needle-spraying antipersonnel weapons against rural villages in which guerrillas are suspected to be hiding, or from which small-arms fire has been received. The majority of those killed and wounded in these aerial attacks are reported to be women and children, even when some combatants are caught as well. However, the government regards these civilian casualties as a regrettable side effect of what is a legitimate attack against an armed enemy.

It might be thought easy to dismiss this as sophistry: if one bombs, burns, or strafes a village containing a hundred people, twenty of whom one believes to be guerrillas, so that by killing most of them one will be statistically likely to kill most of the guerrillas, then isn't one's attack on the group of one hundred a *means* of destroying the guerrillas, pure and simple? If one makes no attempt to discriminate between guerrillas and civilians, as is impossible in a aerial attack on a small village, then one cannot regard as a mere side effect the deaths of those in the group that one would not have bothered to kill if more selective means had been available.

The difficulty is that this argument depends on one particular description of the act, and the reply might be that the means used against the guerrillas is not: killing everybody in the village—but rather: obliteration bombing of the *area* in which the twenty guerrillas are known to be located. If there are civilians in the area as well, they will be killed as a side effect of such action.[5]

Because of casuistical problems like this, I prefer to stay with the original, unanalyzed distinction between what one does to people and what merely happens to them as a result of what one does. The law of double effect provides an approximation to that distinction in many cases, and perhaps it can be sharpened to the point where it does better than that. Certainly the original distinction itself needs clarification, particularly since some of the things we do to people involve things happening to them as a result of other things we do. In a case like the one discussed, however, it is clear that by bombing the village one slaughters and maims the civilians in it. Whereas by giving the only available medicine to one of two sufferers from a disease, one does not kill the other, even if he dies as a result.

The second technical point to take up concerns a possible misinterpretation of this feature of the position. The absolutist focus on actions rather than outcomes does not merely introduce a new, outstanding item into the catalogue of evils. That is, it does not say that the worst thing in the world is the deliberate murder of an innocent person. For if that were all, then one could presumably justify one such murder on the ground that it would prevent several others, or ten thousand on the ground that they would prevent a hundred thousand more. That is a familiar argument. But if this is allowable, then there is no absolute prohibition against murder after all. Absolutism requires that we *avoid* murder at all costs, not that we *prevent* it at all costs.[6]

---

5 This counterargument was suggested by Rogers Albritton.

6 Someone might of course acknowledge the *moral relevance* of the distinction between deliberate

Finally, let me remark on a frequent criticism of absolutism that depends on a misunderstanding. It is sometimes suggested that such prohibitions depend on a kind of moral self-interest, a primary obligation to preserve one's own moral purity, to keep one's hands clean no matter what happens to the rest of the world. If this were the position, it might be exposed to the charge of self-indulgence. After all, what gives one man a right to put the purity of his soul or the cleanness of his hands above the lives or welfare of large numbers of other people? It might be argued that a public servant like Truman has no right to put himself first in that way; therefore if he is convinced that the alternatives would be worse, he must give the order to drop the bombs, and take the burden of those deaths on himself, as he must do other distasteful things for the general good.

But there are two confusions behind the view that moral self-interest underlies moral absolutism. First, it is a confusion to suggest that the need to preserve one's moral purity might be the *source* of an obligation. For if by committing murder one sacrifices one's moral purity or integrity, that can only be because there is *already* something wrong with murder. The general reason against committing murder cannot therefore be merely that it makes one an immoral person. Secondly, the notion that one might sacrifice one's moral integrity justifiably, in the service of a sufficiently worthy end, is an incoherent notion. For if one were justified in making such a sacrifice (or even morally required to make it), then one would not be sacrificing one's moral integrity by adopting that course: one would be preserving it.

Moral absolutism is not unique among moral theories in requiring each person to do what will preserve his own moral purity in all circumstances. This is equally true of utilitarianism, or of any other theory which distinguishes between right and wrong. Any theory which defines the right course of action in various circumstances and asserts that one should adopt that course, ipso facto asserts that one should do what will preserve one's moral purity, simply because the right course of action *is* what will preserve one's moral purity in those circumstances. Of course utilitarianism does not assert that this is *why* one should adopt that course, but we have seen that the same is true of absolutism.

V

It is easier to dispose of false explanations of absolutism than to produce a true one. A positive account of the matter must begin with the observation that war, conflict, and aggression are relations between persons. The view that it can be wrong to consider merely the overall effect of one's actions on the general welfare comes into prominence when those actions involve relations with others. A man's acts usually affect more people than he deals with directly, and those effects must naturally be

and nondeliberate killing, without being an absolutist. That is, he might believe simply that it was *worse* to bring about a death deliberately than as a secondary effect. But that would be merely a special assignment of value, and not an absolute prohibition.

considered in his decisions. But if there are special principles governing the manner in which he should *treat* people, that will require special attention to the particular persons toward whom the act is directed, rather than just to its total effect.

Absolutist restrictions in warfare appear to be of two types: restrictions on the class of persons at whom aggression or violence may be directed and restrictions on the manner of attack, given that the object falls within that class. These can be combined, however, under the principle that hostile treatment of any person must be justified in terms of something *about that person* which makes the treatment appropriate. Hostility is a personal relation, and it must be suited to its target. One consequence of this condition will be that certain persons may not be subjected to hostile treatment in war at all, since nothing about them justifies such treatment. Others will be proper objects of hostility only in certain circumstances, or when they are engaged in certain pursuits. And the appropriate manner and extent of hostile treatment will depend on what is justified by the particular case.

A coherent view of this type will hold that extremely hostile behavior toward another is compatible with treating him as a person—even perhaps as an end in himself. This is possible only if one has not automatically stopped treating him as a person as soon as one starts to fight with him. If hostile, aggressive, or combative treatment of others always violated the condition that they be treated as human beings, it would be difficult to make further distinctions on that score *within* the class of hostile actions. That point of view, on the level of international relations, leads to the position that if complete pacifism is not accepted, no holds need be barred at all, and we may slaughter and massacre to our hearts' content, if it seems advisable. Such a position is often expressed in discussions of war crimes.

But the fact is that ordinary people do not believe this about conflicts, physical or otherwise, between individuals, and there is no more reason why it should be true of conflicts between nations. There seems to be a perfectly natural conception of the distinction between fighting clean and fighting dirty. To fight dirty is to direct one's hostility or aggression not at its proper object, but at a peripheral target which may be more vulnerable, and through which the proper object can be attacked indirectly. This applies in a fist fight, an election campaign, a duel, or a philosophical argument. If the concept is general enough to apply to all these matters, it should apply to war—both to the conduct of individual soldiers and to the conduct of nations.

Suppose that you are a candidate for public office, convinced that the election of your opponent would be a disaster, that he is an unscrupulous demagogue who will serve a narrow range of interests and seriously infringe the rights of those who disagree with him; and suppose you are convinced that you cannot defeat him by conventional means. Now imagine that various unconventional means present themselves as possibilities: you possess information about his sex life which would scandalize the electorate if made public; or you learn that his wife is an alcoholic or that in his youth he was associated for a brief period with a proscribed political party, and you believe that this information could be used to blackmail him into withdrawing his candidacy; or you can have a team of your supporters flatten the tires of a crucial subset of his supporters on election day; or you are in a position to stuff the ballot boxes; or, more simply, you can have him assassinated. What is wrong with these methods, given that they will achieve an overwhelmingly desirable result?

There are, of course, many things wrong with them: some are against the law; some infringe the procedures of an electoral process to which you are presumably committed by taking part in it; very importantly, some may backfire, and it is in the interest of all political candidates to adhere to an unspoken agreement not to allow certain personal matters to intrude into a campaign. But that is not all. We have in addition the feeling that these measures, these methods of attack are *irrelevant* to the issue between you and your opponent, that in taking them up you would not be directing yourself to that which makes him an object of your opposition. You would be directing your attack not at the true target of your hostility, but at peripheral targets that happen to be vulnerable.

The same is true of a fight or argument outside the framework of any system of regulations or law. In an altercation with a taxi driver over an excessive fare, it is inappropriate to taunt him about his accent, flatten one of his tires, or smear chewing gum on his windshield; and it remains inappropriate even if he casts aspersions on your race, politics, or religion, or dumps the contents of your suitcase into the street.[7]

The importance of such restrictions may vary with the seriousness of the case; and what is unjustifiable in one case may be justified in a more extreme one. But they all derive from a single principle: that hostility or aggression should be directed at its true object. This means both that it should be directed at the person or persons who provoke it and that it should aim more specifically at what is provocative about them. The second condition will determine what form the hostility may appropriately take.

It is evident that some idea of the relation in which one should stand to other people underlies this principle, but the idea is difficult to state. I believe it is roughly this: whatever one does to another person intentionally must be aimed at him as a subject, with the intention that he receive it as a subject. It should manifest an attitude to *him* rather than just to the situation, and he should be able to recognize it and identify himself as its object. The procedures by which such an attitude is manifested need not be addressed to the person directly. Surgery, for example, is not a form of personal confrontation but part of a medical treatment that can be offered to a patient face to face and received by him as a response to his needs and the natural outcome of an attitude toward *him*.

---

7 Why, on the other hand, does it seem appropriate, rather than irrelevant, to punch someone in the mouth if he insults you? The answer is that in our culture it is an insult to punch someone in the mouth, and not just an injury. This reveals, by the way, a perfectly unobjectionable sense in which convention may play a part in determining exactly what falls under an absolutist restriction and what does not. I am indebted to Robert Fogelin for this point.

Hostile treatment, unlike surgery, is already addressed *to* a person, and does not take its interpersonal meaning from a wider context. But hostile acts can serve as the expression or implementation of only a limited range of attitudes to the person who is attacked. Those attitudes in turn have as objects certain real or presumed characteristics or activities of the person which are thought to justify them. When this background is absent, hostile or aggressive behavior can no longer be intended for the reception of the victim as a subject. Instead it takes on the character of a purely bureaucratic operation. This occurs when one attacks someone who is not the true object of one's hostility—the true object may be someone else, who can be attacked through the victim; or one may not be manifesting a hostile attitude toward anyone, but merely using the easiest available path to some desired goal. One finds oneself not facing or addressing the victim at all, but operating on him—without the larger context of personal interaction that surrounds a surgical operation.

If absolutism is to defend its claim to priority over considerations of utility, it must hold that the maintenance of a direct interpersonal response to the people one deals with is a requirement which no advantages can justify one in abandoning. The requirement is absolute only if it rules out any calculation of what would justify its violation. I have said earlier that there may be circumstances so extreme that they render an absolutist position untenable. One may find then that one has no choice but to do something terrible. Nevertheless, even in such cases absolutism retains its force in that one cannot claim *justification* for the violation. It does not become *all right*.

As a tentative effort to explain this, let me try to connect absolutist limitations with the possibility of justifying *to the victim* what is being done to him. If one abandons a person in the course of rescuing several others from a fire or a sinking ship, one *could* say to him, "You understand, I have to leave you to save the others." Similarly, if one subjects an unwilling child to a painful surgical procedure, one can say to him, "If you could understand, you would realize that I am doing this to help you." One could *even* say, as one bayonets an enemy soldier, "It's either you or me." But one cannot really say while torturing a prisoner, "You understand, I have to pull out your fingernails because it is absolutely essential that we have the names of your confederates"; nor can one say to the victims of Hiroshima, "You understand, we have to incinerate you to provide the Japanese government with an incentive to surrender."

This does not take us very far, of course, since a utilitarian would presumably be willing to offer justifications of the latter sort to his victims, in cases where he thought they were sufficient. They are really justifications to the world at large, which the victim, as a reasonable man, would be expected to appreciate. However, there seems to me something wrong with this view, for it ignores the possibility that to treat someone else horribly puts you in a special relation to him, which may have to be defended in terms of other features of your relation to him. The suggestion needs much more development; but it may help us to understand how there may be requirements which are absolute in the sense that there can be no justification for violating them. If the justification for what one did to another person had to be such that it could be offered to him specifically, rather than just to the world at large, that would be a significant source of restraint.

If the account is to be deepened, I would hope for some results along the following lines. Absolutism is associated with a view of oneself as a small being interacting with others in a large world. The justifications it requires are primarily interpersonal. Utilitarianism is associated with a view of oneself as a benevolent bureaucrat distributing such benefits as one can control to countless other beings, with whom one may have various relations or none. The justifications it requires are primarily administrative. The argument between the two moral attitudes may depend on the relative priority of these two conceptions.[8]

VI

Some of the restrictions on methods of warfare which have been adhered to from time to time are to be explained by the mutual interests of the involved parties: restrictions on weaponry, treatment of prisoners, etc. But that is not all there is to it. The conditions of directness and relevance which I have argued apply to relations of conflict and aggression apply to war as well. I have said that there are two types of absolutist restrictions on the conduct of war: those that limit the legitimate targets of hostility and those that limit its character, even when the target is acceptable. I shall say something about each of these. As will become clear, the principle I have sketched does not yield an unambiguous answer in every case.

First let us see how it implies that attacks on some people are allowed, but not attacks on others. It may seem paradoxical to assert that to fire a machine gun at someone who is throwing hand grenades at your emplacement is to treat him as a human being. Yet the relation with him is direct and straightforward.[9] The attack is aimed specifically against the threat presented by a dangerous adversary, and not against a peripheral target through which he happens to be vulnerable but which has nothing to do with that threat. For example, you might stop him by machine-gunning his wife and children, who are standing nearby, thus distracting him from his aim of blowing you up and enabling you to capture him. But if his wife and children are not threatening your life, that would be to treat them as means with a vengeance.

This, however, is just Hiroshima on a smaller scale. One objection to weapons of mass annihilation—nuclear, thermonuclear, biological, or chemical—is that their indiscriminateness disqualifies them as direct instruments for the expression of

---

8 Finally, I should mention a different possibility, suggested by Robert Nozick: that there is a strong general presumption against benefiting from the calamity of another, whether or not it has been deliberately inflicted for that or any other reason. This broader principle may well lend its force to the absolutist position.

9 It has been remarked that according to my view, shooting at someone establishes an I-thou relationship.

hostile relations. In attacking the civilian population, one treats neither the military enemy nor the civilians with that minimal respect which is owed to them as human beings. This is clearly true of the direct attack on people who present no threat at all. But it is also true of the character of the attack on those who *are* threatening you, viz., the government and military forces of the enemy. Your aggression is directed against an area of vulnerability quite distinct from any threat presented by them which you may be justified in meeting. You are taking aim at them through the mundane life and survival of their countrymen, instead of aiming at the destruction of their military capacity. And of course it does not require hydrogen bombs to commit such crimes.

This way of looking at the matter also helps us to understand the importance of the distinction between combatants and noncombatants, and the irrelevance of much of the criticism offered against its intelligibility and moral significance. According to an absolutist position, deliberate killing of the innocent is murder, and in warfare the role of the innocent is filled by noncombatants. This has been thought to raise two sorts of problems: first, the widely imagined difficulty of making a division, in modern warfare, between combatants and noncombatants; second, problems deriving from the connotation of the word "innocence."

Let me take up the latter question first.[10] In the absolutist position, the operative notion of innocence is not moral innocence, and it is not opposed to moral guilt. If it were, then we would be justified in killing a wicked but noncombatant hairdresser in an enemy city who supported the evil policies of his government, and unjustified in killing a morally pure conscript who was driving a tank toward us with the profoundest regrets and nothing but love in his heart. But moral innocence has very little to do with it, for in the definition of murder "innocent" means "currently harmless," and it is opposed not to "guilty" but to "doing harm." It should be noted that such an analysis has the consequence that in war we may often be justified in killing people who do not deserve to die, and unjustified in killing people who do deserve to die, if anyone does.

So we must distinguish combatants from noncombatants on the basis of their immediate threat or harmfulness. I do not claim that the line is a sharp one, but it is not so difficult as is often supposed to place individuals on one side of it or the other. Children are not combatants even though they may join the armed forces if they are allowed to grow up. Women are not combatants just because they bear children or offer comfort to the soldiers. More problematic are the supporting personnel, whether in or out of uniform, from drivers of munitions trucks and army cooks to civilian munitions workers and farmers. I believe they can be plausibly classified by applying the condition that the prosecution of conflict must direct itself to the cause of danger, and not to what is peripheral. The threat presented by an army and its

---

10 What I say on this subject derives from Anscombe.

members does not consist merely in the fact that they are men, but in the fact that they are armed and are using their arms in the pursuit of certain objectives. Contributions to their arms and logistics are contributions to this threat; contributions to their mere existence as men are not. It is therefore wrong to direct an attack against those who merely serve the combatants' needs as human beings, such as farmers and food suppliers, even though survival as a human being is a necessary condition of efficient functioning as a soldier.

This brings us to the second group of restrictions: those that limit what may be done even to combatants. These limits are harder to explain clearly. Some of them may be arbitrary or conventional, and some may have to be derived from other sources; but I believe that the condition of directness and relevance in hostile relations accounts for them to a considerable extent.

Consider first a case which involves both a protected class of noncombatants and a restriction on the measures that may be used against combatants. One provision of the rules of war which is universally recognized, though it seems to be turning into a dead letter in Vietnam, is the special status of medical personnel and the wounded in warfare. It might be more efficient to shoot medical officers on sight and to let the enemy wounded die rather than be patched up to fight another day. But someone with medical insignia is supposed to be left alone and permitted to tend and retrieve the wounded. I believe this is because medical attention is a species of attention to completely general human needs, not specifically the needs of a combat soldier, and our conflict with the soldier is not with his existence as a human being.

By extending the application of this idea, one can justify prohibitions against certain particularly cruel weapons: starvation, poisoning, infectious diseases (supposing they could be inflicted on combatants only), weapons designed to maim or disfigure or torture the opponent rather than merely to stop him. It is not, I think, mere casuistry to claim that such weapons attack the men, not the soldiers. The effect of dum-dum bullets, for example, is much more extended than necessary to cope with the combat situation in which they are used. They abandon any attempt to discriminate in their effects between the combatant and the human being. For this reason the use of flamethrowers and napalm is an atrocity in all circumstances that I can imagine, whoever the target may be. Burns are both extremely painful and extremely disfiguring—far more than any other category of wound. That this well-known fact plays no (inhibiting) part in the determination of US weapons policy suggests that moral sensitivity among public officials has not increased markedly since the Spanish Inquisition.[11]

---

11 Beyond this I feel uncertain. Ordinary bullets, after all, can cause death, and nothing is more permanent than that. I am not at all sure why we are justified in trying to kill those who are trying to kill us (rather than merely in trying to stop them with force which may also result in their deaths). It is often argued that incapacitating gases are a relatively humane weapon (when not used, as in Vietnam, merely to make people easier to shoot). Perhaps the legitimacy of restrictions

Finally, the same condition of appropriateness to the true object of hostility should limit the scope of attacks on an enemy country: its economy, agriculture, transportation system, and so forth. Even if the parties to a military conflict are considered to be not armies or governments but entire nations (which is usually a grave error), that does not justify one nation in warring against every aspect or element of another nation. That is not justified in a conflict between individuals, and nations are even more complex than individuals, so the same reasons apply. Like a human being, a nation is engaged in countless other pursuits while waging war, and it is not in those respects that it is an enemy.

The burden of the argument has been that absolutism about murder has a foundation in principles governing all one's relations to other persons, whether aggressive or amiable, and that these principles, and that absolutism, apply to warfare as well, with the result that certain measures are impermissible no matter what the consequences.[12] I do not mean to romanticize war. It is sufficiently utopian to suggest that when nations conflict they might rise to the level of limited barbarity that typically characterizes violent conflict between individuals, rather than wallowing in the moral pit where they appear to have settled, surrounded by enormous arsenals.

VII

Having described the elements of the absolutist position, we must now return to the conflict between it and utilitarianism. Even if certain types of dirty tactics become acceptable when the stakes are high enough, the most serious of the prohibited acts, like murder and torture, are not just supposed to require unusually strong justification. They are supposed *never* to be done, because no quantity of resulting benefit is thought capable of *justifying* such treatment of a person.

---

against them must depend on the dangers of escalation, and the great utility of maintaining *any* conventional category of restriction so long as nations are willing to adhere to it.

Let me make clear that I do not regard my argument as a defense of the moral immutability of the Hague and Geneva Conventions. Rather, I believe that they rest partly on a moral foundation, and that modifications of them should also be assessed on moral grounds.

But even this connection with the actual laws of war is not essential to my claims about what is permissible and what is not. Since completing this paper I have read an essay by Richard Wasserstrom entitled "The Laws of War" (forthcoming in *The Monist*), which argues that the existing laws and conventions do not even attempt to embody a decent moral position: that their provisions have been determined by other interests, that they are in fact immoral in substance, and that it is a grave mistake to refer to them as standards in forming moral judgments about warfare. This possibility deserves serious consideration, and I am not sure what to say about it, but it does not affect my view of the moral issues.

12 It is possible to draw a more radical conclusion, which I shall not pursue here. Perhaps the technology and organization of modern war are such as to make it impossible to wage as an acceptable form of interpersonal or even international hostility. Perhaps it is too impersonal and large-scale for that. If so, then absolutism would in practice imply pacifism, given the present state of things. On the other hand, I am skeptical about the unstated assumption that a technology dictates its own use.

The fact remains that when an absolutist knows or believes that the utilitarian cost of refusing to adopt a prohibited course will be very high, he may hold to his refusal to adopt it, but he will find it difficult to feel that a moral dilemma has been satisfactorily resolved. The same may be true of someone who rejects an absolutist requirement and adopts instead the course yielding the most acceptable consequences. In either case, it is possible to feel that one has acted for reasons insufficient to justify violation of the opposing principle. In situations of deadly conflict, particularly where a weaker party is threatened with annihilation or enslavement by a stronger one, the argument for resorting to atrocities can be powerful, and the dilemma acute.

There may exist principles, not yet codified, which would enable us to resolve such dilemmas. But then again there may not. We must face the pessimistic alternative that these two forms of moral intuition are not capable of being brought together into a single, coherent moral system, and that the world can present us with situations in which there is no honorable or moral course for a man to take, no course free of guilt and responsibility for evil.

The idea of a moral blind alley is a perfectly intelligible one. It is possible to get into such a situation by one's own fault, and people do it all the time. If, for example, one makes two incompatible promises or commitments—becomes engaged to two people, for example—then there is no course one can take which is not wrong, for one must break one's promise to at least one of them. Making a clean breast of the whole thing will not be enough to remove one's reprehensibility. The existence of such cases is not morally disturbing, however, because we feel that the situation was not unavoidable: one had to do something wrong in the first place to get into it. But what if the world itself, or someone else's actions, could face a previously innocent person with a choice between morally abominable courses of action, and leave him no way to escape with his honor? Our intuitions rebel at the idea, for we feel that the constructibility of such a case must show a contradiction in our moral views. But it is not in itself a contradiction to say that someone can do X or not do X, and that for him to take either course would be wrong. It merely contradicts the supposition that *ought* implies *can*—since presumably one ought to refrain from what is wrong, and in such a case it is impossible to do so.[13] Given the limitations on human action, it is naïve to suppose that there is a solution to every moral problem with which the world can face us. We have always known that the world is a bad place. It appears that it may be an evil place as well.

---

13 This was first pointed out to me by Christopher Boorse.

Recommended Reading

Anscombe, G.E. (1970). "War and Murder." In R. Wasserstrom (ed.), *War and Morality*. Belmont, CA: Wadsworth.

Clausewitz, C. von. (1995). *On War*. (A. Rapoport, Trans.) Harmondsworth, UK: Penguin.

Holmes, R. (1989). *On War and Morality*. Princeton: Princeton UP.

Kissinger, H. (1994). *Diplomacy*. New York: Simon & Schuster.

Morgenthau, H. (1973). *Politics Among Nations* (5th ed.). New York: Knopf.

Nagel, T. (1971–72). "War and Massacre." *Philosophy and Public Affairs* 1(2): 123–43.

Narveson, J. (1970). "Pacifism: A Philosophical Analysis." In R. Wasserstrom, ed., *War and Morality*. Belmont, CA: Wadsworth.

Norman, R. (1995). *Ethics, Killing and War*. Cambridge: Cambridge UP.

Orend, B. (2006). *The Morality of War*. Peterborough, ON: Broadview.

Teichman, J. (1986). *Pacifism and the Just War*. Oxford: Basil Blackwell.

Walzer, M. (2000). *Just and Unjust Wars: A Moral Argument with Historical Illustrations*, 3rd ed. New York: Basic Books.

Wasserstrom, R., ed. (1970). *War and Morality*. Belmont, CA: Wadsworth.

VI

Population and the Environment: Introduction

Intrinsic and Instrumental Value

Why should we put ourselves out to preserve the environment? The most obvious reason is that it is in our interests to do so. The United Nations' most recent Global Environment Outlook, published in 2007, surveys the state and trends in the condition of the environment, atmosphere, land, water, and biodiversity, includes a discussion of the human dimensions of environmental change, and projects the environmental outlook toward 2015 and beyond, as well as the impact these changes are likely to have on human populations. The most compelling and least controversial reason to combat environmental degradation is self-interest. We depend on the environment. Without clean air and water, without land capable of supporting agriculture, we will die.

These goods are of *instrumental value*; that is, they are valuable as means to further ends. Clean air and water are of instrumental value because they support our survival and well-being—an end that most of us take to be of great importance. We may also ask whether a healthy ecosystem is also of *intrinsic value*, that is, of worth in and of itself in addition to or apart from any value it may have as a means to some further end. It is controversial whether the health of the ecosystem is of intrinsic value. It is, however, relatively uncontroversial that human well-being is, and that a healthy environment is of instrumental value insofar as it is a means to that end.

But not all environmental projects seem to be directly concerned with furthering human interests; indeed, some appear to be contrary to our interests. Preserving African grasslands and the endangered species they support imposes restrictions on local farmers, pastoralists, and hunters. Conservation programs prevent the extraction of fossil fuels and minerals from wilderness areas. We preserve some wilderness areas in their pristine state, prohibiting all human use, including tourism. We protect the tiger, an endangered species, even though within their Asian habitat tigers kill farm animals and humans. Why should we support environmental projects that do us no good?

The first, and starkest, response is that we shouldn't. Pristine wilderness does us no good and, in addition to the direct costs of preserving it, there are opportunity costs: old-growth forests can be harvested for human consumption and, once logging is complete, farmed to provide cheaper, more abundant food for hungry people; alternatively, wilderness areas can be opened for hiking, hunting, and other recreational purposes. As for the tiger, a dangerous animal that kills and maims humans and destroys their property, there is no more reason to preserve it than there is to preserve the smallpox bacillus: neither of these species serves our interests.

The second answer, diametrically opposed to the first, is the response of *deep ecology*, according to which the flourishing of all natural things, not merely humans or other animals, is of intrinsic and not merely instrumental value. Some critics, however, have accused deep ecology of being elitist:

> The Indian writer Ramachandra Guha for instance, depicts the activities of many western-based conservation groups as a new form of cultural imperialism, aimed at securing converts to conservationism. "Green missionaries," as Guha calls them, represent a movement aimed at further dispossessing the world's poor and indigenous people. "Putting deep ecology in its place," he writes, "is to recognize that the trends it derides as 'shallow' ecology might in fact be varieties of environmentalism that are more apposite, more representative and more popular in the countries of the South." ... Guha's criticism raises important questions about the application of deep ecological principles in different social, economic and cultural contexts.[1]

Yet deep ecology is not the only environmentalist alternative. There may be other reasons to preserve pristine wilderness, tigers, and other features of the environment that do not seem to serve our interests in any obvious way. First, prudence dictates that we be conservative when it comes to managing the environment: unless interplanetary colonization becomes feasible, this is the only world we've got. Second, the preservation of environmental features that do not contribute to our well-being in any obvious way may nevertheless benefit us to the extent that it satisfies widespread human preferences. Even if we do not hike through pristine wilderness and assiduously steer clear of tigers, we want there to *be* wilderness and tigers. For

---

1 *Stanford Encyclopedia of Philosophy*, <http://plato.stanford.edu/entries/ethics-environmental/>.

the preference utilitarian, who understands well-being as preference satisfaction, states of affairs beyond our experience can harm or benefit us. If the world is the way I want it to be, if there are tigers and wilderness, I am benefitted even if I never directly experience either.

Environmental concerns nevertheless pose a range of moral dilemmas. Resources are finite, and there is an irreconcilable conflict of interests amongst earth's stakeholders, which include humans around the world, rich and poor, animals of innumerable species and, if deep ecology advocates are to be believed, the Earth itself. And there are no easy answers, as the following sample of moral dilemmas suggest.

Moral Dilemmas

Venice Sinking

In 2011, readers of Arthur Frommer's *Budget Travel* magazine voted Venice the most world's most beautiful city. Built on a cluster of islands and laced with canals, it is a unique living museum of spectacular cityscapes and glorious architecture. But Venice is sinking because of natural processes accelerated by the rise of sea level due to climate change. Seawater from the Adriatic regularly washes over St. Mark's Square to the doors of the cathedral, the most sumptuous of Byzantine churches, where one can hear a Gabrieli mass in Latin, sung from separated balconies, under 42,000 square feet of mosaics. Saving St. Mark's, and Venice, if it is technologically feasible, will be very expensive. And whenever there is expense there are *opportunity costs*, the costs of pursuing that option measured in terms of the best foregone alternative. The money we spend on keeping Venice (more or less) dry is money that could be put to use for education, health care, or social services, for feeding the hungry and saving the lives of millions of our fellow human beings who are now dying of easily preventable and treatable diseases.

To complicate matters further, Venice sits on a salt marsh, a fragile ecosystem that could be destroyed by efforts to save the city. Tourists do not make the pilgrimage to Venice to see the mud flats or the fish and sea birds. But Venice and its environs are an ecosystem, and further human interference will likely disrupt it. We humans have an interest in preserving Venetian cityscapes, art, and architecture. But our interference directed to that end could have adverse effects on the natural environment.

What shall we do? Shall we please the environmentalists, who want to preserve the salt marsh, at the expense of the aesthetes who want to preserve St. Mark's and the other architectural delights, or vice versa? Life is full of hard choices. Maybe we can have it all: the art, the salt marsh, and the money to fund education, health care, social services, and other good deeds—but more likely we can't. And if we can't, how shall we make principled decisions about which goals take precedence and what trade-offs should be made? *Is it worth trading off the health, or life, of low-status individuals to preserve a salt marsh—or an aesthetic attraction for wealthy tourists? If so, why?*

Slash-and-Burn Farming

Venice is a wealthy European city and the choices posed by its ecological plight are not as pressing as the dilemmas posed by environmental concerns in the developing world. Conservationists clamor for the preservation of animals that endanger the lives and livelihoods of farmers. Landless peasants reclaim jungle through slash-and-burn techniques; environmentalists deplore the destruction of rain forests in order to provide land for subsistence agriculture.

Almost half of tropical deforestation is caused by transient settlers using slash-and-burn techniques to clear land for subsistence farming.[2] After cutting trees for building material, settlers clear undergrowth and burn down forest trees not used for construction. They plant crops like bananas, palms, manioc, maize, or rice and, after a year or two, when the thin rainforest soils are depleted, move on. They contribute to the ongoing deforestation of the planet—which has been estimated as proceeding at a rate of 80,000 acres (32,000 hectares) per day.[3]

It would be satisfying to lay the blame for environmental degradation entirely on greedy capitalists, exploiting natural resources for gain and victimizing the poor. But that is not the way it is. Subsistence farmers, with no other viable options, as well as rapacious commercial developers and loggers, contribute to the destruction of rain forests. In the short run, conservation, which is vital for the long-term survival of humans as well as other species, sets back the interests of impoverished peasants as well as profit-seeking entrepreneurs.

Earth as a Common

In the long run, however, environmental degradation will likely have the most serious consequences for individuals and countries with the fewest resources, those least able to cope with its consequences. Climate change is likely to have the most adverse effects in poor countries of the Global South. Wealthy European countries have the resources to deal with rising sea levels. The Netherlands, much of which is already below sea level, maintains a system of expensive, technologically sophisticated dikes to keep the sea out. Italy has undertaken a range of expensive, technologically sophisticated projects to protect Venice from the encroaching Adriatic, including the MOSE project, which involves the construction of an artificial island and a total of 78 sea gates, projected to cost 4.7 billion Euros by the time it is completed in 2014.[4]

Low-lying islands and coastal areas in poor countries are also vulnerable to rising sea levels, but such countries cannot afford the same expensive solutions. And rising sea levels are not the only consequences of climate change. Desertification in marginal areas, induced by man-made climate change, is likely to have the greatest

---

2 <http://rainforests.mongabay.com/0804.htm>.
3 <http://rainforests.mongabay.com/0804.htm>.
4 John Keahey, *Venice against the Sea: A City Besieged* (New York: St. Martin's, Thomas Dunne Books, 2002), cited in Wikipedia: <http://en.wikipedia.org/wiki/MOSE_Project>.

.impact on poor countries in the Global South, deepening the ongoing food crisis for many of the world's poorest people, many of whom will become "climate change refugees," and precipitating violence and political instability.[5]

The moral of this story is that we are all of us, rich and poor, playing out the "tragedy of the commons," which arises when individuals acting to further their own interests deplete a shared, limited resource—and ultimately make things worse for everyone, including themselves. Climate change, a consequence of releasing greenhouse gases into the atmosphere to drive industry and clear land for farming for our benefit harms us all. "Think of the atmosphere as a giant global sink into which we can pour our waste gases," writes Peter Singer. "The atmosphere's capacity to absorb our gases has become a finite resource on which various parties have competing claims. The problem is to allocate those claims justly."[6]

In his classic article, "Living on a Lifeboat," Garrett Hardin argues that increasing the food supply in poor countries, through aid and improved agricultural technology, will only promote increased population growth in poor countries, which already have high fertility rates. "A world food bank," he argues, "is a commons in disguise.... The less provident and less able will multiply at the expense of the abler and more provident, bringing eventual ruin upon all who share in the commons."[7] We now know that Hardin was wrong about population growth. Food security and improved standards of living have dramatically *reduced* birth rates in developing countries rather than inducing the "less provident" to reproduce more abundantly. In the years since the publication of Hardin's article in 1974, estimates of world population growth have been revised downwards. Humans do not have a fixed, unqualified desire to maximize progeny. They do, however, have robust desires for more comfort, security, and entertainment, for more farmland and other real property, and for more manufactured goods. So, unless policies are established to allocate environmental resources fairly and stop environmental degradation, they will exploit environmental commons to satisfy those desires.

Rich and Poor... Again

Environmental sensitivity, however, may be a luxury that developing countries cannot afford. The ongoing debate over genetically modified food crops displays the complexity of this issue. Advocates argue that genetic modification produces high yields, cuts down on the need for expensive pesticides, and may be used to deliver drugs and vaccines to individuals in developing countries. Affluent consumers in Japan, Australia, and EU countries, however, shun GM foods and demand labeling, if not outright bans. As a consequence, agrarian nations in the developing world are pressed to eschew GM crops for fear of undermining their opportunities to export

---

5 <http://www.scientificamerican.com/article.cfm?id=climate-change-refugees-extended>.
6 Peter Singer, "One Atmosphere," pp. 440–64 in this volume.
7 Garrett Hardin, "Living on a Lifeboat," pp. 423–38 in this volume.

agricultural products. So, in 2002–03, faced with drought and severe famine conditions that put some 30 per cent of its population in danger of starvation, Zambia, in the supposed interests of preventing health risks to its population, blocked food aid that was "tainted" by genetic modification from entering the country. Whatever concerns the Zambian government may have had about the health of its starving citizens, it was clear that if there were any suspicion that Zambian agricultural products were tainted by genetic modification, it would be more difficult for Zambia to market them for export to ecologically fastidious consumers in affluent countries.

Environmental activist Vandana Shiva's Open Letter to Oxfam and Thomas DeGregori's response represent the debate between opponents and advocates of genetically modified foods. Shiva argues that the environmental projects she favors benefit the poor, and that by promoting genetically modified crops, Oxfam "risks betraying the [Global] South." DeGregori, however, notes that many citizens of the Global South want no part of her program.

Should we be environmentalists? Of course we should! It is an indisputable scientific fact that the earth's climate is changing as a consequence of human activity, and that this will have serious, long-term consequences, many of which will be harmful to humans and other animals. At the same time we should recognize that some efforts to address environmental concerns will benefit some people at the expense of others. In the end we must be selective: we cannot have it all. Allocating resources fairly will mean sacrificing some degree of our own well-being to benefit others. Preserving the environment for future generations will mean making tough choices that make us, and our contemporaries, worse off. Going green—reducing consumption and striving to achieve a smaller ecological footprint—will make our lives less convenient, deprive us of a range of pleasures, and undermine our quality of life.

31. Global Environment Outlook 4 (selections)[*]

United Nations Environmental Programme

Introduction

Imagine a world in which environmental change threatens people's health, physical security, material needs and social cohesion. This is a world beset by increasingly intense and frequent storms, and by rising sea levels. Some people experience extensive flooding, while others endure intense droughts. Species extinction occurs at rates never before witnessed. Safe water is increasingly limited, hindering economic activity. Land degradation endangers the lives of millions of people.

This is the world today. Yet, as the World Commission on Environment and Development (Brundtland Commission) concluded 20 years ago "humanity has the ability to make development sustainable." The fourth *Global Environment Outlook* highlights imperative steps needed to achieve this vision.

[...]

Our Common Future: Evolution of Ideas and Actions

Two decades ago the Brundtland Commission report—*Our Common Future*—addressed the links between development and environment, and challenged policymakers to consider the interrelationships among environment, economic and social issues when it comes to solving global problems. The report examined emerging global challenges in:

- population and human resources;
- food security;
- species and ecosystems;
- energy;
- industry; and
- urbanization.

---

[*] Source: UNEP, *Global Environment Outlook 4* (Nairobi: UNEP, 2007).

The commission recommended institutional and legal changes in six broad areas to address these challenges:

- getting at the sources;
- dealing with the effects;
- assessing global risks;
- making informed choices;
- providing the legal means; and
- investing in our future.

Recommendations emphasized the expansion of international institutions for cooperation, and the creation of legal mechanisms for environmental protection and sustainable development, and also stressed the links between poverty and environmental degradation. They also called for increased capacity to assess and report on risks of irreversible damage to natural systems, as well as threats to human survival, security and well-being.

[...]

Environment as the foundation for development

[...]

While a healthy environment can support development, the relationship is not always reciprocal. Many alternative views exist on the benefits and disadvantages of modern development (Rahnema 1997). It has been argued that development is destructive, even violent, to nature (Shiva 1991). As *GEO-4* [i.e., this publication: *Global Environment Outlook 4*] illustrates, past development practices have often not been beneficial to the environment. However, opportunities exist to make development sustainable.

Environmental degradation due to development raises deep ethical questions that go beyond economic cost-benefit ratios. The question of justice is perhaps the greatest moral question emerging in relation to environmental change and sustainable development. Growing evidence indicates that the burden of environmental change is falling far from the greatest consumers of environmental resources, who experience the benefits of development. Often, people living in poverty in the developing world, suffer the negative effects of environmental degradation. Furthermore, costs of environmental degradation will be experienced by humankind in future generations. Profound ethical questions are raised when benefits are extracted from the environment by those who do not bear the burden.

Barriers to sustainable development

Despite changes in environmental governance, and greater understanding of the links between environment and development, real progress towards sustainable development has been slow. Many governments continue to create policies concerned with environmental, economic and social matters as single issues. There is a continued failure to link environment and development in decision making (Dernbach 2002). As a result, development strategies often ignore the need to maintain the very ecosystem services on which long-term development goals depend. A notable example, made apparent in the aftermath of the 2005 Hurricane Katrina, is the failure of some government agencies to see the link between destruction of coastal wetlands and the increased vulnerability of coastal communities to storms (Fischetti 2005). For many, acknowledging that environmental change could endanger future human well-being is inconvenient, as it requires an uncomfortable level of change to individual and working lives (Gore 2006).

International negotiations on solutions to global environmental problems have frequently stalled over questions of equity (Brown 1999). For instance, in the case of climate change, international negotiations have slowed down over the question on of how to share responsibilities and burden among nations, given different historic and current levels of national emissions.

Providing widespread participation in sustainable development decision making called for by Agenda 21 has also raised significant challenges. The enormous diversity of issues that need to be considered in sustainable development policy making, together with aspirations for transparency, make public participation design daunting. If participation is treated superficially, and embodied merely as a quota of specified groups in decision making processes, it could easily be no more than "lip service." The task of designing modern, cross-cutting, transparent, evidence-based interdisciplinary decision making is not only conceptually challenging, but also necessitates a huge increase in local capacity for democracy and decision making (MacDonald and Service 2007).

Many social, economic and technological changes described later in this chapter have made implementation of the recommendations in *Our Common Future* difficult. […] changes such as a growing population and increased consumption of energy have had a huge impact on the environment, challenging society's ability to achieve sustainable development.

Finally, the nature of the environmental problems has influenced the effectiveness of past responses. Environmental problems can be mapped along a continuum from "problems with proven solutions" to "less known emerging (or persistent) problems" (Speth 2004). With problems with proven solutions, the cause-and-effect relationships are well known. The scale tends to be local or national. Impacts are highly visible and acute, and victims are easily identified. During the past 20 years, workable solutions have been identified for several such problems, for example industrial air and water pollution, local soil erosion, mangrove clearance for aquaculture, and vehicle exhaust emissions.

However, progress has been limited on harder-to-manage environmental issues, which can also be referred to as "persistent" problems (Jänicke and Volkery 2001). These are deeply rooted structural problems, related to the ways production and consumption are conducted at the household, national, regional and global levels. Harder to manage problems tend to have multiple dimensions and be global in scale. Some of the basic science of cause-and-effect relationships is known, but often not enough to predict when a tipping point or a point of no return will be reached. There is often a need to implement measures on a very large-scale. Examples of such problems include global climate change, persistent organic pollutants and heavy metals, ground-level ozone, acid rain, large-scale deterioration of fisheries, extinction of species, or introductions of alien species.

Awareness of the nature of an environmental problem provides a basis for creating strategies, targeting efforts, and finding and implementing a sustainable solution. Possible solutions to different types of environmental problems are introduced in the last section of this chapter [and elsewhere in the report].

Human Well-being and the Environment

For sustainable development to be achieved, links between the environment and development must be examined. It is also important to consider the end point of development: human well-being. The evolution of ideas on development has made the concept of human well-being central to the policy debate. Human well-being is the outcome of development. Human well-being and the state of the environment are strongly interlinked. Establishing how environmental changes have impacts on human well-being, and showing the importance of environment for human well-being, are among the core objectives of this report.

Defining human well-being

Defining human well-being (see Box 31.1) is not easy, due to alternative views on what it means. Simply put, human well-being can be classified according to three views, each of which has different implications for the environment:

- The resources people have, such as money and other assets. Wealth is seen as conducive to well-being. This view is closely linked to the concept of weak sustainability, which argues that environmental losses can be compensated for by increases in physical capital (machines) (Solow 1991). The environment can only contribute to development as a means to promote economic growth.
- How people feel about their lives (their subjective views). Individuals' assessments of their own living conditions take into account the intrinsic importance that environment has for life satisfaction. According to this view, people value

Box 31.1   Human well-being

Human well-being is the extent to which individuals have the ability and the opportunity to live the kinds of lives they have reason to value.

People's ability to pursue the lives that they value is shaped by a wide range of instrumental freedoms. Human well-being encompasses personal and environmental security, access to materials for a good life, good health and good social relations, all of which are closely related to each other, and underlie the freedom to make choices and take action:

■ Health is a state of complete physical, mental and social well-being, and not merely the absence of disease or illness. Good health not only includes being strong and feeling well, but also freedom from avoidable disease, a healthy physical environment, access to energy, safe water and clean air. What one can be and do include among others, the ability to keep fit, minimize health-related stress, and ensure access to medical care.

■ Material needs relate to access to ecosystem goods-and-services. The material basis for a good life includes secure and adequate livelihoods, income and assets, enough food and clean water at all times, shelter, clothing, access to energy to keep warm and cool, and access to goods.

■ Security relates to personal and environmental security. It includes access to natural and other resources, and freedom from violence, crime and wars (motivated by environmental drivers), as well as security from natural and human-caused disasters.

■ Social relations refer to positive characteristics that define interactions among individuals, such as social cohesion, reciprocity, mutual respect, good gender and family relations, and the ability to help others and provide for children.

Increasing the real opportunities that people have to improve their lives requires addressing all these components. This is closely linked to environmental quality and the sustainability of ecosystem services. Therefore, an assessment of the impact of the environment on individuals' well-being can be done by mapping the impact of the environment on these different components of well-being.

Sources: MA 2003, Sen 1999

the environment for its traditional or cultural aspects (Diener 2000, Frey and Stutzer 2005).

• What people are able to be and to do. This view focuses on what the environment allows individuals to be and to do (Sen 1985, 1992, 1999). It points out that the environment provides the basis for many benefits, such as proper nourishment, avoiding unnecessary morbidity and premature mortality, enjoying security and self-respect, and taking part in the life of the community. The environment is appreciated beyond its role as income generator, and its impacts on human well-being are seen as multidimensional.

The evolution of these ideas has progressed from the first to the third, with increasing importance being given to the real opportunities that people have to achieve what they wish to be and to do. This new understanding of human well-being has several important aspects. First, multidimensionality is viewed as an important feature of human well-being. Consequently, the impact of the environment on human well-being is seen according to many different dimensions.

Second, autonomy is considered a defining feature of people, and of well-being. Autonomy can be defined broadly as allowing people to make individual or collective choices. In other words, to know whether an individual is well requires considering his or her resources, subjective views, and the ability to choose and act. This concept of human well-being highlights the importance of understanding whether individuals are simply passive spectators of policy interventions, or, in fact, active agents of their own destiny.

Context of human well-being

The potential for individuals, communities and nations to make their own choices, and maximize opportunities to achieve security and good health, meet material needs and maintain social relations is affected by many interlinked factors, such as poverty, inequality and gender. It is important to note how these factors relate to each other, and to the environment.

Poverty and inequality

Poverty is understood as a deprivation of basic freedoms. It implies a low level of well-being, with such outcomes as poor health, premature mortality and morbidity, and illiteracy. It is usually driven by inadequate control over resources, discrimination (including by race or gender), and lack of access to material assets, health care and education (UN 2004).

Inequality refers to the skewed distribution of an object of value, such as income, medical care or clean water, among individuals or groups. Unequal access to environmental resources remains an important source of inequality among individuals. Equity is the idea that a social arrangement addresses equality in terms of something of value. Distributive analysis is used to assess features of human well-being that are unequally distributed among individuals according to arbitrary factors, such as gender, age, religion and ethnicity. When an analysis of this distribution focuses on its lower end, it refers to poverty.

Mobility

When seen in a dynamic perspective, inequality and poverty are better understood through the concepts of social mobility and vulnerability. Mobility relates to the ability of people to move from one social group, class or level to another. Environmental degradation may be responsible for locking individuals within low-mobility paths, limiting opportunities to improve their own well-being.

Vulnerability

Vulnerability involves a combination of exposure and sensitivity to risk, and the inability to cope or adapt to environmental change. Most often, the poor are more vulnerable to environmental change. Broad patterns of vulnerability to environmental and socio-economic changes can be identified so that policy-makers can respond, providing opportunities for reducing vulnerability, while protecting the environment. Chapter 7 [of this report] assesses the vulnerability of the human-environment system to multiple stresses (drivers and pressures).

Gender inequality

An analysis of distributive impacts of the environment on human well-being cannot ignore features such as gender. Gender inequality is one of the most persistent inequalities in both developed and developing countries, with the majority of people living in poverty being women (UNDP 2005b). Women and girls often carry a disproportionate burden from environmental degradation compared to men. Understanding the position of women in society, and their relationship with the environment is essential for promoting development. In many cases, women and girls assume greater responsibilities for environmental management, but have subordinate positions in decision making (Braidotti et al. 1994). Women need to be at the centre of policy responses (Agarwal 2000). At the same time, it is important to avoid stereotyping these roles, and to base responses on the complexities of local realities (Cleaver 2000).

Environmental change and human well-being

One of the main findings of the Millennium Ecosystem Assessment is that the relationship between human well-being and the natural environment is mediated by services provided by ecosystems (see Box 31.2). Changes to these services, as a result of changes in the environment, affect human well-being through impacts on security, basic material for a good life, health, and social and cultural relations (MA 2003). All people—rich and poor, urban and rural, and in all regions—rely on natural capital.

Box 31.2   Ecosystem services

Ecosystem services include *provisioning services*, such as food and water; *regulating services*, such as flood and disease control; *cultural services*, such as spiritual, recreational and cultural benefits; and *supporting services*, such as nutrient cycling that maintain the conditions for life on Earth.

Source: MA 2005a

The world's poorest people depend primarily on environmental goods and services for their livelihoods, which makes them particularly sensitive and vulnerable to environmental changes (WRI 2005). Furthermore, many communities in both developing and developed countries derive their income from environmental resources, which include fisheries, non-timber forest products and wildlife.

Health

Shortly before the publication of *Our Common Future*, the nuclear accident at Chernobyl illustrated the catastrophic impact pollution can have on health. Twenty years later, as victims of Chernobyl still struggle with disease, the health of countless other people around the world continues to be affected by human-induced changes to the environment. Changes affecting provisioning services, including water, can influence human health. Changes affecting regulating services influence health via the distribution of disease transmitting insects or pollutants in water and air (MA 2003). Almost one-quarter of all diseases are caused by environmental exposure (WHO 2006).

As described in Chapter 2 [of this report], urban air pollution is one of the most widespread environmental problems, affecting health in almost all regions of the world. While air pollution has decreased in many industrialized countries, it has increased in other regions, particularly in Asia. Here, rapid population growth, economic development and urbanization have been associated with increasing use of fossil fuels, and a deterioration of air quality. WHO estimates that more than 1 billion people in Asian countries are exposed to air pollutant levels exceeding their guidelines (WHO 2000). In 2002, WHO estimated that more than 800,000 people died prematurely due to PM_{10} (particulate matter with a diameter less than 10 micrometers) outdoor pollution and 1.6 million due to PM_{10} indoor air pollution (WHO 2002) (see Chapter 2 [of this report]).

Chapter 4 [of this report] highlights how the overexploitation and pollution of freshwater ecosystems—rivers, lakes, wetlands and groundwater—has direct impacts on human well-being. Although access to clean water and sanitation has improved, in 2002 more than 1.1 billion people lacked access to clean water, and 2.6 billion lacked access to improved sanitation (WHO and UNICEF 2004). Annually, 1.8 million children die from diarrhoea, making the disease the world's second biggest killer of children (UNDP 2006).

Many heavy metals, such as mercury and lead, are found in water and sediments, and are a major concern as they can accumulate in the tissues of humans and other organisms (UNESCO 2007). Numerous activities contribute to heavy metal contamination. Burning coal, incineration, urban and agricultural run-off, industrial discharges, small-scale industrial activities, mining, and landfill leakages are among the main ones described in Chapters 2, 3 and 4 [of this report].

Changes in the environment have also resulted in the emergence of diseases. Since 1980, more than 35 infectious diseases have emerged or taken on new importance. These include previously unknown, emerging diseases, such as HIV, SARS and avian influenza (H5N1), as well as diseases once thought controllable, such as dengue fever, malaria and bubonic plague (Karesh et al. 2005, UNEP 2005a). Human-induced changes to the environment, such as climate change, land-use change and interaction with wildlife […] have driven this recent epidemiological transition (McMichael 2001, 2004). Growing human contact with wildlife, caused by population pressure on remaining relatively undisturbed environmental resources, increases the opportunity for pathogen exchange (Wolfe et al. 1998). Globalization, in turn, has an effect on disease emergence as disease agents have the opportunity to move into new niches, and meet new, vulnerable populations. A recent UNEP report on Avian Influenza and the Environment states: "If the transfer of Asian lineage H5N1 between domestic flocks and wild birds is to be reduced, it will become essential to take measures to minimize their contact. Restoring wetland health will reduce the need for migrating wild birds to share habitat with domestic poultry" (UNEP 2006).

Material needs
People depend on natural resources for their basic needs, such as food, energy, water and housing. In many communities, particularly in developing countries, environmental resources, including fisheries, timber, non-timber forest products and wildlife, directly contribute to income and other material assets required to achieve a life that one values. The ability to meet material needs is strongly linked to the provisioning, regulating and supporting services of ecosystems (MA 2003).

More than 1.3 billion people depend on fisheries, forests and agriculture for employment—close to half of all jobs worldwide... (FAO 2004a). In Asia and the Pacific, small-scale fisheries contributed 25 per cent to the total fisheries production of Malaysia, the Philippines, and Thailand for the decade ending in 1997 (Kura and others 2004). In Africa, more than 7 in 10 people live in rural areas, with most engaged in resource-dependent activities (IFAD 2001). The corresponding small-scale production accounts for a significant percentage of the GDP in many African countries (IFPRI 2004). Moreover, small-scale agriculture accounts for more than 90 per cent of Africa's agricultural production (Spencer 2001). A study of households in the Masvingo province in southeast Zimbabwe indicates that 51 per cent of incomes are from agriculture, and that the total income from the environment averages 66 per cent (Campbell and others 2002). Where resources are degraded, livelihoods are placed at risk. Forest loss may reduce the availability of food, energy resources and other forest products, which, in many communities, support trade and income earning opportunities.

Increasing evidence shows that investment in ecosystem conservation, such as watershed management, results in increased income for the rural poor. In the Adgaon watershed in India, the annual days of employment (wage labour) per worker increased from 75 days before watershed rehabilitation to 200 days after restoration was completed (Kerr, Pangare and Pangare 2002). In Fiji, strengthening the traditional "no-take" management system to promote recovery of marine life has resulted in a 35–43 per cent increase in income over a period of three years... (WRI 2005). In a pioneering people-led watershed management project in India, the implementation of a participatory restoration scheme led to halving the distance to the water table, a doubling of land under irrigation, and an increase in the total agricultural income of the village from about US$55,000 in 1996, before watershed regeneration, to about US$235,000 in 2001 (D'Souza and Lobo 2004, WRI 2005).

Security
Security incorporates economic, political, cultural, social and environmental aspects (Dabelko, Lonergan, and Matthew 2000). It includes freedom from threats of bodily

harm, and from violence, crime and war. It means having stable and reliable access to resources, the ability to be secure from natural and human disasters, and the ability to mitigate and respond to shocks and stresses. Environmental resources are a critical part of the livelihoods of millions of people, and when these resources are threatened through environmental change, people's security is also threatened. "At the centre of sustainable development is the delicate balance between human security and the environment" (CHS 2006).

The Earth has shown clear signs of warming over the past century. Eleven of the last 12 years (1995–2006) rank among the 12 warmest years in the instrumental record of global surface temperature (since 1850) (IPCC 2007). As Chapter 2 [of this report] describes, climate change is very likely to affect ecological regulating services, resulting in increased frequency and intensity of extreme weather hazards in many regions around the globe (IPCC 2007), and greater insecurity for much of the world's population (Conca and Dabelko 2002). The impacts of extreme weather events will fall disproportionately upon developing countries, such as Small Island Developing States (SIDS)... as well as on the poor in all countries (IPCC 2007). During Hurricane Katrina in the United States in 2005, impoverished people without access to private transportation were unable to leave the city. People in poor health or lacking bodily strength were less likely to survive the Indian Ocean tsunami in 2004. For example, in villages in North Aceh, Indonesia, women constituted up to 80 per cent of deaths (Oxfam 2005). In Sri Lanka, a high mortality rate was also observed among other vulnerable groups: children and the elderly (Nishikiori et al. 2006).

Environmental change can also affect security through changes in provisioning services, which supply food and other goods. Scarcity of shared resources has been a source of conflict and social instability (deSombre and Barkin 2002). Disputes over water quantity and quality are ongoing in many parts of the world. The apparent degradation of Easter Island's natural resources by its Polynesian inhabitants, and the ensuing struggle between clans and chiefs, provides a graphic illustration of a society that destroyed itself by overexploiting scarce resources (Diamond 2005). Natural resources can play an important role in armed conflicts. They have often been a means of funding war.... Armed conflicts have also been used as a means to gain access to resources (Le Billion 2001), and they can destroy environmental resources.

Insecurity caused by bad governance or war can contribute to environmental degradation. Security requires the current and future availability of environmental goods and services, through good governance, mechanisms for conflict avoidance and resolution, and for disaster prevention, preparedness and mitigation (Dabelko, Lonergan and Matthew 2000; Huggins, Chenje and Mohamed-Katerere 2006; Maltais, Dow and Persson 2003). Inequitable governance and institutions may prevent people from having secure livelihoods, as illustrated by land tenure conflicts in Southern Africa (Katerere and Hill 2002), and by poor management in Indonesia's peat swamps (Hecker 2005). In both examples, the resource is closely linked to local livelihoods, and insecurity is a result not so much of scarcity but of unequal access to and distribution of these vital resources. In other cases, as illustrated [above], degradation may result from changes in settlement patterns as people are forced to flee an area due to hostilities or war.

Social relations

The environment also affects social relations by providing cultural services, such as the opportunity to express aesthetic, cultural or spiritual values associated with ecosystems (MA 2005a). The natural world provides opportunities for observation and education, recreation and aesthetic enjoyment, all of which are of value to a given society. In some communities, the environment underpins the very structure of social relations. As described in Chapter 5 [of this report], many cultures, particularly indigenous ones, are deeply interwoven with the local environment.

Climate change is a major concern for SIDS and their high cultural diversity; SIDS are imperilled by sea-level rise and increases in the intensity and number of storms (Watson, Zinyower and Dokken 1997) (see Chapter 7 [of this report]). Tuvalu is an example of an island vulnerable to environmental change. Even though its culture is strongly related to the local environment, the islanders may have to consider relocating to other countries to escape rising sea level as a result of climate change. Coping mechanisms embedded in such cultures might be lost, making society less resilient to future natural disasters (Pelling and Uitto 2001).

A diet of traditional foods plays a particularly important role in the social, cultural, nutritional and economic health of indigenous peoples living in the Arctic (Donaldson 2002). Hunting, fishing, and the gathering of plants and berries are associated with important traditional values and practices that are central to their identity as indigenous peoples. Their traditional food is compromised by environmental contaminants...and climate change (see Chapter 6 [of this report]), and this affects all dimensions of indigenous well-being. The issue becomes magnified in light of the lack of accessible, culturally acceptable and affordable alternatives. Store food is expensive, and lacks cultural significance and meaning. Long-term solutions require that Arctic lifestyles be considered when development choices are made in industrial and agricultural regions around the world (Doubleday 2005).

Drivers of Change and Pressures

Environmental changes and the effects on human well-being are induced by various drivers and pressures. Drivers such as demographic changes, economic demand and trade, science and technology, as well as institutional and socio-political frameworks induce pressures which, in turn, influence the state of the environment with impacts on the environment itself, and on society and economic activity. Most pressures on ecosystems result from, for example, changes in emissions, land use and resource extraction. Analyses of the linkages shown by the drivers-pressures-state-impacts-responses (DSPIR) framework...form the foundation on which the *GEO-4* assessment is constructed. In the two decades since the Brundtland Commission, these drivers and pressures have changed, often at an increasing rate. The result is that the environment has changed dramatically. No region has been spared the reality of a changing environment, and its immediate, short- and long-term impacts on human well-being.

Population

Population is an important driver behind environmental change, leading to increased demand for food, water and energy, and placing pressure on natural resources. Today's population is three times larger than it was at the beginning of the 20th century. During the past 20 years global population has continued to rise, increasing from 5 billion in 1987 to 6.7 billion in 2007..., with an average annual growth rate of 1.4 per cent. However, large differences in growth are evident across regions, with Africa and West Asia recording high growth rates, and the European population stabilizing.... Although the world population is increasing, the rate of increase is slowing....

Forced and economic migrations influence demographic changes and settlement patterns, particularly at the regional level. There were 190 million international migrants in 2005, compared to 111 million in 1985. About one-third of migrants in the world have moved from one developing country to another, while another third have moved from a developing country to a developed country (UN 2006). Many migrants are refugees, internally displaced or stateless persons. At the end of 2005, more than 20.8 million people were classified as "of concern" to the UN High Commission for Refugees (UNHCR 2006b). These included refugees, internally displaced and stateless persons. Worldwide refugee numbers have decreased since 2000, but there has been an upward trend in numbers of other displaced groups (UNHCR 2006b).

The term *ecomigrant* has been used to describe anyone whose need to migrate is influenced by environmental factors (Wood 2001). It has been claimed that during the mid-1990s up to 25 million people were forced to flee as a result of environmental change, and as many as 200 million people could eventually be at risk of displacement (Myers 1997). Other analyses indicated that while the environment may play a role in forced migration, migration is usually also linked to political divisions, economic interests and ethnic rivalries (Castles 2002). A clear separation between factors is often difficult.

Urbanization continues around the world, particularly in developing countries, where rural migration continues to fuel urban growth.... By the end of 2007, more people will be living in cities than in rural areas for the first time in history (UN-HABITAT 2006). In North East Asia and South East Asia, the population living in urban areas increased from 28–29 per cent in 1985 to 44 per cent in 2005, and is projected to reach 59 per cent by 2025 (GEO Data Portal, from UNPD 2005). In some places, the urban area is increasing faster than the urban population, a process known as urban sprawl. For example, between 1970 and 1990, the total area of the 100 largest urban areas in the United States increased by 82 per cent. Only half of this increase was caused by population growth (Kolankiewicz and Beck 2001).... A growing number of people living in urban areas are living in slums—inadequate housing with no or few basic services (UN-HABITAT 2006). In many sub-Saharan African cities, children living in slums are more likely to die from water-borne and respiratory illnesses than rural children. For 2005, the number of slum dwellers was estimated at almost 1 billion (UN-HABITAT 2006).

Migration and urbanization have complex relationships with environmental change. Natural disasters, and degradation of land and local ecosystems are among the causes of migration (Matutinovic 2006). Changing demographic patterns, caused by migration or urbanization, alter land use and demand for ecosystem services....

Urbanization in particular can exert significant pressure on the environment (see Chapter 6 [of this report]). Coastal urban areas often cause offshore water pollution. Coastal populations alone are expected to reach 6 billion by 2025 (Kennish 2002). In these areas, large-scale development results in excessive nutrient inputs from municipal and industrial waste. As described in Chapter 4 [of this report], eutrophication contributes to the creation of dead zones, areas of water with low or no dissolved oxygen. Fish cannot survive, and aquatic ecosystems are destroyed. Dead zones are an emerging problem in Asia, Africa and South America, but are present around the world. With population growth, and increasing industrialization and urbanization, dead zones can only continue to expand. Properly managed, cities can also become a solution for some of the environmental pressures. They provide economies of scale, opportunities for sustainable transport and efficient energy options.

Economic growth

Global economic growth has been spectacular during the last two decades. Gross domestic product per capita (at purchasing power parity) increased by almost 1.7 per cent annually, but this growth was unevenly spread.... People in Africa, Eastern Europe and Central Asia, and certain areas of Latin America and the Caribbean are worse off than those in North America and Central and Western Europe. Many countries in these regions experienced no growth and some even a clear economic decline between 1987 and 2004. Especially in Africa there are large differences within the region, and even where there is growth, countries are faced with a heavy debt burden.... Income in Asia and the Pacific is still well below the global average, but its growth rate was twice the global average....

Economic growth and unsustainable consumption patterns represent a growing pressure on the environment, though this pressure is often distributed unequally. Dasgupta (2002) argues that economic growth is unsustainable in poor countries, partly because it is sustainable in wealthy countries. Countries that export resources are subsidizing the consumption of importing countries (Dasgupta 2002). However, consumption patterns among regions are changing with the emergence of new economies and powers such as China, India, Brazil, South Africa and Mexico. China, for example, is expected to become the world's largest economy between 2025 and 2035. Its rapid economic development is influencing global patterns of resource production and consumption, with both environmental and geopolitical consequences (Grumbine 2007). Vehicle ownership patterns illustrate the impact of changing consumption patterns (see Chapter 2 [of this report]). China had some 27.5 million passenger vehicles and 79 million motorcycles in use by 2004 (China Statistics Bureau 1987–2004). The growing trend in vehicle ownership affects urban air quality, which has clear consequences for human health.

Globalization

The world's economy has been characterized by growing globalization, which is spurring the increasing integration of the global economy through trade and financial flows, and in the integration of knowledge through the transfer of information, culture and technology (Najam, Runnalls and Halle 2007). Governance has also become globalized, with increasingly complex interstate interactions, and with a growing role for non-state actors. International companies have become influential economic actors in a global governance context traditionally dominated by nations. While states "rule the world," corporations have publicly sought the global political stage at gatherings such as the World Economic Forum and at multilateral negotiations, such as the Multilateral Agreement on Investment (De Grauwe and Camerman 2003, Graham 2000). Advances in technology and communications, such as the Internet, have also boosted the role of individuals and organizations as key players in a globalized world (Friedman 2005).

Globalization raises both fears and expectations. Some suggest that increasing interdependence is good for cooperation, peace and solving common problems (Bhagwati 2004, Birdsall and Lawrence 1999, Russett and Oneal 2001). Economic integration may offer dynamic benefits, such as higher productivity. The exchange of goods and services also helps the exchange of ideas and knowledge. A relatively open economy is better able to learn and adopt foreign, state-of-the-art technologies than is a relatively closed economy (Coe and Helpman 1995, Keller 2002). Others, however, view growing economic interdependence as destabilizing. They say that rapid flows of investment into and out of countries cause job losses, increase inequality, lower wages (Haass and Litan 1998) and result in harm to the environment. It is argued that globalization is exploitative, and is creating a murkier future for global cooperation and justice (Falk 2000, Korten 2001, Mittelman 2000).

The environment and globalization are intrinsically linked. The globalization of trade has facilitated the spread of exotic species, including the five most important freshwater suspension feeding invaders (*Dressena polymorpha, D. bugensis, Corbicula fluminea, C. fluminalis, and Limoperna fortunei*). The zebra mussel (*Dressena polymorpha*) has spread through North America during the last 20 years, resulting in significant ecological and economic impacts. Its introduction corresponds with dramatic increase in wheat shipments between the US, Canada, and the former Soviet Union (Karatayev et al. 2007). In a globalized world, important decisions related to environmental protection may have more to do with corporate management and market outcomes than with state-level, political factors. Countries may be reluctant to enforce strict environmental laws, fearing that companies would relocate elsewhere. However, it is often forgotten that the environment itself can have an impact on globalization. Resources fuel global economic growth and trade. Solutions to environmental crises, such as climate change, require coordinated global action and greater globalization of governance (Najam, Runnalls and Halle 2007).

Trade

World trade has continued to grow over the past 20 years, as a result of lower transport and communication costs, trade liberalization and multilateral trade agreements, such as the North American Free Trade Agreement. Between 1990 and 2003, trade in goods increased from 32.5 to 41.5 per cent of world GDP. Differences exist between regions. In North East Asia, trade in goods increased from 47 to 70.5 per cent of GDP, and high technology exports increased from 16 to 33 per cent of manufactured exports. By contrast, trade in goods in West Asia and Northern Africa only increased from 46.6 per cent to 50.4 per cent of GDP. High technology exports only accounted for 2 per cent of manufactured exports in 2002 (World Bank 2005). Since 1990, least developed countries (LDC) have increased their share of world merchandise trade, but still accounted for only 0.6 per cent of world exports and 0.8 per cent of world imports in 2004 (WTO 2006).

As with globalization, a two-way relationship exists between the environment and trade. Transport has increased as a result of increasing flows of goods and global production networks. Transport is now one of the most dynamic sectors in a modern economy, and has strong environmental impacts (Button and Nijkamp 2004) (see Chapters 2 and 6 [of this report]). Trade itself can exert pressures on the environment. Increases in international grain prices may increase the profitability of agriculture, and result in the expansion of farming into forested areas in Latin America and the Caribbean, for example.... The wildlife trade in Mongolia, valued at US$100 million annually, is contributing to the rapid decline of species such as saiga antelope (World Bank and WCS 2006). In the presence of market or intervention failures, international trade may also exacerbate environmental problems indirectly. For example, production subsidies in the fishing sector can promote overfishing (OECD 1994). Natural disasters, in turn, can have an impact on trade at the national level, when exports fall as a result of physical damage.

One example of this linkage is the hurricane damage to oil refineries in the Gulf of Mexico in 2005. Oil production in the Gulf of Mexico, which supplies 2 per cent of the world's crude oil, slowed following Hurricane Katrina, and crude oil prices jumped to over US$70 a barrel (WTO 2006).

Trade may also be positive for the environment. Debate rages over whether or not free trade will raise incomes to a point where environmental protection becomes a priority (Gallagher 2004). At the 2002 WSSD in Johannesburg, commitments were made to expand markets for environmental goods and services. Liberalization of trade in goods that protect the environment may help spur the creation of industry dedicated to environmental improvements (OECD 2005). Consumer preferences can influence production standards, which can be used to improve environmental conditions. In 2006, a large grain distributor imposed a moratorium on the purchase of soy produced on deforested areas of the Amazon, as a result of a Greenpeace campaign in Europe (Cargill 2006, Greenpeace 2006).

Energy

The world is facing twin threats: inadequate and insecure supplies of energy at affordable prices, and environmental damage due to overconsumption of energy (IEA 2006a). Global demand for energy keeps growing, placing an ever-increasing burden on natural resources and the environment. For about three decades, world primary energy demand grew by 2.1 per cent annually, rising from 5,566 million tonnes oil equivalent (Mtoe) in 1971 to 11,204 Mtoe in 2004 (IEA 2006b). Over two-thirds of this increase came from developing countries, but OECD countries still account for almost 50 per cent of world energy demand. In 2004, primary energy use per capita in OECD countries was still 10 times higher than in sub-Saharan Africa....

Global increases in carbon dioxide emissions are primarily due to fossil fuel use (IPCC 2007), the fuels that met 82 per cent of the world's energy demand in 2004. Traditional biomass (firewood and dung) remains an important energy source in developing countries, where 2.1 billion people rely on it for heating and cooking (IEA 2002). Use of cleaner energy sources, such as solar and wind power, remains minimal overall. The need to curb growth in energy demand, increase fuel supply diversity and mitigate climate destabilizing emissions is more urgent than ever (IEA 2006a). However, expansion of alternative energy sources, such as biofuels, must also be carefully planned. Brazil expects to double the production of ethanol, a "modern" biofuel, in the next two decades (Government of Brazil 2005). In order to produce enough crops to reach production targets, the cultivated area is increasing rapidly. The growth of farming jeopardizes entire ecoregions, like the Cerrado, one of the world's biodiversity hot spots (Klink and Machado 2005).

Technological innovation

Advances in agriculture, energy, medicine and manufacturing have offered hope for continued human development and a cleaner environment. New farming technologies and practices related to water use, fertilizer and plant breeding have transformed agriculture, increasing food production and addressing undernutrition and chronic famine in some regions. Since 1970, food consumption is increasing in all regions, and is expected to continue to increase as a result of economic development and population growth. Concerns have been raised over the ability to meet future demand: 11 per cent of the world's land is already used for agriculture, and in many places little room exists for agricultural expansion due to land or water shortages. Biotechnology, including genetic modification, as well as nanotechnology, has the potential to increase production in agriculture and contribute to advances in human health (UNDP 2004), but remains subject to much controversy over effects on health and the environment. Earlier lessons from new technologies show the importance of applying the precautionary approach (CIEL 1991), because unintended effects of technological advances can lead to the degradation of ecosystem services. For example, eutrophication of freshwater systems and hypoxia in coastal marine ecosystems result from excess application of inorganic fertilizers. Advances in fishing technologies have contributed significantly to the depletion of marine fish stocks.

Communications and cultural patterns have also been revolutionized in the last 20 years, with the exponential growth of the Internet and telecommunications…. Worldwide, mobile phone subscribers increased from 2 per 1,000 people in 1990 to 220 per 1,000 in 2003 and worldwide Internet use increased from 1 in 1,000 in 1990 to 114 per 1,000 in 2003 (GEO Data Portal, from ITU 2005). Many developed countries lead the way in the number of Internet users, hosts and secure servers, prompting some to claim that there is a digital divide between different regions of the world. In Australia and New Zealand, for example, only 4 per cent of the population used the Internet in 1996, but by 2003, that had risen to 56 per cent of the population. By contrast in 2003, in poor countries such as Bangladesh, Burundi, Ethiopia, Myanmar and Tajikistan only 1 or 2 people per 1,000 used the Internet (GEO Data Portal, from ITU 2005).

Governance

The global and regional political context has changed considerably since the Brundtland Commission, with the end of the Cold War triggering renewed optimism in multilateral and global governance. The 1990s was a decade of global summits on a diversity of issues, including children (1990), sustainable development (1992), human rights (1994), population (1994), social development (1995), gender equality (1995) and human settlements (1996). The new millennium has been equally active and agenda-setting, starting with the Millennium Summit in 2000, and its follow-up in 2005. Normative declarations and ambitious action plans from all these summits illustrate an emerging unity in how governments and the international community understand complex and global problems and formulate appropriate responses. The establishment of the World Trade Organization in 1994 strengthened global governance through its considerable authority in the areas of trade, while the establishment of the International Criminal Court of Justice in 2002 attempted to do the same for crimes against humanity. Some important reforms have happened within the UN system, including an approach that increasingly uses partnerships (such as the Global Water Partnership) and institutionalized processes to strengthen the participation of civil society (such as the UNEP's Global Civil Society Forum and Global Women's Assembly on Environment).

At the regional level, countries have expanded or established institutions to enhance cooperation, including the European Union (EU), the North American Free Trade Agreement (NAFTA), the Southern Common Market (MERCOSUR), the Association of Southeast Asian Nations (ASEAN) and the African Union (AU). Regions became more visible in global deliberations, through, for example, the emphasis on regional preparation meetings for the World Summit on Sustainable Development.

The national level remains central in governance, despite discussions in the context of globalization and regionalization. Some countries are adopting innovative governance systems and there has been a trend towards both political and fiscal decentralization of governance to sub-national levels. This does not necessarily mean that local authorities have been empowered. It has been argued that decentralization without devolution of power can be a way to strengthen the presence of the central authority (Stohr 2001). Local governments have also engaged much more widely in international cooperation in various arenas, and their role has been strengthened at the global level through the establishment in 2000 of the UN Advisory Committee of Local Authorities (UNACLA) and the World Urban Forum in 2002, as well as the founding of the United Cities and Local Governments Organization in 2004.

Responses

Interactions between drivers and pressures, and their consequent impacts on ecosystem services and human well-being present challenges that could not be foreseen in 1987. There is an urgent need for effective policy responses at all levels—international, regional, national and local. As highlighted in the other chapters of this report, the range and scope of response options available to policy-makers has progressively evolved over the past 20 years (see Box 31.3), with a diversity of multilateral environmental agreements and institutions now involved in trying to address the challenges. The increase in governance regimes has brought about its own challenges, including competition and overlap. An interlinkages approach is essential to managing the environment, not in its individual parts but more holistically. This approach recognizes that the environment itself is interlinked; land, water and atmosphere are connected in many ways, particularly through the carbon, nitrogen and water cycles.

[...]

For conventional, well-known environmental problems with proven solutions, it is necessary to continue to apply, and to further improve upon previously successful approaches. Countries that have yet to address such problems should apply these proven, workable solutions to current problems. Previously successful approaches have generally addressed changes to pressures, for example by regulating emission levels, land use or resource extraction. In order to address less-known persistent (or emerging) problems, transformative policies are needed. These policies address the drivers of environmental problems, such as demographic change and consumption patterns. Adaptive management is essential, to enable policy-makers to learn from previous experience as well as to make use of a variety of new tools that may be needed.

Economic instruments

Today, greater emphasis is being placed on the potential use of economic instruments to help correct market failures. These instruments were promoted by Principle 16 of the Rio Declaration: "National authorities should endeavour to promote the internalization of environmental costs and the use of economic instruments."

Natural resources can be seen as a capital asset belonging to a general portfolio, which is comprised of other assets and capitals, including material, financial, human and social. Managing this portfolio in a good and sustainable manner to maximize its returns and benefits over time is good investment. It is also central to sustainable development.

A variety of economic instruments exist, including property rights, market creation, fiscal instruments, charge systems, financial instruments, liability systems, and bonds and deposits. There is a mix of so-called market-based instruments (MBIs) and command-and-control instruments to enable policy-makers to better manage and get more accurate information regarding the portfolio of capital assets. Table 31.1 summarizes different economic instruments, and how they can be applied to different environmental sectors. One of the tools is valuation, which can be used to help better assess the value of ecosystem services, and the costs of human-induced changes to the environment.

Valuation

Environmental ministries and agencies are often the last to benefit from investments, because economics and growth generation take precedence in government spending decisions. This is often due to lack of information on the value and carrying limits of the Earth's ecosystems. Measurement of economic development and progress has often been linked to measures of economic output such as Gross National Product (GNP). Such aggregate measurements do not consider the depletion of natural

Table 31.1   Economic instruments and applications

	Property rights	Market creation	Fiscal instruments	Charge systems	Financial instruments	Liability systems	Bonds and deposits
Forests	Communal rights	Concession building	Taxes and royalties		Reforestation incentives	Natural resource liability	Reforestation bonds, forest management bonds
Water resources	Water rights	Water shares	Capital gains tax	Water pricing Water protection charges			
Oceans and seas		Fishing rights, Individual transferable quotas Licensing					Oil spill bonds
Minerals	Mining rights		Taxes and royalties				Land reclamation bonds
Wildlife		Access fees				Natural resource liability	
Biodiversity	Patents Prospecting rights	Transferable development rights		Charges for scientific tourism		Natural resource liability	
Water pollution		Tradeable effluent permits	Effluent charges	Water treatment fees	Low-interest loans		
Land and soils	Land rights, use rights		Property taxes, land-use taxes		Soil conservation incentives (such as loans)		Land reclamation bonds
Air pollution		Tradeable emission permits	Emission charges	Technology subsidies, low-interest loans			
Hazardous waste				Collection charges			Deposit refund systems
Solid waste			Property taxes	Technology subsidies, low-interest loans			
Toxic chemicals			Differential taxation			Legal liability, liability insurance	Deposit refund
Climate	Tradeable emission entitlements Tradeable forest protection obligations	Tradeable CO_2 permits Tradeable CFC quotas CFC quota auction Carbon offsets	Carbon taxes BTU tax		CFC replacement incentives Forest compacts		
Human settlements	Land rights	Access fees Tradeable development quotas Transferable development rights	Property taxes, land-use taxes	Betterment charges Development charges Land-use charges Road tolls Import fees			Development completion bonds

Source: Adapted from Panayotou 1994

capital caused by the consumption and production of goods and services. National accounting systems need revision to better include the value of the changes in the environmental resource base due to human activities (Mäler 1974, Dasgupta and Mäler 1999).

Valuing different goods and services involves comparisons across different sets of things. How these things are accounted for, and how the services provided by the ecosystems, for example, improve well-being is called the accounting price. Table 31.2 illustrates different approaches to valuation, and how these approaches might be used to help assess the impact of policies on environmental change and human well-being.

A "set of institutions capable of managing the natural resources, legal frameworks, collecting resource rents, redirecting these rents into profitable investments" is key to effective use of valuation (World Bank 2006a). Valuing natural resources and evaluating policies where institutions such as markets do not exist, and where there is a lack of individual property rights, pose challenges. Under such uncertainties, and where divergent sets of values exist, the economic value of common resources can be measured by the maximum amount of other goods and services that individuals are willing to give up to obtain a given good or service. Therefore, it is possible to weigh the benefits from an activity such as the construction of a dam against its negative impacts on fishing, livelihoods of nearby communities, and changes to scenic and aesthetic values. Box 31.3 provides an example of non-market valuation using the contingent valuation method (CVM).

Valuation presents a set of challenges beyond conflicting value systems or lack of existing market institutions. It uses notional and proxy measures to estimate the economic values of tangible and intangible services provided by the environment. An increasing body of valuation work has been undertaken on provisioning services of ecosystems. It has produced estimates of the value of non-timber forest products, forestry, and the health impacts of air pollution and water-borne diseases. However, studies on less tangible but yet important services, such as water purification and the prevention of natural disasters, as well as recreational, aesthetic and cultural services, have been hard to get. To get objective monetary estimates of these services remains a challenge. Market data is limited to a small number of services provided by ecosystems. Furthermore, methodologies such as cost-benefit analysis and CVM may raise problems of bias.

The use of market and non-market-based instruments has also shown gaps in addressing distributional and intergenerational equity issues (MA 2005b), notably with regard to poverty-related issues. Finally, many valuation studies estimating the impact of policies or projects on human well-being fail due to the lack of sufficiently precise estimates of the consequences of these policies or projects now and in the future. Despite these flaws, valuation may be a useful tool with which to examine the complex relationships and feedback involving the environment, economic growth and human well-being.

Table 31.2 Purpose and application of different valuation approaches

Approach	Why is it done	How is it done
Determining the total value of the current flow of benefits from an ecosystem.	To understand the contribution that ecosystems make to society and to human well-being.	Identify all mutually compatible services provided. Measure the quantity of each service provided, and multiply by the value of each service.
Determining the net benefits of an intervention that alters ecosystem conditions.	To assess whether the intervention is worthwhile.	Measure how the quantity of each service would change as a result of the intervention, as compared to their quantity without the intervention. Multiply by the marginal value of each service.
Examining how the costs and benefits of an ecosystem (or an intervention) are distributed.	To identify winners and losers, for ethical and practical reasons.	Identify relevant stakeholder groups. Determine which specific services they use, and the value of those services to that group (or changes in values resulting from an intervention).
Identifying potential financing sources for conservation.	To help make ecosystem conservation financially self-sustaining.	Identify groups that receive large benefit flows from which funds could be extracted, using various mechanisms.

Source: Adapted from Stephano 2004

Box 31.3 Valuing the removal of the Elwha and Glines Dams

An environmental impact analysis using CVM was conducted in the 1990s to explore the removal of the Elwha and Glines dams in Washington State in the United States. These two 30- and 60-metre-high dams, respectively, are old, and block the migration of fish to 110 km of pristine water located in the Olympic National Park. The dams also harm the Lower Elwha Klallam Tribe which relies on the salmon and river for their physical, spiritual and cultural well-being. Dam removal could bring substantial fishing benefits, more than tripling the salmon populations. The cost of removing the dams, and especially the sediment build-up is estimated at about US$100–$125 million. Recreational and commercial fishing benefits resulting from dam removal would not be sufficient to cover these costs.

A CVM survey was conducted and yielded a 68 per cent response in Washington State, and 55 per cent response for the rest of the United States. Willingness to pay for dam removal ranged from US$73 per household for Washington to US$68 for the rest of the United States. If every household in Washington State were to pay US$73, the cost of dam removal and river restoration could be covered. If the return stemming from Washington residents' willingness to pay was added to the rest of the US willingness to pay (the 86 million households and their willingness to pay an average of US$68 per head) in excess of US$1 billion dollars would result.

After years of negotiations it has been decided that the dams will be removed, and the Elwha Restoration Project will go forward. This is the biggest dam-removal project in history, and an event of national significance in the United States. It is expected that the two dams will be removed in stages over the course of three years, between 2009 and 2011.

Source: American Rivers 2006, Loomis 1997, USGS 2006

Non-economic instruments
In addition to economic instruments, a variety of non-economic instruments have been employed to address both well-known proven and less clear emerging (or persistent) environmental problems. Today, the emerging understanding of human well-being increasingly influences our choice of instruments.

Public participation
Human well-being depends on the unconstrained ability of people to participate in decisions, so that they can organize society in a way that is consistent with their highest values and aspirations. In other words, public participation is not only a

matter of procedural justice, but also a precondition for achieving well-being. While this is challenging, managers should involve civil society in policy interventions. The Convention on Biological Diversity offers several examples of possible stakeholder engagement in decision making. These include CBD VII/12, The Addis Ababa Guidelines on the sustainable use of the components of biodiversity; CBD VII/14 guidelines on sustainable tourism development; and the CBD VII/16 Akwe, on voluntary guidelines for the conduct of cultural, environmental and social impact assessments for development proposals on sacred sites, lands and waters traditionally occupied or used by indigenous and local communities. The development of similar agreements and protocols that enhance effective engagement of all sectors of society should be encouraged.

Education
Access to information and education is a basic human right, and an important aspect of human well-being. It is also an important tool for generating knowledge that links ecological analyses to societal challenges, and is critical to the decision making process. Women and marginalized communities must be ensured access to education. The United Nations launched its Decade of Education for Sustainable Development (DESD) in 2005 and designated UNESCO as lead agency for the promotion of the Decade....

Justice and ethics
Since the environment affects the very basis of human well-being, it is a matter of justice to consider the impacts of environmental degradation on others, and attempt to minimize harm for both current and future generations. It has been argued that a "global ethic" is required to address the problems of the 21st century (Singer 2002). The intrinsic value of species has also been recognized (IUCN, UNEP and WWF 1991). The pursuit of some people's opportunities and freedoms may harm or limit those of others. It is important that policy-makers consider the adverse effects their decisions have on people and the environment in other areas or regions, since such communities do not participate in local decision making.

Scenario development
The use of scenarios to inform policy processes is growing, providing policy-makers with opportunities to explore the likely impacts and outcomes of various policy decisions. The goal of developing scenarios "is often to support more informed and rational decision making that takes both the known and unknown into account" (MA 2005c). Their purpose is to widen perspectives and illuminate key issues that might otherwise be missed or dismissed. Chapter 9 [of this report] uses four plausible scenarios to explore the impact of different policy decisions on environmental change and future human well-being.

Conclusion

Two decades after *Our Common Future* emphasized the urgency of sustainable development, environmental degradation continues to threaten human well-being, endangering health, physical security, social cohesion and the ability to meet material needs. Analyses throughout *GEO-4* also highlight rapidly disappearing forests, deteriorating landscapes, polluted waters and urban sprawl. The objective is not to present a dark and gloomy scenario, but an urgent call for action.

While progress towards sustainable development has been made through meetings, agreements and changes in environmental governance, real change has been slow. Since 1987, changes to drivers, such as population growth, consumption patterns and energy use, have placed increasing pressure on the state of the environment. To effectively address environmental problems, policy-makers should design policies that tackle both pressures and the drivers behind them. Economic instruments such as market creation and charge systems may be used to help spur environmentally sustainable behaviour. Valuation can help policy-makers make informed decisions about the value of changes to ecosystem services. Non-economic instruments should be used to address both well-known problems with proven solutions and less clear emerging problems. [...]

Imagine a world in which human well-being for all is secure. Every individual has access to clean air and water, ensuring improvements in global health. Global warming has been addressed, through reductions in energy use, and investment in clean technology. Assistance is offered to vulnerable communities. Species flourish as ecosystem integrity is assured. Transforming these images into reality is possible, and it is this generation's responsibility to start doing so.

References

Agarwal, B. (2000). Conceptualizing Environmental Collective Action: Why Gender Matters. In *Cambridge Journal of Economics* 24(3): 283–310

AMAP (2002). *Persistent Organic Pollutants, Heavy Metals, Radioactivity, Human Health, Changing Pathways*. Arctic Monitoring and Assessment Programme, Oslo.

American Rivers (2006). *Elwha River Restoration*. http://www.americanrivers.org/site/PageServer?pagename=AMR_elwharestoration (accessed 12 June 2007)

Bass, S. (2006). *Making poverty Reduction Irreversible: Development Implications of the Millennium Ecosystem Assessment*. IIED Environment for the MDGs' Briefing Paper. International Institute on Environment and Development, London

Bell, D., Robertson, S. and Hunter, P. (2004). Animal origins of SARS Coronavirus: Possible Links with the International Trade of Small Carnivores. In *Philosophical Transactions of the Royal Society London* 359: 1107–14

Bhagwati, J. (2004). *In Defense of Globalization*. Oxford UP, Oxford

Birdsall, N. and Lawrence, R. (1999). Deep Integration and Trade Agreements: Good for Developing Countries? In Grunberg, K. and Stern, M. (eds.) *Global Public*

Goods: International Cooperation in the 21st Century. Oxford UP, New York

Braidotti, R., Charkiewicz, E., Hausler, S. and Wieringa, S. (1994). *Women, the Environment and Sustainable Development.* Zed, London

Brown, D. (1999). Making CSD Work. In *Earth Negotiations Bulletin* 3(2): 2–6

Brown, S. (2006). The West Develops a Taste for Bushmeat. In *New Scientist* 2559: 8

Button, K. and Nijkamp, P. (2004). Introduction: Challenges in Conducting Transatlantic Work on Sustainable Transport and the STELLA/STAR Initiative. In *Transport Reviews* 24 (6): 635–43

Campbell, B., Jeffrey, S., Kozanayi, W., Luckert, M., Mutamba, M. and Zindi, C. (2002). *Household Livelihoods in Semi-arid Regions:Options and Constraints.* Center for International Forestry Research, Bogor

Cargill (2006). *Brazilian Soy Industry Announces Initiative Designed to Curb Soy-Related Deforestation in the Amazon.* http://www.cargill.com/news/issues/ issues_soyannouncement_en.htm (last accessed 11 June 2007)

Carothers, T. and Barndt, W. (2000). Civil Society. In *Foreign Policy* (11):18–29

Castles, S. (2002). *Environmental Change and Forced Migration: Making Sense of the Debate.* New Issues in Refugee Research, Working Paper No. 70. United Nations High Commission for Refugees, Geneva

China Statistical Bureau (1987–2004). *China Statistical Yearbook (1987–2004).* China 28 Statistics Press (in Chinese), Beijing

Christian Reformed Church (2005). *Global Debt. An OSJHA Fact Sheet.* Office of Social Justice and Hunger Action. http://www.crcna.org/site_uploads/uploads/factsheet_ globaldebt.doc (accessed 21 April 2007)

CHS (2006). *Outline of the Report of the Commission on Human Security.* Commission on Human Security. http://www.humansecurity-chs.org/finalreport/Outlines/outline. pdf (accessed 1 May 2007)

CIEL (1991). *The Precautionary Principle: A Policy for Action in the Face of Uncertainty.* King's College, London

Cleaver, F. (2000). Analysing Gender Roles in Community Natural Resource Management: Negotiation, Life Courses, and Social Inclusion. In *IDS Bulletin* 31(2): 60–67

Coe, D.T. and Helpman, E. (1995). *International R&D Spillovers.* NBER Working Papers 4444. National Bureau of Economic Research, Inc, Cambridge, MA

Conca, K. and Dabelko, G. (2002). *Environmental Peacemaking.* Woodrow Wilson Center Press, Washington, DC

Dabelko, D., Lonergan, S. and Matthew, R. (2000). *State of the Art Review of Environmental Security and Co-operation.* Organisation for Economic Cooperation and Development, Paris

Dasgupta, P. (2002). Is Contemporary Economic Development Sustainable? In *Ambio* 31(4): 269–71

Dasgupta, P. and Mäler, K.G. (1999). Net National Product, Wealth, and Social Well-Being. In *Environment and Development Economics* 5: 69–93

DATA (2007). *The DATA Report 2007: Keep the G8 Promise to Africa*. Debt AIDS Trade Africa, London

De Grauwe, P. and Camerman, F. (2003). Are Multinationals Really Bigger Than Nations? In *World Economics* 4 (2): 23–37

Delgado, C., Wada, N., Rosegrant, M., Meijer, S. and Ahmed, M. (2003). Outlook for fish to 2020. In *Meeting Global Demand. A 2020 Vision for Food, Agriculture, and the Environment Initiative*, International Food Policy Research Institute, Washington, DC

Dernbach, J. (2002). *Stumbling Toward Sustainability*. Environmental Law Institute, Washington, DC

DeSombre, E.R. and Barkin, S. (2002). Turbot and Tempers in the North Atlantic. In Matthew, R., Halle, M. and Switzer, J (eds.) *Conserving the Peace: Resources, Livelihoods, and Security*, 325–60. International Institute for Sustainable Development and the World Conservation Union, Winnipeg

Diamond, J. (2005). *Collapse: How Societies Choose to Fail or Survive*. Penguin Books, London

Diener, E. (2000). Subjective Well-being. The Science of Happiness and a Proposal for a National Index. In *The American Psychologist* 55: 34–43

Dodds, F. and Pippard, T. (eds.) (2005). *Human and Environmental Security: An Agenda for Change*. Earthscan, London

Donaldson, S. (2002). Re-thinking the Mercury Contamination Issue in Arctic Canada. MA Thesis (Unpublished). Carleton University, Ottawa, ON

Doubleday, N. (1996). "Commons" Concerns in Search of Uncommon Solutions: Arctic Contaminants, Catalyst of Change? In *The Science of the Total Environment* 186: 169–79

Doubleday, N. (2005). Sustaining Arctic Visions, Values and Ecosystems: Writing Inuit Identity, Reading Inuit Art. In Williams, M. and Humphrys, G. (eds.) *Cape Dorset, Nunavut in Presenting and Representing Environments: Cross-Cultural and Cross-Disciplinary Perspectives*. Springer, Dordrecht

D'Souza, M. and Lobo, C. (2004). Watershed Development, Water Management and the Millennium Development Goals. Paper presented at the Watershed Summit, Chandigarh, 25–27 November 2004. Watershed Organization Trust, Ahmednagar

EM-DAT (undated). *Emergency Events Database: The OFDA/CRED International Disaster Database* (in GEO Data Portal). Université Catholique de Louvain, Brussels

Fa, J., Albrechtsen, L. and Brown. D. (2007). Bushmeat: The Challenge of Balancing Human and Wildlife Needs in African Moist Tropical Forests. In Macdonald, D. and Service, K. (eds.) *Key Topics in Conservation Biology* 206–21. Blackwell Publishing, Oxford

Falk, R. (2000). *Human Rights Horizons: The Pursuit of Justice in a Globalizing World*. Routledge, New York

FAO (2004a). *The State of Food and Agriculture 2003–2004: Agriculture Biotechnology-Meeting the Needs of the Poor?* Food and Agriculture Organization of the United Nations, Rome. http://www.fao.org/WAICENT/FAOINFO/ECONOMIC/ESA/en/ pubs_sofa.htm (accessed 11 June 2007)

FAO (2004b). *The State of the World's Fisheries and Aquaculture 2004.* Food and Agriculture Organization of the United Nations, Rome

Fischetti, M. (2005). Protecting Against the Next Katrina: Wetlands Mitigate flooding, But Are They Too Damaged in the Gulf? In *Scientific American* October 24

Frey, B. and Stutzer, A. (2005). Beyond Outcomes: Measuring Procedural Utility. In *Oxford Economic Papers* 57(1): 90–111

Friedman, T. (2005). *The World is Flat: A Brief History of the Twenty-First Century.* Farrar, Straus, and Giroux, New York

Gallagher, K. (2004). *Free Trade and the Environment: Mexico, NAFTA and Beyond.* Stanford UP, Stanford

GEF (2006). *What Is the GEF?* The Global Environment Facility, Washington, DC http://www.gefweb.org/What_is_the_GEF/what_is_the_gef.html (accessed 1 May 2007)

GEO Data Portal. UNEP's online core database with national, sub-regional, regional and global statistics and maps, covering environmental and socio-economic data and indicators. United Nations Environment Programme, Geneva. http://www.unep.org/geo/data or http://geodata.grid.unep.ch (accessed 12 June 2007)

Goodall, J. (2005). Introduction. In Reynolds, V. (ed.) *The Chimpanzees of the Budongo Forest.* Oxford UP, Oxford

Gore, A. (2006). *An Inconvenient Truth: The Planetary Emergency of Global Warming and What We Can Do About It.* Bloomsbury, London

Government of Brazil (2005). *Diretrizes de Política de Agroenergia 2006–2011.* Ministério da Agricultura, Pecuária e Abastecimento, Ministério da Ciência e Tecnologia, Ministério de Minas e Energia, Ministério do Desenvolvimento, Indústria e Comércio Exterior, Brasilia

Graham, E. (2000). *Fighting the Wrong Enemy: Antiglobal Activists and Multinational Enterprises.* Institute of International Economics, Washington, DC

Greenpeace (2006). *The Future of the Amazon Hangs in the Balance.* http://www.greenpeace.org/usa/news/mcvictory (accessed 11 June 2007)

Grumbine, R. (2007). China's emergence and the Prospects for Global Sustainability. In *BioScience* 57 (3): 249–55

Haass, R. and Litan, R. (1998). Globalization and Its Discontents: Navigating the Dangers of a Tangled World. In *Foreign Affairs* 77(3): 2–6

Hecker, J.H. (2005). *Promoting Environmental Security and Poverty Alleviation in the Peat Swamps of Central Kalimantan, Indonesia.* Institute of Environmental Security, The Hague

Huggins, C., Chenje, M. and Mohamed-Katerere, J.C. (2006). Environment for Peace and Regional Cooperation. In UNEP (2006). *Africa Environment Outlook 2. Our Environment, Our Wealth*. United Nations Environment Programme, Nairobi

IEA (2002). *World Energy Outlook 2003*. International Energy Agency, Paris

IEA (2006a). *World Energy Outlook 2006*. International Energy Agency, Paris

IEA (2006b). *Key Energy Statistics*. International Energy Agency, Paris

IFAD (2001). *Rural Poverty Report 2001. The Challenge of Ending Rural Poverty*. International Fund for Agricultural Development, Rome. http://www.ifad.org/poverty/index.htm (accessed 1 May 2007)

IFPRI (2004). *Ending Hunger in Africa: Prospects for the Small Farmer*. International Food Policy Research Institute, Washington, DC http://www.ifpri.org/pubs/ib/ib16.pdf (accessed 1 May 2007)

IPCC (2001). Technical Summary, *Climate Change 2001: Impacts, Adaptation and Vulnerability*. Contribution of Working Group II to the Third Assessment Report of the Intergovernmental Panel on Climate Change. Intergovernmental Panel on Climate Change. Cambridge UP, New York

IPCC (2007). *Climate Change 2007: The Physical Science Basis. Summary for Policymakers*. Contribution of Working Group 1 to the Fourth Assessment Report of the Intergovernmental Panel on Climate Change, Geneva

ITU (2005). *ITU Yearbook of Statistics*. International Telecommunication Union (in GEO Data Portal)

IUCN, UNEP and WWF (1991). *Caring for the Earth: A Strategy for Sustainable Living*. The World Conservation Union, United Nations Environment Programme and World Wide Fund for Nature, Gland

Jänicke, M. and Volkery, A. (2001). Persistente Probleme des Umweltschutzes. In *Natur und Kultur* 2 (2001): 45–59

Karatayev, A., Padilla, D., Minchin, D., Boltovskoy, D. and Burlakova, L. (2007). Changes in Global Economies and Trade: The Potential Spread of Exotic Freshwater Bivalves. In *Bio Invasions* 9: 161–80

Karesh, W., Cook, R., Bennett, E. and Newcomb, J. (2005). Wildlife Trade and Global Disease Emergence. In *Emerging Infectious Diseases* 11 (7): 1000–02

Katerere, Y. and Hill, R. (2002). Colonialism and Inequality in Zimbabwe. In Matthew, R., Halle, M. and Switzer, J. (eds.) *Conserving the Peace: Resources, Livelihoods, and Security*. International Institute for Sustainable Development and The World Conservation Union, Winnipeg and Gland

Katerere, Y. and Mohamed-Katerere, J. (2005). From Poverty to Prosperity: Harnessing the Wealth of Africa's Forests. In Mery, G., Alfaro, R., Kanninen, M. and Lobovikov, M. (eds.) *Forests in the Global Balance—Changing Paradigms*. IUFRO World Series Vol. 17. International Union of Forest Research Organizations, Helsinki

Keller, W. (2002). Trade and the Transmission of Technology. In *Journal of Economic Growth* 7: 5–24

Kennish, M. (2002). Environmental Threats and Environmental Future of Estuaries. In *Environmental Conservation* 29 (1): 78–107

Kerr J., Pangare G. and Pangare V. (2002). Watershed development projects in India: An evaluation. In *Research Report of the International Food Policy Research Institute* 127: 1–90

Klink, C. and Machado, R. (2005). Conservation of the Brazilian Cerrado. In *Conservation Biology* 19 (3): 707–13

Kolankiewicz, L. and Beck, R. (2001). Weighing Sprawl Factors in Large U.S. Cities, Analysis of U.S. Bureau of the Census Data on the 100 Largest Urbanized Areas of the United States. http://www.sprawlcity.org (accessed 1 May 2007)

Korten, D. (2001). *When Corporations Rule the World*, 2nd edition. Kumarian, Bloomfield

Kura, Y., Revenga, C., Hoshino, E. and Mock, G. (2004). *Fishing for Answers: Making Sense of the Global Fish Crisis*. World Resources Institute, Washington, DC

Langhelle, O. (1999). Sustainable development: exploring the ethics of Our Common Future. In *International Political Science Review* 20 (2): 129–49

Le Billion, P. (2001). The political Ecology of war: natural resources and armed conflict. In *Political Geography* 20: 561–84

LeRoy, E., Rouquet, P., Formenty, P., Souquière, S., Kilbourne, A., Froment, J., Bermejo, M., Smit, S., Karesh, W., Swanepoel, R., Zaki, S. and Rollin, P. (2004). Multiple Ebola virus transmission events and rapid decline of central African wildlife. In *Science* 303: 387–90

Li, W., Shi, Z., Yu, M., Ren, W., Smith, C., Epstein, J., Wang, H., Crameri, G., Hu., Z., Zhang, H., Zhang, J., McEachern, J., Field, H., Daszak, P., Eaton, B., Zhang, S. and Wang, L. (2005). Bats are natural reservoirs of SARS-like coronaviruses. In *Science* 310: 676–79

Loomis, J. (1997). Use of Non-Market Valuations Studies. Water Resources Management Assessments. In *Water Resources Update* 109: 5–9

MA (2003). *Ecosystems and Human Well-being; a framework for assessment*. Millennium Ecosystem Assessment. Island, Washington, DC

MA (2005a). *Ecosystems and Human Well-being: Biodiversity Synthesis*. Millennium Ecosystem Assessment. World Resources Institute. Island, Washington, DC

MA (2005b). *Ecosystems and Human Well-being: Synthesis Report*. Millennium Ecosystem Assessment. Island, Washington, DC

MA (2005c). *Ecosystems and Human Well-being: Volume 2—Scenarios*. Millennium Ecosystem Assessment. Island, Washington, DC

MacDonald, D. and Service, K. (2007). *Key Topics in Conservation Biology*. Blackwell Publications, Oxford

Mäler, K-G. (1974). *Environmental Economics: A Theoretical Enquiry*. John Hopkins UP, Baltimore

Maltais, A., Dow, K. and Persson, A. (2003). *Integrating Perspectives on Environmental Security*. SEI Risk and Vulnerability Programme, Report 2003–1. Stockholm Environment Institute, Stockholm

Matthew, R., Halle, M. and Switzer, J. (eds.) (2002). *Conserving the Peace: Resources, Livelihoods and Security*. International Institute for Sustainable Development, Winnipeg

Matthews, D. (1995). Common versus open access. The collapse of Canada's east coast fishery. In *The Ecologist* 25: 86–96

Matutinovic, I. (2006). Mass migrations, income inequality and ecosystem health in the second wave of globalization. In *Ecological Economics* 59: 199–203

McMichael, A. (2001). Human culture, ecological change and infectious disease: are we experiencing history's fourth great transition? In *Ecosystem Health* 7: 107–15

McMichael, A. (2004). Environmental and social influences on emerging infectious disease: past, present and future. *Philosophical Transactions of the Royal Society of London Biology* 10: 1–10

Meredith, M. (2005). *The State of Africa: A history of fifty years of independence*. Free Press, London

Mittelman, J. (2000). *Capturing Globalization*. Carfax, Abingdon

Myers, N. (1997). Environmental Refugees. In *Population and Environment* 19(2): 167–82

Najam, A., Runnalls, D. and Halle, M. (2007). *Environment and Globalization: Five Propositions*. International Institute for Sustainable Development, Winnipeg

Nishikiori, N., Abe, T., Costa, D., Dharmaratne, S., Kunii, O. and Moji, K. (2006). Who died as a result of the tsunami? Risk factors of mortality among internally displaced persons in Sri Lanka: a retrospective cohort analysis. In *BMC Public Health* 6: 73

OECD (1994). *The Environmental Effects of Trade*. Organisation for Economic Co-operation and Development, Paris

OECD (2005). *Trade that Benefits the Environment and Development: Opening Markets for Environmental Goods and Services*. Organisation for Economic Co-operation and Development, Paris

Oxfam (2005). *The Tsunami's Impact on Women*. Oxfam Briefing Note. http://www.oxfam.org.uk/what_we_do/issues/conflict_disasters/bn_tsunami_women.htm (accessed 11 June 2007)

Panayotou, T. (1994). *Economic Instruments for environmental Management and Sustainable Development*. Environmental Economics series Paper No.1, United Nations Environment Programme, Nairobi

Peiris, J., Guan, Y. and Yuen, K. (2004). Severe acute respiratory syndrome. In *Nature Medicine* 10 (12): S88–S97

Pelling, M. and Uitto, J. (2001). Small island developing states: natural disaster vulnerability and global change. In *Environmental Hazards* 3: 49–62

Peterson, D. (2003). *Eating Apes*. University of California Press, London

Prakash, A. (2000). Responsible Care: An Assessment. In *Business and Society* 39(2): 183–209

Rahnema, M. (ed.) (1997). *The Post-Development Reader*. Zed Books, London

Russett, B. and Oneal, J. (2001). *Triangulating Peace: Democracy, Interdependence, and International Organizations*, The Norton Series in World Politics. W.W. Norton and Company, London

Sen, A. (1985). *Commodities and Capabilities*, Oxford UP, Oxford

Sen, A. (1992). *Inequality Re-examined*. Clarendon, Oxford

Sen, A. (1999). *Development as Freedom*. Oxford UP, Oxford

Shiva, V. (1991). *The Violence of the Green Revolution: Third World Agriculture, Ecology and Politics*. Zed Books, London

Singer, P. (2002). *One World*. Yale UP, London

Smith, K. (2006). Oil from Bombed Plant Left to Spill. In *Nature* 442: 609

Solow, R.M. (1991). Sustainability: An Economist's Perspective. The Eighteen J. Seward Johnson Lecture to the Marine Policy Center, Woods Hole Oceanographic Institution. In Dorfman, R. and Dorfman, N.S. (eds.) *Economics of the Environment: Selected Readings*. Norton, New York

Spencer, D. (2001). Will They Survive? Prospects for Small Farmers in sub-Saharan Africa. *Paper Presented in Vision 2020: Sustainable Food Security for All by 2020*. International Conference Organized by the International Food Policy Research Institute (IFPRI), September 4–6, 2001, Bonn

Speth, J. (2004). *Red Sky at Morning: America and the Crisis of the Global Environment*. Yale UP, New Haven and London

Stefano, P., Von Ritter, K. and Bishop, J. (2004). *Assessing the Economic Value of Ecosystem Conservation*. Environment Development Paper No.101. The World Bank, Washington, DC

Stohr, W. (2001). Introduction. In Stohr, W., Edralin, J. and Mani, D. (eds.) *New Regional Development Paradigms: Decentralization, Governance and the New Planning for Local-Level Development*. (ed.). Contributions in Economic History Series (225). Published in cooperation with the United Nations and the United Nations Centre for Regional Development. Greenwood Press, Westport, CT

UN (2000). *United Nations Millennium Declaration*. United Nations, New York. http://www.un.org/millennium/declaration/ares552e.htm (accessed 1 May 2007)

UN (2002). *Report of the World Summit on Sustainable Development*. Johannesburg, South Africa, 26 August–4 September. A/CONF.199/20. United Nations, New York

UN (2004). *Human Rights and Poverty Reduction. A Conceptual Framework*. United Nations Office of the High Commissioner for Human Rights. United Nations, New York and Geneva

UN (2006). *Trends in Total Migrant Stock: The 2005 Revision*. Population Division of the Department of Economic and Social Affairs of the United Nations Secretariat, New

York. http://www.un.org/esa/population/publications/migration/UN_Migrant_Stock_Documentation_2005.pdf (accessed 1 May 2007)

UNAIDS (2006). *2006 Report on Global AIDS Epidemic.* United Nations Programme on HIV/AIDS, Geneva

UNDP (2004). *Human Development Report 2001: Making New Technologies Work for Human Development.* United Nations Development Programme, New York

UNDP (2005a). *Environmental Sustainability in 100 Millennium Development Goals Country Report.* United Nations Development Programme, New York

UNDP (2005b). *Human Development Report 2005: International Cooperation at a Crossroads.* United Nations Development Programme, New York

UNDP (2006) *Human Development Report 2006. Beyond Scarcity: Power, Poverty and the Global Water Crisis.* United Nations Development Programme, New York

UNEP (2002). *Global Environment Outlook (GEO-3).* United Nations Environment Programme, Nairobi

UNEP (2004b). *GEO Year Book 2003.* United Nations Environment Programme, Nairobi

UNEP (2005a). *GEO yearbook 2004/2005.* United Nations Environment Programme, Nairobi

UNEP (2005b). *One Planet Many People: Atlas of Our Changing Environment.* United Nations Environment Programme, Nairobi

UNEP (2006). Avian Influenza and the Environment: An Ecohealth Perspective. Paper prepared by David J. Rapport on behalf of UNEP, United Nations Environment Programme and EcoHealth Consulting, Nairobi

UNESCO (2007). *United Nations Decade of Education for Sustainable Development (2005–2014).* http://portal.unesco.org/education/en/ev.php-URL_ID=27234&URL_DO=DO_TOPIC&URL_SECTION=201.html/ (accessed 25 June 2007)

UNESCO-WWAP (2006*). Water for People. Water for Life: The United Nations World Water Development Report.* United Nations Educational, Scientific and Cultural Organization, Paris and Berghahn Books, Oxford and New York

UN-Habitat (2006). *State of the World's Cities 2006/7.* United Nations-Habitat, Nairobi

UNHCR (2006a). *Statistical Yearbook 2004 Country Data Sheets: Guinea.* United Nations High Commission for Refugees, Geneva

UNHCR (2006b). *2005 Global Refugee Trends Statistical Overview of Populations of Refugees, Asylum-seekers, Internally Displaced Persons, Stateless Persons, and Other Persons of Concern to UNHCR.* United Nations High Commission for Refugees, Geneva

UNICEF (2006). *Pneumonia: The Forgotten Killer of Children.* United Nations Children's Fund and World Health Organization, New York

UNPD (2005). *World Urbanisation Prospects: The 2005 Revision* (in GEO Data Portal). UN Population Division, New York. http://www.un.org/esa/population/unpop.htm (accessed 4 June 2007)

UNPD (2007). *World Population Prospects: The 2006 Revision* (in GEO Data Portal). UN Population Division, New York. http://www.un.org/esa/population/unpop. htm (accessed 4 June 2007)

USGS (2006). Studying the Elwha River, Washington, in Preparation for Dam Removal. In *Sound Waves Monthly Newsletter*. US Geological Survey, Washington, DC. http://soundwaves.usgs.gov/2006/11/fieldwork3.html (accessed 12 June 2007)

Van Oostdam, J., Donaldson, S., Feeley, M., Arnold, D., Ayotte, P., Bondy, G., Chan, L., Dewaily, E., Furgal, C.M., Kuhnlein, H., Loring, E., Muckle, G., Myles, E., Receveur, O., Tracy, B., Gill, U., Kalhok, S. (2005). Human health implications of environmental contaminants in Arctic Canada: A review. In *Science of the Total Environment* 351–52: 165–246

Watson, R., Zinyower, M. and Dokken, D. (eds.) (1997). *The Regional Impacts of Climate Change: An Assessment of Vulnerability. Summary for Decision Makers*. Special Report of IPCC Working Group II. Intergovernmental Panel on Climate Change

WBCSD (2007). Then & Now: Celebrating the 20th Anniversary of the "Brundtland Report"—2006 WBCSD Annual Review. World Business Council for Sustainable Development, Geneva

WCED (1987). *Our Common Future*. Oxford UP, Oxford

WHO (2000). *Guidelines for Air Quality*. WHO/SDE/OEH/00.02, World Health Organization, Geneva

WHO (2002). *The World Health Report: Reducing Risks, Promoting Healthy Life*. World Health Organization, Geneva

WHO (2006). *Preventing Disease Through Healthy Environments: Towards an Estimate of the Environmental Burden of Disease*. World Health Organization, Geneva

WHO and UNICEF (2004). *Meeting the MDG Drinking-water and Sanitation Target: A Mid-term Assessment of Progress*. World Health Organization and United Nations Children's Fund, Geneva and New York

Wolfe, N., Escalante, A., Karesh, W., Kilbourn, A., Spielman, A. and Lal, A. (1998). Wild Primate Populations in Emerging Infectious Disease Research: The Missing Link? In *Emerging Infectious Diseases* 4 (2):148–59

Wolfe, N., Heneine, W., Carr, J., Garcia, A., Shanmugam, V., Tamoufe, U., Torimiro, J., Prosser, T., LeBreton, M., Mpoudi-Ngole, E., McCutchan, F., Birx, D., Folks, T., Burke, D. and Switzer, W. (2005). Emergence of Unique Primate T-lymphotropic Viruses Among Central African Bushmeat hunters. In *Proceedings of the National Academy of Sciences* 102 (22): 7994–99

Wolfe, N., Switzer, W., Carr, J., Bhullar, V., Shanmugam, V., Tamoufe, U., Prosser, A., Torimiro, J., Wright, A., Mpoudi-Ngole, E., McCutchan, F., Birx, D., Folks, T., Burke, D. and Heneine, W. (2004). Naturally Acquired Simian Retrovirus Infections in Central African Hunters. In *The Lancet* 363:932–37

Wood, W.B. (2001). Ecomigration: Linkages between environmental change and Migration. In Zolberg, A.R. and Benda, P.M. (eds.) *Global Migrants, Global Refugees*. Berghahn, Oxford

World Bank (2005). *The Little Data Book 2005*. The World Bank, Washington, DC

World Bank (2006a). *Where Is the Wealth of Nations? Measuring Capital for the 21st Century*. The World Bank, Washington, DC

World Bank (2006b). *World Development Indicators 2006* (in GEO Data Portal). The World Bank, Washington, DC

World Bank and Wildlife Conservation Society (2006). *The Silent Steppe: The Illegal Wildlife Trade Crisis*. The World Bank, Washington, DC

WRI (2005). *World Resources 2005: The Wealth of the Poor—Managing Ecosystems to Fight Poverty*. World Resources Institute in Collaboration with the United Nations Development Programme, the United Nations Environment Programme and The World Bank. World Resources Institute, Washington, DC

WTO (2006). *World Trade Report 2006: Exploring the Links between Subsidies, Trade and the WTO*. World Trade Organization, Geneva

32. Living on a Lifeboat*

Garrett Hardin

Susanne Langer (1942) has shown that it is probably impossible to approach an unsolved problem save through the door of metaphor. Later, attempting to meet the demands of rigor, we may achieve some success in cleansing theory of metaphor, though our success is limited if we are unable to avoid using common language, which is shot through and through with fossil metaphors. (I count no less than five in the preceding two sentences.)

Since metaphorical thinking is inescapable it is pointless merely to weep about our human limitations. We must learn to live with them, to understand them, and to control them. "All of us," said George Eliot in Middlemarch, "get our thoughts entangled in metaphors, and act fatally on the strength of them." To avoid unconscious suicide we are well advised to pit one metaphor against another. From the interplay of competitive metaphors, thoroughly developed, we may come closer to metaphor-free solutions to our problems.

No generation has viewed the problem of the survival of the human species as seriously as we have. Inevitably, we have entered this world of concern through the door of metaphor. Environmentalists have emphasized the image of the earth as a spaceship—Spaceship Earth. Kenneth Boulding (1966) is the principal architect of this metaphor. It is time, he says, that we replace the wasteful "cowboy economy" of the past with the frugal "spaceship economy" required for continued survival in the limited world we now see ours to be. The metaphor is notably useful in justifying pollution control measures. Unfortunately, the image of a spaceship is also used to promote measures that are suicidal. One of these is a generous immigration policy, which is only a particular instance of a class of policies that are in error because they lead to the tragedy of the commons (Hardin 1968). These suicidal policies are attractive because they mesh with what we unthinkingly take to be the ideals of "the best people." What is missing in the idealistic view is an insistence that rights and responsibilities

---

* Source: *BioScience* 24.10 (October 1974).

must go together. The "generous" attitude of all too many people results in asserting inalienable rights while ignoring or denying matching responsibilities.

For the metaphor of a spaceship to be correct the aggregate of people on board would have to be under unitary sovereign control (Ophuls 1974). A true ship always has a captain. It is conceivable that a ship could be run by a committee: But it could not possibly survive if its course were determined by bickering tribes that claimed rights without responsibilities.

What about Spaceship Earth? It certainly has no captain, and no executive committee. The United Nations is a toothless tiger, because the signatories of its charter wanted it that way. The spaceship metaphor is used only to justify spaceship demands on common resources without acknowledging corresponding spaceship responsibilities.

An understandable fear of decisive action leads people to embrace "incrementalism"—moving toward reform by tiny stages. As we shall see, this strategy is counterproductive in the area discussed here if it means accepting rights before responsibilities. Where human survival is at stake, the acceptance of responsibilities is a precondition to the acceptance of rights, if the two cannot be introduced simultaneously.

Lifeboat Ethics

Before taking up certain substantive issues let us look at an alternative metaphor, that of a lifeboat. In developing some relevant examples the following numerical values are assumed. Approximately two-thirds of the world is desperately poor, and only one third is comparatively rich. The people in poor countries have an average per capita GNP (Gross National Product) of about $200 per year; the rich, of about $3,000. (For the United States it is nearly $5,000 per year.) Metaphorically, each rich nation amounts to a lifeboat full of comparatively rich people. The poor of the world, are in other, much more crowded lifeboats. Continuously, so to speak, the poor fall out of their lifeboats and swim for a while in the water outside, hoping to be admitted to a rich lifeboat, or in some other way to benefit from the "goodies" on board. What should the passengers on a rich lifeboat do? This is the central problem of "the ethics of a lifeboat."

First we must acknowledge that each lifeboat is effectively limited in capacity. The land of every nation has a limited carrying capacity. The exact limit is a matter for argument, but the energy crunch is convincing more people every day that we have already exceeded the carrying capacity of the land. We have been living on "capital"—stored petroleum and coal—and soon we must live on income alone.

Let us look at only one lifeboat—ours. The ethical problem is the same for all, and is as follows. Here we sit, say, 50 people in a lifeboat. To be generous, let us assume our boat has a capacity of 10 more, making 60. (This, however, is to violate the engineering principle of the "safety factor." A new plant disease or a bad change in the weather may decimate our population if we don't preserve some excess capacity as a safety factor.)

The 50 of us in the lifeboat see 100 others swimming in the water outside, asking for admission to the boat, or for handouts. How shall we respond to their calls? There are several possibilities.

One. We may be tempted to try to live by the Christian ideal of being "our brother's keeper," or by the Marxian ideal (Marx 1875) of "from each according to his abilities, to each according to his needs." Since the needs of all are the same, we take all the needy into our boat, making a total of 150 in a boat with a capacity of 60. The boat is swamped, and everyone drowns. Complete justice, complete catastrophe.

Two. Since the boat has an unused excess capacity of 10, we admit just 10 more to it. This has the disadvantage of getting rid of the safety factor, for which action we will sooner or later pay dearly. Moreover, *which* 10 do we let in? "First come, first served?" The best 10? The neediest 10? How do we *discriminate*? And what do we say to the 90 who are excluded?

Three. Admit no more to the boat and preserve the small safety factor. Survival of the people in the lifeboat is then possible (though we shall have to be on our guard against boarding parties).

The last solution is abhorrent to many people. It is unjust, they say. Let us grant that it is.

"I feel guilty about my good luck," say some. The reply to this is simple: *Get out and yield your place to others.* Such a selfless action might satisfy the conscience of those who are addicted to guilt but it would not change the ethics of the lifeboat. The needy person to whom a guilt-addict yields his place will not himself feel guilty about his sudden good luck. (If he did he would not climb aboard.) The net result of conscience-stricken people relinquishing their unjustly held positions is the elimination of their kind of conscience from the lifeboat. The lifeboat, as it were, purifies itself of guilt. The ethics of the lifeboat persist, unchanged by such momentary aberrations.

This then is the basic metaphor within which, we must work out our solutions. Let us enrich the image step by step with substantive additions from the real world.

Reproduction

The harsh characteristics of lifeboat ethics are heightened by reproduction, particularly by reproductive differences. The people inside the lifeboats of the wealthy nations are doubling in numbers every 87 years; those outside are doubling every 35 years, on the average. And the relative difference in prosperity is becoming greater.

Let us, for a while, think primarily of the US lifeboat. As of 1973 the United States had a population of 210 million people, who were increasing by 0.8% per year, that is, doubling in number every 87 years.

Although the citizens of rich nations are outnumbered two to one by the poor, let us imagine an equal number of poor people outside our lifeboat—a mere 210 million poor people reproducing at a quite different rate. If we imagine these to be the combined populations of Colombia, Venezuela, Ecuador, Morocco, Thailand, Pakistan, and the Philippines, the average rate of increase of the people "outside" is 3.3% per year. The doubling time of this population is 21 years.

Suppose that all these countries, and the United States, agreed to live by the Marxian ideal, "to each according to his needs," the ideal of most Christians as well. Needs, of course, are determined by population size, which is affected by reproduction. Every nation regards its rate of reproduction as a sovereign right. If our lifeboat were big enough in the beginning it might be possible to live *for a while* by Christian-Marxian ideals.

Might.

Initially, in the model given, the ratio of non-Americans to Americans would be one to one. But consider what the ratio would be 87 years later. By this time Americans would have doubled to a population of 420 million. The other, group (doubling every 21 years) would now have swollen to *3,540* million. Each American would have more than eight people to share with. How could the lifeboat possibly keep afloat?

All this involves extrapolation of current trends into the future, and is consequently suspect. Trends may change. Granted: but the change will not necessarily be favorable. If—as seems likely—the rate of population increase falls faster in the ethnic group presently inside the lifeboat than it does among those now outside, the future will turn out to be even worse than mathematics predicts, and sharing will be even more suicidal.

Ruin in the Commons

The fundamental error of the sharing ethics is that it leads to the tragedy of the commons. Under a system of private property the man (or group of men) who own property recognize their responsibility to care for it, for if they don't they will eventually suffer. A farmer, for instance, if he is intelligent, will allow no more cattle in a pasture than its carrying capacity justifies. If he overloads the pasture, weeds take over, erosion sets in, and the owner loses in the long run.

But if a pasture is run as a commons open to all, the right of each to use it is not matched by an operational responsibility to take care of it. It is no use asking independent herdsmen in a commons to act responsibly, for they dare not. The considerate herdsman who refrains from overloading the commons suffers more than a selfish one who says his needs are greater. (As Leo Durocher says, "Nice guys finish last.") Christian-Marxian idealism is counterproductive. That it *sounds* nice is no excuse. With distribution systems, as with individual morality, good intentions are no substitute for good performance.

A social system is stable only if it is insensitive to errors. To the Christian-Marxian idealist a selfish person is a sort of "error." Prosperity in the system of the commons cannot survive errors. If *everyone* would only restrain himself, all would be well; but it takes *only one less than everyone* to ruin a system of voluntary restraint. In a crowded world of less than perfect human beings—and we will never know any other—mutual ruin is inevitable in the commons. This is the core of the tragedy of the commons.

One of the major tasks of education today is to create such an awareness of the dangers of the commons that people will be able to recognize its many varieties, however disguised. There is pollution of the air and water because these media are treated as commons. Further growth of population and growth in the per capita conversion of natural resources into pollutants require that the system of the commons be modified or abandoned in the disposal of "externalities."

The fish populations of the oceans are exploited as commons, and ruin lies ahead. No technological invention can prevent this fate: in fact, all improvements in the art of fishing merely hasten the day of complete ruin. Only the replacement of the system of the commons with a responsible system can save oceanic fisheries.

The management of western range lands, though nominally rational, is in fact (under the steady pressure of cattle ranchers) often merely a government-sanctioned system of the commons, drifting toward ultimate ruin for both the rangelands and the residual enterprisers.

World Food Banks

In the international arena we have recently heard a proposal to create a new commons, namely an international depository of food reserves to which nations will contribute according to their abilities, and from which nations may draw according to their needs. Nobel laureate Norman Borlaug has lent the prestige of his name to this proposal.

A world food bank appeals powerfully to our humanitarian impulses. We remember John Donne's celebrated line, "Any man's death diminishes me." But before we rush out to see for whom the bell tolls let us recognize where the greatest political push for international granaries comes from, lest we be disillusioned later. Our experience with Public Law 480 clearly reveals the answer. This was the law that moved billions of dollars worth of U.S. grain to food-short, population-long countries during the past two decades. When P.L. 480 first came into being, a headline in the business magazine *Forbes* (Paddock and Paddock 1970) revealed the power behind it: "Feeding the World's Hungry Millions: How it will mean billions for U.S. business."

And indeed it did. In the years 1960 to 1970 a total of $7.9 billion was spent on the "Food for Peace" program, as P.L. 480 was called. During the years 1948 to

1970 an additional $49.9 billion were extracted from American taxpayers to pay for other economic aid programs, some of which went for food and food-producing machinery. (This figure does *not* include military aid.) That P.L. 480 was a give-away program was concealed. Recipient countries went through the motions of paying for P.L. 480 food—with IOU's. In December 1973 the charade was brought to an end as far as India was concerned when the United States "forgave" India's $3.2 billion debt (Anonymous 1974). Public announcement of the cancellation of the debt was delayed for two months: one wonders why.

"Famine—1974!" (Paddock and Paddock 1970) is one of the few publications that points out the commercial roots of this humanitarian attempt. Though all U.S. taxpayers lost by P.L. 480, special interest groups gained handsomely. Farmers benefited because they were not asked to contribute the grain—it was bought from them by the taxpayers. Besides the direct benefit there was the indirect effect of increasing demand and thus raising prices of farm products generally. The manufacturers of farm machinery, fertilizers, and pesticides benefited by the farmers' extra efforts to grow more food. Grain elevators profited from storing the grain for varying lengths of time. Railroads made money hauling it to port, and shipping lines by carrying it overseas. Moreover, once the machinery for P.L. 480 was established an immense bureaucracy had a vested interest in its continuance regardless of its merits.

Very little was ever heard of these 'selfish' interests when P.L. 480 was defended in public. The emphasis was always on its humanitarian effects. The combination of multiple and relatively silent selfish interests with highly vocal humanitarian apologists constitutes a powerful lobby for extracting money from taxpayers. Foreign aid has become a habit that can apparently survive in the absence of any known justification. A news commentator in a weekly magazine (Lansner 1974), after exhaustively going over all the conventional arguments for foreign aid—self-interest, social justice, political advantage, and charity—and concluding that none of the known arguments really held water, concluded: "So the search continues for some logically compelling reasons for giving aid..." In other words. *Act now, Justify later*—if ever. (Apparently a quarter of a century is too short a time to find the justification for expending several billion dollars yearly.)

The search for a rational justification can be short-circuited by interjecting the word "emergency." Borlaug uses this word. We need to look sharply at it: What is an "emergency"? It is surely something like an accident, which is correctly defined as *an event that is certain to happen, though with a low frequency* (Hardin 1972a). A well-run organization prepares for everything that is certain, including accidents and emergencies. It budgets for them. It saves for them. It expects them—and mature decision-makers do not waste time complaining about accidents when they occur.

What happens if some organizations budget for emergencies and others do not? If each organization is solely responsible for its own well-being, poorly managed ones will suffer. But they should be able to learn from experience. They have a chance to mend their ways and learn to budget for infrequent but certain emergencies. The weather, for instance, always varies and periodic crop failures are certain. A wise and competent government saves out of the production of the good years in anticipation of bad years that are sure to come. This is not a new idea. The Bible tells us that Joseph taught this policy to Pharaoh in Egypt more than 2,000 years ago. Yet it is literally true that the vast majority of the governments of the world today have no such policy. They lack either the wisdom or the competence, or both. Far more difficult than the transfer of wealth from one country to another is the transfer of wisdom between sovereign powers or between generations.

"But it isn't their fault! How can we blame the poor people who are caught in an emergency? Why must we punish them?" The concepts of blame and punishment are irrelevant. The question is, what are the operational consequences of establishing a world food bank? If it is open to every country every time a need develops, slovenly rulers will not be motivated to take Joseph's advice. Why should they? Others will bail them out whenever they are in trouble.

Some countries will make deposits in the world food bank and others will withdraw from it: there will be almost no overlap. Calling such a depository-transfer unit a "bank" is stretching the metaphor of *bank* beyond its elastic limits. The proposers, of course, never call attention to the metaphorical nature of the word they use.

The Ratchet Effect

An "international food bank" is really, then, not a true bank but a disguised oneway transfer device for moving wealth from rich countries to poor. In the absence of such a bank, in a world inhabited by individually responsible sovereign nations, the population of each nation would repeatedly go through a cycle of the sort shown in Figure 1. P2 is greater than P1, either in absolute numbers or because a deterioration of the food supply has removed the safety factor and produced a dangerously low ratio of resources to population. P2 may be paid to represent a state of overpopulation, which becomes obvious upon the appearance of an "accident," e.g., a crop failure. If the "emergency" is not met by outside help, the population drops back to the "normal" level—the "carrying capacity" of the environment—or even below. In the absence of population control by a sovereign, sooner or later the population grows to P2 again and the cycle repeats. The long-term population curve (Hardin 1966) is an irregularly fluctuating one, equilibrating more or less about the carrying capacity.

A demographic cycle of this sort, obviously involves great suffering in the restrictive phase, but such a cycle is normal to any independent country with inadequate population control. The third century theologian Tertullian (Hardin 1969a) expressed what must have been the recognition of many wise men when he wrote: "The scourges of pestilence, famine, wars, and earthquakes have come to be regarded as a blessing to overcrowded nations, since they serve to prune away the luxuriant growth of the human race."

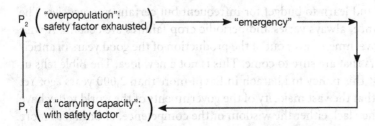

Fig. 1 The population cycle of a nation that has no effective, conscious population control, and which receives no aid from the outside. P2 is greater than P1.

Only under a strong and farsighted sovereign—which theoretically could be the people themselves, democratically organized—can a population equilibrate at some set point below the carrying capacity, thus avoiding the pains normally caused by periodic and unavoidable disasters. For this happy state to be achieved it is necessary that those in power be able to contemplate with equanimity the "waste" of surplus food in times of bountiful harvests. It is essential that those in power resist the temptation to convert extra food into extra babies. On the public relations level it is necessary that the phrase "surplus food" be replaced by "safety factor."

But wise sovereigns seem not to exist in the poor world today. The most anguishing problems are created by poor countries that are governed by rulers insufficiently wise and powerful. If such countries can draw on a world food bank in times of "emergency," the population *cycle* of Figure 1 will be replaced by the population *escalator* of Figure 2. The input of food from a food bank acts as the pawl of a ratchet, preventing the population from retracing its steps to a lower level. Reproduction pushes the population upward; inputs from the world bank prevent its moving downward. Population size escalates, as does the absolute magnitude of "accidents" and "emergencies." The process is brought to an end only by the total collapse of the whole system, producing a catastrophe of scarcely imaginable proportions.

Such are the implications of the well-meant sharing of food in a world of irresponsible reproduction.

I think we need a new word for systems like this. The adjective "melioristic" is applied to systems that produce continual improvement; the English word is derived from the Latin *meliorare*, to become or make better. Parallel with this it would be useful to bring in the word *pejoristic* (from the Latin *pejorare*, to become or make worse). This word can be applied to those systems which, by their very nature, can be relied upon to make matters worse. A world food bank coupled with sovereign state irresponsibility in reproduction is an example of a pejoristic system.

This pejoristic system creates an unacknowledged commons. People have more motivation to draw from than to add to the common store. The license to make such

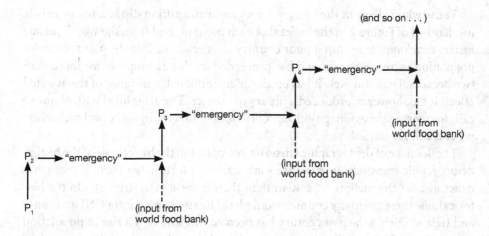

Fig. 2 The population escalator. Note that input from a world food bank acts like the pawl of a ratchet, preventing the normal population cycle shown in Figure 1 from being completed. Pn+1 is greater than Pn, and the absolute magnitude of the "emergencies" escalates. Ultimately the entire system crashes. The crash is not shown, and few can imagine it.

withdrawals diminishes whatever motivation poor countries might otherwise have to control their populations. Under the guidance of this ratchet, wealth can be steadily moved in one direction only, from the slowly-breeding rich to the rapidly-breeding poor, the process finally coming to a halt only when all countries are equally and miserably poor.

All this is terribly obvious once we are acutely aware of the pervasiveness and danger of the commons. But many people still lack this awareness and the euphoria of the "benign demographic transition" (Hardin 1973) interferes with the realistic appraisal of pejoristic mechanisms. As concerns public policy, the deductions drawn from the benign demographic transition are these:

1) If the per capita GNP rises the birth rate will fall; hence, the rate of population increase will fall, ultimately producing ZPG (Zero Population Growth).

2) The long-term trend all over the world (including the poor countries) is of a rising per capita GNP (for which no limit is seen).

3) Therefore, all political interference in population matters is unnecessary; all we need to do is foster economic "development"—*note the metaphor*—and population problems will solve themselves.

Those who believe in the benign demographic transition dismiss the pejoristic mechanism of Figure 2 in the belief that each input of food from the world outside fosters development within a poor country thus resulting in a drop in the rate of population increase. Foreign aid has proceeded on this assumption for more than two decades. Unfortunately it has produced no indubitable instance of the asserted effect. It has, however, produced a library of excuses. The air is filled with plaintive calls for more massive foreign aid appropriations so that the hypothetical melioristic process can get started.

The doctrine of demographic laissez-faire implicit in the hypothesis of the benign demographic transition is immensely attractive. Unfortunately there is more evidence against the melioristic system than there is for it (Davis 1963). On the historical side there are many counter-examples. The rise in per capita GNP in France and Ireland during the past century has been accompanied by a rise in population growth. In the 20 years following the Second World War the same positive correlation was noted almost everywhere in the world. Never in world history before 1950 did the worldwide population growth reach 1% per annum. Now the average population growth is over 2% and shows no signs of slackening.

On the theoretical side, the denial of the pejoristic scheme of Figure 2 probably springs from the hidden acceptance of the "cowboy economy" that Boulding castigated. Those who recognize the limitations of a spaceship, if they are unable to achieve population control at a safe and comfortable level, accept the necessity of the corrective feedback of the population cycle shown in Figure 1. No one who knew in his bones that he was living on a true spaceship would countenance political support of the population escalator shown in Figure 2.

Eco-Destruction via the Green Revolution

The demoralizing effect of charity on the recipient has long been known. "Give a man a fish and he will eat for a day: teach him how to fish and he will eat for the rest of his days." So runs an ancient Chinese proverb. Acting on this advice the Rockefeller and Ford Foundations have financed a multipronged program for improving agriculture in the hungry nations. The result, known as the "Green Revolution," has been quite remarkable. "Miracle wheat" and "miracle rice" are splendid technological achievements in the realm of plant genetics.

Whether or not the Green Revolution can increase food production is doubtful (Harris 1972, Paddock 1970, Wilkes 1972), but in any event not particularly important. What is missing in this great and well-meaning humanitarian effort is a firm grasp of fundamentals. Considering the importance of the Rockefeller Foundation in this effort it is ironic that the late Alan Gregg, a much-respected vice-president of the Foundation, strongly expressed his doubts of the wisdom of all attempts to increase food production some two decades ago. (This was before Borlaug's work—supported by Rockefeller—had resulted in the development of "miracle wheat.") Gregg (1955) likened the growth and spreading of humanity over the surface of the earth to the metastasis of cancer in the human body, wryly remarking that "Cancerous growths demand food; but, as far as I know, they have never been cured by getting it."

"Man does not live by bread alone"—the scriptural statement has a rich meaning even in the material realm. Every human being born constitutes a draft on all aspects of the environment—food, air, water, unspoiled scenery, occasional and optional solitude, beaches, contact with wild animals, fishing, hunting—the list is long and incompletely known. Food can, perhaps, be significantly increased: but what about clean beaches, unspoiled forests, and solitude? If we satisfy the need for food in a growing population we necessarily decrease the supply of other goods, and thereby increase the difficulty of equitably allocating scarce goods (Hardin 1969b, 1972b).

The present population of India is 600 million, and it is increasing by 15 million per year. The environmental load of this population is already great. The forests of India are only a small fraction of what they were three centuries ago. Soil erosion, floods, and the psychological costs of crowding are serious. Every one of the net 15 million lives added each year stresses the Indian environment more severely. *Every life saved this year in a poor country diminishes the quality of life for subsequent generations.*

Observant critics have shown how much harm we wealthy nations have already done to poor nations through our well-intentioned but misguided attempts to help them (Paddock and Paddock 1973). Particularly reprehensible is our failure to carry out postaudits of these attempts (Farvar and Milton 1972). Thus have we shielded our tender consciences from knowledge of the harm we have done. Must we Americans continue to fail to monitor the consequences of our external "do-gooding?" If, for instance, we thoughtlessly make it possible for the present 600 million Indians to swell to 1,200 million by the year 2001—as their present growth rate promises—will posterity in India thank *us* for facilitating an even greater destruction of *their* environment? Are good intentions ever a sufficient excuse for bad consequences?

Immigration Creates a Commons

I come now to the final example of a commons in action, one for which the public is least prepared for rational discussion. The topic is at present enveloped by a great silence which reminds me of a comment made by Sherlock Holmes in A. Conan Doyle's story, "Silver Blaze." Inspector Gregory had asked, "Is there any point to which you would wish to draw my attention?" To this Holmes responded:

"To the curious incident of the dog in the night-time."

"The dog did nothing in the night-time," said the Inspector.

"That was the curious incident," remarked Sherlock Holmes.

By asking himself what would repress the normal barking instinct of a watch dog Holmes realized that it must be the dog's recognition of his master as the criminal trespasser. In a similar way we should ask ourselves what repression keeps us from discussing something as important as immigration?

It cannot be that immigration is numerically of no consequence. Our government acknowledges a *net* inflow of 400,000 a year. Hard data are understandably lacking on the extent of illegal entries, but a not implausible figure is 600,000 per year (Buchanan 1973). The natural increase of the resident population is now about 1.7 million per year. This means that the yearly gain from immigration is at least 19%, and may be 37%, of the total increase. It is quite conceivable that educational campaigns like that of Zero Population Growth, Inc., coupled with adverse social and economic factors—inflation, housing shortage, depression, and loss of confidence in national leaders—may lower the fertility of American women to a point at which all of the yearly increase in population would be accounted for by immigration. Should we not at least ask if that is what we want? How curious it is that we so seldom discuss immigration these days!

Curious, but understandable—as one finds out the moment he publicly questions the wisdom of the status quo in immigration. He who does so is promptly charged with *isolationism, bigotry, prejudice, ethnocentrism, chauvinism,* and *selfishness.* These are hard accusations to beat. It is pleasanter to talk about other matters, leaving immigration policy to wallow in the cross-currents of special interests that take no account of the good of the whole—*or of the interests of posterity.*

We Americans have a bad conscience because of things we said in the past about immigrants. Two generations ago the popular press was rife with references to *Dagos, Wops, Pollacks, Japs, Chinks,* and *Krauts*—all pejorative terms which failed to acknowledge our indebtedness to Goya, Leonardo, Copernicus, Hiroshige, Confucius, and Bach. Because the implied inferiority of foreigners was *then* the justification for keeping them out, it is *now* thoughtlessly assumed that restrictive policies can only be based on the assumption of immigrant Inferiority. *This is not so.*

Existing immigration laws exclude idiots and known criminals; future laws will almost certainly continue this policy. But should we also consider the quality of the average immigrant, as compared with the quality of the average resident? Perhaps we should, perhaps we shouldn't. (What is "quality" anyway?) But the quality issue is not our concern here.

From this point on, *it will be assumed that immigrants and native-born citizens are of exactly equal quality,* however quality may be defined. The focus is only on quantity. The conclusions reached depend on nothing else, so all charges of ethnocentrism are irrelevant.

World food banks move food to the people, thus facilitating the exhaustion of the environment of the poor. By contrast, unrestricted immigration moves people to the food, thus speeding up the destruction of the environment in rich countries. Why poor people should want to make this transfer is no mystery: but why should rich hosts encourage it? This transfer, like the reverse one, is supported by both selfish interests and humanitarian impulses.

The principal selfish interest in unimpeded immigration is easy to identify; it is the interest of the employers of cheap labor, particularly that needed for degrading jobs. We have been deceived about the forces of history by the lines of Emma Lazarus inscribed on the Statue of Liberty:

> Give me your tired, your poor
> Your huddled masses yearning to breathe free,
> The wretched refuse of your teeming shore,
> Send these, the homeless, tempest-tossed, to me:
> I lift my lamp beside the golden door.

The image is one of an infinitely generous earth-mother, passively opening her arms to hordes of immigrants who come here on their own initiative. Such an image may have been adequate for the early days of colonization, but by the time these lines were written (1886) the force for immigration was largely manufactured inside our own borders by factory and mine owners who sought cheap labor not to be found among laborers already here. One group of foreigners after another was thus enticed into the United States to work at wretched jobs for wretched wages.

At present, it is largely the Mexicans who are being so exploited. It is particularly to the advantage of certain employers that there be many illegal immigrants. Illegal immigrant workers dare not complain about their working conditions for fear of being repatriated. Their presence reduces the bargaining power of all Mexican-American laborers. Cesar Chavez has repeatedly pleaded with congressional committees to close the doors to more Mexicans so that those here can negotiate effectively for higher wages and decent working conditions. Chavez understands the ethics of a lifeboat.

The interests of the employers of cheap labor are well served by the silence of the intelligentsia of the country. WASPS—White Anglo-Saxon Protestants—are particularly reluctant to call a closing of the doors to immigration for fear of being called ethnocentric bigots. It was, therefore, an occasion of pure delight for this particular WASP to be present at a meeting when the points he would like to have made were made better by a non-WASP speaking to other non-WASPS. It was in Hawaii, and most of the people in the room were second-level Hawaiian officials of Japanese ancestry. All Hawaiians are keenly aware of the limits of their environment, and the speaker had asked how it might be practically and constitutionally possible to close the doors to more immigrants to the islands. (To Hawaiians, immigrants from the other 49 states are as much of a threat as those from other nations. There is only so much room in the islands, and the islanders know it. Sophistical arguments that imply otherwise do not impress them.)

Yet, the Japanese-Americans of Hawaii have active ties with the land of their origin. This point was raised by a Japanese-American member of the audience who asked the Japanese-American speaker: "But how can we shut the doors now? We have many friends and relations in Japan that we'd like to bring to Hawaii some day so that they can enjoy this beautiful land."

The speaker smiled sympathetically and responded slowly: "Yes, but we have children now and someday we'll have grandchildren. We can bring more people here from Japan only by giving away some of the land that we hope to pass on to our grandchildren some day. What right do we have to do that?"

To be generous with one's own possessions is one thing; to be generous with posterity's is quite another. This, I think, is the point that must be gotten across to those who would, from a commendable love of distributive justice, institute a ruinous system of the commons, either in the form of a world food bank or that of unrestricted immigration. Since every speaker is a member of some ethnic group it is always possible to charge him with ethnocentrism. But even after purging an argument of ethnocentrism the rejection of the commons is still valid and necessary if we are to save at least some parts of the world from environmental ruin. Is it not desirable that at least some of the grandchildren of people now living should have a decent place in which to live?

The Asymmetry of Door-Shutting

We must now answer this telling point: "How can you justify slamming the door once you're inside? You say that immigrants should be kept out. But aren't we all immigrants, or the descendants of immigrants? Since we refuse to leave, must we not, as a matter of justice and symmetry, admit all others?"

It is literally true that we Americans of non-Indian ancestry are the descendants of thieves. Should we not, then, "give back" the land to the Indians; that is, give it to the now-living Americans of Indian ancestry? As an exercise in pure logic I see no way to reject this proposal. Yet I am unwilling to live by it; and I know no one who is. Our reluctance to embrace pure justice may spring from pure selfishness. On the other hand, it may arise from an unspoken recognition of consequences that have not yet been clearly spelled out.

Suppose, becoming intoxicated with pure justice, we "Anglos" should decide to turn our land over to the Indians. Since all our other wealth has also been derived from the land, we would have to give that to the Indians, too. Then what would we non-Indians do? Where would we go? There is no open land in the world on which men without capital can make their living (and not much unoccupied land on which men with capital can either). Where would 209 million putatively justice-loving, non-Indian, Americans go? Most of them—in the persons of their ancestors—came from Europe, but they wouldn't be welcomed back there. Anyway, Europeans have no better title to their land than we to ours. They also would have to give up their homes. (But to whom? And where would *they* go?)

Clearly, the concept of pure justice produces an infinite regress. The law long ago invented statutes of limitations to justify the rejection of pure justice, in the interest of preventing massive disorder. The law zealously defends property rights—but only *recent* property rights. It is as though the physical principle of exponential decay applies to property rights. Drawing a line in time may be unjust, but any other action is practically worse.

We are all the descendants of thieves, and the world's resources are inequitably distributed, but we must begin the journey to tomorrow from the point where we are today. We cannot remake the past. We cannot, without violent disorder and suffering, give land and resources back to the "original" owners—who are dead anyway.

We cannot safely divide the wealth equitably among all present peoples, so long as people reproduce at different rates, because to do so would guarantee that our grandchildren—everyone's grandchildren—would have only a ruined world to inhabit.

Must Exclusion Be Absolute?

To show the logical structure of the immigration problem I have ignored many factors that would enter into real decisions made in a real world. No matter how convincing the logic may be it is probable that we would want, from time to time, to admit a few people from the outside to our lifeboat. Political refugees in particular are likely to cause us to make exceptions: We remember the Jewish refugees from Germany after 1933, and the Hungarian refugees after 1956. Moreover, the interests of national defense, broadly conceived, could justify admitting many men and women of unusual talents, whether refugees or not. (This raises the quality issue, which is not the subject of this essay.)

Such exceptions threaten to create runaway population growth inside the lifeboat, i.e., the receiving country. However, the threat can be neutralized by a population policy that includes immigration. An effective policy is one of flexible control.

Suppose, for example, that the nation has achieved a stable condition of ZPG, which (say) permits 1.5 million births yearly. We must suppose that an acceptable system of allocation birthrights to potential parents is in effect. Now suppose that an inhumane regime in some other part of the world creates a horde of refugees, and that there is a widespread desire to admit some to our country. At the same time, we do not want to sabotage our population control system. Clearly, the rational path to pursue is the following. If we decide to admit 100,000 refugees this year we should compensate for this by reducing the allocation of birth-rights in the following year by a similar amount, that is downward to a total of 1.4 million. In that way we could achieve both humanitarian and population control goals. (And the refugees would have to accept the population controls of the society that admits them. It is not inconceivable that they might be given proportionately fewer rights than the native population.)

In a democracy, the admission of immigrants should properly be voted on. But by whom? It is not obvious. The usual rule of a democracy is votes for all. But it can be questioned whether a universal franchise is the most just one in a case of this sort. Whatever benefits there are in the admission of immigrants presumably accrue to everyone. But the costs would be seen as falling most heavily on potential parents, some of whom would have to postpone or forego having their (next) child because of the influx of immigrants. The double question *Who benefits? Who pays?* suggests that a restriction of the usual democratic franchise would be appropriate and just in this case. Would our particular quasi-democratic form of government be flexible enough to institute such a novelty? If not, the majority might, out of humanitarian motives, impose an unacceptable burden (the foregoing of parenthood) on a minority, thus producing political instability.

Plainly many new problems will arise when we consciously face the immigration question and seek rational answers. No workable answers can be found if we ignore population problems. And—if the argument of this essay is correct—so long as there is not true world government to control reproduction everywhere it is impossible to survive in dignity if we are to be guided by Spaceship ethics. Without a world government that is sovereign in reproductive matters mankind lives, in fact, on a number of sovereign lifeboats. For the foreseeable future survival demands that we govern our actions by the ethics of a lifeboat. Posterity will be ill served if we do not.

References

Anonymous. 1974. *Wall Street Journal* 19 Feb.

Borlaug, N. 1973. Civilization's future: a call for international granaries. *Bull. At. Sci.* 29: 7-15.

Boulding, K. 1966. The economics of the coming Spaceship earth. In H. Jarrett, ed. *Environmental Quality in a Growing Economy*. Johns Hopkins UP, Baltimore.

Buchanan, W. 1973. Immigration statistics. *Equilibrium* 1(3): 16-19.

Davis, K. 1963. Population. *Sci. Amer.* 209(3): 62-71.

Farvar, M.T., and J.P. Milton. 1972. *The Careless Technology*. Natural History, Garden City, NY.

Greg, A. 1955. A medical aspect of the population problem. *Science* 121: 681-82.

Hardin, G. 1966. Chap. 9 in *Biology: Its Principles and Implications*, 2nd ed. Freeman, San Francisco.

———. 1968. The tragedy of the commons. *Science* 162: 1243-48.

———. 1969a Page 18 in *Population, Evolution, and Birth Control*, 2nd ed. Freeman, San Francisco.

———. 1969b. The economics of wilderness, *Nat. Hist.* 78(6): 20-27.

———. 1972a. Pages 81-82 in *Exploring New Ethics for Survival: The Voyage of the Spaceship Beagle*. Viking, NY.

———. 1972b. Preserving quality on Spaceship Earth. In J.B. Trefethen, ed. *Transactions of the Thirty-Seventh North American Wildlife and Natural Resources Conference*. Wildlife Management Institute, Washington, DC.

————. 1973. Chap. 23 in *Stalking the Wild Taboo*. Kaufmann, Los Altos, CA.

Harris, M. 1972. How green the revolution. *Nat. Hist.* 81(3): 28-30.

Langer, S.K. 1942. *Philosophy in a New Key*. Harvard UP, Cambridge.

Lansner, K. 1974. Should foreign aid begin at home? *Newsweek,* 11 Feb., p. 32.

Marx, K. 1875. Critique of the Gotha program. Page 388 in R.C. Tucker, ed. *The Marx-Engels Reader*. Norton, NY, 1972.

Ophuls, W. 1974. The scarcity society. *Harpers* 248(1487): 47-52.

Paddock, W.C. 1970. How green is the green revolution? *BioScience* 20: 897-902.

Paddock, W., and E. Paddock. 1973. *Don't Know How*. Iowa State UP, Ames, IA.

Paddock, W., and P. Paddock. 1967. *Famine—1975!* Little, Brown, Boston.

Wilkes, H.G. 1972. The green revolution. *Environment* 14(8): 32-39.

33. One Atmosphere[*]

Peter Singer

The Problem

There can be no clearer illustration of the need for human beings to act globally than the issues raised by the impact of human activity on our atmosphere. That we all share the same planet came to our attention in a particularly pressing way in the 1970s when scientists discovered that the use of chlorofluorocarbons (CFCs) threatens the ozone layer shielding the surface of our planet from the full force of the sun's ultraviolet radiation. Damage to that protective shield would cause cancer rates to rise sharply and could have other effects, for example, on the growth of algae. The threat was especially acute to the world's southernmost cities, since a large hole in the ozone was found to be opening up each year over Antarctica, but in the long term, the entire ozone shield was imperiled. Once the science was accepted, concerted international action followed relatively rapidly with the signing of the Montreal Protocol in 1985. The developed countries phased out virtually all use of CFCs by 1999, and the developing countries, given a ten-year period of grace, are now moving toward the same goal.

Getting rid of CFCs has turned out to be just the curtain raiser: the main event is climate change, or global warming. Without belittling the pioneering achievement of those who brought about the Montreal Protocol, the problem was not so difficult, for CFCs can be replaced in all their uses at relatively little cost, and the solution to the problem is simply to stop producing them. Climate change is a very different matter.

The scientific evidence that human activities are changing the climate of our planet has been studied by a working group of the Intergovernmental Panel on Climate Change, or IPCC, an international scientific body intended to provide policymakers with an authoritative view of climate change and its causes. The group released its Third Assessment Report in 2001, building on earlier reports and incorporating new evidence accumulated over the previous five years. The Report is the work of 122 lead authors and 515 contributing authors, and the research on which

---

[*] Source: *One World: The Ethics of Globalization* (New Haven, CT: Yale UP, 2002), pp. 14–50.

it was based was reviewed by 337 experts. Like any scientific document it is open to criticism from other scientists, but it reflects a broad consensus of leading scientific opinion and is by far the most authoritative view at present available on what is happening to our climate.

The Third Assessment Report finds that our planet has shown clear signs of warming over the past century. The 1990s were the hottest decade, and 1998 the hottest year, recorded over the 140 years for which meteorological records have been kept. As 2001 drew to a close, the World Meteorological Organization announced that it would be second only to 1998 as the hottest year recorded. In fact nine of the ten hottest years during this period have occurred since 1990, and temperatures are now rising at three times the rate of the early 1900s.[1] Sea levels have risen by between 10 and 20 centimeters (4 to 8 inches) over the past century. Since the 1960s snow and ice cover has decreased by about 10 percent, and mountain glaciers are in retreat everywhere except near the poles. In the past three decades the El Niño effect in the southern hemisphere has become more intense, causing greater variation in rainfall. Paralleling these changes is an unprecedented increase in concentrations of carbon dioxide, methane, and nitrous oxide in the atmosphere, produced by human activities such as burning fossil fuels, the clearing of vegetation, and (in the case of methane) cattle and rice production. Not for at least 420,000 years has there been so much carbon dioxide and methane in the atmosphere.

How much of the change in climate has been produced by human activity, and how much can be explained by natural variation? The Third Assessment Report finds "new and stronger evidence that most of the warming observed over the last 50 years is attributable to human activities," and, more specifically, to greenhouse gas emissions. The report also finds it "very likely" that most of the rise in sea levels over the past century is due to global warming.[2] Those of us who have no expertise in the scientific aspects of assessing climate change and its causes can scarcely disregard the views held by the overwhelming majority of those who do possess that expertise. They could be wrong—the great majority of scientists sometimes are—but in view of what is at stake, to rely on that possibility would be a risky strategy.

What will happen if we continue to emit increasing amounts of greenhouse gases and global warming continues to accelerate? The Third Assessment Report

1 "This Year Was the 2nd Hottest, Confirming a Trend, UN Says," *New York Times*, December 19, 2001, p. A5.

2 J.T. Houghton et al., eds., *Climate Change 2001: The Scientific Basis: Contribution of Working Group I to the Third Assessment Report of the Intergovernmental Panel on Climate*, United Nations Environment Program and Intergovernmental Panel on Climate Change (Cambridge UP, Cambridge, 2001), Summary for Policymakers; available at www.ipcc.ch/pub/tar/wgi/index.htm. See also *Reconciling Observations of Global Temperature Change*, Panel on Reconciling Temperature Observations, National Research Council, National Academy of Sciences, Washington, D.C., 2000, available at www.nap.edu/books/0309068916/html. For another example of recent research indicating that anthropogenic climate change is real, see Thomas J. Crowley, "Causes of Climate Change over the Past 1000 Years," *Science* 289 (July 14, 2000): 270–277.

estimates that between 1990 and 2100, average global temperatures will rise by at least 1.4°C (2.5°F), and perhaps by as much as 5.8°C (10.4°F).[3] Although these average figures may seem quite small—whether tomorrow is going to be 20°C (69°F) or 22°C (72°F) isn't such a big deal—even a 1°C rise in average temperatures would be greater than any change that has occurred in a single century for the past 10,000 years. Moreover, some regional changes will be more extreme and are much more difficult to predict. Northern landmasses, especially North America and Central Asia, will warm more than the oceans or coastal regions. Precipitation will increase overall, but there will be sharp regional variations, with some areas that now receive adequate rainfall becoming arid. There will also be greater year-to-year fluctuations than at present—which means that droughts and floods will increase. The Asian summer monsoon is likely to become less reliable. It is possible that the changes could be enough to reach critical tipping points at which the weather systems alter or the directions of major ocean currents, such as the Gulf Stream, change.

What will the consequences be for humans?

- As oceans become warmer, hurricanes and tropical storms that are now largely confined to the tropics will move farther from the equator, hitting large urban areas that have not been built to cope with them. This is a prospect that is viewed with great concern in the insurance industry, which has already seen the cost of natural disasters rise dramatically in recent decades.[4]
- Tropical diseases will become more widespread.
- Food production will rise in some regions, especially in the high northern latitudes, and fall in others, including sub-Saharan Africa.
- Sea levels will rise by between 9 and 88 centimeters (between 4 and 35 inches).

Rich nations may, at considerable cost, be able to cope with these changes without enormous loss of life. They are in a better position to store food against the possibility of drought, to move people away from flooded areas, to fight the spread of disease-carrying insects and to build seawalls to keep out the rising seas. Poor nations will not be able to do so much. Bangladesh, the world's most densely populated large country, has the world's largest system of deltas and mudflats, where mighty rivers like the Ganges and the Brahmaputra reach the sea. The soil in these areas is fertile, but the hazards of living on such low-lying land are great. In 1991 a cyclone hit the coast of Bangladesh, coinciding with high tides that left 10 million people homeless and killed 139,000. Most of these people were living on mudflats in the deltas. People

3 Houghton et al., eds., *Climate Change 2001: The Scientific Basis.*
4 Munich Reinsurance, one of the world's largest insurance companies, has estimated that the number of major natural disasters has risen from 16 in the 1960s to 70 in the 1990s. Cited by Christian Aid, Global Advocacy Team Policy Position Paper, *Global Warming, Unnatural Disasters and the World's Poor*, November 2000, <www.christianaid.org.uk/indepth/ooiiglob.globwarm.htm>.

continue to live there in large numbers because they have nowhere else to go. But if sea levels continue to rise, many peasant farmers will have no land left. As many as 70 million people could be affected in Bangladesh, and a similar number in China. Millions more Egyptian farmers on the Nile delta also stand to lose their land. On a smaller scale, Pacific island nations that consist of low-lying atolls face even more drastic losses. Kiribati, placed just to the west of the International Date Line, was the first nation to enter the new millennium. Ironically, it may also be the first to leave it, disappearing beneath the waves. High tides are already causing erosion and polluting fragile sources of fresh water, and some uninhabited islands have been submerged.

Global warming would lead to an increase in summer deaths due to heat stress, but these would be offset by a reduced death toll from winter cold. Much more significant than either of these effects, however, would be the spread of tropical diseases, including diseases carried by insects that need warmth to survive. The Third Assessment Report considers several attempts to model the spread of diseases like malaria and dengue, but finds that the research methodology is, at this stage, inadequate to provide good estimates of the numbers likely to be affected.[5]

If the Asian monsoon becomes less reliable, hundreds of millions of peasant farmers in India and other countries will go hungry in the years in which the monsoon brings less rain than normal. They have no other way of obtaining the water needed for growing their crops. In general, less reliable rainfall patterns will cause immense hardship among the large proportion of the world's population who must grow their own food if they want to eat.

The consequences for non-human animals and for biodiversity will also be severe. In some regions plant and animal communities will gradually move farther from the equator, or to higher altitudes, following climate patterns. Elsewhere that option will not be available. Australia's unique alpine plants and animals already survive only on the country's highest alpine plains and peaks. If snow ceases to fall on their territory, they will become extinct. Coastal ecosystems will change dramatically, and warmer waters may destroy coral reefs. These predictions look ahead only as far as 2100, but even if greenhouse gas emissions have been stabilized by that time, changes in climate will persist for hundreds, perhaps thousands of years. A small change in average global temperatures could, over the next millennium, lead to the melting of the Greenland ice cap which, added to the partial melting of the West Antarctic ice sheet, could increase sea levels by 6 meters, or nearly 20 feet.[6]

All of this forces us to think differently about our ethics. Our value system evolved in circumstances in which the atmosphere, like the oceans, seemed an unlimited

5 James McCarthy et al., eds., *Climate Change 2001: Impacts, Adaptation, and Vulnerability, Contribution of Working Group II to the Third Assessment Reports of the Intergovernmental Panel on Climate Change*, United Nations Environment Program and Intergovernmental Panel on Climate Change (Cambridge UP, Cambridge, 2001), chapter 9.7; available at <www.ipcc.ch/pub/tar/wg2/index.htm>.
6 Houghton et al., eds., *Climate Change 2001: The Scientific Basis*.

resource, and responsibilities and harms were generally clear and well defined. If someone hit someone else, it was clear who had done what. Now the twin problems of the ozone hole and of climate change have revealed bizarre new ways of killing people. By spraying deodorant at your armpit in your New York apartment, you could, if you use an aerosol spray propelled by CFCs, be contributing to the skin cancer deaths, many years later, of people living in Punta Arenas, Chile. By driving your car, you could be releasing carbon dioxide that is part of a causal chain leading to lethal floods in Bangladesh.[7] How can we adjust our ethics to take account of this new situation?

Rio and Kyoto

That seemingly harmless and trivial human actions can affect people in distant countries is just beginning to make a significant difference to the sovereignty of individual nations. Under existing international law, individuals and companies can sue for damages if they are harmed by pollution coming from another country, but nations cannot take other nations to court. In January 2002, Norway announced that it would push for a binding international "polluter-pays" scheme for countries. The announcement followed evidence that Britain's Sellafield nuclear power plant is emitting radioactive wastes that are reaching the Norwegian coastline. Lobsters and other shellfish in the North Sea and the Irish Sea have high levels of radioactive technetium-99.[8]

The Sellafield case has revealed a gap in environmental legislation on a global basis. Norway is seeking an international convention on environmental pollution, first at the European level, and then, through the United Nations, globally. The principle is one that is difficult to argue against, but if Norway can force Britain to pay for the damage its leaking nuclear plant causes to their coastline, will not nations like Kiribati be able to sue America for allowing large quantities of carbon dioxide to be emitted into the atmosphere, causing rising sea levels to submerge their island homes? Although the link between rising sea levels and a nation's emissions of greenhouse gases is much more difficult to prove than the link between Britain's nuclear power plant and technetium-99 found along the Norwegian coast, it is hard to draw a clear line of principle between the two cases. Yet accepting the right of Kiribati to sue for damages for American greenhouse gas emissions makes us one world in a new and far more sweeping sense than we ever were before. It gives rise to a need for concerted international action.

Climate change entered the international political arena in 1988, when the United Nations Environment Program and the World Meteorological Office jointly set up

---

7 See Dale Jamieson, "Ethics, Public Policy, and Global Warming," *Science, Technology, and Human Values* 17.2 (Spring 1992): 139–153, and "Global Responsibilities: Ethics, Public Health, and Global Environmental Change," *Indiana Journal of Global Legal Studies* 5.1 (Fall 1997): 99–119.

8 "Norway Wants Sanctions for Cross Border Polluters," *Reuters News Service*, 1 February 2002, <www.planetark.org/dailynewsstory.cfm/newsid/14316/story.htm>.

the Intergovernmental Panel on Climate Change. In 1990 the IPCC reported that the threat of climate change was real, and a global treaty was needed to deal with it. The United Nations General Assembly resolved to proceed with such a treaty. The United Nations Framework Convention on Climate Change was agreed to in 1992, and opened for signature at the Earth Summit, or more formally, the United Nations Conference on Environment and Development, which was held in Rio de Janeiro in the same year. This "framework convention" has been accepted by 181 governments. It is, as its name suggests, no more than a framework for further action, but it calls for greenhouse gases to be stabilized at safe levels, and it says that the parties to the convention should do this "on the basis of equity and in accordance with their common but differentiated responsibilities and respective capabilities." Developed nations should "take the lead in combating climate change and the adverse effects thereof." The developed nations committed themselves to 1990 levels of emissions by the year 2000, but this commitment was not legally binding.[9] For the United States and several other countries, that was just as well, because they came nowhere near meeting it. In the United States, for example, by 2000 carbon dioxide emissions were 14 percent higher than they were in 1990. Nor was the trend improving, for the increase between 1999 and 2000 was 3.1 percent, the biggest one-year increase since the mid 1990s.[10]

The framework convention builds in what is sometimes called "the precautionary principle," calling on the parties to act to avoid the risk of serious and irreversible damage even in the absence of full scientific certainty. The convention also recognizes a "right to sustainable development," asserting that economic development is essential for addressing climate change. Accordingly, the Rio Earth Summit did not set any emissions reduction targets for developing countries to meet.

The framework convention set up a procedure for holding "conferences of the parties" to assess progress. In 1995, this conference decided that more binding targets were needed. The result, after two years of negotiations, was the 1997 Kyoto Protocol, which set targets for 39 developed nations to limit or reduce their greenhouse gas emissions by 2012. The limits and reductions were designed to reduce total emissions from the developed nations to a level at least 5 percent below 1990 levels. The national targets vary, however, with the European Union nations and the United States having targets of 8 percent and 7 percent, respectively, below 1990 levels, and other nations, such as Australia, being allowed to go over their 1990 levels. These targets were arrived at through negotiations with government leaders, and they were not based on any general principles of fairness, nor much else that can be defended

9   *United Nations Framework Convention on Climate Change*, Article 4, section 2, subsections (a) and (b), available at <www.unfccc.int/resource/conve/conv.html>; *Guide to the Climate Change Negotiation Process*, <www.unfccc.int/resource/process/components/response/respconv.html>.

10 "US Carbon Emissions Jump in 2000," *Los Angeles Times*, 11 November 2001, p. A36, citing figures released by the US Department of Energy's Energy Information Administration on 9 November 2001.

on any terms other than the need to get agreement.[11] This was necessary since under the prevailing conception of national sovereignty, countries cannot be bound to meet their targets unless they decide to sign the treaty that commits them to do so. To assist countries in reaching their targets, the Kyoto Protocol accepted the principle of "emissions trading," by which one country can buy emissions credits from another country that can reach its target with something to spare.

The Kyoto conference did not settle the details of how countries could meet their targets, for example, whether they would be allowed credits for planting forests that soak up carbon dioxide from the atmosphere, and how emissions trading was to operate. After a meeting at The Hague failed to reach agreement on these matters, they were resolved at further meetings held in Bonn and Marrakech in July and November 2001, respectively. There, 178 nations reached an historic agreement that makes it possible to put the Kyoto Protocol into effect. American officials, however, were merely watching from the sidelines. The United States was no longer a party to the agreement.

The Kyoto agreement will not solve the problem of the impact of human activity on the world's climate. It will only slow the changes that are now occurring. For that reason, some skeptics have argued that the likely results do not justify the costs of putting the agreement into effect. In an article in *The Economist*, Bjorn Lomborg writes:

> Despite the intuition that something drastic needs to be done about such a costly problem, economic analyses clearly show that it will be far more expensive to cut carbon-dioxide emissions radically than to pay the costs of adaptation to the increased temperatures.[12]

Lomborg is right to raise the question of costs. It is conceivable, for example, that the resources the world is proposing to put into reducing greenhouse gas emissions could be better spent on increasing assistance to the world's poorest people, to help them develop economically and so cope better with climate change. But how likely is it that the rich nations would spend the money in this manner? As we shall see in Chapter 5 [of *One World*] their past record is not encouraging. A comparatively inefficient way of helping the poor may be better than not helping them at all.

Significantly, Lomborg's highly controversial book, *The Skeptical Environmentalist*, offers a more nuanced picture than the bald statement quoted above. Lomborg himself points out that, even in a worst-case scenario in which Kyoto is implemented in an inefficient way, "there is no way that the cost will send us to the poorhouse." Indeed, he says, one could argue that whether we choose to implement the Kyoto Protocol or to go beyond it, and actually stabilize greenhouse gases,

---

11 Eileen Claussen and Lisa McNeilly, *The Complex Elements of Global Fairness*, Pew Center on Global Climate Change, Washington, DC, 29 October 1998, <www.pewclimate.org/projects/pol_equity.cfm>.

12 Bjorn Lomborg, "The Truth about the Environment," *The Economist*, 2 August 2001, available at < http://www.economist.com/topics/bjorn-lomborg>.

The total cost of managing global warming ad infinitum would be the same as deferring the [economic] growth curve by less than a year. In other words we would have to wait until 2051 to enjoy the prosperity we would otherwise have enjoyed in 2050. And by that time the average citizen of the world will have become twice as wealthy as she is now.[13]

Lomborg does claim that the Kyoto Protocol will lead to a net loss of $150 billion. This estimate assumes that there will be emissions trading within the developed nations, but not among all nations of the world. It also assumes that the developing nations will remain outside the Protocol—in which case the effect of the agreement will be only to delay, by a few years, the predicted changes to the climate. But if the developing nations join in once they see that the developed nations are serious about tackling their emissions, and if there is global emissions trading, then Lomborg's figures show that the Kyoto pact will bring a net benefit of $61 billion.

These estimates all assume that Lomborg's figures are sound—a questionable assumption, for how shall we price the increased deaths from tropical diseases and flooding that global warming will bring? How much should we pay to prevent the extinction of species and entire ecosystems? Even if we could answer these questions, and agree on the figures that Lomborg uses, we would still need to consider his decision to discount all future costs at an annual rate of 5 percent. A discount rate of 5 percent means that we consider losing $100 today to be the equivalent of losing $95 in a year's time, the equivalent of losing $90.25 in two years' time, and so on. Obviously, then, losing something in, say, 40 years' time isn't going to be worth much, and it wouldn't make sense to spend a lot now to make sure that you don't lose it. To be precise, at this discount rate, it would only be worth spending $14.20 today to make sure that you don't lose $100 in 40 years' time. Since the costs of reducing greenhouse gas emissions will come soon, whereas most of the costs of not doing anything to reduce them fall several decades into the future, this makes a huge difference to the cost/benefit equation. Assume that unchecked global warming will lead to rising sea levels, flooding valuable land in 40 years' time. With an annual discount rate of 5 percent, it is worth spending only $14.20 to prevent flooding that will permanently inundate land worth $100. Losses that will occur a century or more hence dwindle to virtually nothing. This is not because of inflation—we are talking about costs expressed in dollars already adjusted for inflation. It is simply discounting the future. Lomborg justifies the use of a discount rate by arguing that if we invest $14.20 today, we can get a (completely safe) return of 5 percent on it, and so it will grow to $100 in 40 years. Though the use of a discount rate is a standard economic practice, the decision about which rate should be used is highly speculative, and assuming different interest rates, or even acknowledging uncertainty about

---

13 Bjorn Lomborg, *The Skeptical Environmentalist* (Cambridge UP, Cambridge, 2001), p. 323.

interest rates, would lead to very different cost/benefit ratios.[14] There is also an ethical issue about discounting the future. True, our investments may increase in value over time, and we will become richer, but the price we are prepared to pay to save human lives, or endangered species, may go up just as much. These values are not consumer goods, like TVs or dishwashers, which drop in value in proportion to our earnings. They are things like health, something that the richer we get, the more we are willing to spend to preserve. An ethical, not an economic, justification would be needed for discounting suffering and death, or the extinction of species, simply because these losses will not occur for 40 years. No such justification has been offered.

It is important to see Kyoto not as the solution to the problem of climate change, but as the first step. It is reasonable to raise questions about whether the relatively minor delay in global warming that Kyoto would bring about is worth the cost. But if we see Kyoto as a necessary step for persuading the developing countries that they too should reduce greenhouse gas emissions, we can see why we should support it. Kyoto provides a platform from which a more far-reaching and also more equitable agreement can be reached. Now we need to ask what that agreement would need to be like to satisfy the requirement of equity or fairness.

What Is an Equitable Distribution?

In the second of the three televised debates held during the 2000 US presidential election, the candidates were asked what they would do about global warming. George W Bush said:

> I'll tell you one thing I'm not going to do is I'm not going to let the United States carry the burden for cleaning up the world's air, like the Kyoto treaty would have done. China and India were exempted from that treaty. I think we need to be more even-handed.

There are various principles of fairness that people often use to judge what is fair or "even-handed." In political philosophy, it is common to follow Robert Nozick in distinguishing between "historical" principles and "time-slice" principles.[15] An historical principle is one that says: we can't decide, merely by looking at the present situation, whether a given distribution of goods is just or unjust. We must also ask how the situation came about; we must know its history. Are the parties entitled, by an originally justifiable acquisition and a chain of legitimate transfers, to the holdings they now have? If so, the present distribution is just. If not, rectification or compensation will be needed to produce a just distribution. In contrast, a time-slice principle

14 See Richard Newell and William Pizer, *Discounting the Benefits of Future Climate Change Mitigation: How Much Do Uncertain Rates Increase Valuations?* Pew Center on Global Climate Change, Washington, DC, December 2001. Available at <www.pewclimate.org/projects/econ_discounting.cfm>.
15 Robert Nozick, *Anarchy, State and Utopia* (Basic Books, New York, 1974), p. 153.

looks at the existing distribution at a particular moment and asks if that distribution satisfies some principles of fairness, irrespective of any preceding sequence of events. I shall look at both of these approaches in turn.

A Historical Principle: "The Polluter Pays" or "You Broke It, Now You Fix It"
Imagine that we live in a village in which everyone puts their wastes down a giant sink. No one quite knows what happens to the wastes after they go down the sink, but since they disappear and have no adverse impact on anyone, no one worries about it. Some people consume a lot, and so have a lot of waste, while others, with more limited means, have barely any, but the capacity of the sink to dispose of our wastes seems so limitless that no one worries about the difference. As long as that situation continues, it is reasonable to believe that, in putting waste down the sink, we are leaving "enough and as good" for others, because no matter how much we put down it, others can also put as much as they want, without the sink overflowing. This phrase "enough and as good" comes from John Locke's justification of private property in his *Second Treatise on Civil Government*, published in 1690. In that work Locke says that "the earth and all that is therein is given to men for the support and comfort of their being." The earth and its contents "belong to mankind in common." How, then, can there be private property? Because our labor is our own, and hence when we mix our own labor with the land and its products, we make them our own. But why does mixing my labor with the common property of all humankind mean that I have gained property in what belongs to all humankind, rather than lost property in my own labor? It has this effect, Locke says, as long as the appropriation of what is held in common does not prevent there being "enough and as good left in common for others."[16] Locke's justification of the acquisition of private property is the classic historical account of how property can be legitimately acquired, and it has served as the starting point for many more recent discussions. Its significance here is that, if it is valid and the sink is, or appears to be, of limitless capacity, it would justify allowing everyone to put what they want down the sink, even if some put much more than others down it.

Now imagine that conditions change so that the sink's capacity to carry away our wastes is used up to the full, and there is already some unpleasant seepage that seems to be the result of the sink's being used too much. This seepage causes occasional problems. When the weather is warm, it smells. A nearby water hole where our children swim now has algae blooms that make it unusable. Several respected figures in the village warn that unless usage of the sink is cut down, all the village water supplies will be polluted. At this point, when we continue to throw our usual wastes down the sink we are no longer leaving "enough and as good" for others, and hence our right to unchecked waste disposal becomes questionable. For the sink belongs to us

---

16 John Locke, *Second Treatise on Civil Government*, C.B. Macpherson, ed. (Hackett, Indianapolis, 1980), sec. 27, p. 19.

all in common, and by using it without restriction now, we are depriving others of their right to use the sink in the same way without bringing about results none of us wants. We have an example of the well-known "tragedy of the commons."[17] The use of the sink is a limited resource that needs to be shared in some equitable way. But how? A problem of distributive justice has arisen.

Think of the atmosphere as a giant global sink into which we can pour our waste gases. Then once we have used up the capacity of the atmosphere to absorb our gases without harmful consequences, it becomes impossible to justify our usage of this asset by the claim that we are leaving "enough and as good" for others. The atmosphere's capacity to absorb our gases has become a finite resource on which various parties have competing claims. The problem is to allocate those claims justly.

Are there any other arguments that justify taking something that has, for all of human history, belonged to human beings in common, and turning it into private property? Locke has a further argument, arguably inconsistent with his first argument, defending the continued unequal distribution of property even when there is no longer "enough and as good" for others. Comparing the situation of American Indians, where there is no private ownership of land, and hence the land is not cultivated, with that of England, where some landowners hold vast estates and many laborers have no land at all, Locke claims that "a king of a large and fruitful territory there [i.e., in America] feeds, lodges, and is clad worse than a day laborer in England."[18] Therefore, he suggests, even the landless laborer is better off because of the private, though unequal, appropriation of the common asset, and hence should consent to it. The factual basis of Locke's comparison between English laborers and American Indians is evidently dubious, as is its failure to consider other, more equitable ways of ensuring that the land is used productively. But even if the argument worked for the landless English laborer, we cannot defend the private appropriation of the global sink in the same way. The landless laborer who no longer has the opportunity to have a share of what was formerly owned in common should not complain, Locke seems to think, because he is better off than he would have been if inegalitarian private property in land had not been recognized. The parallel argument to this in relation to the use of the global sink would be that even the world's poorest people have benefited from the increased productivity that has come from the use of the global sink by the industrialized nations. But the argument does not work, because many of the world's poorest people, whose shares of the atmosphere's capacity have been appropriated by the industrialized nations, are not able to partake in the benefits of this increased productivity in the industrialized nations—they cannot afford to buy its products—and if rising sea levels inundate their farm lands, or cyclones destroy their homes, they will be much worse off than they would otherwise have been.

---

17 See Garrett Hardin, "The Tragedy of the Commons," *Science* 162 (1968): 1243–1248.
18 Locke, *Second Treatise on Civil Government*, sec. 41.

Apart from John Locke, the thinker most often quoted in justifying the right of the rich to their wealth is probably Adam Smith. Smith argued that the rich did not deprive the poor of their share of the world's wealth, because

> The rich only select from the heap what is most precious and agreeable. They consume little more than the poor, and in spite of their natural selfishness and rapacity, though they mean only their own convenience, though the sole end which they propose from the labours of all the thousands whom they employ, be the gratification of their own vain and insatiable desires, they divide with the poor the produce of all their improvements.[19]

How can this be? Because, Smith tells us, it is as if an "invisible hand" brings about a distribution of the necessaries of life that is "nearly the same" as it would have been if the world had been divided up equally among all its inhabitants. By that Smith means that in order to obtain what they want, the rich spread their wealth throughout the entire economy. But while Smith knew that the rich could be selfish and rapacious, he did not imagine that the rich could, far from consuming "little more" than the poor, consume many times as much of a scarce resource as the poor do. The average American, by driving a car, eating a diet rich in the products of industrialized farming, keeping cool in summer and warm in winter, and consuming products at a hitherto unknown rate, uses more than fifteen times as much of the global atmospheric sink as the average Indian. Thus Americans, along with Australians, Canadians, and to a lesser degree Europeans, effectively deprive those living in poor countries of the opportunity to develop along the lines that the rich ones themselves have taken. If the poor were to behave as the rich now do, global warming would accelerate and almost certainly bring widespread catastrophe.

The putatively historical grounds for justifying private property put forward by its most philosophically significant defenders—writing at a time when capitalism was only beginning its rise to dominance over the world's economy—cannot apply to the current use of the atmosphere. Neither Locke nor Smith provides any justification for the rich having more than their fair share of the finite capacity of the global atmospheric sink. In fact, just the contrary is true. Their arguments imply that this appropriation of a resource once common to all humankind is not justifiable. And since the wealth of the developed nations is inextricably tied to their prodigious use of carbon fuels (a use that began more than 200 years ago and continues unchecked today), it is a small step from here to the conclusion that the present global distribution of wealth is the result of the wrongful expropriation by a small fraction of the world's population of a resource that belongs to all human beings in common.

---

19 Adam Smith, *A Theory of the Moral Sentiments* (Prometheus, Amherst, NY, 2000), IV, i. 10.

For those whose principles of justice focus on historical processes, a wrongful expropriation is grounds for rectification or compensation. What sort of rectification or compensation should take place in this situation?

One advantage of being married to someone whose hair is a different color or length from your own is that, when a clump of hair blocks the bath outlet, it's easy to tell whose hair it is. "Get your own hair out of the tub" is a fair and reasonable household rule. Can we, in the case of the atmosphere, trace back what share of responsibility for the blockage is due to which nations? It isn't as easy as looking at hair color, but a few years ago researchers measured world carbon emissions from 1950 to 1986 and found that the United States, with about 5 percent of the world's population at that time, was responsible for 30 percent of the cumulative emissions, whereas India, with 17 percent of the world's population, was responsible for less than 2 percent of the emissions.[20] It is as if, in a village of 20 people all using the same bathtub, one person had shed 30 percent of the hair blocking the drain hole and three people had shed virtually no hair at all. (A more accurate model would show that many more than three had shed virtually no hair at all. Indeed, many developing nations have per capita emissions even lower than India's.) In these circumstances, one basis of deciding who pays the bill for the plumber to clear out the drain would be to divide it up proportionately to the amount of hair from each person that has built up over the period that people have been using the tub, and has caused the present blockage.

There is a counterargument to the claim that the United States is responsible for more of the problem, per head of population, than any other country. The argument is that because the United States has planted so many trees in recent decades, it has actually soaked up more carbon dioxide than it has emitted.[21] But there are many problems with this argument. One is that the United States has been able to reforest only because it earlier cut down much of its great forests, thus releasing the carbon into the atmosphere. As this suggests, much depends on the time period over which the calculation is made. If the period includes the era of cutting down the forests, then the United States comes out much worse than if it starts from the time in which the forest had been cut, but no reforestation had taken place. A second problem is that forest regrowth, while undoubtedly desirable, is not a long-term solution to the emissions problem but a temporary and one-shot expedient, locking up carbon only while the trees are growing. Once the forest is mature and an old tree dies and rots for every new tree that grows, the forest no longer soaks up significant amounts of carbon from the atmosphere.[22]

20 Peter Hayes and Kirk Smith eds., *The Global Greenhouse Regime: Who Pays?* (Earthscan, London, 1993, chapter 2, table 2.4; available at <www.unu.edu/unupress/unupbooks/80836e/80836E08.htm>.
21 See S. Fan, M. Gloor, J. Mahlman, S. Pacala, J. Sarmiento, T. Takahashi, and P. Tans, "A Large Terrestrial Carbon Sink in North America Implied by Atmospheric and Oceanic Carbon Dioxide Data and Models," *Science* 282 (16 October 1998): 442–446.
22 William Schlesinger and John Lichter, "Limited Carbon Storage in Soil and Litter of Experimental Forest Plots under Increased Atmospheric CO2," *Nature* 411 (24 May 2001): 466–469.

At present rates of emissions—even including emissions that come from changes in land use like clearing forests—contributions of the developing nations to the atmospheric stock of greenhouse gases will not equal the built-up contributions of the developed nations until about 2038. If we adjust this calculation for population—in other words, if we ask when the contributions of the developing nations per person will equal the per person contributions of the developed nations to the atmospheric stock of greenhouse gases—the answer is: not for at least another century.[23]

If the developed nations had had, during the past century, per capita emissions at the level of the developing nations, we would not today be facing a problem of climate change caused by human activity, and we would have an ample window of opportunity to do something about emissions before they reached a level sufficient to cause a problem. So, to put it in terms a child could understand, as far as the atmosphere is concerned, the developed nations broke it. If we believe that people should contribute to fixing something in proportion to their responsibility for breaking it, then the developed nations owe it to the rest of the world to fix the problem with the atmosphere.

Time-Slice Principles

The historical view of fairness just outlined puts a heavy burden on the developed nations. In their defense, it might be argued that at the time when the developed nations put most of their cumulative contributions of greenhouse gases into the atmosphere, they could not know of the limits to the capacity of the atmosphere to absorb those gases. It would therefore be fairer, it may be claimed, to make a fresh start now and set standards that look to the future, rather than to the past.

There can be circumstances in which we are right to wipe the slate clean and start again. A case can be made for doing so with respect to cumulative emissions that occurred before governments could reasonably be expected to know that these emissions might harm people in other countries. (Although, even here, one could argue that ignorance is no excuse and a stricter standard of liability should prevail, especially since the developed nations reaped the benefits of their early industrialization.) At least since 1990, however, when the Intergovernmental Panel on Climate Change published its first report, solid evidence about the hazards associated with emissions has existed.[24] To wipe the slate clean on what happened since 1990 seems unduly favorable to the industrialized nations that have, despite that evidence, continued to emit a disproportionate share of greenhouse gases. Nevertheless, in order to see

23 Duncan Austin, José Goldemberg, and Gwen Parker, "Contributions to Climate Change: Are Conventional Metrics Misleading the Debate?," World Resource Institute Climate Protection Initiative, Climate Notes, <www.igc.org/wri/cpi/notes/metrics.html>.

24 The Intergovernmental Panel on Climate Change, *First Assessment Report* was published in three volumes. See especially J.T. Houghton, G.J. Jenkins, and J.J. Ephraums, eds., *Scientific Assessment of Climate Change—Report of Working Group I* (Cambridge UP, Cambridge, 1990). For details of the other volumes see <www.ipcc.ch/pub/reports.htm>.

whether there are widely held principles of justice that do not impose such stringent requirements on the developed nations as the "polluter pays" principle, let us assume that the poor nations generously overlook the past. We would then need to look for a time-slice principle to decide how much each nation should be allowed to emit.

An Equal Share for Everyone

If we begin by asking, "Why should anyone have a greater claim to part of the global atmospheric sink than any other?" then the first, and simplest response is: "No reason at all." In other words, everyone has the same claim to part of the atmospheric sink as everyone else. This kind of equality seems self-evidently fair, at least as a starting point for discussion, and perhaps, if no good reasons can be found for moving from it, as an end point as well.

If we take this view, then we need to ask how much carbon each country would be allowed to emit and compare that with what they are now emitting. The first question is what total level of carbon emission is acceptable. The Kyoto Protocol aimed to achieve a level for developed nations that was 5 percent below 1990 levels. Suppose that we focus on emissions for the entire planet and aim just to stabilize carbon emissions at their present levels. Then the allocation per person conveniently works out at about 1 metric ton per year. This therefore becomes the basic equitable entitlement for every human being on this planet.

Now compare actual per capita emissions for some key nations. The United States currently produces more than 5 tons of carbon per person per year. Japan and Western European nations have per capita emissions that range from 1.6 tons to 4.2 tons, with most below 3 tons. In the developing world, emissions average 0.6 tons per capita, with China at 0.76 and India at 0.29.[25] This means that to reach an "even-handed" per capita annual emission limit of 1 ton of carbon per person, India would be able to increase its carbon emissions to more than three times what they now are. China would be able to increase its emissions by a more modest 33 percent. The United States, on the other hand, would have to reduce its emissions to no more than one-fifth of present levels.

One objection to this approach is that allowing countries to have allocations based on the number of people they have gives them insufficient incentive to do anything about population growth. But if the global population increases, the per capita amount of carbon that each country is allocated will diminish, for the aim is to keep total carbon emissions below a given level. Therefore a nation that increases its population would be imposing additional burdens on other nations. Even nations with zero population growth would have to decrease their carbon outputs to meet the new, reduced per capita allocation.

---

25 See G. Marland, T.A. Boden, and R.J. Andres, *Global, Regional, and National Fossil Fuel CO_2 Emissions* (Carbon Dioxide Information Analysis Center, Oak Ridge, TN), available at <cdiac.esd.ornl. gov/trends/emis/top96.cap>. These are 1996 figures.

By setting national allocations that are tied to a specified population, rather than allowing national allocations to rise with an increase in national population, we can meet this objection. We could fix the national allocation on the country's population in a given year, say 1990, or the year that the agreement comes into force. But since different countries have different proportions of young people about to reach reproductive age, this provision might produce greater hardship in those countries that have younger populations than in those that have older populations. To overcome this, the per capita allocation could be based on an estimate of a country's likely population at some given future date. For example, estimated population sizes for the next 50 years, which are already compiled by the United Nations, might be used.[26] Countries would then receive a reward in terms of an increased emission quota per citizen if they achieved a lower population than had been expected, and a penalty in terms of a reduced emission quota per citizen if they exceeded the population forecast—and there would be no impact on other countries.

Aiding the Worst-off

Giving everyone an equal share of a common resource like the capacity of the atmosphere to absorb our emissions is, I have argued, a fair starting point, a position that should prevail unless there are good reasons for moving from it. Are there such reasons? Some of the best-known accounts of fairness take the view that we should seek to improve the prospects of those who are worst off. Some hold that we should assist the worst-off only if their poverty is due to circumstances for which they are not responsible, like the family, or country, into which they were born, or the abilities they have inherited. Others think we should help the worst-off irrespective of how they have come to be so badly off. Among the various accounts that pay special attention to the situation of the worst-off, by far the most widely discussed is that of John Rawls. Rawls holds that, when we distribute goods, we can only justify giving more to those who are already well off if this will improve the position of those who are worst off. Otherwise, we should give only to those who are, in terms of resources, at the lowest level.[27] This approach allows us to depart from equality, but only when doing so helps the worst-off.

Whereas the strict egalitarian is vulnerable to the objection that equality can be achieved by "leveling down," that is, by bringing the rich down to the level of the poor without improving the position of the poor, Rawls's account is immune

26 Paul Baer et al., "Equity and Greenhouse Gas Responsibility," *Science* 289 (29 September 2000): 2287; Dale Jamieson, "Climate Change and Global Environmental Justice," in P. Edwards and C. Miller, eds., *Changing the Atmosphere: Expert Knowledge and Global Environmental Governance* (MIT, Cambridge, MA, 2001), pp. 287–307.
27 See John Rawls, *A Theory of Justice*, especially pp. 65-83. For a different way of giving priority to the worst-off, see Derek Parfit, "Equality or Priority?," The Lindley Lecture, University of Kansas, 21 November 1991, reprinted in Matthew Clayton and Andrew Williams, eds., *The Ideal of Equality* (Macmillan, London, 2000).

to this objection. For example, if allowing some entrepreneurs to become very rich will provide them with incentives to work hard and set up industries that provide employment for the worst-off, and there is no other way to provide that employment, then that inequality would be permissible.

That there are today very great differences in wealth and income between people living in different countries is glaringly obvious. It is equally evident that these differences depend largely on the fact that people are born into different circumstances, rather than because they have failed to take advantage of opportunities open to them. Hence if in distributing the atmosphere's capacity to absorb our waste gases without harmful consequences, we were to reject any distribution that fails to improve the situation of those who, through no fault of their own, are at the bottom of the heap, we would not allow the living standard in poor countries to be reduced while rich countries remain much better off.[28] To put this more concretely: if, to meet the limits set for the United States, taxes or other disincentives are used that go no further than providing incentives for Americans to drive more fuel-efficient cars, it would not be right to set limits on China that prevent the Chinese from driving cars at all.

In accordance with Rawls's principle, the only grounds on which one could argue against rich nations bearing all the costs of reducing emissions would be that to do so would make the poor nations even worse off than they would have been if the rich nations were not bearing all the costs. It is possible to interpret President George W. Bush's announcement of his administration's policy on climate change as an attempt to make this case. Bush said that his administration was adopting a "greenhouse gas intensity approach" which seeks to reduce the amount of greenhouse gases the United States emits per unit of economic activity. Although the target figure he mentioned—an 18 percent reduction over the next 10 years—sounds large, if the US economy continues to grow as it has in the past, such a reduction in greenhouse gas intensity will not prevent an increase in the total quantity of greenhouse gases that the United States emits. But Bush justified this by saying "economic growth is the solution, not the problem" and "the United States wants to foster economic growth in the developing world, including the world's poorest nations."[29]

Allowing nations to emit in proportion to their economic activity—in effect, in proportion to their Gross Domestic Product—can be seen as encouraging efficiency, in the sense of leading to the lowest possible level of emissions for the amount produced. But it is also compatible with the United States continuing to emit more emissions, because it is producing more goods. That will mean that other nations

---

28 This is Rawls's "difference principle," applied without the restriction to national boundaries that are difficult to defend in terms of his own argument....

29 "President Announces Clear Skies and Global Climate Change Initiative," Office of the Press Secretary, White House, 14 February 2002, <www.whitehouse.gov/news/releases/2002/02/20020214-5. html>. For amplification of the basis of the administration's policy, see Executive Office of the President, Council of Economic Advisers, *2002 Economic Report of the President*, US Government Printing Office, Washington, DC, 2002, chapter 6, pp. 244-249, <http://w3.access.gpo.gov/eop/>.

must emit less, if catastrophic climate change is to be averted. Hence for Bush's "economic growth is the solution, not the problem" defense of a growth in US emissions to succeed as a Rawlsian defense of continued inequality in per capita emissions, it would be necessary to show that United States production not only makes the world as a whole better off, but also makes the poorest nations better off than they would otherwise be.

The major ethical flaw in this argument is that the primary beneficiaries of US production are the residents of the United States itself. The vast majority of the goods and services that the United States produces—89 percent of them—are consumed in the United States.[30] Even if we focus on the relatively small fraction of goods produced in the United States that are sold abroad, US residents benefit from the employment that is created and, of course, US producers receive payment for the goods they sell abroad. Many residents of other countries, especially the poorest countries, cannot afford to buy goods produced in the United States, and it isn't clear that they benefit from US production.>

Figure 33.1

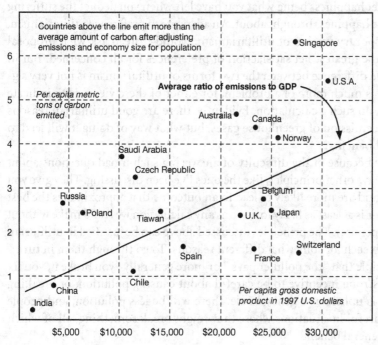

Source: CIA: Carbon Dioxide Information Analysis Center.

30 National Council on Economic Education, "A Case Study: United States International Trade in Goods and Services—May 2001," <www.econedlink.org/lessons/index.cfm?lesson=EM196>.

The factual basis of the argument is also flawed: the United States does not produce more efficiently, in terms of greenhouse gas emissions, than other nations. Figures published by the U.S. Central Intelligence Agency show that the United States is well above average in the amount of emissions per head it produces in proportion to its per capita GDP. (See Figure 33.1.) On this basis the United States, Australia, Canada, Saudi Arabia, and Russia are relatively inefficient producers, whereas developing countries like India and China join European nations like Spain, France, and Switzerland in producing a given value of goods per head for a lower than average per capita level of emissions.[31]

Because the efficiency argument fails, we must conclude that a principle that requires us to distribute resources so as to improve the level of the worst-off would still, given the huge resource gap between rich and poor nations, make the rich nations bear all of the costs of the required changes.

The Greatest Happiness Principle

Classical utilitarians would not support any of the principles of fairness discussed so far. They would ask what proposal would lead to the greatest net happiness for all affected—net happiness being what you have left when you deduct the suffering caused from the happiness brought about. An advocate of preference utilitarianism, a more contemporary version of utilitarianism, would instead ask what proposal would lead to the greatest net satisfaction of preferences for all concerned. But in this context, the difference between the two forms of utilitarianism is not very significant. What is much more of a problem, for either of these views, is to indicate how one might do such a calculation. Evidently, there are good utilitarian reasons for capping the emission of greenhouse gases, but what way of doing it will lead to the greatest net benefits?

Perhaps it is because of the difficulty of answering such broad questions about utility that we have other principles, like the ones I've been discussing. They give you easier answers and are more likely to lead to an outcome that approximates the best consequences (or is at least as likely to do so as any calculation we could make without using those principles). The principles discussed above can be justified in utilitarian terms, although each for somewhat different reasons. To go through them in turn:

1. The principle that "the polluter pays," or more generally "you broke it, you fix it," provides a strong incentive to be careful about causing pollution, or breaking things. So if it is upheld as a general rule, there will be less pollution, and people will be more careful in situations where they might break something, all of which will be to the general benefit.

2. The egalitarian principle will not, in general, be what utilitarians with perfect knowledge of all the consequences of their actions would choose. Where there is no

---

31 Andrew Revkin, "Sliced Another Way: Per Capita Emissions," *New York Times*, 17 June 2001, section 4, p. 5.

other clear criterion for allocating shares, however, it can be an ideal compromise that leads to a peaceful solution, rather than to continued fighting. Arguably, that is the best basis for defending "one person, one vote" as a rule of democracy against claims that those who have more education, or who pay more taxes, or who have served in the military, or who believe in the one true God, or who are worse off should have additional votes because of their particular attributes.[32]

3. In practice, utilitarians can often support the principle of distributing resources to those who are worst off, because when you already have a lot, giving you more does not increase your utility as much as when you have only a little. One of the 1.2 billion people in the world living on $1 per day will get much more utility out of an additional $100 than will someone living on $60,000 per year. Similarly, if we have to take $100 from someone, we will cause much less suffering if we take it from the person earning $60,000 than if we take it from the person earning $365 a year. This is known as "diminishing marginal utility." When compared with giving resources to meet someone's core needs, giving further resources "at the margin" to someone else whose core needs have already been satisfied will lead to diminished utility. Hence a utilitarian will generally favor the worst-off when it comes to distributing resources. In contrast to Rawls, however, a utilitarian does not consider this principle to be absolute. The utilitarian always seeks the greatest overall benefit, and it is only a broad rule of thumb that this will generally be obtained by adding to the stock of resources of those who have the least.

The utilitarian would also have to take into account the greater hardship that might be imposed on people living in countries that have difficulty in complying with strict emission standards because their geography or climate compels their citizens to use a greater amount of energy to achieve a given level of comfort than do people living elsewhere. Canadians, for example, could argue that it would simply not be possible to live in many parts of their country without using above average quantities of energy to keep warm. Residents of rich countries might even advance the bolder claim that, since their affluent residents have become used to traveling by car, and keeping their houses cool in warm humid weather, they would suffer more if they have to give up their energy-intensive lifestyle than poorer people will suffer if they never get the chance to experience such comforts.

The utilitarian cannot refuse to consider such claims of hardship, even when they come from those who are already far better off than most of the world's people. As we shall see, however, these claims can be taken into account in a way that is compatible with the general conclusion to which the utilitarian view would otherwise lead: that the United States and other rich nations should bear much more of the burden of reducing greenhouse gas emissions than the poor nations—perhaps even the entire burden.

---

32 For discussion of equal votes as a compromise, see my *Democracy and Disobedience* (Clarendon, Oxford, 1973), pp. 30-41.

Fairness: A Proposal

Each of the four principles of fairness I have considered could be defended as the best one to take, or we could take some in combination. I propose, both because of its simplicity, and hence its suitability as a political compromise, and because it seems likely to increase global welfare, that we support the second principle, that of equal per capita future entitlements to a share of the capacity of the atmospheric sink, tied to the current United Nations projection of population growth per country in 2050.

Some will say that this is excessively harsh on industrialized nations like the United States, which will have to cut back the most on their output of greenhouse gases. But we have now seen that the equal per capita shares principle is much more indulged in the United States and other developed nations than other principles for which there are strong arguments. If, for example, we combined "the polluter pays" principle with the equal share principle, we would hold that until the excessive amounts of greenhouse gases in the atmosphere that the industrialized nations have put there have been soaked up, the emissions of industrialized nations ought to be held down to much less than a per capita equal share. As things stand now, even on an equal per capita share basis, for at least a century the developing nations are going to have to accept lower outputs of greenhouse gases than they would have had to, if the industrialized nations had kept to an equal per capita share in the past. So by saying, "forget about the past, let's start anew," the pure equal per capita share principle is a lot more favorable to the developed countries than an historically based principle would be.

The fact that 178 nations, including every major industrial nation in the world except the United States, have now indicated their intention to ratify the Kyoto Protocol makes the position of the United States particularly odious from an ethical perspective. The claim that the Protocol does not require the developing nations to do their share does not stand up to scrutiny. Americans who think that even the Kyoto Protocol requires America to sacrifice more than it should are really demanding that the poor nations of the world commit themselves to a level that gives them, in perpetuity, lower levels of greenhouse gas production per head of population than the rich nations have. How could that principle be justified? Alternatively, if that is not what the US Government is proposing, what exactly is it proposing?

It is true that there are some circumstances in which we are justified in refusing to contribute if others are not doing their share. If we eat communally and take turns cooking, then I can justifiably feel resentment if there are some who eat but never cook or carry out equivalent tasks for the good of the entire group. But that is not the situation with climate change, in which the behavior of the industrialized nations has been more like that of a person who has left the kitchen tap running but refuses either to turn it off, or to mop up the resulting flood, until you—who spilt an insignificant half-glass of water onto the floor—promise not to spill any more water. Now the other industrialized nations have agreed to turn off the tap (to be strictly accurate, to restrict the flow), leaving the United States, the biggest culprit, alone in its refusal to commit itself to reducing emissions.

Although it is true that the Kyoto Protocol does not initially bind the developing nations, it is generally understood that the developing countries will be brought into the binding section of the agreement after the industrialized nations have begun to move toward their targets. That was the procedure with the successful Montreal Protocol concerning gases that damage the ozone layer, and there is no reason to believe that it will not also happen with the Kyoto Protocol. China, by far the largest greenhouse gas emitter of the developing nations and the only one with the potential to rival the total—not, of course, per capita—emissions of the United States in the foreseeable future, has already, even in the absence of any binding targets, achieved a substantial decline in fossil-fuel CO_2 emissions, thanks to improved efficiency in coal use. Emissions fell from a high of 909 million metric tons of carbon in 1996 to 848 million metric tons of carbon in 1998. Meanwhile US emissions reached an all-time high of 1,906 million metric tons of carbon in 2000 an increase of 2.5 percent over the previous year.[33]

The real objection to allocating the atmosphere's capacity to absorb greenhouse gases to nations on the basis of equal per capita shares is that it would be tremendously dislocating for the industrialized nations to reduce their emissions so much that, within 5, 10, or 15 years, they were not producing more than their share, on a per capita basis, of some acceptable level of greenhouse gases. But fortunately there is a mechanism that, while fully compatible with the equal per capita share principle, can make this transition much easier for the industrialized nations, while at the same time producing great benefits for the developing nations. That mechanism is emissions trading. Emissions trading works on the same simple economic principle of trade in general: if you can buy something from someone else more cheaply than you can produce it yourself, you are better off buying it than making it. In this case, what you can buy will be a transferable quota to produce greenhouse gases, allocated on the basis of an equal per capita share. A country like the United States that is already producing more gases than its share will need its full quota, and then some, but a country like Russia that is below its share will have excess quota that it can sell. If the quota were not transferable, the United States would immediately have to reduce its output to about 20 percent of what it now produces, a political impossibility. In contrast, Russia would have no incentive to maintain its levels of greenhouse gas emissions well below its allowable share. With emissions trading, Russia has an incentive to maximize the amount of quota it can sell, and the United States has, at

33 Energy Information Administration, *Emissions of Greenhouse Gases in the United States 2000*, DOE/ EIA-0573 (2000), US Department of Energy, Washington, DC, November 2001, page vii, <www. cia/doe.gov/pub/oiaf/1605/cdrom/pdf/ggrpt/057300.pdf>.

some cost, an opportunity to acquire the quotas it needs to avoid total disruption of the economy.[34]

Although some may think that emissions trading allows the United States to avoid its burdens too easily, the point is not to punish nations with high emissions, but to produce the best outcome for the atmosphere. Permitting emissions trading gives us a better hope of doing this than prohibiting emissions trading does. The Kyoto Protocol as agreed to in Bonn and Marrakech allows emissions trading between states that have binding quotas. Thus Russia will have quota to sell, but countries like India, Bangladesh, Mozambique, Ethiopia, and many others will not. Emissions trading would be much more effective, and have far better consequences, if all nations were given binding quotas based on their per capita share of the designated total emissions. As we saw earlier in this chapter, even the environmental skeptic Bjorn Lomborg accepts that with global emissions trading, the Kyoto Protocol produces a net economic benefit. Moreover, global emissions trading would give the world's poorest nations something that the rich nations very much want. They would have, at last, something that they can trade in exchange for the resources that will help them to meet their needs. This would be, on most principles of justice or utility, a very good thing indeed. It could also end the argument about making the developing nations part of a binding agreement on emissions, because the developing nations would see that they have a great deal to gain from binding quotas.

Since global emissions trading is both possible and desirable, it also answers two objections to allocating greenhouse gas emissions quotas on the basis of equal per capita shares. First, it answers the objection raised when discussing a utilitarian approach to these problems, that countries like Canada might suffer undue hardship if forced to limit emissions to the same per capita count as, say, Mexico, because Canadians need to use more energy to survive their winters. But global emissions trading means that Canada would be able to buy the quota it requires from other countries that do not need their full quota. Thus the market would provide a measure of the additional burden put on the world's atmosphere by keeping one's house at a pleasant temperature when it is too cold, or too hot, outside. Citizens of rich countries could choose to pay that price and keep themselves warm, or cool, as the case may be. They would not, however, be claiming a benefit for themselves that they were not prepared to allow poor countries to have, because the poor countries would benefit by having emission quotas to sell. The claim of undue hardship therefore does not justify allowing rich countries to have a higher per capita emissions quota than poor countries.

Second, global emissions trading answers the objection that equal per capita shares would lead to inefficient production because countries with little industrialization would be able to continue to manufacture goods even though they emit more

---

34 See Jae Edmonds et al., *International Emissions Trading and Global Climate Change: Impacts on the Cost of Greenhouse Gas Mitigation.* A report prepared for the Pew Center on Global Climate Change, December 1999, available at <www.pewclimate.org/projects/econ_emissions.cfm>.

greenhouse gases per unit of economic activity than highly industrialized nations, while the highly industrialized nations would have to cut back on their manufacturing capacity, even though they produce fewer emissions per unit of economic activity. But as we have seen, the present laissez-faire system allows emitters to reap economic benefits for themselves, while imposing costs on third parties who may or may not share in the benefits of the polluters' high productivity. That is neither a fair nor an efficient outcome. A well-regulated system of per capita entitlements combined with global emissions trading would, by internalizing the true costs of production, lead to a solution that is both fair and efficient.

There are two serious objections, one scientific and one ethical, to global emissions trading. The scientific objection is that we do not have the means to measure emissions accurately for all countries. Hence it would not be possible to know how much quota these countries have to sell, or need to buy. This is something that needs more research, but it should not prove an insuperable obstacle in the long run. As long as estimates are fair, they do not need to be accurate to the last ton of carbon. The ethical objection is that while emissions trading would benefit poor countries if the governments of those countries used it for the benefit of their people, some countries are run by corrupt dictators more interested in increasing their military spending, or adding to their Swiss bank accounts. Emissions trading would simply give them a new way of raising money for these purposes.

The ethical objection is similar to a problem discussed in [the next chapter of *One World*] on trade, legitimacy, and democracy, and my proposed solution may be clearer after reading that section. It is to refuse to recognize a corrupt dictatorial regime, interested only in self-preservation and self-enrichment, as the legitimate government of the country that has excess quota to sell. In the absence of any legitimate government that can receive payments for quota, the sale of quota could be managed by an international authority answerable to the United Nations. That authority could hold the money it receives in trust until the country has a government able to make a credible claim that the money will be used to benefit the people as a whole.

Down from the Clouds?

To cynical observers of the Washington scene, all this must seem absurdly lacking in political realism. George W. Bush's administration has spurned the Kyoto Protocol, which allows the United States to continue to produce at least four times its per capita share of carbon dioxide. Since 1990 US emission levels have already risen by 14 percent. The half-hearted measures for energy conservation proposed by the Bush administration will, at best, slow that trend. They will not reverse it. So what is the point of discussing proposals that are far less likely to be accepted by the US Government than the Kyoto Protocol?

The aim of this chapter is to help us to see that there is no ethical basis for the present distribution of the atmosphere's capacity to absorb greenhouse gases without drastic climate change. If the industrialized countries choose to retain this distribution (as the United States does), or to use it as the starting point for a new allocation of the capacity of the global sink (as the countries that accept the Kyoto Protocol do), they are standing simply on their presumed rights as sovereign nations. That claim, and the raw military power these nations yield, makes it impossible for anyone else to impose a more ethically defensible solution on them. If we, as citizens of the industrialized nations, do not understand what would be a fair solution to global warming, then we cannot understand how flagrantly self-serving the position of those opposed to signing even the Kyoto Protocol is. If, on the other hand, we can convey to our fellow citizens a sense of what would be a fair solution to the problem, then it may be possible to change the policies that are now leading the United States to block international cooperation on something that will have an impact on every being on this planet.

Let us consider the implications of this situation a little further. Today the overwhelming majority of nations in the world are united in the view that greenhouse gas emissions should be significantly reduced, and all the major industrial nations but one have committed themselves to doing something about this. That one nation, which happens to be the largest emitter of them all, has refused to commit itself to reducing its emissions. Such a situation gives impetus to the need to think about developing institutions or principles of international law that limit national sovereignty. It should be possible for people whose lands are flooded by sea-level rises due to global warming to win damages from nations that emit more than their fair share of greenhouse gases. Another possibility worth considering is sanctions. There have been several occasions on which the United Nations has used sanctions against countries that have been seen as doing something gravely wrong. Arguably the case for sanctions against a nation that is causing harm, often fatal, to the citizens of other countries is even stronger than the case for sanctions against a country like South Africa under apartheid, since that government, iniquitous as its policies were, was not a threat to other countries.... Is it inconceivable that one day a reformed and strengthened United Nations will invoke sanctions against countries that do not play their part in global measures for the protection of the environment?

34. An Open Letter to Oxfam[*]

Vandana Shiva

Dear Friends at Oxfam,

I have just received a copy of your position on GMOs and WTO and it has saddened and disappointed me.

While Oxfam has been an NGO leader on food security issues, and it has been part of the mobilisation for a moratorium on GM crops in UK, it is now calling for donor support for developing of GM technologies in developing countries.

Oxfam sees the "need for public investment and incentives to promote private investment in GM research and innovation benefiting poor farmers and low income consumers."

In its position paper on "GM crops, WTO and Food Security," Oxfam recommends, "Donor governments and agencies commit resources for investment in research into the potential opportunities presented by applications of GM to deliver environmental and health benefits pertaining to small holder agriculture in adverse agroecological zones."

We feel that Oxfam risks betraying the South, the poor and food security objectives by calling for support for promotion of GM crops in the South instead of calling for support for ecological and sustainable agriculture which is much better suited to the small farmers in adverse agroecological zones.

Research from our own programmes in India and studies worldwide are countering the myth that ecological agriculture has low productivity and low returns. Farmers

---

* Source: <http://members.iinet.net.au/~rabbit/vanlatest.htm>.

in fact have a tripling of incomes by getting off the chemical treadmill and getting out of the debt trap created by purchase of costly seeds and chemicals.

Because GE free agriculture is good for the poor and good for the environment. We have launched the "Bija Satyagraha" which includes the creation of GE free zones in agriculture as part of the National Food Rights Campaign in India, in which more than 2,500 groups participate.

As a leading NGO funder and development agency, we hope Oxfam will join our call for freedom from GE in the South. Oxfam should join the worldwide campaign for promoting alternatives to both chemical agriculture and genetic engineering while calling for a moratorium on GM crops.

The focus on promotion of GM crops in the Third World, and the total absence of recommendations relating to the promotion of sustainable, ecological agriculture will on the one hand deprive the poor of ecological, decentralised production systems. On the other hand it carries a major risk of creating a nutritional apartheid—with northern consumers having GE free foods and the poor in the South being condemned to a future based on GE crops and foods.

At this juncture in history, we need a joining of environment and development concerns, we need a combining of producer and consumer interests, we need North South solidarity. With such a joining of forces, people's power will be successful in controlling the corporate Biotechnology giants and promoting ecological options for small farmers.

We hope Oxfam will review its GM policy for the Third World and be part of the global movement for a sustainable and equitable agriculture.

Oxfam spends £13m a year on projects linked to crop production. It provides £10m assistance for food aid and trades in 60 food products through the Oxfam Fair Trade Company. It, therefore, has an influential role in setting food security agendas.

Oxfam will definitely be assisting to provide relief in the recent disaster caused by the super cyclone in Orissa. We hope your food aid will be GE free and that in the rehabilitation programmes you will help distribute open pollinated varieties and indigenous varieties of seeds so that farmers are not made dependent on costly inputs.

We look forward to working with Oxfam on these urgent issues.
Yours sincerely,

Vandana Shiva

35. Shiva the Destroyer?[*][1]

Thomas R. DeGregori

Postmodernist anti-science thought was once primarily associated with European and North American academics in the humanities. Now not only has its influence become international, but it has become integrally intertwined with a number of other issues such as anti-globalization, anti-transgenic technology in agriculture, and conservation. Nobody can fault the prevailing internationalism of postmodernists and their respect for different cultures and peoples (except for the culture of those who are committed to modern science/technology and its benefits). Nor can we fault their argument that all of us have biases, though they fail to comprehend the vital role that scientific method plays in helping to overcome the limitations which personal and cultural biases impose. Their belief in the worth and dignity of all human beings is unexceptionable. Some of us critics would suspect, however, that in going global, postmodernist thought does not necessarily impact on other political/cultural traditions in a way which upholds the worthy ideas that most postmodernists claim to espouse. To the extent that these postmodernist ideas have become part of the globalization debates, there is a legitimate issue of consistency if in fact what is being forcefully advocated produces adverse outcomes contrary to what its proponents claim for them.

None of us are totally consistent in all our beliefs, nor can we find total consistency in the various political or social movements we may be committed to. Life and the world of ideas are messy, and so we can take heart with Ralph Waldo Emerson's

---

* Source: http://www.mobot.org/plantscience/resbot/Phil/shiva.htm.

1 The article is largely drawn from the author's book manuscript, *Origins of the Organic Agriculture Debate* (Ames: Iowa State P, A Blackwell Scientific Publisher [in press], <http://store.yahoo.com/isupress/0813805139.html>. Additional material is taken from two recently published books: Thomas R. DeGregori, *The Environment, Our Natural Resources, and Modern Technology* (Ames: Iowa State P, A Blackwell Scientific Publisher), and Thomas R. DeGregori, *Bountiful Harvest: Technology, Food Safety, and the Environment* (Washington, DC: Cato Institute), which was originally published as *Agriculture and Modern Technology: A Defense* (Ames: Iowa State UP). Author's homepage is <www.uh.edu/~trdegreg>.

467

strictures against that foolish consistency which is the hobgoblin of petty minds. A little untidiness and a few gaps in our knowledge here and there are probably healthy, and facilitate the emergence of new ideas. However, the argument to be pursued here is that there is a basic inconsistency, or more accurately, a *fundamental contradiction* between what has been advocated by a type of postmodernist thought, and its practical outcome in developing countries. It is a contradiction that is often so blatant as to undermine whatever merit there may be in the avowed postmodernist respect for other cultures. Stated baldly, the respect for Postmodernist anti-science thought was once primarily associated with European and North American academics in the humanities. Local ways of knowing, rather than promoting multi-culturalism, ends up instead promoting crass forms of cultural chauvinism and intolerance that can devolve into violence. In our internet/information age, there is no excuse for those who have entered various globalization debates without knowing the outcomes and implications of their advocacy.

Local Knowledge and Reactionary Politics

Dr. Vandana Shiva is likely the world's most celebrated holistic ecofeminist, deep ecologist, postmodernist luddite, anti-globalizer, and spokesperson for those she claims are without a voice. Because she has advanced degrees in science, Shiva is useful for providing legitimacy to a range of anti-science views on the part of those who mistrust scientific inquiry (except where they think that it will promote their ideological agenda). Contemporary ecofeminist literature is almost unreadable, particularly on the Green Revolution, which ecofeminists deem to be a failure, and on "organic" agriculture, which they favor. Being able to cite Shiva as a presumed authority allows them to talk about global agriculture without any substantive knowledge of how peoples around the world raise crops and feed their families. One wonders how many academics obtained tenure on the basis of books and articles for which Shiva was a major source.

One leader does not fully define a movement, to be sure, but Shiva with her condemnation of "scientific reductionism" has become so pre-eminent in the global deep ecology/ecofeminist movement against modern science that raising serious questions about her does in many respects raise questions about the entire movement. Shiva's ideas, which are shared and promoted in the West by ecofeminists and others as radical and revolutionary, often turn out to have reactionary consequences where they are practiced in India.

This may come as a shock to the true believers, but for many the faith in the fundamental rightness of Shiva's message is so firm that it would be a near impossibility to convince them otherwise. The philosopher of science Meera Nanda shows that the much revered "holistic way of knowing... lies at the very heart of caste and gender hierarchy in India" (Nanda 2002, 54). "The role that the goddesses and the idea of sacredness of nature have played (and still play) in perpetuating the oppression of actual women is not adequately understood by the enthusiasts for alternative sciences" (Nanda 2003a). It is the much venerated "local knowledge" of the Hindu cosmology of "Karma and caste" which was used to justify the repression of Dalits (the crushed or oppressed—untouchable). The liberation of women is "linked" to overcoming the "kind of cultural assumptions about sacredness and holism" that are promoted by Shiva (Nanda 2003b).

Many of those now promoting the virtues of "local ways of knowing" were, we hope, opponents of it in its pre-postmodernist manifestations. From 1948, with the election of the National Party in South Africa, to the early 1990s, a similar reverence for "local ways of knowing" appropriate to the culture was proclaimed and promoted as "Bantu education." It was called Apartheid and many of us spent most of our adult life in active opposition to it, as, undoubtedly, did many of today's activists who tout the special virtues of local knowledge.

Among the many reasons for opposition to Apartheid and its repressive policies, was that the so-called "Bantu education" would handicap the student even in a non-Apartheid society by not providing her or him with the knowledge necessary to survive economically. Today we have what is misnamed as "Science Studies" promoting a "Navajo way of knowing" (which is "assuredly more spiritual and holistic than European ways") in learning mathematics by "teaching calculus before fractions" (Olson 1999). Among many problems with this method of teaching is the "difficulty of expressing the slope of a line, one of the fundamentals of calculus, in any way other than by using a fraction or decimal" (Olson 1999). Thus, "while well-meaning teachers puzzle out such difficulties, Navajo children are...to grow up without learning how to compute sales tax" (Olson 1999). From the elite precincts of Western universities, "multi-culturalism" has spread to other parts of the world. Across the border from where Shiva's ecofeminism lends support to Hindu chauvinism, Pakistani proponents of "Islamic science" and "Islamic epistemology" have been

> citing the work of feminist science critics in their campaign to purge many Western ideas from the schools, and certain feminist professors in the West—perhaps caught up in the thrill of having their work cited half a world away—have favorably cited the Islamicists right back. (Olson 1999)

Not to be outdone by Shiva's Indian advocacy, in the United States there are advocates of a mysterious entity called "feminist algebra" (Bookchin 1995, 212). When the right-wing Bharatiya Janata Party (BJP) came to power in Uttar Pradesh, India, in 1992, they sought to awaken "national pride" by making "Vedic mathematics compulsory for high school students" (Nanda 1996b). "Hindu ways of knowing" involved government-approved texts replacing standard algebra and calculus with sixteen Sanskrit verses. Leading Indian mathematicians and historians examined the verses and found "nothing Vedic about them," thinking them merely a "set of clever formulas for quick computation" and not a "piece of ancient wisdom" (Nanda 1996b). According to Meera Nanda (1996b), "in the name of national pride, students are being deprived of conceptual tools that are crucial in solving real-world mathematical problems they will encounter as scientists and engineers."

Hinduization extends beyond mathematics to promoting the "Aryan race" together with a disdain for all "foreigners including Muslims." The BJP along with the VHP (Vishva Hindu Parishad or World Hindu Council) are offsprings of the RSS (Rashtirya Svyamsevak Sangh or Organization of National Volunteers) which has been actively promoting hatred of Muslims and Christians in India, and has been involved in the destruction of Muslim and Christian places of worship and fostering deadly riots against non-Hindus. Postmodernist/ecofeminist multi-culturalism might be a worthy idea in some ways, but when it is integrated with a "suspicion of modern science as a metanarrative of binary dualism, reductionism and consequently domination of nature, women and Third World people" it supports Hindu reactionary modernists who claim the "same holist, non-logocentric ways of knowing not as a standpoint of the oppressed but for the glory of the Hindu nation itself" (Nanda 2000, 2001).

The Chipko "Movement"
Many activists like Shiva, who are promoted in the West by the anti-globalization Greens and who receive uncritical acclaim, are often the object of very severe criticism in their own countries, a fact which goes largely unreported. After an article in a Malaysian newspaper talked about Shiva in highly flattering terms, claiming that she was a leader of the famed Chipko (tree huggers) movement in India, the Chipko local activists sent a letter of protest to the editor, arguing that the interview was based on false claims and noting that it had angered many people. Those writing the letter saw themselves as being the "real activists," who do not understand why Shiva is "reportedly publishing wrong claims about Chipko in the foreign press."

Shiva uses Chipko as a model for Green ideologies from deep ecology to ecofeminism. Jayanta Bandyopadhyay, a distinguished scientist and environmentalist, examines each of these ideologies and deems them myths without any basis in fact (1999). He is an active supporter of the Chipko villages, in which he finds "a movement rooted in economic conflicts over mountain forests," and a "social movement based on gender collaboration" and not a "feminist movement based on gender conflicts" (Bandyopadhyay 1999).

Chipko is but one example where external activists, even those who may be well intentioned idealists, in effect hijack a movement and use it to promote an ideological agenda. The original motivation for "participating in Chipko protests" was to gain local control of forest resources in order to create a forest-based industry which offered the Himalayan villagers the possibility that their kinsmen who had to migrate to find work, might be employed closer to home. Further, increased local access to forest resources might "have offered women the possibility of adding to their meagre incomes and insuring themselves from potential crisis if remittances ceased or became intermittent" (Rangan 2000, 199–200).

Chipko is one of many cases of environmental groups in developed countries co-opting a cause like wildlife or habitat conservation, or a local movement with legitimate grievances, and then subverting them. In the case of Chipko, the co-option was initially by people from the urban elite in India, who received international acclaim as a result. As with other cases that I have examined, in places like Africa and the Americas, not only do local concerns get brushed aside, but often the locals are worse off because of the external "support." This is particularly true in case after case that I have examined for conservation projects, be they in Africa, Central America or India, where local interests are swept aside in favor of saving the environment from those who live there (DeGregori, 2004, Chapters 4, 10 & 11; DeGregori 2002, Chapter 2).

One of Shiva's "Chipko women" from the Pindar Valley in Chamoli District, Gayatri Devi, bitterly states that the movement has made life worse in the valley:

> Now they tell me that because of Chipko the road cannot be built [to her village], because everything has become parovarian [environment].... We cannot get even wood to build a house...our ha-haycock [rights and concessions] have been snatched away. (Rangan 2000, 42)

This helps to answer the questions which Rangan raises:

> Why do words like environment and ecology make so many people living in the Garhwal Himalayas see red? Why do so many of them make derisive comments when the Chipko movement figures in any discussion? Why is it that in most parts of Garhwal today, local populations are angry and resentful of being held hostage by Chipko, an environmental movement of their own making? (Rangan 1993, 155)

When the world community was ready to hear the claims of the Garhwal Himalayan villages,

> their voice in the Chipko movement had all but ceased to exist. The brief love affair between Chipko's activists and the state had resulted in the romantic ideal that the Himalayan environment by itself mattered more than the people who eked out their existence within it.

Rangan adds that:

> if some of the communities are ready to banish their axes today, it must be seen as yet another attempt to affirm themselves and give voice to the difficulties of sustaining livelihoods within their localities. (174–75)

From Agarwal and Narain, we learn that the situation has driven some to advocate practices that violate laws which the urban conservationists have imposed: "Uttarkhand, the land which gave birth to the Chipko movement, now even has a Jungle Kato Andolan (cut the forest movement). Thanks to the ministry of environment, 'environment' is no longer a nice word in Uttarkhand" (1991). Rangan argues that the Chipko today is a "fairy tale," a myth sustained and propagated by a few self-appointed spokespeople through conferences, books, and journal articles that eulogize it as a social movement, peasant movement, environmental movement, women's movement, Ghandian movement—in short, an all-encompassing movement (Rangan 1993, 158).

The Green Revolution

Dr. Vandana Shiva, in a book-length diatribe against the Green Revolution, frequently refers to its voracious demand for chemical fertilizers and indicates that there are alternative ways, more benign, of achieving these outputs (Shiva 1991). Plants need ingredients (nutrients) in order to grow. If a molecule is in the plant, it or its constituent elements must come from somewhere. Except for carbon dioxide from the atmosphere, plants derive their nutrients from the soil, or in the case of nitrogen from atmospheric nitrogen mediated by cyanobacteria (other than that from fertilizer). More plant output means more nutrient input. The often repeated claim that Green Revolution plants need more fertilizer has about as much meaning as saying that it takes more food to raise three children than it does to raise one. If sufficient nutrient is not in the soil, it must be added. Shiva's argument in essence is that one can grow plants without nutrients or that one can achieve the same output as Green Revolution seeds yield without providing nutrient input other than available "organic" sources. This is patently nonsensical and violates our fundamental knowledge of physics.

Shiva has made a number of preposterous statements over the years about yields in traditional Indian agriculture or traditional agriculture elsewhere such as among the Maya. Even before the Green Revolution dramatically increased the demand for and use of synthetic fertilizer, there was a large difference between the nutrients extracted from the soil in India and the "organic" nutrients available to be returned to it. In fact, nearly twice as much nutrient was being withdrawn from the soil as was being returned. Contrary to Shiva's assertions, this process was not sustainable. Given the dramatic increases in Indian agricultural output over the last four decades (which more than accommodated a doubling of the population), the deficit in "organic" nutrient must be vastly greater today. Shiva cites Sir Albert Howard, whose vitalist ideas on "organic" agriculture were developed in colonial India (Howard 1940). But though he was a strong proponent of composting ("Indore method"), Howard recognized the need for additional synthetic fertilizer and improved seeds, which means he might have favored GM crops if he were alive today.

Shiva has a belief that "food crops for local needs" are "water prudent" (Shiva 2000). For the Green Revolution grains, the primary output is a larger percentage of the plant (harvest index) and therefore requires less nutrient input per unit of output. These gains in agricultural efficiency and in yields per hectare, particularly for the Green Revolution grains, has accommodated a doubling of the world's population, with about a 30% increase in per capita food consumption with only a slight increase in land under cultivation (about 4% for grains). For rice, the gains in water use efficiency have been nothing less than astounding. According to a recent FAO (UN Food and Agriculture Organization) report, "the modern rice varieties have about a threefold increase in water productivity compared with traditional varieties" (FAO 2003, 28). Overall, for water use in agriculture, "water productivity increased by at least 100 percent between 1961 and 2001" while water use per capita was falling about in half (FAO 2003, 25–26). What the FAO is primarily describing is the yield increases and greater plant efficiency of the Green Revolution technologies so sharply criticized by Shiva.

Biotechnologists are working to create even more efficient plants, a goal which is opposed by Shiva and her followers. In her paeans in praise of cow dung, Shiva's pre-Green Revolution Indian agriculture is one of a healthy, self-sufficient, calorically adequate, nutritious food supply produced in an ecologically sustainable manner (Avery 2000; for a critique of Shiva by an Indian scholar, see Nanda 1991, 1997, 1998). Why hundreds of millions of peasant agriculturalists in India and around the world have forsaken this utopian existence and adopted the Green Revolution's crops and modern agricultural technologies is never explained. Maybe those actually raising crops and feeding their families know something about agriculture that Shiva and her fellow activists don't?

Equally unexplained is why, if, as Shiva argues, modern technology is pauperizing populations and in many cases driving people to suicide, life expectancies have risen so dramatically throughout Asia for both rural and urban populations. Even more difficult to explain is why those in developed countries, who are presumed to be educated and informed, uncritically accept her musings and pay her homage, including selecting her to give prestigious presentations such as the Reith Lecture (Shiva 2000 and Scruton 2000).

Contradictions, Mistakes and Double Standards

Contradictions and mistakes are all too prevalent in the work of Shiva and those who revere her. For example, in a public lecture in Toronto, Canada, she claimed both that the price level of food in India was doubling and that it was falling. Arguing that the technologies of the Green Revolution have failed, she has the price of food in India doubling so that consumers can no longer afford it. But when she wishes to criticize the United States for "dumping" food on the Indian market, pushing Indian farmers to commit suicide, she claims that subsidized foreign food is "driving down prices" (O'Hara 2000; Oakley 2000).

The following excerpt from a news item on Shiva's visit to Houston in October of 2000 is indicative. Shiva appears not to know the difference between a field of rice and one of weeds:

> Shiva walked across the road and looked out into a shaggy field. "They look unhappy," she said. "The rice plants. Ours at home look very happy." "That," RiceTec reports, "is because it's not rice. That's our test field, it was harvested in August. That's weeds." (Tyer 2000)

Shiva-inspired anti-technology criticism reached its true nadir when humanitarian aid for people in need was attacked because of the technology used to produce it. In India, following a "super-cyclone," a team from Vandana Shiva's "research foundation" gathered samples of donated grain while involved in "relief work" and had them tested in the United States to see if they were genetically modified. Claiming that they were genetically modified, *Diverse Women for Diversity* then demanded that the government of India "immediately withdraw the corn-soya blend from Orissa," seemingly preferring starvation for the cyclone victims to a presumed but unproven contamination from GM food (RFSTE 2000, Devraj 2000, Lean 2000 and Jayarsman 2000).

Possibly, Shiva could arrange for "organic" agriculturalists like Prince Charles to provide famine relief using funds from Greenpeace and other environmental groups with annual budgets into the tens of millions of dollars. And once again, it is appropriate to ask how many poor farmers have Shiva's *Diverse Women for Diversity* or *The Research Foundation for Science, Technology and Ecology* helped to grow more food? How many of those in need have they helped to feed? And in the name of transparency, what are the sources of its funding?

These questions are legitimate because too many groups that raise and spend significant amounts of money and help feed no one, demand transparency from others and criticize groups and individuals who have assisted those in need by helping them to grow more food or by providing relief food that modern agricultural surpluses facilitate. Many "Civil Society" groups in developing countries are largely and in some cases fully funded by developed country NGOs, so one can legitimately ask questions about the independence of their judgements in much the same way that one would question the independence of a statement by a developing country employee of a multinational corporation (see DeGregori 2002).

Nanda accuses "populist intellectuals like Shiva" of being "guilty of hypocrisy and double standards" for failing to recognize that "their own growth as intellectuals and activists owes a tremendous debt" to the very ideas that they disparage (Nanda 1991, 55). It has not gone unobserved that those like Shiva who are most critical of modern science have gained favor in Western universities and have often benefited greatly as a result:

> Furthermore, the jet-setting, globe-trotting neopopulist intellectuals' propensity to project the life style of the poor as being morally superior and socially richer than that of the Western oppressors is hypocritical to say the least... [and] fails to offer a progressive and feasible program for change. (Nanda 1991, 39)

Local Knowledge versus Modern Knowledge

We talked earlier about the Chipko movement in the Himalayan Garhwal region of Uttar Pradesh, India for whom Shiva presumes to speak and for which she has won international acclaim. When the Chipko movement's battle for local control of vital forest resources was taken up by Shiva and other "deep ecologists," the local struggles for resources and development were sacrificed to global environmental concerns by groups that "tacitly support coercive conservation tactics that weaken local claims to resource access for sustaining livelihoods" (Rangan 2000, 239; see also Peluso 1993).

Those who champion local wisdom too often respect it only so long as it is in line with their ideological agenda. Ideas that are presumed to liberate end up being instruments of oppression. Their advocates in developed countries seem to live in a virtual Potemkin village, blissfully unaware that local knowledge and control privileges traditional elites who tend to be dominating upper class males who find the rhetoric of ecofeminism useful, but not its desire for equality of classes, races and genders. Anyone who has been involved in economic development is aware of the importance of local knowledge and the need to use it along with any other available knowledge. But there is a very big difference between using local knowledge and being dominated by it. And it is important to distinguish between local knowledge and local myth, particularly myths of domination that deny some people access to productive resources.

Intellectual elites in some developing countries such as Mexico promote local use and custom (usos y costumbres) with the same outcome of male domination. The modernism which opened up society and allowed racial and other minorities to demand equal rights and women to challenge male domination is being denied those who are most in need of change in poorer countries: "The oppressed Others do not need patronizing affirmations of their ways of knowing, as much as they need ways to challenge these ways of knowing" (Nanda 1996a, 2003b).

Modern knowledge allowed Nanda to escape from such practices as forced marriage and other forms of domination but still allowed her to retain a sense of shared identity with the culture of her origin. It is the rationality of the Enlightenment, science and modernity that were instrumental in the creation of more tolerant multi-cultural societies. As Nanda states it, "We Are All Hybrids Now" (Nanda 2001). I would add that we have been hybrids for some time. Over 60 years ago, the anthropologist Ralph Linton had a sketch of a "solid American citizen" awakening in a "bed built on a pattern which originated in the Near East" traversing the day taking for granted the diverse global origins of the items of his daily routine, ending it by thanking a "Hebrew deity in an Indo-European language that he is 100% American" (Linton 1963, 326–27).

More important, modernity allows one the freedom to participate fully in modernity while still being able to retain a more localized personal identity. This is a tolerance for diversity which is rare in the traditional societies that Shiva seeks to promote. Modern science and technology are central to this hybridity. As many of us (including Nanda) have long argued, calling science and technology "Western" is to accept the 19th century claim of exclusive authorship to what has been and remains a universal endeavor to which all peoples have contributed just as they contributed to the artifacts of Linton's 100% American.

Shiva and others can call modern science logophallocentric reductionism and any number of other pejorative slogans in contrast to Prakriti or the feminine principle, but, in fact, modern knowledge is liberating. Shiva and her cohorts may feel "victimized" by "alien" ideas, but it is doubtful that this is the case for many throughout the world who have benefited from it, whether by a larger crop or lives saved by immunization or antibiotics. Nanda suggests that it would be "interesting" to see the reaction of "untouchables" to the "knowledge that DNA material...has the same composition in all living beings, be it brahmin or bacterium. Or what would a woman do with the knowledge that it is the chromosome in sperm that determines the sex of the new born?" (1991, 38).

May we add that over 99.9% of the human genome is shared by all human beings and that of the less than 0.1% that differentiate us, only about 3 to 5% of it is between groups, with about 95% being intra group variation (Rosenberg et al. 2002). If Shiva wishes to help women and those in need in India, she should be promoting an understanding of DNA and molecular biology and its liberating implications rather than fostering false fears of its use for human betterment. Not only is the genome that unites us as humans vastly greater than that which differentiates us, but the portion of the genome that defines our individual biological differences within our culture is vastly greater than the minuscule portion of the genome, 0.05%, that defines differences between groups (Rosenberg et al. 2002; King and Motulsky 2002; Wade 2002).

We can argue as to how far we have come on the road to a more just society or how much farther we have to go, but it is undeniable that in countries like the United States, the rights of minorities and women have been greatly expanded over the last decades. Shiva has been promoting a road to a past that never existed and to a future where nobody really wants to go, including those who blindly follow her.

References

Agarwal, Anil and Sunita Narain. 1991. "Chipko People Driven to Jungle Kato [Cut the Forests] Stir." *Economic Times* (India), 31 March.

Avery, Alex. 2000. "Vandana Shiva Antoinette: Let Them Eat Weeds!" *Global Food Quarterly* 30.6 (Spring).

Bandyopadhyay, Jayanta. 1999. *Chipko Movement: Of Floated Myths and Flouted Realities.* "Mountain People, Forests, and Trees," Mountain Forum's on-line library, <http://www.mtnforum.org/resources/library/bandj99a.htm>.

Bookchin, Murray. 1995. *Re-enchanting Humanity: A Defense of the Human Spirit Against Antihumanism, Misanthropy, Mysticism, and Primitivism.* London and New York: Cassell.

DeGregori, Thomas R. 2002. "NGOs Don't Speak for the Hungry," American Council on Science and Health, *Health Facts and Fears*, 26 August, <http://www.health-factsandfears.com/featured_articles/aug2002/ngo082602.html>.

DeGregori, Thomas R. 2004. *Origins of the Organic Debate: Vitalist Junkscience vs. Scientific Inquiry.* Ames: Iowa State P, A Blackwell Scientific Publisher (in press).

Devraj, Ranjit. 2000. *Cyclone Victims Are Guinea Pigs for Mutant Food.* Inter Press Service, atimes.com online, 13 June.

FAO (Food and Agriculture Organization of the United Nations). 2003. *Unlocking the Water Potential of Agriculture.* Rome: Food and Agriculture Organization of the United Nations, <http://www.fao.org/ag/AGL/aglw/aquastat/kyoto/index.stm>.

Howard, Sir Albert. 1940. *Agricultural Testament.* Oxford: Oxford UP.

Jayarman, K.S. 2000. "GM Food Dumped on India as Food Aid." *Nature* 405 (6789): 875, 22 June.

King, Mary-Claire, and Arno G. Motulsky. 2002. "Human Genetics: Mapping Human History." *Science* 298 (5602): 2342–43, 20 December.

Lean, Geoffrey. 2000. "Rejected GM Food Dumped on the Poor." *The Independent* (London), 18 June.

Linton, Ralph. 1963. *The Study of Man.* New York: Appleton-Century-Crofts.

Nanda, Meera. 1991. "Is Modern Science a Western Patriarchal Myth? A Critique of the Populist Orthodoxy." *South Asian Bulletin* XI (1&2): 32–61.

Nanda, Meera. 1996a. "The Science Question in Postcolonial Feminism." In *The Flight from Science and Reason*, ed. Paul R. Gross, Norman Levitt and Martin W. Lewis, pp. 420–36. New York: The New York Academy of Sciences.

Nanda, Meera. 1996b. "The Science Wars in India." *Dissent* 44 (1), Winter.

Nanda, Meera. 1997. "History Is What Hurts: A Materialist Feminist Perspective on the Green Revolution and Its Ecofeminist Critics." In *Materialist Feminism: A Reader in Class, Difference, and Women's Lives*, ed. Rosemary Hennessy and Chrys Ingraham, pp. 364–94. New York: Routledge.

Nanda, Meera. 1998. "The Episteme Charity of the Social Constructivist Critics of Science and Why the Third World Should Refuse the Offer." In *A House Built on Sand: Exposing Postmodernist Myths About Science*, ed. Noretta Koertge, pp. 286–311. New York: Oxford UP.

Nanda, Meera. 2000. *Dharma and the Bomb: Post-Modern Critiques of Science and the Rise of Reactionary Modernism in India*, paper read at the American Sociological Association, August.

Nanda, Meera. 2001. "We Are All Hybrids Now: The Dangerous Epistemology of Post-Colonial Populism." *The Journal of Peasant Studies* 28(2): 162–87.

Nanda, Meera. 2002. *Breaking the Spell of Dharma: A Case for Indian Enlightenment*. Delhi: Three Essays.

Nanda, Meera. 2003a. "Anti-Science." In *The Oxford Companion to the History of Modern Science*. New York: Oxford UP.

Nanda, Meera. 2003b. "Do the Marginalized Valorize the Margins: Exploring the Dangers of Difference." In *Development or Post Development: Which Way for Women in the 21st Century*, ed. Kriemild Sunders. London: Zed Books. (In press in an edited book; citations taken from manuscript provided by the author.)

Oakley, Aaron. 2000. "Hating Modern Agriculture." *The New Australian* 151 (10–16 April).

O'Hara, Kathleen. 2000. "The Stolen Harvest." *The New Australian* 151 (10–16 April).

Olson, Walter. 1999. "Benighted Elite: Postmodernist Critics of Science Get Their Comeuppance." *Reason online*, June.

Peluso, N. 1993. "Coercing Conservation: The Politics of State Resource Control." *Global Environmental Change* 4 (2): 199–217.

Rangan, Haripriya. 1993. "Romancing the Environment: Popular Environmental Action in Garhwal Himalayas." In *In Defense of Livelihood: Comparative Studies on Environmental Action*, ed. John Friedmann and Haripriya Rangan, pp. 155–81. West Hartford, CT: Kumarian.

Rangan, Haripriya. 2000. *Of Myths and Movements: Rewriting Chipko into Himalayan History*. London; New York: Verso.

RFSTE. 2000. *US Government Dumping Genetically Engineered Corn-soya Mix on Victims of Orissa Super-cyclone*. New Delhi: Press Release, Diverse Women for Diversity, The Research Foundation for Science, Technology and Ecology, 2 June.

Rosenberg, Noah A., Jonathan K. Pritchard, James L. Weber, Howard M. Cann, Kenneth K. Kidd, Lev A. Zhivotovsky, and Marcus W. Feldman. 2002. "Genetic Structure of Human Populations." *Science* 298 (5602): 2381–85, 20 December.

Scruton, Roger. 2000. "Herbicide, Pesticide, Suicide: Seed Merchants Prosper and Farmers Wither; That's the Truth of Global Agribusiness." *Business, Weekend FT Magazine, Financial Times*, London, 6 June.

Shiva, Vandana. 1991. *The Violence of the Green Revolution: Third World Agriculture, Ecology, and Politics*. London: Zed Books.

Shiva, Vandana. 2000. BBC Reith Lectures 2000, *BBC online network*, 12 May.

Tyer, Brad. 2000. RiceTec Paddy Whack, *Houston Press*, 23 November.

Wade, Nicholas. 2002. "Gene Study Identifies 5 Main Human Populations." *Science* 298 (5602): 2381–85, 20 December.

Recommended Reading

Carson, R. (1963). *The Silent Spring.* Boston: Houghton Mifflin, 2002.

Collier, P. (2010). *The Plundered Planet: Why We Must—and How We Can—Manage Nature for Global Prosperity.* New York: Oxford UP.

Constanza, R., Graumlich, L.J., and Steffen, W. (eds.). (2011). *Sustainability or Collapse: An Integrated History and Future of People on Earth.* Cambridge, MA: MIT.

DeGregori, T.R. (2002). *Bountiful Harvest.* Washington, DC: Cato Institute.

Diamond, J. (2005). *Collapse: How Societies Choose to Fail or Succeed.* New York: Viking.

Grey, W. (1993). "Anthropocentrism and Deep Ecology." *Australasian Journal of Philosophy* 71.4: 463–75.

Hardin, G. (1968). "The Tragedy of the Commons." *Science* 162: 1243–48.

Jamison, D. (2008). *Ethics and the Environment: An Introduction.* Cambridge: Cambridge UP.

Lovelock, J. (2000). *Gaia: A New Look at Life on Earth.* New York: Oxford UP.

US Environmental Protection Agency. (2011). *Climate Change Basic Information.* <http://www.epa.gov/climatechange/basicinfo.html>.

VII

Gender: Introduction

Preference-satisfaction, Well-being, and Choice

As academic advisors we help students make career decisions and choose majors that will qualify them for their chosen occupations. It isn't easy. Some students have clear goals but lots are less sure.

In a primitive hunter-gatherer society our advisor job would be a no-brainer. You're a guy? Hunt! You're a gal? Gather! That's it. And it wouldn't be much harder in most pre-modern societies where, with few exceptions, individuals' occupations are determined by sex, class, family of origin, and other unchosen characteristics. The very idea that individuals should *choose* their occupations, and more particularly the idea that being male or female shouldn't determine their occupation or opportunities would have been amazing to most of our ancestors, and is still alien to many of our fellow humans.

We value choice—with good reason. Getting what we want usually makes us better off. Indeed, on one plausible account, that of *preference utilitarianism*, well-being consists in the satisfaction of our (informed and rationally considered) preferences. All other things being equal, the more choices we have, the more likely we are to satisfy our preferences. Therefore, the more options people have, the better off they are.

But maybe all other things are not equal. Some of my advisees have no clear preferences: they agonize about majors and career choices. They might be better off without all those confusing possibilities. Even assuming that preference-satisfaction makes us better off, having choices doesn't do us any good if it provides us with options we don't even want. If men prefer hunting and women prefer gathering, the hunter-gatherer arrangement may be perfectly fine: women are not better off for having the chance to hunt if that is not what they want to do, and men are no better off for having the gathering option if they prefer to hunt.

Most societies exhibit significant levels of occupational sex segregation. If, however, gendered differences in occupation reflect differences in male and female preferences, then, the preferentist says, there is no problem: so long as everyone gets what he or she wants, there is nothing to complain about. If all women prefer to gather and all men prefer to hunt then the best possible state of affairs is one in which all women gather and all men hunt—and it does not benefit anyone if men and women have the chance to do otherwise if that is something they do not want. If such sex differences exist, whether they are a result of nature or nurture, the division of labor is best for all concerned.

Individual and Statistical Differences

However, when people talk about sex differences, confusion sets in: they do not distinguish between on-the-average (or statistical) differences and across-the-board differences. "Elephants are bigger than fleas," we say. That is an across-the-board difference: every elephant is bigger than any flea. We also say, "men are taller than women." But that does not mark an across-the-board difference: it expresses an on-the-average, or statistical, difference. *On the average* men are taller than women, but some women are taller than some men.

There are statistical differences between men and women when it comes to skills, preferences, and other psychological characteristics too. It is controversial whether these differences are a result or nature of nurture or some combination of both. But it is uncontroversial that these psychological differences are statistical, on-the-average differences—not individual differences. It is not the case that every man is better at math or more aggressive than any woman or that every woman is better at languages and more nurturing than any man. It is also generally agreed that the statistical male–female differences in most psychological characteristics are much smaller than the statistical difference in heights. Research concerning differences in mathematical aptitude, for example, suggests that if there is a difference at all it is quite small.[1]

There are also statistical differences in male and female preferences, which may be a result of nature or nurture, or both. But once again there is significant overlap: there is much greater diversity amongst women and amongst men than between men and women on the average. And this means that, all other things being equal, a system that enforces sex roles, which restrict men to some roles and occupations and women to others, will undermine preference-satisfaction.

To see this, suppose the curves for hunting preference and gathering preference overlap, like the curves for height, so that on the average men prefer hunting to

---

1   Other studies suggest it is non-existent and there is reason to believe that at least some differences in math performance are a consequence of environment rather than innate aptitude. See, e.g., <http://web.mit.edu/newsoffice/2009/math-gender.html>.

gathering, while women on the average prefer gathering to hunting. If all men hunt and all women gather, then there will be some men and some women who happen to be well-suited to their assigned roles, who are perfectly delighted with the arrangement. There will be others who are indifferent between hunting and gathering or have only mild preferences for one activity or the other, who will find their assigned roles satisfactory—or can be socialized to prefer their socially appropriate roles. But there will also be men who would strongly prefer gathering to hunting and women who just can't stand gathering and would love to hunt, whom no amount of socialization would adjust to their assigned roles. And they will be miserable. Assuming an overlap in preferences, therefore, sex roles are costly. Moreover, if we assume significant overlap in skills and aptitudes as well, sex roles are costly not only to misfits who dislike their assigned roles but to the entire society, which misses out on the contribution they could make to the common good.

Yet sex roles are pervasive. And even in societies in which hunting and gathering aren't the only available jobs, occupational sex segregation remains the norm. Everywhere, to a greater or lesser extent, women are both differently off and worse off compared to men. Women have different options from men, fewer options, and, for the most part, less desirable options. Moreover, gender inequality is greatest in low-income countries and impedes development.

The Role of Gender in Development

The World Bank report "Engendering Development" is a comprehensive look at the status of women throughout the world, including an analysis of the causes and effects of gender inequality, which impedes development. Gender equality, the report notes, is a core development issue. Though women and girls bear the most direct costs of gender inequality, the costs cut more broadly across society, harming everyone. One study estimates that if the countries in South Asia, Africa, and the Middle East had started with the gender gap in average years of schooling that East Asia had in 1960 and had subsequently closed that gender gap at the same rate as East Asian countries, their per-capita income growth could have been substantially higher. Another notes that in sub-Saharan Africa a more equal control of inputs and farm income by women and men would raise farm yields by as much as a fifth of current output.

Gender equality is not a "women's issue" or a luxury item that can wait until we deal with the important business of economic development. Inequality impedes development; educating and improving the status of women lowers birth rates and promotes economic growth.

The economic emergence of women is a global phenomenon. Throughout the world gender inequalities in education, health, and employment have decreased substantially, but important gaps persist and in many areas progress has been slow and uneven. Gender disparities are greatest amongst the poor—and greater in poor countries than in rich countries. Women fare poorly in "traditional societies" of the

Global South and among immigrant groups who bring their cultures with them to the North.

This is, as Susan Okin notes in her classic essay "Is Multiculturalism Bad for Women," a hard saying. Liberal pluralists balk at "blaming the victim": they are hesitant to assess the cultures of disadvantaged groups critically and averse to imposing their values, practices, and social arrangements, including, some argue, "Western feminism." Some Communitarians urge the recognition of group rights and the accommodation of diverse cultural practices, including those that support traditional sex roles. Okin notes, however, that traditional societies embody norms and practices that not only impede development but are also seriously harmful to women. It is difficult, therefore, to avoid Okin's conclusion that multiculturalism is bad for women.

Adaptive Preference

Critics nevertheless note that within traditional societies women embrace and perpetuate practices that are, from the liberal Western perspective, demeaning or harmful to women. Liberals, in the interests of supporting individual rights and expanding the scope of individual choice, oppose the subordination of women; but women in traditional societies, it seems, willingly play subordinate roles and approve of practices that constrain their options and undermine their well-being.

Martha Nussbaum considers this dilemma in her essay on "adaptive preference." Telling the stories of impoverished women in India whose preferences, she claims, have been "deformed" by poverty and oppression, Nussbaum argues that we should therefore reject preference welfarism, the doctrine that getting what we want is good for us espoused by utilitarians who understand utility as desire-satisfaction. She argues that preference utilitarianism, and other "subjectivist welfarist" accounts of well-being, cannot explain why the conditions of these women's lives are morally unacceptable or why they should move us to criticize the social injustices with which poor women in developing countries contend. "Embraced as a normative position," she writes, "subjective welfarism makes it impossible to conduct a radical critique of unjust institutions."[2]

In the final reading in this section, H.E. Baber responds to Nussbaum in defense of preference utilitarianism. She argues that in cases of the sort Nussbaum considers there is in fact no evidence to suggest that the women involved prefer the conditions of their lives to more favorable states of affairs, which are, for them, unattainable. Individuals in deprived circumstances are, quite reasonably, pessimistic—something that privileged observers such as Nussbaum fail to appreciate. There is no compelling reason to believe that they prefer the conditions of their lives to what we should regard as better alternatives: they simply believe—rightly or wrongly, but

---

2 Martha Nussbaum, "Adaptive Preference and Women's Options," pp. 516–18 in this volume.

with justification—that these alternatives are unattainable. Political oppression, social constraints and poverty restrict women to a narrow range of options, most of which are low on their preference rankings. Their acquiescence is not a consequence of irrational fatalism or low self-esteem, as Nussbaum suggests, but an expression of reasonable pessimism. According to the preference-utilitarian account they would be better off if they could get goods that ranked higher on their preference rankings because they would prefer to do better. This is the preferentist's radical critique of unjust institutions, which lock in poverty and limit people's options.

36. Engendering Development*

World Bank

Gender discrimination remains pervasive in many dimensions of life—worldwide. This is so despite considerable advances in gender equality in recent decades. The nature and extent of the discrimination vary considerably across countries and regions. But the patterns are striking. In no region of the developing world are women equal to men in legal, social, and economic rights. Gender gaps are widespread in access to and control of resources, in economic opportunities, in power, and political voice. Women and girls bear the largest and most direct costs of these inequalities—but the costs cut more broadly across society, ultimately harming everyone.

For these reasons, gender equality is a core development issue—a development objective in its own right. It strengthens countries' abilities to grow, to reduce poverty, and to govern effectively. Promoting gender equality is thus an important part of a development strategy that seeks to enable *all people*—women and men alike—to escape poverty and improve their standard of living.

Economic development opens many avenues for increasing gender equality in the long run. A considerable body of evidence around the world supports this assertion. But growth alone will not deliver the desired results. Also needed are an institutional environment that provides equal rights and opportunities for women and men and policy measures that address persistent inequalities. This report argues for a three-part strategy for promoting gender equality:

- *Reform institutions to establish equal rights and opportunities for women and men.* Reforming legal and economic institutions is necessary to establish a foundation of equal rights and equal opportunities for women and men. Because the law in many countries continues to give unequal rights to women and men, legal

---

* Source: *Engendering Development* (New York: Oxford UP, 2001), pp. 1–28.

reforms are needed, particularly in family law, protection against violence, land rights, employment, and political rights.

- *Foster economic development to strengthen incentives for more equal resources and participation.* Rising income and falling poverty levels tend to reduce gender disparities in education, health, and nutrition. Higher productivity and new job opportunities often reduce gender inequalities in employment. And investments in basic water, energy, and transportation infrastructure help reduce gender disparities in workloads.

- *Take active measures to redress persistent disparities in command over resources and political voice.* Because institutional reforms and economic development may not be sufficient—or forthcoming—active measures are needed to redress persistent gender disparities in the short to medium term.

Gender Equality—in Rights, Resources, and Voice

Gender refers to socially constructed roles and socially learned behaviors and expectations associated with females and males. Women and men are different biologically—but all cultures interpret and elaborate these innate biological differences into a set of social expectations about what behaviors and activities are appropriate, and what rights, resources, and power they possess. While these expectations vary considerably among societies, there are also some striking similarities. For example, nearly all societies give the primary responsibility for the care of infants and young children to women and girls, and that for military service and national defense to men.

Like race, ethnicity, and class, gender is a social category that largely establishes one's life chances, shaping one's participation in society and in the economy. Some societies do not experience racial or ethnic divides, but all societies experience gender asymmetries—differences and disparities—to varying degrees. Often these asymmetries take time to change, but they are far from static. In fact, they can at times change quite rapidly in response to policy and changing socioeconomic conditions.

The term *gender equality* has been defined in a variety of ways in the context of development. This report defines gender equality in terms of equality under the law, equality of opportunity (including equality of rewards for work and equality in access to human capital and other productive resources that enable opportunity), and equality of voice (the ability to influence and contribute to the development process). It stops short of defining gender equality as equality of outcomes for two reasons. First, different cultures and societies can follow different paths in their pursuit of gender equality. Second, equality implies that women and men are free to choose different (or similar) roles and different (or similar) outcomes in accordance with their preferences and goals.

This report uses a variety of types of data and analyses to discuss issues related to gender inequality across the developing world. But measuring and assessing the many dimensions of gender inequality are tricky and difficult, and the lack of gender-differentiated data and analyses in several important aspects of gender equality is a real obstacle. Since empirical evidence is often richer and more available for more developed countries than for less developed countries, the report also reviews the experience of industrialized countries. It presents a combination of micro, country-level, and cross-country analyses, and reviews empirical work from several social science disciplines.

Despite Progress, Gender Disparities Remain in All Countries

The last half of the 20th century saw great improvement in the absolute status of women and in gender equality in most developing countries.

- With few exceptions female education levels improved considerably. The primary enrollment rates of girls about doubled in South Asia, Sub-Saharan Africa, and the Middle East and North Africa, rising faster than boys' enrollment rates. This substantially reduced large gender gaps in schooling.
- Women's life expectancy increased by 15–20 years in developing countries. With greater investments in girls and women and better access to health care, the expected biological pattern in female and male longevity has emerged in all developing regions; for the first time, in the 1990s, women in South Asia are living longer than men, on average.
- More women have joined the labor force. Since 1970 women's labor force participation has risen on average by 15 percentage points in East Asia and Latin America. This growth was larger than for men, thus narrowing the gender gap in employment. Gender gaps in wages have also narrowed.

Despite the progress significant gender inequalities in rights, resources, and voice persist in all developing countries—and in many areas the progress has been slow and uneven. Moreover, socioeconomic shocks in some countries have brought setbacks, jeopardizing hard-won gains.

Rights

In no region do women and men have equal social, economic, and legal rights (Figure 36.1).[1] In a number of countries women still lack independent rights to own land, manage property, conduct business, or even travel without their husband's consent. In much of Sub-Saharan Africa, women obtain land rights chiefly through their

---

1 The rights indicator used in [this and other figures] is an average of three indexes of gender equality in rights collected for more than 100 countries by Humana (1992). The individual rights indexes focus on gender equality of political and legal rights, social and economic rights, and rights in marriage and in divorce proceedings. The indexes are constructed using a consistent methodology across countries in which the extent of rights is evaluated (on a scale from 1 to 4) against rights as specified in several human rights instruments of the United Nations....

Figure 36.1 Gender Inequalities in Basic Rights Persist in All Regions

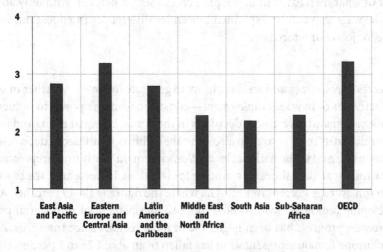

Index of gender equality

Note: A value of 1 indicates low gender equality in rights, a value of 4 high equality.
Source: Rights data from Humana (1992); population weights from World Bank (1999).

husband as long as the marriage endures, and they often lose those rights when they are divorced or widowed. Gender disparities in rights constrain the sets of choices available to women in many aspects of life—often profoundly limiting their ability to participate in or benefit from development.

Resources

Women continue to have systematically poorer command over a range of productive resources, including education, land, information, and financial resources. In South Asia women have only about half as many years of schooling as men, on average, and girls' enrollment rates at the secondary level are still only two-thirds of boys'. Many women cannot own land, and those who do generally command smaller landholdings than men. And in most developing regions female-run enterprises tend to be undercapitalized, having poorer access to machinery, fertilizer, extension information, and credit than male-run enterprises. Such disparities, whether in education or other productive resources, hurt women's ability to participate in development and to contribute to higher living standards for their families. Those disparities also translate into greater risk and vulnerability in the face of personal or family crises, in old age, and during economic shocks.

Despite recent increases in women's educational attainment, women continue to earn less than men in the labor market—even when they have the same education and years of work experience as men. Women are often limited to certain occupations in developing countries and are largely excluded from management positions in the formal sector. In industrial countries women in the wage sector earn an average of 77 percent of what men earn; in developing countries, 73 percent. And only about a fifth of the wage gap can be explained by gender differences in education, work experience, or job characteristics.

Voice
Limited access to resources and weaker ability to generate income—whether in self-employed activities or in wage employment—constrain women's power to influence resource allocation and investment decisions in the home. Unequal rights and poor socioeconomic status relative to men also limit their ability to influence decisions in their communities and at the national level. Women remain vastly underrepresented in national and local assemblies, accounting for less than 10 percent of the seats in parliament, on average (except in East Asia where the figure is 18–19 percent). And in no developing region do women hold more than 8 percent of ministerial positions. Moreover, progress has been negligible in most regions since the 1970s. And in Eastern Europe female representation has fallen from about 25 to 7 percent since the beginning of economic and political transition there.

Gender Disparities Tend to Be Greatest among the Poor
Gender disparities in education and health are often greatest among the poor. A recent study of boys' and girls' school enrollments in 41 countries indicates that within countries gender disparities in school enrollment rates are commonly greater among the poor than among the nonpoor. Similar patterns across poor and nonpoor households are seen with respect to boys' and girls' mortality rates for children under 5.

Similar patterns also emerge when comparing poor and nonpoor countries. While gender equality in education and health has increased noticeably over the past 30 years in today's low-income countries, disparities between females and males in school enrollments are still greater in those countries than in middle-income and high-income countries (Figure 36.2). And despite the links between economic development and gender equality, women's representation in parliaments remains minimal. A few low-income countries, such as China and Uganda, have made special efforts to open parliamentary seats to women, achieving levels of female representation even higher than those in high-income countries. They demonstrate the potential impact of a social mandate for gender equality.

It is important to note that these indicators are only a few measurable markers of gender equality. More systematic information is needed on other dimensions—from control of physical and financial assets to autonomy—to better understand how much has been accomplished and how far there is to go.

Figure 36.2   Gender Equality Has Increased over Time in Low- and Middle-Income Countries—Except in Political Participation

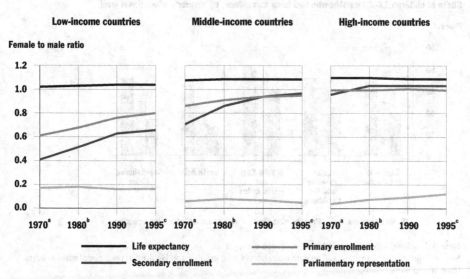

Note: The gross enrollment rate is total enrollment in a school level, regardless of students' age, expressed as a percentage of the official school-age population corresponding to that level in a given school year. The female to male enrollment ratio is the female gross enrollment ratio divided by the male gross enrollment ratio. For parliamentary representation the ratio is seats held by women to seats held by men. All values are population-weighted averages.
a. Parliamentary data are from 1975.
b. Parliamentary data are from 1985.
c. Life expectancy data are from 1997.
Source: Parliamentary data from WISTAT (1998); income data from World Bank (1999).

Gender Inequalities Harm Well-Being, Hinder Development

Gender inequalities impose large costs on the health and well-being of men, women, and children, and affect their ability to improve their lives. In addition to these personal costs, gender inequalities reduce productivity in farms and enterprises and thus lower prospects for reducing poverty and ensuring economic progress. Gender inequalities also weaken a country's governance—and thus the effectiveness of its development policies.

Well-Being

Foremost among the costs of gender inequality is its toll on human lives and the quality of those lives. Identifying and measuring the full extent of these costs are difficult—but a wealth of evidence from countries around the world demonstrates that societies with large, persistent gender inequalities pay the price of more poverty, malnutrition, illness, and other deprivations.

491

Figure 36.3 Child Immunization Rates Rise with Mother's Education

Share of children 12–23 months who had been immunized, by mother's educational level

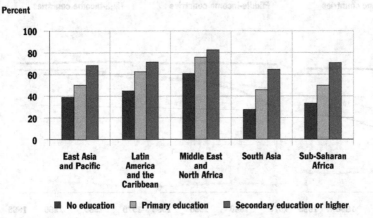

Note: All regional values are population-weighted averages....
Source: Education and immunization data from latest Demographic and Health Surveys; population weights from World Bank (1999).

- China, Korea, and South Asia have excessively high female mortality. Why? Social norms that favor sons, plus China's one-child policy, have led to child mortality rates that are higher for girls than for boys. Some estimates indicate that there are 60–100 million fewer women alive today than there would be in the absence of gender discrimination.
- Mothers' illiteracy and lack of schooling directly disadvantage their young children. Low schooling translates into poor quality of care for children and then higher infant and child mortality and malnutrition. Mothers with more education are more likely to adopt appropriate health-promoting behaviors, such as having young children immunized (Figure 36.3). Supporting these conclusions are careful analyses of household survey data that account for other factors that might improve care practices and related health outcomes.
- As with mothers' schooling, higher household income is associated with higher child survival rates and better nutrition. And putting additional incomes in the hands of women within the household tends to have a larger positive impact than putting that income in the hands of men, as studies of Bangladesh, Brazil, and Côte d'Ivoire show. Unfortunately, rigid social norms about the appropriate gender division of labor and limited paid employment for women restrict women's ability to earn income.

- Gender inequalities in schooling and urban jobs accelerate the spread of HIV. The AIDS epidemic will spread rapidly over the next decade—until up to one in four women and one in five men become HIV infected, already the case in several countries in Sub-Saharan Africa.
- While women and girls, especially the poor, often bear the brunt of gender disparities, gender norms and stereotypes impose costs on males, too. In the transition economies of Eastern Europe men have experienced absolute declines in life expectancies in recent years. Increases in male mortality rates—the largest registered in peacetime—are associated with growing stress and anxiety due to rapidly worsening unemployment among men.

Productivity and Economic Growth

The toll on human lives is a toll on development—since improving the quality of people's lives is development's ultimate goal. But gender inequalities also impose costs on productivity, efficiency, and economic progress. By hindering the accumulation of human capital in the home and the labor market, and by systematically excluding women or men from access to resources, public services, or productive activities, gender discrimination diminishes an economy's capacity to grow and to raise living standards.

- Losses in output result from inefficiencies in the allocation of productive resources between men and women within households. In households in Burkina Faso, Cameroon, and Kenya more equal control of inputs and farm income by women and men could raise farm yields by as much as a fifth of current output.
- Low investment in female education also reduces a country's overall output. One study estimates that if the countries in South Asia, Sub-Saharan Africa, and the Middle East and North Africa had started with the gender gap in average years of schooling that East Asia had in 1960 and had closed that gender gap at the rate achieved by East Asia from 1960 to 1992, their income per capita could have grown by 0.5–0.9 percentage points higher per year—substantial increases over actual growth rates. Another study estimates that even for middle- and high-income countries with higher initial education levels, an increase of 1 percentage point in the share of women with secondary education is associated with an increase in per capita income of 0.3 percentage point. Both studies control for other variables commonly found in the growth literature.

Governance

Greater women's rights and more equal participation in public life by women and men are associated with cleaner business and government and better governance. Where the influence of women in public life is greater, the level of corruption is lower.

This holds even when comparing countries with the same income civil liberties, education, and legal institutions. Although still only suggestive, these findings lend additional support for having more women in the labor force and in politics—since women can be an effective force for rule of law and good government.

Women in business are less likely to pay bribes to government officials, perhaps because women have higher standards of ethical behavior or greater risk aversion. A study of 350 firms in the republic of Georgia concludes that firms owned or managed by men are 10 percent more likely to make unofficial payments to government officials than those owned or managed by women. This result holds regardless of the characteristics of the firm, such as the sector in which it operates and firm size, and the characteristics of the owner or manager, such as education. Without controlling for these factors, firms managed by men are twice as likely to pay bribes.

Why Do Gender Disparities Persist?

If gender inequalities harm people's well-being and a country's prospects for development, why do harmful gender disparities persist in so many countries? Why are some gender inequalities much more difficult to eliminate than others? For example, improvements have been rapid in such dimensions as health and access to schooling, but much slower in political participation and equal rights to property. What factors stand in the way of transforming gender relations and eliminating gender inequalities? Institutions, households, and the economy.

Societal institutions—social norms, customs, rights, laws—as well as economic institutions, such as markets, shape roles and relationships between men and women and influence what resources women and men have access to, what activities they can or cannot undertake, and in what forms they can participate in the economy and in society. They embody incentives that can encourage or discourage prejudice. Even when formal and informal institutions do not distinguish explicitly between males and females, they are generally informed (either explicitly or implicitly) by social norms relating to appropriate gender roles. These societal institutions have their own inertia and can be slow and difficult to change—but they are far from static.

Like institutions, households play a fundamental role in shaping gender relations from early in life and in transmitting these from one generation to the next. People make many of life's most basic decisions within their households—about having and raising children, engaging in work and leisure, and investing in the future. How tasks and productive resources are allocated among sons and daughters, how much autonomy they are given, whether expectations differ among them—all this creates, reinforces, or mitigates gender disparities. But families do not make decisions in a vacuum. They make them in the context of communities and in ways that reflect the influence of incentives established by the larger institutional and policy environment.

And because the economy determines many of the opportunities people have to improve their standard of living, economic policy and development critically affect gender inequality. Higher incomes mean fewer resource constraints within the household that force parents to choose between investing in sons or in daughters. But how precisely women and men are affected by economic development depends on what income-generating activities are available, how they are organized, how effort and skills are rewarded, and whether women and men are equally able to participate.

Indeed, even apparently gender-neutral development policies can have gender-differentiated outcomes—in part because of the ways in which institutions and household decisions combine to shape gender roles and relations. The gender division of labor in the home, social norms and prejudice, and unequal resources prevent women and men from taking equal advantage of economic opportunities—or from coping equally with risk or economic shocks. Failure to recognize these gender-differentiated constraints when designing policies can compromise the effectiveness of those policies, both from equity and efficiency perspectives.

So, societal institutions, households, and the broader economy together determine people's opportunities and life prospects, by gender. They also represent important entry points for public policy to address persistent gender inequalities.

A Three-Part Strategy to Promote Gender Equality

That gender inequalities exact high human costs and constrain countries' development prospects provides a compelling case for public and private action to promote gender equality. The state has a critical role in improving the well-being of both women and men and, by so doing, in capturing the substantial social benefits associated with improving the absolute and relative status of women and girls. Public action is particularly important since social and legal institutions that perpetuate gender inequalities are extremely difficult, if not impossible, for individuals alone to change. Market failures, too, mean insufficient information about women's productivity in the labor market (because they spend a greater part of their work hours in nonmarket activities or because labor markets are absent or undeveloped) and are clear obstacles.

Improving the effectiveness of societal institutions and achieving economic growth are widely accepted as key elements of any long-term development strategy. But successful implementation of this strategy does not guarantee gender equality. To promote gender equality, policies for institutional change and economic development need to consider and address prevailing gender inequalities in rights, resources, and voice. And active policies and programs are needed to redress long-standing disparities between women and men. The evidence argues for a three-part strategy for promoting gender equality.

1. Reforming Institutions to Establish Equal Rights and Opportunities for Women and Men

Because social, legal, and economic institutions shape women's and men's access to resources, their opportunities, and their relative power, a critical element in promoting gender equality is establishing a level institutional "playing field" for women and men.

Ensuring equality in basic rights. Gender equality in rights is an important development goal in its own right. Legal, social, and economic rights provide an enabling environment in which women and men can participate productively in society, attain a basic quality of life, and take advantage of the new opportunities that development affords. Greater equality in rights is also consistently and systematically associated with greater gender equality in education, health, and political participation—effects independent of income.

If countries in South Asia, Sub-Saharan Africa, and the Middle East and North Africa were to increase gender equality in rights to the level of the "most equal" country in their respective regions, the ratio of women to men in parliament would more than double in the Middle East and North Africa and would increase by more than 60 percent in the other two regions. Although increasing gender equality in rights would have more modest impacts (at the margin) on gender equality in education, significant rights improvements could go far toward achieving parity between boys and girls in school enrollments. Only in South Asia would sizable gender gaps in enrollments be expected to persist in the face of large improvements in rights. There is thus a critical role for legal reforms that accord equal rights and equal protection to women and men.

But statutory reform is seldom enough. In many developing countries the capacity to implement legal reforms remains weak, complicated by multiple—and inconsistent—legal systems. For example, civil law in Uganda provides for equal rights in divorce—but customary law prevails in the division of conjugal property, and divorced women are unable to retain access to land. In cases of gender-based violence, heavy evidentiary requirements and other procedural barriers (as well as the attitudes of enforcers) stand in the way of justice in a number of countries. In such contexts efforts to strengthen the enforcement capabilities of the country's judicial and administrative agencies are critical to achieving greater gender equality in basic rights. In almost all cases political leadership is decisive.

Establishing incentives that discourage discrimination by gender. The structure of economic institutions also affects gender equality in important ways. Markets embody a powerful set of incentives that influence decisions and actions for work, saving, investment, and consumption. The relative wages of men and women, the returns to productive assets, and the prices of goods and services are all largely determined by the structure of markets. Evidence from Mexico and the United States suggests that firms operating in competitive environments discriminate less against women in hiring and pay practices than do firms with significant market power in protected environments. Similarly, in both urban and rural China, women face greater wage discrimination in jobs that have been administratively assigned to them than in jobs obtained through competitive channels.

More broadly, policies and investments that deepen markets and redress gender disparities in access to information—combined with sanctions against those who discriminate—all help strengthen incentives for gender equality in the labor market. In China and Vietnam, for example, the deepening of rural labor markets has brought with it substantial increases in demand for female labor in nonfarm enterprises, opening up new employment and earnings opportunities for women.

Designing service delivery to facilitate equal access. The design of program delivery—such as school systems, health care centers, financial organizations, and agricultural extension programs—can facilitate or inhibit equitable access for females and males. Moreover, involving the community in the design of service delivery helps to address specific demands within local contexts, often with positive effects on female access and use.

In Bangladesh, Kenya, and Pakistan, for example, girls' enrollments are more sensitive than boys' to school quality and to specific delivery attributes—such as the presence of female teachers, sex-segregated schools and facilities, and safe transport to and from the school. Addressing such considerations can significantly increase parents' demand for educating daughters. In parts of West Africa "mobile bankers" (known as *susu* collectors in Ghana) bring financial services to local markets, workplaces, and homes, eliminating the need for women to travel long distances to save or borrow. And in Bangladesh, group-based lending programs use support groups and peer pressure as a substitute for traditional bank collateral to ensure repayment. Both designs have increased women's access to financial resources.

2. Fostering Economic Development to Strengthen Incentives for More Equal Resources and Participation

In most settings economic development is associated with improved circumstances for women and girls and with greater gender equality—through several channels:

- Households decide about work, consumption, and investments partly in response to price levels and other market signals. Shifts in these signals tend to bring about reallocation of resources. When economic development improves the availability and quality of public services, such as health clinics and schools, it lowers the cost of investments in human capital for the household. If costs decline more for females than for males, or if investments in females are more sensitive to price changes than investments in males as evidence suggests, females benefit more.
- When economic development raises incomes and reduces poverty, gender inequalities often narrow. Since low-income families are forced to ration

spending on education, health care, and nutrition, with women and girls bearing much of the costs, as household incomes rise, gender disparities in human capital tend to fall.

As with basic rights, higher incomes generally translate into greater gender equality in resources, whether in health or in education. In education, simulations suggest that the largest improvements from income growth are likely to occur in the poorest regions: South Asia and Sub-Saharan Africa. Moreover, the effects of income appear particularly strong at the secondary level. But simulation analysis also suggests that very large increases in income—say, to average OECD levels—would be required to reach equality or near-equality in secondary enrollments in these regions. Such increases are not realistic in the short or medium term. Very large increases in income also would be necessary to induce noticeable gains in gender equality in parliamentary representation.

- When economic development expands work opportunities, it raises the expected rate of return to human capital, strengthening the incentives for families to invest in girls' health and education and for women to participate in the labor force. By changing incentives for work, economic development affects gender equality.
- Economic development leads to the emergence of labor markets where none has existed. In so doing, it not only creates or strengthens market signals about the returns to labor but also eliminates some economic inefficiencies. For example, where active labor markets exist, hired labor provides a substitute for female family labor, whether on farms or in household maintenance and care activities. This allows households to use time more efficiently, perhaps reducing women's workload. Where labor markets are absent or do not function well, such substitution is not possible.
- Economic growth is typically accompanied by an expansion of investments in infrastructure—for safe water, roads, transport, and fuel. This too tends to reduce the time women and girls need to dedicate to household maintenance and care activities. In Burkina Faso, Uganda, and Zambia, for example, women and girls could save hundreds of hours a year if walking times to sources of fuel and potable water were reduced to 30 minutes or less. The development of economic infrastructure significantly reduces females' time on domestic chores, with potential benefits for their health, their participation in income-generating activities, and for girls, in schooling.

Although economic development tends to promote gender equality, its impact is neither sufficient nor immediate. Nor is it automatic. The impact of economic development on gender equality depends in large part on the state of rights, access to and control of productive resources (such as land and credit), and political voice.

And social policies that combat labor market discrimination or support child care supplement what economic development alone cannot achieve in reducing gender inequalities—as experience shows in the transition economies, the high-growth countries in East Asia, and the adjusting countries in Latin America and Sub-Saharan Africa. Social protection policies that recognize gender differences in market-based and household work and in risks are also important to protect women (and men) from economic shocks or prolonged economic downturns.

Recent debates on gender and development have tended to pit growth-oriented approaches to development against rights-based or institutional approaches. But the evidence suggests that both economic development and institutional change are key elements of a long-term strategy to promote gender equality. For example, where per capita income and gender equality in rights are low, increasing either equality in rights or incomes would raise gender equality in education levels. Improving both rights and incomes would yield even greater gain.

Institutional reforms that strengthen basic rights and policies that foster economic development can be mutually reinforcing. In Sub-Saharan Africa establishing land rights for women raises productivity on female-managed plots—increasing women's as well as their families' incomes. Similarly, providing women greater access to savings institutions and credit enhances their economic status and security and helps improve household welfare. In Bangladesh, as women's abilities to borrow capital in microcredit programs increase, their status and bargaining power in the family rise, as does household consumption (income).

3. Taking Active Policy Measures to Redress Persistent Gender Disparities in Command over Resources and Political Voice

Because the combined effects of institutional reform and economic development usually take time to be realized, active measures are often warranted in the short to medium term. Active measures are concrete steps aimed at redressing specific forms of gender discrimination and exclusion—whether in the home, the community, or the workplace. Such measures accelerate progress in redressing persistent gender inequalities—and they are useful in targeting specific subpopulations, such as the poor, for whom gender disparities can be particularly acute.

Since the nature and extent of gender inequality differ considerably across countries, the interventions that will be most relevant will also differ across contexts. Decisions on whether the state should intervene and which active measures should be adopted must be based on an understanding and analysis of local realities. Since active measures have real resource costs, policymakers will need to be selective about which measures to undertake, focusing strategically on where government intervention has the largest social benefits. This implies focusing on areas where market failure and spillover effects are likely to be greatest. This also implies focusing on areas that the private sector is unlikely to take on independently—or to take on well.

Beyond assessing whether particular interventions are warranted, choices need to be made on how precisely the state should intervene. For example, is direct public provision of goods or services required? Or can similar objectives be fulfilled more cost effectively through greater availability of information, regulatory and enforcement efforts, or through public subsidies to private providers?

The report focuses on four key areas of active policy.

Promoting gender equality in access to productive resources and earnings capacity. Efforts to promote greater equality of access to and control of productive resources—whether education, financial resources, or land—and to ensure fair and equal access to employment opportunities can advance gender equality as well as enhance economic efficiency. Policymakers have a number of potential entry points for intervention:

- Reducing the costs of schooling, addressing parental concerns about female modesty or safety, and increasing returns to families from investing in female schooling through improvements in school quality can overcome social and economic barriers to girls' education, even in highly gender-stratified societies.
- Designing financial institutions in ways that account for gender-specific constraints—whether by using peer pressure to substitute for traditional forms of collateral, by simplifying banking procedures, or by delivering financial services closer to homes, markets, and workplaces—can increase female access to savings and credit.
- Land reforms that provide for joint titling of husband and wife or that enable women to hold independent land titles can increase women's control of land where statutory law predominates. Where customary and statutory laws operate side-by-side, their interactions must be taken into account if efforts to strengthen female access to land are to succeed.
- In countries with relatively developed labor markets and law enforcement capabilities, affirmative action employment programs can increase female access to formal sector jobs. Where there is serious discrimination in hiring and promotions, affirmative action can also raise productivity in firms and in the economy.

Reducing the personal costs to women of their household roles. In almost all societies gender norms dictate that women and girls take primary responsibility for household maintenance and care activities. In developing countries household responsibilities often require long hours of work that limit girls' ability to continue their education and constrain mothers' capacity to participate in market work. Several types of interventions can reduce the personal costs of household roles to women and girls.

- Interventions that increase education, wages, and labor market participation—coupled with adequate access to basic reproductive health and family planning services—all strengthen women's role in making reproductive decisions. But since women and men may have different preferences for family size and contraceptive use, family planning services need to target men as well as women.

- Providing public support for out-of-home child care services can reduce the costs of care, enabling greater economic participation for women and more schooling for adolescent girls. In Kenya reducing the price of child care significantly increases mothers' wage employment and older girls' schooling.
- Protective labor market legislation is often a two-edged sword, generating costs as well as benefits for women working in the formal sector. For example, when firms bear all the costs of maternity leave, they may bias hiring decisions against women. When women bear all the costs, the incentives for women to continue work are weakened. Measures that help spread the costs of maternity and other care provisions across employers, workers, and even the state can raise the benefits relative to costs for women and their families.
- Selected investments in water, fuel, transport, and other time-saving infrastructure can hasten reductions in women's and girls' domestic workloads, particularly in poor, rural areas—freeing girls to attend school and women to undertake other activities, whether related to income generation or community affairs.

Providing gender-appropriate social protection. Women and men face gender-specific risks during economic shocks or policy reforms. Women command fewer resources with which to cushion shocks—while men, as the traditional breadwinners, are particularly vulnerable to stress associated with large changes in, or uncertain, employment. Taking gender differences in risk and vulnerability into account in designing social protection is particularly important because women and men in the same household may not pool risk.

- To protect both women and men social protection programs need to account for factors that can result in gender bias in participation and benefits. For example, safety net programs have frequently (if inadvertently) excluded women by failing to account for gender differences in labor supply behavior, information access, or the types of work that women and men consider appropriate.
- Old-age security programs that do not account for gender differences in employment, earnings, and life expectancy risk leaving women—especially widows—particularly vulnerable to poverty in old age. A recent study of Chile shows that women's pension benefits relative to men's are highly sensitive to the specific design features of the old-age security system (Figure 36.4).

Strengthening women's political voice and participation. Institutional changes that establish gender equality in basic rights are the cornerstone of greater equality in political participation and voice. Similarly, policies and programs that promote

Figure 36.4 Pension Design Affects the Relative Benefits to Elderly Women and Men

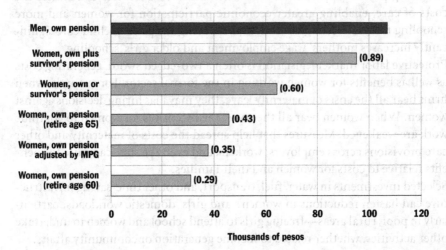

Monthly pension income for female and male workers with incomplete primary education in Chile (female to male ratio in parentheses)

- Men, own pension
- Women, own plus survivor's pension (0.89)
- Women, own or survivor's pension (0.60)
- Women, own pension (retire age 65) (0.43)
- Women, own pension adjusted by MPG (0.35)
- Women, own pension (retire age 60) (0.29)

0   20   40   60   80   100   120

Thousands of pesos

Note: These estimates assume that men retire at 65, women at 60—the statutory retirement ages for men and women—unless otherwise noted. *MPG* stands for the government-supported minimum pension guarantee. The figures are calculated as monthly annuities to urban contributors, assuming a 5 percent rate of return with 2 percent secular wage growth. Males are assumed to survive for 15 years after retirement (at 65) and to make provisions for a survivor's pension for 6 years at 60 percent of their own annuity. If females retire at 60, they are assumed to survive for 23 years, and if they retire at 65, they are assumed to survive for 19 years.
Source: Adapted from Cox-Edwards (2000).

equality in education and access to information (including legal literacy) can strengthen women's agency and thus their capacity to participate in the political arena. But like the impact of economic development more broadly, these approaches take time to reap observable benefits.

Recent experience from more than 30 countries, including Argentina, Ecuador, India, the Philippines, and Uganda, suggests that political "reservation" can be effective in increasing political participation and representation in local and national assemblies in a relatively short period of time. "Reservation" legislation takes different forms in different countries, but generally stipulates that a minimum number (or proportion) of political parties' candidates or of electoral seats in national or local assemblies be reserved for women.

Challenges for the Future—the Way Forward
The evidence presented in this report makes a compelling case for the state to intervene in promoting gender equality. Indeed, the state, civil society groups, and the

international community all have critical roles to play in fighting gender discrimination, thus enabling societies to reap considerable benefits. But there remain several important challenges.

Sharpening Policy through Gender Analysis

How to deepen understanding of the links between gender equality and development and how to reflect these links in policy decisions are key challenges for the present and the future. This report brings together extensive evidence on these links, but much remains to be discovered and understood, implying the need for collecting more and better data and for analyses disaggregated by gender. Two areas for more analysis:

- What are the gender impacts of specific macro and sectoral policies? And how do public expenditure choices promote or inhibit gender equality and economic efficiency? Policymakers face numerous competing demands for public resources and attention, with tight fiscal and administrative budgets. Under these constraints, information and analysis help governments achieve the maximum social gains from the gender-related interventions they choose. Moreover, because the nature of gender disparities differs among societies, effective policy needs to be grounded in analysis that integrates local and national gender concerns.
- Increasingly, it will be important to look beyond how policies and programs affect our usual development markers (such as education, health, or labor force indicators) to how specific interventions improve female autonomy, leadership, and voice—both within the household and in society more broadly. Understanding which interventions are most effective in achieving this requires more gender analysis.

Addressing Emerging Issues

A related challenge is for policymakers to be forward-looking in the face of rapidly changing circumstances. Indeed, many emerging issues require greater attention by policymakers and policy researchers from a gender perspective, including globalization, decentralization in government, the spread of HIV/AIDS, and the aging of the world's population. For example:

- With birth rates declining and people living longer, the world's population is aging. Among other things, this will result in a substantial rise in the number of widows worldwide during the 21st century. What does this demographic shift imply for social protection, health, and other areas of public policy? Understanding the policy implications of this demographic trend will be an important challenge for research in the coming years.

- Similarly, globalization and new information technologies are transforming the way that production is organized and information shared around the world. Will these changes accelerate progress toward gender equality or widen gender gaps in economic opportunity? Better understanding of the opportunities and risks associated with these forces represents another challenge for researchers and policymakers.

Broadening Partnerships

A third critical challenge is for policymakers—in their efforts to promote gender equality—to broaden their partnerships with civil society groups, donors, and others in the international community. While policymakers have an important leadership role to play, efforts to combat gender inequalities can be enhanced by active collaboration with civic and international organizations. The donor community can contribute by supporting the collection and analysis of gender-disaggregated data, by incorporating gender analysis into their dialogues with national policymakers, and by sharing "good practice" based on international experience. Similarly, civic groups and local researchers can contribute critical information and analysis based on local knowledge that will enrich the government's policy dialogue.

Fostering broader participation and transparency in policymaking has the potential for tremendous payoffs, both for gender equality and for national development as a whole. Opening public deliberations and policymaking to greater participation by women's groups can directly empower women—and can enhance the impact of policies and programs. The research findings on the links between greater female participation in public life and lower levels of corruption are intriguing. They suggest that facilitating broader exchanges of ideas and greater transparency in policymaking—and enabling greater female participation in the public domain—can strengthen a country's governance and the effectiveness of its development policy. The world cannot forgo salutary effects as remarkable as these.

References

Cox-Edwards, Alejandra. 2000. "Pension Projections for Chilean Men and Women: Estimates from Social Security Contributions." Background paper for *Engendering Development*. World Bank. Washington, DC.

Humana, Charles. 1992. *World Human Rights Guide*. 3rd ed. New York: Oxford UP.

WISTAT (Women's Indicators and Statistics Database). 1998. Version 3. Prepared by the United Nations Statistical Division. New York.

World Bank. 1999. *World Development Indicators 1999*. Washington, DC.

37. Is Multiculturalism Bad for Women?*

Susan Moller Okin

Until the past few decades, minority groups—immigrants as well as indigenous peoples—were typically expected to assimilate into majority cultures. This assimilationist expectation is now often considered oppressive, and many Western countries are seeking to devise new policies that are more responsive to persistent cultural differences. The appropriate policies vary with context: Countries such as England with established churches or state supported religious education find it hard to resist demands to extend state support to minority religious schools; countries such as France with traditions of strictly secular public education struggle over whether the clothing required by minority religions may be worn in the public schools. But one issue recurs across all contexts, though it has gone virtually unnoticed in current debate: What should be done when the claims of minority cultures or religions clash with the norm of gender equality that is at least formally endorsed by liberal states (however much they continue to violate it in their practice)?

In the late 1980s, for example, a sharp public controversy erupted in France about whether Maghrébin girls could attend school wearing the traditional Muslim headscarves regarded as proper attire for post-pubescent young women. Staunch defenders of secular education lined up with some feminists and far-right nationalists against the practice; much of the old left supported the multiculturalist demands for flexibility and respect for diversity, accusing opponents of racism or cultural imperialism. At the very same time, however, the public was virtually silent about a problem of vastly greater importance to many French Arab and African immigrant women: polygamy.

During the 1980s, the French government quietly permitted immigrant men to bring multiple wives into the country, to the point where an estimated 200,000 families in Paris are now polygamous. Any suspicion that official concern over

---

* Source: *Is Multiculturalism Bad for Women?*, ed. Joshua Cohen, Matthew Howard, and Martha C. Nussbaum (Princeton: Princeton UP, 1999).

headscarves was motivated by an impulse toward gender equality is belied by the easy adoption of a permissive policy on polygamy, despite the burdens this practice imposes on women and the warnings issued by women from the relevant cultures.[1] On this issue, no politically effective opposition galvanized. But once reporters finally got around to interviewing the wives, they discovered what the government could have learned years earlier: that the women affected by polygamy regarded it as an inescapable and barely tolerable institution in their African countries of origin, and an unbearable imposition in the French context. Overcrowded apartments and the lack of each wife's private space lead to immense hostility, resentment, even violence both among the wives and against each other's children.

In part because of the strain on the welfare state caused by families with 20–30 members, the French government has recently decided to recognize only one wife and consider all the other marriages annulled. But what will happen to all the other wives and children? Having neglected women's view on polygamy for so long, the government now seems to be abdicating its responsibility for the vulnerability that women and children incurred because of its rash policy.

The French accommodation of polygamy illustrates a deep and growing tension between feminism and multiculturalist concerns to protect cultural diversity. I think we—especially those of us who consider ourselves politically progressive and opposed to all forms of oppression—have been too quick to assume that feminism and multiculturalism are both good things which are easily reconciled. I shall argue instead that there is considerable likelihood of tension between them—more precisely, between feminism and a multiculturalist commitment to group rights for minority cultures.

A few words to explain the terms and focus of my argument. By "feminism," I mean the belief that women should not be disadvantaged by their sex, that they should be recognized as having human dignity equally with men, and the opportunity to live as fulfilling and as freely chosen lives as men can. "Multiculturalism" is harder to pin down, but the particular aspect that concerns me here is the claim, made in the context of basically liberal democracies, that minority cultures or ways of life are not sufficiently protected by ensuring the individual rights of their members and as a consequence should also be protected with special *group* rights or privileges. In the French case, for example, the right to contract polygamous marriages clearly constituted a group right, not available to the rest of the population. In other cases, groups claim rights to govern themselves, have guaranteed political representation, or be exempt from generally applicable law.

Demands for such group rights are growing—from indigenous native populations, minority ethnic or religious groups, and formerly colonized peoples (at least, when the latter immigrate to the former colonial state). These groups, it is argued, have

---

1 *International Herald Tribune,* 2 February 1996, News section.

their own "societal cultures" which—as Will Kymlicka, the foremost contemporary defender of cultural group rights, says—provide "members with meaningful ways of life across the full range of human activities, including social, educational, religious, recreational, and economic life, encompassing both public and private spheres."[2] Because societal cultures play so pervasive and fundamental a role in the lives of members, and because such cultures are threatened with extinction, minority cultures should be protected by special rights: That, in essence, is the case for group rights.

Some proponents of group rights argue that even cultures that "flout the rights of [their individual members] in a liberal society"[3] should be accorded group rights or privileges if their minority status endangers the culture's continued existence. Others do not claim that all minority cultural groups should have special rights, but rather that such groups—even illiberal ones, that violate their individual members' rights, requiring them to conform to group beliefs or norms—have the right to be "let alone" in a liberal society.[4] Both claims seem clearly inconsistent with the basic liberal value of individual freedom, which entails that group rights should not trump the individual rights of their members; thus, I will not address the problems they present for feminists here.[5] But some defenders of multiculturalism largely confine their defense of group rights to groups that are internally liberal.[6] Even with these restrictions, feminists—anyone, that is, who endorses the moral equality of men and women—should remain skeptical. So I will argue.

Gender and Culture

Most cultures are suffused with practices and ideologies concerning gender. Suppose, then, that a culture endorses and facilitates the control of men over women in various ways (even if informally, in the private sphere of domestic life). Suppose, too, that there are fairly clear disparities of power between the sexes, such that the more powerful, male members are those who are generally in a position to determine and articulate the group's beliefs, practices, and interests. Under such conditions, group rights are potentially, and in many cases actually, antifeminist. They substantially limit the capacities of women and girls of that culture to live with human dignity equal to that of men and boys, and to live as freely chosen lives as they can.

---

2 Will Kymlicka, *Multicultural Citizenship: A Liberal Theory of Minority Rights* (Oxford: Oxford UP, 1995), pp. 89, 76. See also Kymlicka, *Liberalism, Community, and Culture* (Oxford: Clarendon, 1989). It should be noted that Kymlicka himself does not argue for extensive or permanent group rights for those who have voluntarily immigrated.

3 Avishai Margalit and Moshe Halbertal, "Liberalism and the Right to Culture," *Social Research* 61.3 (Fall, 1994): 491.

4 For example, Chandran Kukathas, "Are There Any Cultural Rights?" *Political Theory* 20.1 (1992): 105–39.

5 Okin, "Feminism and Multiculturalism: Some Tensions," *Ethics* (1998).

6 For example, Kymlicka, *Liberalism, Community, and Culture* and *Multicultural Citizenship*, especially chap. 8. Kymlicka does not apply his requirement that groups be internally liberal to those he terms "national minorities," but I will not address this aspect of his theory here.

Advocates of group rights for minorities within liberal states have not adequately addressed this simple critique of group rights, for at least two reasons. First, they tend to treat cultural groups as monoliths—to pay more attention to differences between and among groups than to differences within them. Specifically, they give little or no recognition to the fact that minority cultural groups, like the societies in which they exist (though to a greater or lesser extent), are themselves *gendered*, with substantial differences of power and advantage between men and women. Second, advocates of group rights pay no or little attention to the private sphere. Some of the best liberal defenses of group rights urge that individuals need "a culture of their own," and that only within such a culture can people develop a sense of self-esteem or self-respect, or the capacity to decide what kind of life is good for them. But such arguments typically neglect both the different roles that cultural groups require of their members and the context in which persons' senses of themselves and their capacities are first formed *and* in which culture is first transmitted—the realm of domestic or family life.

When we correct for these deficiencies by paying attention to internal differences and to the private arena, two particularly important connections between culture and gender come into sharp relief, both of which underscore the force of the simple critique. First, the sphere of personal, sexual, and reproductive life provides a central focus of most cultures, a dominant theme in cultural practices and rules. Religious or cultural groups are often particularly concerned with "personal law"—the laws of marriage, divorce, child custody, division and control of family property, and inheritance.[7] As a rule, then, the defense of "cultural practices" is likely to have much greater impact on the lives of women and girls than those of men and boys, since far more of women's time and energy goes into preserving and maintaining the personal, familial, and reproductive side of life. Obviously culture is not only about domestic arrangements, but they do provide a major focus of most contemporary cultures. Home is, after all, where much of culture is practiced, preserved, and transmitted to the young. In turn, the distribution of responsibilities and power at home has a major impact on who can participate in and influence the more public parts of the cultural life, where rules and regulations about both public and private life are made.

Second, most cultures have as one of their principal aims the control of women by men.[8] Consider, for example, the founding myths of Greek and Roman antiq-

---

7 See for example Krit Singh, "Obstacles to Women's Rights in India," in *Human Rights of Women: National and International Perspectives*, ed. Rebecca J. Cook (Philadephia: U of Pennsylvania P, 1994), pp. 375–96, especially 378–89.

8 I cannot discuss here the roots of this male preoccupation, except to say (following feminist theorists Dorothy Dinnerstein, Nancy Chodorow, Jessica Benjamin and, before them, Jesuit anthropologist Walter Ong) that it seems to have a lot to do with female primary parenting. It is also clearly related to the uncertainty of paternity, which technology has now changed. If these issues are at the root of it, then the cultural preoccupation with controlling women is not an inevitable fact of human life, but a contingent factor that feminists have a considerable interest in changing.

uity, and of Judaism, Christianity, and Islam: they are rife with attempts to justify the control and subordination of women. These myths consist of a combination of denials of women's role in reproduction, appropriations by men of the power to reproduce themselves, characterizations of women as overly emotional, untrustworthy, evil, or sexually dangerous, and refusals to acknowledge mothers' rights over the disposition of their children.[9] Think of Athena, sprung from the head of Zeus, and of Romulus and Remus, reared without a human mother. Or Adam, made by a male God, who then (at least according to one of the two biblical versions of the story) made Eve out of part of Adam. Consider Eve, whose weakness led Adam astray. Think of all those endless "begats" in Genesis, where women's primary role in reproduction is completely ignored, or of the textual justifications for polygamy, once practiced in Judaism, still practiced in many parts of the Islamic world and (though illegally) by Mormons in some parts of the United States. Consider, too, the story of Abraham, a pivotal turning point in the development of monotheism.[10] God commands Abraham to sacrifice "his" greatly loved son. Abraham prepares to do exactly what God asks of him, without even telling, much less asking, Isaac's mother, Sarah. Abraham's absolute obedience to God makes him the central, fundamental model of faith, for all three religions.

While the powerful drive to control women—and to blame and punish them for men's difficulty controlling their own sexual impulses—has been softened considerably in the more progressive, reformed versions of Judaism, Christianity, and Islam, it remains strong in their more orthodox or fundamentalist versions. Moreover, it is by no means confined to Western or monotheistic cultures. Many of the world's traditions and cultures, including those practiced within formerly conquered or colonized nation states—certainly including most of the peoples of Africa, the Middle East, Latin America and Asia—are quite distinctly patriarchal. They too have elaborate patterns of socialization, rituals, matrimonial customs, and other cultural practices (including systems of property ownership and control of resources) aimed at bringing women's sexuality and reproductive capabilities under men's control. Many such practices make it virtually impossible for women to choose to live independently of men, to be celibate or lesbian, or not to have children.

Those who practice some of the most controversial of such customs—clitoridectomy, the marriage of children or marriages that are otherwise coerced, or polygamy—sometimes explicitly defend them as necessary for controlling women, and openly acknowledge that the customs persist at men's insistence. In an interview with *New York Times* reporter Celia Dugger, practitioners of clitoridectomy in Côte

---

9   See, for example, Arvind Sharma, ed., *Women in World Religions* (Albany: SUNY P, 1987); John Stratton Hawley, ed., *Fundamentalism and Gender* (Oxford: Oxford UP, 1994).

10 See Carol Delaney, *Abraham on Trial: Paternal Power and the Sacrifice of Children* (Princeton: Princeton UP, 1997). Note that in the Qur'anic version, it is not Isaac but Ishmael whom Abraham prepares to sacrifice.

d'Ivoire and Togo explained that the practice "helps insure a girl's virginity before marriage and fidelity afterward by reducing sex to a marital obligation." As a female exciser said, "[a] woman's role in life is to care for her children, keep house and cook. If she has not been cut, [she] might think about her own sexual pleasure."[11] In Egypt, where a law banning female genital cutting was recently overturned by a court, supporters of the practice say it "curbs a girl's sexual appetite and makes her more marriageable."[12] Moreover, in such contexts, many women have no economically viable alternative to marriage. Men in polygamous cultures, too, readily acknowledge that the practice accords with their self-interest and is a means of controlling women. As a French immigrant from Mali said in a recent interview: "When my wife is sick and I don't have another, who will care for me?... [O]ne wife on her own is trouble. When there are several, they are forced to be polite and well behaved. If they misbehave, you threaten that you'll take another wife." Women apparently see polygamy very differently. French African immigrant women deny that they like polygamy, and say not only that they are given "no choice" in the matter, but that their female forebears in Africa did not like it either.[13] As for child or otherwise coerced marriage: this practice is clearly a way not only of controlling whom the girls or young women marry, but also of ensuring that they are virgins at the time of marriage and, often, enhancing the husband's power by creating a significant age difference between husbands and wives.

Consider, too, the practice—common in much of Latin America, rural South East Asia and parts of West Africa—of encouraging or even requiring a rape victim to marry the rapist. In many such cultures—including fourteen countries of Latin America—rapists are legally exonerated if they marry or (in some cases) even offer to marry their victims. Clearly, rape is not seen in these cultures primarily as a violent assault on the girl or woman herself, but rather as a serious injury to her family and its honor. By marrying his victim, the rapist can help restore the family's honor and relieve it of a daughter who, as "damaged goods," has become unmarriageable. In Peru, this barbaric law was amended for the worse in 1991: the co-defendants in a gang rape are now all exonerated if one of them offers to marry the victim (feminists are fighting to get the law repealed). As a Peruvian taxi driver explained: "Marriage is the right and proper thing to do after a rape. A raped woman is a used item. No one wants her. At least with this law the woman will get a husband."[14] It is hard to imagine a worse fate for a woman than being pressured into marrying the man who has raped her. But worse fates do exist in some cultures—notably in Pakistan and parts of the Arab Middle East, where women who bring rape charges

---

11 *New York Times*, 5 October 1996, A4. The role that older women in such cultures play in perpetuating them is important but complex, and cannot be addressed here.
12 *New York Times*, 26 June 1997, A9.
13 *International Herald Tribune*, 2 February 1997, News section.
14 *New York Times*, 12 March 1997, A8.

are quite frequently charged with the serious Muslim offense of *zina*, or sex outside of marriage. Law allows for the whipping or imprisonment of such a woman, and culture condones the killing or pressuring into suicide of a raped woman by relatives concerned to restore the family's honor.[15]

Thus, many culturally based customs aim to control women and render them, especially sexually and reproductively, servile to men's desires and interests. Sometimes, moreover, "culture" or "traditions" are so closely linked with the control of women that they are virtually equated. In a recent news report about a small community of Orthodox Jews living in the mountains of Yemen—ironically, from a feminist point of view, the story was entitled "Yemen's small Jewish community thrives on mixed traditions"—the elderly leader of this small polygamous sect is quoted as saying: "We are Orthodox Jews, very keen on our traditions. If we go to Israel, we will lose hold over our daughters, our wives and our sisters." One of his sons added: "We are like Muslims, we do not allow our women to uncover their faces."[16] Thus the servitude of women is presented as virtually synonymous with "our traditions." (Only blindness to sexual servitude can explain the title; it is inconceivable that the article would have carried such a title if it were about a community that practiced any kind of slavery but sexual slavery.)

While virtually all of the world's cultures have distinctly patriarchal pasts, some—mostly, though by no means exclusively, Western liberal cultures—have departed far further from them than others. Western cultures, of course, still practice many forms of sex discrimination. They place far more stress on beauty, thinness, and youth in females and on intellectual accomplishment, skill, and strength in males; they expect women to perform for no economic reward far more than half of the unpaid work of their families, whether or not they also work for wages; partly as a consequence of this and partly because of workplace discrimination, women are far more likely than men to become poor; girls and women are also subjected by men to a great deal of (illegal) violence, including sexual violence. But women in more liberal cultures are, at the same time, legally guaranteed many of the same freedoms and opportunities as men. In addition, most families in such cultures, with the exception of some religious fundamentalists, do not communicate to their daughters that they are of less value than boys, that their lives are to be confined to domesticity and service to men and children, and that the only positive value of their sexuality is that it be strictly confined to marriage, the service of men, and reproductive ends. This, as we have seen, is quite different from women's situation in many of the world's other cultures, including many of those from which immigrants to Europe and Northern America come.

---

15 This practice is discussed in Henry S. Richardson, *Practical Reasoning About Final Ends* (Cambridge: Cambridge UP, 1994), especially pp. 240–43, 262–63, 282–84.

16 *Agence France Presse*, 18 May 1997, International News section.

Group Rights?

Most cultures are patriarchal, then, and many (though not all) of the cultural minorities that claim group rights are more patriarchal than the surrounding cultures. So it is no surprise that the cultural importance of maintaining control over women shouts out to us in the examples given in the literature on cultural diversity and group rights within liberal states. Yet, though it shouts out, it is seldom explicitly addressed.[17]

A 1986 paper about the legal rights and culture-based claims of various immigrant groups and gypsies in contemporary Britain mentions the roles and status of women as "one very clear example" of the "clash of cultures."[18] In it, Sebastian Poulter discusses claims put forward by members of such groups for special legal treatment on account of their cultural differences. A few are non-gender-related claims: about a Muslim schoolteacher's being allowed to be absent part of Friday afternoons in order to pray, and gypsy children having less stringent schooling requirements than others on account of their itinerant lifestyle. But the vast majority of the examples concern gender inequalities: child marriages, forced marriages, divorce systems biased against women, polygamy, and clitoridectomy. Almost all of the legal cases discussed stemmed from women's or girls' claims that their individual rights were being truncated or violated by the practices of their cultural groups. In a recent article by political philosopher Amy Gutmann, "The Challenge of Multiculturalism in Political Ethics," fully half the examples have to do with gender issues—polygamy, abortion, sexual harassment, clitoridectomy, and purdah.[19] This is quite typical in the literature on subnational multicultural issues. Moreover, the same phenomenon occurs in practice in the international arena, where women's human rights are often rejected by the leaders of countries or groups of countries as incompatible with their various cultures.[20]

Similarly, the overwhelming majority of "cultural defenses" that are increasingly being invoked in US criminal cases concerning members of cultural minorities are connected with gender—in particular with male control over women and children.[21] Occasionally, cultural defenses come into play in explaining expectable violence

---

17 See, however, Bhikhu Parekh's "Minority Practices and Principles of Toleration," *International Migration Review* (April 1996): 251–84, in which he directly addresses and critiques a number of cultural practices that devalue the status of women.

18 Sebastian Poulter, "Ethnic Minority Customs, English Law, and Human Rights," *International and Comparative Law Quarterly* 36.3 (1987): 589–615.

19 Amy Gutmann, "The Challenge of Multiculturalism in Political Ethics," *Philosophy and Public Affairs* 22.3 (Summer 1993): 171–204.

20 Mahnaz Afkhami, ed., *Faith and Freedom: Women's Human Rights in the Muslim World* (Syracuse: Syracuse UP, 1995); Valentine M. Moghadam, ed., *Identity Politics and Women: Cultural Reassertions and Feminisms in International Perspective* (Boulder, CO: Westview, 1994); Susan Moller Okin, "Culture, Religion, and Female Identity Formation" (unpublished manuscript, 1997).

21 For one of the best and most recent accounts of this, and for legal citations for the cases mentioned below, see Doriane Lambelet Coleman, "Individualizing Justice Through Multiculturalism: The Liberals' Dilemma," *Columbia Law Review* 96.5 (1996): 1093–1167.

among men, or the ritual sacrifice of animals. Much more common, however, is the argument that, in the defendant's cultural group, women are not human beings of equal worth but subordinates whose primary (if not only) functions are to serve men sexually and domestically. Thus, the four types of case in which cultural defenses have been used most successfully are: kidnap and rape by Hmong men who claim that their actions are part of their cultural practice of *zij poj niam* or "marriage by capture"; wife-murder by immigrants from Asian and Middle Eastern countries whose wives have either committed adultery or treated their husbands in a servile way; mothers who have killed their children but failed to kill themselves, and claim that because of their Japanese or Chinese backgrounds the shame of their husbands' infidelity drove them to the culturally condoned practice of mother-child suicide; and—in France, though not yet in the United States, in part because the practice was criminalized only in 1996—clitoridectomy. In a number of such cases, expert testimony about the accused's or defendant's cultural background has resulted in dropped or reduced charges, culturally based assessments of *mens rea*, or significantly reduced sentences. In a well-known recent case, an immigrant from rural Iraq married his two daughters, aged 13 and 14, to two of his friends, aged 28 and 34. Subsequently, when the older daughter ran away with her 20-year-old boyfriend, the father sought the help of the police in finding her. When they located her, they charged the father with child abuse, and the two husbands and boyfriend with statutory rape. The Iraqis' defense is based in part, at least, on their cultural marriage practices.[22]

As these examples show, the defendants are not always male, nor the victims always female. Both a Chinese immigrant man in New York who battered his wife to death for committing adultery and a Japanese immigrant woman in California who drowned her children and tried to drown herself because her husband's adultery had shamed the family, relied on cultural defenses to win reduced charges (from murder to second degree or involuntary manslaughter). It might seem, then, that cultural defense was biased toward the male in the first case, and the female in the second. But no such asymmetry exists. In both cases, the cultural message is similarly gender-biased: women (and children, in the second case) are ancillary to men, and should bear the blame and the shame for any departure from monogamy. Whoever is guilty of the infidelity, the wife suffers: in the first case, by being brutally killed on account of her husband's rage at her shameful infidelity; in the second, by being so shamed and branded a failure by his infidelity that she is driven to kill herself and her children. Again, the idea that girls and women are first and foremost sexual servants of men whose virginity before marriage and fidelity within it are their preeminent virtues emerges in many of the statements made in defense of cultural practices.

Western majority cultures, largely at the urging of feminists, have recently made substantial efforts to avoid or limit excuses for brutalizing women. Well within living

---

22 *New York Times*, 2 December 1996, A6.

memory, American men were routinely held less accountable for killing their wives if they explained their conduct as a crime of passion, driven by jealousy on account of the wife's infidelity. Also not long ago, women who did not have completely celibate pasts or who did not struggle—even so as to endanger themselves—were routinely blamed when raped. Things have now changed to some extent, and doubts about the turn toward cultural defenses undoubtedly come in part from a concern to preserve recent advances. Another concern is that such defenses can distort perceptions of minority cultures by drawing excessive attention to negative aspects of them. But perhaps the primary concern is that, by failing to protect women and sometimes children of minority cultures from male and sometimes maternal violence, cultural defenses violate their rights to the equal protection of the laws.[23] When a woman from a more patriarchal culture comes to the United States (or some other Western, basically liberal, state), why should she be less protected from male violence than other women are? Many women from minority cultures have protested the double standard that is being applied to their aggressors.[24]...

Part of the Solution?

It is by no means clear, then, from a feminist point of view, that minority group rights are "part of the solution." They may well exacerbate the problem. In the case of a more patriarchal minority culture in the context of a less patriarchal majority culture, no argument can be made on the basis of self-respect or freedom that the female members of the culture have a clear interest in its preservation. Indeed, they *may* be much better off if the culture into which they were born were either to become extinct (so that its members would become integrated into the less sexist surrounding culture) or, preferably, to be encouraged to alter itself so as to reinforce the equality of women—at least to the degree to which this is upheld in the majority culture. Other considerations would, of course, need to be taken into account, such as whether the minority group speaks a different language that requires protection, and whether the group suffers from prejudices such as racial discrimination. But it would take significant factors weighing in the other direction to counterbalance evidence that a culture severely constrained women's choices or otherwise undermined their well-being.

What some of the examples discussed above show us is how culturally endorsed practices that are oppressive to women can often remain hidden in the private or domestic sphere. In the Iraqi child marriage case mentioned above, if the father himself had not called in agents of the state, his daughters' plight might well not have become public. And when Congress in 1996 passed a law criminalizing clitoridec-

---

23 See Coleman, "Individualizing Justice Through Multiculturalism."
24 See for example Nilda Rimonte, "A Question of Culture: Cultural Approval of Violence Against Women in the Asian-Pacific Community and the Cultural Defense," *Stanford Law Review* 43 (1991): 1311-26.

tomy, a number of US doctors objected to the law as unjustified, since it concerned a private matter which, as one said, "should be decided by a physician, the family, and the child."[25] It can take more or less extraordinary circumstances for such abuses of girls or women to become public or for the state to be able to intervene protectively.

Thus it is clear that many instances of private sphere discrimination against women on cultural grounds are never likely to emerge in public, where courts can enforce their rights and political theorists can label such practices as illiberal and therefore unjustified violations of women's physical or mental integrity. Establishing group rights to enable some minority cultures to preserve themselves may not be in the best interests of the girls and women of the culture, even if it benefits the men.

When liberal arguments are made for the rights of groups, then, special care must be taken to look at within-group inequalities. It is especially important to consider inequalities between the sexes, since they are likely to be less public, and less easily discernible. Moreover, policies aiming to respond to the needs and claims of cultural minority groups must take seriously the need for adequate representation of less powerful members of such groups. Since attention to the rights of minority cultural groups, if it is to be consistent with the fundamentals of liberalism, must be ultimately aimed at furthering the well-being of the members of these groups, there can be no justification for assuming that the groups' self-proclaimed leaders—invariably mainly composed of their older and their male members—represent the interests of all of the groups' members. Unless women—and, more specifically, young women, since older women often become co-opted into reinforcing gender inequality—are fully represented in negotiations about group rights, their interests may be harmed rather than promoted by the granting of such rights.

---

25 *New York Times*, 12 October 1996, A6. Similar views were expressed on public radio.

38. Adaptive Preference and Women's Options*

Martha Nussbaum

> *The doctor was rightly upset about [the unsanitary conditions in the women's quarters]: but he was wrong in one respect. He thought that it was a source of constant pain for us. Quite the contrary.... To those with low self-regard, neglect does not seem unjust, and so it does not cause them pain. That is why women feel ashamed to be upset about the injustice they encounter. If a woman must accept so much injustice in the life ordered for her, then it is perhaps less painful for her to be kept in total neglect; otherwise she is bound to suffer, and suffer pointlessly, the pain of injustice, if she cannot change the rules governing her life. Whatever the condition that you kept us in, it rarely occurred to me that there was pain and deprivation in it.*
>
> Rabindranath Tagore, "Letter from a Wife"[1]

Any defense of universal norms involves drawing distinctions among the many things people actually desire. If it is to have any content at all, it will say that some objects of desire are more central than others for political purposes, more necessary to a human being's quality of life. A wise approach will go even further, holding that some existing preferences are actually bad bases for social policy....

Vasanti stayed for years in an abusive marriage. Eventually she did leave, and by now she has very firm views about the importance of her bodily integrity: indeed, she and Kokila spend a lot of their time helping other battered women report their cases to the police and goading the police to do something about the problem. But there was a time when Vasanti did not think this way—especially before her husband's vasectomy, when she thought she might still have children. Like many women, she seems to have thought that abuse was painful and bad, but still a part of women's lot in life, just something women have to put up with as part of being

---

* Source: *Women and Human Development* (Cambridge: Cambridge UP, 2000), pp. 111–66.
1 Kalpana Bardhan, ed. *Of Women, Outcastes, Peasants, and Rebels: A Selection of Bengali Short Stories* (Berkeley and Los Angeles: U of California P, 1990), 99.

516

women dependent on men, and entailed by having left her own family to move into a husband's home. The idea that it was a violation of rights, of law, of justice, and that *she herself* has rights that are being violated by her husband's conduct—these ideas she didn't have at that time, and many many women all over the world don't have them now. My universalist approach seems to entail that there is something wrong with the preference (if that's what we should call it) to put up with abuse, that it just shouldn't have the same role in social policy as the preference to protect and defend one's bodily integrity. It also entails that there is something wrong with not seeing oneself in a certain way, as a bearer of rights and a citizen whose dignity and worth are equal to that of others.

Or consider Jayamma, a great defender of her bodily integrity, but very acquiescent in a discriminatory wage structure and a discriminatory system of family income sharing. When women were paid less for heavier work at the brick kiln and denied chances for promotion, Jayamma didn't complain or protest. She knew that this was how things were and would be. Like Tagore's character in my epigraph, she didn't even waste mental energy getting upset, since these things couldn't be changed. Again, when her husband took his earnings and spent them on himself in somewhat unthrifty ways, leaving Jayamma to support the children financially through her labor, as well as doing all of the housework, this didn't strike her as wrong or bad, it was just the way things were, and she didn't waste time yearning for another way. Unlike Vasanti, Jayamma seemed to lack not only the concept of herself as a person with rights that could be violated, but also the sense that what was happening to her was wrong.

Finally, let me introduce one new example, to show the way entrenched preferences can clash with universal norms even at the level of basic nutrition and health. In the desert area outside Mahabubnagar, Andhra Pradesh, I talked with women who were severely malnourished, and whose village had no reliable clean water supply. Before the arrival of a government consciousness-raising program, these women apparently had no feeling of anger or protest about their physical situation. They knew no other way. They did not consider their conditions unhealthful or unsanitary, and they did not consider themselves to be malnourished. Now their level of discontent has gone way up: they protest to the local government, asking for clean water, for electricity, for a health visitor. They protect their food supplies from flies, they wash their bodies more often. Asked what was the biggest change that the government program had brought to their lives, they immediately said, as if in chorus, "We are cleaner now." The consciousness-raising program has clearly challenged entrenched preferences and satisfactions, taking a normative approach based on an idea of good human functioning....

[F]eminists who challenge entrenched satisfactions are frequently charged with being totalitarian and antidemocratic for just this way of proceeding. Who are they to tell real women what is good for them, or to march into an area shaped by tradition and custom with universal standards of what one should demand and what one should desire? Aren't they just brainwashing women, who already had their own ideas of what was right and proper?[2]

It is easy to make a rhetorical connection between the feminist critique of desire and discredited totalitarian ideologies—in part because Marx was among the most interesting and influential developers of a view of "false consciousness," and because feminist strategies of consciousness raising, in the developing world as in the West, frequently show the influence of Marx's account. And yet, the idea that some preferences are deformed by ignorance, malice, injustice, and blind habit has deep roots in the liberal tradition of political philosophy as well: in Adam Smith's ideas about greed and anger, in Mill's ideas about the sexes, in Kant's ideas about the many ways in which people get accustomed to treating one another as means rather than ends, in John Rawls's ideas about the ways in which unjust background conditions shape desire and choice. More recently, the idea of preference deformation has become central in mainstream economic and political thought, in the writings of people as otherwise diverse as Amartya Sen, Jon Elster, and Gary Becker....

In the debate about how preferences should figure in social choice we can identify two extreme positions, between which I shall situate my own. The first position can be called *subjective welfarism*.[3] This position holds that all existing preferences are on a par for political purposes, and that social choice should be based on some sort of aggregation of all of them.... Welfarism springs from respect for people and their actual choices, from a reluctance to impose something alien upon them, or even to treat the desires of different people unequally... [But] embraced as a normative position, subjective welfarism makes it impossible to conduct a radical critique of unjust institutions; it forces us to say, for example, that because Jayamma has accepted an unjust wage structure as the way things must be, that's the way they should remain; that because the women in Andhra Pradesh don't agitate for medical care and clean water, they don't need those things; that so long as Vasanti puts up with an abusive marriage, that's just her lot.

---

2 See Christina Hoff Sommers, *Who Stole Feminism?* (New York: Simon and Schuster, 1994), discussed in Chapter 5 of my *Sex and Social Justice* (New York: Oxford UP, 2000), and in Chapter 6 of my *Cultivating Humanity: A Classical Defense of Reform in Higher Education* (Cambridge MA: Harvard UP, 1997).

3 See Cass R. Sunstein, *The Partial Constitution* (Cambridge, MA: Harvard UP, 1993), Chapter 5, 162–66.

39. Adaptive Preference*

H.E. Baber

Martha Nussbaum argues that *preferentism*, or "subjective welfarism," the doctrine that a person's good consists in the satisfaction of her informed preferences, fails to explain our intuitions in cases of "adaptive preference," where the preferences of individuals in deprived circumstances are "deformed" by poverty, adverse social conditions and political oppression. Nussbaum argues that the satisfaction of such "deformed" preferences does not contribute to well-being, and hence the preference utilitarian's account of well-being is false. Furthermore, she claims, it undermines the motivation for projects intended to improve the material, social, and political life circumstances of individuals who are badly off: since the preferentist account suggests that these conditions are best for them if they are what such individuals prefer, it would seem that there is no reason to work for change.

"Subjective welfarism," writes Nussbaum, "holds that all existing preferences are on a par for political purposes, and that social choice should be based on some sort of aggregation of all of them." Thus she concludes:

> Embraced as a normative position, subjective welfarism makes it impossible to conduct a radical critique of unjust institutions.... This limitation is especially grave when we are in the process of selecting basic political principles that can be embodied in constitutional guarantees.... [T]he problem of preference deformation requires us to depart altogether from the utilitarian framework.[1]

I argue, first, that the deprived individuals whose predicaments Nussbaum cites as examples of "adaptive preference" do not in fact prefer the conditions of their lives to what we should regard as more desirable alternatives, indeed, that we believe they are badly off precisely because they are *not* living the lives they would prefer to live if they had other options and were aware of them. Second, I argue that even where

---

* Source: *Social Theory and Practice* 33.1 (January 2007).

1 Martha Nussbaum, *Women and Human Development* (Cambridge: Cambridge UP, 2000), pp. 116–18.

individuals in deprived circumstances acquire tastes for conditions that we regard as bad, they are typically better off having their acquired preferences satisfied. If they are badly off it is because they cannot get what we, and they, would regard as more desirable alternatives.

Preference utilitarianism explains why individuals in such circumstances are badly off whether they have adapted to their deprived circumstances or not. Even if they prefer the conditions of their lives to all other available alternatives, most would prefer alternatives that are not available to them that would, on the preferentist account, make them better off. And that, on the preferentist account, is the basis for a radical critique of unjust institutions that limit people's options and prevent them from getting what they want.

Subjective Welfarism

As *welfarists*, utilitarians are committed to the doctrine that "the correct way to assess or assign value to states of affairs ... [is] welfare, satisfaction, or people getting what they prefer." Preference utilitarians hold that preference satisfaction alone is what matters, thus J.C. Harsanyi writes:

> [P]reference utilitarianism is the only form of utilitarianism consistent with the important philosophical principle of *preference autonomy* ... the principle that, in deciding what is good and what is bad for a given individual, the ultimate criterion can only be his own wants and his own preferences.[2]

Harsanyi notes that for the principle of preference autonomy to yield plausible results, the utilitarian must idealize the notion of preference: since this notion has work to do in articulating our concepts of rational choice and the social good, it cannot be understood crudely in terms of either drives or actual choices.

> All we have to do is distinguish between a person's manifest preferences and his true preferences. His manifest preferences are his actual preferences as manifested by his observed behavior, including preferences possibly based on erroneous factual beliefs, or on careless logical analysis, or on strong emotions that at the moment greatly hinder rational choice. In contrast, a person's true preferences are the preferences he *would* have if he had all the relevant factual information, always reasoned with the greatest possible care and were in a state of mind most conducive to rational choice ... social utility must be defined in terms of people's true preferences rather than in terms of their manifest preferences.[3]

---

2 J.C. Harsanyi, "Morality and the Theory of Rational Behavior," in Amartya Sen and Bernard Williams (eds.), *Utilitarianism and Beyond* (Cambridge: Cambridge UP, 1982), pp. 39–62, at p. 55.
3 Ibid.

Preference is inextricably linked to choice but, as Harsanyi notes, when it comes to giving a plausible account of welfare in terms of preference satisfaction our choices do not always represent what we prefer in the requisite sense.

First, in order to reflect our true preferences, our choices must be informed. Was choosing S good for me? Not if I didn't know what I was getting into. In cases like this I deny that my choice represents a "real" preference: "I didn't really want S—I didn't know what it would be like, I didn't know what the consequences of getting it would be, I didn't know what alternatives were available, I didn't have an accurate picture of the costs, benefits, or probabilities."

Second, our choices must be free in the broadest sense: they must issue from a state of mind conducive to rational choice. Unreflective or impulsive choices, or choices individuals make when in the grip of an addiction, do not count. In such cases, once again, we deny that our choices reflect what we "really" want: "I didn't really want to do A—I wasn't thinking about it, I did it out of habit," or again, "I didn't really want S—I just couldn't resist."

Finally, in addition to the conditions cited by Harsanyi, arguably a plausible account of preference should not ascribe preferences to us on the basis of choices we make in response to feelings of moral obligation. Where we act out of a sense of moral obligation, again, we commonly deny that our actions reflect our desires. People quite often choose to do things that they do not want to do, and, given the commonsensical notion of preference we say, without worrying about contradiction or paradox: "I didn't do A because I *wanted* to—I would have much *preferred* that things be otherwise. But I *had* to do it [because I promised, because I put the good of my country ahead of my own, because I put my children's welfare ahead of my own, because it was a religious commitment, because it was my duty, because it was the right thing to do...]"; "I don't really want S but I put up with it because I don't deserve better," or more commonly, "I don't really want S but *you* deserve it and delivering it is going to hurt me even more than it hurts you." In spite of a venerable tradition according to which virtue is good for us and is the state we would act to achieve if we were rational and fully informed, common sense suggests otherwise. While some individuals have a taste for virtue and aim to cultivate it, most of us do not, and for us, doing what we believe is the right thing is usually doing precisely what we do *not* want to do. So as a further condition we shall define a person's "true" preferences as those he would have apart from any feelings of moral obligation to do some action or bring about some state of affairs.[4]

These restrictions on what are to count as "true" preferences for the purposes of judging individual welfare handle some of the most troublesome putative counter-examples to preferentism: the choices of individuals who, acting in ignorance or on

---

4 Sorting out moral from nonmoral motivations may be problematic: see, e.g., J. David Velleman, "Motivation by Ideal," *Philosophical Explorations* 5 (2002): 89–104.

impulse, wreak havoc on their own lives and individuals who, acting out of a sense of moral obligation, sacrifice their own well-being.

Nevertheless, on an informed preference account, even given these restrictions, neither the content nor the origin of preferences matters, but only that they are satisfied. Nussbaum and others argue that this by itself renders preferentism vulnerable to a further range of hard cases posed by the phenomenon of "adaptive preference." Our preferences, they note, are influenced by our perceived options and life circumstances. Thus, Nussbaum notes, reflecting on the plight of poor women in developing countries, individuals in deprived circumstances scale down their aspirations:

> "Quiet acceptance of deprivation and bad fate affects the scale of dissatisfaction generated, and the utilitarian calculus gives sanctity to that distortion"...this makes utility quite inadequate as a basis of social choice.[5]

Satisfying desires distorted by deprivation, she argues, does not contribute to the social good, and indeed, consciousness-raising to induce dissatisfaction is in order, particularly where such desires are a consequence of individuals' response to unfair practices.[6]

Nussbaum's case turns upon stories of women in deprived circumstances who, she claims, have come to prefer the conditions of their lives to what we should regard as better alternatives, and are worse off for having such preferences satisfied. To make her case she has to show that the choices they make reflect their preferences but she has not done this: in her rendition of their predicament, Nussbaum ignores the dispositional nature of preference, the trade-offs and prudential calculations rational agents make that lead them to choose goods that they do not ceteris paribus prefer, and the distinction between merely manifest and true preferences.

In general, preferentist theories are vulnerable on two counts. Some are implausible because they incorporate inadequate accounts of what preference is. So, accounts that assume that preference is strictly "revealed" in choice are unsatisfactory because the notion of "revealed preference," introduced in order to avoid reference to unquantifiable, unobservable, subjective states, is remote from the folk-psychological notion of preference.[7] Incorporating the revealed preference doctrine into a preferentist account of well-being, unsurprisingly, yields counterintuitive results.

---

5 Nussbaum here cites Amartya Sen, "Rational Fools: A Critique of the Behavioral Foundations of Economic Theory," *Philosophy and Public Affairs* 6 (1977): 317–44. See *Women and Human Development*, p. 139.

6 Martha Nussbaum, "Adaptive Preferences and Women's Options," *Economics and Philosophy* 17 (2001): 67–88.

7 For the classic attempt to cash out preference as choice, see P.A. Samuelson, "A Note on the Pure Theory of Consumers' Behaviour," *Economica* 5.17 (1938): 61–71. On Harsanyi's account cited earlier, "true" preference, the satisfaction of which contributes to well-being, does not cash out as choice. Other writers note that the revealed preference account is a nonstarter for a variety of

All preferentist accounts, however, are vulnerable to the extent that preference, *however it is understood,* can be pulled apart from welfare—and this is where the argument from adaptive preference is supposed to drive the wedge. To deploy this argument effectively, critics need to cite cases in which states of affairs that do not contribute to individuals' well-being are *clearly and uncontroversially preferred.* If, for example, the cases cited are ones in which individuals count as preferring states of affairs only if we assume the revealed preference doctrine, the argument from adaptive preference loses its force: these are precisely the cases in which ascribing preferences for such states is unintuitive.

Now it is not clear from Nussbaum's text whether her adaptive preference argument is specifically directed against preferentist accounts that incorporate the revealed preference doctrine. If it is, her argument from adaptive preference is superfluous and ineffective. It is superfluous because there are compelling independent reasons for rejecting preferentist theories that assume the revealed preference doctrine, and ineffective because the revealed preference doctrine undermines the effectiveness of the adaptive preference argument. If it is not, her argument fails because, as I shall show, on any reasonable, intuitive understanding of preference incorporating the conditions suggested above, the poor women whose stories she tells do not have the preferences she ascribes to them.[8]

If arguments from adaptive preference fail, it does not get informed preference accounts off the hook. Some of our informed and rationally considered desires, for example, do not involve us in a sufficiently intimate fashion to be pertinent to our well-being. Apart from any moral agendas, I may wish for peace in the world or for the well-being of a stranger I meet even though I do not benefit from the satisfaction

---

reasons. Daniel Hausman, for example, argues that "[c]hoice could not possibly reveal preference, as preference is understood in 'folk psychology,' because choice depends on both preference and belief. The binary relation among objects of choice, which is revealed by choice and is misleadingly called 'preference' by economists, is not a satisfactory replacement. Revealed-preference theory is particularly destructive in game theory, where it empties the theory of all predictive and normative content, but in truth revealed-preference theory serves no useful purpose at all and ought to be given up." See D.M. Hausman, "Revealed Preference, Belief, and Game Theory," *Economics and Philosophy* 16 (2000): 99–115. Hausman, Pettit, and others argue also that rejecting the folk-psychological notion of preference in favor of preference understood as choice renders accounts of well-being as preference satisfaction completely implausible: we often make choices that are bad for us, either because we are unaware of the range of our options or the consequences of our actions, or because we believe that in making such choices we are doing the right thing. See, e.g., Philip Pettit, "Preference, Deliberation and Satisfaction," Princeton Law and Public Affairs Working Paper Series, Working Paper No. 04-021, Fall 2004.

8 In fact it is worse: even assuming the revealed preference account and other assumptions of orthodox welfare economics, the women whose cases she considers do not have the preferences she ascribes to them. Even apart from information requirements, we assume that preference is a dispositional, that individuals' preferences are complete, that choosing a bundle of goods does not imply that the agent prefers each item in the bundle to any item in any other bundle or that rational individuals making decisions under uncertainty always make choices intended to bring about the states of affairs they most prefer.

of such desires. More fundamentally, critics of full information accounts of well-being suggest that the informed, idealized self of such accounts is, in effect, not the self whose welfare is of interest. David Sobel, for example, notes:

> [T]he full information account is not adequate for us because some of the limitations which are idealized away by the full information account play a fundamental role in shaping our capacity to value in the ways that we do. In order to have many experiences one must be a particular kind of person. The idealized self which the full information theorist recommends is not the kind of person who could have some of the experiences which could be ours.[9]

The current discussion, however, is not intended to vindicate informed preference accounts of welfare *tout court* but only to defend them against objections that invoke the phenomenon of adaptive preference. I claim that where those choices individuals make as a consequence of adaptation to deprived circumstances do not benefit them, it is because these choices do not manifest authentic preferences, and that where those choices individuals make as a consequence of adaptation to their life circumstances manifest authentic, informed, and rationally considered preferences, they are better off for having them satisfied. "Adaptation" is irrelevant: if I want something, getting it is good for me regardless of how I came by that desire; if getting what I choose does not benefit me, it is because what I chose is not something that I want.

Martha Nussbaum cites a range of cases in which, she claims, poor women whose desires have been formed through adaptation to deprived circumstances get what they want but are not better off for it insofar as their desires are "deformed." I argue that given an adequate account of preference, even though the women whose stories she tells are reconciled to their life circumstances and do not believe that it would be worthwhile to try for anything better, they do not *prefer* the conditions of their lives to what we, or Nussbaum, would regard as better alternatives. To make this out, let us reflect upon the stories of Jayamma, who stoically put up with poor working conditions and low pay, Vasanti, who endured years of abuse before leaving her husband, and Saida, who chose to marry off her daughter at the age of 12 instead of sending her to school.

Jayamma

"[C]onsider Jayamma," writes Nussbaum, "acquiescent in a discriminatory wage structure and a discriminatory system of family income sharing."

When women were paid less for heavier work at the brick kiln and denied

---

9 David Sobel, "Full Information Accounts of Well-Being," *Ethics* 104 (1994): 784–810, pp. 808–09. See also Connie Rosati, "Persons, Perspectives, and Full Information Accounts of the Good," *Ethics* 105 (1995): 296–325.

chances for promotion, Jayamma didn't complain or protest. She knew that this was how things were and would be...she didn't even waste mental energy getting upset, since these things couldn't be changed...and she didn't waste time yearning for another way.[10]

"Jayamma," Nussbaum speculates, "seemed to lack not only the concept of herself as a person with rights that could be violated, but also the sense that what was happening to her was a wrong."[11]

Nussbaum does not, however, produce any evidence to suggest that Jayamma would reject a raise in salary if one were offered or that she would forgo a promotion in order to continue in her current position, viz., hauling bricks. Indeed, it seems likely that if she were offered a promotion or a raise she would jump at it, since there is no reason to think that she is any different from most people who prefer more money to less money and would rather not spend their days hauling bricks if other options were available. If so, then, even though Jayamma does not *experience* frustration, her preferences are not satisfied.

Preference is not an occurrent, qualitative state: a person may prefer a state of affairs without ever experiencing an occurrent craving, and often it is only when people get what they prefer that they realize that it was what they "wanted all along." While people typically prefer to avoid unpleasant qualitative states associated with the thwarting of desires, we cannot assume that agents who cease to feel frustration have ceased to have the desires that are thwarted.

The proverbial fox wants grapes but knows that they are inaccessible. He also prefers serenity to felt frustration.

Fox's Utility Function

Grapes + no felt frustration	>> 3
No grapes + no felt frustration	>> 2
No grapes + felt frustration	>> 1

Given that he cannot get the grapes, the best he can do is to extinguish frustration—either by practicing self-deception to persuade himself that he does not want the grapes, by modifying his preferences through what Jon Elster calls "character planning," or by avoiding further rumination on the grape problem.[12]

---

10 Nussbaum, *Women and Human Development*, p. 113.
11 Ibid.
12 See Jon Elster, *Sour Grapes: Studies in the Subversion of Rationality* (Cambridge: Cambridge UP, 1983). For a contemporary case, consider official US statements regarding the importance of capturing bin Laden—currently, in light of his apparent escape, assigned a significantly lower priority than initially.

Elster, who takes the story of the fox to be a paradigm case of adaptive preference, remarks that it is characteristic of such cases that the preferences individuals acquire in response to their circumstances are "unstable"—so that if the grapes should come within reach, the fox would jump at them. Given any reasonable dispositional account of preference, however, such an "unstable" preference is no preference at all. If the fox is disposed to jump at the grapes as soon as they become available, then we should say that he has wanted them all along even if he has succeeded in extinguishing feelings of frustration and persuading himself that he does not in fact want them: his problem is not adaptive preference but self-deception. What constitutes his preference is not occurrent feelings but behavioral dispositions, in particular those determining what he would choose if given the opportunity. The inaccessibility of the grapes has not changed his preferences. Arguably there is no compelling reason to believe that poverty, unfair treatment, and bad working conditions have affected the preferences of the poor women whose stories Nussbaum tells, either. Nussbaum confuses the absence of occurrent frustration with preference satisfaction. If Jayamma would, as seems likely, jump at a raise in salary and promotion if they were offered, then we should say that although she does not experience feelings of frustration or moral outrage, she would prefer higher wages and better working conditions and that as things stand this preference is not satisfied. Like the fox, Jayamma settles for second best.

Jayamma's Utility Function

Better job + no feelings of outrage or frustration	>> 3
Current lousy job + no feelings of outrage or frustration	>> 2
Current lousy job + feelings of outrage and frustration	>> 1

Neither the proverbial story of the fox and the grapes nor the true stories of women in developing countries is, on the most plausible interpretation, a case of adaptive preference. The preference utilitarian therefore has no difficulty in explaining what is wrong with institutions that support low wages, discriminatory practices, and poor working conditions for Jayamma and others like her. Because of such institutions and practices, Jayamma cannot get what she most prefers, the state she would choose if it were available and which, on the preference utilitarian account, is therefore what is best for her.

The moral of Jayamma's story: the absence of felt frustration is not the same thing as desire satisfaction.

Vasanti

While preferring a thing is not a matter of the presence, or absence, of feely psychological states, it would nevertheless not be quite right to say that choosing x, or voluntarily doing an action, a, with the intention of bringing about x, is tantamount to preferring it. First, states of affairs are neither baldly preferred nor baldly rejected by agents—they are ranked. A person may prefer x to y and y to z but be perfectly happy to get any one of them even if neither y nor z could be understood simply as "what he wants." Secondly, agents rank bundles rather than isolated goods, so an agent may choose y over x even though ceteris paribus he would prefer x, because x has concomitants that he wants to avoid. Finally, when rational agents choose which policies of action to pursue, they consider not only the utility of the desired outcomes, but the probability of success in achieving them and also the risks and opportunity costs of pursuing their most preferred goals. An agent may pursue y, a sure thing, in preference to x, which he would prefer, all other things being equal, because the odds of his getting x are low.

Consider the case of Vasanti, who, Nussbaum suggests, stayed for years in an abusive marriage because of "desire-deformation" induced by intimidation, contempt, and neglect. Nussbaum writes:

> Like many women, she seems to have thought that abuse was painful and bad, but, still, a part of women's lot…. The idea that it was a violation of rights…and that *she herself* had rights that were being violated by his conduct—she did not have these ideas at that time, and many, many women all over the world still do not have them. My Universalist approach seems to entail that there is something wrong with the preference (if this is what we should call it) to put up with abuse.[13]

Nussbaum's construal of Vasanti's motivation is speculative. If, however, speculation is in order, we might with equal justification understand Vasanti's decision as the result of a utility calculation given a reasonable assessment of her options and the probabilities of various outcomes. Vasanti recognizes that given her circumstances, staying in an abusive marriage is her best bet if she wants to have a home and basic necessities: even if she would rather avoid getting beaten, she is prepared to take on that cost in order to avoid her least preferred outcome—homelessness and destitution.

Vasanti's Utility Function

Home and basic necessities + no beatings	>> 3
Home and basic necessities + occasional beatings	>> 2
No home + begging in the street + no beatings	>> 1

Vasanti does not have a preference for abuse: she prefers having a home and being beaten to not having a home and not being beaten because she is more averse to homelessness and destitution than to abuse.[14]

---

13 Nussbaum, "Adaptive Preferences and Women's Options," pp. 68–69.
14 Women in regions of sub-Saharan Africa where female genital mutilation is the norm are in a position comparable to Vasanti's. In many rural areas, "uncircumcised" girls are unmarriageable

Unless there is more to the story than Nussbaum reveals, there does not seem to be any reason to assume that Vasanti was in a "slumberous state induced by years of contempt and neglect." All the evidence presented suggests that she was behaving prudently. Vasanti preferred a bundle of goods that included being beaten up to one that did not include being beaten up. It does not, however, follow that she preferred being beaten to not being beaten, or that she failed to recognize that it violated her rights, or that she suffered from "desire-deformation."

The moral of Vasanti's story: preferring a bundle that includes x to one that includes y is not the same thing as preferring x to y.

Saida

Neither Jayamma's story nor Vasanti's is a hard case for subjective welfarism, since there is no reason to read either as a case of adaptive preference. Jayamma knew she had no viable options. Vasanti thought she had no acceptable alternative to sticking with her abusive husband. Making the best of a raw deal when no other alternatives are available is not the same as preferring it.

Moreover, where an individual chooses a given policy of action over others that appear to be available, it does not follow that this choice represents her ceteris paribus preference. Even where a person enjoys a better than nil chance of getting her most preferred outcome, x, she may reasonably pursue a less preferred outcome, y, because the likelihood of success in getting y is higher than the probability of getting x, and because she knows that if she pursues x and fails she diminishes her chances of getting y and risks getting z, her least preferred outcome. This is the structure of the game of Hearts. Few players "shoot the moon"—go for a big win—not only because success is unlikely, but because going for the big win substantially diminishes their chances of getting a little win and puts them at risk of losing outright.

The Game of Hearts

In the game of hearts,

1. The probability of getting a little win by playing it safe is higher than the probability of getting a big win by shooting the moon, and

---

and spinsterhood is not a viable option. Even if a woman might prefer that her daughter be uncircumcised and respectably married, that alternative is not, for all practical purposes available, so, like Vasanti, she may reasonably opt for second best in order to avoid her least preferred outcome: an unmarriageable daughter whose only available career path is prostitution. The literature on FGM is extensive. For discussions that include material on the social circumstances that perpetuate the practice, see especially Frances A. Althaus, "Female Circumcision: Rite of Passage or Violation of Rights?" *International Family Planning Perspectives* 23.3 (1997): 130–33, and World Health Organization Fact Sheet No. 241, June 2000.

2. The probability of getting a loss if you shoot the moon is higher than the probability of getting a loss if you play it safe.

Often people play it safe, aiming for a less preferred outcome rather than shooting the moon, because of the low probability they assign, whether rightly or wrongly, to achieving their most preferred outcomes and the opportunity costs of actively pursuing the goal they most prefer. This was Saida's policy.

In a recent interview, a group of traditional Afghan women held that formal education was a waste for girls:

> Like the others, Saida, 27, received no formal education.... Saida says her eldest daughter Nahid, 12, is getting ready for her betrothal to a 26-year-old farmer and does not have much time to spare for morning instruction.... Saida teaches her girls the really important things—how to cook, sew and soothe a husband's ego. "Teaching my daughters how to make their husbands comfortable is the most important thing," she says, "because if a husband is not comfortable, then the woman's life is hell."[15]

This is a rational decision given her assessment of the options girls in Afghanistan have and the probability of success in achieving various goals. It is unlikely that any lower-class Afghan girl, or boy, will become a teacher, doctor, or engineer. Statistically, the overwhelming likelihood is that a girl will eventually marry and be totally dependent on her husband's good will for financial support and a decent life. So, in the manner of American mothers who, 30 years ago, advised their daughters to forgo "unrealistic" career goals that might hinder them in the marriage market, Afghan mothers are "realistic." Such "realism" is not a manifestation of low self-esteem or adaptive preference—it is a matter of rationally playing the odds.[16]

Saida thinks that making a husband comfortable is the most important thing because she believes that the only realistic alternative her daughters have is *failing* to make their husbands comfortable and suffering the consequences. It does not follow that she thinks that marriage at age 12 and domestic servitude is preferable to education and a career. Rather, she recognizes that it is highly unlikely that her

---

15 Richard Lacayo, "About Face for Afghan Women," *Time Magazine*, 17 January 2002.

16 Vasanti, it seems, was also playing the odds. Initially she believed, with justification, that the probability of getting her most preferred outcome was low. Most Indian women whose marriages fail are blamed for the failure by their families of origin and rejected. Knowing how things ordinarily worked in her society, she only left after her husband had a vasectomy (in order to take advantage of the Indian government's financial incentive program for voluntary sterilization). Prior to that, she calculated, reasonably, that having children would improve her status and open up the possibility of future financial support from them. So long as the possibility of having children was open, carrying with it the prospect of improved treatment, she did not think it worthwhile to take the risk of entering into negotiations with her family of origin. Once the prospect of improvement disappeared, she judged the risk of approaching her family worthwhile and, happily, achieved a good outcome.

daughters will be able to achieve any degree of financial independence or have lives significantly different from her own. She calculates that the risk of shooting the moon is unwarranted.

The moral of Saida's story: rational choosers do not just consider the desirability of outcomes; they also calculate the probability of achieving them and the opportunity costs of trying for them. Adopting a policy of action intended to get x rather than one intended to get y is not the same thing as preferring x to y.

Rational Choice

Nussbaum cites a range of cases in which women voluntarily remain in abusive marriages, work at bad jobs, put up with poor living conditions, or otherwise engage in behavior that she regards as undignified or demeaning. She does not, however, provide any compelling reason to read these stories as cases in which women have come to *prefer* the conditions they tolerate to what she, or we, should regard as better options. Poor women in developing countries do not have these options.

Poor, unskilled women put up with discriminatory treatment at work because they know that regulations forbidding such practices and protecting workers who protest are never taken seriously and that they can be easily replaced. They put up with abusive husbands because they prefer having basic necessities, even at the cost of getting beaten up, to being homeless and destitute. Some may indeed be overly pessimistic about their prospects and only learn, from seeing the benefits that come from the establishment of women's co-ops or micro-credit schemes, that efforts to improve their lot could pay off. Their pessimism, however, is the consequence of inadequate information and factual error rather than distorted preference: there is nothing in the anecdotal material Nussbaum provides to favor one reading over the other, and maximum charity suggests that we regard these women as pessimistic but rational choosers who may adopt more proactive policies given additional information.

Nussbaum also ignores the extent to which feedback effects lock in poverty and bad treatment. Jayamma knows that isolated protests do no good. So long as her coworkers put up with low wages and poor working conditions, she knows her best option is to put up with adverse conditions and unfair treatment—because she knows her fellow workers know that that is their best option too, given that they know that they are all in the same boat. And their employer knows that they know. The phenomenon is familiar: even where everyone gets what she most prefers, given the choices of others, and to that extent what is best for them in the circumstances, everyone might prefer the outcome of everyone's having chosen differently. Second-guessing and feedback effects lock in suboptimal equilibria. And poor women in developing nations are especially vulnerable to being caught in such vicious circles because they are less able to assume risk than individuals who have economic cushions or fallback positions.

There are indeed hard cases for preference utilitarianism of the sort Nussbaum has in mind, for the most part fictional cases in which individuals are manipulated through brainwashing, psychosurgery, or genetic engineering, and their preferences are, by hypothesis, changed. Nussbaum has not, however, shown that the cases she cites are instances of adaptive preference or that they are hard cases for preference utilitarianism. The preference utilitarian does not claim that what is best for a person *tout court* is his getting what he prefers from amongst available options, but that it is the best he can do for himself from amongst available options. Where an individual prefers options that are not on offer, she holds that it would be better for him if they were.[17] This is what motivates the preference utilitarian's critique of unjust institutions that restrict opportunities for desire satisfaction and support for efforts to provide needy individuals with material assistance rather than rights, self-esteem, dignity, or other cheap goods.[18]

[…]

---

17 Axiomatic utility theory assumes that individuals' preferences are *complete* such that, for any states of affairs, bundles of goods, or "things" in the world x and y, *if* a person is given a choice between x and y, then either she prefers x to y or prefers y to x or is indifferent between the two. This means that the ordering of a person's preferences includes preferences for states, bundles of goods, and things that she cannot get as well as those that are available to her, among them states, bundles of goods, and things that she may never even have heard of. The completeness assumption is not far out of line with our folk-psychological notion of preference. I give people creative Christmas presents from the "Things You Never Knew Existed" catalogue (http://www.johnsonsmith.com/website/aspfiles/home. asp). Even though I'm certain that the people on my list have never even thought of the things I give them, I choose things I think they would prefer. The subjunctive idiom does not make any substantive difference: intuitively, we believe that we can rank things people never knew existed among their desiderata. Arguably, when Jayamma chooses to put up with poor working conditions and low wages, she is getting what she prefers from amongst her available options and what is best for her given her circumstances and lack of viable alternatives. It does not follow that these conditions are morally acceptable, and there is no need to show that her preferences have been "distorted" in order to make the case that her prospects should be improved: she would be better off getting *unavailable* options that she prefers, including options that she has never even thought about.

18 I am grateful to the anonymous reviewer for this journal who notes: "Nussbaum may also be subtly appealing to Mill's idea of higher pleasures: better to be Socrates dissatisfied than a pig satisfied. If, once one has the idea that one is entitled to human rights, one regards one's former state as degraded, even though one feels more frustration once one recognizes the gap between what one has and what one is entitled to, then arguably it is better to be Socrates dissatisfied."

I am skeptical about the notion of "higher pleasures" and about the idea that rights, self-esteem, and "dignity" are inherently good. People who are well off develop expensive tastes, and, when their ordinary wants are satisfied, acquire new desires for various psychological goods and intangibles. I do not see why developing such expensive tastes is a good thing. More importantly, I worry when privileged social reformers fuss about providing less privileged people with self-esteem, dignity, and other intangibles because these goods are cheap whereas material improvement and changes to the policies and social practices that lock people into lives of poverty and drudgery are expensive and difficult to achieve.

If consciousness-raising and other ploys for giving poor women the idea that they are "dignified persons with rights, entitled to more than they have" is, as the reviewer suggests, "a path to a better future"—a future in which they can get the material benefits they want—then these practices are no doubt instrumentally good. But social action agendas in which they figure as distractions or cheap substitutes for material improvement are vile.

Preference, Choice, and Commitment

[...]

Nussbaum and other members of elites in affluent countries do not fully appreciate how few options most people have, how little they know about even the few options available to them and the extent to which the precarious circumstances of their lives make it difficult for them to assume risk. They are, consequently, inclined to construe rational responses to such conditions as symptoms of "preference-deformation." I have argued that given a reasonable informed preference account, the choices less privileged people make do not represent their ceteris paribus preferences.

First, individuals in adverse circumstances with no economic cushions or safety nets cannot afford to assume risk. All other things being equal, Saida may well have preferred to send her daughter to school: she trained Nahid for domestic servitude because she knew that her chances of a better life even with the schooling available were negligible and that the costs Nahid would incur as an uppity wife, unwilling or unable to make her husband "comfortable," were too great to warrant the risk. Saida and Nahid do not need their preferences fixed: they need reasonably safe, viable options.

Second, illiterate rural folk in developing countries are quite often very short on factual information about even the few options they have and the feasibility of pursuing them, so their choices do not reflect their true preferences—the choices they would make if they were adequately informed. As Nussbaum herself notes, for example, in spite of laws according men and women equal rights in India, women put up with discrimination and poor treatment because they do not know about these laws or how to go about getting them enforced:

> [I]n the absence of programs targeted at increasing female literacy, economic empowerment, and employment opportunities, those rights are not real to them. As a recent report on laws addressing violence against women puts it, "For the vast majority of Indian women, these statutes are meaningless.... Lack of basic knowledge about the law and procedures, delays and insensitivity of the judicial system, the cost involved in getting justice have all contributed to this."[19]

Even if the "vast majority of Indian women" put up with discrimination, domestic violence, and poor living conditions, it does not follow that these choices reflect their "true" preferences. We imagine that if we were in their place we would report abusive husbands, demand clean water, and form women's co-ops to better ourselves.

---

19 Nussbaum, *Women and Human Development*, p. 54.

But rural women in Andhra Pradesh do not know that wife-beating is illegal or that their water supply is contaminated, and it has never occurred to them to form co-ops. They do not need consciousness-raising or self-esteem enhancement: they need factual information.

Finally, even when we are fully informed, reason with the greatest care, and are in a state of mind conducive to rational choice, we do not always choose what we most prefer, because sometimes we act out of what Sen calls "commitment" rather than out of an interest in promoting our own well-being.[20] Achieving what we believe to be good through our voluntary actions does not always make us better off: the idea of principled, rationally considered *sacrifice* is not incoherent, and sacrifice is precisely something the agent knows is *not* good for her but does anyway because she believes that it is right.

Sometimes our commitments are wrong-headed: as Nussbaum suggests, some individuals "internalize" oppressive ideologies and come to believe that behavior we regard as morally wrong is legitimate. In many traditional societies, for example, where wife-beating is the norm, both men and women regard the practice as morally permissible.

> About 80% of Zambian wives find it acceptable to be beaten by their husbands "as a form of chastisement," according to the latest Zambia Demographic Health Survey. Out of 5,029 women interviewed countrywide, 79% said they should be beaten if they went out without their husband's permission. 61% said a beating was acceptable if they denied their husbands sex, while 45% said a beating was in order if they cooked "bad" food.[21]

Zambian women live in a society where wife-beating is commonplace and socially acceptable: most believe that in exchange for financial support, or simply in virtue of being female, they are obliged to provide sex on demand and good cooked food, and that it is morally permissible for men to beat wives who fail to perform these duties.

Nevertheless, from the fact that a woman believes that she ought to knuckle under to men and that she and others similarly situated deserve to be beaten if they are remiss in their duties, it does not follow that she *prefers* to knuckle under or get beaten. Our moral beliefs and commitments do not always reflect our preferences. There is no contradiction in saying that an individual believes that doing an action, *a*, would be the right thing to do and chooses to do *a*, but does not want to do *a*—or even *want to* want to do *a*.[22]

---

20 See especially Sen, "Rational Fools."

21 Lusaka, "Wife-beating in Zambia a 'Natural Consequence'" *East African Mail and Guardian*, 3 December 2003.

22 Arguably, appealing to higher-order preferences to explain committed choice is an ad hoc move to back the doctrine that where there is voluntary action or rational choice there is preference

There is in any case no compelling reason to believe that most Zambian women, whatever their moral convictions, prefer the lives they live either, or even that they would prefer to prefer them. Choosing to do something because we believe, whether correctly or incorrectly, that it is the right thing is not the same thing as preferring it. Zambian women do not need to be cured of "preference-deformation": they need information about alternative domestic arrangements and moral education.

Preferentism and Social Change

Life is tough. We rarely, if ever, get what we most want: we settle for second, third, and nth best. We are constrained, and the fault is not in ourselves but in our stars: many options are too costly or risky to be worth pursuing; most are just not gettable, regardless of how much we are willing to pay or how much risk we are prepared to assume.

For elite individuals in affluent countries, the boundaries of practical possibility are remote and there is room for maneuver. Within the bounds we can make substantial changes in our lives through our own efforts and, at least, satisfice. So, we imagine that individuals whose lives are by our standards profoundly unsatisfactory are also getting what they want, and, depending on our politics, either infer that they are getting what is best for them (and what they deserve) or conclude that their preferences are "deformed" and that the satisfaction of such preferences does not contribute to their well-being.

I have argued that there is no compelling reason to believe that the deprived individuals cited by Nussbaum [and other writers] and popular writers like Kristof as victims of "preference deformation" *prefer* the conditions of their lives to what we should regard as better alternatives. Political oppression, social constraints and poverty restrict women like [...] Jayamma, Vasanti, and Saida and her daughter to a narrow range of options most of which are low on their preference rankings. Their acquiescence is not a consequence of irrational fatalism or low self-esteem but an expression of reasonable pessimism. According to the preferentist account of well-being, they would do better if they had a wider range of options and so could get goods that rank higher on their preference orderings, including items of which they are unaware.

That is the basis for the preference utilitarian's radical critique of unjust institutions, which lock in poverty and limit people's options. "Adaptive preference" is a red

---

lurking somewhere, even if only at one or more removes. Compare cases in which we act out of commitment to those where higher-order preferences do seem to be at work. I would prefer to be more fastidious. Being dirty doesn't bother me, but I am bothered by the fact that it doesn't bother me. I shower and brush my teeth to avoid social opprobrium but I don't want to. And I am embarrassed about not wanting to: even though I don't want to maintain higher standards of personal hygiene and grooming, I want to want to—such is my higher-order preference.

Is moral commitment like this? Do people generally want to be the sort of people who want to do the right thing? I don't. I want to be fastidious, and I want to have good taste but I have no real desire to be dutiful, altruistic, morally upright, or virtuous.

herring and we do not need to appeal to it or to Nussbaum's list of central human capabilities to explain why the subjects of her stories are badly off. Moreover, unlike Nussbaum, who repeatedly suggests that the subjects of her stories are irrational, subsisting in a "slumberous state," unaware of their rights, beaten down, victimized, and psychologically damaged, the preference utilitarian can make the case for improving the conditions of their lives while recognizing that they are rational choosers, coping as best as they can and making the best of a raw deal.[23]

---

23 I am grateful to Timothy Hall, who commented on an earlier version of this paper read at the American Philosophical Association Pacific Division Mini-Conference on Global Justice, Portland, Oregon, March 2006. I am also grateful for comments from participants at that session, and for comments by anonymous reviewers for this journal.

Recommended Reading

Bergmann, B. (1997). *In Defense of Affirmative Action*. New York: Basic Books.

Blau, F.D., & Ferber, M.A. (1992). *The Economics of Women, Men, and Work*. Englewood Cliffs, NJ: Prentice-Hall.

de Beauvoir, S. (1989 [1949]). *The Second Sex*. New York: Vintage.

Friedan, B. (1974 [1963]). *The Feminine Mystique*. New York: Norton.

Jaggar, A. (1983). *Feminist Politics and Human Nature*. Totowa, NJ: Rowman & Allanheld.

Kavane, M. (2004). *Women and Development in Africa*. Boulder, CO: Lynne Rienner.

Mill, J.S. (1989 [1869]). *On the Subjugation of Women*. Cambridge: Cambridge UP.

Murphy, E.F. (2005). *Getting Even*. New York: Touchstone.

Nussbaum, M. (2000). *Women and Human Development*. Cambridge: Cambridge UP.

Tavris, C. (1993). *The Mismeasure of Woman*. New York: Touchstone.

Valian, V. (1999). *Why So Slow?* Cambridge, MA: MIT.

VIII

Cultural Relativism and Its Critics: Introduction

"America is awash in tolerance," writes William B. Irvine.

> In my own life I confront this epidemic of tolerance every time I discuss value theory in the college philosophy classes that I teach. Relativism runs rampant among the undergraduates, and those undergraduates who cling to absolutes often do so surreptitiously, fearing the scorn of the relativists around them.... The first task in any college ethics class, then, is to confront relativism.[1]

Cultural relativism

Cultural relativism means different things, but here are three ways in which it has traditionally been understood:

(1) **Descriptive Cultural Relativism:** People's beliefs, attitudes, tastes, etc. are significantly affected by their culture—and people in different cultures have very different beliefs, attitudes, tastes, etc.

(2) **Methodological Cultural Relativism:** cultures should be studied on their own terms.

(3) **Normative Cultural Relativism:** Actions are right or wrong to the extent that they conform or don't conform to cultural norms.

---

1 William B. Irvine, "Confronting Relativism," in *Academic Questions* 14.1 (2000): 42–49, <http://www.springerlink.com.sally.sandiego.edu/content/mw7jqntd16fc6y53/?p=b885ed17be2641b693daa3cdff9c5168&pi=8>.

(1) is of course true. The study of different cultures over the past centuries has shown us the extent of human diversity.

(2) is also true, and it is what anthropologists usually mean when they talk about cultural relativism. The idea is that we should study cultures on their own terms and not try to squeeze them into a template provided by our own culture. This is just good science.

Adopting our own culture as a model distorts our understanding of other cultures in much the way that taking the grammar of one language as a universal model makes it difficult to make sense of the way in which other languages work. This is why, for example, English prescriptive grammar is peculiar. When the formal grammar of English was developed, the model was Latin—a bad model since English is a Germanic language and adopting Latin as the model meant squeezing English into a grammatical structure suitable for Romance languages. So, for example, we are not supposed to "split infinitives," i.e., to say things like "to never stop trying" or "to always remember." There is no good English reason why we shouldn't say things like this. But prescriptive grammarians forbid us because in Latin, and Romance languages, infinitives can't be "split."

Good linguistics and good anthropology understand other languages and cultures on their own terms. But that doesn't mean (3)—holding that actions are right or wrong to the extent that they conform or don't conform to cultural norms. So we happily accept (1) and (2) but reject (3).

Is this a problem? Let us consider some worries people have about the rejection of cultural relativism in the sense of (3). We note the following:

(i) Actions that are wrong may be excusable so that people who do them are not *blameworthy*.

Lots of cultures practiced human sacrifice because they believed that the deaths of some were necessary to insure the life and well-being of many more. Their goal was reasonable even if their means to achieving it was ridiculous. Arguably we should not blame them: they were doing what they thought best, given their ignorance and misinformation. What they did was wrong but, on this account, not blameworthy.

(ii) Even if an action is wrong, it does not follow that it would be right to stop people from doing it.

James Fergusson, author of several books on Afghanistan, asks whether Western soldiers should be dying for the rights of Afghan women—and answers that they should not. "The case of Bibi Sanubar, the Afghan widow brutally flogged and shot dead by the Taliban for the crime of being pregnant," he writes, "caused outrage in the west. Earlier in the month, *Time* magazine published a truly shocking picture of Aisha, an 18-year-old girl whose nose had been cut off because she had run away from her in-laws." He continues:

> [But] Taliban leadership did not see themselves as oppressors of women but as their defenders.... The Taliban's first purpose was to bring law and order to a country that had been devastated by five years of vicious civil war and in those areas that came under their control, they succeeded brilliantly.... To many Afghans, including many Afghan women, oppression was a small price to pay in exchange for an end to the wholesale rape and slaughter of the preceding years.... Women's suffrage in Britain was achieved not by imposition from abroad but through long internal social debate, which is as it should be in so obviously sovereign a matter.[2]

Fergusson argues that even though Pashtun treatment of women is morally wrong, it would be wrong also for Western countries to intervene. In this, and a range of other cases, it is an open question whether intervention is morally justified. In general, even if an action is morally wrong it does not follow that we are justified in trying to stop it.

(iii) Practices that produce good results in one culture may not produce good results in another.

"During the 1980s," Susan Okin writes,

> the French government quietly permitted immigrant men to bring multiple wives into the country, to the point where an estimated 200,000 families in Paris are now polygamous.... Overcrowded apartments and the lack of each wife's private space led to immense hostility, resentment, even violence both among the wives and against each other's children. In part because of the strain on the welfare state caused by families with 20-30 members, the French government has recently decided to recognize only one wife and consider all the other marriages annulled.[3]

In an agrarian society, outside of the money economy, where wives and children work the farmstead, polygamy is a viable arrangement. Co-wives share the work, so the more wives and children there are to work the land, the better off the family is. As Okin notes, however, polygamy plays out differently in urban European settings. This shouldn't worry ethical universalists, who hold that there are *some*

---

2 <http://www.guardian.co.uk/commentisfree/2010/aug/15/james-fergusson-afghanistan-women-west>.

3 Susan Moller Okin, "Is Multiculturalism Bad for Women?", pp. 505–68 in this volume.

moral standards that hold universally since we are not committed to holding that polygamy is always morally permissible or always morally prohitibed. We can hold that polygamy in circumstances where it promotes human happiness is right but is wrong in circumstances where it results in hostility, resentment, and violence.

The "Paradox of Tolerance"

Normative cultural relativism is attractive because it seems to promote tolerance. But, arguably, there are some practices that we should not tolerate. Moreover, it generates the so-called Paradox of Tolerance.

Cultural relativists hold that an action is right insofar as it is in conformity with the mores of the culture in which it is done. In plain English that means, "when in Rome do as the Romans do."[4] We should remember, however, that the Romans did perfectly awful things. They crucified Christians—starting with Jesus. They owned slaves and enjoyed blood sports in which slaves were made to kill one another for the entertainment of citizens. Christianity didn't significantly improve the Romans: Constantine fought to secure and maintain power, killed off his rivals, and had both his wife and son from an earlier liaison executed for unknown reasons. Subsequent Byzantine emperors blinded, mutilated, tortured, and executed competitors, waged endless war and, reversing Constantine's policy of religious toleration, persecuted pagans, heretics, and Jews.

No one in his right mind would, from a moral point of view, recommend doing as these Romans did.

Advocates imagine that normative cultural relativism supports tolerance. But it does not support *any* universal moral principles, including the principle of tolerance. Moreover, if we are cultural relativists, committed to the view that the mores of our culture determine what is right for us, we shall have to hold that members of intolerant cultures, like the culture of the medieval Eastern Roman Empire, are morally obliged to be intolerant.

The United Nations Declaration of Universal Human Rights, adopted in 1948 and reprinted in most applied ethics textbooks since then, "proclaims...a common standard of achievement for all peoples and all nations" including rights to life, liberty, and security of person, and the right not to be enslaved or tortured.

The United Nations Declaration and a variety of other recommendations for supporting human rights which, prima facie, seem uncontroversial have been challenged by some social scientists. Anthropologist Carolyn Fluehr-Lobban notes that in 1947 the executive board of the American Anthropological Association withdrew from the discussions of the UN Declaration that led to its adoption. Anthropolo-

---

4 The origin of this phrase is as follows. St. Augustine went to Rome and discovered that the liturgical practices there were different from those of his native Carthage. He wrote to his mentor, St. Ambrose, to inquire what to do. Ambrose's response is generally paraphrased as "When in Rome, do as the Romans do."

gists, committed to cultural relativism, did so in the belief that no such declaration would be applicable to all human beings. Fluehr-Lobban's short article, originally published in the *Chronicle of Higher Education*, poses in the starkest terms the case against ethical relativism.

James Rachels offers an accessible, comprehensive philosophical critique of cultural relativism, including a discussion of the consequences of taking cultural relativism seriously. "What would it be like if it [cultural relativism] were true?" asks Rachels.

> Suppose a society waged war on its neighbors for the purpose of taking slaves. Or suppose a society was violently anti-Semitic and its leaders set out to destroy the Jews.... [I]f we took Cultural Relativism seriously, we would have to regard these social practices as also immune from criticism.... Cultural Relativism would not only forbid us from criticizing the codes of other societies; it would stop us from criticizing our own.... Usually, we think that at least some social changes are for the better.... If Cultural Relativism is correct... [o]ur idea of social reform will also have to be reconsidered.[5]

Carol Williams describes a striking test case for cultural relativism. After the internationally notorious honor killing of Fadime Sahindal, a member of a Kurdish immigrant family in Sweden, it was Kurdish immigrants and immigrant organizations that objected most vigorously to well-meaning Swedish policies intended to accommodate the cultural practices of immigrant groups:

> "The message this should send to Swedish people, especially the Social Democrats who have been in power for 40 years, is that the system isn't working," said Dilsa Demirbag-Sten, a former government advisor on integration affairs whose Kurdish family came to Sweden from eastern Turkey when she was 7. She accuses authorities of arrogance in their view that certain rights and freedoms accorded Nordic residents, such as gender equality and protection from forced marriage, are not necessarily applicable to immigrants.[6]

As a descriptive account of diverse cultures, cultural relativism is correct, and as a methodological principle for the study of these cultures it is invaluable. But as a normative theory, arguably, it runs afoul of the hard cases. There are some practices that are embedded into the fabric of other cultures, and of our own, that violate human rights and undermine well-being. And only the recognition of some universal ethical standards can justify our deploring these practices and working for their elimination.

---

5 James Rachels, "The Challenge of Cultural Relativism," pp. 553–63 in this volume.
6 Carol Williams, "The Price of Freedom, in Blood," pp. 564–68 in this volume.

40. Universal Declaration of Human Rights[*]

United Nations

Adopted and proclaimed by General Assembly resolution 217 A (III) of 10 December 1948

On December 10, 1948 the General Assembly of the United Nations adopted and proclaimed the Universal Declaration of Human Rights the full text of which appears in the following pages. Following this historic act the Assembly called upon all Member countries to publicize the text of the Declaration and "to cause it to be disseminated, displayed, read and expounded principally in schools and other educational institutions, without distinction based on the political status of countries or territories."

Preamble

Whereas recognition of the inherent dignity and of the equal and inalienable rights of all members of the human family is the foundation of freedom, justice and peace in the world,

Whereas disregard and contempt for human rights have resulted in barbarous acts which have outraged the conscience of mankind, and the advent of a world in which human beings shall enjoy freedom of speech and belief and freedom from fear and want has been proclaimed as the highest aspiration of the common people,

Whereas it is essential, if man is not to be compelled to have recourse, as a last resort, to rebellion against tyranny and oppression, that human rights should be protected by the rule of law,

Whereas it is essential to promote the development of friendly relations between nations,

---

[*] Source: <http://www.un.org/en/documents/udhr/index.shtml>.

Whereas the peoples of the United Nations have in the Charter reaffirmed their faith in fundamental human rights, in the dignity and worth of the human person and in the equal rights of men and women and have determined to promote social progress and better standards of life in larger freedom,

Whereas Member States have pledged themselves to achieve, in co-operation with the United Nations, the promotion of universal respect for and observance of human rights and fundamental freedoms,

Whereas a common understanding of these rights and freedoms is of the greatest importance for the full realization of this pledge,

Now, Therefore THE GENERAL ASSEMBLY proclaims THIS UNIVERSAL DEC-LARATION OF HUMAN RIGHTS as a common standard of achievement for all peoples and all nations, to the end that every individual and every organ of society, keeping this Declaration constantly in mind, shall strive by teaching and education to promote respect for these rights and freedoms and by progressive measures, national and international, to secure their universal and effective recognition and observance, both among the peoples of Member States themselves and among the peoples of territories under their jurisdiction.

Article 1.
All human beings are born free and equal in dignity and rights. They are endowed with reason and conscience and should act towards one another in a spirit of brotherhood.

Article 2.
Everyone is entitled to all the rights and freedoms set forth in this Declaration, without distinction of any kind, such as race, colour, sex, language, religion, political or other opinion, national or social origin, property, birth or other status. Furthermore, no distinction shall be made on the basis of the political, jurisdictional or international status of the country or territory to which a person belongs, whether it be independent, trust, non-self-governing or under any other limitation of sovereignty.

Article 3.
Everyone has the right to life, liberty and security of person.

Article 4.
No one shall be held in slavery or servitude; slavery and the slave trade shall be prohibited in all their forms.

Article 5.
No one shall be subjected to torture or to cruel, inhuman or degrading treatment or punishment.

Article 6.
Everyone has the right to recognition everywhere as a person before the law.

Article 7.
All are equal before the law and are entitled without any discrimination to equal protection of the law. All are entitled to equal protection against any discrimination in violation of this Declaration and against any incitement to such discrimination.

Article 8.
Everyone has the right to an effective remedy by the competent national tribunals for acts violating the fundamental rights granted him by the constitution or by law.

Article 9.
No one shall be subjected to arbitrary arrest, detention or exile.

Article 10.
Everyone is entitled in full equality to a fair and public hearing by an independent and impartial tribunal, in the determination of his rights and obligations and of any criminal charge against him.

Article 11.
1. Everyone charged with a penal offence has the right to be presumed innocent until proved guilty according to law in a public trial at which he has had all the guarantees necessary for his defence.

2. No one shall be held guilty of any penal offence on account of any act or omission which did not constitute a penal offence, under national or international law, at the time when it was committed. Nor shall a heavier penalty be imposed than the one that was applicable at the time the penal offence was committed.

Article 12.
No one shall be subjected to arbitrary interference with his privacy, family, home or correspondence, nor to attacks upon his honour and reputation. Everyone has the right to the protection of the law against such interference or attacks.

Article 13.

1. Everyone has the right to freedom of movement and residence within the borders of each state.

2. Everyone has the right to leave any country, including his own, and to return to his country.

Article 14.

1. Everyone has the right to seek and to enjoy in other countries asylum from persecution.

2. This right may not be invoked in the case of prosecutions genuinely arising from non-political crimes or from acts contrary to the purposes and principles of the United Nations.

Article 15.

1. Everyone has the right to a nationality.

2. No one shall be arbitrarily deprived of his nationality nor denied the right to change his nationality.

Article 16.

1. Men and women of full age, without any limitation due to race, nationality or religion, have the right to marry and to found a family. They are entitled to equal rights as to marriage, during marriage and at its dissolution.

2. Marriage shall be entered into only with the free and full consent of the intending spouses.

3. The family is the natural and fundamental group unit of society and is entitled to protection by society and the State.

Article 17.

1. Everyone has the right to own property alone as well as in association with others.

2. No one shall be arbitrarily deprived of his property.

Article 18.

Everyone has the right to freedom of thought, conscience and religion; this right includes freedom to change his religion or belief, and freedom, either alone or in community with others and in public or private, to manifest his religion or belief in teaching, practice, worship and observance.

Article 19.
Everyone has the right to freedom of opinion and expression; this right includes freedom to hold opinions without interference and to seek, receive and impart information and ideas through any media and regardless of frontiers.

Article 20.
1. Everyone has the right to freedom of peaceful assembly and association.

2. No one may be compelled to belong to an association.

Article 21.
1. Everyone has the right to take part in the government of his country, directly or through freely chosen representatives.

2. Everyone has the right of equal access to public service in his country.

3. The will of the people shall be the basis of the authority of government; this will shall be expressed in periodic and genuine elections which shall be by universal and equal suffrage and shall be held by secret vote or by equivalent free voting procedures.

Article 22.
Everyone, as a member of society, has the right to social security and is entitled to realization, through national effort and international co-operation and in accordance with the organization and resources of each State, of the economic, social and cultural rights indispensable for his dignity and the free development of his personality.

Article 23.
1. Everyone has the right to work, to free choice of employment, to just and favourable conditions of work and to protection against unemployment.

2. Everyone, without any discrimination, has the right to equal pay for equal work.

3. Everyone who works has the right to just and favourable remuneration ensuring for himself and his family an existence worthy of human dignity, and supplemented, if necessary, by other means of social protection.

4. Everyone has the right to form and to join trade unions for the protection of his interests.

Article 24.
Everyone has the right to rest and leisure, including reasonable limitation of working hours and periodic holidays with pay.

Article 25.

1. Everyone has the right to a standard of living adequate for the health and well-being of himself and of his family, including food, clothing, housing and medical care and necessary social services, and the right to security in the event of unemployment, sickness, disability, widowhood, old age or other lack of livelihood in circumstances beyond his control.

2. Motherhood and childhood are entitled to special care and assistance. All children, whether born in or out of wedlock, shall enjoy the same social protection.

Article 26.

1. Everyone has the right to education. Education shall be free, at least in the elementary and fundamental stages. Elementary education shall be compulsory. Technical and professional education shall be made generally available and higher education shall be equally accessible to all on the basis of merit.

2. Education shall be directed to the full development of the human personality and to the strengthening of respect for human rights and fundamental freedoms. It shall promote understanding, tolerance and friendship among all nations, racial or religious groups, and shall further the activities of the United Nations for the maintenance of peace.

3. Parents have a prior right to choose the kind of education that shall be given to their children.

Article 27.

1. Everyone has the right freely to participate in the cultural life of the community, to enjoy the arts and to share in scientific advancement and its benefits.

2. Everyone has the right to the protection of the moral and material interests resulting from any scientific, literary or artistic production of which he is the author.

Article 28.

Everyone is entitled to a social and international order in which the rights and freedoms set forth in this Declaration can be fully realized.

Article 29.

1. Everyone has duties to the community in which alone the free and full development of his personality is possible.

2. In the exercise of his rights and freedoms, everyone shall be subject only to such limitations as are determined by law solely for the purpose of securing due recognition and respect for the rights and freedoms of others and of meeting the just requirements of morality, public order and the general welfare in a democratic society.

3. These rights and freedoms may in no case be exercised contrary to the purposes and principles of the United Nations.

Article 30.
Nothing in this Declaration may be interpreted as implying for any State, group or person any right to engage in any activity or to perform any act aimed at the destruction of any of the rights and freedoms set forth herein.

41. Anthropologists, Cultural Relativism, and Universal Rights[*]

Carolyn Fluehr-Lobban

Cultural relativism, long a key concept in anthropology, asserts that since each culture has its own values and practices, anthropologists should not make value judgments about cultural differences. As a result, anthropological pedagogy has stressed that the study of customs and norms should be value-free, and that the appropriate role of the anthropologist is that of observer and recorder.

Today, however, this view is being challenged by critics inside and outside the discipline, especially those who want anthropologists to take a stand on key human-rights issues. I agree that the time has come for anthropologists to become more actively engaged in safeguarding the rights of people whose lives and cultures they study.

Historically, anthropology as a discipline has declined to participate in the dialogue that produced international conventions regarding human rights. For example, in 1947, when the executive board of the American Anthropological Association withdrew from discussions that led to the "Universal Declaration of Human Rights," it did so in the belief that no such declaration would be applicable to all human beings. But the world and anthropology have changed. Because their research involves extended interaction with people at the grassroots, anthropologists are in a unique position to lend knowledge and expertise to the international debate regarding human rights.

Doing so does not represent a complete break with the traditions of our field. After all, in the past, anthropologists did not hesitate to speak out against such reprehensible practices as Nazi genocide and South African apartheid. And they have testified in US courts against government rules that impinge on the religious traditions or sacred lands of Native Americans, decrying government policies that treat groups of people unjustly.

---

[*] Source: *Chronicle of Higher Education*, 9 June 1995.

However, other practices that violate individual rights or oppress particular groups have not been denounced. Anthropologists generally have not spoken out, for example, against the practice in many cultures of female circumcision, which critics call a mutilation of women. They have been unwilling to pass judgment on such forms of culturally based homicide as the killing of infants or the aged. Some have withheld judgment on acts of communal violence, such as clashes between Hindus and Muslims in India or Tutsis and Hutus in Rwanda, perhaps because the animosities between those groups are of long standing.

Moreover, as a practical matter, organized anthropology's refusal to participate in drafting the 1947 human-rights declaration has meant that anthropologists have not had much of a role in drafting later human-rights statements, such as the United Nations' "Convention on the Elimination of All Forms of Discrimination Against Women," approved in 1979. In many international forums discussing women's rights, participants have specifically rejected using cultural relativism as a barrier to improving women's lives.

The issue of violence against women throws the perils of cultural relativism into stark relief. Following the lead of human-rights advocates, a growing number of anthropologists and others are coming to recognize that violence against women should be acknowledged as a violation of a basic human right to be free from harm. They believe that such violence cannot be excused or justified on cultural grounds.

Let me refer to my own experience. For nearly 25 years, I have conducted research in the Sudan, one of the African countries where the practice of female circumcision is widespread, affecting the vast majority of females in the northern Sudan. Chronic infections are a common result, and sexual intercourse and childbirth are rendered difficult and painful. However, cultural ideology in the Sudan holds that an uncircumcised woman is not respectable, and few families would risk their daughter's chances of marrying by not having her circumcised. British colonial officials outlawed the practice in 1946, but this served only to make it surreptitious and thus more dangerous. Women found it harder to get treatment for mistakes or for side effects of the illegal surgery.

For a long time I felt trapped between, on one side, my anthropologist's understanding of the custom and of the sensitivities about it among the people with whom I was working, and, on the other, the largely feminist campaign in the West to eradicate what critics see as a "barbaric" custom. To ally myself with Western feminists and condemn female circumcision seemed to me to be a betrayal of the value system and culture of the Sudan, which I had come to understand. But as I was asked over the years to comment on female circumcision because of my expertise in the Sudan, I came to realize how deeply I felt that the practice was harmful and wrong.

In 1993, female circumcision was one of the practices deemed harmful by delegates at the international Human Rights Conference in Vienna. During their discussions, they came to view circumcision as a violation of the rights of children as well as of the women who suffer its consequences throughout life. Those discussions made me realize that there was a moral agenda larger than myself, larger than Western culture or the culture of the northern Sudan or my discipline. I decided to join colleagues from other disciplines and cultures in speaking out against the practice.

Some cultures are beginning to change, although cause and effect are difficult to determine. Women's associations in the Ivory Coast are calling for an end to female circumcision. In Egypt, the Cairo Institute for Human Rights has reported the first publicly acknowledged marriage of an uncircumcised woman. In the United States, a Nigerian woman recently was granted asylum on the ground that her returning to her country would result in the forcible circumcision of her daughter, which was deemed a violation of the girl's human rights.

To be sure, it is not easy to achieve consensus concerning the point at which cultural practices cross the line and become violations of human rights. But it is important that scholars and human-rights activists discuss the issue. Some examples of when the line is crossed may be clearer than others. The action of a Japanese wife who feels honor-bound to commit suicide because of the shame of her husband's infidelity can be explained and perhaps justified by the traditional code of honor in Japanese society. However, when she decides to take the lives of her children as well, she is committing murder, which may be easier to condemn than suicide.

What about "honor" killings of sisters and daughters accused of sexual misconduct in some Middle Eastern and Mediterranean societies? Some anthropologists have explained this practice in culturally relativist terms, saying that severe disruptions of the moral order occur when sexual impropriety is alleged or takes place. To restore the social equilibrium and avoid feuds, the local culture requires the shedding of blood to wash away the shame of sexual dishonor. The practice of honor killings, which victimizes mainly women, has been defended in some local courts as less serious than premeditated murder, because it stems from long-standing cultural traditions. While some judges have agreed, anthropologists should see a different picture: a pattern of cultural discrimination against women.

As the issue of domestic violence shows, we need to explore the ways that we balance individual and cultural rights. The "right" of a man to discipline, slap, hit, or beat his wife (and often, by extension, his children) is widely recognized across many cultures in which male dominance is an accepted fact of life. Indeed, the issue of domestic violence has only recently been added to the international human-rights agenda, with the addition of women's rights to the list of basic human rights at the Vienna conference.

The fact that domestic violence is being openly discussed and challenged in some societies (the United States is among the leaders) helps to encourage dialogue in societies in which domestic violence has been a taboo subject. This dialogue is relatively new, and no clear principles have emerged. But anthropologists could inform and enrich the discussion, using their knowledge of family and community life in different cultures.

Cases of genocide may allow the clearest insight into where the line between local culture and universal morality lies. Many anthropologists have urged the Brazilian and Venezuelan governments to stop gold miners from slaughtering the Yanomami people, who are battling the encroachment of miners on their rain forests. Other practices that harm individuals or categories of people (such as the elderly, women, and enslaved or formerly enslaved people) may not represent genocide *per se,* and thus may present somewhat harder questions about the morality of traditional practices. We need to focus on the harm done, however, and not on the scale of the abuse. We need to be sensitive to cultural differences but not allow them to override widely recognized human rights.

The exchange of ideas across cultures is already fostering a growing acceptance of the universal nature of some human rights, regardless of cultural differences. The right of individuals to be free from harm or the threat of harm, and the right of cultural minorities to exist freely within states, are just two examples of rights that are beginning to be universally recognized—although not universally applied.

Fortunately, organized anthropology is beginning to change its attitude toward cultural relativism and human rights. The theme of the 1994 convention of the American Anthropological Association was human rights. At the sessions organized around the topic, many anthropologists said they no longer were absolutely committed to cultural relativism. The association has responded to the changing attitude among its members by forming a Commission for Human Rights, charged with developing a specifically anthropological perspective on those rights, and with challenging violations and promoting education about them.

Nevertheless, many anthropologists continue to express strong support for cultural relativism. One of the most contentious issues arises from the fundamental question: What authority do we Westerners have to impose our own concept of universal rights on the rest of humanity? It is true that Western ideas of human rights have so far dominated international discourse. On the other hand, the cultural relativists' argument is often used by repressive governments to deflect international criticism of their abuse of their citizens. At the very least, anthropologists need to condemn such misuse of cultural relativism, even if it means that they may be denied permission to do research in the country in question.

Personally, I would go further: I believe that we should not let the concept of relativism stop us from using national and international forums to examine ways to protect the lives and dignity of people in every culture. Because of our involvement in local societies, anthropologists could provide early warnings of abuses—for example, by reporting data to international human-rights organizations, and by joining the dialogue at international conferences. When there is a choice between defending human rights and defending cultural relativism, anthropologists should choose to protect and promote human rights. We cannot just be bystanders.

42. The Challenge of Cultural Relativism[*]

James Rachels

Morality differs in every society, and is a convenient term for socially approved habits.
—Ruth Benedict, Patterns of Culture (1934)

2.1. How Different Cultures Have Different Moral Codes

Darius, a king of ancient Persia, was intrigued by the variety of cultures he encountered in his travels. He had found, for example, that the Callatians (a tribe of Indians) customarily ate the bodies of their dead fathers. The Greeks, of course, did not do that—the Greeks practiced cremation and regarded the funeral pyre as the natural and fitting way to dispose of the dead. Darius thought that a sophisticated understanding of the world must include an appreciation of such differences between cultures. One day, to teach this lesson, he summoned some Greeks who happened to be present at his court and asked them what they would take to eat the bodies of their dead fathers. They were shocked, as Darius knew they would be, and replied that no amount of money could persuade them to do such a thing. Then Darius called in some Callatians, and while the Greeks listened asked them what they would take to burn their dead fathers' bodies. The Callatians were horrified and told Darius not even to mention such a dreadful thing.

This story, recounted by Herodotus in his *History*, illustrates a recurring theme in the literature of social science: different cultures have different moral codes. What is thought right within one group may be utterly abhorrent to the members of another group, and vice versa. Should we eat the bodies of the dead or burn them? If you were a Greek, one answer would seem obviously correct; but if you were a Callatian, the opposite would seem equally certain.

It is easy to give additional examples of the same kind. Consider the Eskimos. They are a remote and inaccessible people. Numbering only about 25,000, they live in small, isolated settlements scattered mostly along the northern fringes of North

---

* Source: *The Elements of Moral Philosophy*, 4th ed. (Boston: McGraw-Hill, 2002), pp. 20–36.

America and Greenland. Until the beginning of this century, the outside world knew little about them. Then explorers began to bring back strange tales.

Eskimo customs turned out to be very different from our own. The men often had more than one wife, and they would share their wives with guests, lending them for the night as a sign of hospitality. Moreover, within a community, a dominant male might demand—and get—regular sexual access to other men's wives. The women, however, were free to break these arrangements simply by leaving their husbands and taking up with new partners—free, that is, so long as their former husbands chose not to make trouble. All in all, the Eskimo practice was a volatile scheme that bore little resemblance to what we call marriage.

But it was not only their marriage and sexual practices that were different. The Eskimos also seemed to have less regard for human life. Infanticide, for example, was common. Knud Rasmussen, one of the most famous early explorers, reported that he met one woman who had borne twenty children but had killed ten of them at birth. Female babies, he found, were especially liable to be destroyed, and this was permitted simply at the parents' discretion, with no social stigma attached to it. Old people also, when they became too feeble to contribute to the family, were left out in the snow to die. So there seemed to be, in this society, remarkably little respect for life.

To the general public, these were disturbing revelations. Our own way of living seems so natural and right that for many of us it is hard to conceive of others living so differently. And when we do hear of such things, we tend immediately to categorize those other peoples as "backward" or "primitive." But to anthropologists and sociologists, there was nothing particularly surprising about the Eskimos. Since the time of Herodotus, enlightened observers have been accustomed to the idea that conceptions of right and wrong differ from culture to culture. If we assume that our ideas of right and wrong will be shared by all peoples at all times, we are merely naive.

2.2. Cultural Relativism
To many thinkers, this observation—"Different cultures have different moral codes"—has seemed to be the key to understanding morality. The idea of universal truth in ethics, they say, is a myth. The customs of different societies are all that exist. These customs cannot be said to be "correct" or "incorrect," for that implies we have an independent standard of right and wrong by which they may be judged. But there is no such independent standard; every standard is culture-bound. The great pioneering sociologist William Graham Sumner, writing in 1906, put the point like this:

> The "right" way is the way which the ancestors used and which has been handed down. The tradition is its own warrant. It is not held subject to verification by experience. The notion of right is in the folkways. It is not outside of them, of independent origin, and brought to test them. In the folkways,

whatever is, is right. This is because they are traditional, and therefore contain in themselves the authority of the ancestral ghosts. When we come to the folkways we are at the end of our analysis.

This line of thought has probably persuaded more people to be skeptical about ethics than any other single thing. Cultural Relativism, as it has been called, challenges our ordinary belief in the objectivity and universality of moral truth. It says, in effect, that there is no such thing as universal truth in ethics; there are only the various cultural codes, and nothing more. Moreover, our own code has no special status; it is merely one among many.

As we shall see, this basic idea is really a compound of several different thoughts. It is important to separate the various elements of the theory because, on analysis, some parts of the theory turn out to be correct, whereas others seem to be mistaken. As a beginning, we may distinguish the following claims, all of which have been made by cultural relativists:

1. Different societies have different moral codes.
2. There is no objective standard that can be used to judge one societal code better than another.
3. The moral code of our own society has no special status; it is merely one among many.
4. There is no "universal truth" in ethics—that is, there are no moral truths that hold for all peoples at all times.
5. The moral code of a society determines what is right within that society; that is, if the moral code of a society says that a certain action is right, then that action is right, at least within that society.
6. It is mere arrogance for us to try to judge the conduct of other peoples. We should adopt an attitude of tolerance toward the practices of other cultures.

Although it may seem that these six propositions go naturally together, they are independent of one another, in the sense that some of them might be true even if others are false. In what follows, we will try to identify what is correct in Cultural Relativism, but we will also be concerned to expose what is mistaken about it.

2.3. The Cultural Differences Argument

Cultural Relativism is a theory about the nature of morality. At first blush it seems quite plausible. However, like all such theories, it may be evaluated by subjecting it to rational analysis; and when we analyze Cultural Relativism we find that it is not so plausible as it first appears to be.

The first thing we need to notice is that at the heart of Cultural Relativism there is a certain form of argument. The strategy used by cultural relativists is to argue from facts about the differences between cultural outlooks to a conclusion about the status of morality. Thus we are invited to accept this reasoning:

1. The Greeks believed it was wrong to eat the dead, whereas the Callatians believed it was right to eat the dead.
2. Therefore, eating the dead is neither objectively right nor objectively wrong. It is merely a matter of opinion, which varies from culture to culture.

Or, alternatively:

1. The Eskimos see nothing wrong with infanticide, whereas Americans believe infanticide is immoral.
2. Therefore, infanticide is neither objectively right nor objectively wrong. It is merely a matter of opinion, which varies from culture to culture.

Clearly, these arguments are variations of one fundamental idea. They are both special cases of a more general argument, which says:

1. Different cultures have different moral codes.
2. Therefore, there is no objective "truth" in morality. Right and wrong are only matters of opinion, and opinions vary from culture to culture.

We may call this the *Cultural Differences Argument*. To many people, it is very persuasive. But from a logical point of view, is it a sound argument?

It is not sound. The trouble is that the conclusion does not really follow from the premise—that is, even if the premise is true, the conclusion still might be false. The premise concerns what people believe: in some societies, people believe one thing; in other societies, people believe differently. The conclusion, however, concerns what really is the case. The trouble is that this sort of conclusion does not follow logically from this sort of premise.

Consider again the example of the Greeks and Callatians. The Greeks believed it was wrong to eat the dead; the Callatians believed it was right. Does it follow, from the mere fact that they disagreed, that there is no objective truth in the matter? No, it does not follow; for it could be that the practice was objectively right (or wrong) and that one or the other of them was simply mistaken.

To make the point clearer, consider a very different matter. In some societies, people believe the earth is flat. In other societies, such as our own, people believe the earth is (roughly) spherical. Does it follow, from the mere fact that they disagree, that there is no "objective truth" in geography? Of course not; we would never draw such a conclusion because we realize that, in their beliefs about the world, the members of some societies might simply be wrong. There is no reason to think that if the world is round everyone must know it. Similarly, there is no reason to think that if there is moral truth everyone must know it. The fundamental mistake in the Cultural Differences Argument is that it attempts to derive a substantive conclusion about a subject (morality) from the mere fact that people disagree about it.

It is important to understand the nature of the point that is being made here. We are not saying (not yet, anyway) that the conclusion of the argument is false. Insofar as anything being said here is concerned, it is still an open question whether the conclusion is true. We are making a purely logical point and saying that the conclusion does not follow from the premise. This is important, because in order to determine whether the conclusion is true, we need arguments in its support. Cultural Relativism proposes this argument, but unfortunately the argument turns out to be fallacious. So it proves nothing.

2.4. The Consequences of Taking Cultural Relativism Seriously

Even if the Cultural Differences Argument is invalid, Cultural Relativism might still be true. What would it be like if it were true?

In the passage quoted above, William Graham Sumner summarizes the essence of Cultural Relativism. He says that there is no measure of right and wrong other than the standards of one's society: "The notion of right is in the folkways. It is not outside of them, of independent origin, and brought to test them. In the folkways, whatever is, is right."

Suppose we took this seriously. What would be some of the consequences?

1. We could no longer say that the customs of other societies are morally infe-
    rior to our own. This, of course, is one of the main points stressed by Cul-
    tural Relativism. We would have to stop condemning other societies merely
    because they are "different." So long as we concentrate on certain examples,
    such as the funerary practices of the Greeks and Callatians, this may seem to
    be a sophisticated, enlightened attitude.

However, we would also be stopped from criticizing other, less benign practices. Suppose a society waged war on its neighbors for the purpose of taking slaves. Or suppose a society was violently anti-Semitic and its leaders set out to destroy the Jews. Cultural Relativism would preclude us from saying that either of these practices was wrong. We would not even be able to say that a society tolerant of Jews is better than the anti-Semitic society, for that would imply some sort of transcultural standard of comparison. The failure to condemn these practices does not seem "enlightened"; on the contrary, slavery and anti-Semitism seem wrong wherever they occur. Never-theless, if we took Cultural Relativism seriously, we would have to admit that these social practices also are immune from criticism.

2. We could decide whether actions are right or wrong just by consulting the
    standards of our society. Cultural Relativism suggests a simple test for deter-
    mining what is right and what is wrong: all one has to do is ask whether the
    action is in accordance with the code of one's society. Suppose a resident of
    South Africa is wondering whether his country's policy of apartheid—rigid
    racial segregation—is morally correct. All he has to do is ask whether this
    policy conforms to his society's moral code. If it does, there is nothing to
    worry about, at least from a moral point of view.

This implication of Cultural Relativism is disturbing because few of us think that our society's code is perfect—we can think of ways it might be improved. Yet Cultural Relativism would not only forbid us from criticizing the codes of other societies; it would stop us from criticizing our own. After all, if right and wrong are relative to culture, this must be true for our own culture just as much as for others.

3. The idea of moral progress is called into doubt. Usually, we think that at least some changes in our society have been for the better. (Some, of course, may have been changes for the worse.) Consider this example: Throughout most of Western history the place of women in society was very narrowly circum-scribed. They could not own property; they could not vote or hold political office; with a few exceptions, they were not permitted to have paying jobs; and generally they were under the almost absolute control of their husbands. Recently much of this has changed, and most people think of it as progress.

If Cultural Relativism is correct, can we legitimately think of this as progress? Progress means replacing a way of doing things with a better way. But by what stan-dard do we judge the new ways as better? If the old ways were in accordance with the social standards of their time, then Cultural Relativism would say it is a mistake to judge them by the standards of a different time. Eighteenth-century society was, in effect, a different society from the one we have now. To say that we have made progress implies a judgment that present-day society is better, and that is just the sort of transcultural judgment that, according to Cultural Relativism, is impermissible.

Our idea of social reform will also have to be reconsidered. A reformer such as Martin Luther King, Jr., seeks to change his society for the better. Within the constraints imposed by Cultural Relativism, there is one way this might be done. If a society is not living up to its own ideals, the reformer may be regarded as acting for the best: the ideals of the society are the standard by which we judge his or her proposals as worthwhile. But the "reformer" may not challenge the ideals themselves, for those ideals are by definition correct. According to Cultural Relativism, then, the idea of social reform makes sense only in this very limited way.

These three consequences of Cultural Relativism have led many thinkers to reject it as implausible on its face. It does make sense, they say, to condemn some practices, such as slavery and anti-Semitism, wherever they occur. It makes sense to think that our own society has made some moral progress, while admitting that it is still imperfect and in need of reform. Because Cultural Relativism says that these judg-ments make no sense, the argument goes, it cannot be right.

2.5. Why There Is Less Disagreement than It Seems

The original impetus for Cultural Relativism comes from the observation that cul-tures differ dramatically in their views of right and wrong. But just how much do they differ? It is true that there are differences. However, it is easy to overestimate the extent of those differences. Often, when we examine what seems to be a dramatic difference, we find that the cultures do not differ nearly as much as it appears.

Consider a culture in which people believe it is wrong to eat cows. This may even be a poor culture, in which there is not enough food; still, the cows are not to be touched. Such a society would appear to have values very different from our own. But does it? We have not yet asked why these people will not eat cows. Suppose it is because they believe that after death the souls of humans inhabit the bodies of animals, especially cows, so that a cow may be someone's grandmother. Now do we want to say that their values are different from ours? No; the difference lies elsewhere. The difference is in our belief systems, not in our values. We agree that we shouldn't eat Grandma; we simply disagree about whether the cow is (or could be) Grandma.

The general point is this. Many factors work together to produce the customs of a society. The society's values are only one of them. Other matters, such as the religious and factual beliefs held by its members and the physical circumstances in which they must live, are also important. We cannot conclude, then, merely because customs differ, that there is a disagreement about values. The difference in customs may be attributable to some other aspect of social life. Thus there may be less disagreement about values than there appears to be.

Consider the Eskimos again. They often kill perfectly normal infants, especially girls. We do not approve of this at all; a parent who did this in our society would be locked up. Thus there appears to be a great difference in the values of our two cultures. But suppose we ask why the Eskimos do this. The explanation is not that they have less affection for their children or less respect for human life. An Eskimo family will always protect its babies if conditions permit. But they live in a harsh environment, where food is often in short supply. A fundamental postulate of Eskimo thought is: "Life is hard, and the margin of safety small." A family may want to nourish its babies but be unable to do so.

As in many "primitive" societies, Eskimo mothers will nurse their infants over a much longer period of time than mothers in our culture. The child will take nourishment from its mother's breast for four years, perhaps even longer. So even in the best of times there are limits to the number of infants that one mother can sustain. Moreover, the Eskimos are a nomadic people—unable to farm, they must move about in search of food. Infants must be carried, and a mother can carry only one baby in her parka as she travels and goes about her outdoor work. Other family members can help, but this is not always possible.

Infant girls are more readily disposed of because, first, in this society the males are the primary food providers—they are the hunters, according to the traditional division of labor—and it is obviously important to maintain a sufficient number of food gatherers. But there is an important second reason as well. Because the hunters suffer a high casualty rate, the adult men who die prematurely far outnumber the women who die early. Thus if male and female infants survived in equal numbers, the female adult population would greatly outnumber the male adult population. Examining the available statistics, one writer concluded that "were it not for female infanticide... there would be approximately one-and-a-half times as many females in the average Eskimo local group as there are food-producing males."

So among the Eskimos, infanticide does not signal a fundamentally different attitude toward children. Instead, it is a recognition that drastic measures are sometimes needed to ensure the family's survival. Even then, however, killing the baby is not the first option considered. Adoption is common; childless couples are especially happy to take a more fertile couple's "surplus." Killing is only the last resort. I emphasize this in order to show that the raw data of the anthropologists can be misleading; it can make the differences in values between cultures appear greater than they are. The Eskimos' values are not all that different from our values. It is only that life forces upon them choices that we do not have to make.

2.6. How All Cultures Have Some Values in Common
It should not be surprising that, despite appearances, the Eskimos are protective of their children. How could it be otherwise? How could a group survive that did not value its young? This suggests a certain argument, one which shows that all cultural groups must be protective of their infants:

1. Human infants are helpless and cannot survive if they are not given extensive care for a period of years.
2. Therefore, if a group did not care for its young, the young would not survive, and the older members of the group would not be replaced. After a while the group would die out.
3. Therefore, any cultural group that continues to exist must care for its young. Infants that are not cared for must be the exception rather than the rule.

Similar reasoning shows that other values must be more or less universal. Imagine what it would be like for a society to place no value at all on truth telling. When one person spoke to another, there would be no presumption at all that he was telling the truth—for he could just as easily be speaking falsely. Within that society, there would be no reason to pay attention to what anyone says. (I ask you what time it is, and you say "Four o'clock." But there is no presumption that you are speaking truly; you could just as easily have said the first thing that came into your head. So I have no reason to pay attention to your answer—in fact, there was no point in my asking you in the first place!) Communication would then be extremely difficult, if not impossible. And because complex societies cannot exist without regular communication among their members, society would become impossible. It follows that in any complex society there must be a presumption in favor of truthfulness. There may of course be exceptions to this rule: there may be situations in which it is thought to be permissible to lie. Nevertheless, these will be exceptions to a rule that is in force in the society.

Let me give one further example of the same type. Could a society exist in which there was no prohibition on murder? What would this be like? Suppose people were free to kill other people at will, and no one thought there was anything wrong with it. In such a "society," no one could feel secure. Everyone would have to be constantly on guard. People who wanted to survive would have to avoid other people as much as possible. This would inevitably result in individuals trying to become as self-sufficient as possible—after all, associating with others would be dangerous. Society on any large scale would collapse. Of course, people might band together in smaller groups with others that they could trust not to harm them. But notice what this means: they would be forming smaller societies that did acknowledge a rule against murder. The prohibition of murder, then, is a necessary feature of all societies.

There is a general theoretical point here, namely, that there are some moral rules that all societies will have in common, because those rules are necessary for society to exist. The rules against lying and murder are two examples. And in fact, we do find these rules in force in all viable cultures. Cultures may differ in what they regard as legitimate exceptions to the rules, but this disagreement exists against a background of agreement on the larger issues. Therefore, it is a mistake to overestimate the amount of difference between cultures. Not every moral rule can vary from society to society.

2.7. What Can Be Learned from Cultural Relativism

At the outset, I said that we were going to identify both what is right and what is wrong in Cultural Relativism. Thus far I have mentioned only its mistakes: I have said that it rests on an invalid argument, that it has consequences that make it implausible on its face, and that the extent of cultural disagreement is far less than it implies. This all adds up to a pretty thorough repudiation of the theory. Nevertheless, it is still a very appealing idea, and the reader may have the feeling that all this is a little unfair. The theory must have something going for it, or else why has it been so influential? In fact, I think there is something right about Cultural Relativism, and now I want to say what that is. There are two lessons we should learn from the theory, even if we ultimately reject it.

1. Cultural Relativism warns us, quite rightly, about the danger of assuming that all our preferences are based on some absolute rational standard. They are not. Many (but not all) of our practices are merely peculiar to our society, and it is easy to lose sight of that fact. In reminding us of it, the theory does a service.

Funerary practices are one example. The Callatians, according to Herodotus, were "men who eat their fathers"—a shocking idea, to us at least. But eating the flesh of the dead could be understood as a sign of respect. It could be taken as a symbolic act that says: We wish this person's spirit to dwell within us. Perhaps this was the understanding of the Callatians. On such a way of thinking, burying the dead could be seen as an act of rejection, and burning the corpse as positively scornful. If this is hard to imagine, then we may need to have our imaginations stretched. Of course we may feel a visceral repugnance at the idea of eating human flesh in any circumstances. But what of it? This repugnance may be, as the relativists say, only a matter of what is customary in our particular society.

There are many other matters that we tend to think of in terms of objective right and wrong, but that are really nothing more than social conventions. Should women cover their breasts? A publicly exposed breast is scandalous in our society, whereas in other cultures it is unremarkable. Objectively speaking, it is neither right nor wrong—there is no objective reason why either custom is better. Cultural Relativism begins with the valuable insight that many of our practices are like this—they are only cultural products. Then it goes wrong by concluding that, because some practices are like this, all must be.

2. The second lesson has to do with keeping an open mind. In the course of growing up, each of us has acquired some strong feelings: we have learned to think of some types of conduct as acceptable, and others we have learned to regard as simply unacceptable. Occasionally, we may find those feelings challenged. We may encounter someone who claims that our feelings are mistaken. For example, we may have been taught that homosexuality is immoral, and we may feel quite uncomfortable around gay people and see them as alien and "different." Now someone suggests that this may be a mere prejudice; that there is nothing evil about homosexuality; that gay people are just people, like anyone else, who happen, through no choice of their own, to be attracted to others of the same sex. But because we feel so strongly about the matter, we may find it hard to take this seriously. Even after we listen to the arguments, we may still have the unshakable feeling that homosexuals must, somehow, be an unsavory lot.

Cultural Relativism, by stressing that our moral views can reflect the prejudices of our society, provides an antidote for this kind of dogmatism. When he tells the story of the Greeks and Callatians, Herodotus adds:

> For if anyone, no matter who, were given the opportunity of choosing from amongst all the nations of the world the set of beliefs which he thought best, he would inevitably, after careful consideration of their relative merits, choose that of his own country. Everyone without exception believes his own native customs, and the religion he was brought up in, to be the best.

Realizing this can result in our having more open minds. We can come to understand that our feelings are not necessarily perceptions of the truth—they may be nothing more than the result of cultural conditioning. Thus when we hear it suggested that some element of our social code is not really the best and we find ourselves instinctively resisting the suggestion, we might stop and remember this. Then we may be more open to discovering the truth, whatever that might be.

We can understand the appeal of Cultural Relativism, then, even though the theory has serious shortcomings. It is an attractive theory because it is based on a genuine insight—that many of the practices and attitudes we think so natural are really only cultural products. Moreover, keeping this insight firmly in view is important if we want to avoid arrogance and have open minds. These are important points, not to be taken lightly. But we can accept these points without going on to accept the whole theory.

43. The Price of Freedom, in Blood[*]

Carol J. Williams

BOTKYRKA, Sweden—When Fadime Sahindal told police her life had been threatened, they gave her an alarm system. When she approached politicians for help, they told her to make peace with her parents.

And when she appealed in television interviews for aid in escaping a death sentence imposed by her father after she refused an arranged marriage, she provoked sympathy among Swedes—whose more liberal outlook she shared—but little willingness to get involved in a family matter.

Now that she's dead, shot in the head by her father, the 26-year-old victim of an "honor killing" is drawing attention to the cultural double standards she battled during the last four years of her life.

Neither the first nor likely the last immigrant daughter to shame her hidebound clan simply by acting Swedish, Sahindal has become a martyr among women who came to this liberal country from patriarchal cultures. Her death was a warning to officials that they ignore at great peril the dangers of not integrating immigrant communities.

Although Sahindal's father, Rahmi, came to Sweden from Turkey 20 years ago, he still was guided more by pressure from his Kurdish clansmen than by the rule of law or love for his daughter. When Fadime braved a visit to her mother and sister Jan. 21 in the clan stronghold in Uppsala, about 40 miles north of Stockholm, her father got wind of it.

Police say Rahmi, who is in jail awaiting trial, told them he felt he had no choice but to make good on his vow to kill her.

No comprehensive statistics exist to show the extent of such honor killings here and elsewhere in Scandinavia, where whole communities of Kurds and other Muslim groups have found refuge. But although such slayings are believed to be infrequent, Sahindal's death has exposed the region's failure to integrate immigrants, with their

[*] Source: *Los Angeles Times*, 7 March 2002, <http://articles.latimes.com/2002/mar/07/news/mn-31584>.

often fundamentally different values, into these societies. Having long looked the other way when religious and cultural clashes came to public attention, Swedes are pondering what more they could and should have done.

"The message this should send to Swedish people, especially the Social Democrats who have been in power for 40 years, is that the system isn't working," said Dilsa Demirbag-Sten, a former government advisor on integration affairs whose Kurdish family came to Sweden from eastern Turkey when she was 7.

She accuses authorities of arrogance in their view that certain rights and freedoms accorded Nordic residents, such as gender equality and protection from forced marriage, are not necessarily applicable to immigrants.

"Fadime's brother told police that honor killing is part of our culture. But most Kurds don't believe that," said the 33-year-old activist, wife, mother and recording industry executive. "There is a package you buy when you come to Sweden, and that should include respect for the law."

Immigrants have been coming to Sweden in increasing numbers in the last decade to fill a persistent labor shortage. They also take advantage of the country's liberal asylum policy, which grants refuge from the conflicts occurring in many of the immigrants' homelands.

But institutional flaws—such as the two years on average that it takes to get a decision on asylum requests—encourage those waiting for permanent refuge to band together in bleak housing projects in what amounts to self-imposed segregation while awaiting the right to citizenship and work.

At least 15% of Sweden's 9 million residents are non-Nordic and heavily concentrated in volatile ghettos of Somalis, Kurds, Bosnians and dozens of other ethnic groups. Scandinavia's liberal values curry little favor in many of those quarters.

"There are places just outside of Stockholm where the entire population is foreign. These people aren't living in Sweden at all," said Keya Izol, head of the Federation of Kurdish Assns. in Sweden, referring to towns and suburbs such as Botkyrka, a 30-minute drive from central Stockholm.

Generation Gap

"It is a mistake to have too many people from the same town or village or clan together," Izol added. "It is the habit of exiles to want to protect their way of life, and in such places they hear no Swedish, they see no Swedish television and they have no jobs that bring them in contact with Swedish people."

A 1995 reform of laws on refugees and immigration has worsened the situation, Izol said, by focusing training and jobs on the younger generation, causing strains within families as well as between immigrants and Swedes.

"We have been too slow to integrate the older generation and too fast in integrating the younger ones," former Danish Justice Minister Erling Olsen said of the Scandinavian countries, which are all experiencing social pressures amid recent immigration.

"We in Denmark have tended to ignore incidents in the immigrant communities that contradict our own understanding of human rights, but we have a responsibility to ensure our values are respected," he added. Some arranged marriages between young immigrant women and men in their homelands are tantamount to illegal visa sales, he said, as the grooms are then eligible for family reunification, immigrant aid and a speedier path to Danish citizenship.

National Outcry

Nalin Pekgul, a Social Democratic legislator of Kurdish origin in Sweden, shares the revulsion over Sahindal's killing but cautions against interpreting an act of criminal extremism as typical of fundamentalist immigrants.

"Sweden has done a better job than most countries with integration, which is why this case has caused such strong reaction," Pekgul said. Other governments simply avert their eyes when immigrant girls and women are shipped home, where they face possible death, she said.

"People ask if the Swedish government could have prevented this killing. I say no, but the Kurds in Uppsala could have prevented it," Pekgul said, blaming backwardness and illiteracy for creating an atmosphere in which patriarchs are held in disgrace when their wives or daughters embrace Swedish culture.

As a figure of respect in Sweden's 40,000-strong Kurdish community, Pekgul tried to intervene on Sahindal's behalf. The young woman had given interviews to Swedish media about the death threats from her father and brother, Masud, a level of defiance that Pekgul feared was only enhancing the danger.

The lawmaker negotiated a compromise in 1998 by which Sahindal agreed to stay away from Uppsala and her father promised not to stalk her outside their hometown while she was living in seclusion near Stockholm.

In recent years, Sahindal had been pursuing a sociology degree and become an outspoken advocate of the opportunities Nordic immigration presented for women from fundamentalist backgrounds.

She braved the fatal visit to her mother and sister to say farewell ahead of her departure for Kenya, where she was to spend this year writing her master's thesis. Her sister is mentally disabled and suffered Sahindal's long absence in sadness and confusion, say friends trying to explain what might appear a reckless action. Attractive and Westernized in her dress and demeanor, Sahindal apparently was spotted upon arrival in Uppsala by someone in her father's entourage.

Pekgul said Sahindal underestimated the danger of clan mentality.

"People who come to such a level of despair that they can kill must feel cornered in this society," said Annick Sjogren, a sociologist directing an integration program in Botkyrka, where more than 80% of the 30,000 residents are immigrants and refugees.

"They aren't used to women being equal to men or nakedness being taken as natural instead of sexual or the idea that you can choose your own partner. They get scared and become defensive and much more fundamentalist than they would be at home."

Sjogren and Aina Bigestans, her colleague at the Multicultural Development Center, defend the notion of honoring cultural practices, including arranged marriage, more strongly than is popular in the wake of Sahindal's killing.

Recalling a recent conversation with an Indian friend, Bigestans said she was compelled to agree that a marriage arranged by caring parents with an offspring's best interests in mind might be seen as more "rational" than partnerships forged in the delirium of young love.

Women's advocacy groups concede that there are profound contradictions in the way Swedes, and Scandinavians in general, balance tolerance of ethnic traditions with a commitment to human rights.

"Fadime was a role model for young women in this society. She was beautiful and intelligent and brave and spoke perfect Swedish," said Angela Beausang, chairwoman of the National Organization of Battered Women's Shelters in Sweden. "But now she stands as a scary example. The message from her killing is that this could happen to you too."

But Beausang believes Sahindal's death has forced Swedes of all backgrounds to examine their behavior and values and discuss what kind of multicultural society they should be working toward.

If any good is to come of the slaying, Beausang said, laws and practices that reflect a double standard must be changed to prevent such honor killings.

Law Bows to Tradition

Swedish law allows girls from immigrant families to marry as young as 15, while marriage for Swedish citizens is permitted only at 18 or older. That de facto bow to immigrant cultural practice is expected to be legislated out of existence as momentum gathers in a national campaign to prevent forced marriage.

Sahindal was not the first case of honor killing to come to national attention. Three years ago, during a visit with family members to her Kurdish homeland in Iraq, 19-year-old Pela Atroshi was shot in the head by her uncle on the orders of her father and brother for having refused to marry a cousin. A few months earlier, here in Sweden, she had been scalded with boiling water and denounced by her clan.

The uncle received a one-year sentence in Iraq for an action that was viewed there with greater acceptance. Atroshi's sister, now in hiding, gave testimony to Swedish prosecutors, which led to the three men's conviction and sentencing to terms upward of 15 years when they returned last year to Sweden, said an activist familiar with her case.

Sara Mohammad, a 34-year-old Iraqi Kurd who changed her name after immigrating here eight years ago to avoid creating problems for her family back home, estimates that there are 30 to 40 young women in Sweden hiding from male relatives who have vowed to kill them.

Clash of Values

Mohammad, an outspoken activist and founder of Never Forget Pela, a movement to empower Muslim women, accuses Swedes of misguided liberalism in their tolerance of immigrant behavior that would be considered repressive among Nordic peoples.

"The Swedish government is to blame because they respect the culture and religion of immigrants but not the people themselves or their basic human rights," Mohammad said. "This isn't about religious freedoms in Sweden, but about religious values clashing with women's and children's rights. It's not about Swedish culture, but about human values and norms."

Mohammad's group, to be renamed Never Forget Pela and Fadime, plans a memorial gathering Friday on International Women's Day to raise awareness about the dangers facing immigrant women.

She has sent a list of demands for legislative change to Mona Sahlin, the government official in charge of integration policy. They include support for raising the minimum age for marriage to 18 for all women, advisory sessions for new arrivals on the vast differences in gender relations they will encounter and must respect, prohibition of head scarves or veils for girls under 16, and equal opportunity in all aspects of education. (Parents from conservative religious backgrounds currently can opt to remove their children from sex education classes, swimming and other coeducational sports, and field trips.)

While her compatriots across the ethnic spectrum lament her death and the social ills it exposes, Sahindal had the last word in her familial clash of cultures. Aware of the risks she faced, she told friends she wanted to be buried in the graveyard of Uppsala's Lutheran cathedral—alongside her Swedish boyfriend, Patrik Lindesjo, who was killed in a car crash in June 1998. Six young female friends carried her coffin.

Recommended Reading

American Anthropological Association Executive Board. (1947). Statement on Human Rights. *American Anthropologist* 49: 539–43.

Benedict, R. (1934). *Patterns of Culture*. Boston, MA: Houghton Mifflin.

Blackburn, S. (2007, August 27). *Simon Blackburn on Moral Relativism*. Philosophy Bites: <http://www.philosophybites.libsyn.com/simon_blackburn_on_moral_relativism>.

Gardner, M. (1950). *Beyond Cultural Relativism*. Ethics 61(1): 38–45.

Gowans, C. (21 March 2011). "Moral Relativism." E.N. Zalta, ed. *Stanford Encyclopedia of Philosophy*: <http://plato.stanford.edu/archives/spr2011/entries/moral-relativism/>.

Harman, G. (1985). "Is There a Single Pure Morality?" In D. Copp, & D. Zimmerman Eds., *Morality, Reason and Truth: New Essays in the Foundations of Ethics*. Totowa, NJ: Rowman and Allenheld.

Harman, G., & Thomson, J. (1996). *Moral Relativism and Moral Objectivity*. Malden, MA: Wiley-Blackwell.

Okin, S. (1997, October/November). "Is Multiculturalism Bad for Women?" *Boston Review*.

Williams, B. (1974). *The Truth in Relativism*. Proceedings of the Aristotelian Society 75: 215–28.

Immigration, Integration, and Diversity: Introduction

Too Diverse?

Are modern multicultural societies "too diverse" and, if so, too diverse for what? David Goodhart worries that diversity of culture and lifestyle within a nation makes it more difficult to sustain a risk-pooling welfare state. This is the progressive dilemma: "Progressives," writes Goodhart, "want diversity but they thereby undermine part of the moral consensus on which a large welfare state rests."[1]

Goodhart speculates that there is a trade-off between ethnic diversity and social solidarity. Noting that Scandinavian countries, with the strongest welfare states, are among the least ethnically diverse nations in the developed world while America, with a minority population he reckoned at 30%, was the least committed to social programs identified with the welfare state, he suggested that progressives faced a dilemma: liberal immigration policies, by increasing cultural diversity and "thinning out" the national culture would inevitably undermine social solidarity. "And therein," Goodhart writes, "lies one of the central dilemmas of political life."

People do hesitate to enter into risk-pooling schemes that they believe are likely to benefit individuals who are culturally alien and either unwilling or unable to buy into shared values and a shared culture. However, immigration and ethnic diversity do not inevitably undermine cultural homogeneity or cultural cohesion. Americans have traditionally assumed that immigrants could, should, and would become Americans—indeed, as Teddy Roosevelt famously proclaimed, "unhyphenated Americans."

---

1 David Goodhart, "Too Diverse?", pp. 576–85 in this volume.

A century ago, during mass immigration from European countries, Americans supported schools, settlement houses, and other programs that benefited immigrants under the rubric of "Americanization." Even if anti-immigrant sentiment bubbled under the surface, the melting pot was official ideology: Goodhart may be correct in suggesting that where the native population assumes that immigrants or minorities cannot be absorbed or actively reject the fundamental values of the dominant culture, social solidarity suffers. But where they assume that immigrants and minorities can and will assimilate—an assumption that, arguably, is warranted—they work to promote integration.

Goodhart is also correct in suggesting that "absorbing outsiders into a community that is worthy of the name takes time"—and effort. Oddly, considering his worries about the difficulties of promoting support for a welfare state in America, he cites "the old US melting pot" as a model for integrating immigrants. But the American melting pot did melt—and the most striking evidence for that is the fact that Goodhart puts the "minority population" of the United States at 30% as distinct from the 70% he characterizes as "non-Hispanic whites." A century ago, the grandparents and great-grandparents of many members of that 70% were themselves classified as minorities, and native-born Americans (whose grandparents and great-grandparents had immigrated a century earlier) worried about the ability of the United States to absorb mass immigration.

Assimilation: E Pluribus Unum?

Nevertheless, even if assimilation is virtually inevitable, in the short run diversity undermines *social capital*, the system of social networks and the associated norms of reciprocity and trustworthiness identified by political scientist Robert Putnam that promote social cohesion. In his recent and extensively documented study "E Pluribus Unum," Putnam notes that immigration and ethnic diversity do not merely reduce social trust and cohesion between different communities, or "bridging social capital," but also undermine "bonding social capital" *within* communities. "Diversity," he writes, "seems to trigger *not* in-group/out-group division but anomie or social isolation. In colloquial language, people living in ethnically diverse settings appear to 'hunker down'—that is to pull in like a turtle ... inhabitants of diverse communities tend to withdraw from collective life, to distrust their neighbours, regardless of the colour of their skin, to withdraw even from close friends, to expect the worst from their community and its leaders."[2]

Putnam argues, however, that in the long run new "cross-cutting" forms of social solidarity overcome such fragmentation. Looking only at a time slice, we see ethnically diverse communities that are fragmented and, in a variety of ways, less congenial than more homogeneous social milieus. But, as Putnam notes, over time

---

2 Robert Putnam, "*E Pluribus Unum*: Diversity and Community in the Twenty-first Century," pp. 586–626 in this volume.

ethnicity has becomes less socially salient: in the US, appearance and ancestry have ceased to signal significant cultural difference; ethnic groups have assimilated and ethnic differences have become don't-cares—for friendship, marriage, and other social affiliations. And social solidarity has re-emerged: the US, a nation of immigrants, has become from many, one.

Elsewhere, within African nations, cobbled together for administrative convenience by colonial powers, social fragmentation seems unavoidable. Alexis Rawlinson, however, argues that the "tribalism" driving inter-ethnic rivalries and chronic warfare is in fact constructed and managed by elites in the interest of gaining influence in the state and control of its resources. Indeed, he suggests, "today's bounded and mutually antagonistic ethnic groups are largely the creation of elites and colonial masters." Colonial administrators, without adequate staff, Rawlinson writes, created "tribes" and elevated "big men" as chiefs in order to maintain a system of "indirect rule."[3] Since independence, big men in government have used cultural diversity to serve their ends, exploiting ethnic communities' mutual distrust to promote their political interests and maintain power.

Advocates of multiculturalist policies, which support cultural diversity, often suggest that even if diversity undermines social solidarity, such policies support individual freedom. Immigrants and indigenous ethnic minorities, they hold, should be free to maintain their customs and languages within a pluralistic society, which recognizes diverse cultural identities. Amartya Sen argues, to the contrary, that multiculturalism as it is commonly understood and practiced, or *plural monoculturalism* as he calls it, restricts individual freedom by locking individuals into unchosen identities. "One of the central issues," he writes, "concerns how human beings are seen":

> Should they be categorized in terms of inherited traditions, particularly the inherited religion, of the community in which they happen to have been born, taking that unchosen identity to have automatic priority over other affiliations involving politics, profession, class, gender, language, literature, social involvement, and many other connections? Or should they be understood as persons with many affiliations and associations, whose relative priorities they must themselves choose...?[4]

Anthony Appiah, in broad agreement with Sen, argues that the collective identities promoted by multiculturalist policies imposed "scripts" on individuals identified with those collectives that constrain individual freedom and from which members of "visible" minority groups cannot opt out. Social color-consciousness imposes burdens on ethnically identified individuals. Nevertheless, arguably, color-conscious policies are necessary in order, ultimately, to achieve a color-blind society. Amy

---

3 Alexis Rawlinson, "The Political Manipulation of Ethnicity in Africa," pp. 627–37 in this volume.
4 Amartya Sen, "Chili and Liberty," pp. 638–47 in this volume.

Gutmann argues compellingly that color-conscious and gender-conscious policies, including affirmative action, are important in the interests of achieving a just and ultimately color-blind society.[5]

Multiculturalism

"Multiculturalism" is in any case an ambiguous term. In one sense it refers to a family of policies intended to accommodate, or promote, a diversity of "cultures," values or lifestyles: the promotion of Sen's "plural monoculturalism." In another sense, however, it simply refers to the fact of racial or ethnic diversity—what might be better described as "multiethnicity." Currently, that ambiguity has been exploited to promote exclusionary policies and restrictions on immigration. At the time of this writing, Anders Behring Breivik, perpetrator of a terrorist attack in Norway that killed dozens of people, most of them teenagers, has been captured and has explained that his act was "cruel but necessary" in order to stop the spread of "cultural Marxism," Islam, and multiculturalism. Breivik frequented right-wing anti-immigrant blogs and took up their theme, namely that immigration to Europe from the Middle East and elsewhere, in particular from Muslim countries, would undermine "European Civilization." They identified the generous immigration policies, and multiethnicity, with multiculturalism—understood as the accommodation or promotion of diverse "cultures."

But this is to confuse culture with race or ancestry, or at the very least to assume that immigrants prefer to retain their ancestral cultures and aim to impose them on others in their host nations. Conservatives opposed to immigration assume that immigrants from majority-Muslim countries are keen to impose Shari'ia and transform Europe into Eurabia. But there is no compelling evidence for this thesis and very good reason to think that it is false. Immigrants—and if not they, then their children—do assimilate. And when they—or, more often, their acculturated, native-born children—affirm ancestral cultures or demand accommodation it is most often because they are not accepted as full-fledged citizens of the countries in which they, or their children, live.[6] Arguably, for the most part, when immigrants and other minorities engage in politically motivated violence it is on the principle that "if we can't join you, we will beat you."

In 2010, German Chancellor Angela Merkel declared that multiculturalism has "utterly failed."[7] Since then, former French president Nicolas Sarkozy and British Prime Minister David Cameron have echoed her sentiments. And there does indeed

---

5 Amy Gutmann, *Color Conscious: The Political Morality of Race*, Introduction by David Wilkins (Princeton, NJ: Princeton UP, 1996).

6 For further discussion, and substantiation, see H.E. Baber, *The Multicultural Mystique: The Liberal Case Against Diversity* (Peterborough, ON: Broadview, 2008).

7 <http://www.dailymail.co.uk/news/article-1321277/Angela-Merkel-Multiculturalism-Germany-utterly-failed.html>.

seem to be some reason to worry about multiculturalism understood as a program for accommodating cultural diversity. Cultural diversity drains human capital and undermines social cohesion. It promotes mutual distrust among ethnically defined groups that unscrupulous politicians can exploit. It threatens members of the indigenous, majority population who worry that immigrants are undermining their culture. Worst of all it imposes scripts on members of ethnic minorities, in many cases locking them into ancestral cultures that are alien to them and with which they do not want to be identified.

Cultural diversity is not the inevitable concomitant of ethnic diversity. Culture is not genetically coded. Assimilation is not only possible—in the long run it is inevitable. Multiculturalist policies promoting cultural diversity have failed, but, arguably, the response to that failure is not exclusion but assimilation.

44. Too Diverse?*

David Goodhart

Is Britain becoming too diverse to sustain the mutual obligations behind a good society and the welfare state?

Britain in the 1950s was a country stratified by class and region. But in most of its cities, suburbs, towns and villages there was a good chance of predicting the attitudes, even the behaviour, of the people living in your immediate neighbourhood.

In many parts of Britain today that is no longer true. The country has long since ceased to be Orwell's "family" (albeit with the wrong members in charge). To some people this is a cause of regret and disorientation—a change which they associate with the growing incivility of modern urban life. To others it is a sign of the inevitable, and welcome, march of modernity. After three centuries of homogenisation through industrialisation, urbanisation, nation-building and war, the British have become freer and more varied. Fifty years of peace, wealth and mobility have allowed a greater diversity in lifestyles and values. To this "value diversity" has been added ethnic diversity through two big waves of immigration: first the mainly commonwealth immigration from the West Indies and Asia in the 1950s and 1960s, followed by asylum-driven migrants from Europe, Africa and the greater middle east in the late 1990s.

The diversity, individualism and mobility that characterise developed economies—especially in the era of globalisation—mean that more of our lives is spent among strangers. Ever since the invention of agriculture 10,000 years ago, humans have been used to dealing with people from beyond their own extended kin groups. The difference now in a developed country like Britain is that we not only live among stranger citizens but we must share with them. We share public services and parts of our income in the welfare state, we share public spaces in towns and cities where we are squashed together on buses, trains and tubes, and we share in a democratic

---

* Source: *Prospect Magazine* 95 (20 February 2004), <http://www.prospectmagazine.co.uk/2004/02/too-diverse-david-goodhart-multiculturalism-britain-immigration-globalisation/>.

conversation—filtered by the media—about the collective choices we wish to make. All such acts of sharing are more smoothly and generously negotiated if we can take for granted a limited set of common values and assumptions. But as Britain becomes more diverse that common culture is being eroded.

And therein lies one of the central dilemmas of political life in developed societies: sharing and solidarity can conflict with diversity. This is an especially acute dilemma for progressives who want plenty of both solidarity—high social cohesion and generous welfare paid out of a progressive tax system—and diversity—equal respect for a wide range of peoples, values and ways of life. The tension between the two values is a reminder that serious politics is about trade-offs. It also suggests that the left's recent love affair with diversity may come at the expense of the values and even the people that it once championed.

It was the Conservative politician David Willetts who drew my attention to the "progressive dilemma." Speaking at a roundtable on welfare reform (*Prospect*, March 1998), he said: "The basis on which you can extract large sums of money in tax and pay it out in benefits is that most people think the recipients are people like themselves, facing difficulties which they themselves could face. If values become more diverse, if lifestyles become more differentiated, then it becomes more difficult to sustain the legitimacy of a universal risk-pooling welfare state. People ask, 'Why should I pay for them when they are doing things I wouldn't do?' This is America versus Sweden. You can have a Swedish welfare state provided that you are a homogeneous society with intensely shared values. In the US you have a very diverse, individualistic society where people feel fewer obligations to fellow citizens. Progressives want diversity but they thereby undermine part of the moral consensus on which a large welfare state rests."

These words alerted me to how the progressive dilemma lurks beneath many aspects of current politics: national tax and redistribution policies; the asylum and immigration debate; development aid budgets; EU integration and spending on the poorer southern and east European states; and even the tensions between America (built on political ideals and mass immigration) and Europe (based on nation states with core ethnic-linguistic solidarities).

Thinking about the conflict between solidarity and diversity is another way of asking a question as old as human society itself: who is my brother? With whom do I share mutual obligations? The traditional conservative Burkean view is that our affinities ripple out from our families and localities, to the nation and not very far beyond. That view is pitted against a liberal universalist one which sees us in some sense equally obligated to all human beings from Bolton to Burundi—an idea associated with the universalist aspects of Christianity and Islam, with Kantian universalism and with left-wing internationalism. Science is neutral in this dispute, or rather it stands on both sides of the argument. Evolutionary psychology stresses both the universality of most human traits and—through the notion of kin selection and reciprocal altruism—the instinct to favour our own. Social psychologists also argue that the tendency to perceive in-groups and out-groups, however ephemeral, is innate. In any case, Burkeans claim to have common sense on their side. They argue that we feel more comfortable with, and are readier to share with, and sacrifice for, those with whom we have shared histories and similar values. To put it bluntly—most of us prefer our own kind.

The category "own kind" or in-group will set alarm bells ringing in the minds of many readers. So it is worth stressing what preferring our own kind does not mean, even for a Burkean. It does not mean that we are necessarily hostile to other kinds or cannot empathise with outsiders. (There are those who do dislike other kinds but in Britain they seem to be quite a small minority.) In complex societies, most of us belong simultaneously to many in-groups—family, profession, class, hobby, locality, nation—and an ability to move with ease between groups is a sign of maturity. An in-group is not, except in the case of families, a natural or biological category and the people who are deemed to belong to it can change quickly, as we saw so disastrously in Bosnia. Certainly, those we include in our in-group could be a pretty diverse crowd, especially in a city like London.

Moreover, modern liberal societies cannot be based on a simple assertion of group identity—the very idea of the rule of law, of equal legal treatment for everyone regardless of religion, wealth, gender or ethnicity, conflicts with it. On the other hand, if you deny the assumption that humans are social, group-based primates with constraints, however imprecise, on their willingness to share, you find yourself having to defend some implausible positions: for example that we should spend as much on development aid as on the NHS [National Health Service], or that Britain should have no immigration controls at all. The implicit "calculus of affinity" in media reporting of disasters is easily mocked—two dead Britons will get the same space as 200 Spaniards or 2,000 Somalis. Yet everyday we make similar calculations in the distribution of our own resources. Even a well-off, liberal-minded Briton who already donates to charities will spend, say, £200 on a child's birthday party, knowing that such money could, in the right hands, save the life of a child in the third world. The extent of our obligation to those to whom we are not connected through either kinship or citizenship is in part a purely private, charitable decision. But it also has policy implications, and not just in the field of development aid. For example, significant NHS resources are spent each year on foreign visitors, especially in London. Many of us might agree in theory that the needs of desperate outsiders are often greater than our own. But we would object if our own parent or child received inferior treatment because of resources consumed by non-citizens.

Is it possible to reconcile these observations about human preferences with our increasingly open, fluid and value-diverse societies? At one level, yes. Our liberal democracies still work fairly well; indeed it is one of the achievements of modernity that people have learned to tolerate and share with people very unlike themselves.

(Until the 20th century, today's welfare state would have been considered contrary to human nature.) On the other hand, the logic of solidarity, with its tendency to draw boundaries, and the logic of diversity, with its tendency to cross them, do at times pull apart. Thanks to the erosion of collective norms and identities, in particular of class and nation, and the recent surge of immigration into Europe, this may be such a time.

The modern idea of citizenship goes some way to accommodating the tension between solidarity and diversity. Citizenship is not an ethnic, blood and soil concept but a more abstract political idea—implying equal legal, political and social rights (and duties) for people inhabiting a given national space. But citizenship is not just an abstract idea about rights and duties; for most of us it is something we do not choose but are born into—it arises out of a shared history, shared experiences, and, often, shared suffering; as the American writer Alan Wolfe puts it: "Behind every citizen lies a graveyard."

Both aspects of citizenship imply a notion of mutual obligation. Critics have argued that this idea of national community is anachronistic—swept away by globalisation, individualism and migration—but it still has political resonance. When politicians talk about the "British people" they refer not just to a set of individuals with specific rights and duties but to a group of people with a special commitment to one another. Membership in such a community implies acceptance of moral rules, however fuzzy, which underpin the laws and welfare systems of the state.

In the rhetoric of the modern liberal state, the glue of ethnicity ("people who look and talk like us") has been replaced with the glue of values ("people who think and behave like us"). But British values grow, in part, out of a specific history and even geography. Too rapid a change in the make-up of a community not only changes the present, it also, potentially, changes our link with the past. As Bob Rowthorn wrote (*Prospect*, February 2003), we may lose a sense of responsibility for our own history—the good things and shameful things in it—if too many citizens no longer identify with it.

[...]

Greater diversity can produce real conflicts of values and interests, but it also generates unjustified fears. Exposure to a wider spread of lifestyles, plus more mobility and better education, has helped to combat some of those fears—a trend reinforced by popular culture and the expansion of higher education (graduates are notably more tolerant than non-graduates). There is less overt homophobia, sexism or racism (and much more racial intermarriage) in Britain than 30 years ago and racial discrimination is the most politically sensitive form of unfairness. But 31 per cent of people still admit to being racially prejudiced. Researchers such as Isaac Marks at London's Institute of Psychiatry warn that it is not possible to neatly divide the population between a small group of xenophobes and the rest. Feelings of suspicion and hostility towards outsiders are latent in most of us.

The visibility of ethnic difference means that it often overshadows other forms of diversity. Changes in the ethnic composition of a city or neighbourhood can come to stand for the wider changes of modern life. Some expressions of racism, especially by old people, can be read as declarations of dismay at the passing of old ways of life (though this makes it no less unpleasant to be on the receiving end). The different appearance of many immigrants is an outward reminder that they are, at least initially, strangers. If welfare states demand that we pay into a common fund on which we can all draw at times of need, it is important that we feel that most people have made the same effort to be self-supporting and will not take advantage. We need to be reassured that strangers, especially those from other countries, have the same idea of reciprocity as we do. Absorbing outsiders into a community worthy of the name takes time.

Negotiating the tension between solidarity and diversity is at the heart of politics. But both left and right have, for different reasons, downplayed the issue. The left is reluctant to acknowledge a conflict between values it cherishes; it is ready to stress the erosion of community from "bad" forms of diversity such as market individualism but not from "good" forms of diversity such as sexual freedom and immigration. And the right, in Britain at least, has sidestepped the conflict, partly because it is less interested in solidarity than the left, but also because it is still trying to prove that it is comfortable with diversity.

But is there any hard evidence that the progressive dilemma actually exists in the real world of political and social choices? In most EU states the percentage of GDP taken in tax is still at historically high levels, despite the increase in diversity of all kinds. Yet it is also true that Scandinavian countries with the biggest welfare states have been the most socially and ethnically homogeneous states in the west. By the same token the welfare state has always been weaker in the individualistic, ethnically divided US compared with more homogeneous Europe. And the three bursts of welfarist legislation that the US did see—Franklin Roosevelt's New Deal, Harry Truman's Fair Deal and Lyndon Johnson's Great Society—came during the long pause in mass immigration between the World War I and 1968. (They were also, clearly, a response to the depression and two world wars.)

In their 2001 Harvard Institute of Economic Research paper "Why Doesn't the US Have a European-style Welfare State?" Alberto Alesina, Edward Glaeser and Bruce Sacerdote argue that the answer is that too many people at the bottom of the pile in the US are black or Hispanic. Across the US as a whole, 70 per cent of the population are non-Hispanic whites—but of those in poverty only 46 per cent are non-Hispanic whites. So a disproportionate amount of tax income spent on welfare is going to minorities. The paper also finds that US states that are more ethnically fragmented than average spend less on social services. The authors conclude that Americans think of the poor as members of a different group, whereas Europeans still think of the poor as members of the same group. Robert Putnam, the analyst of social capital, has also found a link between high ethnic mix and low trust in the US. There is some British evidence supporting this link too. Researchers at Mori found that the average level of satisfaction with local authorities declines steeply as the extent of ethnic fragmentation increases. Even allowing for the fact that areas of high ethnic mix tend to be poorer, Mori found that ethnic fractionalisation still had a substantial negative impact on attitudes to local government.

[...]

What are the main objections, at least from the left, to this argument about solidarity and diversity? Multiculturalists stress Britain's multiple diversities, of class and region, which preceded recent waves of immigration. They also argue that all humans share similar needs and a common interest in ensuring they are met with minimum conflict; this, they say, can now be done through human rights laws. And hostility to diversity, they conclude, is usually a form of "false consciousness."

Critics of the dilemma also say, rightly, that the moral norms underpinning a community need not be hard for outsiders to comply with: broad common standards of right and wrong, some agreement on the nature of marriage and the family, respect for law, and some consensus about the role of religion in public life. Moreover, they add, there are places such as Canada (even Australia) which are happily combining European-style welfare with an officially multicultural politics. London, too, has US levels of ethnic diversity but is the most left-wing part of Britain.

[...]

A further point made by the multiculturalists is more telling. They argue that a single national story is not a sound base for a common culture because it has always been contested by class, region and religion. In Britain, the left traces democracy back to the peasants' revolt, the right back to Magna Carta, and so on. But while that is true, it is also the case that these different stories refer to a shared history. This does not imply a single narrative or national identity any more than a husband and wife will describe their married life together in the same way. Nor does it mean that the stress on the binding force of a shared history (or historical institutions like parliament) condemns immigrants to a second-class citizenship. Newcomers can and should adopt the history of their new country as well as, over time, contributing to it—moving from immigrant "them" to citizen "us." Helpfully, Britain's story includes, through empire, the story of many of our immigrant groups—empire soldiers, for example, fought in many of the wars that created modern Britain.

[...]

When solidarity and diversity pull against each other, which side should public policy favour? Diversity can increasingly look after itself—the underlying drift of social and economic development favours it. Solidarity, on the other hand, thrives at times of adversity, hence its high point just after the second world war and its steady decline ever since as affluence, mobility, value diversity and (in some areas) immigration have loosened the ties of a common culture. Public policy should therefore tend to favour solidarity in four broad areas.

Immigration and asylum About 9 per cent of British residents are now from ethnic minorities, rising to almost one third in London. On current trends about one fifth of the population will come from an ethnic minority by 2050, albeit many of them fourth or fifth generation. Thanks to the race riots in northern English towns in 2001, the fear of radical Islam after 9/11, and anxieties about the rise in asylum-led immigration from the mid-1990s (exacerbated by the popular press), immigration has shot up the list of voter concerns, and according to Mori 56 per cent of people (including 90 per cent of poor whites and even a large minority of immigrants) now believe there are too many immigrants in Britain. This is thanks partly to the over-burdened asylum system, which forces refugees on to welfare and prevents them from working legally for at least two years—a system calculated to provoke maximum hostility from ordinary Britons with their acute sensitivity to free riding.... As soon as the system is under control and undeserving applicants are swiftly removed or redirected to legitimate migration channels, the ban on working should be reduced to six months or abolished. A properly managed asylum system will sharply reduce the heat in the whole race and immigration debate.

Immigrants come in all shapes and sizes. From the American banker or Indian software engineer to the Somali asylum seeker—from the most desirable to the most burdensome, at least in the short term. Immigrants who plan to stay should be encouraged to become Britons as far as that is compatible with holding on to some core aspects of their own culture. In return for learning the language, getting a job and paying taxes, and abiding by the laws and norms of the host society, immigrants must be given a stake in the system and incentives to become good citizens. (While it is desirable to increase minority participation at the higher end of the labour market, the use of quotas and affirmative action seems to have been counter-productive in the US.) Immigrants from the same place are bound to want to congregate together but policy should try to prevent that consolidating into segregation across all the main areas of life: residence, school, workplace, church. In any case, the laissez-faire approach of the postwar period in which ethnic minority citizens were not encour-aged to join the common culture (although many did) should be buried. Citizen-ship ceremonies, language lessons and the mentoring of new citizens should help to create a British version of the old US melting pot. This third way on identity can be distinguished from the coercive assimilationism of the nationalist right, which rejects any element of foreign culture, and from multiculturalism, which rejects a common culture.

Is there a "tipping point" somewhere between Britain's 9 per cent ethnic minor-ity population and America's 30 per cent, which creates a wholly different US-style society—with sharp ethnic divisions, a weak welfare state and low political participation? No one knows, but it is a plausible assumption. And for that tipping point to be avoided and for feelings of solidarity towards incomers not to be overstretched it is important to reassure the majority that the system of entering the country and becoming a citizen is under control and that there is an honest debate about the scale, speed and kind of immigration. It is one thing to welcome smart, aspiring Indians or east Asians. But it is not clear to many people why it is such a good idea to welcome people from poor parts of the developing world with little experience of urbanisation, secularism or western values.

Welfare policy A generous welfare state is not compatible with open borders and possibly not even with US-style mass immigration. Europe is not America. One of the reasons for the fragmentation and individualism of American life is that it is a vast country. In Europe, with its much higher population density and planning controls, the rules have to be different. We are condemned to share—the rich cannot ignore the poor, the indigenous cannot ignore the immigrant—but that does not mean people are always happy to share. A universal, human rights-based approach to welfare ignores the fact that the rights claimed by one group do not automatically generate the obligation to accept them, or pay for them, on the part of another group.... If we want high tax and redistribution, especially with the extra welfare demands of an ageing population, then in a world of stranger citizens taxpayers need reassurance that their money is being spent on people for whose circumstances they would have some sympathy. For that reason, welfare should become more overtly conditional. The rules must be transparent and blind to ethnicity, religion, sexuality and so on, but not blind to behaviour. People who consistently break the rules of civilised behaviour should not receive unconditional benefits.

The "localisation" of more tax and redistribution would make it possible to see how and on whom our taxes are spent. More controversially, there is also a case—as Meghnad Desai has argued—for introducing a two-tier welfare system. Purely economic migrants or certain kinds of refugees could be allowed temporary residence, the right to work (but not to vote) and be given access to only limited parts of the welfare state, while permanent migrants who make the effort to become citizens would get full access to welfare. A two-tier welfare state might reduce pressure on the asylum system and also help to deracialise citizenship—white middle-class bankers and Asian shopkeepers would have full British citizenship, while white Slovenian temporary workers would not. Such a two-tier system is emerging in Denmark. Indeed it already applies to some extent in Britain: migrants on work permits and spouses during the two-year probationary period cannot get most benefits. If we want to combine social solidarity with relatively high immigration, there is also a strong case for ID cards both on logistical grounds and as a badge of citizenship that transcends narrower group and ethnic loyalties.

Culture Good societies need places like London and New York as well as the more homogeneous, stable, small and medium-size towns of middle Britain or the American midwest. But the emphasis, in culture and the media, should be on maintaining a single national conversation at a time when the viewing and listening public is becoming more fragmented. In Britain, that means strong support for the "social glue" role of the BBC. (The glue once provided by religion no longer works, and in any case cannot include immigrants of different faiths.) The teaching of multi-ethnic citizenship in schools is a welcome step. But too many children leave school with no sense of the broad sweep of their national history. The teaching of British history, and in particular the history of the empire and of subsequent immigration into Britain, should be a central part of the school curriculum. At the same time, immigrants should be encouraged to become part of the British "we," even while bringing their own very different perspective on its formation.

Politics and Language Multiculturalists argue that the binding power of the liberal nation state has been eroded from within by value diversity and from without by the arrival of immigrant communities with other loyalties. But the nation state remains irreplaceable as the site for democratic participation and it is hard to imagine how else one can organise welfare states and redistribution except through national tax and public spending. Moreover, since the arrival of immigrant groups from non-liberal or illiberal cultures it has become clear that to remain liberal the state may have to prescribe a clearer hierarchy of values. The US has tried to resolve the tension between liberalism and pluralism by developing a powerful national myth. Even if this were desirable in Britain, it is probably not possible to emulate. Indeed, the idea of fostering a common culture, in any strong sense, may no longer be possible either. One only has to try listing what the elements of a common culture might be to realise how hard it would be to legislate for. That does not mean that the idea must be abandoned; rather, it should inform public policy as an underlying assumption rather than a set of policies. Immigration and welfare policies, for example, should be designed to reduce the fear of free riding, and the symbolic aspects of citizenship should be reinforced; they matter more in a society when tacit understandings and solidarities can no longer be taken for granted. Why not, for example, a British national holiday or a state of the union address?

Lifestyle diversity and high immigration bring cultural and economic dynamism but can erode feelings of mutual obligation, reducing willingness to pay tax and even encouraging a retreat from the public domain. In the decades ahead European politics itself may start to shift on this axis, with left and right being eclipsed by value-based culture wars and movements for and against diversity. Social democratic parties risk being torn apart in such circumstances, partly on class lines: recent British Social Attitudes reports have made clear the middle class and the working class increasingly converge on issues of tax and economic management, but diverge on diversity issues.

The anxieties triggered by the asylum seeker inflow into Britain now seem to be fading. But they are not just a media invention; a sharp economic downturn or a big inflow of east European workers after EU enlargement might easily call them up again. The progressive centre needs to think more clearly about these issues to avoid being engulfed by them. And to that end it must try to develop a new language in which to address the anxieties, one that transcends the thin and abstract language of universal rights on the one hand and the defensive, nativist language of group identity on the other. Too often the language of liberal universalism that dominates public debate ignores the real affinities of place and people. These affinities are not obstacles to be overcome on the road to the good society; they are one of its foundation stones. People will always favour their own families and communities; it is the task of a realistic liberalism to strive for a definition of community that is wide enough to include people from many different backgrounds, without being so wide as to become meaningless.

45. *E Pluribus Unum*: Diversity and Community in the Twenty-first Century[*]

Robert D. Putnam

One of the most important challenges facing modern societies, and at the same time one of our most significant opportunities, is the increase in ethnic and social heterogeneity in virtually all advanced countries. The most certain prediction that we can make about almost any modern society is that it will be more diverse a generation from now than it is today. This is true from Sweden to the United States and from New Zealand to Ireland. In this article, I want to begin to explore the implications of that transition to a more diverse, multicultural society for "social capital"—the concept for which I have been honored by the Skytte Prize committee.[1]

I begin with a word or two about this concept, which has been the subject of an exponentially expanding and controversial literature over the last fifteen years. I prefer a "lean and mean" definition: social networks and the associated norms of reciprocity and trustworthiness.[2] The core insight of this approach is extremely simple: like tools (physical capital) and training (human capital), social networks have value. Networks have value, first, to people who are in the networks. For example, economic sociologists have shown repeatedly that labor markets are thoroughly permeated by networks so that most of us are as likely to get our jobs through whom we know as through what we know. Indeed, it has been shown that our lifetime income is powerfully affected by the quality of our networks (Granovetter 1973, 1974; Burt 1992, 1997; Lin 1999, 2001). Similarly, much evidence is accumulating about the health benefits of social ties (House et al. 1988; Berkman 1995; Seeman 1996; Berkman & Glass 2000).

---

[*] Source: *Scandinavian Political Studies* 30:2 June 2007: pp. 137–74.

1 This article summarizes initial results from a longer-term project. My colleagues and I will elaborate on our evidence and argument in subsequent publications. My intention here is to provide enough evidence that others can evaluate our argument and provide instructive commentary and criticism.

2 See Putnam (2000, 18–24) for a discussion of the concept of "social capital."

What makes social networks even more interesting, however, is that they also have implications for bystanders. For example, criminologists have taught us the power of neighbourhood networks to deter crime (Sampson et al. 1997; Sampson 2001). My wife and I have the good fortune to live in a neighbourhood of Cambridge, Massachusetts, that has a good deal of social capital: barbecues and cocktail parties and so on. I am able to be in Uppsala, Sweden, confident that my home is being protected by all that social capital, even though—and this is the moment for confession—I actually never go to the barbecues and cocktail parties. In other words, I benefit from those social networks even though I am not actually in them myself. In the language of economics, social networks often have powerful externalities.

Social capital comes in many forms, not all fungible. Not all networks have exactly the same effects: friends may improve health, whereas civic groups strengthen democracy. Moreover, although networks can powerfully affect our ability to get things done, nothing guarantees that what gets done through networks will be socially beneficial. Al Qaeda, for instance, is an excellent example of social capital, enabling its participants to accomplish goals they could not accomplish without that network. Nevertheless, much evidence suggests that where levels of social capital are higher, children grow up healthier, safer and better educated, people live longer, happier lives, and democracy and the economy work better (Putnam 2000, Section IV). So it seems worthwhile to explore the implications of immigration and ethnic diversity for social capital.

In this article, I wish to make three broad points:

- Ethnic diversity will increase substantially in virtually all modern societies over the next several decades, in part because of immigration. Increased immigration and diversity are not only inevitable, but over the long run they are also desirable. Ethnic diversity is, on balance, an important social asset, as the history of my own country demonstrates.
- In the short to medium run, however, immigration and ethnic diversity challenge social solidarity and inhibit social capital. In support of this provocative claim I wish to adduce some new evidence, drawn primarily from the United States. In order to elaborate on the details of this new evidence, this portion of my article is longer and more technical than my discussion of the other two core claims, but all three are equally important.
- In the medium to long run, on the other hand, successful immigrant societies create new forms of social solidarity and dampen the negative effects of diversity by constructing new, more encompassing identities. Thus, the central challenge for modern, diversifying societies is to create a new, broader sense of "we."

The Prospects and Benefits of Immigration and Ethnic Diversity

Figure 45.1 provides illustrative evidence that immigration has grown remarkably across the advanced nations of the world over the last half century. This chart shows

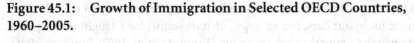

Figure 45.1: Growth of Immigration in Selected OECD Countries, 1960–2005.

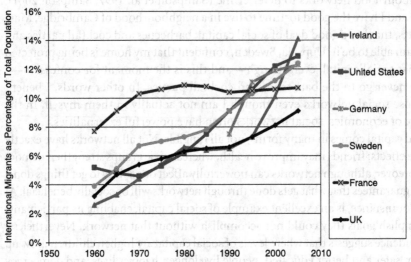

Source: Population Division of the Department of Economic and Social Affairs of the United Nations Secretariat, "Trends in Total Migrant Stock: The 2005 Revision," <http://esa.un.org/migration> 27 September 2006.

the trends in six different countries, selected more or less at random, with quite different historical trajectories: the United States, Ireland, Sweden, Germany, Britain and France. Although these countries began at somewhat different starting points in the 1960s (France relatively higher, Ireland relatively lower), the general pattern is a clear convergence toward a much higher number of immigrants as a fraction of the total population.

Of course, not all immigrants are ethnically different from the native population: Danish immigrants do not significantly alter the ethnic mix in Sweden, nor do Canadian immigrants in the United States. Conversely, much of the ethnic diversity in the United States, especially black-white diversity, is entirely unrelated to immigration since the ancestors of most African-Americans have been in the United States longer than the ancestors of most white Americans. So diversity and immigration are not identical, and in our subsequent, more detailed analyses we will need to make that distinction more explicit and rigorous. Nonetheless, as a general rule, the mounting wave of immigration depicted in Figure 45.1 has increased ethnic diversity in the receiving countries. Moreover, because immigrant groups typically have higher fertility rates than native-born groups, ethnic diversity in virtually all of these countries would still increase in the years ahead, even if all new immigration were somehow halted (Smith & Edmonston 1997).

So our societies will inevitably be more ethnically diverse tomorrow than they are today. And that diversity will be a valuable national asset.[3] It is not merely that national cuisine is enhanced by immigration, or even that culture of all sorts is enhanced by diversity, though culture and cuisine in my own country provide powerful evidence of those benefits.

- Creativity in general seems to be enhanced by immigration and diversity (Simonton 1999). Throughout history, for example, immigrants have accounted for three to four times as many of America's Nobel Laureates, National Academy of Science members, Academy Award film directors and winners of Kennedy Center awards in the performing arts as native-born Americans (Lerner & Roy 1984; Simonton 1999, Chapter 6; Smith & Edmonston 1997, 384–85). If we were to include second-generation immigrants (i.e., the children of immigrants), the contribution of immigrants would be even greater. Many (though not all) of the scores of studies of collective creativity in work groups (in business, education and so on) find that diversity fosters creativity (Webber & Donahue 2001; O'Reilly et al. 1997; Williams & O'Reilly 1998). Scott Page (2007) has powerfully summarized evidence that diversity (especially intellectual diversity) produces much better, faster problem-solving.
- Immigration is generally associated with more rapid economic growth. The economics profession has debated the short-run economic consequences of immigration for native workers. While there are important distributional effects to be considered, especially the impact of immigration on low-wage native workers in the US, the weight of the evidence suggests that the net effect of immigration is to increase national income. One recent study, for example, suggests that the income of native-born Americans rises more rapidly, *ceteris paribus*, if they are living in places with more immigrants than if they are living in places with fewer immigrants.[4]
- In advanced countries with aging populations, immigration is important to help offset the impending fiscal effects of the retirement of the baby-boom generation (Smith & Edmonston 1997, Chapters 6 and 7). In my country, for example, young immigrant workers (documented and undocumented) contribute financially to our Social Security system, but will not draw benefits for several decades, if at all, thus mitigating the otherwise unsustainable imbalance in the medium term

---

3 For a thorough, nuanced analysis of diversity as a social and political value, see Schuck (2003).

4 Smith and Edmonston (1997, Chapters 4 and 5); Ottaviano and Peri (2006a, 2006b). The two poles in the debate about the wage impact of immigration on natives are George Borjas (immigration reduces low-skilled native wages) and David Card (immigration raises all Americans' wages). Some key cites from this literature are: Borjas and Aydemir (2006); Borjas (1987, 2003, 2005); Card (1990, 2001, 2005); Card and DiNardo (2000); Engerman and Jones (1997); Borjas et al. (1992, 1996); Friedberg and Hunt (1995); Butcher and Card (1991). For a broader review of the economic consequences of ethnic diversity, see Alesina and La Ferrara (2005).

between outflow and inflow into our national coffers.[5] This effect is even more important in the more rapidly aging nations of Europe and East Asia.

- New research from the World Bank has highlighted yet another benefit from immigration, one of special relevance to the Nordic countries that have long played a disproportionate role on issues of global development. This new research suggests that immigration from the global South to the richer North greatly enhances development in the South, partly because of remittances from immigrants to their families back home and partly because of the transfer of technology and new ideas through immigrant networks. So powerful is this effect that despite "brain drain" costs, increasing annual northward immigration by only three percentage points might produce net benefits greater than meeting all our national targets for development assistance *plus* cancelling all Third World debt *plus* abolishing all barriers to Third World trade (World Bank 2005; Pritchett 2006).

In short, immigration and multicultural diversity have powerful advantages for both sending and receiving countries. Yet what about the effects on social capital?

Immigration and Diversity Foster Social Isolation

In the theoretical toolkit of social science we find two diametrically opposed perspectives on the effects of diversity on social connections. The first, usually labelled the "contact hypothesis," argues that diversity fosters interethnic tolerance and social solidarity. As we have more contact with people who are unlike us, we overcome our initial hesitation and ignorance and come to trust them more. Some of the most striking evidence in support of the contact hypothesis came originally from a famous study of the American soldier during the Second World War. White soldiers were asked how they would feel about having black soldiers serving in the same platoon with them. As Table 45.1 shows, among white soldiers who in fact had no contact with black soldiers, most opposed the idea. On the other hand, white soldiers who had been assigned to units with black soldiers were much more relaxed about the idea of racial integration (Stouffer 1949).

Evidence of this sort suggested to social psychologists, beginning with Gordon Allport in the 1950s, the optimistic hypothesis that if we have more contact with people of other ethnic and racial backgrounds (or at least more contact in the right circumstances), we will all begin to trust one another more.[6] More formally, accord-

---

5 This fiscal effect is off-set in part by the cost of educating the children of immigrants. Since in the US education is mostly financed at the state and local levels, the net fiscal effect at these levels is typically negative.

6 Four conditions are often said to be necessary for the contact theory to hold: common goals, intergroup cooperation, equal status, and authority sanction and support. The classic explication of the contact theory is Allport (1954). For recent developments of the theory, see Pettigrew and Tropp (2000, 2006); Tropp and Pettigrew (2005a, 2005b). See also Pettigrew (1998); Sigelman and Welch (1993); Stein et al. (2000). For critiques of contact theory, see Dixon et al. (2005); Dovidio et al. (2003).

ing to this theory, diversity reduces ethnocentric attitudes and fosters out-group trust and solidarity. If black and white children attend the same schools, for example, race relations will improve. This logic (and the sort of evidence presented in Table 45.1) was an important part of the legal case that led the United States Supreme Court to require racial desegregation in the famous *Brown v. Board of Education* case in 1954. For progressives, the contact theory is alluring, but I think it is fair to say that most (though not all) empirical studies have tended instead to support the so-called "conflict theory," which suggests that, for various reasons—but above all, contention over limited resources—diversity fosters out-group distrust and in-group solidarity. On this theory, the more we are brought into physical proximity with people of another race or ethnic background, the more we stick to "our own" and the less we trust the "other" (Blumer 1958; Blalock 1967; Giles & Evans 1986; Quillian 1995, 1996; Brewer & Brown 1998; Taylor 1998; Bobo 1999; Bobo & Tuan 2006).

Table 45.1   Attitudes of White Soldiers in United States Army in the Second World War toward Racial Integration.

Extent of contact with black troops	Percentage opposed to mixing black and white platoons in their company	Percentage opposed to a general policy of mixing black and white platoons
No contact	62	82
Same division, but not same regiment as black troops	24	50
Same regiment, but not same company as black troops	20	44
Same company as black troops	7	46

The evidence that diversity and solidarity are negatively correlated (controlling for many potentially confounding variables) comes from many different settings:

- Across workgroups in the United States, as well as in Europe, internal heterogeneity (in terms of age, professional background, ethnicity, tenure and other factors) is generally associated with lower group cohesion, lower satisfaction and higher turnover (Jackson et al. 1991; Cohen & Bailey 1997; Keller 2001; Webber & Donahue 2001).

- Across countries, greater ethnic heterogeneity seems to be associated with lower social trust (Newton & Delhey 2005; Anderson & Paskeviciute 2006; but see also Hooghe et al. 2006).
- Across local areas in the United States, Australia, Sweden, Canada and Britain, greater ethnic diversity is associated with lower social trust and, at least in some cases, lower investment in public goods (Poterba 1997; Alesina et al. 1999; Alesina & La Ferrara 2000, 2002; Costa & Kahn 2003b; Vigdor 2004; Glaeser & Alesina 2004; Leigh 2006; Jordahl & Gustavsson 2006; Soroka et al. 2007; Pennant 2005; but see also Letki forthcoming).
- Among Peruvian micro-credit cooperatives, ethnic heterogeneity is associated with higher default rates; across Kenyan school districts ethno-linguistic diversity is associated with less voluntary fundraising; and in Himalayan Pakistan, clan, religious, and political diversity are linked with failure of collective infrastructure maintenance (Karlan 2002; Miguel & Gugerty 2005; Khwaja 2006).
- Across American census tracts, greater ethnic heterogeneity is associated with lower rates of car-pooling, a social practice that embodies trust and reciprocity (Charles & Kline 2002).
- Within experimental game settings such as prisoners-dilemma or ultimatum games, players who are more different from one another (regardless of whether or not they actually know one another) are more likely to defect (or "cheat"). Such results have been reported in many countries, from Uganda to the United States (Glaeser et al. 2000; Fershtman & Gneezy 2001; Eckel & Grossman 2001; Willinger et al. 2003; Bouckaert & Dhaene 2004; Johansson-Stenman et al. 2005; Gil-White 2004; Habyarimana et al. 2006).
- Within the Union (northern) Army in the American Civil War, the casualty rate was very high and the risks of punishment for desertion were very low, so the only powerful force inhibiting the rational response of desertion was loyalty to one's fellow soldiers, virtually all of whom were other white males. Across companies in the Union Army, the greater the internal heterogeneity (in terms of age, hometown, occupation, etc.), the higher the desertion rate (Costa & Kahn 2003a).

Advocates of the conflict and contact theories clearly disagree about the balance of the empirical evidence, but in their shared focus on ethnocentric attitudes, they share one fundamental assumption—namely that in-group trust and out-group trust are negatively correlated. I believe this assumption is unwarranted and may have obscured some of the most interesting and unexpected consequences of diversity for social capital. In order to explain why, I need to remind you of an important distinction now commonly made in the field of social capital—that is, the distinction between "bonding" social capital (ties to people who are *like* you in some important way) and "bridging" social capital (ties to people who are *unlike* you in some important way). So, my bonding social capital consists of my ties to other white, male, elderly professors, and my bridging social capital reflects my ties to people of a different generation or a different race or a different gender.

Too often, without really thinking about it, we assume that bridging social capital and bonding social capital are inversely correlated in a kind of zero-sum relationship: if I have lots of bonding ties, I must have few bridging ties, and vice versa. As an empirical matter, I believe that assumption is often false. In other words, high bonding might well be compatible with high bridging, and low bonding with low bridging.[7] In the United States, for example, whites who have more non-white friends *also* have more white friends.[8] This article is not the place for an extended discussion of that empirical issue, but the theoretical point helps to clarify the relationship between diversity and social capital.

Contact theory suggests that diversity erodes the in-group/out-group distinction and enhances out-group solidarity or bridging social capital, thus lowering ethnocentrism. Conflict theory suggests that diversity enhances the in-group/out-group distinction and strengthens in-group solidarity or bonding social capital, thus increasing ethnocentrism. However, virtually none of the hundreds of empirical studies of this broad topic has ever actually measured in-group attitudes. Instead, researchers have typically measured out-group attitudes (positive or negative) and have simply *assumed* that in-group attitudes must vary inversely. Thus, they have presumed (without evidence) that their measures of out-group attitudes were straightforward measures of ethnocentrism.[9] However, once we recognize that in-group and out-group attitudes need not be reciprocally related, but can vary independently, then we need to allow, logically at least, for the possibility that diversity might actually reduce *both* in-group *and* out-group solidarity—that is, both bonding *and* bridging social capital. We might label this possibility "constrict theory" (a term suggested by my colleague, Abby Williamson).

I now present some initial evidence from the United States on the issue of how diversity (and by implication, immigration) affects social capital. The evidence comes from a large nationwide survey, the Social Capital Community Benchmark Survey, carried out in 2000, with a total sample size of roughly 30,000. Embedded within the nationwide sample is a representative national sample of 3,000, as well as smaller samples representative of 41 very different communities across the United States, ranging from large metropolitan areas like Los Angeles, Chicago, Houston and Boston to small towns and rural areas like Yakima, Washington, rural South Dakota and the Kanawha Valley in the mountains of West Virginia. While these 41 sites vary with respect to geographic

---

7 Of course, one can artificially create a zero-sum relationship between bridging and bonding by asking what *proportion* of, say, friendships are bridging or bonding, or about *relative* trust of in-groups and out-groups, but the result is a mathematical trick, not an empirical finding.

8 This generalization is based on our extensive analysis of the 2000 Social Capital Community Benchmark Survey described later in this article.

9 An important exception to this critique is Brewer (1999), who emphasizes that in-group and out-group attitudes can be independent of one another.

Figure 45.2   Social Capital Benchmark Survey Locations.

scope from two inner city neighbourhoods to several largely rural states, for the most part they represent metropolitan areas.[10] These sites are shown in Figure 45.2 and Table 45.2. These community sites differ in many ways (size, economic profile, region, educational levels, etc.), but for our purposes it is important that they differ greatly in their ethnic diversity. For example, Los Angeles and San Francisco (roughly 30–40 percent white) are among the most ethnically diverse human habitations in history, whereas in our rural South Dakota county (95 percent white) celebrating "diversity" means inviting a few Norwegians to the annual Swedish picnic.

---

10 The 41 community sites were not chosen strictly randomly, but reflected our ability to raise local funds to cover local costs in as wide an array of communities as we could manage. Nevertheless, extensive analysis has failed to unearth any significant differences between the nationally representative sample of 3,000 and the aggregate of the 41 local sites (N~27,000), either in frequency distributions or in relations among variables. Thus, for practical purposes, we treat the entire sample of 30,000 as a single nationwide sample, while confirming key generalizations on the nationally representative sample of 3,000. Several sites, as well as the national sample, over-sampled African-Americans and Latinos. We used both English- and Spanish-speaking interviewers, so we have an unusually broad sample of Latino respondents. All analyses reported here are based on data weighted to reflect population cross-distributions on race, age, education and gender. The AAPOR RR3 response rate was 27.4 percent across all communities, fairly typical for random-digit dialing telephone interviews nowadays. On the effects (often surprisingly small) of response rates on response bias, see Groves (2006). Having explored the representativeness of these data, we believe that the only significant defect is that the responses are modestly (5–10 percent) biased in a "pro-community" direction, probably due to a contextual effect that enhanced normal social desirability bias—that is, since the interview spent 30 minutes on questions of trust and community involvement, some respondents focused on the attractions and duties of community more than they otherwise might have done.

Table 45.2   Social Capital Community Benchmark Survey Sites.

Site	State	N
National sample		3,003
Atlanta Metro	GA	510
Baton Rouge	LA	500
Birmingham Metro	AL	500
Bismarck	ND	506
Boston	MA	604
Boulder	CO	500
Central Oregon (mid-sized town)	OR	500
Charlotte region/14 county	NC	1,500
Chicago Metro	IL	750
Cincinnati Metro	OH	1,001
Cleveland/Cuyahoga County	OH	1,100
Delaware (statewide)	DE	1,383
Denver (city/County)	CO	501
Detroit Metro/7 county	MI	501
East Bay (urban neighbourhood)	CA	500
East Tennessee (rural region)	TN	500
Fremont/Newaygo County	MI	753
Grand Rapids (city)	MI	502
Greensboro/Guilford County	NC	752
Houston/Harris County	TX	500
Indiana (selected counties)	IN	1,001
Kalamazoo County	MI	500
Kanawha Valley	WV	500
Lewiston-Auburn	ME	523
Los Angeles County	CA	515
Minneapolis	MN	501
Montana (statewide)	MT	502
New Hampshire (statewide)	NH	711
North Minneapolis (urban neighbourhood)	MN	452
Peninsula-Silicon Valley	CA	1,505
Phoenix/Maricopa County	AZ	501
Rochester Metro	NY	988
Rural SE South Dakota county	SD	368
San Diego County	CA	504
San Francisco (city)	CA	500
Seattle	WA	502

St Paul Metro	MN	503
Syracuse/Onondaga County	NY	541
Winston-Salem/Forsyth County	NC	750
Yakima	WA	500
York	PA	500
Total sample size		29,739

Another important methodological feature of this survey is that it was conducted simultaneously with the national census of 2000, and virtually every interview in our survey was "geo-coded" (i.e., for the vast majority of our respondents, we know exactly where they live, and thus we know the demographic characteristics of the census tract within which they live).[11] Thus, we know not only the race, education, income, marital status and so on of our respondents, but also the race, education, income, marital status and so on of their neighbours. The variability of the thousands of census tracts within which our respondents live is even greater than the variability across the 41 sample communities. Some respondents live in neighbourhoods that are almost completely homogeneous, while others live in neighbourhoods that are extremely diverse in every respect. For our detailed and most sophisticated analyses presented below, we use the individual as the unit of analysis, linking his or her attitudes and behavior to the characteristics of his or her neighbourhood. For expository purposes, however, I begin by using the community as the unit of analysis, showing how the diversity of a community is linked to the average level of social capital in that community.

One last methodological preliminary: For present purposes, we adopt the basic fourfold categorization of race and ethnicity that was used in the concurrent census: Hispanic, non-Hispanic white, non-Hispanic black and Asian. This classification scheme, like all such schemes, is "socially constructed"—that is, it is not God-given, or biological, or timeless and unchanging, or uniquely defensible. Indeed, the social construction of ethnicity will be an important part of my concluding remarks. However, this typology has two advantages for present purposes. First, it is widely used in public and private discourse in contemporary America, and second, it allows us to treat respondents (from our survey) and their neighbours (from the census) in parallel ways.

I begin with probably the least surprising, but in some respects most misleading, finding from our survey. Figure 45.3 arrays our 41 communities according to their ethnic diversity and the average level of *inter-racial trust* expressed by our respondents in those communities. We asked every respondent how much he or she

11 A United States census tract has an average of roughly 4,000 inhabitants, so it can be thought of as a large neighbourhood. Census tract boundaries are generally drawn to reflect local opinion about real neighbourhoods, though inevitably there is slippage in this effort.

Figure 45.3   Racial Homogeneity and Inter-racial Trust.

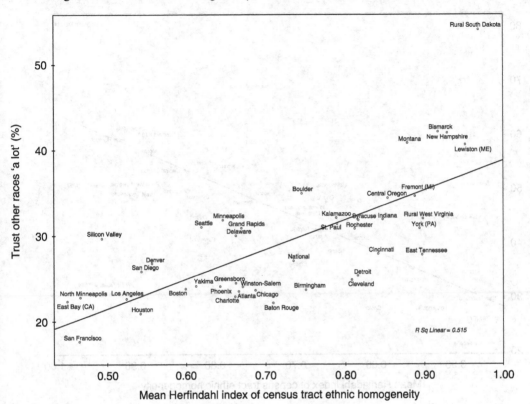

trusted whites, blacks, Asian-Americans and Hispanics (or Latinos), and we know the respondent's own ethnicity, so this measure is simply the average trust expressed toward the other three ethnic categories.[12] Obviously, Figure 45.3 shows a strong positive relationship between inter-racial trust and ethnic homogeneity.[13] Inter-racial trust is relatively high in homogeneous South Dakota and relatively low in heterogeneous San Francisco or Los Angeles. The more ethnically diverse the people we live around, the less we trust them. This pattern may be distressing normatively, but

12 Respondents were asked: "(How about) *White people* (would you say you can you trust them a lot, some, only a little, or not at all)?" "How about *African-Americans or blacks*?" "How about *Hispanics or Latinos*?" "How about *Asian people*?" Question order was randomized.

13 Our measure of ethnic homogeneity is a Herfindahl index calculated across the four basic ethnic categories. This standard measure is best interpreted as the likelihood that any two individuals randomly selected from a given community will be from the same category. We replicated our results using another plausible measure of ethnic diversity, García-Montalvo and Reynal-Querol's (2005) index of polarization, and the results are virtually identical.

Figure 45.4   Racial Homogeneity and Trust of Neighbours.

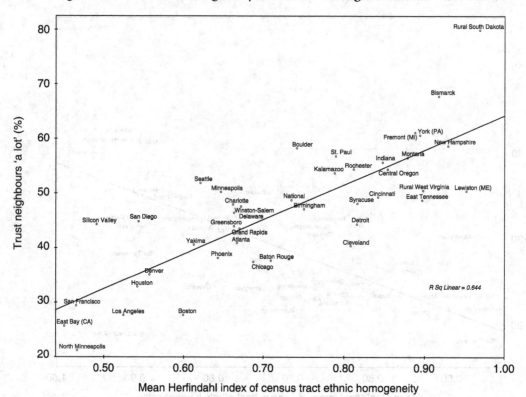

it seems to be consistent with conflict theory. Had we stopped our inquiry at this point (as previous studies of conflict and contact theory have done), we would have rejected contact theory, at least in its simplest form,[14] and accepted conflict theory. However, as we shall see momentarily, the story is actually more complicated.

Figure 45.4 is directly comparable to Figure 45.3, except that here our measure of social capital is trust in "people who live in your neighbourhood." Because of *de facto* residential segregation, most Americans' neighbours are of the same race as their own. And yet Figure 45.4 shows virtually the same pattern. The differences across our 41 sites are very substantial in absolute terms. In highly diverse Los Angeles or San Francisco, for example, roughly 30 percent of the inhabitants say that they trust their neighbours "a lot," whereas in the ethnically homogeneous communities of

---

14 I say "in its simplest form," because the more complicated version of contact theory maintains that contact enhances trust only under highly specific conditions: common goals, inter-group cooperation and so forth. As those conditions are narrowed, however, contact theory itself approaches tautology.

Figure 45.5   Racial Homogeneity and Intra-racial Trust.

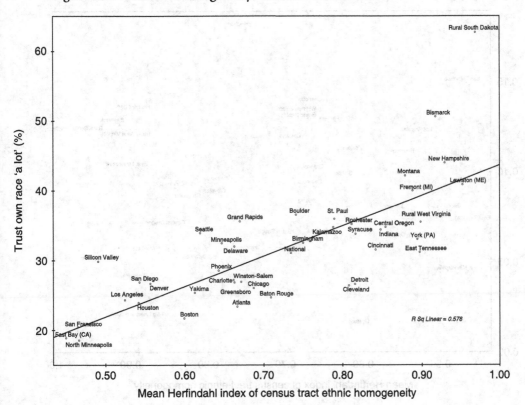

North and South Dakota, 70–80 percent of the inhabitants say the same. In more diverse communities, people trust their neighbours less.

Figure 45.5 repeats the story, but with one important difference. Now we ask about trust in people of the respondent's *own* race: how much do whites trust other whites, blacks other blacks, Hispanics other Hispanics, and Asians other Asians? This figure charts an entirely unexpected correlation for it shows that in-group trust, too, is lower in more diverse settings. Whereas Figures 45.3 and 45.4 are inconsistent with contact theory, Figure 45.5 is inconsistent with conflict theory. In other words, in more diverse settings, Americans distrust not merely people who do not look like them, but even people who *do*.

Finally, Figure 45.6 completes the story by arraying community diversity and "ethnocentric trust"—that is, trust in one's own race *minus* trust in other races.[15] This figure clearly shows that ethnocentric trust is completely uncorrelated with

15 Figure 45.6 is based on subtracting "other" from "own" racial trust, each as measured on a 4-point scale.

Figure 45.6   Racial Homogeneity and Ethnocentric Trust.

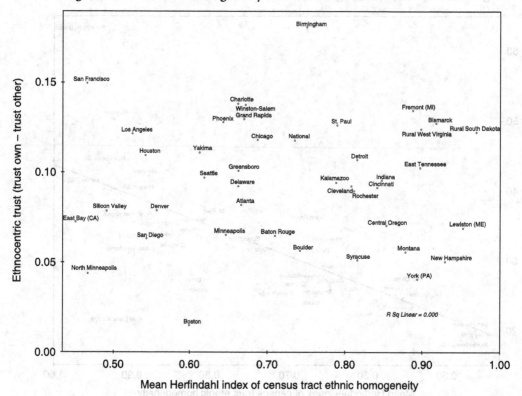

ethnic diversity. Thus, it suggests that *neither* conflict theory *nor* contact theory corresponds to social reality in contemporary America. Diversity seems to trigger *not* in-group/out-group division, but anomie or social isolation. In colloquial language, people living in ethnically diverse settings appear to "hunker down"—that is, to pull in like a turtle. Figures 45.3 to 45.6, taken together, suggest support for what I earlier tentatively labelled "constrict theory."

So far I have limited my presentation to evidence regarding social trust, and it is true that the most impressive and substantial patterns we have so far discovered involve trust of various sorts, including even trust of shop clerks. However, a wide array of other measures of social capital and civic engagement are also negatively correlated with ethnic diversity.[16] In areas of greater diversity, our respondents demonstrate:

16 Each of the following generalizations is based not merely on the sort of bivariate aggregate analysis presented in Figures 45.3 to 45.6, but on exhaustive multivariate, individual-level analyses as described below.

- Lower confidence in local government, local leaders and the local news media.[17]
- Lower political efficacy—that is, confidence in their own influence.[18]
- Lower frequency of registering to vote, but more interest and knowledge about politics and more participation in protest marches and social reform groups.[19]
- Less expectation that others will cooperate to solve dilemmas of collective action (e.g., voluntary conservation to ease a water or energy shortage).[20]
- Less likelihood of working on a community project.[21]
- Lower likelihood of giving to charity or volunteering.[22]
- Fewer close friends and confidants.[23]
- Less happiness and lower perceived quality of life.[24]
- More time spent watching television and more agreement that "television is my most important form of entertainment."[25]

---

17 The questions were: "How much of the time do you think you can trust the local government to do what is right—just about always, most of the time, only some of the time, or hardly ever?" "Do you agree strongly, agree somewhat, disagree somewhat, or disagree strongly: The people running my community don't really care much what happens to me?" "Would you say you can trust the local news media a lot, some, only a little, or not at all?" Census tract diversity is *not* related to trust in *national* government, implying that people distinguish (sensibly) between the effects of local diversity on local institutions and the non-effects of local diversity on national institutions.

18 The question was: "Overall, how much impact do you think people like you can have in making your community a better place to live—no impact at all, a small impact, a moderate impact, or a big impact?"

19 The questions were: "Are you currently registered to vote?" "How interested are you in politics and national affairs—very interested, somewhat interested, only slightly interested, or not at all interested?" "Could you tell me the names of the two US Senators from your state?" "Have you in the last twelve months participated in any demonstrations, protests, boycotts, or marches?" "Did any of the groups that you are involved with take any local action for social or political reform in the past 12 months?"

20 The question was: "Now I'd like to ask you a few questions about the local community where you live. If public officials asked everyone to conserve water or electricity because of some emergency, how likely is it that people in your community would cooperate—very likely, likely, unlikely, or very unlikely?"

21 The question was: "Have you in the last twelve months…worked on a community project?"

22 The measure here is a factor score index combining questions about contributions to charity and frequency of volunteering.

23 The questions were: "Right now, how many people do you have in your life with whom you can share confidences or discuss a difficult decision—nobody, one, two, or three or more?" "About how many close friends do you have these days? These are people you feel at ease with, can talk to about private matters, or call on for help. Would you say that you have no close friends, one or two, three to five, six to ten, or more than that?"

24 The questions were: "Overall, how would you rate your community as a place to live—excellent, good, only fair, or poor?" "All things considered, would you say you are very happy, happy, not very happy, or not happy at all?" In recent years, psychologists and economists have produced a sophisticated literature on the determinants of happiness. It is generally agreed that social connectivity (family, friends and community involvement) is a powerful determinant, so this simple question turns out to be a good, indirect measure of social capital. For overviews of this burgeoning field, see Diener (2000); Layard (2005); Kahneman et al. (1999); Myers and Diener (1995); Blanchflower and Oswald (2004); Powdthavee (2006); Helliwell (2006); Helliwell and Putnam (2004).

25 The questions were: "How many hours per day do you spend watching television on an average weekday, that is, Monday through Friday?" "Do you agree/disagree with the statement that 'Television is my most important form of entertainment'?"

To be sure, some dimensions of social capital and civic engagement seem relatively unaffected by ethnic diversity in American communities. For example, organizational activity of various sorts, including religious activity, is essentially uncorrelated with diversity, once we control for confounding variables, and as I have already noted, several measures of political engagement are positively correlated with diversity.[26] Nevertheless, a reasonably coherent, consistent image emerges from this analysis.[27]

Diversity does *not* produce "bad race relations" or ethnically defined group hostility, our findings suggest. Rather, inhabitants of diverse communities tend to withdraw from collective life, to distrust their neighbours, regardless of the colour of their skin, to withdraw even from close friends, to expect the worst from their community and its leaders, to volunteer less, give less to charity and work on community projects less often, to register to vote less, to agitate for social reform *more*, but have less faith that they can actually make a difference, and to huddle unhappily in front of the television. Note that this pattern encompasses attitudes and behaviour, bridging and bonding social capital, public and private connections. Diversity, at least in the short run, seems to bring out the turtle in all of us.

This conclusion is provocative, but the graphic evidence presented thus far (bivariate, aggregate analysis) is open to numerous objections. The first and most important is that so far I have used community as the unit of analysis, but that approach obscures a crucial issue—namely, is it *who* is living in a community that matters (a compositional effect), or who they are living *around* (a contextual effect)? This question can be resolved only by moving to the individual level of analysis, in which we seek to predict an individual's social connectedness from *both* his or her personal characteristics (race, age, geographic mobility, etc.) *and* his or her neighbours' characteristics (age, race, mobility, etc.).

Second, the diverse communities in our study are clearly distinctive in many other ways apart from their ethnic composition. Diverse communities tend to be larger, more mobile, less egalitarian, more crime-ridden and so on. Moreover, indi-

---

26 For a recent empirical assessment of the links between ethnic diversity and political engagement (or "citizenship behavior"), including a review of previous political science treatments of that issue, see Anderson & Paskeviciute (2006). For the argument that heterogeneity enhances some forms of political engagement, while dampening others, see Campbell (2006).

27 I set aside for fuller analysis in a subsequent publication one important dimension of social capital—namely, inter-racial friendships. At first glance, ethnic diversity is *positively* correlated with inter-racial friendships. However, to some extent, that correlation represents a quasi-tautological "pool" effect: It is obviously much easier, even randomly, for whites who live in Harlem to have black friends than it is for whites who live in virtually all-white Duluth, Minnesota. When we control for that structural constraint (e.g., by calculating the odds that any respondent would encounter people of other races simply randomly in their local community), then inter-racial friendships (apart from that structural constraint on opportunities for contact) appear to be actually more common in less diverse settings. The statistical methodology for this analysis is, however, far from straightforward, so I forebear from pursuing the issue here. For a useful introduction to this general issue, see McPherson et al. (2001).

viduals who live in ethnically diverse places are different in many ways from people who live in homogeneous areas. They tend to be poorer, less educated, less likely to own their home, less likely to speak English and so on. In order to exclude the possibility that the seeming "effect" of diversity is spurious, we must control, statistically speaking, for many other factors. Our ability to control simultaneously and reliably for many factors, both individual and aggregate, is enhanced by our much larger sample of respondents than is typical in social surveys. Yakima, Washington, for example, is highly diverse, but relatively small, so our sample there helps distinguish the effects of size and diversity.

These first two methodological objections can be dealt with most efficiently in the context of multivariate analysis. In our "standard model" we have included simultaneously controls at *both* the individual *and* the census tract level for:

Age	Affluence/poverty	Citizenship
Ethnicity	Language	Commuting time
Education	Residential mobility	Homeownership

In addition, we control for region of the country; the respondent's gender, financial satisfaction and work hours; the population density and the Gini index of income inequality in his or her census tract; and two measures of the crime rate in the respondent's county.[28] Obviously, it is impossible here to present the full array of statistical evidence for each of the dozens of dependent variables we have examined, but the multivariate analysis we carried out is illustrated in Table 45.3.

Here we seek to predict trust in neighbours (as measured on the full 4-point scale) from our standard array of individual and aggregate-level variables. Not surprisingly, the strongest predictors (controlling for everything else) are individual-level variables: age (younger people are less trusting), ethnicity (blacks and Hispanics are less trusting) and socioeconomic class (the educated, the well-off, and homeowners are more trusting). All of these individual-level patterns are well-established from past research. Next in importance are several contextual variables: poverty (less trust among inhabitants of poorer neighbourhoods), crime (less trust in high-crime areas) and ethnic diversity (less trust among inhabitants of ethnically heterogeneous neighbourhoods).

It is sadly true in the United States that poverty, crime and diversity are themselves intercorrelated, but Table 45.3 shows that even comparing two *equally* poor (or equally rich), *equally* crime-ridden (or equally safe) neighbourhoods, greater ethnic diversity is associated with less trust in neighbours. We should take the precise numeric estimates here with more than a grain of salt, but in round numbers Table 45.3 implies that in terms of the effect on neighbourly trust, the difference

---

28 The county is the lowest geographical level at which crime rates in America are consistently reported.

Table 45.3   Predicting Trust in Neighbours from Individual and Contextual Variables.

	B	S.E.	Beta	t	Sig.
(Constant)	0.79	0.11		7.0	0.0000
R's age	0.01	0.00	0.15	21.4	0.0000
R owns home (v. rent)	0.25	0.01	0.13	19.7	0.0000
R's education (years)	0.04	0.00	0.13	19.1	0.0000
R's ethnicity: black	−0.31	0.02	−0.12	−18.6	0.0000
Census tract poverty rate	−0.66	0.09	−0.08	−7.1	0.0000
R's satisfaction with current finances	0.10	0.01	0.08	12.4	0.0000
R's ethnicity: Latino	−0.24	0.02	−0.07	−9.8	0.0000
R's household income ($100,000)	0.14	0.02	0.05	7.5	0.0000
County: Non-violent Crimes per Capita	−2.57	0.41	−0.05	−6.2	0.0000
Census tract Herfindahl Index of Ethnic	**0.18**	**0.04**	**0.04**	**5.1**	**0.0000**

Homogeneity

	B	S.E.	Beta	t	Sig.
Census Tract Population Density (100,000 per sq. mi)	−0.39	0.08	−0.04	−4.8	0.0000
Census Tract Percent Living Same Town as	−0.24	0.04	−0.04	−5.4	0.0000

Five Years Earlier

	B	S.E.	Beta	t	Sig.
R's decades in this community	.020	.004	0.04	5.3	0.0000
Census Tract Percent Renters	−0.14	0.04	−0.04	−3.5	0.0006
Census Tract Percent Bachelor's Degree	0.29	0.07	0.03	4.3	0.0000
R is Spanish-speaker	−0.13	0.03	−0.03	−4.1	0.0001
R is female	0.05	0.01	0.03	4.7	0.0000
Census Tract Gini Coefficient for Household	0.39	0.15	0.02	2.7	0.0069

Income

	B	S.E.	Beta	t	Sig.
Census Tract Average Commute Time (hours)	−0.21	−0.06	−0.02	−3.4	0.0006
R's ethnicity: Asian	−0.09	0.03	−0.02	−3.3	0.0011
Census Tract Percent United States Citizens	0.21	0.09	0.02	2.2	0.0264
County: Violent Crimes per Capita	6.59	3.35	0.02	2.0	0.0489
Census Tract Percent Over 65	0.21	0.10	0.01	2.1	0.0364

R is a citizen	0.06	0.03	0.01	2.1	0.0356
R's average monthly work hours	.002	.001	0.01	1.8	0.0732
R is resident of South	−0.02	0.02	−0.01	−1.2	0.2182
R is resident of Midwest	−0.02	0.02	−0.01	−1.0	0.3296
R is resident of West	0.01	0.02	0.01	0.8	0.4238
R's commuting time (hours)	−0.00	0.01	0.00	−0.2	0.8069

Notes: Question was "How much can you trust people in your neighbourhood?" N = 23,260. Adj. R^2 = 0.26.

between living in an area as homogeneous as Bismarck, North Dakota, and one as diverse as Los Angeles is roughly as great as the difference between an area with a poverty rate of 7 percent and one with a poverty rate of 23 percent, or between an area with 36 percent college graduates and one with none. Even holding constant affluence and poverty, diversity *per se* has a major effect. *Every one of the correlates of ethnic homogeneity listed above (civic collaboration, altruism, personal friendship, confidence in local institutions, happiness, television-watching and so on) passes this same stringent multivariate, multilevel test.*

Methodologically speaking, the analysis of contextual effects is one of the thorniest thickets in contemporary social science. I do not have time or space here to elaborate on all the serious threats to the validity of these claims that my colleagues and I have considered, or to adduce all the evidence that has led us (at least so far) to reject those threats. Nevertheless, it may be useful simply to list several prominent issues and briefly indicate our verdict.

Self-selection

People mostly choose where to live, and that simple fact opens up a hornets' nest of methodological problems with correlational analysis since people with a certain characteristic may *choose* to live in distinctive areas. For example, the fact that people with children live nearer to schools does not mean that proximity to a school caused them to become parents. In our case, however, selection bias is *prima facie* implausible as an explanation for our results. For selection bias to produce a negative correlation between diversity and sociability, paranoid, television-watching introverts would have to choose disproportionately to live in mixed neighbourhoods. Phrased differently, a self-selection interpretation of our results would require, for example, that when non-whites move into a previously all-white neighbourhood, the *first* whites to flee (or the most reluctant to move in) would be the *most* trusting, and the *last* to flee would be the *least* trusting; or alternatively, that ethnic minorities and immigrants would selectively choose to move into neighbourhoods in which the majority residents are most irascible and misanthropic. Common sense suggests that the opposite is more likely; if anything, selection bias probably artificially mutes the underlying causal pattern. In short, taking self-selection into account, our findings may *underestimate* the real effect of diversity on social withdrawal.[29]

Different Strokes for Different Folks?

We considered the possibility that the effects of diversity on social capital might vary from group to group. Perhaps people in poor neighbourhoods are more sensitive to diversity than people in upscale neighbourhoods (or the reverse). Perhaps women are more likely to hunker in the presence of diversity than men (or the reverse). Perhaps conservatives are more allergic to diversity than liberals (or the reverse). Perhaps the basic relationship is different for different racial and ethnic groups. Perhaps younger people are less upset by diversity than older generations. Our base model directly controls for most of these variables, but the more subtle question here involves interaction effects: Does the relationship between diversity and sociability vary between men and women, upscale and downscale neighbourhoods, liberals and conservatives, whites and non-whites, young people and older generations?

The short answer is basically "no." The same pattern appears within each of these demographic groups. To be sure, the strength of the core patterns varies somewhat from group to group, partly perhaps as a function of sample size and reduced variance. Thus, for example, the impact of diversity on trust and sociability seems to be somewhat greater in lower-status neighbourhoods, but for measures of altruism the negative impact of diversity seems somewhat greater in upper-status areas. Diversity seems to affect men and women equally, though with minor variation across different indicators of sociability. The impact of diversity on sociability seems somewhat greater among conservatives, but it is significant among liberals, too. The impact of diversity is definitely greater among whites, but is visible as well among non-whites.

Broadly speaking, contemporary ethnic diversity in American communities reflects (in roughly equal measure) two quite different historical processes: the African slave trade of the seventeenth and eighteenth centuries and the growing immigration of Latinos and Asians into the United States in the twentieth and twenty-first centuries. Although all four racial-ethnic categories are represented in all parts of the country, African-Americans are disproportionately represented in the

---

29 We have also undertaken some empirical tests of selection bias. For example, since higher SES people are less constrained in housing markets, any selection bias should be concentrated among them. However, our core findings are equally found among upper and lower SES respondents. We also used our respondents' reported likelihood of staying in their community over the next five years to explore whether low-trust individuals are poised to flee homogeneous communities, as the selection-bias story implies. In general, low-trust people say they are less likely to stay put, but this is equally true in homogeneous and heterogeneous neighbourhoods. Finally, for some indicators, such as trust and friendship, the effects of diversity are higher among long-term residents. In no case are the effects higher among recent arrivals. This, too, argues against a selection bias explanation for our key findings.

Southeast and the urban areas of the North, whereas Latinos and Asian-Americans are concentrated in the Southwest and West. Thus, in gross terms, variance in our basic measure of ethnic diversity can be partitioned into two distinct factors: the percentage of blacks in a given area and the percentage of immigrants in a given area. It is important to ask whether these two different types of diversity, with their very different historical matrices, have different effects on social capital.

Thus, we replicated our multivariate, multilevel analyses, but included both "percent black" and "percent immigrant" in place of our core measure of ethnic diversity. For the primary indicators of social capital discussed earlier (i.e., social trust, community attachment and sociability) each of these two separate measures of diversity has a significant and independent negative effect, though percent immigrant seems to have a somewhat more consistent and powerful effect. In the interests of parsimony, therefore, I have presented our findings in this article simply in terms of ethnic diversity, rather than distinguishing among different types of diversity. In subsequent work it will be desirable to seek to decompose the underlying patterns much further: what is the effect (for example) of Latino neighbours on blacks' trust of Asians? And what is the effect of (say) Mexican neighbours on Cubans' trust of whites? On the other hand, these further decompositions will be complicated by increasingly severe problems of sample size and multicollinearity. At this stage in our work, we have discovered no patterns at this level of disaggregation that would call into question our core finding that ethnic diversity itself seems to encourage hunkering.

We initially suspected that the effects of diversity might be greater for older generations raised in a less multicultural era, whereas younger cohorts would be less discombobulated by diversity. Among twenty-something respondents in 2000, diversity appears to lower trust somewhat less than it does among older respondents. However, every successively older cohort from age 30 to age 90 showed essentially equal effects, so Americans raised in the 1970s seem fully as unnerved by diversity as those raised in the 1920s. Moreover, people in their 20s are exceptionally mobile (as they go to college and take jobs), so their current residence is probably a noisier proxy for their actual social context. Consequently, even their slightly lower contextual sensitivity might well be merely a passing life cycle effect, not a harbinger of enduring change. We have unearthed no convincing evidence of generational differences in reactions to diversity.

Defining Context
In claiming that ethnically diverse neighbourhoods produce hunkering, we use the census tract as a proxy for "neighbourhood." However, the real neighbourhoods in which people experience their daily lives likely vary from census tracts. Obviously, no nationwide survey could gather contextual data on personally defined "neighbourhoods" for all respondents, so it is difficult to address this issue empirically.

However, insofar as the error introduced by this mismatch between objectively and subjectively defined contexts is more or less random, the net effect is that our results underestimate the real effects of diversity. Moreover, we have replicated all our key findings using *county* as the contextual variable, and the results are virtually identical, though slightly less sharp, like a photograph that is slightly out of focus.[30] That is precisely what we would expect if the error introduced by mismatch were random because the mismatch is undoubtedly greater when context is defined at the more gross level of county than at the finer-grained level of census tract.[31] Moreover, the fact that we find the same contextual effect using two such different measures of context suggests that the pattern is impressively robust. The presumption is that if we could magically define the boundaries of each respondent's neighbourhood personally and attach relevant neighbourhood characteristics, the negative effects of diversity might look even more pronounced.

To confirm the robustness of the relationship between social capital and ethnic diversity, we exploited an entirely different dataset: a measurement of social capital for every county in America compiled by Anil Rupasingha, Stephen J. Goetz and David Freshwater (RGF) at Pennsylvania State University (Rupasingha et al. 2006). The RGF measure, based on the density of civic and non-profit organizations, voting turnout and cooperation with the census, includes no measures of individual attitudes and behaviour, but it is strongly correlated with an independent survey-based measure of social trust.[32] The advantage of the RGF dataset is that it covers all 3,111 counties in the continental United States. Controlling for education levels, poverty, urbanization, commuting time, total population (logged), residential mobility and region, the RGF social capital measure is strongly negatively correlated with both immigration and ethnic diversity.[33] This entirely independent confirmation strengthens our confidence that our core finding is not dependent upon a restrictive definition of "context."

Non-linearity and Inequality?

We suspected that the effects of ethnic diversity might be non-linear, perhaps reflecting "tipping point" effects, so that an increase of non-white immigrants (for example) from 0 to 5 percent might not have the same impact as an increase from 10 to

---

30 One partial exception to this generalization involves religious involvement. Using our standard multivariate, multilevel model, tract-level homogeneity tends to predict slightly *higher* religious involvement, whereas county-level homogeneity tends to predict *lower* religious involvement. This anomalous pattern appears to reflect regional differences in religiosity.

31 Whereas the average census tract has a population of roughly 4,000, the average county has a population of roughly 80,000.

32 Necessarily our survey measure of trust (based on the aggregated DDB survey agree-disagree item "most people are honest") under-represents less populous counties nationwide, so this confirmatory analysis is limited to the 444 most populous counties. Given the noise in both measures, the correlation between the RGF measure and the DDB measure is quite strong (r = 0.37).

33 Details available upon request from the author.

15 percent or from 47.5 to 52.5 percent. In fact, we found no empirical evidence for such non-linear effects of diversity in our analyses.

In exploring the effects of diversity, we have obviously concentrated on *ethnic* diversity. However, an equally important and directly analogous set of questions might be—indeed, should be—posed about the effects of *economic* diversity. What is the relationship between neighbourhood economic inequality and social capital? This query is especially important because (as I have explained elsewhere) the correlation between economic equality and social capital is virtually ubiquitous, both across space and across time, both in the United States and around the world (Putnam 2000, 358–60; Costa & Kahn 2003b).

Our standard statistical model includes measures of economic inequality, particularly the Gini index of income inequality, and its effects are often quite parallel to, and independent of, the effects of ethnic diversity. Generally speaking, people who live in neighbourhoods of greater economic inequality also tend to withdraw from social and civic life. On the other hand, the relationships involving economic diversity seem to be somewhat more complex than those involving ethnic diversity, which are the focus of our concern in this article. First, the correlations between social capital and economic inequality are less consistent than those between social capital and ethnic diversity. Second, the correlations we find between economic inequality and social capital appear to be non-linear, with some pronounced tipping points, unlike the patterns involving ethnic diversity. Third, unlike ethnic diversity, the effects of income inequality seem to be interactive at the tract and county levels.

Most fundamentally, however, economic inequality does not appear to be a significant confounding variable in our analyses of ethnic diversity. First, as I have already noted, our standard model directly controls for both income inequality and poverty. Second, we have been able to discover no significant interactive effects between economic inequality and ethnic diversity—that is, our core finding that diversity produces hunkering is equally true both in communities with great economic disparities and in those that are relatively egalitarian. Economic inequality is very important, but it does not appear to cause, amplify or obscure the apparent effects of ethnic diversity on social capital.

Pot-holes and Playgrounds

We considered the possibility that public amenities might be rarer in more diverse neighbourhoods, perhaps for political reasons, and that this absence of amenities (not diversity itself) might undermine social capital. Ethnically homogeneous neighbourhoods might have a more congenial ratio of playgrounds to pot-holes. We have found no perfect nationwide measures of local amenities within each census tract, but we were able to construct several ZIP-code-level measures of schools, libraries, civic associations, small shops, sports clubs, religious institutions, day care facilities and other sites of social interaction.[34] If anything, such community resources turn out to be *positively* correlated with ethnic diversity, so they cannot account for our core finding, and in fact, when added to our standard model, do not.

Hierarchical Modelling

Our data set has a complicated, nested structure, including one large national sample and 41 smaller community samples. One of the methodological challenges is that the nested structure introduces the possibility of biased standard errors since observations within each community are not independent.[35] Moreover, conventional multiple regression assumes that the effect of the key explanatory variable (diversity, in our case) does not vary from community to community, whereas, in fact, variation in reactions to diversity from one community to another community is an open and interesting question. To address this issue, we pursued four strategies:

- We replicated the analysis on the (N = 3,003) national sample alone. The core results are fully confirmed, although the significance levels are obviously attenuated by the smaller sample size.
- We ran the standard model separately *within* each community sample. These samples are much smaller (and therefore more vulnerable to random error). Moreover, variation in ethnic diversity is much lower within any community than nationwide, and multicollinearity among contextual variables is a more serious problem within any given community. (Bismarck has no rich, transient, Asian-American neighbourhoods, for example, and Los Angeles has no poor, low-crime, all-white neighbourhoods.) Consequently, standard errors are much higher in this setting. Nevertheless, within 26 of the 41 community samples, diversity was associated with low trust, controlling for all standard covariates, although the link achieved conventional statistical significance in only a few cases.
- We estimated a random-intercept, random-coefficient Hierarchical Linear Model (HLM) for the pooled, 41-site sample. This approach produces an estimate of the diversity effect that is essentially a weighted average of the coefficients within each community. This estimate is highly significant, though slightly lower than the full-sample OLS coefficient.
- Based on the estimated HLM model, we calculated the empirical Bayes or shrinkage estimate of the effect of diversity on trust within each community,

---

34 I am grateful to Mario Luis Small for pointing us to these data.
35 On analyzing clustered data and hierarchical linear modelling, see Singer (1998); Raudenbush and Bryk (2002); Gelman and Hill (2007). In addition to the strategies outlined in the text, we have adjusted standard errors for intragroup correlation within each community sample and with the exception of one composite measure of volunteering and giving to charity, census tract ethnic heterogeneity remains a highly significant predictor across a dozen diverse indicators of trust and sociability.

and that effect is negative in 39 of the 41 communities. To be sure, the negative effects of diversity seem to be more pronounced in some communities than in others, and those differences across communities should be quite instructive, so we intend to explore them more fully in subsequent work. Nevertheless, the core finding that diversity encourages hunkering seems highly robust.

In short, we have tried to test every conceivable artifactual explanation for our core finding, and yet the pattern persists. Many Americans today are uncomfortable with diversity.

One powerful limitation on this analysis, however, deserves more substantial discussion, for it sheds an entirely new light on our central concern about the effects of immigration and ethnic diversity on modern societies. All our empirical analysis to this point has involved "comparative statics"—that is, we have compared people living in places with different ethnic mixes *at one point in time*—namely different American communities in the year 2000.[36] Although our evidence does suggest that it is the *level* of diversity that matters, not the rate of change, we have not yet considered any "dynamic" evidence about the effects of immigration and diversity *over long periods of time within a single place* (whether a single community or the nation as a whole). Exploring the dynamics, as opposed to the comparative statics, of diversity and social capital requires entirely different methods, and my research group has only begun to explore those avenues. For example, several of my colleagues have undertaken case studies of the effects of immigration and diversity over time on the social and political life of various local communities in the United States.[37] Moreover, we have only begun to explore highly relevant evidence from such distant domains as experimental social psychology and the history of previous waves of immigration. Thus, my comments in the final third of this article are necessarily preliminary. However, these ideas are, I believe, crucial to any final interpretation of our "comparative statics" evidence.

---

36 We have explored whether "old" diversity is different from "new" diversity by examining differences between neighbourhoods that were already diverse in the 1980 and 1990 censuses and neighbourhoods that had become diverse only in 2000. Although our examination of such "lagged" effects is incomplete, we have so far discovered no evidence that over a span of these two decades "older" diversity has become any less likely to trigger the "hunkering" reaction than more recent diversity.

37 Benjamin Deufel has explored the impact of Latino immigration into five mid-sized towns in Minnesota, Iowa and North Carolina—so-called "new destination" immigration. Abby Williamson is exploring the impact of both sudden and gradual immigration on the social and political life of a half dozen towns from Lewiston, Maine, to Yakima, Washington. Their work, though still in progress, makes clear that the effects of immigration and diversity over time vary widely from place to place and that those effects depend in part on policies, public and private, within the receiving communities.

Becoming Comfortable with Diversity

Social psychologists and sociologists have taught us that people find it easier to trust one another and cooperate when the social distance between them is less.[38] "When social distance is small, there is a feeling of common identity, closeness, and shared experiences. But when social distance is great, people perceive and treat the other as belonging to a different category" (Alba & Nee 2003, 32). Social distance depends in turn on social identity: our sense of who we are. Identity itself is socially constructed and can be socially de-constructed and re-constructed. Indeed, this sort of social change happens all the time in any dynamic and evolving society. For example, religious evangelism, social mobilization and political campaigning all involve the intentional transformation of identities.

Changed identity can also lead to changed behaviour. For example, the more university graduates identify with their *alma mater*, the greater their alumni donations (Mael & Ashforth 1992, as cited in Kramer 2006). Although the linkage between identity and social capital is only beginning to be explored, it is an important frontier for research. The relationship between the two is almost certainly powerful and reciprocal: Whom you hang out with probably affects who you think you are, and who you think you are probably affects whom you hang out with.

Diversity itself can only be conceived in terms of socially constructed identities. We saw that earlier when we were forced to define "diversity" in our research in terms of the currently canonical four ethno-racial categories in the United States Census. However, how people are assigned by others to racial and ethnic categories has varied greatly over time and space. Thus, adapting over time, dynamically, to immigration and diversity requires the reconstruction of social identities, not merely of the immigrants themselves (though assimilation is important), but also of the newly more diverse society as a whole (including the native born).

Please allow me several personal anecdotes to illustrate that identities are socially constructed and malleable. Several of my grandchildren were raised in Costa Rica, the children of an American mother (my daughter) and a Costa Rican father. A few years ago they moved to Pittsburgh and at the end of the first week of school, my granddaughter Miriam came home and asked my daughter: "People keep calling me 'Hispanic.' What do they mean? I tell them 'No, I'm Costa Rican.'" My daughter, a social historian by profession, but also a mom, knew she had to answer the question seriously, and she replied: "'Hispanic' is how North Americans refer to people whose parents came from Latin America." "Oh," asked Miriam, "is Daddy Hispanic?"

---

38 Social psychology also suggests that neighbourhood heterogeneity may lead to lower predictability of social behavior and thus to "information overload." (This literature builds on Milgram (1970). I am grateful to Daniel Gilbert for pointing me to this literature.) Information overload in turn leads to systemic shutdown, the physiological counterpart of "hunkering down." In short, unfamiliar difference in the social environment may lead to withdrawal. We intend to explore this avenue in subsequent research.

"Yes," replied my daughter. After a pause, Miriam asked: "Are you Hispanic?" and my daughter replied "No." After a much longer pause came Miriam's inevitable question: "Am I Hispanic?" "That's a difficult question, isn't it?" replied my daughter. Miriam was learning about the complicated way in which Americans today divide up the world, and in the process she was reconstructing her own social identity.

A second story: I grew up in a small town in the Midwest in the 1950s. Of the 150 students in my senior class, I knew the religion of virtually every one. Even now, when I have long forgotten their names, I can generally remember who was a Catholic, who was a Methodist and so on. Nor was that some personal quirk of mine, because in fact most of my classmates knew everyone else's religion. My own children, who went to high school in the 1980s, knew the religion of hardly any of their classmates. Why the difference? To solve the mystery, you need to know that over those thirty years religious endogamy (the practice of marrying only within one's faith) has largely faded in America, at least among mainline Protestants and Catholics and Jews. In the 1950s, for the most important aspect of any adolescent's life—mating—it was essential to keep track of one's peers' religious affiliations. By the 1980s, religion was hardly more important than left- or right-handedness to romance. Very few of us keep track of the handedness of other people because it seldom matters to our social interactions. People know whether they themselves are left- or right-handed, but it is not an important badge of social identity. Similarly, though most Americans know their own religious affiliation, for younger Americans that affiliation is less salient socially.

In that sense, Americans have more or less deconstructed religion as a salient line of social division over the last half century, even though religion itself remains personally important. In fact, our own survey evidence suggests that for most Americans their religious identity is actually more important to them than their ethnic identity, but the salience of religious differences as lines of social identity has sharply diminished. As our religious identities have become more permeable, we have gained much religiously bridging social capital, while not forsaking our own religious loyalties. To be sure, deconstructing divisive racial and ethnic identities will not be so quick and simple, but an extraordinary achievement of human civilization is our ability to redraw social lines in ways that transcend ancestry. It is my hypothesis that a society will more easily reap the benefits of immigration, and overcome the challenges, if immigration policy focuses on the reconstruction of ethnic identities, reducing their social salience without eliminating their personal importance. In particular, it seems important to encourage permeable, syncretic, "hyphenated" identities; identities that enable previously separate ethnic groups to see themselves, in part, as members of a shared group with a shared identity.[39]

---

39 My approach here is akin to the "post-ethnic" perspective offered by Hollinger (2000). For a useful overview of this process, see Foner and Alba (2006).

To illustrate that this is not a purely platitudinous prescription, let me mention briefly some historical success stories from my own country. First, the United States Army today has become a relatively colour-blind institution. Systematic surveys have shown that the average American soldier has many closer inter-racial friendships than the average American civilian of the same age and social class (United States Department of Defense 1997; Moskos & Butler 1996). Yet barely thirty years ago the Army was *not* a race-relations success story. During the Vietnam War, one heard frequently of inter-racial "fragging"—that is, deadly attacks with fragmentation hand grenades among soldiers of different races. We need to learn more details about this case, but even this brief sketch suggests that something that the Army has actually *done* during the last thirty years has had the effect of reconstructing social identities and increasing social solidarity even in the presence of ethnic diversity. Strict enforcement of anti-discrimination and anti-defamation policies is a key part of the story, but I suspect that a new emphasis on shared identities that cross racial lines may also have been important.

A second example is equally striking. Historically, Americans worshipped in such complete racial segregation that it was proverbial among sociologists of religion that "11:00 am Sunday is the most segregated hour in the week." In recent years, however, many churches, especially evangelical megachurches, have become substantially more integrated in racial terms. During ongoing research on the changing role of religion, my colleagues and I have attended numerous services over the last several years in churches across America. In many large evangelical congregations, the participants constituted the largest thoroughly integrated gatherings we have ever witnessed. It remains true that most church-goers in America (53 percent) report that all or almost all of the people in their congregation are of the same race. However, younger people and those who attend evangelical megachurches (and Catholic parishes) report significantly more racial integration.[40] It seems likely that this undoing of past segregation is due, at least in part, to the construction of religiously based identities that cut across (while not effacing) conventional racial identities.

A last example is historically more complicated, but ultimately more relevant to our contemporary interests. A century ago America also experienced a large, sustained wave of immigration that massively increased our ethnic diversity in traditional terms, with the arrival of millions of immigrants of different "races"—a term that then referred to the Italian and Polish Catholics, Russian Jews and others who were swarming into a previously White Anglo Saxon Protestant (WASP)-dominated society. Though I have not found any comparable survey evidence for that period, my strong suspicion is that that period also witnessed a good deal of hunkering,

---

40 I shall provide detailed evidence on racial integration in American churches in a forthcoming book on the changing role of religion in American society. The quantitative evidence I report here is drawn from a national survey on religion and civic life conducted in 2006 among 3,000 Americans.

even within the immigrant communities. Yet fifty years later, the grandchildren of the WASPs and of the immigrants were comfortable in one another's presence.

The best quantitative evidence concerns ethnic endogamy. At the turn of the last century in-marriage was "castelike for new ethnics from east and southern Europe," whereas by 1990 only "one-fifth [of white Americans] have spouses with identical [ethnic] backgrounds."[41] Conversely, the cultures of the immigrant groups permeated the broader American cultural framework, with the Americanization of St Patrick's Day, pizza and "Jewish" humour. In some ways "they" became like "us," and in some ways our new "us" incorporated "them." This was no simple, inevitable, friction-less "straight-line" assimilation, but over several generations the initial ethnic differences became muted and less salient so that assimilation became the master trend for these immigrant groups during the twentieth century.[42]

Recounting exactly how that happened would require another article longer than this one. Such an essay would not tout the American experience in the twentieth century as an undiluted triumph, but America has been, as the historian David Hollinger (2000, 208) argues, "a formidable engine of ethno-racial change."[43] "American identity," observes Charles Hirschman, "is rooted not in nationhood but rather in the welcoming of strangers," as embodied in the Statue of Liberty (Hirschman 2005, 595).

That longer article would also have to address the complicated racial dynamics raised by so-called "whiteness studies," or in the words of one leading scholar: "how America's immigrants became white."[44] This accommodation of the immigrants is sometimes said to have coincided with increased prejudice and discrimination against African-Americans, but was that link causally necessary or merely coincidental? Such an article would need to address the question of how the pace of assimilation was affected, if at all, by the long pause in American immigration between 1924 and 1964. It would explore the intriguing and unexpected history of American flag worship and the Pledge of Allegiance, a civic practice that was sought by (among other groups) American socialists as a way to symbolize that embracing American ideals ("one nation indivisible with liberty and justice for all") made you a perfectly good American even if you were not a WASP (Ellis 2005). Such an article would explore the effects of "Americanization" in public schools, as well as the transition in American nationalism during the 1930s and 1940s from "ethnic nationalism" to "civic nationalism" (Mirel 2002). It would reckon with the effects of the Second

---

41 Paginini and Morgan (1990) and Alba (1995), both as cited in Smith and Edmonston (1997, 369).

42 On this assimilation process, see Gordon (1964); Hirschman (2005); Lieberson (1980); Alba and Nee (2003).

43 Greeley (1976) described the integration of white ethnics into the changing American mix over the first half of the twentieth century as an "ethnic miracle".

44 See Roediger (1991, 2005); King (2000); Ignatiev (1996); Jacobson (1998). A useful review of the whiteness studies is McDermott and Samson (2005). Critical responses include Arnesen (2001); Kolchin (2002); Guglielmo (2003); and Alba and Tsao (2007).

World War on American popular culture, including the ubiquitous movie foxhole that always seemed (and not by accident) to contain a Jew from Brooklyn, an Italian from Chicago and a Swede from North Dakota. It would explore the role played by political parties and religious institutions, especially the Catholic Church. It would grapple with the divergent meanings of assimilation, and the fact that Americans today are far more comfortable than Europeans with hyphens (Alba & Nee 2003; Alba 2005). It would weigh potential differences between the twentieth- and twenty-first-century waves of immigration, such as the possibly more visible distinctiveness of contemporary migrants, the structural economic differences, the increase of transnational ties, and the ideological and policy differences (such as affirmative action) between the two eras.

And most fundamentally and most controversially, that longer historical analysis would need to re-open one of the questions that I earlier set aside: To what extent are the two different forms of diversity in America today (i.e., that involving recent immigrants and that involving African-Americans) really analogous? I have argued that the *effects* of these two forms of diversity on social capital seem largely similar in contemporary America. The historical *origins* of the two forms are, however, obviously different, and that might well mean that the most effective public responses to the underlying issues must also be different.

Some tough research questions have been raised by my analysis that I have not yet answered. We need to learn more about the many possible mechanisms—from physiological to political—that link diversity and hunkering. We need to chart the conditions under which this linkage is strong, weak, or even non-existent. Is it equally true in all countries, for example? Even within the US, does diversity in the workplace or in church or in school have the same effects as the neighbourhood diversity I have examined in this article? We need to explore whether and when bonding and bridging social capital might be negatively related, because in such circumstances diversity could well produce a more classic in-group/out-group divide that I have *not* found in the contemporary US. We need to examine more closely the interaction between economic and ethnic diversity, asking whether diversity may have a more deleterious effect when ethnic divisions coincide more fully with economic ones. And most fundamentally, we need much more systematic research to confirm the hypotheses in this third section of my essay linking institutions, identity, and social capital.

So, this article is but a prolegomenon to a larger project on how to manage the challenge that immigration and diversity pose to social capital and solidarity. Nevertheless, my hunch is that at the end we shall see that the challenge is best met not by making "them" like "us," but rather by creating a new, more capacious sense of "we," a reconstruction of diversity that does not bleach out ethnic specificities, but creates overarching identities that ensure that those specificities do not trigger the allergic, "hunker down" reaction.[45] In this I share the view expressed by Trevor Phillips, chair of the British Commission on Equality and Human Rights, who has been quoted as saying: "We need to respect people's ethnicity but also give them, at some point in the week, an opportunity to meet and want to be with people with whom they have something in common that is not defined by their ethnicity" (Easton 2006).

My argument here is that in the short run there is a tradeoff between diversity and community, but that over time wise policies (public and private) can ameliorate that tradeoff. Even while pressing forward with research to confirm and clarify these arguments, we must also begin to ask about their implications for public policy. This is surely not the place for a comprehensive proposal for immigration reform, but a few comments may illustrate the policy directions suggested by my analysis.

Immigration policy is not just about numbers and borders. It is also about fostering a sense of shared citizenship. Whatever decisions we reach on numbers and borders, America is in the midst of renewing our historical identity as a nation of immigrants, and we must remind ourselves how to be a successful immigrant nation.

- Tolerance for difference is but a first step. To strengthen shared identities, we need more opportunities for meaningful interaction across ethnic lines where Americans (new and old) work, learn, recreate, and live. Community centers, athletic fields, and schools were among the most efficacious instruments for incorporating new immigrants a century ago, and we need to reinvest in such places and activities once again, enabling us all to become comfortable with diversity.

- Most immigrants want to acculturate—to learn English, for example. Expanding public support for English-language training, especially in settings that encourage ties among immigrants and natives of diverse ethnic backgrounds, should be a high priority.

- Since the long-run benefits of immigration and diversity are often felt at the national level (scientific creativity, fiscal dividends, and so forth), whereas the short-run costs (fragile communities, educational and health costs, for example) are often concentrated at the local level, there is a strong case for national aid to affected localities.

- Our field studies suggest that locally based programs to reach out to new immigrant communities are a powerful tool for mutual learning. Religious institutions—and in our era, as a century ago, especially the Catholic church—have a major role to play in incorporating new immigrants and then forging shared identities across ethnic boundaries. Ethnically defined social groups (such as

---

45 For a historically sophisticated account of these issues, see Hollinger (2000). My argument that the effects of diversity on social capital may be moderated by policies that transform and reinforce national identity is consistent with Miguel (2004), who finds that ethnic diversity dampens the provision of public goods in Kenya, but *not* in Tanzania, which pursued more serious nation-building policies.

the Sons of Norway or the Knights of Columbus or Jewish immigrant aid societies) were important initial steps toward immigrant civic engagement a century ago. Bonding social capital can thus be a prelude to bridging social capital, rather than precluding it. To force civic and religious groups who work with immigrants to serve as enforcement tools for immigration laws, as some have suggested, would be exceptionally counterproductive to the goal of creating an integrated nation of immigrants.

But we need to work toward bridging, as well as bonding. Senator Barack Obama, whose life story embodies ties between immigrant and native-born America, has called for

> ...an America where race is understood in the same way that the ethnic diversity of the white population is understood. People take pride in being Irish-American and Italian-American. They have a particular culture that infuses the (whole) culture and makes it richer and more interesting. But it's not something that determines people's life chances and there is no sense of superiority or inferiority.... [I]f we can expand that attitude to embrace African-Americans and Latino-Americans and Asian-Americans, then...all our kids can feel comfortable with the worlds they are coming out of, knowing they are part of something larger. (Obama 2007)

Scientific examination of immigration, diversity and social cohesion easily could be inflamed as the results of research become part of the contemporary political debate, but that debate needs to be informed by our best efforts to ascertain the facts. It would be unfortunate if a politically correct progressivism were to deny the reality of the challenge to social solidarity posed by diversity. It would be equally unfortunate if an ahistorical and ethnocentric conservatism were to deny that addressing that challenge is both feasible and desirable. Max Weber instructed would-be political leaders nearly a century ago that "Politics is a slow boring of hard boards." The task of becoming comfortable with diversity will not be easy or quick, but it will be speeded by our collective efforts and in the end well worth the effort. One great achievement of human civilization is our ability to redraw more inclusive lines of social identity. The motto on the Great Seal of the United States (and on our dollar bill) and the title of this essay—*e pluribus unum*—reflects precisely that objective—namely to create a novel "one" out of a diverse "many."

Acknowledgements

The roster of colleagues who have made important contributions to this project is too long to list here, but crucial roles have been played by Tom Sander, Chris Achen, Mahzarin Banaji, Amy Bates, Mark Beissinger, Josh Bolian, Xavier de Souza Briggs,

Tami Buhr, Karena Cronin, Ben Deufel, John DiIulio, Sarah Dryden-Peterson, Lew
Feldstein, Shaylyn Romney Garrett, Marty Gilens, Dan Hopkins, Darby Jack, Louise
Kennedy, Andrew Leigh, Chaeyoon Lim, Gabriel Loiacono, Sean McGraw, Byron
Miller, Matt Pehl, Lara Putnam, Pedro Ramos-Pinto, Steve Resch, Nate Schwartz,
Thomas Soehl, Anant Thaker, Van Tran, Jessica Wellburn, Abby Williamson and
Catherine Wreyford. I am also grateful for the generous support of the Carnegie
Corporation, the Ford Foundation, the William and Flora Hewlett Foundation, the
Lilly Endowment, the Rockefeller Brothers Fund, the Rockefeller Foundation and
more than three dozen community foundations that funded the 2000 Social Capital
Community Benchmark Survey.

References

Alba, R. 1995. "Assimilation's Quiet Tide," *The Public Interest* 119, 1–18.

Alba, R. 2005. "Bright vs Blurred Boundaries: Second-generation Assimilation and
Exclusion in France, Germany and the United States," *Ethnic and Racial Studies*
28, 20–49.

Alba, R. & Nee, V. 2003. *Remaking the American Mainstream: Assimilation and Contemporary Immigration*. Cambridge, MA: Harvard UP.

Alba, R. & Tsao, H-S. 2007. "Connecting Past, Present and Future: Reflections on
Immigration and the Possibilities for Racial and Ethnic Change in the US,"
unpublished, Albany, SUNY.

Alesina, A., Baqir, R. & Easterly, W. 1999. "Public Goods and Ethnic Divisions,"
Quarterly Journal of Economics 114, 1243–84.

Alesina, A. & La Ferrara, E. 2000. "Participation in Heterogeneous Communities,"
Quarterly Journal of Economics 115, 847–904.

Alesina, A. & La Ferrara, E. 2002. "Who Trusts Others?" *Journal of Public Economics* 85, 207–34.

Alesina, A. & La Ferrara, E. 2005. "Ethnic Diversity and Economic Performance,"
Journal of Economic Literature 43, 762–800.

Allport, G. 1954. *The Nature of Prejudice*. Reading, MA: Addison-Wesley.

Anderson, C.J. & Paskeviciute, A. 2006. "How Ethnic and Linguistic Heterogeneity
Influence the Prospects for Civil Society: A Comparative Study of Citizenship
Behavior," *Journal of Politics* 68, 783–802.

Arnesen, E. 2001. "Whiteness and the Historians' Imagination," *International Labor
and Working-class History* 60, 3–32.

Berkman, L.F. 1995. "The Role of Social Relations in Health Promotion," *Psychoso-
matic Medicine* 57, 245–54.

Berkman, L.F. & Glass, T. 2000. "Social Integration, Social Networks, Social Support and Health," in Berkman, L.F. & Kawachi, I., eds., *Social Epidemiology*. New
York: Oxford UP.

Blalock, H.M., Jr. 1967. *Toward a Theory of Minority-group Relations*. New York: John Wiley & Sons.

Blanchflower, D.G. & Oswald, A.J. 2004. "Well-being Over Time in Britain and the USA," *Journal of Public Economics* 88, 1359–86.

Blumer, H. 1958. "Race Prejudice as a Sense of Group Position," *Pacific Sociological Review* 1, 3–7.

Bobo, L.D. 1999. "Prejudice as Group Position: Microfoundations of a Sociological Approach to Racism and Race Relations," *Journal of Social Issues* 55, 445–72.

Bobo, L.D. & Tuan, M. 2006. *Prejudice in Politics: Group Position, Public Opinion and the Wisconsin Treaty Rights Dispute*. Cambridge, MA: Harvard UP.

Borjas, G.J. 1987. "Immigrants, Minorities and Labor Market Competition," *Industrial and Labor Relations Review* 40, 382–92.

Borjas, G.J. 2003. "The Labor Demand Curve Is Downward Sloping: Reexamining the Impact of Immigration on the Labor Market," *Quarterly Journal of Economics* 118, 1335–74.

Borjas, G.J. 2005. *Native Internal Migration and the Labor Market Impact of Immigration*. NBER Working Paper 11610. Cambridge, MA: National Bureau of Economic Research.

Borjas, G.J. & Aydemir, A. 2006. *A Comparative Analysis of the Labor Market Impact of International Migration: Canada, Mexico and the United States*. NBER Working Paper 12327. Cambridge, MA: National Bureau of Economic Research.

Borjas, G.J., Freeman, R.B. & Katz, L.F. 1992. "On the Labor Market Effects of Immigration and Trade," in Borjas, G.J. & Freeman, R.B., eds., *Immigration and the Work Force: Economic Consequences for the United States and Source Areas*. Chicago: U of Chicago P.

Borjas, G.J., Freeman, R.B. & Katz, L.F. 1996. "Searching for the Effect of Immigration on the Labor Market," *American Economic Review* 86, 246–51.

Bouckaert, J. & Dhaene, G. 2004. "Inter-ethnic Trust and Reciprocity: Results of an Experiment with Small Businessmen," *European Journal of Political Economy* 20, 869–86.

Brewer, M. 1999. "The Psychology of Prejudice: Ingroup Love or Outgroup Hate," *Journal of Social Issues* 55, 429–44.

Brewer, M.B. & Brown, R.J. 1998. "Intergroup Relations," in Gilbert, D.T., Fiske, S.T. & Lindzey, G., eds., *Handbook of Social Psychology*, 4th ed. New York: Oxford UP.

Burt, R.S. 1992. *Structural Holes: The Social Structure of Competition*. Cambridge, MA: Harvard University Press.

Burt, R.S. 1997. "The Contingent Value of Social Capital," *Administrative Science Quarterly* 42, 339–65.

Butcher, K.F. & Card, D. 1991. "Immigration and Wages: Evidence from the 1980s," *American Economic Review* 81, 292–96.

Campbell, D.E. 2006. *Why We Vote: How Schools and Communities Shape Our Civic Life*. Princeton, NJ: Princeton UP.

Card, D. 1990. "The Impact of the Mariel Boatlift on the Miami Labor Market," *Industrial and Labor Relations Review* 43, 245–57.

Card, D. 2001. "Immigrant Inflows, Native Outflows and the Local Labor Market Impacts of Higher Immigration," *Journal of Labor Economics* 19, 22–64.

Card, D. 2005. *Is the New Immigration Really So Bad?* NBER Working Paper 11547. Cambridge, MA: National Bureau of Economic Research.

Card, D. & DiNardo, J. 2000. "Do Immigrant Inflows Lead to Native Outflows?," *American Economic Review* 90, 360–67.

Charles, K. & Kline, P. 2002. *Relational Costs and the Production of Social Capital: Evidence from Carpooling*. NBER Working Paper 9041. Cambridge, MA: National Bureau of Economic Research.

Cohen, S.G. & Bailey, D.E. 1997. "What Makes Teams Work: Group Effectiveness Research from the Shop Floor to the Executive Suite," *Journal of Management* 23, 239–90.

Costa, D.L. & Kahn, M.E. 2003a. "Cowards and Heroes: Group Loyalty in the American Civil War," *Quarterly Journal of Economics* 118, 519–48.

Costa, D.L. & Kahn, M.E. 2003b. "Civic Engagement and Community Heterogeneity: An Economist's Perspective," *Perspectives on Politics* 1, 103–11.

Diener, E. 2000. "Subjective Well-being: The Science of Happiness and a Proposal for a National Index," *American Psychologist* 55, 34–43.

Dixon, J., Durrheim, K. & Tredoux, C. 2005. "Beyond the Optimal Contact Strategy: A Reality Check for the Contact Hypothesis," *American Psychologist* 60, 697–711.

Dovidio, J.R., Gaertner, S.L. & Kawakami, K. 2003. "Intergroup Contact: The Past, Present and the Future," *Group Processes & Intergroup Relations* 6, 5–21.

Easton, M. 2006. "Does Diversity Make Us Unhappy?" *BBC News*, 26 June. Interview of Trevor Phillips for the BBC's *The Happiness Formula*.

Eckel, C. & Grossman, P. 2001. "Chivalry and Solidarity in Ultimatum Games," *Economic Inquiry* 39, 171–88.

Ellis, R.J. 2005. *To the Flag: The Unlikely History of the Pledge of Allegiance*. Lawrence: UP of Kansas.

Engerman, S.L. & Jones, R.W. 1997. "International Labor Flows and National Wages," *American Economic Review* 87, 200–04.

Fershtman, C. & Gneezy, U. 2001. "Discrimination in a Segmented Society: An Experimental Approach," *Quarterly Journal of Economics* 116, 351–77.

Foner, N. & Alba, R. 2006. "The Second Generation from the Last Great Wave of Immigration: Setting the Record Straight." *Migration Information Source*. http://www.migrationinformation.org/feature/display.cfm?ID=439.

Friedberg, R.M. & Hunt, J. 1995. "The Impact of Immigrants on Host Country Wages, Employment and Growth," *Journal of Economic Perspectives* 9, 23–45.

García-Montalvo, J. & Reynal-Querol, M. 2005. "Ethnic Diversity and Economic Development," *Journal of Development Economics* 76, 293–323.

Gelman, A. & Hill, J. 2007. *Data Analysis Using Regression and Multilevel/Hierarchical Models*. New York: Cambridge UP.

Giles, M.W. & Evans, A. 1986. "The Power Approach to Intergroup Hostility," *Journal of Conflict Resolution* 30, 469–85.

Gil-White, F. 2004. "Ultimatum Game with an Ethnicity Manipulation: Results from Kohvdiin Bulgan Sum, Mongolia," in Henrich, J. et al., eds., *Foundations of Human Sociality: Economic Experiments and Ethnographic Evidence from Fifteen Small-scale Societies*. New York: Oxford UP.

Glaeser, E. & Alesina, A. 2004. *Fighting Poverty in the US and Europe: A World of Difference*. Oxford: Oxford UP.

Glaeser, E.L. et al. 2000. "Measuring Trust," *Quarterly Journal of Economics* 115, 811–46.

Gordon, M.M. 1964. *Assimilation in American Life: The Role of Race, Religion, and National Origins*. New York: Oxford UP.

Granovetter, M.S. 1973. "The Strength of Weak Ties," *American Journal of Sociology* 78, 1360–80.

Granovetter, M.S. 1974. *Getting a Job: A Study of Contacts and Careers*. Cambridge, MA: Harvard UP.

Greeley, A.M. 1976. *Ethnicity, Denomination and Inequality*. Beverly Hills, CA: Sage.

Groves, R.M. 2006. "Nonresponse Rates and Nonresponse Bias in Household Surveys," *Public Opinion Quarterly* 70, 646–75.

Guglielmo, T.A. 2003. *White on Arrival: Race, Color and Power in Chicago, 1890–1945*. New York: Oxford UP.

Habyarimana, J.P. et al. 2006. *Why Does Ethnic Diversity Undermine Public Goods Provision? An Experimental Approach*. IZA Discussion Paper 2272. Bonn: Institute for the Study of Labor.

Helliwell, J.F. 2006. "Well-being, Social Capital and Public Policy: What's New?" *Economic Journal* 116, C34–C45.

Helliwell, J.F. & Putnam, R.D. 2004. "The Social Context of Well-being," *Philosophical Transactions of the Royal Society B: Biological Studies* 359, 1435–46. Reprinted in Huppert, F.A., Kaverne, B. & Baylis, N., eds. 2005. *The Science of Well-being*. London: Oxford UP.

Hirschman, C. 2005. "Immigration and the American Century," *Demography* 42, 595–620.

Hollinger, D. 2000. *Postethnic America: Beyond Multiculturalism*. New York: Basic Books.

Hooghe, M. et al. 2006. "Ethnic Diversity, Trust and Ethnocentrism and Europe: A Multilevel Analysis of 21 European Countries." Unpublished paper presented at American Political Science Association Annual Meeting.

House, J.S., Landis, K.R. & Umberson, D. 1988. "Social Relationships and Health," *Science* 241, 540–45.

Ignatiev, N. 1996. *How the Irish Became White*. New York: Routledge.

Jackson, S. et al. 1991. "Some Differences Make a Difference: Individual Dissimilarity and Group Heterogeneity as Correlates of Recruitment, Promotions and Turnover," *Journal of Applied Psychology* 76, 675–89.

Jacobson, M.F. 1998. *Whiteness of a Different Color: European Immigrants and the Alchemy of Race*. Cambridge, MA: Harvard UP.

Johansson-Stenman, O., Martinsson, P. & Mahmud, M. 2005. *Trust, Trust Games and Stated Trust: Evidence from Rural Bangladesh*. Working Paper 166. Goteborg: Goteborg University.

Jordahl, H. & Gustavsson, M. 2006. *Inequality and Trust in Sweden: Some Inequalities Are More Harmful Than Others*. Ratio Working Paper 106. Stockholm: Ratio.

Kahneman, D., Diener, E. & Schwarz, N., eds. 1999. *Well-being: The Foundations of Hedonic Psychology*. New York: Russell Sage.

Karlan, D. 2002. "Social Capital and Group Banking." Unpublished manuscript, Massachusetts Institute of Technology.

Keller, R.T. 2001. "Cross-functional Project Groups in Research and New Product Development: Diversity, Communications, Job Stress and Outcomes," *Academy of Management Journal* 44, 547–55.

Khwaja, A.I. 2006. "Can Good Projects Succeed in Bad Communities?" Harvard University, Kennedy School of Government Working Papers. http://ksghome. harvard.edu/~akhwaja/papers/BaltNov06.pdf.

King, D. 2000. *Making Americans: Immigration, Race and the Origins of the Diverse Democracy*. Cambridge, MA: Harvard UP.

Kolchin, P. 2002 "Whiteness Studies: The New History of Race in America," *Journal of American History* 89, 154–73.

Kramer, R. 2006. "Social Identity and Social Capital: The Collective Self at Work," *International Journal of Public Management* 9, 25–45.

Layard, P.R.G. 2005. *Happiness: Lessons from a New Science*. New York: Penguin.

Leigh, A. 2006. "Trust, Inequality and Ethnic Heterogeneity," *Economic Record* 82, 268–80.

Lerner, J. & Roy, R. 1984. "Numbers, Origins, Economic Value and Quality of Technically Trained Immigrants into the United States," *Scientometrics* 6, 243–59.

Letki, N. forthcoming. "Does Diversity Erode Social Cohesion? Social Capital and Race in British Neighbourhoods," *Political Studies*.

Lieberson, S. 1980. *A Piece of the Pie: Blacks and White Immigrants Since 1880*. Berkeley: U of California P.

Lin, N. 1999. "Social Networks and Status Attainment," *Annual Review of Sociology* 25, 467–87.

Lin, N. 2001. *Social Capital: A Theory of Social Structure and Action*. New York: Cambridge UP.

Mael, F. & Ashforth, B.E. 1992. "Alumni and Their Alma Mater: A Partial Test of the Reformulated Model of Organizational Identification," *Journal of Organizational Behavior* 13, 103–23.

McDermott, M. & Samson, F.L. 2005. "White Racial and Ethnic Identity in the United States," *Annual Review of Sociology* 31, 245–61.

McPherson, M., Smith-Lovin, L. & Cook, J.M. 2001. "Birds of a Feather: Homophily in Social Networks," *Annual Review of Sociology* 27, 415–44.

Miguel, E. 2004. "Tribe or Nation? Nation Building and Public Goods in Kenya versus Tanzania," *World Politics* 56, 327–62.

Miguel, E. & Gugerty, M.K. 2005. "Ethnic Diversity, Social Sanctions and Public Goods in Kenya," *Journal of Public Economics* 89, 2325–68.

Milgram, S. 1970. "The Experience of Living in Cities," *Science* 167, 1461–68.

Mirel, J. 2002. "Civic Education and Changing Definitions of American Identity, 1900–1950," *Educational Review* 54, 143–52.

Moskos, C.C. & Butler, J.S. 1996. *All That We Can Be: Black Leadership and Racial Integration the Army Way*. New York: Basic Books.

Myers, D.G. & Diener, E. 1995. "Who Is Happy?" *Psychological Science* 6, 10–19.

Newton, K. & Delhey, J. 2005. "Predicting Cross-national Levels of Social Trust: Global Pattern or Nordic Exceptionalism?," *European Sociological Review* 21, 311–27.

Obama, B. 2007. "I Have the Potential of Bringing People Together." *Politico* 8 February. <http://www.politico.com/news/stories/0207/2689.html>.

O'Reilly, C., Williams, R.K. & Barsage, S. 1997. "Group Demography and Innovation: Does Diversity Help?," in Mannix, E. & Neale, M., eds., *Research in the Management of Groups and Teams, vol. 1*. Greenwich, CT: JAI Press.

Ottaviano, G.I.P. & Peri, G. 2006a. "The Economic Value of Cultural Diversity: Evidence from US Cities," *Journal of Economic Geography* 6, 9–44.

Ottaviano, G.I.P. & Peri, G. 2006b. *Rethinking the Effects of Immigration on Wages*. NBER Working Paper 12497. Cambridge, MA: National Bureau of Economic Research.

Page, S. 2007. *The Difference: How the Power of Diversity Creates Better Groups, Firms, Schools and Societies*. Princeton, NJ: Princeton UP.

Paginini, D.L. & Morgan, S.P. 1990. "Intermarriage and Social Distance among US Immigrants at the Turn of the Century," *American Journal of Sociology* 96, 405–32.

Pennant, R. 2005. *Diversity, Trust and Community Participation in England*. Home Office Findings 253, Research, Development and Statistics Directorate. <http://www.blink.org.uk/docs/ho_findings_diversity_trust.pdf>.

Pettigrew, T.F. 1998. "Intergroup Contact Theory," *Annual Review of Psychology* 49, 68–85.

Pettigrew, T.F. & Tropp, L.R. 2000. "Does Intergroup Contact Reduce Prejudice? Recent Meta-analytic Findings," in Oskamp, S., ed., *Reducing Prejudice and Discrimination*. Mahwah, NJ: Lawrence Erlbaum Associates.

Pettigrew, T.F. & Tropp, L.R. 2006. "A Meta-analytic Test of Intergroup Contact Theory," *Journal of Personality and Social Psychology* 90, 751–83.

Poterba, J.M. 1997. "Demographic Structure and the Political Economy of Public Education," *Journal of Policy Analysis and Management* 16, 48–66.

Powdthavee, N. 2006. "Putting a Price Tag on Friends, Relatives and Neighbours: Using Surveys of Life Satisfaction to Value Social Relationships." Unpublished manuscript, Institute of Education, University of London.

Pritchett, L. 2006. *Let Their People Come: Breaking the Gridlock on International Labor Mobility.* Washington, DC: Center for Global Development.

Putnam, R.D. 2000. *Bowling Alone: The Collapse and Revival of American Community.* New York: Simon & Schuster.

Quillian, L. 1995. "Prejudice as a Response to Perceived Group Threat: Population Composition and Anti-immigrant and Racial Prejudice in Europe," *American Sociological Review* 60, 586–611.

Quillian, L. 1996. "Group Threat and Regional Change in Attitudes towards African Americans," *American Journal of Sociology* 102, 816–60.

Raudenbush, S.W. & Bryk, A.S. 2002. *Hierarchical Linear Models: Applications and Data Analysis Methods.* Thousand Oaks, CA: Sage.

Roediger, D.R. 1991. *The Wages of Whiteness: Race and the Making of the American Working Class.* London: Verso.

Roediger, D.R. 2005. *Working Toward Whiteness: How American Immigrants Became White.* New York: Basic Books.

Rupasingha, A., Goetz, S.J. & Freshwater, D. 2006. "The Production of Social Capital in US Counties," *Journal of Socio-Economics* 35, 83–101.

Sampson, R.J. 2001. "Crime and Public Safety: Insights from Community-level Perspectives on Social Capital," in Saegert, S., Thompson, J.P. & Warren, M.R., eds., *Social Capital and Poor Communities.* New York: Russell Sage.

Sampson, R.J., Raudenbush, S.W. & Earls, F. 1997. "Neighbourhoods and Violent Crime: A Multilevel Study of Collective Efficacy," *Science* 277, 918–24.

Schuck, P. 2003. *Diversity in America.* Cambridge, MA: Belknap.

Seeman, T.E. 1996. "Social Ties and Health: The Benefits of Social Integration," *Annals of Epidemiology* 6, 442–51.

Sigelman, L. & Welch, S. 1993. "The Contact Hypothesis Revisited: Black-White Interaction and Positive Racial Attitudes," *Social Forces* 71, 781–95.

Simonton, D.K. 1999. *Origins of Genius.* New York: Oxford UP.

Singer, J.D. 1998. "Using SAS PROC MIXED to Fit Multilevel Models, Hierarchical Models and Individual Growth Models," *Journal of Educational and Behavioral Statistics* 24, 323–55.

Smith, J.P. & Edmonston, B., eds. 1997. *The New Americans: Economic, Demographic and Fiscal Effects of Immigration.* Washington, DC: National Academy Press.

Soroka, S.N., Helliwell, J.F. & Johnston, R. 2007. "Measuring and Modeling Inter-personal Trust," in Kay, F.M. & Johnston, R., eds., *Social Capital, Diversity and the Welfare State*. Vancouver: UBC P.

Stein, R.M., Post, S.S. & Rinden, A.L. 2000. "Reconciling Context and Contact Effects on Racial Attitudes," *Political Research Quarterly* 53, 285–303.

Stouffer, S. 1949. *American Soldier*. Princeton, NJ: Princeton UP.

Taylor, M. 1998. "Local Racial/Ethnic Proportions and White Attitudes: Numbers Count," *American Sociological Review* 63, 512–35.

Tropp, L.R. & Pettigrew, T.F. 2005a. "Differential Relationships between Intergroup Contact and Affective and Cognitive Dimensions of Prejudice," *Personality and Social Psychology Bulletin* 31, 1145–58.

Tropp, L.R. & Pettigrew, T.F. 2005b. "Relationships between Intergroup Contact and Prejudice among Minority and Majority Status Groups," *Psychological Science* 16, 951–57.

Tyack, D. 2001. "School for Citizens: The Politics of Civic Education from 1790 to 1990," in Gerstle, G. & Mollenkopf, J. eds., *E Pluribus Unum? Contemporary and Historical Perspectives on Immigrant Political Incorporation*. New York: Russell Sage Foundation.

United States Department of Defense. 1997. *Armed Forces Equal Opportunity Survey*. Available online at: http://www.dod.mil/prhome/docs/r97_027.pdf.

Vigdor, J.L. 2004. "Community Composition and Collective Action: Analyzing Initial Mail Response to the 2000 Census," *Review of Economics and Statistics* 86, 303–12.

Webber, S.S. & Donahue, L.M. 2001. "Impact of Highly and Less Job-related Diversity on Work Group Cohesion and Performance: A Meta-analysis," *Journal of Management* 27, 141–62.

Williams, K.Y. & O'Reilly, C.A. 1998. "Demography and Diversity in Organizations: A Review of 40 Years of Research," in Staw, B.M. & Cummings, L.L., eds., *Research in Organizational Behavior, vol. 20*. Greenwich, CT: JAI Press.

Willinger, M. et al. 2003. "A Comparison of Trust and Reciprocity Between France and Germany: Experimental Investigation Based on the Investment Game," *Journal of Economic Psychology* 24, 447–66.

World Bank. 2005. *Global Economic Prospects: Economic Implications of Remittances and Migration*. Washington, DC: World Bank.

46. The Political Manipulation of Ethnicity in Africa[*]

Alexis Rawlinson

The new civil war in Côte d'Ivoire, more than just a rebellion by demobilised soldiers, is the latest manifestation of politicised inter-ethnic rivalries that are present throughout the African continent south of the Sahara. Indeed, ethnic mobilisation has been the main source of conflict in sub-Saharan Africa since independence (from 1957 onwards) and one of the major barriers to human and economic development in African societies. This essay seeks to explain why and how the ethnic dimension of society in Africa has been so prominent and so conflictive. The generalisations that are put forward about "Africa" are of course to be handled with care, as they cannot hope to take account of the wide variety of particular contexts and individual situations in such a large continent and over a long time period: the ambition here is only to provide a general model for understanding the core mechanisms at play. The key idea is that what often seems a bewildering primordial and uncontrollable source of instability, "tribalism," is in fact more a political contest, led and managed by elites, for influence in the state and control of its resources—"who gets what, when, how," as Harold Lasswell puts it. This instrumental use of ethnicity dominates political contestation at the expense of other cleavages, and it undermines efforts at nation-building; since it is largely an artificial construct, this "tribalism" may be reduced through responsible conduct by elites.

★ ★ ★

Competition for control of the state has been dominated by issues of ethnicity at the expense of class cleavages and other issues.

In Africa, the main criterion according to which socio-political groups define and identify themselves is rooted in ethnicity rather than in class. It is through ethnic

---

[*] Source: <http://www.scribd.com/doc/6512059/Rawlinson-The-political-manipulation-of-eth-nicity-in-Africa>.

identification that competition for influence in the state and in the allocation of resources takes place, instead of it being a contest between the "haves" and the "have nots" as in most Western societies. While ethnic tension usually results from the perception of inequitable access to resources among groups and the fear of marginalisation from power (as demonstrated in Nigeria, for example, by the mutual distrust between the Igbo and other groups that led to the 1967–70 Biafran civil war and by the sectarian clashes between Hausas and Tivs in Nasawara state in 2001), in reality disparities in access to resources and policy influence are generally far more pronounced within ethnic communities than across them. The "big men" of every group lead a lifestyle very far removed from the vast majority of their followers, whose support for their community leaders is conditional on favours and special advantages bestowed on them through client-patron relationships.

This system is replicated at every level, forming a dense trickle-down network of patronage sustained by channelling the state's revenues to one's own group through pork barrelling, rent-seeking and corruption. When access to resources and power is not monopolised by one dominant group but shared out equitably between competing ethnic groups, as epitomised by the ethnic balancing acts of presidents Jomo Kenyatta in Kenya (1963–78) and Félix Houphouët-Boigny in Côte d'Ivoire (1960–93), the system is politically stable and socially cohesive within the self-identifying ethnic communities, though economically inefficient and ultimately unsustainable. Donald Rothchild identifies such relationships between state and ethnic groups as situations of "hegemonial exchange." He argues that "as an ideal type, hegemonial exchange is a form of state-facilitated co-ordination in which a somewhat autonomous central state and a number of considerably less autonomous ethnoregional (and other) interests engage in a process of mutual accommodation on the basis of commonly accepted procedural norms, rules, or understandings."

Unfortunately, all too often the temptation not to abide by the unwritten rules is too strong: sectarian leaders use numerical or strategic advantages to favour their own support base, upsetting the delicate balance and fomenting conflict. This has been particularly tempting in cases where full-blown racial differences have been evident, such as with Idi Amin's expulsion of the wealthy Asian merchant class from Uganda in 1972 or Robert Mugabe's expropriation of white farmers' land in Zimbabwe in 2001–02. In other cases, such as in Côte d'Ivoire from 1994 or in Zambia in 1995, the concept of nationality has been manipulated to exclude a proportion of the citizens (and in particular popular leaders such as Alassane Ouattara and Kenneth Kaunda) from a share in decision-making. In yet more cases, such as throughout Daniel arap Moi's rule in Kenya (1978–2003), or Mobutu Sese Seko's reign in Zaire (1965–97), ethnic groups have deliberately been played against each other to prevent the emergence of a broad, unified opposition movement likely to challenge for overall power. In states where certain ethnic groupings are powerful, even dominant, national stability has been extremely precarious. The political power of the Baganda in Uganda has traditionally far exceeded that of any other ethnic grouping, and was reflected in the special status of the Baganda in the post-independence constitutional settlement. This created resentment among other groups, and three consecutive leaders, Milton Obote, Idi Amin and Tito Okello, none of them Baganda, sought to minimise the influence of the dominant "tribe," resulting in decades of repression and civil war.

It is not the case that all elites are unprincipled profiteers who purposefully exploit ethnic appeals for personal advantage and with total disregard for the wider consequences. It is enough that some are: as Sam Nolutshungu writes, "once one party opts for 'tribalism' or ethnic chauvinism, it becomes rational for any would-be rival to define and consolidate an ethnic base." Parties, and indeed whole ethnic groups, are faced with a Prisoner's Dilemma, in which, "whilst the outcome may be catastrophic for all concerned, no party can abstain from using ethnic strategies for fear of losing out to the ethnic mobilisation of an opponent." As such, issues and interests are either couched in ethnic terms or end up marginalised from the political scene.

The instrumental use of ethnic ties—"political tribalism" in John Lonsdale's language—is successful because it goes hand in hand with a strong cultural identification with the ethnic group on the part of followers—"moral ethnicity." Citizens have a deep-seated allegiance to traditional and cultural leaders—the "tribal" chiefs—who, often as a result, are also the political, social and economic elites. This link works both ways: political, social and economic leaders, conscious of the appeal of cultural ties, often portray themselves as "tribal" chiefs even when their claims are dubious, or seek the symbolic support of cultural leaders: Mangosuthu Buthelezi of the Inkatha Freedom Party in South Africa exemplifies both these trends, dressing in ostentatious chieftaincy robes to promote his chieftaincy and wheeling out the Zulu king at political rallies.

This politicisation of ethnicity is parasitic on class mobilisation. According to Sam Nolutshungu, it involves the "necessary displacement of class politics." Leroy Vail remarks that ordinary Africans are prey to a "false consciousness" due to elites' "instrumental mobilisation" of the population along ethnic lines. One might wonder if it is ever possible for individuals' consciousness of ethnic belonging to be subjectively "false"; what is certain is that, objectively, it runs against what is in their material interest, which is to undermine prebendal and clientelist politics and demand transparency, the rule of law and the delivery of efficient government services. Ordinary Africans continue to favour ethnic appeals instead of focusing on class or other interests. Tom Mboya, trade union leader and first Minister of Labour in Kenya, argued that "no class problems exist today [the 1960s] amongst Africans." This was not meant to imply that Africa was a continent of societies with no status differentiation, which was and remains obviously false, but that it was not considered a salient issue. Only in heavily industrialised or urbanised states and regions, such as in South Africa or in the Zambian copper belt, is class-based political mobilisation a significant factor.

A good example of the artificial use of ethnicity to simplify and amplify political issues revolving around status and resources is the Rwandan genocide of 1994. It was portrayed, even within Rwanda, as an act of vengeance by the Hutu "tribe" on the Tutsi "tribe" for previous domination and repression: this was a simple and, sadly, highly appealing framework for fostering violence. But such a reading of the massacre is grossly misleading. In fact, Hutus and Tutsis share their language and their culture, and by and large have the same genetic origins. What differentiates a Hutu from a Tutsi above all is his lower social status. As René Lemarchand explains, "a Tutsi cast in the role of client vis-à-vis a wealthier patron would be referred to as 'Hutu,' even though his cultural identity remained Tutsi." During the Rwandan massacre, ethnicity was used as a vehicle for creating a "minimum winning coalition" (though not in the usual democratic sense of the phrase) around issues of status and class. Large numbers of moderate and materially comfortable Hutus were also killed alongside the Tutsis: they were not quite "Hutu" enough, which is to say that their social status was too high.

★ ★★

The instrumental use of ethnicity has undermined the emergence of cohesive national identities.

As a result of the largely arbitrary colonial partition of Africa, in most independence-era African states ethnic identities have not been contiguous with national borders. For example, Nigeria contains over 250 ethnic groups, of which three, the Igbo, the Yoruba and the Hausa-Fulani, are usually regarded as the major "tribes." Strong ethnic allegiances dilute national identification, a matter not helped by the relative youth of most states.

The resulting lack of inherent legitimacy of the state has been a problem for generations of African leaders. A nation-state has fewer social cleavages, which, all other things equal, entails greater stability. The "nation," with its attendant attributes of (relative, sometimes imagined) homogeneity, unity and solidarity, is a source of great strength to the state. As a result nation-building has been identified by many post-independence African leaders as an important dimension in their development strategies. But the cohesive nation buttressed by a shared consciousness among its citizens, which Benedict Anderson defines as an "imagined community," has in general proved to be an elusive dream for those post-independence African leaders who have aspired to that ideal.

It might seem surprising that national identification has been such a weak current, and that ethnic rivalries have so dominated post-independence Africa, given that African independence movements, whether in the first wave in the 1950s or later, were largely based on nationalist appeals. On closer analysis, however, African nationalism can in most cases be shown to have been hollow. Indeed, the parallels between pre-independence nationalism and post-independence ethnic mobilisation are very strong, as both have made instrumental appeals to identity, ideology and culture which, below the surface, hide issues of access to resources and power. Recent religious tensions between Muslims and Christians in Nigeria (such as during the Miss World contest in 2003) are a further expression of this same phenomenon.

The emergence of African nationalism during the colonial era was, in most cases, the product of the small African middle classes which the colonisers had created in order to help with the administration of the colonies. Socialised in a European context (educated, clerical or professional, urban, Christian...), these men found that they could not break through the glass ceiling of racial prejudice. Frantz Fanon suggests that the middle class nationalist's dream was to "set himself up in the settler's place." A more charitable interpretation of middle-class nationalist motivation in the lead-up to independence is that, whereas it was perceived that Europeans were interested in exploiting rather than developing Africa and did not understand African ways, they, as Africans themselves, were more able and more willing to develop their state's potential and that of its people. Perhaps both interpretations contain a germ of truth.

In most cases, colonial administrations toppled fairly easily in the late 1950s and the 1960s in the face of increasing international and domestic pressure, both moral and economic, to dismantle empires. There was no need, therefore, for a mass nationalist movement to have coherent aims and be well organised prior to decolonisation: it was enough to clamour the catch-phrase "Africa for the Africans." Nationalism was as good an excuse as any to fan the flames of protest and lay a claim to resources.

The real challenge for nationalism came at the onset of independence. Once the removal of the colonial masters had been achieved, the nationalist movement lost much of its appeal. Leroy Vail remarks that "African nationalist movements, ideologically shaped by the basically negative sentiments of anti-colonialism and with little substantive philosophical content relevant to the day-to-day life of ordinary Africans living in post-colonial states, were simply unable to provide them with compelling intellectual, social, and political visions." Competition for resources was no longer with the white man: now it was with other Africans, and in this context ethnic appeals became tempting. Nationalist leaders such as Julius Nyerere in Tanzania or Léopold Senghor in Senegal attempted to keep the nationalist flame alive, but it became increasingly irrelevant. A state without a co-extensive nation must, in order to retain its legitimacy and foster a sense of belonging, produce tangible rewards for the citizen. But the huge social, economic and environmental challenges faced by African governments past and present have not favoured the distribution of sufficient rewards for the citizen. All too often, in competing for the allocation of scarce resources, regional—and national—leaders have therefore resorted to exclusionary ethnic appeals.

Ethnic mobilisation, then, has been a political instrument of the African elites in the post-independence period in much the same way that the phenomenon of nationalism was in the decolonisation years. As a result, the emergence of cohesive national identities which are essential for the implementation of cooperative development strategies has been stymied. Samora Machel, Mozambique's President between 1975 and 1986, highlighted the tensions between the different tiers of ethno-territorial allegiances in stark terms: "for the nation to live, the tribe must die." For Mahmood Mamdani, interactions between the state and the "tribes" are the key to understanding the political volatility that has plagued African politics since independence. The process of nation-building has been fraught by the artificiality of the parameters of nationality and by the failure of African governments to produce the tangible rewards required to induce African societies to accept the legitimacy of the state. Ethnicity has played a destructive role in both of these ways: it has laid competing and more intuitively appealing claims to Africans' allegiance, as compared to nationality, and the political instability it has fostered has been one of the biggest hindrances to the achievement of the potential benefits of a strong state, such as security and economic or social development.

★ ★ ★

Today's bounded and mutually antagonistic ethnic groups are largely the creation of elites and colonial masters.

As John Lonsdale's distinction between "political tribalism" and "moral ethnicity" reveals, ethnic mobilisation is not only an instrument for the control and distribution of the state's resources; it is successful because it carries a powerful emotive appeal. Differentiation through ethnicity has always existed in Africa and humans have a universal propensity to form collective identities, to distinguish outsiders from insiders, along ethnic lines. For example, some African ethnic groups in equatorial Africa willingly cooperated with the pre-colonial slave trade, capturing individuals deemed to belong to other ethnic groups and exchanging them for goods. There were, moreover, some notable pre-colonial kingdoms and nations, such as the Kongo, Zulu or Baganda, whose members had a strong collective consciousness.

Nevertheless, as has been confirmed by countless studies, in much of pre-colonial Africa ethnic identity was fluid and ill-defined, and the largest collective unit conceived of by most Africans was rather parochial, for instance at the level of the lineage group or clan. Aidan Southall notes that pre-colonial African societies were characterised by "interlocking, overlapping, multiple identities" based on ethnic, cultural and geographical communities that were smaller than any "tribe." In most cases

Africans had only a very weak allegiance, if at all, to what might now be classed as a "tribe" according to objective criteria of genetic, linguistic or cultural homogeneity within a geographical region. These objective criteria, in any case, were rarely clearly demarcated, as much of the African continent was marked by a gradual change in customs and ways of life from one village or community to the next, depending on local geographic, agricultural and climatic conditions. Indeed, the process of consolidation of dialects into a single tribal vernacular was often not begun until the arrival of Christian missionaries intent on spreading the (printed) Word. Jean-Loup Amselle goes so far as to claim that "there was nothing that resembled a bounded ethnic group during the pre-colonial period."

Far from being primordial units with defined boundaries, ethnic groups are largely a colonial legacy, which emerged as instruments for the control and distribution of people and resources. European colonists encouraged the assimilation of Africans into groups, via the creation of administrative units which were subsequently labelled in ethnic terms, as occurred in British-run Uganda, and the compulsory classification of local people according to "tribe," as occurred in Belgian-run Rwanda. In British-run Northern Rhodesia (Zambia), an astonishing catalogue of stereotypes was drawn up: the Ngoni were "strong" and "warlike," the Lamba were "lazy and indolent," and so on for the 70-odd "tribes."

Whereas pre-colonial African societies had tended to operate on the basis of limited horizons which did not require a large degree of social organisation, the efficient administration of vast swathes of colonised territory by an external coercive power required categorisation and order, rigid boundaries and parameters. As Mahmood Mamdani comments, the scarcity of colonists in most parts of Africa (though not southern Africa, or, to a lesser extent, parts of East Africa) demanded the creation of a system of "indirect rule." Colonial administrators, too stretched to sort out matters at the village level, wanted to be able to negotiate with a few "big men," the supposed traditional chiefs. These chiefs were to be responsible for the execution of colonial policy in their allocated region. Where existing ethnic communities were fragmented (i.e. in most places), these communities were amalgamated or assigned to other groups, and a single chief was chosen to represent them all. Ethnic groups such as the Yoruba in Nigeria (containing at least 12 important sub-groups within the collective "tribe"), Akan in Ghana or Xhosa in South Africa were largely artificial amalgams of linguistically similar cultural groups. Cultural symbols and ancient customs were identified, and where necessary created, to give ballast to the idea of a unitary and timeless "tribe." It was, to use Terence Ranger and Eric Hobsbawm's idea, the "invention of tradition."

Africans themselves participated in this creation of "tribes" because not to do so would exclude or marginalise them from the bargaining process for state-allocated resources. Ethnicity was promoted and defined "in the pursuit of material advantage,"

to use Crawford Young's description. Robert Bates argues that communities amalgamated not because of an emerging common ethnic consciousness but to profit
from the comparative advantages of size: the larger the "tribe," the more influence
it could wield in negotiations with the colonial administration. Ethnic elites in
particular, as the state's agents in the distribution of the resources allocated to their
"tribe," had a great deal to gain from larger ethno-regional groups, and as opinion-
leaders they were able to influence the acceptance of a tribal consciousness among
ordinary Africans. An excellent example of this process was the creation of a Tiv
"paramount chief" in central Nigeria to represent central Nigerian interests in the
face of an increasingly hegemonic tripartite structure, North (Hausa-Fulani), South-
East (Igbo) and South-West (Yoruba). Conversely, the colonial administrators and, in
those parts of Africa in which Europeans settled, neo-colonial white minority governments, manipulated ethnic rivalries as a form of "divide and rule." Long after the
end of colonial domination elsewhere, apartheid South Africa deliberately fomented
sectarianism, both within its own borders (encouraging Zulu differentiation from
the main black consciousness movement) and among its neighbours (in Angola for
example), in order to prevent the growth of African nationalist sentiment. Both
coloniser and colonised participated in defining and encouraging the emergence
of bounded and mutually antagonistic ethnic identities. J. Iliffe summarises the
situation as one in which "Europeans believed Africans belonged to tribes; Africans
built tribes to belong to."

★ ★ ★

Ethnic mobilisation may be reduced through responsible conduct by elites.
Far from being primordial and a largely uncontrollable source of instability, then,
modern ethnic sectarianism is political and, to a large degree, artificial. By encouraging a clientelist attitude towards the state, whose resources are perceived as a pie from
which each group must try to carve out as large a slice as possible, and by hampering
any efforts at cooperative nation-building, the politicisation of ethnicity is also one
of the major barriers to human and economic development in African societies.
Devising methods to discourage the political calculations that lie at the root of ethnic appeals has exercised nationalist African leaders since independence. President
Milton Obote of Uganda (1962–71, 80–85) complained that Ugandan politicians
always seemed to be playing some curious game of "Tribal Development Monopoly."

All over Africa—and the case of Milton Obote is a particularly clear example of
this—the need to pursue nationalism at the expense of this much decried "tribalism" has been expressed through authoritarianism and the one-party state, parties
being perceived as essentially ethnic associations. It also happened to be the case
that the dangers of ethnic mobilisation were a good excuse for the elimination of
political rivals. In an era in which democratisation and participation have become

key conditions of bilateral and multilateral aid, the same logic has been applied in more subtle forms. The current President of Uganda, Yoweri Museveni (1986–), has pioneered what he calls "no-party democracy" in response to the ethnic partisanship of existing political parties. In addition, in an effort to reduce citizens' identification of their interests with existing ethnic groupings, he has dismantled the old, "tribal" administrative regions and replaced them with a larger number of smaller, town-based districts. In Nigeria, similarly, opposition political parties are allowed but only if they are not associated with any ethnic claims.

More so than any institutional engineering or forcible repression, however, the responsibility for the successful elimination of ethnic manipulation rests with African elites. So long as resources are scarce, there will be tensions between groups competing for a share of them. However, these tensions need not be expressed in ethnic terms, as they overwhelmingly have been in the past, nor do they have to spill over into violence, as has occurred with depressing regularity. Although competing political leaders have repeatedly expressed their commitment to peaceful negotiation and democratic processes of decision-making, when things have not gone their way they have tended to resort to exploiting sectarian sentiment, or have felt obliged to respond to pressure from their client networks and ethnic base for a more favourable distribution by abandoning cooperative strategies at the national level. Current Ivorian President Laurent Gbagbo's use of rioting youths in Abidjan to express disagreement with an attempted compromise solution imposed by France, the former colonial power, at the Paris summit in January 2003 is a typical example of the instrumental use of ethnicity that has blighted African development efforts.

While it is difficult to persuade political leaders to eschew strategies of ethnic manipulation, there is reason to hope that it is possible for new generations of African leaders to adopt successful political strategies that avoid turning issues of status, power and access to resources into issues of ethnicity. In South Africa, Nelson Mandela purposefully avoided resorting to ethnic appeal, neither in terms of the black-white dichotomy despite the obvious injustices of the apartheid system, nor within the black majority despite the repeated provocations of the Inkatha Freedom Party. From the start of his political career, when he symbolically abandoned his royal Xhosa roots, he promoted his vision of a unified "rainbow nation." History rewarded him with 27 years in prison and a Nobel peace prize.

★ ★ ★

Real ethnic tensions exist independently of political leaders. African elites do not create mutual distrust between competing communities but merely harness it. By doing so, however, they perpetuate these tensions and make them worse. Colonial administrators encouraged artificial groupings and divisions between communities in order better to rule over them. Both before and after independence, African elites have contributed to the continuation of this system by encouraging perceptions of national politics as a zero-sum game, and by presenting issues of influence and distribution under an ethnic slant. Manipulating ethnicity for political gain is a dangerous game, however. In its half-century of independence, sub-Saharan Africa has been scarred by multiple internecine conflicts, many of which could have been wholly avoidable. Partly as a result of this, Africa begins the 21st century prey to a crisis of confidence and marginalised from the international scene and the world economy. Promoting an understanding of the roots of ethnic conflict may perhaps contribute, in a small, indirect way, to the human and economic development of the continent.

References

Amselle, Jean-Loup (1998), *Mestizo Logics: Anthropology of Identity in Africa and Elsewhere*, Stanford UP.

Anderson, Benedict (1991) [1983], *Imagined Communities: Reflections on the Origin and Spread of Nationalism*, Verso.

Bayart, Jean-François (1993), *The State in Africa: The Politics of the Belly*, Longman.

Berman, Bruce (1998), "Politics of Uncivil Nationalism: Ethnicity, Patronage and the African State," *African Affairs*, No. 97.

Fanon, Frantz (1967) [1961], *The Wretched of the Earth*, Penguin.

Freund, Bill (1998), *The Making of Contemporary Africa: The Development of African Society Since 1800*, 2nd. ed., Lynne Rienner Publishers.

Hobsbawm, Eric (1990), *Nations and Nationalism Since 1780: Programme, Myth, Reality*, Cambridge UP.

Hobsbawm, Eric & Terence Ranger, eds. (1992) [1983], *The Invention of Tradition*, Cambridge UP.

Hodgkin, Thomas (1956), *Nationalism in Colonial Africa*, Frederick Muller.

Iliffe, J. (1979), *A Modern History of Tanganyika*, Cambridge UP.

Lasswell, Harold (1990) [1936], *Politics: Who Gets What, When, How*, Peter Smith Publishers.

Lemarchand, René (1972), "Political Clientelism and Ethnicity in Tropical Africa: Competing Solidarities in Nation-Building," *American Political Science Review* 64:1.

Lonsdale, John (1994), "Moral Ethnicity and Political Tribalism," in P. Kaarsholm and J. Hultin, eds., *Inventions and Boundaries: Historical and Anthropological Approaches to the Study of Ethnicity and Nationalism*, Institute for Development Studies, Roskilde University.

Mamdani, Mahmood (1996), *Citizen and Subject: Contemporary Africa and the Legacy of Late Colonialism*, Princeton UP.

Marks, Shula & Stan Trapido, eds. (1987), *The Politics of Race, Class and Nationalism in Twentieth Century South Africa*, Longman.

Nnoli, Okwudiba, ed. (1998), *Ethnic Conflicts in Africa*, CODESRIA.

Nolutshungu, Sam (1990), "Fragments of a Democracy: Reflections on Class and Politics in Nigeria," *Third World Quarterly* 12:1.

Rothchild, Donald & Victor Olorunsola, eds. (1983), *State Versus Ethnic Claims: African Policy Dilemmas*, Westview.

Southall, Aidan (1970), "The Illusion of Tribe," *Journal of Asian and African Studies* 5:1.

Vail, Leroy, ed. (1989), *The Creation of Tribalism in Southern Africa*, U of California P.

Young, Crawford (1986), "Nationalism, Class and Ethnicity in Africa: a Retrospective," *Cahiers d'études africaines* 26:3.

47. The Uses and Abuses of Multiculturalism: Chili and Liberty*

Amartya Sen

The demand for multiculturalism is strong in the contemporary world. It is much invoked in the making of social, cultural, and political policies, particularly in Western Europe and America. This is not at all surprising, since increased global contacts and interactions, and in particular extensive migrations, have placed diverse practices of different cultures next to one another. The general acceptance of the exhortation to "Love thy neighbor" might have emerged when the neighbors led more or less the same kind of life ("Let's continue this conversation next Sunday morning when the organist takes a break"), but the same entreaty to love one's neighbors now requires people to take an interest in the very diverse living modes of proximate people. That this is not an easy task has been vividly illustrated once again by the confusion surrounding the recent Danish cartoons of the Prophet Mohammed and the fury they generated. And yet the globalized nature of the contemporary world does not allow the luxury of ignoring the difficult questions that multiculturalism raises.

One of the central issues concerns how human beings are seen. Should they be categorized in terms of inherited traditions, particularly the inherited religion, of the community in which they happen to have been born, taking that unchosen identity to have automatic priority over other affiliations involving politics, profession, class, gender, language, literature, social involvements, and many other connections? Or should they be understood as persons with many affiliations and associations, whose relative priorities they must themselves choose (taking the responsibility that comes with reasoned choice)? Also, should we assess the fairness of multiculturalism primarily by the extent to which people from different cultural backgrounds are "left alone," or by the extent to which their ability to make reasoned choices is positively supported by the social opportunities of education and participation in civil society?

---

* Source: *The New Republic*, 27 February 2006, <http://pierretristam.com/Bobst/library/wf-58.htm>.

There is no way of escaping these rather foundational questions if multiculturalism is to be fairly assessed.

In discussing the theory and the practice of multiculturalism, it is useful to pay particular attention to the British experience. Britain has been in the forefront of promoting inclusive multiculturalism, with a mixture of successes and difficulties, which are of relevance also to other countries in Europe and the United States. Britain experienced race riots in London and Liverpool in 1981, though nothing as large as what happened in France in the fall of 2005, and these led to further efforts toward integration. Things have been fairly stable and reasonably calm over the last quarter-century. The process of integration in Britain has been greatly helped by the fact that all British residents from the Commonwealth countries, from which most non-white immigrants have come to Britain, have full voting rights in Britain immediately, even without British citizenship. Integration has also been helped by largely non-discriminatory treatment of immigrants in health care, schooling, and social security. Despite all this, however, Britain has recently experienced the alienation of a group of immigrants, and also fully homegrown terrorism, when some young Muslims from immigrant families—born, educated, and reared in Britain—killed many people in London through suicide bombings in July 2005.

Discussions of British policies on multiculturalism thus have a much wider reach, and arouse much greater interest and passion, than the boundaries of the ostensible subject matter would lead one to expect. Six weeks after the July terrorist attacks in London, when *Le Monde* published a critical essay called "The British Multicultural Model in Crisis," the debate was immediately joined by a leader of another liberal establishment, James A. Goldston, director of the Open Society Justice Initiative in America, who described the *Le Monde* article as "trumpeting," and replied: "Don't use the very real threat of terrorism to justify shelving more than a quarter-century of British achievement in the field of race relations."[1] There is a general issue of some importance to be debated and evaluated here.

I will argue that the real issue is not whether "multiculturalism has gone too far" (as Goldston summarizes one of the lines of criticism), but what particular form multiculturalism should take. Is multiculturalism nothing other than tolerance of the diversity of cultures? Does it make a difference who chooses the cultural practices—whether they are imposed on young children in the name of "the culture of the community" or whether they are freely chosen by persons with adequate opportunity to learn and to reason about alternatives? What facilities do members of different communities have, in schools as well as in the society at large, to learn about the faiths and non-faiths of different people in the world, and to understand how to reason about choices that human beings must, if only implicitly, make?

---

1 James Goldston,< http://www.nytimes.com/2005/08/29/opinion/29iht-edgoldston.html> *New York Times*, 30 August 2005; the *Le Monde* article appeared on 18 August 2005.

II.

Britain, to which I first came as a student in 1953, has been particularly impressive in making room for different cultures. The distance traveled has been in many ways quite extraordinary. I recollect (with some fondness, I must admit) how worried my first landlady in Cambridge was about the possibility that my skin color might come off in the bath (I had to assure her that my hue was agreeably sturdy and durable), and also the care with which she explained to me that writing was a special invention of Western civilization ("The Bible did it"). For someone who has lived—intermittently but for long periods—through the powerful evolution of British cultural diversity, the contrast between Britain today and Britain half a century ago is just amazing.

The encouragement given to cultural diversity has certainly made many contributions to people's lives. It has helped Britain to become an exceptionally lively place in many different ways. From the joys of multicultural food, literature, music, dancing, and the arts to the befuddling entrapment of the Notting Hill Carnival, Britain gives its people—of all backgrounds—much to relish and to celebrate. Also, the acceptance of cultural diversity (as well as voting rights and largely non-discriminatory public services and social security, referred to earlier) has made it easier for people with very different origins to feel at home.

Still, it is worth recalling that the acceptance of diverse living modes and varying cultural priorities has not always had an easy ride even in Britain. There has been a periodic but persistent demand that immigrants give up their traditional styles of life and adopt the dominant living modes in the society to which they have immigrated. That demand has sometimes taken a remarkably detailed view of culture, involving quite minute behavioral issues, well illustrated by the famous cricket test proposed by Lord Tebbit, the Conservative political leader. His cricket test suggested that the sign of a well-integrated immigrant is that he cheers for England in test matches against the country of his own origin (such as Pakistan) when the two sides play each other.

Tebbit's test has, it must be admitted, the merit of definiteness, and gives an immigrant a marvelously clear-cut procedure for easily establishing his or her integration into British society: "Cheer for the English cricket team and you will be fine!" The immigrant's job in making sure that he or she is really integrated into British society could otherwise be quite exacting, if only because it is no longer easy to identify what actually is the dominant lifestyle in Britain to which the immigrant must conform. Curry, for example, is now so omnipresent in the British diet that it features as "authentic British fare," according to the British Tourist Board. In last year's General Certificate of Secondary Education (GCSE) examinations, taken by graduating schoolchildren around sixteen years old, two of the questions included in the "Leisure and Tourism" paper were: "Other than Indian food, name one other type of food often provided by take-away restaurants" and "Describe what customers need to do to receive a delivery service from an Indian take-away restaurant."

Reporting on the GCSE in 2005, the *Daily Telegraph* complained not about any cultural bias in these nationwide exams, but about the "easy" nature of the questions, which anyone in Britain should be able to answer without any special training.

I also recollect seeing, not long ago, a definitive description of the unquestionable Englishness of an Englishwoman in a London paper: "She is as English as daffodils or chicken tikka masala." Given all this, a South Asian immigrant to Britain might be a bit confused, but for Tebbit's kindly help, about what will count as a surefire test of British identity. The important issue underlying the frivolity of the foregoing discussion is that cultural contacts are currently leading to such a hybridization of behavioral modes across the world that it is exceptionally difficult to identify any local culture as being genuinely indigenous, with a timeless quality. But thanks to Tebbit, the task of establishing Britishness can become nicely algorithmic and wonderfully easy (almost as easy as answering the GCSE questions just cited).

Tebbit has gone on to suggest, more recently, that if his cricket test had been put to use, it would have helped to prevent the terrorist attacks by British-born militants of Pakistani origin: "Had my comments been acted on, those attacks would have been less likely." It is difficult to avoid the thought that this confident prediction perhaps underestimates the ease with which any would-be terrorist—with or without training from Al Qaeda—could pass the cricket test by cheering for the English cricket team without changing his behavior pattern one iota in any other way.

I don't know how much into cricket Tebbit himself is. If you enjoy the game, cheering for one side or the other is determined by a number of varying factors: one's national loyalty or residential identity, of course, but also the quality of play and the overall interest of a series. Wanting a particular outcome often has a contingent quality that would make it hard to insist on unvarying and unfailed rooting for any team (England or any other). Despite my Indian origin and nationality, I must confess that I have sometimes cheered for the Pakistani cricket team, not only against England but also against India. During the Pakistani team's tour of India in 2005, when Pakistan lost the first two one-day matches in the series of six, I cheered for Pakistan for the third match, to keep the series alive and interesting. In the event, Pakistan went well beyond my hopes and won all of the remaining four matches to defeat India soundly by the margin of four to two (another instance of Pakistan's "extremism" of which Indians complain so much!).

A more serious problem lies in the obvious fact that admonitions of the kind enshrined in Tebbit's cricket test are entirely irrelevant to the duties of British citizenship or residence, such as participation in British politics, joining British social life, or desisting from making bombs. They are also quite distant from anything that may be needed to lead a fully cohesive life in the country.

These points were quickly seized upon in post-imperial Britain, and despite the diversions of such invitations as Tebbit's cricket test, the inclusionary nature of British political and social traditions made sure that varying cultural modes within the country could be seen as being entirely acceptable in a multi-ethnic Britain. To be sure, there are many natives who continue to feel that this historical trend is a great mistake, and that disapproval is often combined with severe resentment that Britain has become such a multi-ethnic country at all. (In my last encounter with such a resenter, at a bus stop, I was suddenly told, "I have seen through you all!," but I was disappointed that my informant refused to tell me more about what he had seen.) Yet the weight of British public opinion has been moving, at least until recently, quite strongly in the direction of tolerating—and even celebrating—cultural diversity. All this, and the inclusionary role of voting rights and non-discriminatory public services, have contributed to an interracial calm of a kind that France in particular has not enjoyed recently. Still, it leaves some of the central issues of multiculturalism entirely unresolved, and I want to take them up now.

III.

One important issue concerns the distinction between multiculturalism and what may be called "plural monoculturalism." Does the existence of a diversity of cultures, which might pass one another like ships in the night, count as a successful case of multiculturalism? Since, in the matter of identity, Britain is currently torn between interaction and isolation, the distinction is centrally important (and even has a bearing on the question of terrorism and violence).

Consider a culinary contrast, by noting first that Indian and British food can genuinely claim to be multicultural. India had no chili until the Portuguese brought it to India from America, but it is effectively used in a wide range of Indian food today and seems to be a dominant element in most types of curries. It is plentifully present in a mouth-burning form in vindaloo, which, as its name indicates, carries the immigrant memory of combining wine with potatoes. Tandoori cooking might have been perfected in India, but it originally came to India from West Asia. Curry powder, on the other hand, is a distinctly English invention, unknown in India before Lord Clive, and evolved, I imagine, in the British army mess. And we are beginning to see the emergence of new styles of preparing Indian food, offered in sophisticated subcontinental restaurants in London.

In contrast, having two styles or traditions co-existing side by side, without the twain meeting, must really be seen as plural monoculturalism. The vocal defense of multiculturalism that we frequently hear these days is very often nothing more than a plea for plural monoculturalism. If a young girl in a conservative immigrant family wants to go out on a date with an English boy that would certainly be a multicultural initiative. In contrast, the attempt by her guardians to stop her from doing this (a common enough occurrence) is hardly a multicultural move, since it seeks to keep the cultures separate. And yet it is the parents' prohibition, which contributes to plural monoculturalism, that seems to garner the loudest and most vocal defense from alleged multiculturalists, on the ground of the importance of honoring traditional cultures—as if the cultural freedom of the young woman were of no relevance whatever, and as if the distinct cultures must somehow remain in secluded boxes.

Being born in a particular social background is not in itself an exercise of cultural liberty, since it is not an act of choice. In contrast, the decision to stay firmly within the traditional mode would be an exercise of freedom, if the choice were made after considering other alternatives. In the same way, a decision to move away—by a little or a lot—from the standard behavior pattern, arrived at after reflection and reasoning, would also qualify as such an exercise. Indeed, cultural freedom can frequently clash with cultural conservatism, and if multiculturalism is defended in the name of cultural freedom, then it can hardly be seen as demanding unwavering and unqualified support for staying steadfastly within one's inherited cultural tradition.

The second question relates to the fact that while religion or ethnicity may be an important identity for people (especially if they have the freedom to choose between celebrating or rejecting inherited or attributed traditions), there are other affiliations and associations that people also have reason to value. Unless it is defined very oddly, multiculturalism cannot override the right of a person to participate in civil society, or to take part in national politics, or to lead a socially non-conformist life. No matter how important multiculturalism is, it cannot lead automatically to giving priority to the dictates of traditional culture over all else.

The people of the world cannot be seen merely in terms of their religious affiliations—as a global federation of religions. For much the same reasons, a multi-ethnic Britain can hardly be seen as a collection of ethnic communities. Yet the "federational" view has gained much support in contemporary Britain. Indeed, despite the tyrannical implications of putting persons into rigid boxes of given "communities," that view is frequently interpreted, rather bafflingly, as an ally of individual freedom. There is even a much-aired "vision" of "the future of multi-ethnic Britain" that sees it as "a looser federation of cultures" held together by common bonds of interest and affection and a collective sense of being.

But must a person's relation to Britain be mediated through the culture of the family in which he or she was born? A person may decide to seek closeness with more than one of these pre-defined cultures or, just as plausibly, with none. Also, a person may well decide that her ethnic or cultural identity is less important to her than, say, her political convictions, or her professional commitments, or her literary persuasions. It is a choice for her to make, no matter what her place is in the strangely imagined "federation of cultures."

There would be serious problems with the moral and social claims of multiculturalism if it were taken to insist that a person's identity must be defined by his or her community or religion, overlooking all the other affiliations a person has, and giving automatic priority to inherited religion or tradition over reflection and choice. And yet that approach to multiculturalism has assumed a pre-eminent role in some of the official British policies in recent years.

The state policy of actively promoting new "faith schools," freshly devised for Muslim, Hindu, and Sikh children (in addition to pre-existing Christian schools), illustrates this approach, and not only is it educationally problematic, it also encourages a fragmentary perception of the demands of living in a desegregated Britain. Many of these new educational institutions are coming up precisely at a time when religious prioritization has been a major source of violence in the world (adding to the history of such violence in Britain itself, including Catholic-Protestant divisions in Northern Ireland—themselves not unconnected with segmented schooling). Prime Minister Tony Blair is certainly right to note that "there is a very strong sense of ethos and values in those schools." But education is not just about getting children, even very young ones, immersed in an old inherited ethos. It is also about helping children to develop the ability to reason about new decisions any grown-up person will have to take. The important goal is not some formulaic parity in relation to old Brits with their old-faith schools, but what would best enhance the capability of the children to live "examined lives" as they grow up in an integrated country.

[...]

V.

There is an uncanny similarity between the problems that Britain faces today and those that British India faced, and which Mahatma Gandhi thought were getting direct encouragement from the Raj. Gandhi was critical in particular of the official view that India was a collection of religious communities. When Gandhi came to London for the Indian Round Table Conference called by the British government in 1931, he found that he was assigned to a specific sectarian corner in the revealingly named "Federal Structure Committee." Gandhi resented the fact that he was being depicted primarily as a spokesman for Hindus, in particular "caste Hindus," with the rest of the population being represented by delegates, chosen by the British prime minister, of each of the "other communities."

Gandhi insisted that while he himself was a Hindu, the political movement that he led was staunchly secular and not a community-based movement. It had supporters from all the different religious groups in India. While he saw that a distinction can be made along religious lines, he pointed to the fact that other ways of dividing the population of India were no less relevant. Gandhi made a powerful plea for the British rulers to see the plurality of the diverse identities of Indians. In fact, he said he wanted to speak not for Hindus in particular, but for "the dumb, toiling, semi-starved millions" who constitute "over 85 percent of the population of India." He added that, with some extra effort, he could speak even for the rest, "the Princes...the landed gentry, the educated class."[2]

Gender, as Gandhi pointed out, was another basis for an important distinction that the British categories ignored, thereby giving no special place to considering the problems of Indian women. He told the British prime minister, "You have had, on behalf of the women, a complete repudiation of special representation," and went on to point out that "they happen to be one-half of the population of India." Sarojini Naidu, who came with Gandhi to the Round Table Conference, was the only woman delegate at the conference. Gandhi mentioned the fact that she was elected the president of the Congress Party, overwhelmingly the largest political party in India (this was in 1925, which was exactly fifty years before any woman was elected to preside over any major British political party). Sarojini Naidu could, on the Raj's "representational" line of reasoning, speak for half the Indian people, namely Indian women; and Abdul Qaiyum, another delegate, pointed also to the fact that Naidu, whom he called "the Nightingale of India," was also the one distinguished poet in the assembled gathering, a different kind of identity from being seen as a Hindu politician.

In a meeting arranged at the Royal Institute of International Affairs during his visit, Gandhi insisted that he was trying to resist "the vivisection of a whole nation." He was not ultimately successful, of course, in his attempt at "staying together," though it is known that he was in favor of taking more time to negotiate to prevent the partition of 1947 than the rest of the Congress leadership found acceptable. Gandhi would have been extremely pained also by the violence against Muslims that was organized by sectarian Hindu leaders in his own state of Gujarat in 2002. But he would have been relieved by the massive condemnation that these barbarities received from the Indian population at large, which influenced the heavy defeat, in the Indian general elections that followed in May 2004, of the parties implicated in the violence in Gujarat.

Gandhi would have taken some comfort in the fact, not unrelated to his point at the Round Table Conference in London in 1931, that India, with more than 80 percent Hindu population, is led today by a Sikh prime minister (Manmohan Singh) and headed by a Muslim president (Abdul Kalam), with its ruling party (Congress) being presided over by a woman from a Christian background (Sonia Gandhi). Such mixtures of communities may be seen in most walks of Indian life, from literature and cinema to business and sports, and they are not regarded as anything particularly special. It is not just that a Muslim is the richest businessman—indeed the wealthiest person—living in India (Azim Premji), or the first putative international star in women's tennis (Sania Mirza), or has captained the Indian cricket team

---

2 The Selected Works of Mahatma Gandhi, <http://www.mkgandhi.org/voiceoftruth/roundtable-conference.htm>.

(Pataudi and Azharuddin), but also that all of them are seen as Indians in general, not as Indian Muslims in particular.

During the recent parliamentary debate on the judicial report on the killings of Sikhs that occurred immediately after Indira Gandhi's assassination by her Sikh bodyguard, the Indian prime minister, Manmohan Singh, told the Indian parliament, "I have no hesitation in apologising not only to the Sikh community but to the whole Indian nation because what took place in 1984 is the negation of the concept of nationhood and what is enshrined in our Constitution." Singh's multiple identities are very much in prominence here when he apologized, in his role as prime minister of India and as leader of the Congress Party, to the Sikh community, of which he is a member (with his omnipresent blue turban), and to the whole Indian nation, of which he is a citizen. All this might be very puzzling if people were to be seen in the "solitarist" perspective of only one identity each, but the multiplicity of identities and roles fits very well with the fundamental point Gandhi was making at the London conference.

Much has been written concerning the fact that India, with more Muslim people than almost every Muslim-majority country in the world (and with nearly as many Muslims—more than 145 million—as Pakistan), has produced extremely few home-grown terrorists acting in the name of Islam, and almost none linked with Al Qaeda. There are many causal influences here, including the influence of the growing and integrated Indian economy. But some credit must also go to the nature of Indian democratic politics, and to the wide acceptance in India of the idea, championed by Gandhi, that there are many identities other than religious ethnicity that are relevant to a person's self-understanding, and also to the relations between citizens of diverse backgrounds within the country.

I recognize that it is a little embarrassing for me, as an Indian, to claim that, thanks to the leadership of Mahatma Gandhi and others (including the clearheaded analysis of "the idea of India" by Rabindranath Tagore, the greatest Indian poet, who described his family background as "a confluence of three cultures, Hindu, Mohammedan, and British"), India has been able, to a considerable extent, to avoid indigenous terrorism linked to Islam, which currently threatens a number of Western countries, including Britain. But Gandhi was expressing a very general concern, not one specific to India, when he asked, "Imagine the whole nation vivisected and torn to pieces; how could it be made into a nation?"

That query was motivated by Gandhi's deep worries about the future of India. But the problem is not specific to India. It arises for other nations too, including the country that ruled India until 1947. The disastrous consequences of defining people by their religious ethnicity and giving priority to the community-based perspective over all other identities, which Gandhi thought was receiving support from India's British rulers, may well have come, alas, to haunt the country of the rulers themselves.

In the Round Table Conference in 1931, Gandhi did not get his way, and even his dissenting opinions were only briefly recorded, with no mention of where the dissent came from. In a gentle complaint addressed to the British prime minister, Gandhi remarked, "In most of these reports you will find that there is a dissenting opinion, and in most of the cases that dissent unfortunately happens to belong to me." Yet Gandhi's farsighted refusal to see a nation as a federation of religions and communities did not "belong" only to him or to the secular India he was leading. It also belongs to any country in the world that is willing to see the serious problems to which Gandhi was drawing attention.

48. Race, Culture, Identity: Misunderstood Connections[*]

The Tanner Lectures on Human Values, delivered at University of California at San Diego, 27 and 28 October 1994

K. Anthony Appiah

Identities and Norms

In the liberal tradition, to which I adhere, we see public morality as engaging each of us as individuals with our individual "identities": and we have the notion, which comes (as Charles Taylor has rightly argued) from the ethics of authenticity,[1] that, other things being equal, people have the right to be acknowledged publicly as what they already really are. It is because someone is already authentically Jewish or gay that we deny them something in requiring them to hide this fact, to "pass," as we say, for something that they are not. Taylor has suggested that we call the political issues raised by this fact the politics of recognition: a politics that asks us to acknowledge socially and politically the authentic identities of others. As has often been pointed out, however, the way much discussion of recognition proceeds is strangely at odds with the individualist thrust of talk of authenticity and identity. If what matters about me is my individual and authentic self, why is there so much contemporary talk of identity about large categories—race, gender, ethnicity, nationality, sexuality—that seem so far from individual? What is the relation between this collective language and the individualist thrust of the modern notion of the self? How has social life come to be so bound up with an idea of identity that has deep roots in romanticism with its celebration of the individual over and against society?[2]

The connection between individual identity, on the one hand, and race and other collective identities, on the other, seems to be something like this: Each person's

---

* Source: Anthony Appiah and Amy Gutmann, *Color Conscious: The Political Morality of Race*, Introduction by David Wilkins (Princeton, NJ: Princeton UP, 1996).

1 Charles Taylor, *Multiculturalism and "The Politics of Recognition,"* with commentary by Amy Gutmann, ed., K. Anthony Appiah, Jürgen Habermas, Steven C. Rockefeller, Michael Walzer, and Susan Wolf (Princeton: Princeton UP, 1994).

2 Taylor reminds us rightly of Trilling's profound contributions to our understanding of this history. I discuss Trilling's work in chap. 4 of *In My Father's House*.

individual identity is seen as having two major dimensions. There is a collective dimension, the intersection of their collective identities; and there is what I will call a personal dimension, consisting of other socially or morally important features of the person—intelligence, charm, wit, cupidity—that are not themselves the basis of forms of collective identity. The distinction between these two dimensions of identity is, so to speak, a sociological rather than a logical distinction. In each dimension we are talking about properties that are important for social life. But only the collective identities count as social categories, kinds of person. There is a logical category but no social category of the witty, or the clever, or the charming, or the greedy: people who share these properties do not constitute a social group, in the relevant sense. The concept of authenticity is central to the connection between these two dimensions; and there is a problem in many current understandings of that relationship, a misunderstanding one can find, for example, in Charles Taylor's recent (brilliant) essay on *Multiculturalism and "The Politics of Reconstruction."*

Authenticity

Taylor captures the ideal of authenticity in a few elegant sentences: "There is a certain way of being that is my way. I am called upon to live my life in this way.... If I am not [true to myself], I miss the point of my life."[3] To elicit the problem here, let me start with a point Taylor makes in passing about Herder:

> I should note here that Herder applied his concept of originality at two levels, not only to the individual person among other persons, but also to the culture-bearing people among other peoples. Just like individuals, a Volk should be true to itself, that is, its own culture.[4]

It seems to me that in this way of framing the issue less attention than necessary is paid to the connection between the originality of persons and of nations. After all, in many places nowadays, the individual identity, whose authenticity screams out for recognition, is likely to have an ethnic identity (which Herder would have seen as a national identity) as a component of its collective dimension. It is, among other things, my being, say, an African-American that shapes the authentic self that I seek to express.[5] And it is, in part, because I seek to express my self that I seek recognition of an African-American identity. This is the fact that makes problems: for recognition as an African-American means social acknowledgment of that collective identity, which requires not just recognizing its existence but actually demonstrating respect for it. If, in understanding myself as African-American, I see myself as resisting white norms, mainstream American conventions, the racism (and, perhaps,

---

3 Taylor, *Multiculturalism*, p. 30.
4 Ibid., p. 31.
5 And, for Herder, this would be a paradigmatic national identity.

the materialism or the individualism) of "white culture," why should I at the same time seek recognition from these white others?

There is, in other words, at least an irony in the way in which an ideal—you will recognize it if I call it the Bohemian ideal in which authenticity requires us to reject much that is conventional in our society—is turned around and made the basis of a "politics of recognition."

[...]

Of course, neither the picture in which there is just an authentic nugget of self-hood, the core that is distinctively me, waiting to be dug out, nor the notion that I can simply make up any self I choose should tempt us. We make up selves from a tool kit of options made available by our culture and society: in ways that I pointed out earlier. We do make choices, but we don't determine the options among which we choose.[6] If you agree with this, you will wonder how much of authenticity we should acknowledge in our political morality: and that will depend, I suppose, on whether an account of it can be developed that is neither essentialist nor monological. It would be too large a claim that the identities that claim recognition in the multicultural chorus must be essentialist and monological. But it seems to me that one reasonable ground for suspicion of much contemporary multicultural talk is that the conceptions of collective identity they presuppose are indeed remarkably unsubtle in their understandings of the processes by which identities, both individual and collective, develop. The story I have told for African-American identity has a parallel for other collective identities: in all of them, I would argue, false theories play a central role in the application of the labels; in all of them the story is complex, involves "making up people," and cannot be explained by an appeal to an essence.

Beyond Identity

The large collective identities that call for recognition come with notions of how a proper person of that kind behaves: it is not that there is one way that Blacks should behave, but that there are proper black modes of behavior. These notions provide loose norms or models, which play a role in shaping the life plans of those who make these collective identities central to their individual identities; of the identifications of those who fly under these banners.[7] Collective identities, in short, provide what we might call scripts: narratives that people can use in shaping their lifeplans and in telling their life stories. In our society (though not, perhaps, in the England of Addison and Steele) being witty does not in this way suggest the life-script of "the

---

6 This is too simple, too, for reasons captured in Anthony Giddens's many discussions of "duality of structure."

7 I say "make" here not because I think there is always conscious attention to the shaping of life plans or a substantial experience of choice but because I want to stress the antiessentialist point that there are choices that can be made.

wit." And that is why what I called the personal dimensions of identity work differently from the collective ones.

[...]

How does this general idea apply to our current situation in the multicultural West? We live in societies in which certain individuals have not been treated with equal dignity because they were, for example, women, homosexuals, Blacks, Catholics. Because, as Taylor so persuasively argues, our identities are dialogically shaped, people who have these characteristics find them central—often, negatively central—to their identities. Nowadays there is a widespread agreement that the insults to their dignity and the limitations of their autonomy imposed in the name of these collective identities are seriously wrong. One form of healing of the self that those who have these identities participate in is learning to see these collective identities not as sources of limitation and insult but as a valuable part of what they centrally are. Because the ethics of authenticity requires us to express what we centrally are in our lives, they move next to the demand that they be recognized in social life as women, homosexuals, Blacks, Catholics. Because there was no good reason to treat people of these sorts badly, and because the culture continues to provide degrading images of them nevertheless, they demand that we do cultural work to resist the stereotypes, to challenge the insults, to lift the restrictions.

These old restrictions suggested life-scripts for the bearers of these identities, but they were negative ones. In order to construct a life with dignity, it seems natural to take the collective identity and construct positive life-scripts instead.

An African-American after the Black Power movement takes the old script of self-hatred, the script in which he or she is a "nigger," and works, in community with others, to construct a series of positive black life-scripts. In these life-scripts, being a Negro is recoded as being black: and this requires, among other things, refusing to assimilate to white norms of speech and behavior. And if one is to be black in a society that is racist then one has constantly to deal with assaults on one's dignity. In this context, insisting on the right to live a dignified life will not be enough. It will not even be enough to require that one be treated with equal dignity despite being black: for that will require a concession that being black counts naturally or to some degree against one's dignity. And so one will end up asking to be respected *as a black*.

I hope I seem sympathetic to this story. I am sympathetic. I see how the story goes. It may even be historically, strategically necessary for the story to go this way.[8] But I think we need to go on to the next necessary step, which is to ask whether the

---

8 Compare what Sartre wrote in his "Orphée Noir," in *Anthologie de la Nouvelle Poésie Nègre et Malagache de Langue Française*, ed. L.S. Senghor, p. xiv. Sartre argued, in effect, that this move is a necessary step in a dialectical progression. In this passage he explicitly argues that what he calls an "antiracist racism" is a path to the "final unity...the abolition of differences of race."

identities constructed in this way are ones we can all be happy with in the longer run. What demanding respect for people as Blacks or as gays requires is that there be some scripts that go with being an African-American or having same-sex desires. There will be proper ways of being black and gay: there will be expectations to be met; demands will be made. It is at this point that someone who takes autonomy seriously will want to ask whether we have not replaced one kind of tyranny with another. If I had to choose between Uncle Tom and Black Power, I would, of course, choose the latter. But I would like not to have to choose. I would like other options. The politics of recognition requires that one's skin color, one's sexual body, should be politically acknowledged in ways that make it hard for those who want to treat their skin and their sexual body as personal dimensions of the self. And "personal" doesn't mean "secret" but "not too tightly scripted," "not too constrained by the demands and expectations of others." In short, so it seems to me, those who see potential for conflict between individual freedom and the politics of identity are right.

Why Differences between Groups Matter

But there is a different kind of worry about racial identities; one that has to do not with their being too-tightly scripted but with a consequence of their very existence for social life. We can approach the problem by asking why differences between groups matter.

This is, I think, by no means obvious. If some minority groups—Korean-Americans, say—do especially well, most people feel, more power to them. We worry, then, about the minorities that fail. And the main reason why people currently worry about minorities that fail is that group failure may be evidence of injustice to individuals. That is the respectable reason why there is so much interest in hypotheses, like those of [Charles] Murray and [Richard J.] Herrnstein, that suggest a different diagnosis. But let us suppose that we can get rid of what we might call Sowellian discrimination: discrimination based on false or even unwarranted beliefs about the different average capacities of racial groups.[9]

Even without Sowellian discrimination socioeconomic disparities between groups threaten the fairness of our social arrangements. This issue can be kept clear only if we look at the matter from the point of view of an individual. Suppose I live in a society with two groups, Blacks and Whites. Suppose that, for whatever reason, the Black group, to which I obviously belong, scores averagely low on a test that is genu-

---

9 "Once the possibility of economic performance differences between groups is admitted, then differences in income, occupational 'representation,' and the like do not, in themselves, imply that decision-makers took race or ethnicity into account. However, in other cases, group membership may in fact be used as a proxy for economically meaningful variables, rather than reflecting either mistaken prejudices or even subjective affinities and animosities." Thomas Sowell, *Race and Culture* (New York: Basic Books, 1995), p. 114.

inely predictive of job-performance. Suppose the test is expensive. And suppose I would have, in fact, a high score on this test, and that I would, in fact, perform well.[10]

In these circumstances, it may well be economically rational for an employer, knowing what group I belong to, simply not to give me the test and, thus, not to hire me.[11] The employer has acted in a rational fashion; there is no Sowellian discrimination here. But most people will understand me if I say that I feel that this outcome is unfair. One way of putting the unfairness is to say: what I can do and be with my talents is being held back because others, over whose failings I have no control, happen to have the characteristics they do.

Capitalism—like life—is full of such unfairness: luck—from lotteries to hurricanes—affects profit. And we can't get rid of all unfairness; for if we had perfect insurance, zero risk, there'd be no role for entrepreneurship, no markets, no capitalism. But we do think it proper to mitigate some risks. We think, for example, that we should do something about bad luck when it has large negative effects on individual people, or if it forces them below some socioeconomic baseline—we insure for car accidents, death, loss of home; the government helps those ruined by largescale acts of God. We don't worry much about the chance production of small negative effects on individuals, even large numbers of individuals. It is at least arguable that, in our society, the cost to competent, well-behaved individual Blacks and Hispanics[12] of being constantly treated as if they have to measure up—the cost in stress, in anger, in lost opportunities—is pretty high.[13] It would be consistent with a general attitude of wanting to mitigate risks with large negative consequences for individuals to try to do something about it.[14]

This specific sort of unfairness—where a person who is atypically competent in a group that is averagely less competent—is the result, among other things, of the fact that jobs are allocated by a profit-driven economy and the fact that I was born into a group in which I am atypical. The latter fact may or may not be the consequence of policies adopted by this society. Let's suppose it isn't: so society isn't, so to speak, causally responsible. According to some—for example, Thomas Sowell, again—that means it isn't morally responsible either: you don't have to fix what you didn't break.

---

10 You need both these conditions, because a high score on a test that correlates well for some skill doesn't necessarily mean you will perform well. And, in fact, Sowell discusses the fact that the same IQ score predicts different levels of economic success for different ethnic groups; ibid., pp. 173, 182.

11 Knowing this, I might offer to pay myself, if I had the money: but that makes the job worth less to me than to members of the other groups. So I lose out again.

12 Let me explicitly point out that many of these people are not middle class.

13 I actually think that there is still rather more Sowellian discrimination than Sowell generally acknowledges; but that is another matter.

14 It will seem to some that I've avoided an obvious argument here, which is that the inequalities in resources that result from differences in talents under capitalism need addressing. I agree. But the argument I am making here is meant to appeal to only extremely unradical individualist ideas; it's designed not to rely on arguing for egalitarian outcomes directly.

I'm not so sure. First, we can take collective responsibility, "as a society," for harms we didn't cause, as is recognized in the Americans with Disabilities Act. But second, the labor market is, after all, an institution: in a modern society it is kept in place by such arrangements as the laws of contract, the institution of money, laws creating and protecting private property, health, and safety at work, and equal employment laws. Sowell may disapprove of some of these, but he can't disapprove of all of them; without all of them, there'd be no capitalism. So the outcome is the result not only of my bad luck but of its interaction with social arrangements, which could be different.

Thus, once we grasp the unfairness of this situation, people might feel that something should be done about it. One possible thing would be to try to make sure there were no ethnic minorities significantly below norm in valuable skills. If the explanation for most significant differences between groups is not hereditary, this could be done, in part, by adopting policies that discouraged significant ethnic differentiation, which would gradually produce assimilation to a single cultural norm. Or it could be done by devoting resources most actively to the training of members of disadvantaged groups.

Another—more modest—move would be to pay special attention to finding talented members of minority groups who would not be found when employers were guided purely by profit.

A third—granted once more that the differences in question are not largely hereditary—would be to explore why there are such differences and to make known to people ways of giving themselves or their children whatever aptitudes will maximize their life-changes, given their hereditary endowments.

Fourth, and finally, for those differences that were hereditary it would be possible to do research to seek to remedy the initial distribution by the genetic lottery—as we have done in making it possible for those without natural resistance to live in areas where malaria and yellow fever are endemic.

Each of these strategies would cost something and the costs would be not only financial. Many people believe that the global homogenization of culture impoverishes the cultural fabric of our lives. It is a sentiment, indeed, we find in Arnold: My brother Saxons have, as is well known, a terrible way with them of wanting to improve everything but themselves off the face of the earth; I have no passion for finding nothing but myself everywhere; I like variety to exist and to show itself to me, and I would not for the world have the lineaments of the Celtic genius lost.[15] The first strategy—of cultural assimilation—would undoubtedly escalate that process. And all of these strategies would require more knowledge than we now have to apply in actual cases so as to guarantee their success. Anyone who shares my sense that there is an unfairness here to be met, an unfairness that has something to do with

---

15 Matthew Arnold, *On the Study of Celtic Literature* (London: Smith, Elder and Co., 1867), p. 11.

the idea that what matters is individual merit, should be interested in developing that kind of knowledge.

But I want to focus for a moment on the general effect of these four strategies. They would all lead to producing a population less various in some of the respects that make a difference to major socioeconomic indicators. This would not mean that everybody would be the same as everybody else—but it could lead to a more recreational conception of racial identity. It would make African-American identity more like Irish-American identity for most of those who care to keep the label. And that would allow us to resist one persistent feature of ethno-racial identities: they risk becoming the obsessive focus, the be-all and end-all, of the lives of those who identify with them. They lead people to forget that their individual identities are complex and multifarious—that they have enthusiasms that do not flow from their race or ethnicity, interests and tastes that cross ethno-racial boundaries, that they have occupations or professions, are fans of clubs and groups. And they then lead them, in obliterating the identities they share with people outside their race or ethnicity, away from the possibility of identification with others. Collective identities have a tendency, if I may coin a phrase, to "go imperial," dominating not only people of other identities, but the other identities, whose shape is exactly what makes each of us what we individually and distinctively are.

In policing this imperialism of identity—an imperialism as visible in racial identities as anywhere else—it is crucial to remember always that we are not simply black or white or yellow or brown, gay or straight or bisexual, Jewish, Christian, Muslim, Buddhist, Confucian: but that we are also brothers and sisters; parents and children; liberals, conservatives, and leftists; teachers and lawyers and auto-makers and gardeners; fans of the Padres and the Bruins; amateurs of grunge rock and lovers of Wagner; movie-buffs; MTV-holics; mystery-readers; surfers and singers; poets and pet-lovers; students and teachers; friends and lovers. Racial identity can be the basis of resistance to racism; but even as we struggle against racism—and though we have made great progress, we have further still to go—let us not let our racial identities subject us to new tyrannies.

Recommended Reading

Baber, H.E. (2008). *The Multicultural Mystique: The Liberal Case Against Diversity.* Amherst, NY: Prometheus Books.

Barry, B. (2001). *Culture and Equality: An Egalitarian Critique of Multiculturalism.* Cambridge, MA: Harvard UP.

Ford, R.T. (2005). *Racial Culture: A Critique.* Princeton: Princeton UP.

Hirsi Ali, A. (2007). *Infidel.* New York: Free.

Kymlicka, W. (1996). *Multicultural Citizenship: A Literal Theory of Minority Rights.* New York: Oxford UP.

McWhorter, J. (2001). *Losing the Race.* New York: Harper Perennial.

Portes, A., & Rumbaut, R.G. (2001). *Legacies: The Story of the Immigrant Second Generation.* Berkeley: U of California P.

Roy, O. (2007). *Secularism Confronts Islam.* New York: Columbia UP.

Sandall, R. (2001). *The Culture Cult.* Boulder, CO: Westview.

Schlesinger, A.M. (1992). *The Disuniting of America.* New York: W.W. Norton & Company.

Wellman, C.H. (2010, June 21). "Immigration." *The Stanford Encyclopedia of Philosophy.* <http://plato.stanford.edu/archives/sum2010/entries/immigration>.

from the publisher

A name never says it all, but the word "broadview" expresses a good deal of the philosophy behind our company. We are open to a broad range of academic approaches and political viewpoints. We pay attention to the broad impact book publishing and book printing has in the wider world; we began using recycled stock more than a decade ago, and for some years now we have used 100% recycled paper for most titles. As a Canadian-based company we naturally publish a number of titles with a Canadian emphasis, but our publishing program overall is internationally oriented and broad-ranging. Our individual titles often appeal to a broad readership too; many are of interest as much to general readers as to academics and students.

Founded in 1985, Broadview remains a fully independent company owned by its shareholders—not an imprint or subsidiary of a larger multinational.

If you would like to find out more about Broadview and about the books we publish, please visit us at **www.broadviewpress.com**. And if you'd like to place an order through the site, we'd like to show our appreciation by extending a special discount to you: by entering the code below you will receive a 20% discount on purchases made through the Broadview website.

Discount code: **broadview20%**

Thank you for choosing Broadview.

Please note: this offer applies only to sales of bound books within the United States or Canada.

MIX
Paper from
responsible sources
FSC® C004071
FSC
www.fsc.org